AVIATION WEATHER

4TH EDITION

JEPPESEN
A BOEING COMPANY

By Peter F. Lester

The charts, tables, and graphs used in this publication are for illustration purposes only and cannot be used for navigation or to determine actual aircraft performance.

ISBN: 978-0-88487-594-9

Library of Congress Control Number: 00-134308

Jeppesen
55 Inverness Drive East
Englewood, CO 80112-5498
Web site: www.jeppesen.com
Email: Captain@jeppesen.com
Copyright © Jeppesen
All Rights Reserved.
10001850-004   Published 1995, 1997, 2000, 2001, 2004, 2007, 2013

ACKNOWLEDGMENTS

Producing the 4th Edition of Aviation Weather has been a team effort rather than the work of an individual author. I am indebted to Kimberly Winter-Manes, Senior Project Manager at Jeppesen, who coordinated the effort, keeping our team organized, on task, and on schedule. From the beginning, Chuck Stout, with his keen eye as both editor and pilot, made important suggestions to improve the book, and patiently incorporated those changes into the 4th Edition to produce the best training product. I know that this newest edition also benefits from the talents of the art and production personnel at Jeppesen. I don't know each of you personally, but I know you have been there making the book shine. Thanks!

During the preparation of this book, I have had many helpful discussions with pilots, aviation weather forecasters, and atmospheric scientists on both the public and private sides of meteorology. I thank them for their input and for their ongoing dedication to deliver the most useful meteorological information to the pilot on the ground and in the air.

In preparing for this new edition, I was fortunate to be able to call on three colleagues to review the text and provide important suggestions for improvements. They are Ray Sanchez-Pescador, private pilot; Steve Senderling, commercial pilot, CFI, and Instructor of Ground School and Meteorology at Lane Community College, Eugene, Oregon; and Frank W. Lester, retired Air Force pilot and former Director of Safety and Education for the Idaho Division of Aeronautics. Many improvements and updates to the book are due to their extensive and thoughtful inputs.

My family continues to keep me centered in my writing tasks. I thank them all for understanding my passion for this aviation weather stuff and encouraging me along the way. Thank you Heather, Morgan, and David Rodd; Rachael, Andrew, Elijah, Jasmine, and Leonardo Posada. My wife, Julia, has been my personal support team, listening, providing more synonyms than I ever knew, typing, being away when I needed space and quiet to think, and feeding and encouraging me. She is a sailor who now knows much more about flying weather than she ever expected.

This book is dedicated to the people who got me into this aviation meteorology writing business. Mike Cetinich led me to Jeppesen after I described to him my first ideas about writing meteorology education and training materials both for pilots and aspiring pilots. Dick Snyder, whose extensive editorial experience at Jeppesen and whose ability to manage an author's ego, took me from my first effort, *Turbulence, A New Perspective for Pilots* to this book, *Aviation Weather*. Along the way, he taught me many practical matters about technical writing. Today he is gone but his influence is still strongly felt as, appropriately, my current editor, Chuck Stout, was mentored by Dick.

Peter F. Lester, 2013

TABLE OF CONTENTS

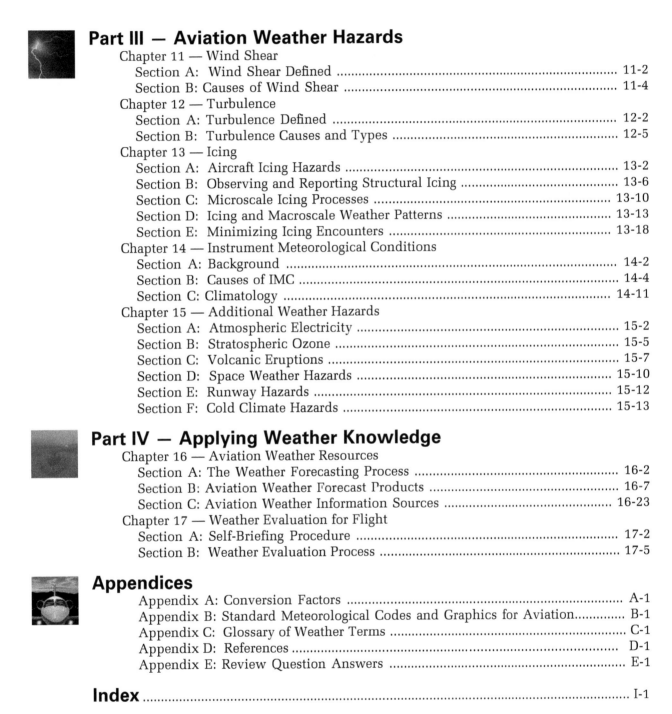

HOW THE SYSTEM WORKS

The Jeppesen Sanderson study/review concept of learning presents information in an uncomplicated way with coordinated text and illustrations. Aviation Weather is designed to facilitate self-study. To get the most out of this textbook in the shortest amount of time, the following self-study procedure is recommended.

1. Review the Chapter Outline at the beginning of each chapter, noting major topics and subtopics.

2. Review the list of Key Terms and Chapter Questions at the end of the chapter.

3. Read the chapter Introduction and Summary Sections.

4. Skim through the chapter, reading the FAA Question Material, Insight Readings, and Illustrations.

5. Read the chapter.

6. Answer the Chapter Questions and check your answers to Review Questions in Appendix E.

7. For a general review, repeat steps 1 through 4.

The key elements in Aviation Weather are presented in color to allow you to review important points and concepts. The major features of the book are presented in the following pages.

PART I
Aviation Weather Basics

Part I provides you with the fundamentals of meteorology. These "basics" are the foundation of the entire study of aviation weather. The time you spend reading and understanding the basics will pay off in later parts of the text when you turn your attention to more complex topics such as the behavior and prediction of weather systems, and weather related flight hazards.

When you complete Part I, you will have developed a vocabulary of aviation weather terms and a knowledge of the essential properties and weather-producing processes of the atmosphere. As a pilot, you must be fully aware of weather and its influences on flight. Your task of understanding these concepts is made much easier with a solid foundation in Aviation Weather Basics.

Learning Objectives

Learning objectives at the beginning of each Part and Chapter help you focus on important concepts.

Chapter Outlines

Chapter outlines help you identify the major topics of the chapter.

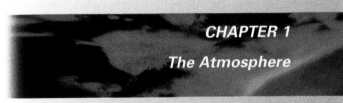

CHAPTER 1
The Atmosphere

Introduction

The formal study of any physical system, such as an engine or an airplane, usually begins with a description of that system. Information about component parts, their location and dimensions, and terminology is necessary background for later examination and understanding of the system design and operation. Our study of aviation weather begins in a similar way. The "system" in this case, is the atmosphere.

When you complete this chapter, you should be able to describe the composition, dimensions, and average vertical structure of the atmosphere using proper technical vocabulary. Furthermore, you will have been introduced to a valuable reference tool, the standard atmosphere.

SECTION A: ATMOSPHERIC COMPOSITION
SECTION B: ATMOSPHERIC PROPERTIES
    Temperature
    Density
    Pressure
    The Gas Law
SECTION C: ATMOSPHERIC STRUCTURE
    Dimensions
    Atmospheric Layers
        Temperature Layers
        Other Layers
        Standard Atmosphere

and true altitude will be equal only if the atmospheric temperatures are standard. If the atmosphere is colder than standard, your true altitude will be lower than your indicated altitude. If the atmosphere is warmer than standard, the true altitude will be higher than your indicated altitude. (Figure 3-12) Temperature errors are generally smaller than those associated with variations in sea level pressure. For example, if the actual temperature was 10C° warmer than standard, the true altitude would be about 4% higher. This is only 40 feet at 1,000 feet MSL. But the error increases with height. At 12,000 feet MSL, it is about 500 feet. Flight over high mountains in bad weather requires close attention to possible temperature errors.

The **third pressure altimeter error** that arises because of nonstandard atmospheric conditions is caused by large and rapid changes in vertical movements of the air. These changes upset the balance of forces (hydrostatic balance) that allows atmospheric pressure to be related directly to altitude. Such errors may be expected in the extreme updrafts of thunderstorms and in strong mountain waves. More on this problem is presented in Part III on aviation weather hazards.

The altimeter errors discussed above are all related to atmospheric conditions. Other errors may arise due to instrument problems. These include improper calibration, friction, lag, improper instrument location, and temperature changes of the instrument. These are beyond the scope of this text and the reader is referred to other sources for details. (Jeppesen, 1999)

> Remember, the pressure altimeter will not automatically show exact altitude in flight. It is the pilot's responsibility to ensure terrain avoidance.

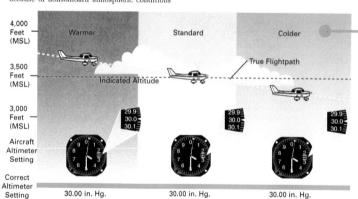

Figure 3-12. Flight cross section from a warmer to a colder airmass. Notice that standard atmospheric conditions only occur near the center of the diagram. The aircraft true altitude is higher than indicated in the warmer air and lower than indicated in the colder air.

On warm days pressure surfaces are raised and the indicated altitude is lower than true altitude.

3-14

Insight Readings

Insight readings are contained in green boxes throughout the text. These readings add insight to the information covered and help you relate to and understand the main topics in the chapter.

Full Color Graphics

Full-color graphics mak learning fun and meaningful. Detailed material is presented in an uncomplicated way. Graphics are carefully planned to complement and expand the concepts in the text.

FAA Questions

FAA question material appears in blue boxes. This material summarizes important concepts behind the weather-related questions on the Private, Instrument, and Commercial airmen knowledge exams. You can review the blue boxes prior to taking your FAA exam.

SUMMARY

The basic properties of horizontal motions of the atmosphere have been examined in this chapter. You should now understand that air responds to pressure gradients by being accelerated toward lower pressure. Furthermore, pressure gradients are caused by temperature gradients and the movement of atmospheric mass by the winds. Once the air is in motion, Coriolis force becomes important, especially in large scale atmospheric circulations.

The wind that results when Coriolis force is exactly in balance with the pressure gradient force is the geostrophic wind. Because the near balance of these two forces is common, the geostrophic wind has proven to be a very useful estimate of actual wind in a variety of applications ranging from the interpretation of isobars and contours on weather charts, to navigation. Friction modifies the geostrophic balance, especially in the atmospheric boundary layer where its effect is apparent in cross-isobar airflow, turbulence, and gusty winds.

Your knowledge of the basic causes and characteristics of wind will be of great value as you examine vertical motions, clouds, and weather in the next two chapters and, subsequently, specific atmospheric circulations.

Chapter Summaries

Chapter summaries are provided at the end of each chapter to help you review the important concepts contained in the chapter.

KEY TERMS

Acceleration
Anticyclone
Anticyclonic Flow
Boundary Layer
Centrifugal Force
Coriolis Force
Cyclone
Cyclonic Flow
Cyclostrophic Balance
Cyclostrophic Winds
D-Value
Differential Heating
Drag
Form Drag
Friction
Geostrophic Balance
Geostrophic Wind
Gust
Horizontal Pressure Gradient Force

Parcel
Peak Wind
Pressure Gradient Force
Return Flow
Scalar
Sea Breeze
Skin Friction
Squall
Surface Friction
Sustained Speed
Thermal Circulat
True North
Vector
Veer
Wind
Wind Direction
Wind Speed
Wind Velocity

Key Terms

Key terms are set off in blue type when they are first used and defined. Key terms are listed at the end of each chapter and included in a glossary at the end of the book.

REVIEW QUESTIONS

1. What is the bearing of the center of a nearby low pressure area (assume it is circular) from your location if your measured wind direction at 2,000 feet AGL is
   1. northwest?
   2. 240°?
   3. south?
   4. 090°?

2. What would your answers to question number 1 be if the wind directions were measured at the airport weather station instead of 2,000 feet?

3. In cyclonic flow in the Southern Hemisphere, which way do winds circulate around the center of the pressure system? Is the central pressure relatively low or high in the cyclonic case?

4. A series of weather reports are listed below. Decode all wind information.

   METAR KDAY 050851Z 03003KT 5SM -RA BR OVC036 07/06 A3000=
   METAR KDAY 051405Z 10020G23KT 3SM BR SCT023 BKN037 OVC065 07/06 A2996=
   METAR KBAB 051755Z 00000KT 15SM FEW100 BKN200 12/03 A3028=
   METAR KSAC 051847Z VRB05KT 20SM BKN160 BKN280 13/02 A3027=
   METAR KVIS 051854Z AUTO 19006KT 10SM CLR 14/06 A3026=
   METAR KFTK 051755Z 21005KT 1 1/4SM -SHRA BR BKN003 OVC005 13/12 A2985=

Chapter Questions

Chapter questions help you evaluate your understanding of the material presented in the chapter. There are two types of Questions: "Review Questions" ask you for very specific details related to concepts, definitions, simple calculations, and terminology. Answers are provided in Appendix E. "Discovery Questions" are more involved, requiring you to integrate ideas, interpret weather conditions, and make flight decisions.

DISCOVERY QUESTIONS

5. With the guidance of your instructor, obtain a surface analysis chart with well-defined high and low pressure systems. Select five or ten widely separated weather reporting stations for which wind data are available. Construct a table to record the answers of each of the questions below for each station.
   1. What are the observed wind speeds and directions?
   2. What is the most likely wind direction at 2,000 feet AGL?
   3. Which of the locations has the strongest surface geostrophic winds?

6. With the guidance of your instructor, select a 700 mb constant pressure chart for, preferably, a winter day. Select five observing stations for which wind data are plotted and in regions where the contours have different directions and gradients. Answer each of the questions below for each station.

1. What are the observed wind speeds and directions?
2. What are the geostrophic wind directions?
3. Which of the locations has the strongest geostrophic winds?
4. What is the approximate flight level of the chart?

7. Do some research on aircraft navigation and document the effects of Coriolis force in detail.

8. If the weather chart in question number 5 was in the Southern Hemisphere and the pressure pattern remained exactly the same, how would the winds be different? Redraw the map to illustrate your answer.

off to the side, the path is still straight. Note that if the direction of rotation is clockwise (cw), the deflection of the ball is to the left.

When we attempt to describe the motion of the atmosphere (or anything else) relative to the rotating earth, we must also consider Coriolis force. However, things become a little more involved because the earth is a rotating sphere, rather than a rotating disk. In the case of the merry-go-round, it did not matter where the thrower and the catcher were located on the rotating platform. For a fixed rotation rate and a constant speed of the ball, Coriolis force was

is not the case with the earth. For a fixed rotation rate and speed of the ball, Coriolis force is different at different latitudes. The variation is illustrated in figure 4-8.

If, as shown in figure 4-8, our merry-go-round is attached to the earth at the North Pole, it rotates counterclockwise. Note that the axis of the earth and the axis of rotation of the merry-go-round are parallel at the pole. If we let the earth's rotation rate and the speed of the ball be the same as in the previous example, then (considering only Coriolis force) we would see the same effect on the ball. At the equator, the situation is different. In that location, the axis of the earth is perpendicular to the axis of the merry-go-round, so the merry-go-round does not rotate about its

the same everywhere on the platform. This is because the axis of rotation of the merry-go-round was vertical; that is, perpendicular to the platform across which the ball was moving. This

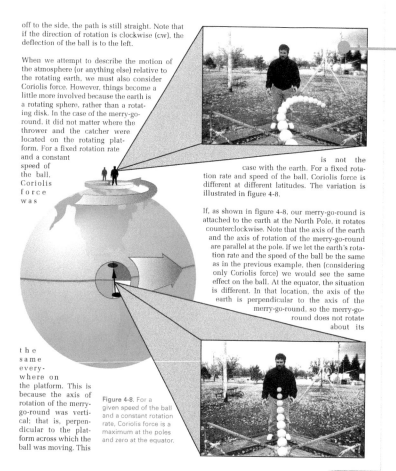

Figure 4-8. For a given speed of the ball and a constant rotation rate, Coriolis force is a maximum at the poles and zero at the equator.

4-11

References

Appendix D helps you find further information on the topics presented in this book by providing a detailed list of reference materials. These resources can provide a much deeper understanding of meteorology and weather processes for those with a desire to know more.

REFERENCES

The references provided here were used in the preparation of this text and/or are given as recommended reading for greater detail on the topics presented in the text. References that are also posted on the Internet are included along with the Internet address (URL) valid at the time the reference was obtained. Many publications listed below are available through the American Meteorological Society (AMS). Information on the availability of AMS publications may be obtained at *http://www.ametsoc.org/AMS* or by writing

American Meteorological Society
45 Beacon St., Boston MA
02108-3693
USA

Ahrens, C.D. *Meteorology Today, An Introduction to Weather, Climate, and the Environment.* Brooks/Cole/Thompson, 2012.

American Meteorological Society. *Preprints, 9th Conference on Aerospace and Aeronautical Meteorology.* Omaha, NE: American Meteorological Society, 1983.

American Meteorological Society. *Preprints, 3rd International Conference on the Aviation Weather System. Anaheim, CA:* American Meteorological Society. *Preprints, 5th ...tion Weather System.* Meteorological Society,

... Society. Preprints, 7th, ...onferences on Aviation, ...eteorology. 1997, 1999,

...ion to Flight, 2nd Ed. ...560pp, 1985.

...dation. *Safety Review, ... Accidents, An Analysis ...gies.* AOPA Air Safety ...on Way, Frederick MD

Atkinson, B.W. *Mesoscale Atmospheric Circulations.* Academic Press, 495pp, 1981.

Atlas, D. (Ed.): *Radar in Meteorology.* Boston: American Meteorological Society, 806pp, 1990.

Bernstein, Ben C., T. Omeron, M. Politovitch, and F. McDonough. "Surface Weather Features associated with freezing precipitation and severe in-flight aircraft icing," *Atmospheric Research*, 46, 57-73. New York, Amsterdam, Tokyo, Singapore: Elsevier Science, 1998.

Bernstein, Ben C., and B. Brown. "A Climatology of Supercooled Large Droplet Conditions based upon Surface Observations and Pilot Reports of Icing," in *Preprints, 7th Conference on Aviation, Range and Aerospace Meteorology*, 82-87. Long Beach, CA: American Meteorological Society, 1997.

Bernstein, Ben C., T.P. Ratvasky, D.R. Miller, F. McDonough. "Freezing Rain as an In-Flight Icing Hazard," *Preprints, 8th Conference on Aviation, Range and Aerospace Meteorology*, 38-42. Dallas, TX: American Meteorological Society, 1999.

Bhangar, S., S. C. Cowlin, B. C. Singer, R. G. Sextro, and W. W. Nazaroff. Environmental Science and Technology, 42, 3938-3943. "Ozone Levels in Passenger Cabins of Commercial Aircraft on North American and Transoceanic Routes." 2008.

Bluestein, H.B. Synoptic-Dynamic Meteorology in Midlatitudes. Volume I: Principles of Kinematics and Dynamics, 431pp. Volume II: Observations and Theory of Weather Systems. 594pp. New York, Oxford: Oxford University Press, 1993.

Bradbury, T.A., and J.P. Kuettner (Eds.). Forecasters Manual for Soaring Flight. Geneva: Organisation Scientifique et Technique International du Vol a Voile (OSTIV), 119pp, 1976.

Buck, R.N. *Weather Flying, 3rd Ed.* New York: MacMillan, 311pp ,1988.

Byers, H.R. *General Meteorology.* New York: McGraw-Hill, 1974.

WIND SHEAR

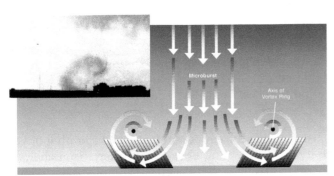

Microburst

Axis of Vortex Ring

Figure 11-5. Microburst cross section. The flight hazards include the strong downdraft, often with heavy precipitation; gusty horizontal winds (shaded); strong horizontal wind shear from one side of the microburst to the other side; and turbulence in the vortex rings. The inset in the upper left is a photograph of the vortex ring of a microburst made visible by condensation. Photograph credit: NOAA Photo Library, NOAA Central Library

Within 100 feet of the ground, only a few seconds may be available for the recognition and recovery from wind shear associated with a microburst.

The peak outflow speed observed in an average microburst is about 25 knots. Winds in excess of 100 knots are possible. More critical is the change in wind speed across a microburst. An aircraft intersecting a typical microburst experiences an average headwind change of about 45 knots. This LLWS exceeds the capabilities of most light aircraft and is about the maximum that can be tolerated by heavy jet transports. The effect is illustrated in figure 11-6.

There are several variations in the formation and appearance of precipitation-induced downdrafts and microbursts. For example, a downdraft does not require a thunderstorm. As discussed

On a July afternoon in 1982, a B-727 departed New Orleans, Louisiana, into a heavy rain shower near the end of the runway. The aircraft soon began sinking despite all the best efforts of the pilots to maintain takeoff climb. Less than twenty seconds after leaving the runway, the aircraft crashed killing 152 persons. An analysis of flight recorder and weather data by Dr. T. Fujita of the University of Chicago showed that the B-727 had flown into a strong precipitation-induced downdraft. During the penetration, a 14-knot <u>head-wind</u> at liftoff became a 27-knot <u>tailwind</u> just prior to the crash. Comprehensive analyses of this and other accidents by Dr. Fujita and his research team led to the identification of the microburst as a critical and identifiable aviation weather hazard. The subsequent development of flight techniques for wind shear situations and the installation of wind shear detection systems at airports received their impetus from Dr. Fujita's pioneering work on microbursts.

The duration of an individual microburst is seldom longer than 15 minutes from the time the burst strikes the ground until dissipation.

Accident/Incident

Brief descriptions of aircraft accidents and incidents appear in red boxes to illustrate the impact of aviation weather hazards and to provide cases for discussion and analysis.

PREFACE

Meteorology is the study of the atmosphere and its phenomena; in many texts, it is simply referred to as atmospheric science. In contrast, weather is technically defined as the state of the atmosphere at an instant in time. Although the study of atmospheric impacts on aviation deals both with meteorology and with weather, it is traditionally referred to as aviation weather. We will use the latter terminology, clarifying differences where necessary.

Meteorology is a relatively "young" science. The vast majority of important developments in the field have only taken place in the last hundred years. Driven by hot and cold war technological breakthroughs and, more recently, by environmental concerns, our understanding of the atmosphere and our ability to predict its behavior have improved dramatically.

In the middle of this rapid growth has been the airplane. Much of the progress in modern meteorology has also been driven by, and for, aviation. As aircraft designs improved and more and more aircraft were able to fly higher, faster, and farther, previously unobserved details of fronts, jet streams, turbulence, thunderstorms, mountain waves, hurricanes, and many other atmospheric phenomena were encountered.

The aviation industry turned to formal atmospheric research for the practical reason that aircraft are extremely vulnerable to certain atmospheric conditions. Aircraft designers needed careful measurements of those conditions; subsequent studies by specially equipped weather research aircraft produced even more details of the weather environment of flight.

In the early days of aviation, it became obvious that a regular supply of weather information was necessary to serve day-to-day operational needs. In the 1920's, many weather stations and the first weather data communication networks were established in the U.S. to serve the growing aviation industry. These were the forerunners of the modern observation, forecast, and data communication systems that now serve a wide variety of public and private users across the entire world.

The strong interdependence of flight and meteorology will be apparent from the beginning of your aviation experience. Whether your connection to flying is as a pilot, or as a controller, dispatcher, scientist, engineer, or interested passenger, you will quickly discover that it is nearly impossible to discuss any aspect of aviation without some reference to the meteorological environment in which the aircraft operates.

The objective of this text is to help the new student of aviation understand the atmosphere for the purpose of maximizing aircraft performance while minimizing exposure to weather hazards.

The book is also meant to provide a review of meteorology basics in preparation for the FAA examinations. It brings together information from a variety of sources and should serve as an up-to-date reference text. It is written with a minimum of mathematics and a maximum of practical information.

The text is divided into four Parts:

Part I (Chapters 1-6) addresses the "basics." This is important background in elementary meteorology that provides concepts and vocabulary necessary to understand aviation weather applications.

Part II (Chapters 7-10) deals with the wide variety of atmospheric circulation systems, their causes, behavior, and their related aviation weather.

Part III (Chapters 11-15) focuses specifically on the flight hazards produced by the circulation systems described in Part II.

Part IV (Chapters 16 and 17) considers the weather forecast process and the task of obtaining and interpreting pertinent weather information. These final chapters provide a framework for putting the information presented in previous chapters to practical use.

As you begin your study of aviation weather, a brief "pretest" is useful to emphasize the importance of the study of aviation meteorology. Given the following meteorological phenomena:

Rain, gusts, whiteout, drizzle, high density altitude, mountain wave, low ceiling, downdrafts, haze, lightning, obscuration, microburst, high winds, snow, thunderstorm

1. Can you define/describe the specific meteorological conditions that produce each of the phenomena listed above?

2. Can you explain why, when, and where the favorable meteorological conditions that produce the phenomena are likely to occur?

3. Can you describe the specific flight hazards associated with each of the phenomena listed above, and explain how to minimize effects of those hazards?

If you cannot answer these questions, consider that each of weather items listed above was cited as a cause or contributing factor in more than 400 General Aviation accidents that occurred in a single year in the U.S. These weather-related accidents accounted for 19% of all General Aviation accidents that occurred that year. Another sobering statistic is that, if only accidents involving fatalities are considered, weather was the cause or a contributing factor in more than 23% of fatal accident cases . . . nearly one in four!

When you complete this study of aviation meteorology, you should be able to return to this page and answer the three questions above with confidence and with respect for the atmosphere and its vagaries.

PREFACE TO THE FOURTH EDITION

Changes to the 4th Edition were driven by a number of factors. Primarily, they reflect an effort to make the book more understandable and relevant through clarifications and updates of descriptions and explanations of basic physical concepts and atmospheric phenomena relevant to aircraft operations.

Since the 3rd Edition was published, there have been important developments in analysis and forecasting products to help pilots make good preflight and inflight decisions. The ability to access specific and current aviation information from new sources and from almost any location—including the cockpit—is a major change that now enables pilots to be literally "on top of the situation." Of course, having the latest devices to obtain and display relevant meteorological information still requires pilots to make sound decisions based on the proper interpretation of that information. Being able to interpret aviation weather information is at the heart of this book.

The 4th Edition includes several new "Insight Readings," that is, "sound bites" that help readers grasp some of the more detailed topics presented in the text. Additionally, at the recommendation of reviewers, more excerpts from NTSB reports of aircraft accidents and incidents appear throughout the book to emphasize relevant flying hazards. Finally, with the encouragement and help of outside readers, a second scenario based on a real weather situation has been added to Chapter 17.

At critical points in the text, readers are reminded that good weather knowledge is only part of good flight planning and smart inflight decision-making. Equally important, if not more so, is that pilots understand and apply the concept of "personal minimums" as well as the use of tools such as the IMSAFE checklist.

Part I

Aviation Weather Basics

PART I
Aviation Weather Basics

Part I provides you with the fundamentals of meteorology. These "basics" are the foundation of the entire study of aviation weather. The time you spend reading and understanding the basics will pay off in later parts of the text when you turn your attention to more complex topics such as the behavior and prediction of weather systems, and weather-related flight hazards.

When you complete Part I, you will have developed a vocabulary of aviation weather terms and a knowledge of the essential properties and weather-producing processes of the atmosphere. As a pilot, you must be fully aware of weather and its influences on flight. Your task of understanding these concepts is made much easier with a solid foundation in Aviation Weather Basics.

CHAPTER 1
The Atmosphere

Introduction

The formal study of any physical system, such as an engine or an airplane, usually begins with a description of that system. Information about component parts, their location and dimensions, and terminology is necessary background for later examination and understanding of the system design and operation. Our study of aviation weather begins in a similar way. The "system" in this case, is the atmosphere.

When you complete this chapter, you should be able to describe the composition, dimensions, and average vertical structure of the atmosphere using proper technical vocabulary. Furthermore, you will have been introduced to a valuable reference tool, the standard atmosphere.

Section A
ATMOSPHERIC COMPOSITION

Each planet in our solar system is different, a product of the planet's original composition as well as its size and distance from the sun. Most planets, including Earth, have an atmosphere; that is, an envelope of gases surrounding the planet.

The earth's atmosphere is a unique mixture of gases along with small amounts of water, ice, and other particulates. The gases are mainly nitrogen and oxygen with only small amounts of a variety of other gases. (Figure 1-1)

Although nitrogen (N_2) takes up

most of the volume of the atmosphere, it doesn't contribute to weather-producing processes under ordinary atmospheric conditions. Exceptions occur when N_2 is subjected to very high temperatures, for example, when air passes through an internal combustion engine. In that case, nitrogen combines with oxygen to form air pollutants known as "oxides of nitrogen" (NO_x).

By and large, the most important role of atmospheric oxygen (O_2) is the support of life as we know it. Because oxygen concentration decreases with altitude, all pilots must be aware of the serious effects of oxygen deprivation on aircrews and passengers. Oxygen supports combustion and contributes to both the formation and the destruction of air pollutants through chemical combinations with other gases.

In figure 1-1, N_2 and O_2 and many of the "other" atmospheric gases are "permanent," which means that their proportions remain about the same, at least in the lower $_2$60,000 feet (about 43 n.m) of the atmosphere. In contrast, water vapor (H_2O) is a "variable" gas; that is, the percentage of water vapor in the atmosphere can vary greatly, depending on the location and source of the air. For example, over the tropical oceans, water vapor may account for 4% of the total volume of gases, while over deserts or at high altitudes, it may be nearly absent.

Water vapor is an important gas for weather production, even though it exists in very small amounts compared to O_2 and N_2. This is because it can also exist as a liquid (water) and as a solid (ice). These contribute to the formation of fog, clouds, precipitation, and icing, well-known aviation weather problems.

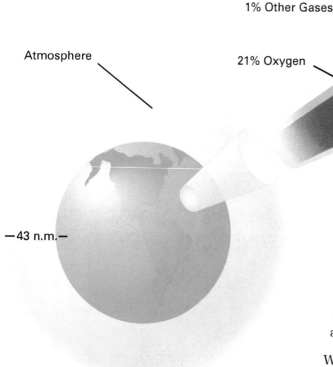

78% Nitrogen

1% Other Gases

Atmosphere

21% Oxygen

—43 n.m.—

Figure 1-1. Primary permanent components of the mixture of gases in the lower atmosphere. Below an altitude of about 43 n.m. (260,000 feet), the ratios of these gases (78:21:1) remain relatively constant. Above this altitude, energy from the sun is great enough to break down molecular structures and change the ratios.

Water vapor also absorbs radiant energy from the earth (terrestrial radiation). This reduces cooling, causing temperatures at the surface to be warmer than would otherwise be expected. Detailed information about this and other characteristics of water vapor, water, and ice are given in later chapters.

Gases that occupy a very small part of the total volume of the atmosphere are generally referred to as "trace gases." Two of the more important of these are also variable gases: carbon dioxide and ozone. Although their concentrations are extremely small, their impact on atmospheric processes may be very large. For example, carbon dioxide (CO_2) also absorbs terrestrial radiation. The concentration of this trace gas has been increasing over the last century due to the worldwide burning of fossil fuels and rain forest depletion, contributing to the long-term warming of the atmosphere.

Ozone (O_3) is a toxic, highly reactive pollutant which is produced in the lower atmosphere by the action of the sun on oxides of nitrogen and by electrical discharges, such as lightning.

Although their concentrations are small, water vapor, carbon dioxide, ozone, and other trace gases have profound effects on weather and climate.

The greatest concentration of ozone is found between 50,000 and 100,000 feet above the earth's surface. The upper ozone layer is beneficial for the most part because ozone absorbs harmful ultraviolet radiation from the sun. This filtering process at high levels protects plants and animals on the earth's surface. However, direct exposure of aircrews and passengers to the toxic properties of O_3 can be a problem during high-altitude flights. These will be discussed in Part III, Aviation Weather Hazards.

Liquid or solid particles that are small enough to remain suspended in the air are known as particulates or aerosols. Some of these are large enough to be seen, but most are not. The most obvious particulates in the atmosphere are water droplets and ice crystals associated with fog and clouds. Other sources of particulates include volcanoes, forest fires, dust storms, industrial processes, automobile and aircraft engines, and the oceans, to name a few. Particulates are important because they intercept solar and terrestrial radiation, provide surfaces for condensation of water vapor, reduce visibility, and, in the worst cases, can foul engines.

Section B

ATMOSPHERIC PROPERTIES

Since the atmospheric "system" is mainly a mixture of gases, its description is commonly given in terms of the state of the gases that make up that mixture. The three fundamental variables used to describe this state are temperature, density, and pressure.

TEMPERATURE

Temperature is defined in a number of ways; for example, as a measure of the direction heat will flow, or as simply a measure of "hotness" or "coldness." Another useful interpretation of temperature is as a measure of the motion of the molecules. Kinetic energy is energy that exists by virtue of motion. A molecule possesses kinetic energy proportional to the square of its speed of movement; temperature is defined as the average of the kinetic energy of the many molecules that make up a substance. The greater the average kinetic energy, the greater the temperature. (Figure 1-2)

A temperature of absolute zero is the point where all molecular motion ceases. The corresponding temperature scale is known as the absolute or Kelvin scale. You will be introduced to the details of the more familiar Fahrenheit and Celsius temperature scales in the next chapter. For the moment, the Kelvin scale will serve our purposes.

On the absolute or Kelvin (°K) temperature scale, the temperature where all molecular motion ceases is 0°K. The melting point of ice is 273°K (0°C) and the boiling point of water is 373°K (100°C).

Higher Kinetic Energy

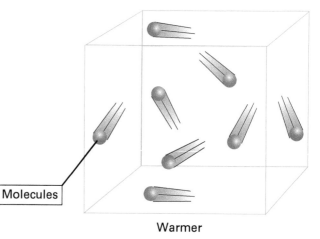

Warmer

Molecules

Lower Kinetic Energy

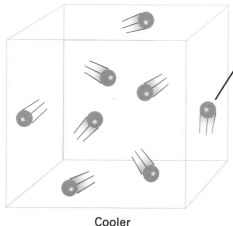

Cooler

Figure 1-2. Temperature is a measure of the average kinetic energy of the molecules of a gas. The red molecules indicate warm temperatures with relatively large speeds (greater kinetic energy). The blue molecules represent cooler temperatures with smaller molecular speeds.

When referring to temperature, the placement of the degree symbol indicates whether the number is an actual temperature (35°C) or a temperature increment (35C°).

DENSITY

Density of a gas is the mass of the molecules in a given volume. If the total mass of molecules in that volume decreases, the density decreases. If the mass remains the same but the volume increases, the density also decreases. The units of density are expressed in terms of mass per unit volume. (Figure 1-3)

PRESSURE

Pressure is the force exerted by the moving molecules of the gas on a given area, for example, a square inch or square meter. Pressure at a point acts equally in all directions. A typical value of atmospheric pressure at sea level is 14.7 pounds per square inch (See table on page 1-7).

THE GAS LAW

A unique characteristic of gases is that they obey a physical principle known as the gas law, which can be written as:

$$\frac{P}{DT} = R$$

In this equation P is pressure, D is density, T is the absolute temperature, and R is a constant number which is known from experiment and theory. The equation above simply states that the ratio of pressure to the product of density and temperature is always the same. For example, if the pressure changes, then either the density or the temperature, or both, must also change in order for the

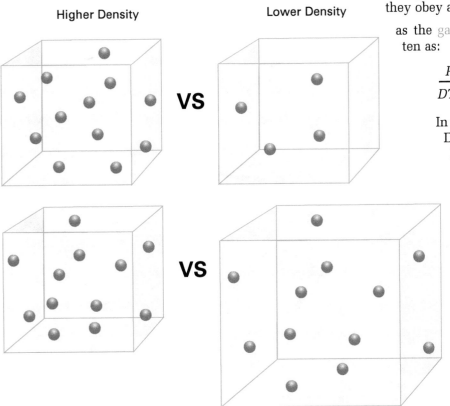

Higher Density   Lower Density

VS

VS

Figure 1-3. In this figure, the mass within each volume is represented by a number of molecules, each with the same mass. The density is equal to the sum of the masses of all of the molecules within the box divided by the total volume. The figure shows that density is decreased when gas molecules are removed or when the volume is increased.

ratio to remain constant. Figure 1-4 illustrates the application of the gas law and three simple ways to lower the pressure in the vessels by varying the temperature or the density.

The gas law makes the measurement of the gaseous state of the atmosphere much simpler. If we know any two of the three variables that describe the gas, we can always calculate the third. In practice, we usually measure pressure and temperature and deduce the density from the gas law.

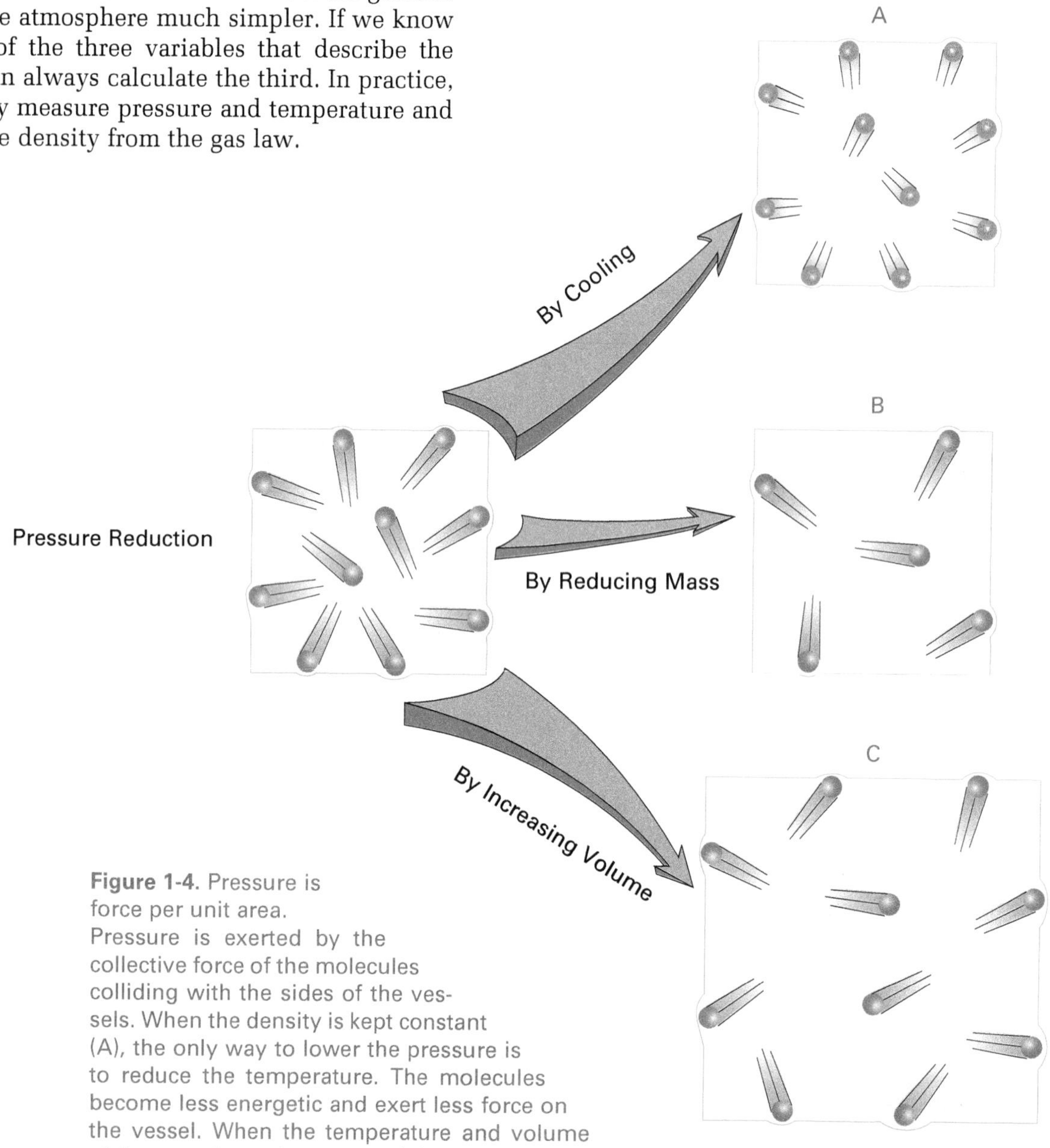

Figure 1-4. Pressure is force per unit area. Pressure is exerted by the collective force of the molecules colliding with the sides of the vessels. When the density is kept constant (A), the only way to lower the pressure is to reduce the temperature. The molecules become less energetic and exert less force on the vessel. When the temperature and volume of the vessel remain constant (B), the pressure can only be reduced by removing gas. Although the molecules remain energetic, there are fewer of them, so the force they exert on the sides of the vessel is reduced. When the temperature and mass of the molecules in the vessel remain the same (C), the pressure can only be lowered by increasing the volume of the vessel. The molecules then exert their collective force over a larger area.

Section C
ATMOSPHERIC STRUCTURE

The brief introduction to the atmospheric composition and the gas law has provided you with some useful vocabulary and some simple physics to examine the structure of the atmosphere.

DIMENSIONS

In much of the material in this and later chapters, we will be concerned with the size of the atmosphere and its phenomena. "How big? How high? How far?" are common questions asked in regard to atmospheric description. In order to keep distances and altitudes in a meaningful context, it is helpful to have some "measuring sticks" for reference. Some of the most useful are the dimensions of the earth. (Figure 1-5)

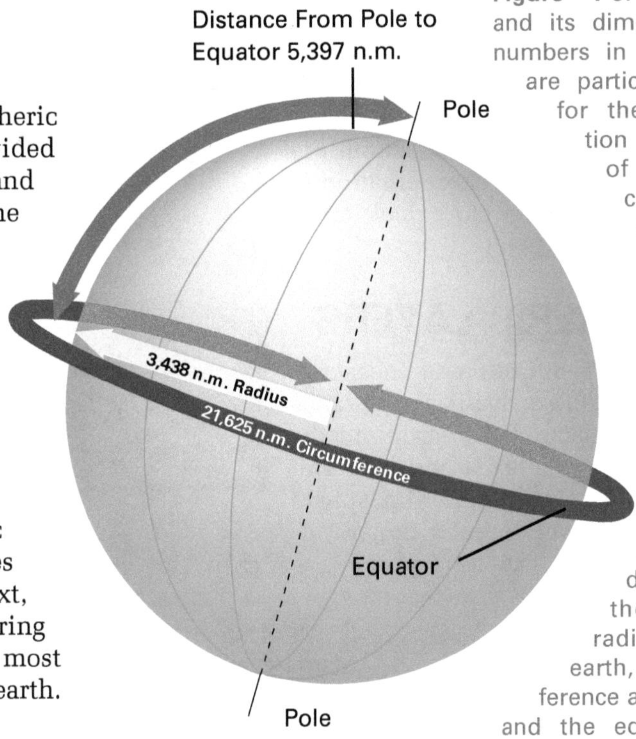

Distance From Pole to Equator 5,397 n.m.

Pole

3,438 n.m. Radius

21,625 n.m. Circumference

Equator

Pole

Figure 1-5. The earth and its dimensions. The numbers in the diagram are particularly useful for the determination of the sizes of atmospheric circulation systems such as the large cyclones that move across the earth's surface. The figure shows the most frequently referenced dimensions: the average radius of the earth, the circumference at the equator, and the equator-to-pole distance.

The units used in this text are those commonly used in aviation meteorology in the United States. These are given below with some useful conversions. Note: stated values are rounded. An expanded table suitable for international conversions is given in Appendix A.

LENGTH
1 degree of latitude
  = 60 n.m.
  = 69 s.m.
  = 111 km
1 nautical mile (n.m.)
  = 1/60 degree of latitude
  = 6,080 ft
  = 1.15 s.m.
  = 1.85 km
  = 1852 m
1 statute mile (s.m.)
  = 5,280 ft
  = 0.87 n.m.
  = 1.61 km = 1609 m
1 foot (ft)
  = 12 in
  = 30.5 cm
  = 0.305 m

AREA
1 square foot (ft^2)
  = 144 in^2
  = 0.093 m^2

SPEED
1 knot (kt)
  = 1 n.m. per hour
  = 1.15 s.m. per hour
  = 101 fpm
  = 0.51 mps
  = 1.85 kph
1 mile per hour (mph)
  = 1 s.m. per hour
  = 0.87 kt
  = 0.45 mps
  = 1.61 kph

VOLUME
1 cubic foot (ft^3)
  = 1728 in^3
  = .028 m^3

PRESSURE
1 standard atmosphere
  = 29.92 in. Hg.
  = 1013.25 mb
  = 1013.25 hPa
  = 14.7 lbs/in^2
1 inch of mercury (in. Hg.)
  = 0.491 lbs/in^2
  = 33.864 mb (hPa)
1 millibar (mb)
  = 1 hPa
  = 0.0295 in. Hg.

The strong influence of gravity causes the vertical dimension of the atmosphere to be much less than the horizontal dimension. (Figure 1-7) This effect causes temperature, density, and pressure to vary much more rapidly in the vertical direction than in the horizontal direction. For this reason, we begin our examination of the atmosphere with a close look at its "typical" vertical structure.

ATMOSPHERIC LAYERS

An important specification of the atmosphere is its thickness; that is, the distance between the surface of the earth and the "top" of the atmosphere. Although technically considered a fluid, the atmosphere does not have a well-defined upper surface as does water. The atmosphere is a highly

Figure 1-7. A view of the atmosphere from space. The colored layers show where air molecules and/or particulates are of sufficient density to scatter light from the sun. Note the relatively small vertical dimension of the layers compared to their great horizontal dimensions (Photo courtesy of Lunar and Planetary Institute, NASA photo.)

compressible fluid, so it just "fades away" with increasing altitude.

We can, however, consider an approximate "top" based on the density of the atmosphere. The density at an altitude of 164,000 feet (about 27 n.m.) is only about one-thousandth of the sea level density. In terms of the total mass of the atmosphere, 99.9% of the mass lies below that altitude. (Figure 1-6) Therefore, this altitude is close to the "top." Note that, in comparison to the circumference of the earth (21,625 n.m.), 27 n.m. is a very small distance. We conclude that the atmosphere is a very thin layer compared to its horizontal extent, analogous to the skin of an apple. Figure 1-7 gives a view from space that dramatically illustrates this characteristic.

TEMPERATURE LAYERS

To further analyze the atmosphere, we can build a reference model by dividing the envelope of gases into layers with similar properties. By far, the most common model of atmospheric structure is one which divides the atmosphere into layers according to the way that temperature changes with altitude. (Figure 1-8)

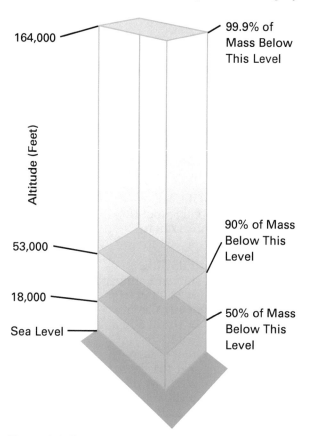

Figure 1-6. Total atmospheric mass below specific altitudes.

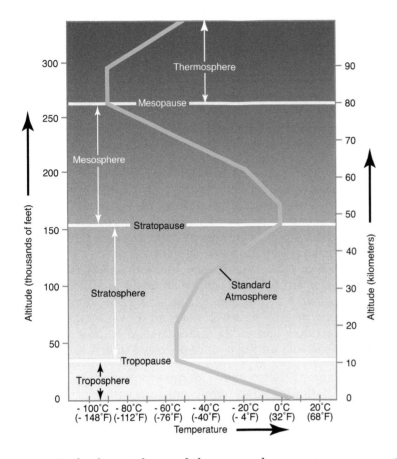

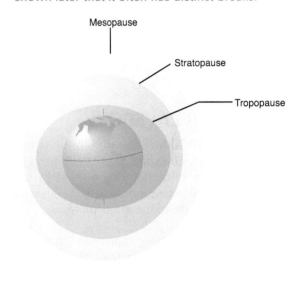

Figure 1-8. Vertical distribution of temperature in the atmosphere. Note that the layer depths around the globe on the right have been greatly exaggerated for clarity. Also, in this simple model, the tropopause is continuous from pole to equator. It will be shown later that it often has distinct breaks.

In the lowest layer of the atmosphere, or troposphere, the average temperature decreases with altitude. The great majority of the clouds and weather occurs in the troposphere.

The top of the troposphere is about 36,000 feet above mean sea level (MSL) in middle latitudes. This upper boundary (a level, not a layer) is known as the tropopause. The tropospheric temperatures often reach a minimum value at this altitude. The tropopause is a very important atmospheric feature for pilots because of its connection to a variety of weather phenomena such as jet streams, clear air turbulence, thunderstorms, and high clouds. The altitude of the tropopause varies with latitude and season. It is lower near the poles and in winter; it is higher near the equator and in summer.

As we move upward from the tropopause into the stratosphere, temperature tends to change slowly at first and then increase with altitude. As evidenced by the name of the layer, air in the stratosphere is confined to move more or less horizontally in "strata" or layers. In contrast, in the troposphere (from the word, trope, meaning "turn" or "change"), there are often strong vertical air motions. We will see in a later chapter that the "stability" of the stratosphere and "instability" of the troposphere are related directly to the variation of temperature with altitude in those layers.

At the top of the stratosphere is the stratopause. It occurs at an altitude of about 160,000 feet MSL. The temperature reaches a maximum value at this height. Immediately above is the mesosphere, a layer where the temperature again decreases with height. The mesosphere extends to a height of slightly more than 280,000 feet MSL, where the mesopause and the coldest temperatures in the diagram are located.

The highest layer in our model atmosphere is the thermosphere. Temperatures generally increase with altitude in this layer. However, the meaning of air temperature is not so clear. The number of air molecules is so small at these very high levels that an "average" kinetic energy of the air molecules doesn't have much meaning. Objects in space at such heights have temperatures that are more closely related to radiation gain on the sun-facing side of the object and radiation loss on the opposite side.

OTHER LAYERS

Figure 1-9 shows the distributions of ozone and ion concentrations with altitude. These curves illustrate other atmospheric layer designations that are also commonly used to describe the vertical structure of the atmosphere.

The ozone layer, sometime called the "ozonosphere," is found in the lower stratosphere. It is characterized by a relatively high concentration of O_3 with maximum concentrations near 80,000 feet MSL. The temperature maximum near the stratopause is due to the absorption of solar radiation by the ozone. (Figure 1-8)

The ozone hole is a region of the ozone layer with lower-than-normal O_3 concentration. It is especially noticeable over the South Pole in spring months (September–December). The ozone hole is created when pollutants, such as man-made chlorofluorocarbons (CFCs), reach stratospheric levels. Solar radiation at those altitudes is intense enough to break the CFCs down so that the chlorine is free to destroy ozone molecules.

The ionosphere is a deep layer of charged particles (ions and free electrons) that extends from the lower mesosphere upward through the thermosphere. (Figure 1-8) The production of charged particles occurs at those altitudes because incoming solar radiation has sufficient energy to strip electrons from atoms and molecules. AM radio waves are reflected and/or absorbed by different sublayers of the ionosphere. Radio communications may be greatly influenced by variations in the lower part of the ionosphere at sunrise and sunset and during periods of greater solar activity.

Figure 1-9 also shows a curve representing the variation of atmospheric pressure with altitude. An important characteristic of pressure is that it always decreases with altitude. This property

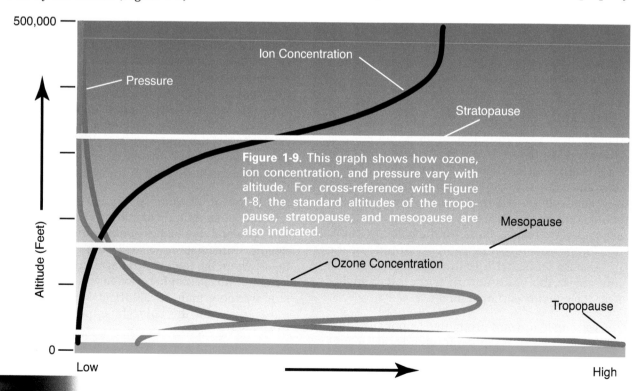

Figure 1-9. This graph shows how ozone, ion concentration, and pressure vary with altitude. For cross-reference with Figure 1-8, the standard altitudes of the tropopause, stratopause, and mesopause are also indicated.

is used to determine aircraft altitude from atmospheric pressure, an important topic of Chapter 3.

Another notable feature of the pressure curve is the rapid decrease in pressure just above the ground and the very gradual decrease at the higher levels. This further demonstrates the compressibility of the atmosphere and the lack of a well-defined upper surface as discussed earlier.

There are several important physiological effects related to flight at high levels because of the decrease in pressure with altitude. The concentration of oxygen in the mixture of atmospheric gases is proportional to total atmospheric pressure. Oxygen concentration therefore decreases with height in the same manner as total pressure. These decreases in pressure and oxygen concentrations with altitude are the basis for the following requirements and recommendations for aircrew and passengers:

For un-pressurized aircraft:

1. Supplemental breathing oxygen is recommended for cabin pressure altitudes above 10,000 feet MSL during the day and 5,000 feet MSL at night.

2. Supplemental oxygen is required for the required minimum flight crew for cabin pressure altitudes above 12,500 feet MSL up to and including 14,000 feet (MSL) on flights of more than 30 minutes duration.

3. At cabin pressure altitudes above 14,000 feet MSL, the required minimum flight crew is required to use suplemental oxygen.

4. At cabin pressure altitudes above 15,000 feet MSL, each occupant of the aircraft must be provided with supplemental oxygen.

> Oxygen is recomended at lower altitudes at night because night vision is affected by a decreased oxygen supply (hypoxia).

For pressurized aircraft:

5. A 10-minute supplemental oxygen supply is required for all aircraft occupants above a flight level of 25,000 feet (FL 250) in case of loss of cabin pressurization.

6. Above a flight level of 35,000 feet (FL 350), one pilot must wear an oxygen mask at all times.

7. For high altitude flights:

8. In an unpressurized environment above approximately 40,000 feet, supplemental oxygen must be supplied under pressure.

9. In an unpressurized environment, the pressure exerted by gases escaping from body fluids exceeds the atmospheric pressure at approximately 63,000 feet. This means the bodily fluids will vaporize. The pilot of an unpressurized aircraft must wear a full pressure suit above 50,000 feet MSL.

> In the lower troposphere, pressure decreases about one inch of mercury (about 34 mb) for each thousand feet of altitude gain.

Similar to pressure, the vertical distribution of atmospheric density doesn't really lend itself to precise layer classifications. In general, density decreases with height, reflecting our earlier observations that most of the mass of the atmosphere is concentrated in the lowest layers. Density is, nonetheless, important in aviation applications. Aircraft performance is directly dependent on the mass of the atmosphere and that performance degrades when the density is low. This is clearly the case at high levels in the atmosphere. But you don't have to fly at stratospheric levels to experience problems due to lower-than-normal density. There are situations when density is critically low near the ground because of very high surface temperatures. An expanded discussion of the effects of these conditions and the concept and use of density altitude is presented in Chapter 3.

STANDARD ATMOSPHERE

The standard atmosphere, also called the international standard atmosphere (ISA), is an idealized atmosphere with specific vertical distributions of pressure, temperature, and density prescribed by international agreement. The standard atmosphere is used for several aerospace applications, not the least of which is determining altitude from pressure altimeters (Chapter 3). The ISA for the lower stratosphere and troposphere is shown graphically in figure 1-10. In the remaining text,

In the ISA troposphere, the temperature decreases 2C° for each 1,000-foot increase in altitude.

we will focus most of our attention on these lowest layers of the atmosphere where the majority of aircraft operations take place.

It is helpful to keep in mind that, although the ISA is a useful tool for aviation, there are large variations from standard conditions in the real atmosphere. The standard atmosphere is most representative of average mid-latitude conditions, at least in the troposphere and lower stratosphere. As shown in figure 1-10, the troposphere is actually colder and the tropopause is lower than ISA over the poles and, respectively, warmer and higher than ISA over the equator. As we describe the atmosphere and its variations in subsequent chapters, the standard atmosphere will serve as a helpful reference.

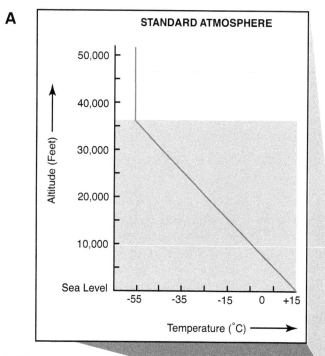

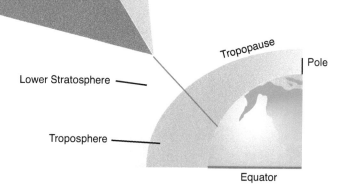

Figure 1-10. The standard atmosphere temperatures in the troposphere and lower stratosphere are plotted versus altitude in diagram A. Diagram B shows the variation of tropopause height between equator and pole. The line through the atmosphere in B indicates the standard atmosphere shown in diagram A is most representative of observed mid-latitude conditions. As in similar diagrams, the vertical dimension of the atmosphere is greatly exaggerated.

SUMMARY

In this chapter, you have started to build the background of basic concepts and vocabulary necessary for the study of aviation weather. You should now be aware of the average composition, structure, and dimensions of the atmosphere. What may have seemed at first to be a rather complicated picture has been simplified by constructing a "model" of the atmospheric structure based mainly on the variation of temperature and pressure with altitude and the effects of those variations on flight. It will soon be clear to the reader that atmospheric models will not only aid in learning and remembering basic atmospheric structures, but will also help the pilot anticipate the occurrence and consequences of many atmospheric phenomena.

KEY TERMS

Absolute Zero
Aerosols
Atmosphere
Carbon Dioxide
Density
Gas Law
International Standard Atmosphere (ISA)
Ionosphere
Kinetic Energy
Mesopause
Mesosphere
Nitrogen
Oxides of Nitrogen

Oxygen
Ozone
Ozone Hole
Ozone Layer
Particulates
Pressure
Stratopause
Stratosphere
Temperature
Thermosphere
Tropopause
Troposphere
Water Vapor

REVIEW QUESTIONS

1. Most clouds and weather occur in what atmospheric layer?

2. In the ISA, the tropopause is found at what altitude?

3. What is the ISA tropopause temperature?

4. You are flying an ER-2 at 65,000 feet. In which atmospheric layer(s) are you located?

5. If you were to fly directly from pole to equator at a groundspeed of 300 knots, how long would it take?

6. Using a reference that describes the ISA, determine the approximate altitudes where atmospheric pressure decreases to one-half and one-quarter of the sea level value.

7. What is the approximate atmospheric pressure at the top of Mt. Everest?

8. You have just taken off from an airport located at sea level. Conditions are exactly the same as prescribed by the International Standard Atmosphere. What will be your outside air temperature (OAT) at the following altitudes:

    1. 1,000 feet?
    2. 1,500 feet?
    3. 3,300 feet?
    4. 7,400 feet?
    5. 32,000 feet?

DISCOVERY QUESTIONS

9. A dry gas is in a closed vessel.

   1. What happens to the pressure of the gas if the density remains the same and the temperature goes up? Why?

   2. How do you keep the pressure inside a vessel constant when you increase the temperature? Why?

   3. How do you decrease the pressure and keep the density constant? Why?

10. You place an empty, one-gallon aluminum can in the unheated cargo compartment of your aircraft. Just before closing the compartment, you place an airtight seal on the can. After takeoff, you climb from sea level to 10,000 feet MSL for the cruise portion of your flight. Your aircraft is unpressurized. What happens to the can? Why?

11. Find a book or manual that deals with the physiology of flight and look up the definitions of "anoxia" and "hypoxia."

    1. What are typical symptoms of hypoxia?

    2. How long can one typically operate without supplementary oxygen at 15,000 feet MSL? 20,000 feet MSL? 30,000 feet MSL?

12. What is the potential impact of supersonic flight on the ozone layer?

13. What is the potential impact of flight in the ozone layer on the pilot of an aircraft?

14. In October 2012, a parachutist jumped from a balloon at an altitude of approximately 124,000 feet. Describe his descent in terms of his meteorological environment (pressure, temperature, density, ozone) and its potential physiological effects.

CHAPTER 2

Atmospheric Energy and Temperature

Introduction

In this chapter, we continue to build a basic reference model of the atmosphere. Now we turn our attention to the energy that drives the atmosphere. Of particular interest is the source of atmospheric energy (the sun). We are interested in the details of energy exchange and resulting atmospheric temperatures. These pieces of information are important parts of the foundation of your understanding of winds and weather.

When you complete this chapter, you will understand important sun-earth relationships and their seasonal and daily variations, modes of energy transfer between the sun and the earth, and between the earth and the atmosphere. You will also learn some practical aspects of measuring temperature and details of global temperature patterns.

Section A

ENERGY TRANSFER

The atmospheric "system" that was briefly described in Chapter 1 operates much like a heat engine. Solar energy enters the system and undergoes a series of energy conversions, finally producing winds, clouds, and precipitation. In order for these processes to be sustained, heat energy must not only be transferred from the sun, but must also be redistributed within the atmosphere. That supply and redistribution is accomplished by three energy transfer processes:

Radiation is the transfer of energy by electromagnetic waves.

Conduction is the transfer of energy through molecular motion.

Convection/Advection refers to the transfer of energy through the movement of mass.

In meteorology, we commonly reserve the term "convection" for vertical movements of the atmosphere and "advection" for horizontal movements. There are other processes that also account for the transfer of heat energy that are explained in later chapters. These include the absorption and release of heat associated with evaporation

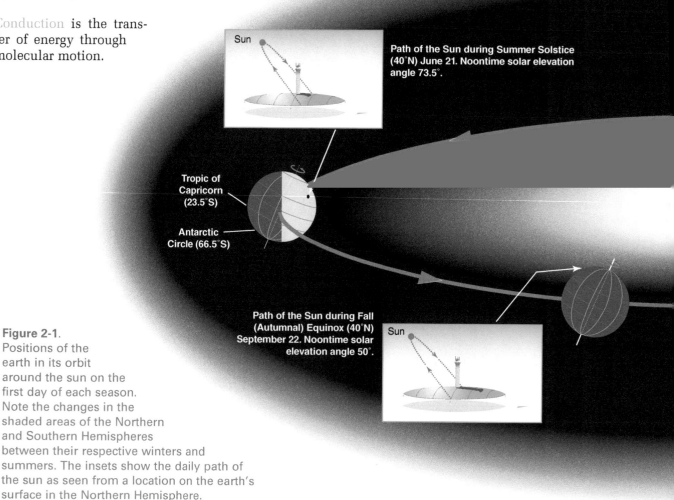

Sun

Path of the Sun during Summer Solstice (40°N) June 21. Noontime solar elevation angle 73.5°.

Tropic of Capricorn (23.5°S)

Antarctic Circle (66.5°S)

Path of the Sun during Fall (Autumnal) Equinox (40°N) September 22. Noontime solar elevation angle 50°.

Sun

Figure 2-1.
Positions of the earth in its orbit around the sun on the first day of each season. Note the changes in the shaded areas of the Northern and Southern Hemispheres between their respective winters and summers. The insets show the daily path of the sun as seen from a location on the earth's surface in the Northern Hemisphere.

and condensation, and the storage and movement of heat by ocean currents.

SOLAR RADIATION

Conduction and convection/advection require mass for energy transfer; therefore, the transfer of energy from the sun across nearly empty space must be accomplished by radiation. In free space, the solar radiation intercepted by the earth is nearly constant over the cross sectional area of the planet, but once it reaches the surface, the amount received varies widely with time and location. Much of the latter variation is due to the shape of the earth and its position relative to the sun; that is, to sun-earth geometry. (Figure 2-1)

SUN-EARTH GEOMETRY

The intensity of solar radiation received at any one point on the earth's surface depends on the location of the sun relative to that point. That location depends on:

1. **Time of day** The earth rotates on its axis once every 24 hours.

2. **Time of year.** The earth orbits the sun once every 365.25 days.

3. **Latitude.** The axis of the earth is tilted 23.5° to the plane of its orbit about the sun.

The geometry of these controls is summarized in figure 2-1. The basic day-night variation in radiation is due to the rotation of the earth each day. But the lengths of the days and nights are not usually equal. The orbit of the earth causes each pole to be tilted toward the sun during half the year and away from the sun during the other half. This causes a variation of the length of the day at each earth latitude. At noon on the first days of spring and fall (the equinoxes), the sun's rays are perpendicular to the earth's surface at the equator.

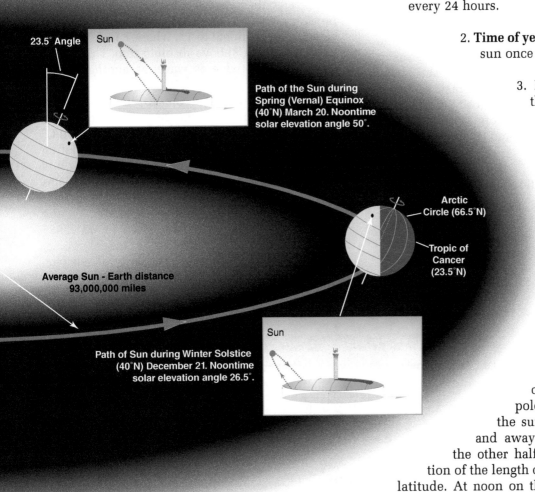

23.5° Angle

Sun

Path of the Sun during Spring (Vernal) Equinox (40°N) March 20. Noontime solar elevation angle 50°.

Arctic Circle (66.5°N)

Tropic of Cancer (23.5°N)

Average Sun - Earth distance 93,000,000 miles

Sun

Path of Sun during Winter Solstice (40°N) December 21. Noontime solar elevation angle 26.5°.

On these dates, the length of daylight is the same (12 hours) everywhere on earth.

On the first day of summer and the first day of winter (the solstices), the noonday sun reaches its highest and lowest latitudes, respectively. The longest day of the year is at summer solstice and the shortest day is at winter solstice. North of 66.5° north latitude (Arctic Circle) and south of 66.5° south latitude (Antarctic Circle) there is at least one day when the sun does not rise and one day when it does not set. This effect reaches a maximum at the poles where there are six months of darkness and six months of light. The low sun angles produce unique visibility hazards at high latitudes.

The influence of the changing position of the sun relative to the earth is illustrated in terms of the solar elevation angle (angle of the sun above the horizon) in figure 2-2. If that angle is small, solar energy is spread over a broad surface area, minimizing heating. This condition is typical near sunrise and sunset, and at high latitudes, especially in winter.

When the solar elevation angle is large, solar energy is concentrated in a smaller area, maximizing heating. These conditions are typical at noon, in the summer, and at low latitudes. In

fact, the noon elevation angle will reach 90° (the sun is directly overhead) twice during the year between latitudes 23.5° north (Tropic of Cancer) and 23.5° south (Tropic of Capricorn).

RADIATION PROCESSES

You were introduced to the concept of absolute zero in Chapter 1. Absolute zero is the temperature where all molecular motion ceases. It is also an important reference point for the understanding of electromagnetic radiation. Electromagnetic energy radiates from any object that has a temperature above absolute zero. The higher the temperature, the greater the radiation. In fact, a basic law of physics is that the total radiation emitted from an object is proportional to T^4, where T is the object's temperature in C° above absolute zero. This means that an object twice as warm as another object will radiate 16 times (2^4) as much radiation. Two good examples of the application of this law are the earth and the sun. The sun has an effective radiating temperature of about 6000 C° above absolute zero while the earth's radiating temperature is only about 288 C° above absolute zero. Therefore, a unit area of the sun radiates 188,379 times the energy of the same area on the cooler earth ($6000^4/288^4$ = 188,379) and, of course, the sun's total surface area is much larger than the earth's.

Radiated energy travels at a speed of 186,000 statute miles per second (about 300,000 kilometers per second) in a vacuum.

Figure 2-2. The influence of solar elevation angle (*e*) on the concentration of energy received at the surface. Light beams indicate parallel rays of energy from the sun near the equinox. While the same amounts of solar energy strike the earth at the equator and near the pole, that energy is spread over a much larger surface area near the pole (small solar elevation angle) than at the equator (large solar elevation angle).

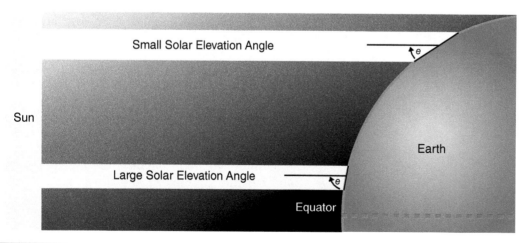

The noontime solar elevation angle (e) for a station at latitude L is given by the following equation.

$$e = 90 - (L - L_p)$$

Where L_p is the solar declination; that is, the latitude where the noon sun is directly overhead. For example, on the first day of Northern Hemisphere summer, the noon sun is overhead at 23.5° north. On that date, the noontime solar elevation angle at Denver (40° north) is

$$e = 90 - (40 - 23.5) = 73.5°$$

On the first day of Northern Hemisphere winter, Denver will have a noontime solar elevation angle of

$$e = 90 - (40 - [-23.5*]) = 90 - (40 + 23.5) = 26.5°$$

*Note: This formula will work for either hemisphere, but if L_p is in the opposite hemisphere from L, then L_p must be negative.

This speed is often referred to as the speed of light even though light is just one of many types of electromagnetic radiation.

In many respects, electromagnetic radiation behaves as collection of waves, each with different characteristics. You may have observed similar combinations of waves in other situations. When observing the surface of the ocean, for example, it is easy to visualize the motion of a particular patch of water as being influenced by a number of distinct waves, all of which are present at the same time. There may be very long swells combined with shorter waves caused by the wind, the passage of a ship, or by the presence of a pier.

With regard to electromagnetic radiation, if you have seen the separation of a beam of white light into its respective colors (red through blue), then you have seen the individual wave components of white light. Each color that makes up the white light may be uniquely described in terms of a wave. Terminology that we use to describe waves is reviewed in figure 2-3.

The speed of any simple wave (c) is related to frequency and wavelength as

$$c = f \times L.$$

With electromagnetic energy, we are fortunate because c is the speed of light. Since it is a constant, we can describe the characteristics of an electromagnetic wave in terms of either wavelength or frequency; that is, given one, the other can always be determined.

Applying these ideas to visible radiation, red light has relatively long wavelengths and low frequencies. Frequencies lower than red are called infrared (IR). Blue light has relatively short wavelengths and high frequencies. Frequencies higher than blue are called ultraviolet (UV).

Figure 2-3. This diagram represents a train of waves on a rope tied to a fixed object. A person standing at the other end of the rope has put wave energy into the rope by moving it vertically. The waves are moving from left to right. Wavelength (L) is the distance between two successive, identical wave features, such as two wave crests. Wave amplitude (A) is half the distance between the lowest and highest points of the wave. The wave frequency (f) is the number of waves that pass some fixed point (for example, point "P") in a given time interval. Units of frequency are cycles per second (cps) or Hertz (Hz).

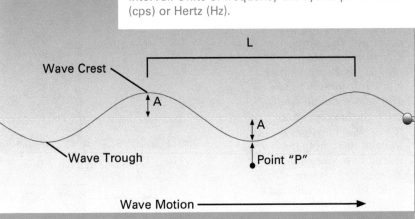

The amplitude (A) of a wave is related to the energy of the wave. To be precise, wave energy is proportional to the square of the amplitude (A^2) of the wave. A useful diagram to illustrate the energy of electromagnetic radiation is a spectrum; that is, a graph of electromagnetic wave energy (A^2) for all electromagnetic waves versus their wavelength. Two examples of energy spectra are shown in figure 2-4.

As we saw earlier, the total energy radiated by any object is proportional to T^4. This property is illustrated in figure 2-4. The areas under the "sun" curve on the left and the "earth" curve on the right are each proportional to the energy emitted by those bodies. The radiation from the sun is hundreds of thousands of times greater than that from the earth.

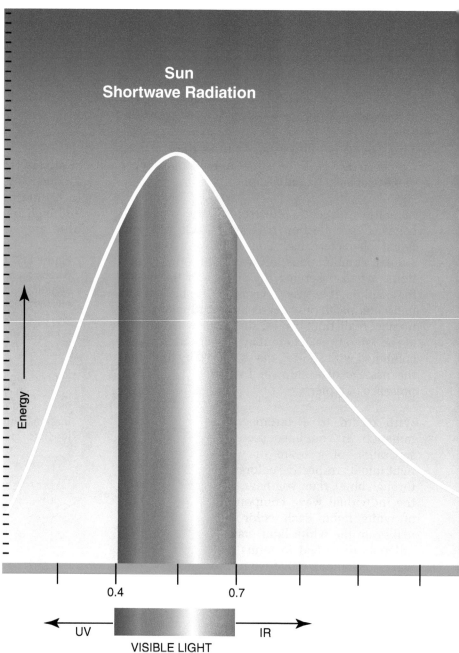

Figure 2-4. Spectra of radiation for the sun and the earth. Note that, in comparison to the solar spectrum, the earth's spectrum has been greatly expanded so that it is large enough to see. The values on the energy scale for the earth are much less than that of the sun. Also note that the earth's spectrum has its maximum energy at much longer wavelengths than that of the sun.

A perfect radiating body emits energy in all possible wavelengths, but the wave energies are not emitted equally in all wavelengths; a spectrum will show a distinct maximum in energy at a particular wavelength depending on the temperature of the radiating body. As the temperature increases, the maximum radiation occurs at shorter and shorter wavelengths. For example, as shown in figure 2-4, the maximum energy radiated in the solar spectrum is at significantly shorter (visible) wavelengths with a large contribution in the UV region. The maximum in the terrestrial spectrum is at longer wavelengths, well into the IR region.

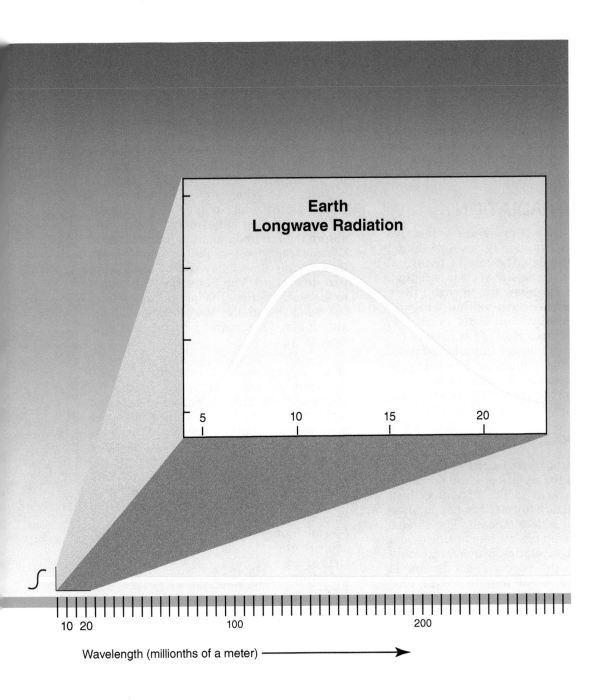

Earth Longwave Radiation

Wavelength (millionths of a meter) ⟶

These properties of solar and terrestrial radiation are important in explaining many temperature variations that occur in the atmosphere. As solar energy enters the earth's atmosphere, nearly 20% is absorbed by the atmospheric gases and clouds. Additionally, there is a loss of approximately 30% of the incoming solar radiation due to reflection and scattering by clouds and other particulates and reflection from the earth's surface. This loss is called the albedo of the earth and its atmosphere. The remaining solar radiation is absorbed by the earth. (Figure 2-5)

The earth's surface then becomes the primary energy source for the atmosphere. Energy is transferred from the earth to the atmosphere by the processes of terrestrial radiation, conduction, convection/advection, evaporation, and the loss of water vapor from plants (transpiration). As we discussed earlier in this chapter, the transfer of heat through evaporation will be covered in Chapter 6.

TERRESTRIAL RADIATION

Because the earth has a temperature well above absolute zero, it is continually losing infrared radiation. During the day, the loss of terrestrial radiation is offset by the receipt of solar radiation, so the temperature increases. But at night, there is no solar input and the earth continues to radiate, cooling significantly. This daily or diurnal variation in the temperature of the surface of the earth is critical in producing important day-to-night changes in wind, ceiling, and visibility. In later chapters on weather hazards, we will also see how radiative processes near the earth's surface can contribute to the production of frost on aircraft wings and to the development of strong low-level wind shear.

An important control of surface temperature is the heat capacity of the surface (ground or water). In general, heat capacity is the amount of heat energy that is necessary to raise the temperature of a substance by a certain amount. The surface of the earth is made up of a variety of substances with different heat capacities which cause substantial temperature differences. A good example is water, which has about four times the heat capacity of typical dry soil. The ability of water to absorb large amounts of solar energy is further increased because radiation can penetrate to a greater depth in water than in soil and, because water can mix easily, the energy is spread around.

This means that if equal amounts of solar radiation fall on equal areas of water and soil, for example along a coastline, the water temperature increases much more slowly than the nearby land temperature. At night, the water, with its great reservoir of heat, cools more slowly than the land. The resulting land-sea temperature differences in both of these cases are crucial in understanding diurnal wind patterns such as sea and land breezes. These types of breezes will be covered in Chapter 4.

The temperature near the earth's surface also depends on other properties of the surface. For example, snow reflects a large fraction of incoming solar radiation and gives up infrared radiation easily; these influences help keep the temperatures low over snow surfaces under clear skies.

Terrestrial radiation behaves differently than solar radiation because it is emitted in the infrared portion of the spectrum. (Figure 2-4) Whereas the atmosphere is highly transparent to much of the solar radiation, certain atmospheric gases easily absorb the infrared radiation from the earth. When these gases are present, they absorb then reemit the energy, part upward and part downward. The IR energy that returns to the earth reduces the loss of energy from the surface and the lowest layers of the atmosphere, maintaining higher temperatures there.

One of the most important of these IR-absorbing gases is water vapor. An example of the influence of water vapor on nighttime cooling is seen in the differences between summertime overnight lows in the humid Southeastern U.S. and the drier West. Although daytime highs may be the same in both locations, nighttime minimum temperatures are often 20 F° or more higher in the Southeast because of the large amounts of water vapor in the air. The presence of clouds at night increases the capture of infrared radiation, further restricting nighttime cooling.

Figure 2-5. The source of energy for the atmosphere is the sun. Only about 51% of the energy striking the top of the atmosphere is actually absorbed at the earth's surface. The solar radiation scattered and reflected into space (30%) is the earth's albedo.

The capture of terrestrial radiation by certain atmospheric gases is called the greenhouse effect, and the gases are called greenhouse gases. Like a greenhouse, once the energy is in the atmosphere, its escape is hindered. The concern over global warming is based upon measured increases of greenhouse gases due to natural and man-made pollutants such as carbon dioxide, methane, and chlorofluorocarbons (CFCs).

CONDUCTION

You have probably experienced the effects of conduction when you have left a spoon in a bowl of hot soup. The energetic molecules in the hot end of the spoon transfer their momentum to the molecules in the cool end of the spoon. As a result, hotter temperatures are conducted up the handle.

Mass is required for conduction, whereas it is not required for radiation.

Since air is a poor conductor, the most significant energy transfer by conduction in the atmosphere occurs at the earth's surface. At night, the ground cools because of radiation; the cold ground then conducts heat away from the air immediately in contact with the ground. During the day, solar radiation heats the ground which heats the air next to it by conduction. These processes are very important in the production of a variety of weather phenomena, including wind, fog, low clouds, and convection.

CONVECTION/ADVECTION

If we were to depend on solar and terrestrial radiation alone for all energy transfer, the earth and atmosphere would become extremely cold in the polar regions and extremely hot near the equator. Fortunately, advection and convection (including the transport of water vapor and its latent heat), and the transfer of heat by ocean currents compensate for the unequal distribution of radiant energy. Advection includes the north-south movements of large warm and cold air masses. Convection includes the large scale ascent and descent of air masses and the smaller scale development of thunderstorms. These topics are examined closely in later chapters.

The most obvious effects of the sun's energy are seen in the distribution of temperatures within the atmosphere.

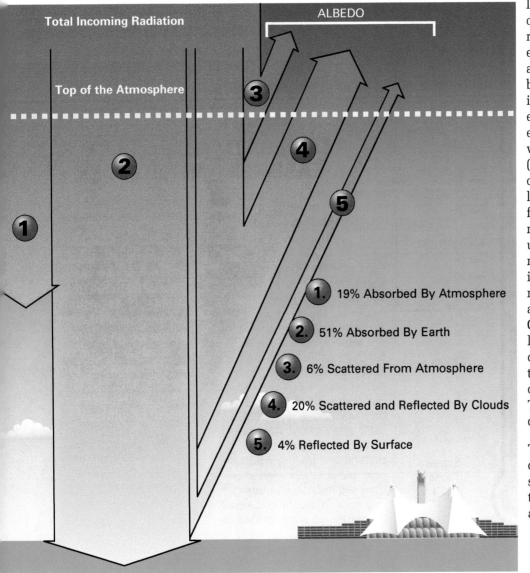

Total Incoming Radiation

ALBEDO

Top of the Atmosphere

1. 19% Absorbed By Atmosphere
2. 51% Absorbed By Earth
3. 6% Scattered From Atmosphere
4. 20% Scattered and Reflected By Clouds
5. 4% Reflected By Surface

Section B

TEMPERATURE

In this section, after a brief introduction to common temperature scales, measurements, and terminology, we examine the global patterns of tropospheric temperatures.

TEMPERATURE SCALES

Temperature scales common to aviation are Fahrenheit (°F) and Celsius (°C). Figure 2-6 shows the relation of these scales to each other.

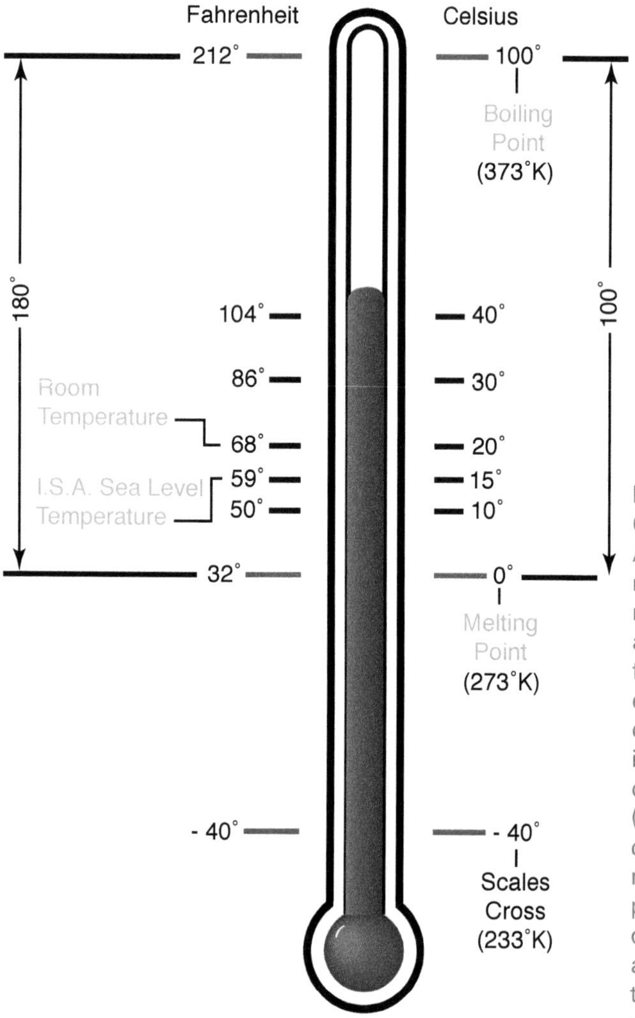

Conversions from Celsius to Fahrenheit are simple if you remember that there are 100 Celsius degrees and 180 Fahrenheit degrees between the melting and boiling points of water at sea level. Knowledge of that ratio, 100/180 or 5/9, and the one point on the scale where temperatures are the same (-40°C = -40°F) allows simple conversions.

$$(\{°C + 40\} \times 9/5) - 40 = °F$$

Example: T = 20°C = ?°F

$$(\{20°C + 40\} \times 9/5) - 40 = 68°F$$

Conversion from Fahrenheit to Celsius:

$$(\{°F + 40\} \times 5/9) - 40 = °C$$

Example: T = 23°F = ?°C

$$(\{23°F + 40\} \times 5/9) - 40 = -5°C$$

Note that both conversions are the same except the factor 9/5 (1.80) is used to convert from °C to °F and 5/9 (0.56) from °F to °C.

TEMPERATURE MEASUREMENTS

A temperature frequently referred to in meteorological applications is the surface air temperature (often called "surface temperature"). This is the temperature of the air measured at 1.5 meters (about 5 feet) above the ground. It is usually measured in a standard instrument shelter ("in the shade") to protect the thermometer from direct solar radiation but allow the free ventilation of outside air. (Figure 2-7)

Other common temperatures used in aviation meteorology are those measured in the "free atmosphere;" that is,

Figure 2-6. Fahrenheit and Celsius temperature scales. Although the conversion formulae are the most direct connections between scales, there are several memory devices for quick estimates. Note for every change of 10 Celsius degrees, there is a corresponding change of 18 Fahrenheit degrees: (0°C + 10) = 10°C = (32°F + 18) = 50°F. Also note common reference points: melting and boiling points of pure water at sea level, standard sea level temperature, and room temperature. Kelvin temperatures are provided as a reference.

above the earth's surface. Such temperatures are usually identified as temperatures aloft, as upper air temperatures, or with reference to the height or pressure level where they are measured, such as "the 300 mb temperature at Miami."

Another aviation-related temperature measurement is indicated air temperature (IAT) which is the temperature of the air as measured by a temperature probe on the outside of an aircraft. Because of friction and heating by compression of the air along the leading edges of a moving aircraft, IAT is greater than the temperature of the surrounding (uncompressed) air. The heating effect increases with speed. At a true airspeed of 180 knots the temperature rise is approximately +4C°. At 500 knots, it is about +29C°. The outside air temperature (OAT) (also called the true air temperature (TAT)) is determined by correcting the measured or indicated air temperature for compression and friction heating. The actual correction depends on the design of the temperature probe and its location.

Temperature Sensor

Courtesy of NWS/NOAA

Figure 2-7. Instrument shelters are shown on the right for Automated temperature measurements. As illustrated in the lower left, upper air temperatures are commonly measured with instruments carried aloft by a sounding balloon.

Upper air temperatures are usually measured directly with freely rising, instrumented balloons (a sounding) or by aircraft. Temperature soundings are also made from weather satellites by relating temperature at various altitudes to measurements of radiant

Courtesy of NWS/NOAA

energy emitted from the earth, clouds, and various atmospheric gases.

In Chapter 6, which covers atmospheric moisture, you will be introduced to three other temperatures (wet bulb, dewpoint, and frostpoint) that will be useful in the explanation of fog, cloud, and precipitation formation.

GLOBAL TEMPERATURE DISTRIBUTION

In Chapter 1, the general features of temperature variations with height in the atmosphere were introduced (for example, troposphere, stratosphere, mesosphere, and thermosphere). Then we looked more closely at the standard atmosphere, a detailed model of the vertical temperature distribution. Now we expand our temperature model by considering another dimension, the horizontal distribution of average temperatures.

SURFACE TEMPERATURES

Figure 2-8 shows surface air temperatures around the world. Notable features of the diagrams are the large changes in temperature from January to July, and the large temperature decrease from the equator to the poles. These patterns are due largely to changes in solar elevation angle with latitude and season.

Ocean currents, land-sea differences, and the presence of mountains tend to modify the large-scale temperature patterns over some areas of the globe. For example, the surface air temperatures over continents are colder than nearby oceans in winter and warmer in summer. For example, the average temperature at Seattle, Washington, in January is 38°F while the average at Chicago, Illinois (which is actually farther south) is 26°F.

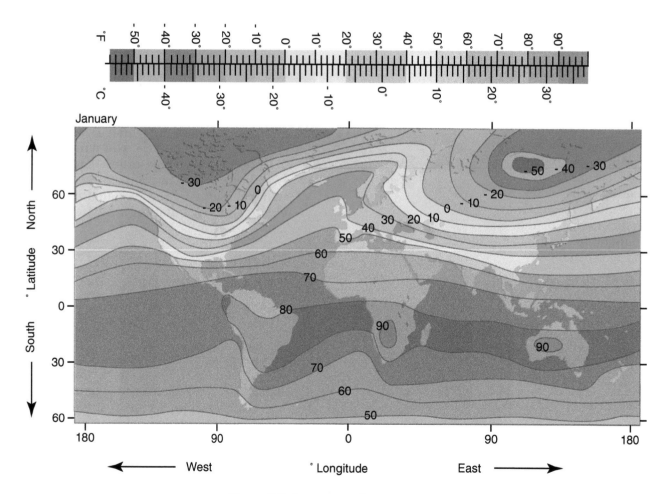

Figure 2-8. Average surface temperatures (°F) for the world, January (Left) and July (Right). The lines of equal temperature are called isotherms.

Other significant patterns in figure 2-8 are temperature gradients. A temperature gradient is defined as the change of temperature divided by the distance over which the change occurs. Where the isotherms are close together, gradients are relatively strong (large temperature change over a small distance). Notice that surface temperatures are not evenly distributed between the cold poles and the warm equator. The largest pole-to-equator temperature gradients occur in midlatitudes (30° to 60° N and S). Furthermore, these gradients are stronger in winter when the polar regions are in darkness. It will be seen that these abrupt transition zones between warm and cold air are favorite locations for the development of large storms.

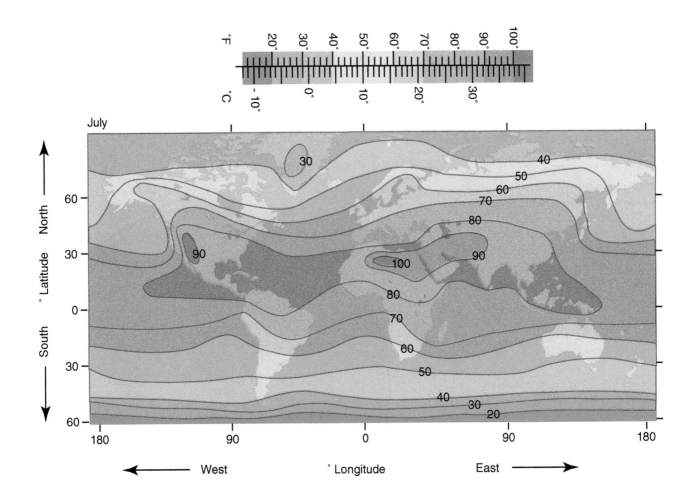

UPPER AIR TEMPERATURES

In the free atmosphere, the impact of the sun-earth geometry on the temperature distribution is large. However, as we move away from the earth, the direct influence of the heating and cooling of the surface becomes less obvious, especially above the tropopause. Advection, convection, and the absorption of radiation by ozone becomes more important in the determination of the temperature distribution. The result is that we see a more symmetrical temperature pattern with respect to the poles. Figure 2-9 illustrates the average horizontal distribution of Northern Hemisphere temperatures near 18,000 feet MSL (500 mb) in the mid-troposphere and near 53,000 feet MSL (100 mb) in the lower stratosphere for January and July. The seasonal variations of temperature shown here are reversed in the Southern Hemisphere.

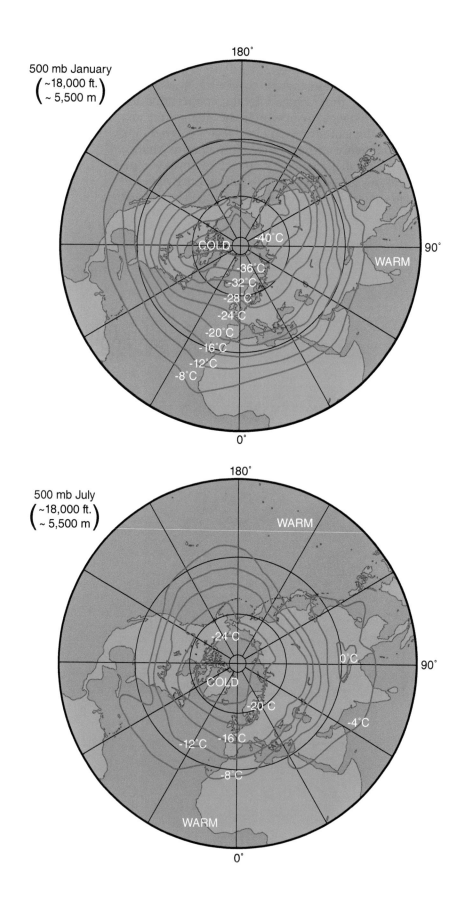

Figure 2-9. Left: Temperatures (°C) at 500 mb (about 18,000 feet, 5,500 meters MSL) for the Northern Hemisphere. Right: Temperatures (°C) at 100 mb (about 53,000 feet, 16,000 meters MSL) for the Northern Hemisphere. Relatively cold and warm regions are labeled.

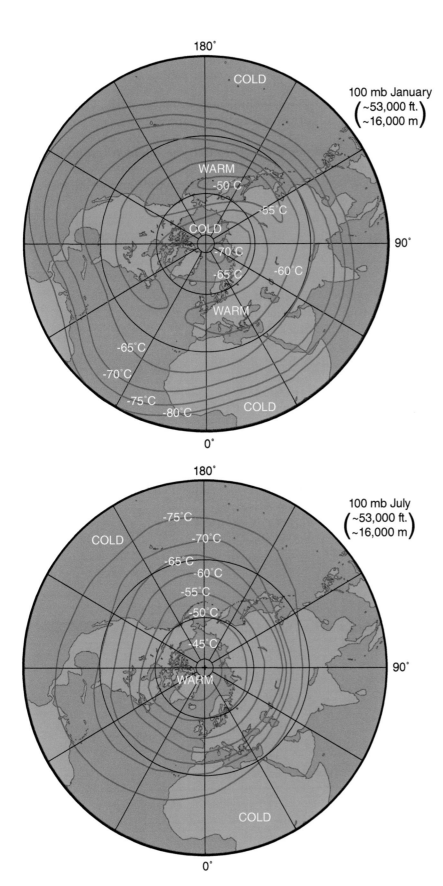

The Northern hemisphere temperature charts at 18,000 feet have features similar to the surface pattern in figure 2-8 (cold poles, warm equator) except, of course, the temperatures are colder aloft. As also expected, temperatures near 53,000 feet are much colder than surface and 500 mb air temperatures. However, there is another significant difference at 53,000 feet. In summer, the stratospheric equatorial temperatures are colder than polar temperatures at that level. The reason for this reversal in temperature pattern is related to the upward slope of the tropopause from the pole to the equator. At the pole, the tropopause is low and the 100 mb level (53,000 feet) is located well up into the warmer stratosphere. At the equator, the cold tropopause is much closer to 53,000 feet (figure 1-8).

As seen in the right-hand maps in figure 2-9, the winter 100 mb temperature pattern is a little more complicated than summer. Because the winter pole is in darkness, the absorption of solar radiation by ozone at that location is nil. The polar stratosphere cools significantly (compare summer and winter temperatures). The result is that *both* equatorial and polar regions are cold at 53,000 feet, while the mid-latitudes are relatively warm. These temperature patterns are important in explaining the characteristics of bands of strong winds (jet streams) found near the tropopause and in the stratosphere.

SUMMARY

The source of energy for the atmosphere is solar radiation. The variety of temperature patterns over the globe is partly the result of the tilt of the earth's axis, the rotation of the earth, and its orbit about the sun. Additionally, many physical processes redistribute heat energy in the atmosphere.

These include terrestrial radiation in the presence of certain radiation-absorbing gases, conduction, and convection/advection. In subsequent chapters we will see that these redistribution processes and resulting temperature patterns are the root causes of atmospheric winds and weather.

KEY TERMS

Absolute Zero
Advection
Albedo
Amplitude
Boiling Point
Celsius
Conduction
Convection
Diurnal Variation
Equinox
Fahrenheit
Frequency
Greenhouse Effect
Heat Capacity
Indicated Air Temperature (IAT)
Infrared (IR)
Melting Point
Outside Air Temperature (OAT)

Radiation
Room Temperature
Solar Declination
Solar Elevation Angle
Solstice
Sounding
Spectrum
Speed of Light
Standard Sea Level Temperature
Surface Air Temperature
Temperature Gradient
Terrestrial Radiation
True Air Temperature (TAT)
Ultraviolet (UV)
Upper Air Temperature
Wavelength

REVIEW QUESTIONS

1. Convert the following temperatures from °C to °F.
   1. -60
   2. -40
   3. -15
   4. 5
   5. 35

2. Convert the following from °F to °C.
   1. -453
   2. -100
   3. 0
   4. 25
   5. 113

3. Compute solar elevation on the first day of Northern Hemisphere winter for the following locations.
   1. Barrow, Alaska.
   2. Seattle, Washington.
   3. Brownsville, Texas.
   4. Mexico City, Mexico.
   5. Panama City, Panama.
   6. Melbourne, Australia.
   7. South Pole.

4. Repeat question number 3, but compute the solar elevation for the first day of the Northern Hemisphere fall (equinox).

5. About how long does it take radiation to reach the earth from the sun?

DISCOVERY QUESTIONS

6. In the next chapter, you will find that differences between ISA temperatures and actual temperatures cause errors in pressure altimeter readings. In order to get an idea of how different ISA can be from real conditions, examine figures 2-8 and 2-9 and determine the maximum positive and negative differences between ISA temperatures and the average temperatures across the globe for the following:

   1. Surface.

   2. 18,000 feet MSL (about 500 mb).

   3. 53,000 feet MSL (about 100 mb).

7. Use an ordinary thermometer to measure the air temperature at heights of 2 inches, 4 inches, 20 inches, and 5 feet above the ground on a hot afternoon (be sure the sun doesn't shine directly on the thermometer) and on a clear, calm night. Plot your results on a piece of graph paper. Contrast and explain the results.

8. On a clear, calm morning, just before sunrise, measure the temperature of the air about an inch above the top surface of the wing of a small aircraft. Note the height of the point of measurement above the ground. Move away from the airplane and measure the air temperature at the same level in the open. Explain the results.

9. The high temperatures at Boston, Massachusetts and at Boise, Idaho were both 85°F on a day where the weather was clear in both locations. The next morning, the low temperature at Boston was 78°F while the low at Boise was 53°F. These were again followed by identical highs of 85°F. There were no major weather changes during the period. Give a reasonable explanation for the temperature differences.

10. Verify that the conversion formulas in the inset on Page 2-10 can also be written as °C=5/9(°F-32) and °F=9/5°C+32

CHAPTER 3

Pressure, Altitude, and Density

Introduction

Pressure and its variations have important applications for aviation, ranging from measurements of altitude and airspeed to the prediction of winds and weather. This chapter focuses on several of these applications. When you complete the chapter, you will have a good physical understanding of atmospheric pressure, altimetry, and density altitude. Furthermore, you will develop important background knowledge about the global patterns of atmospheric pressure. This information will prove useful in the next chapter when we examine the causes and characteristics of atmospheric winds

SECTION A
ATMOSPHERIC PRESSURE

Pressure was defined generally in Chapter 1 as the force exerted by the vibrating molecules of the gas on a given area. This force arises because the molecules are moving about randomly at speeds proportional to their temperature above absolute zero. The pressure exerted by atmospheric gases has the same general meaning; however, because of a special circumstance in the atmosphere, there is an additional, more useful definition. Atmospheric pressure may also be defined as the weight of a column of the atmosphere with a given cross-sectional area. (Figure 3-1)

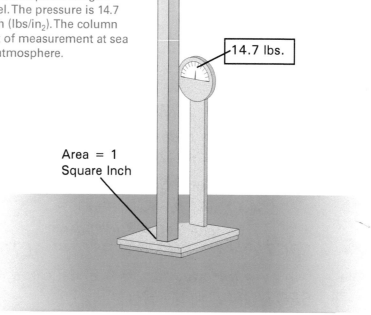

Figure 3-1. Atmospheric pressure as the weight of a single column of air. In the standard atmosphere, a one square inch column of air the height of the atmosphere weighs 14.7 pounds at sea level. The pressure is 14.7 pounds per square inch (lbs/in$_2$). The column extends from the point of measurement at sea level to the top of the atmosphere.

14.7 lbs.

Area = 1 Square Inch

$$\text{Atmospheric Pressure} = \frac{\text{Weight (Force)}}{\text{Area}} = \frac{14.7 \text{ lbs}}{1 \text{ in.}^2} = 14.7 \text{ lbs/in}^2$$

The special circumstance that permits this definition for the atmosphere is the balance between the downward-directed gravitational force and an upward-directed force caused by the decrease of atmospheric pressure with altitude. This is called hydrostatic balance and is illustrated in figure 3-2.

PRESSURE MEASUREMENTS

The definition of atmospheric pressure as the weight of a column of air per unit area is demonstrated nicely in the construction of

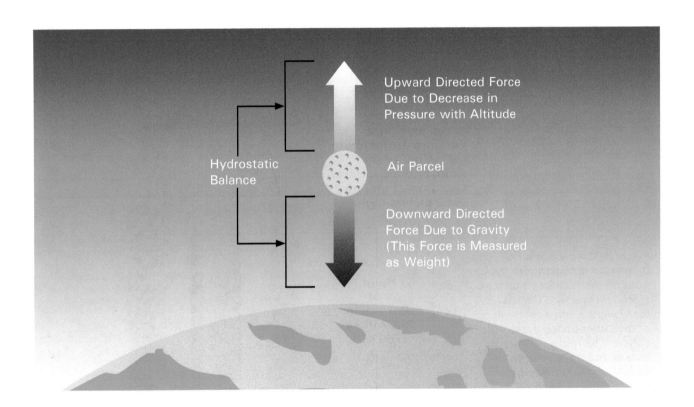

Figure 3-2. Hydrostatic balance. The air parcel resists any change in vertical movement because the forces acting on it tend to be equal and opposite. However, the parcel can still be accelerated horizontally under these circumstances.

one of the most basic devices for the measurement of pressure: the mercurial barometer. We measure atmospheric pressure similar to the way we determine the weight of an object on a familiar balance scale. The pressure (weight) of the atmosphere is balanced against the weight of the mercury. Appropriately, the word barometer is derived from the Greek word *baros* which means weight. As the weight of the atmosphere changes, the height of the mercury column also changes. (Figure 3-3)

Our examination of the structure of the mercurial barometer helps to explain why atmospheric pressure is commonly expressed in units of length (inches or millimeters of mercury) as well as the units of force per area (pounds per square inch [psi] or millibars [mb] or hectoPascals [hPa]). As seen in figure 3-3, "length" refers to the height of the top of the column of mercury above the surface of the mercury reservoir of the barometer. A sea level pressure of 14.7 lbs/in^2 will force the mercury to a height of 29.92 inches above the reference. Recall from Chapter 1 that pressure decreases about one inch of mercury per 1,000 feet. This means that the mercury column would be about 28.92 inches high at an altitude of 1,000 feet MSL.

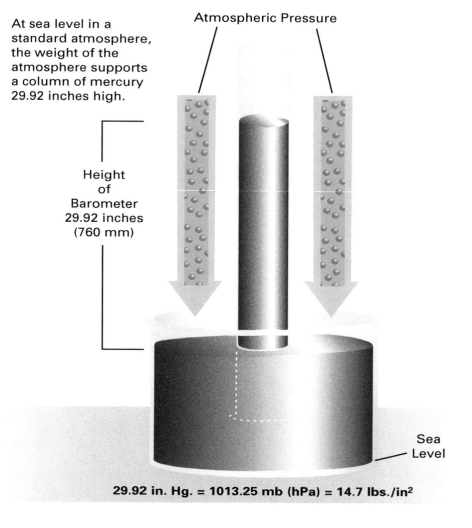

At sea level in a standard atmosphere, the weight of the atmosphere supports a column of mercury 29.92 inches high.

Atmospheric Pressure

Height of Barometer 29.92 inches (760 mm)

Sea Level

29.92 in. Hg. = 1013.25 mb (hPa) = 14.7 lbs./in^2

Figure 3-3. A mercurial barometer is constructed by pouring mercury into a tube closed on one end. The tube is then inverted into a reservoir of mercury open to the atmosphere. The mercury flows back out of the tube until the weight of the remaining mercury column is balanced by the pressure (weight) of the atmosphere over the mercury reservoir.

Liquids other than mercury can be used to construct barometers; however, mercury has the advantage of being very dense, which keeps the size of the barometer manageable. For example, a water barometer would have to be nearly 34 feet high to register standard sea level pressure.

Although it provides accurate measurements, the mercurial barometer is not very useful outside the observatory or laboratory. The instrument is fragile, it must be kept upright, and if the reservoir is ruptured, one must be concerned about the toxicity of mercury. For these reasons, another pressure instrument, known as the aneroid barometer, is more frequently used outside the laboratory. In contrast to the mercurial barometer, the aneroid barometer has no liquid. Rather, it operates on differences in air pressure between the atmosphere and a closed vessel (an aneroid cell). Again, the root of the word helps us remember the principle of operation. Literally, aneroid means "not wet."

As shown in figure 3-4, the aneroid barometer is a closed container under a partial vacuum. It is strong enough not to collapse under pressure, but flexible enough so that its shape will change a specified amount as atmospheric pressure increases or decreases. The change in shape is linked mechanically to an indicator that shows the pressure value. Although not as accurate as the mercurial barometer, the aneroid barometer has several advantages. It is small and rugged; that is, it can be carried in an aircraft where it can withstand strong g-forces due to atmospheric turbulence and maneuvering.

Current atmospheric pressure measurements and altimeter settings reported from automated surface observation stations are based on measurements by digital pressure transducers. The small size, robust construction, high sampling rate, and accuracy of these instruments make them desirable for these and other operational applications.

Figure 3-4. The aneroid barometer. Pressure changes cause the aneroid cell to deform in a predictable manner. The changes are mechanically linked to the pressure scale on the right.

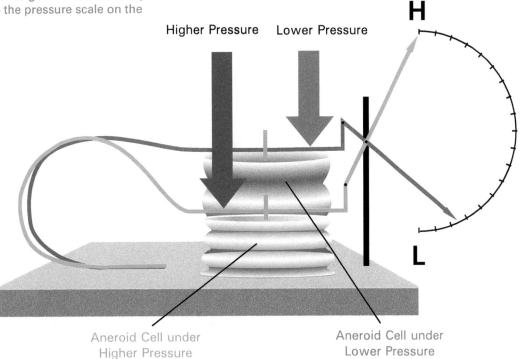

Higher Pressure   Lower Pressure

H

L

Aneroid Cell under
Higher Pressure

Aneroid Cell under
Lower Pressure

SECTION B
CHARTING ATMOSPHERIC PRESSURE

Pilots and meteorologists pay careful attention to the horizontal distribution of atmospheric pressure, because horizontal differences in pressure are related to wind. Also, storms and fair weather areas have distinctive pressure patterns which are important aids for weather diagnosis and prediction. Such pressure patterns are normally identified by inspecting charts which show the horizontal distribution of atmospheric pressure.

STATION AND SEA LEVEL PRESSURE

Surface pressure measurements are most useful if they can be compared with nearby measurements at the same altitude. Over land areas, the direct comparison of station pressures are usually difficult because weather stations are often at different altitudes. (Figure 3-5)

Even slight differences in altitude are important because the change of pressure over a given vertical distance is always much greater than the change of pressure over the same horizontal distance. For example, near sea level, a station elevation difference of only 100 feet will

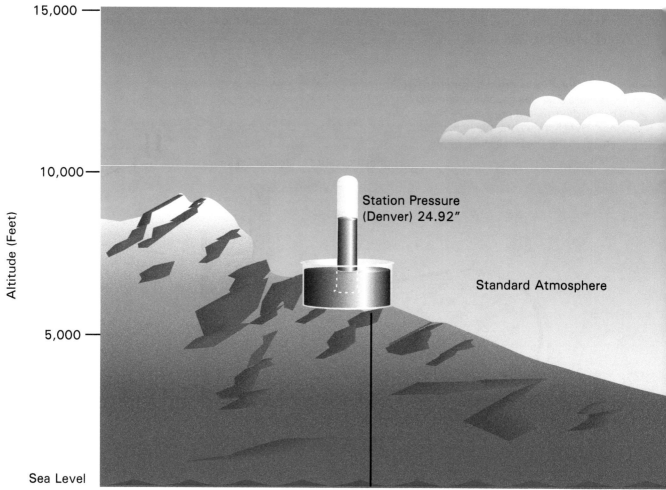

Altitude (Feet)

15,000 —

10,000 —

Station Pressure (Denver) 24.92"

Standard Atmosphere

5,000 —

Sea Level

Denver 29.92"   Sea Level Pressures

cause a difference in station pressure of about 1/10 inch of mercury. If that vertical difference was erroneously reported as a horizontal pressure difference, it would imply an unrealistically strong horizontal wind. In order to correct for such altitude differences, station pressures are extrapolated to sea level pressure. Sea level pressure is the atmospheric pressure measured or estimated at an elevation equal to mean sea level. This extrapolated sea level pressure (station pressure corrected for elevation) is used by pilots to determine altitude. It also is used in aviation reports to depict the atmospheric pressure of a reporting location.

Sea level pressure can be approximated if you know station pressure and elevation. Simply add one inch of mercury to the station pressure for every 1,000 feet of station elevation. For example, if the station pressure is 27.50 inches of mercury and the station elevation is 2,500 feet, the sea level pressure is approximately 30.00 inches of mercury. At National Weather Service stations, calculations of sea level pressure also take into account station temperature. This more precise computation modifies the sea level pressure estimates to account for density differences between the standard atmosphere and actual conditions. Sea level pressures are commonly reported in the U.S. and Canada, but elsewhere, station pressure or some related measurement may be reported.

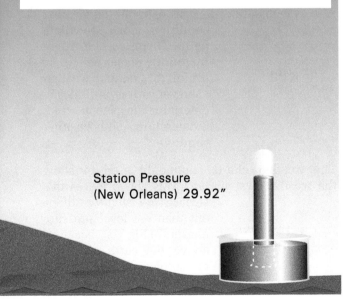

Figure 3-5. Station pressure and sea level pressure. New Orleans, Louisiana, is located near sea level. In the standard atmosphere, the station pressure at New Orleans is equal to the sea level pressure, or about 29.92 in. Hg. In comparison, the altitude of Denver, Colorado, is about 5,000 feet MSL. Since atmospheric pressure decreases one inch of mercury per 1,000 feet, the station pressure at Denver is about 24.92 in. Hg. in the standard atmosphere. Under standard conditions, the sea level pressure at Denver is still 29.92 in. Hg.

Station Pressure
(New Orleans) 29.92"

New Orleans 29.92"

SEA LEVEL PRESSURE PATTERNS

Figure 3-6 shows the global patterns of average sea level pressure for January and July. A chart which shows pressure as well as other meteorological conditions at the surface of the earth is referred to generally as a surface analysis chart.

Some useful terms are shown in figure 3-6. The lines on the charts are isobars, or lines of constant pressure. A high pressure center or a high (H) on a weather chart is a location where the sea level pressure is high compared to its surroundings. A ridge is an elongated region of relatively high pressure. Similarly, a low pressure center or low (L) is a roughly circular area with a lower sea level pressure in the center as compared to the surrounding region; a trough is an elongated region of relatively low pressure. These features are to a surface analysis chart what mountains and valleys are to a topographical chart.

Another important property illustrated in figure 3-6 is the pressure gradient. A pressure gradient is a difference in pressure over a given distance. A pressure difference of 4.0 mb per 100 n.m. is an example of a moderate pressure gradient in mid-latitudes. If the pressure gradient is strong, isobars will be close together; if the gradient is weak, the isobars will be spaced far apart. A pressure gradient on a sea level pressure chart is comparable to the height gradient on a topographical chart; the stronger the height gradient, the steeper the slope. In the next chapter, you will learn how to relate the pressure gradient to wind speed and direction.

Also shown on figure 3-6 are some of the larger semi-permanent pressure systems

and their common geographical names. These include the Bermuda High, the Aleutian Low, the Siberian High, the Icelandic Low, and the Pacific High.

Later in the text, we will examine the unique wind and weather associated with these systems. Notice the range of average sea level pressures in figure 3-6. Values vary from less than 990 mb near Antarctica in July to more than 1032 mb in the Siberian High in January.

Extremely low sea level pressure values are found in hurricanes (lowest reported: 870 mb or 25.69 in. Hg.); extreme high values occur in very cold wintertime high pressure areas (highest reported: 1083.8 mb or 32.00 in. Hg.).

CONSTANT PRESSURE CHARTS

The highs, lows, troughs, and ridges found in the sea level pressure field often extend well above the earth's surface, often well into the stratosphere. But on other occasions, well-defined low and high pressure systems may only exist aloft. In Chapters 7 and 8 we will see that the location, intensity, and vertical extent of atmospheric pressure systems are critical in determining weather conditions along your flight path. Therefore, for flight planning purposes, it is useful to examine weather charts at various altitudes to determine the general wind, temperature, and weather conditions.

The weather charts commonly used to show the weather systems at levels above the earth's surface are slightly different than sea level pressure charts. This is because, above the earth's surface, meteorologists find it easier to deal with heights on

On a surface analysis chart, the solid lines that depict sea-level pressure patterns are called isobars.

On a surface analysis chart, close spacing of the isobars indicates strong pressure gradient.

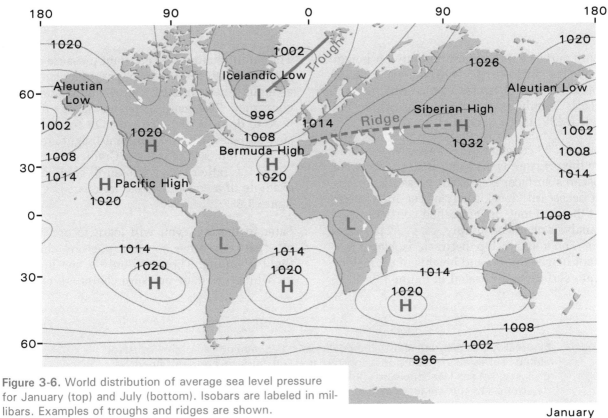

Figure 3-6. World distribution of average sea level pressure for January (top) and July (bottom). Isobars are labeled in millibars. Examples of troughs and ridges are shown.

January

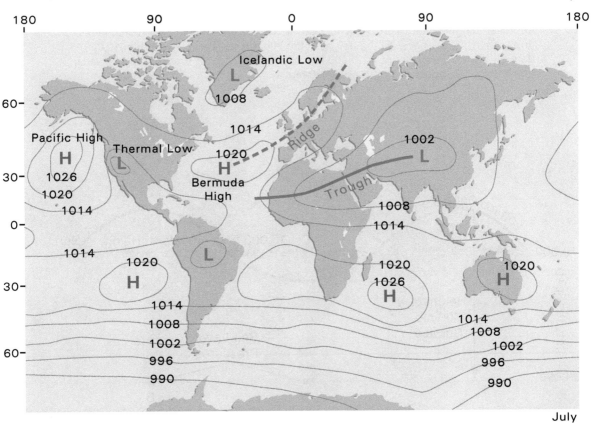

July

pressure surfaces rather than pressure on height surfaces. The difference between the two types of "surfaces" is easy to interpret. A constant height surface is simply a horizontal plane where the altitude (MSL) is the same at all points.

In contrast, a "constant pressure surface" is one where the pressure is the same at all points. Like the ocean's surface, a constant pressure surface is not necessarily level. Many upper air weather charts that you may use are called constant pressure analysis charts or, simply, constant pressure charts. The relationship between isobars on a constant height surface and heights of a constant pressure surface is illustrated in figure 3-7.

The interpretation of a constant pressure chart is identical with the sea level pressure chart as far as highs, lows, troughs, ridges, and gradients are concerned. The main difference is one of terms used to describe the elements. On constant pressure surfaces, lines of constant height are called contours rather than isobars. Gradients are height gradients rather than pressure gradients. An example of a constant pressure chart is given in figure 3-8.

Later in the text, you will learn to use the 500 mb chart and other constant pressure charts for flight planning. There are only a few pressures for which constant pressure charts are regularly

Figure 3-7. This diagram shows the relationship between pressure on a constant altitude surface and heights on a constant pressure surface. From our previous discussion of sea level pressure you know that the pressures at points A and B are determined by the weight of the column of atmosphere above those points. You also know that atmospheric pressure **always** decreases with height. At 10,000 feet MSL, the pressure at points C and D are also determined by the weight of their respective columns above the 10,000-foot level (dashed line). Notice the solid line representing the 700 mb pressure surface. At point C, the pressure at 10,000 feet is lower than 700 mb because the height of the 700 mb surface is lower than 10,000 feet. Similarly, the pressure at 10,000 feet at point D is higher than 700 mb because the 700 mb surface is higher than 10,000 feet.

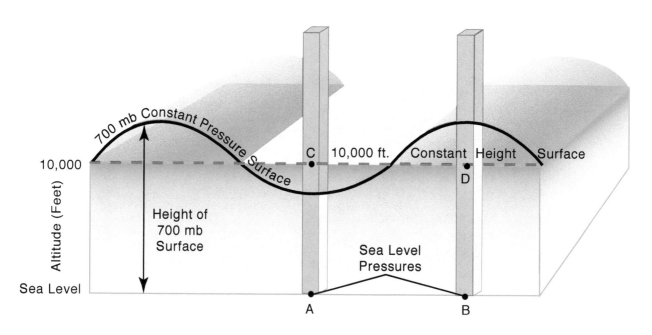

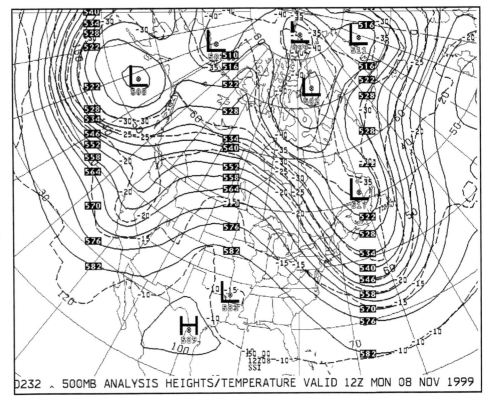

Figure 3-8. Typical 500 mb constant pressure chart. Solid lines are contours labeled in decameters (564dm = 5,640m). Dashed lines are isotherms labeled in °C.

constructed and it would be helpful to learn these and their pressure altitudes for later reference. Pressure altitude is the altitude of a given pressure surface in the standard atmosphere (Figure 3-9). Pilots can determine pressure altitude by setting the standard sea level pressure, 29.92 in. Hg., in the aircraft altimeter (more on this later in this chapter).

> Pressure altitude is the altitude indicated when the altimeter setting is 29.92. If you set your altimeter at 29.92 and fly at 18,289 feet indicated altitude, you will be flying along the 500 mb constant pressure surface.

Pressure	Pressure Altitude		Approximate
Millibars	Feet	Meters	Flight Level
850	4,781	1,457	
700	9,882	3,012	
500	18,289	5,574	~FL180
300	30,065	9,164	~FL300
250	33,999	10,363	~FL340
200	38,662	11,784	~FL390
100	53,083	16,180	~FL530

Figure 3-9. Left: Constant pressure levels for which analysis charts are usually available to pilots. Center: Pressure altitudes indicated in both feet and meters. Right: Approximate Flight Level (FL).

SECTION C

THE PRESSURE ALTIMETER

Perhaps the most important aviation application of the concept of atmospheric pressure is the pressure altimeter. The altimeter is essentially an aneroid barometer that reads in units of altitude rather than pressure. This is possible by using the standard atmosphere to make the conversion from pressure to altitude. A schematic diagram of a pressure altimeter is shown in figure 3-10.

If the actual state of the atmosphere is the same as the standard atmosphere, then the pressure altitude is equivalent to the actual altitude. However, this is usually not the case. Altimeter indications may be inexact if the actual atmospheric conditions are nonstandard. This is true even if the altimeter is in perfect working condition and accurately calibrated. Therefore, you must always be aware of the difference between the altitude measured by your altimeter (indicated altitude) and the actual altitude of your aircraft above mean sea level (true altitude) or above the ground (absolute altitude).

There are three specific altimeter errors caused by nonstandard atmospheric conditions.

1. Sea level pressure different from 29.92 inches of mercury.
2. Temperature warmer or colder than standard temperature.
3. Strong vertical gusts.

The first **pressure altimeter error** arises because the standard atmosphere is based on a fixed sea level pressure of 29.92 inches of mercury (1013.25 mb). This is important because the actual sea level pressure at a given location constantly varies with time due both to daily heating and cooling of the earth and movements of high and low pressure systems through the area. Critical pressure changes may also occur

Figure 3-10. Pressure altimeter and its component parts. Because surface pressures are always changing, a means of changing the altimeter reference pressure (altimeter setting) is necessary. A barometric set knob is provided to change the setting. It is designed to change the altimeter indication approximately 10 feet for each .01 in. Hg. change on the scale. This approximates the rate of pressure change found in the first 10,000 feet of the atmosphere, i.e., 1 in. Hg. for each 1,000 feet.

Increasing the altimeter setting will cause the indicated altitude to increase, while decreasing the altimeter setting will cause the indicated altitude to decrease.

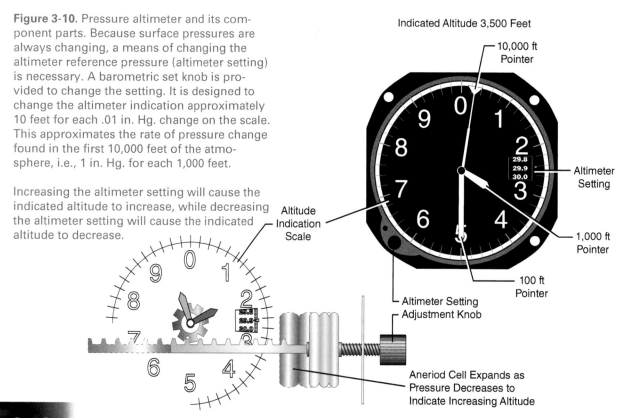

Indicated Altitude 3,500 Feet

10,000 ft Pointer

Altimeter Setting

1,000 ft Pointer

100 ft Pointer

Altimeter Setting Adjustment Knob

Aneriod Cell Expands as Pressure Decreases to Indicate Increasing Altitude

Altitude Indication Scale

Internationally, altimeter settings are given in millibars (hectoPascals, hPa).

along an aircraft's path as it travels across high and low pressure areas.

As shown in figure 3-10, variable sea level pressure is usually taken care of by adjusting the altimeter to the proper altimeter setting. This is the sea level pressure determined from the station pressure and the standard atmosphere. For altitudes below 18,000 feet in the U.S., this adjustment ensures that the altimeter will read the field elevation when the aircraft is on the ground, and it will give an accurate estimate of

must be alert to changes in altimeter setting enroute. With flight levels at and above 18,000 feet in U.S. airspace, altimeters are set to 29.92 inches of mercury.

Figure 3-11 is an example of the differences between true altitude and indicated altitude that could arise when the sea level pressure varies along a flight path while the altimeter is set at a fixed value (30.00 inches in this case). The true altitude will be higher than indicated when the sea level pressure is higher than the altim-

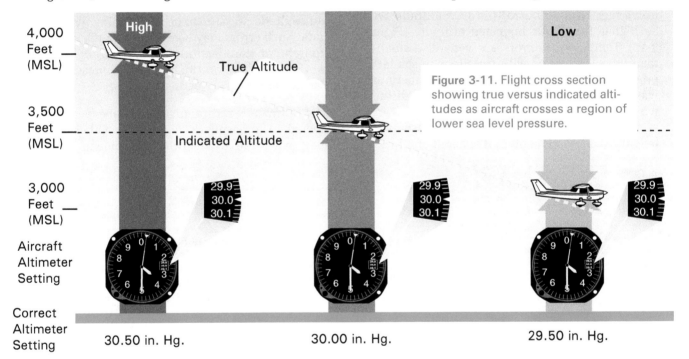

Figure 3-11. Flight cross section showing true versus indicated altitudes as aircraft crosses a region of lower sea level pressure.

Altimeter setting is the value to which the barometric pressure scale on the altimeter is set so the altitude indicates true altitude at field elevation.

altitude above mean sea level when the aircraft is in the air. If the altimeter is set to station pressure, it will read zero on the ground and indicate absolute altitude in the air. Since sea level pressure changes from place to place, you

eter setting. True altitude will be lower than indicated when the sea level pressure is lower than the altimeter setting. These situations are summarized in the well-known rule of thumb: High to low, look out below.

CE 172. One serious injury. During a nighttime approach, a Cessna 172 crashed 2 ½ miles short of the runway. The pilot was unable to activate the runway lights. At the time of the crash the pilot thought he was 900 feet above the ground. NTSB concluded that the pilot failed to correctly set his altimeter.

The **second pressure altimeter error** occurs when atmospheric temperatures are warmer or colder than the standard atmosphere. A problem arises in these cases because atmospheric pressure decreases with altitude more rapidly in cold air than in warm air.

This means that a correct altimeter setting only ensures a correct altitude on the ground. Once you are in the air, the indicated and true altitude will be equal only if the atmospheric temperatures are standard. If the atmosphere is colder than standard, your true altitude will be lower than your indicated altitude. If the atmosphere is warmer than standard, the true altitude will be higher than your indicated altitude. (Figure 3-12) Temperature errors are generally smaller than those associated with variations in sea level pressure. For example, if the actual temperature was 10C° warmer than standard, the true altitude would be about 4% higher. This is only 40 feet at 1,000 feet MSL. But the error increases with height. At 12,000 feet MSL, it is about 500 feet.

Remember, the pressure altimeter will not automatically show exact altitude in flight. It is the pilot's responsibility to ensure terrain avoidance.

Flight over high mountains in bad weather requires close attention to possible temperature errors.

The **third pressure altimeter error** that arises because of nonstandard atmospheric conditions is caused by large and rapid changes in vertical movements of the air. These changes upset the balance of forces (hydrostatic balance) that allows atmospheric pressure to be related directly to altitude. Such errors may be expected in the extreme updrafts of thunderstorms and in strong mountain waves. More on this problem is presented in Part III on aviation weather hazards.

The altimeter errors discussed above are all related to atmospheric conditions. Other errors may arise due to instrument problems. These

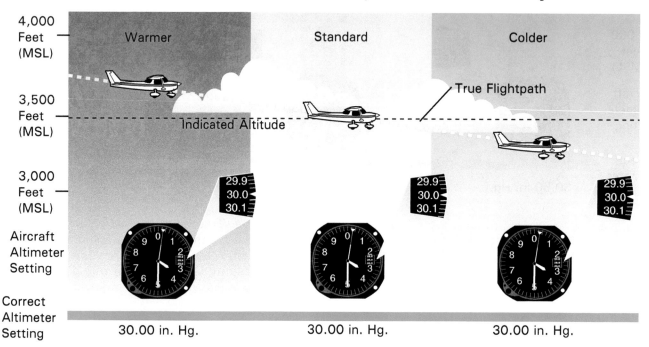

Figure 3-12. Flight cross section from a warmer to a colder airmass. Notice that standard atmospheric conditions only occur near the center of the diagram. The aircraft true altitude is higher than indicated in the warmer air and lower than indicated in the colder air.

On warm days pressure surfaces are raised and the indicated altitude is lower than true altitude.

include improper calibration, friction, lag, improper instrument location, and temperature changes of the instrument. These important details as well as a thorough discussion of altimetry based on radar, sound propagation, and GPS are beyond the scope of this text. The reader is referred to other sources for details. (Jeppesen, 2013)

AN INTRODUCTION TO METAR CODE

Altimeter settings for airports worldwide are reported and transmitted regularly with other weather information in a standard coded format. Known as an aviation routine weather report or METAR, these reports are commonly available to pilots. Learning the code symbols, abbreviations, and contractions will help you to use METAR information during flight planning. (Figure 3-13)

Although report content may vary depending on its source, a typical METAR contains 10 or more separate elements. You will be gradually introduced to the elements of METAR code beginning with those items discussed in this chapter and highlighted in yellow in figure 3-13. In subsequent chapters, you will be introduced to wind, weather elements, clouds, ceiling, and visibility. If you wish to consult the complete code breakdown now, it is given in Appendix B.

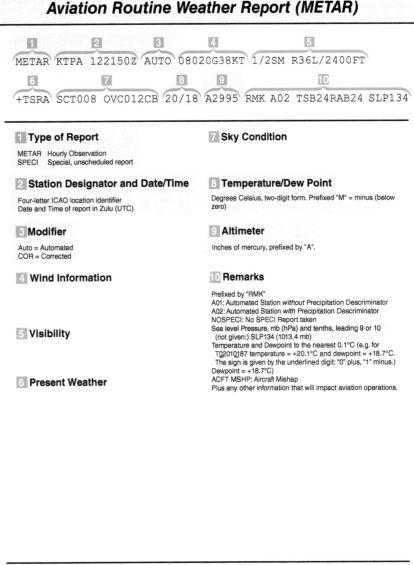

Aviation Routine Weather Report (METAR)

1 METAR 2 KTPA 122150Z 3 AUTO 4 08020G38KT 5 1/2SM R36L/2400FT
6 +TSRA 7 SCT008 OVC012CB 8 20/18 9 A2995 10 RMK A02 TSB24RAB24 SLP134

1 Type of Report

METAR Hourly Observation
SPECI Special, unscheduled report

2 Station Designator and Date/Time

Four-letter ICAO location identifier
Date and Time of report in Zulu (UTC)

3 Modifier

Auto = Automated
COR = Corrected

4 Wind Information

5 Visibility

6 Present Weather

7 Sky Condition

8 Temperature/Dew Point

Degrees Celsius, two-digit form. Prefixed "M" = minus (below zero)

9 Altimeter

Inches of mercury, prefixed by "A".

10 Remarks

Prefixed by "RMK"
A01: Automated Station *without* Precipitation Descriminator
A02: Automated Station *with* Precipitation Descriminator
NOSPECI: No SPECI Report taken
Sea level Pressure, mb (hPa) and tenths, leading 9 or 10 (not given) SLP134 (1013.4 mb)
Temperature and Dewpoint to the nearest 0.1°C (e.g. for T02010187 temperature = +20.1°C and dewpoint = +18.7°C. The sign is given by the underlined digit: "0" plus, "1" minus.)
Dewpoint = +18.7°C)
ACFT MSHP: Aircraft Mishap
Plus any other information that will impact aviation operations.

DECODED REPORT: Routine observation for Tampa, FL, on the 12th day of the month at 2150 UTC. Automated Station. Wind from 080° at 20 knots with gusts to 38 knots. Prevailing visibility 1/2 statute mile, runway 36 Left visual range 2,400 feet. Thunderstorm with heavy rain. Scattered clouds at 800 feet AGL, overcast cumulonimbus clouds with bases of 1,200 feet AGL. Temperature 20°C, dewpoint 18°C. Altimeter setting 29.95 inches of mercury. Remarks: Automated station, precipitation discriminator indicated by A02, thunderstorm began 24 minutes past the hour, rain began 24 minutes past the hour, sea level pressure 1013.4 hectoPascals (Note: 1 hPa = 1 millibar).

Figure 3-13. Reporting code for aviation weather information. Report type, date, time, pressure, temperature, and altimeter settings are explained here. Other items such as wind, sky cover, weather, visibility, and dewpoint will be explained in subsequent chapters. A complete code breakdown is given in Appendix B.

TYPE OF REPORT

The two types of weather reports are the scheduled METAR, which is taken every hour, and the aviation selected special weather report (SPECI). The special METAR weather observation is an unscheduled report indicating a significant change in one or more elements.

STATION DESIGNATOR AND DATE/ TIME OF REPORT

Each reporting station is listed by its four-letter International Civil Aviation Organization (ICAO) identifier. In the contiguous 48 states, the letter "K" prefixes the three-letter domestic location identifier. For example, the domestic identifier for Denver is DEN, and the ICAO identifier is KDEN. In other areas of the world, the first two letters indicate the region, country, or state. Identifiers for Alaska begin with "PA," in Hawaii they begin with "PH," the prefixes in Canada are "CU," "CW," "CY," and "CZ," the United Kingdom is "EG," prefixes in Germany are "ET" and "ED," France is "LF," and Brazil is "SB." A list of station designators is usually available at an FSS or NWS office. You can also use the Airport/Facility Directory, the FAA publication 7350 Location Identifiers, or the ICAO document 7910 Location Indicators to find and decode identifiers.

Following the station identifier is the date (day of the month) and time of the observation. The time is given in UTC or Zulu, as indicated by the Z following the time.

MODIFIER

When a METAR is created by a totally automated weather observation station, the modifier AUTO will follow the date/time element. The modifier COR is used to indicate a corrected METAR which replaces a previously disseminated report. No modifier indicates a manual station or manual input at an automated station.

TEMPERATURE AND DEWPOINT

The current air temperature and dewpoint are reported in two-digit form in degrees Celsius and are separated by a slash. For example, "18/09" indicates a surface temperature of 18°C and a dewpoint of 9°C. Temperatures below 0° Celsius are prefixed with an "M" to indicate minus. For instance 10° below zero would be shown as M10. Temperature and dewpoint also may be added to remarks in an eight-digit format showing tenths of °C. Details as to the meaning and use of dewpoint temperature are presented in Chapter 6.

ALTIMETER

The altimeter setting is reported in inches of mercury in a four digit group without the decimal point, and is prefixed by an "A." An example is A3012, indicating an altimeter setting of 30.12 inches. Internationally, the altimeter setting is reported in millibars (hectoPascals). It is also given in a four-digit group, but preceded by a "Q." For example, Q1013 indicates an altimeter setting of 1013 mb.

REMARKS

The remarks section begins with "RMK." Certain remarks are included to report weather considered significant to aircraft operations. Among this information are the sea level pressure to the nearest tenth of a hectoPascal (millibar) and the temperature/dewpoint in tenths °C. The remark "SLP134" refers to the sea level pressure of 1013.4 hectoPascals (hPa). The leading 9 or 10 is omitted. Prefix the number with a 9 or 10, whichever brings it closer to 1,000.0.

A remark, such as, "T00081016," refers to the temperature and dewpoint in tenths °C. In this example, the first zero in the sequence indicates a plus value for temperature (+.8°C) and the leading "one" in the sequence shows a minus value for dewpoint (−1.6°C).

SECTION D

DENSITY

As you know from your studies of the physics of flight, aircraft performance depends critically on atmospheric density. An aircraft operating at 22,000 feet MSL in the standard atmosphere encounters about one half of the atmospheric density as at sea level. At 40,000 feet MSL, density decreases to approximately one quarter of the sea level value, and to about one tenth near 60,000 feet MSL. At low atmospheric densities, aircraft performance deteriorates.

These problems can be handled to some extent with special aircraft and powerplant designs and by attention to aircraft operation. One example is the ER-2, the stratospheric reconnaissance aircraft. With its glider-like design, it handles much better in a high altitude, low density environment than does a conventionally designed aircraft.

Pressure altitude and density altitude have the same value at standard temperature in the standard atmosphere.

Density altitude increases about 120 feet (above pressure altitude) for every one C° increase in temperature above standard. It can be calculated on your flight computer or from a density altitude chart.

Moisture also has an effect on density altitude because humid air is less dense than dry air at the same pressure and temperature.

DENSITY ALTITUDE

Difficulties with flight in low density conditions are not restricted to extreme altitudes. There is a significant deterioration of performance for aircraft operating in lower-than-normal density conditions caused by high surface temperature. This is especially true at airports with elevations well above sea level. Specifically, longer-than-usual takeoff rolls are required and climbouts are slower than at sea level. These conditions are usually described in terms of the density altitude of the atmosphere in the vicinity of the airport.

Density altitude is the altitude above mean sea level at which a given atmospheric density occurs in the standard atmosphere. It can also be interpreted as pressure altitude corrected for nonstandard temperature differences.

In warmer-than-standard surface conditions, you would say that the density altitude is "high;" that is, operation of your aircraft in a high density altitude condition is equivalent to taking off from a higher airport during standard conditions. In a high density altitude situation, the actual density at the surface is found above the airport elevation in the standard atmosphere. (Figure 3-14)

The precise effects of a given density altitude on takeoff distance and climb rate are presented in most aircraft flight manuals. For example, under the conditions given here, the takeoff distance for a light aircraft (not turbocharged) would be increased by about 60% and the climb rate would be decreased by 40% of that required at sea level. Obviously, a short runway on a hot day in a high, narrow mountain valley offers large problems.

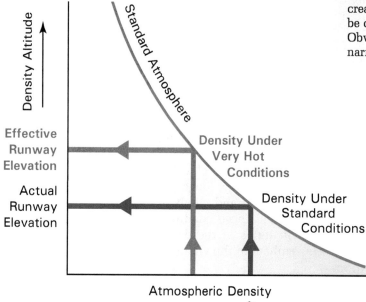

Figure 3-14. The heavy, solid curve shows how density decreases with altitude in the standard atmosphere. Under standard conditions, the surface density would correspond with a density altitude equal to the elevation of the airport. Under very warm conditions, the density is lower and it corresponds with a higher altitude; that is, the density altitude is higher than the elevation of the airport. An example of a density altitude computational graph in given in the most recent version of AC 00-45.

CE U206F. One minor injury. A pilot and four passengers took off from an airport near sea level. After climbing to 400 feet, the pilot could not maintain altitude and subsequently descended to a forced landing in a field where the aircraft collided with some trees. At the time of the takeoff, density altitude was about 2300 feet. The aircraft also had a gross weight that exceeded the maximum allowable weight for the aircraft.

SUMMARY

Atmospheric pressure is an essential component of aviation weather basics. An understanding of pressure is the foundation for understanding such diverse and important topics as altimetry, winds, and storms. In this chapter, you have learned about the useful relationship between atmospheric pressure and the weight of the atmosphere and how that relationship allows us to measure pressure and altitude. Details about the distribution of average sea level pressure around the globe, as well as the terminology and methods for the interpretation of atmospheric pressure charts at the surface and aloft should now be part of your growing knowledge of aviation weather.

You have gained valuable insight into the effects of atmospheric variations in pressure and temperature on the accuracy of pressure altimeter measurements. You have been introduced to standard weather reports available to pilots. In particular, you have learned where to find locations of the reporting stations, times, pressures, temperatures, and altimeter settings in those reports. Finally, you have become familiar with the concept of density altitude and its impact on aircraft performance.

KEY TERMS

Absolute Altitude
Aleutian Low
Altimeter Errors
Altimeter Setting
Aneroid Barometer
Aneroid Cell
Atmospheric Pressure
Bermuda High
Constant Pressure Charts
Contours
Density Altitude
Height Gradient
High
Hydrostatic Balance
Icelandic Low

Indicated Altitude
Isobars
Low
Mercurial Barometer
Pacific High
Pressure Altimeter
Pressure Altitude
Pressure Gradient
Ridge
Sea Level Pressure
Siberian High
Station Pressure
Surface Analysis Chart
Trough
True Altitude

REVIEW QUESTIONS

1. What is the total weight of the atmosphere (in pounds) over an area of one square foot at sea level in the standard atmosphere?

2. You are flying at an indicated altitude of 3,000 feet MSL over a region where there is a strong high pressure area at the surface. Sea level pressure is 1046 mb. Your altimeter is set at 29.92. For simplicity, assume that the atmosphere is at standard temperature and there are no other errors in measurement. Estimate your true altitude.

3. Calculate the density altitude of an airport located at 2,000 feet MSL with an altimeter setting of 29.92 and a temperature of 95°F. Use a flight computer or density altitude chart.

4. Do the computation in problem 3 for the same airport, but for a temperature of 104°F and an altimeter setting of 29.80 in. Hg.

5. If you set your altimeter at 29.92 inches and fly at an indicated altitude of 9,882 feet, what is the atmospheric pressure at flight level?

6. In Question 5, will your true altitude also be 9,882 feet?

7. If your altimeter setting was correct on take-off and the sea level pressure decreased along your flight track, how would your true altitude change relative to your indicated altitude during the flight?

DISCOVERY QUESTIONS

8. Under certain conditions, your ears act as sensitive aneroid barometers and can cause discomfort. Document those conditions and explain the procedures for minimizing the problem.

9. Even if a mercurial barometer could be designed so that it was not so bulky and fragile, it wouldn't work well in an airplane. Discuss.

10. Realistically, the situation in question 2 is commonly associated with a shallow, very cold airmass in winter. Discuss this additional temperature effect on your answer to question 2."

11. Find the range (high and low) of average sea level pressure over the earth's surface from figure 3-6. Convert the pressure to inches of mercury. Now assume that weather disturbances move across an airport (actual field elevation 1,000 feet MSL), causing the pressure to vary between the highest and lowest values of sea level pressure. Except for pressure changes, assume the atmosphere is standard. What errors in field elevation would arise if your altimeter remained at 29.92 inches?

12. For the conditions in questions 3 and 4 determine the increase in takeoff distance and the decrease in climb rate for an aircraft specified by your instructor.

13. Why can't a pump raise water higher than about 34 feet under standard atmospheric conditions?

14. Explain your answer in question 6.

CHAPTER 4

Wind

Introduction

The motion of air is important in many weather-producing processes. Moving air carries heat, moisture, and pollutants from one location to another — at times in a gentle breeze, occasionally in a pure hurricane. Air movements create favorable conditions for the formation and dissipation of clouds and precipitation; in some cases, those motions cause the visibility to decrease to zero; in others, they sweep the skies crystal clear. Winds move atmospheric mass and therefore affect changes in atmospheric pressure. All of these factors create reasons for the changeable nature of not only the wind, but also weather.

In flight, winds can have significant effects on navigation. Chaotic air motions cause turbulence which is, at least, uncomfortable and, at worst, catastrophic. Should atmospheric winds change suddenly over a short distance, flight may not be sustainable. Without question, as a pilot, you must understand air motions for efficient and safe flight.

In this chapter, we consider the causes and characteristics of horizontal motions of the atmosphere. The chapter material provides you with a practical understanding of important relationships between the wind, atmospheric pressure, and the earth's rotation. You will also gain some insight into the important influences of friction between the moving air and the earth's surface. When you complete the chapter, you will not only have an understanding of the fundamental causes of the wind, but you will also know how wind is measured and you will be able to interpret general wind conditions from isobars and contours on weather charts.

Section A

WIND TERMINOLOGY AND MEASUREMENTS

To a pilot, the concept of motion in three dimensions comes much easier than to ground-bound people. For example, after takeoff and during climbout, you are aware of your movement across the ground as well as your change in altitude. Similarly, when air moves from one location to another, it can simultaneously move both horizontally and vertically.

As the pilot finds it convenient to describe and measure aircraft position changes and altitude changes separately, so does the meteorologist find it helpful to separate descriptions of horizontal air movements and vertical air motions. A practical reason for this separation is that horizontal motions are much stronger than vertical motions with the exceptions of a few turbulent phenomena, such as thunderstorms and mountain lee waves. Also, horizontal motions are easier to measure than vertical motions. We separate them here, reserving the term wind for horizontal air motions. Vertical motions will be discussed in the next chapter. (Figure 4-1)

It is common to refer to the "wind velocity" when describing the wind. This term is often erroneously interpreted as "wind speed." This is not the case. Wind velocity is a vector quantity. A vector quantity has a magnitude and a direction, as opposed to scalar quantities, such as temperature and pressure, which only have magnitude. The magnitude of the wind velocity is the wind speed, usually expressed in nautical miles per hour (knots), statute miles per hour (mph), kilometers per hour (kph), or meters per second (mps). The wind direction is the direction from which the wind is blowing, measured in degrees, or to eight or sixteen points of the compass, clockwise from

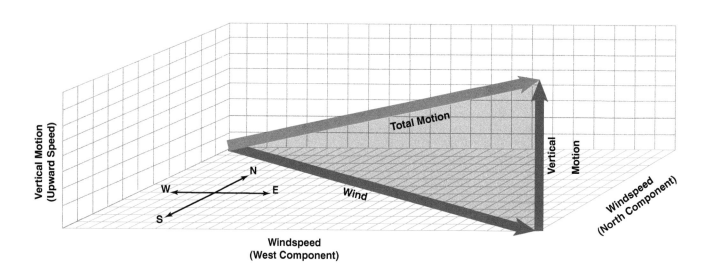

Figure 4-1 The total atmospheric motions are composed of horizontal motions (wind) and vertical motions. In this example, the total motion is composed of a WNW "wind" and an upward "vertical motion." The wind speed is proportional to the length (magnitude) of the horizontal vector labeled "wind" while the magnitude of the vertical motion is proportional to the length of the vertical vector. Note that the length of the vertical motion vector has been exaggerated for clarity (see text for details).

true north (360°). For example, a "westerly" wind blows from the west and has a direction of 270°. Note that meteorologists *always* state their wind directions relative to true north ("true"). Air traffic controllers, on the other hand, always state wind direction in terms of magnetic north ("magnetic"), unless specifically stated otherwise.

Wind velocity is measured at the surface by several different methods. The most common techniques use anemometers and wind vanes. (Figure 4-2) For winds aloft, measurement techniques include the tracking of free balloons, Doppler radar, aircraft navigation systems, and satellite.

A windsock points downwind. When a standard windsock becomes fully inflated, the windspeed equals or exceeds 15 knots.

Figure 4-2. Two surface wind measurement systems. On the left, wind speed is determined from the rotation speed of a cup anemometer while the direction is measured with a wind vane. Note, the vane points *into* the wind. On the right, wind speed and direction are determined from a single airplane-shaped device known as an aerovane. The speed of rotation of the propeller determines the wind speed while the "airplane" also flies *into* the wind. Inset: Standard airport windsock

METAR WIND INFORMATION

In METAR reports of surface weather conditions, several different wind reports may be given. (Figure 4-3) All of these relate to winds measured by a standard instrument which is usually located 30 feet above the ground and away from any obstructions. Reported wind speeds and directions are usually one- or two-minute averages. This average wind speed is also referred to as the sustained speed. A gust is reported when there is at least a ten-knot variation between instantaneous peaks and lulls during the last ten minutes. A squall is reported when there is a sudden increase of wind speed by at least 16 knots to a sustained speed of 22 knots or more for a one-minute period. The peak wind speed is the maximum instantaneous wind speed greater than 25 knots since the last hourly observation.

The two-minute average wind direction and speed are reported in a five digit group, or six digits if the speed is over 99 knots. The first three digits represent the direction from which the wind is blowing, in reference to true north. If the direction is variable, the letters "VRB" are used. The next two (or three) digits show the speed in knots (KT). Calm winds are reported as "00000KT."

If the wind direction varies 60° or more and the speed is above six knots, a variable group follows the wind group. The extremes of wind direction are shown, separated by a "V." For example, if the wind is blowing from 020°, varying to 090°, it is reported as "020V090."

In addition to direction and speed, the character, or type, of wind may be reported. Gusty winds are reported with a "G," followed by the highest gust over the last ten minutes. For example, wind from 080° at 32 knots with gusts to 45 is reported as 08032G45.

REMARKS

Certain wind information is included in the remarks when it is considered significant to aircraft operations. At facilities that have a wind recorder, or an automated weather reporting system, whenever the criteria are met, the annotation "PK WND" (peak wind) is included in the remarks. The peak wind remark includes three digits for direction and two or three digits for speed followed by the time in hours and minutes of the occurrence. If the hour can be inferred from the report time, only the minutes are reported.

Examples

The following shows several examples of wind information as it appears on a METAR. The decoded wind data are shown below.

METAR KSEA 241956Z VRB03KT 10SM FEW080 BKN095 OVC120 09/04 A3035 RMK A02 SLP281 T00940044=

Decoded: Wind direction is variable; wind speed is three knots.

METAR KPUB 241754Z 05016G24KT 10SM CLR 15/M04 A2973 RMK A02 SLP040 VIRGA T01501039=

Decoded: Wind from zero five zero degrees true at sixteen knots, gusting to twenty-four knots.

METAR KDEN 241930Z 36020G27KT 1/4SM +SN FG OVC002 00/00 A2993 RMK A02 PK WND 35035/1915 TWR VIS 1/2 P0002=

Decoded: Wind from three six zero degrees true at twenty knots with gusts to twenty-seven knots. Remarks: Peak wind from three five zero degrees true at thirty-five knots. The time the peak wind occurred was nineteen fifteen Zulu.

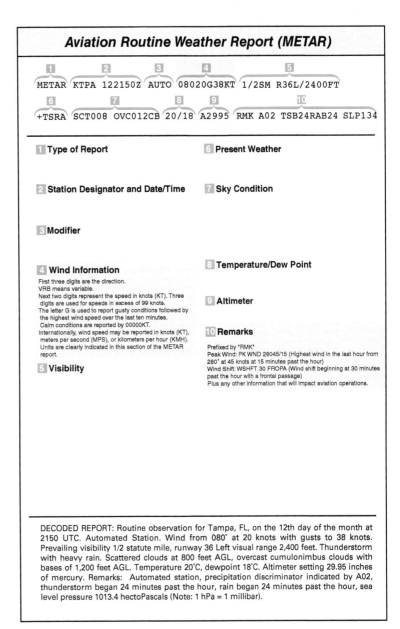

Figure 4-3. Reporting code for aviation weather information. Wind reports are explained here. Other items are explained in previous and subsequent chapters. The complete code is located in Appendix B.

Coded weather observations and forecasts developed many years ago at a time when detailed meteorological information was transmitted over relatively slow communication devices. Also, much of the early operational developments in meteorology occurred during war time when coding of communications was paramount. The abbreviated format of METAR reports is a descendant of those early coded messages. The primary reason that METAR coding continues today is that it is a common international format used by most countries and interpretable by all. In the U.S., both coded and decoded plain language METARS are available through the Aviation Digital Data Service (ADDS). Note: METAR "decoders" are available across the internet through non-governmental sources. Pilots should use FAA approved sources. Other relayed reports may be late and/or "repackaged" such that important weather information has been dropped.

Section B

CAUSES OF WIND

What makes the wind blow? The concise answer is found in the basic physical principle that governs all motions; that is, the conservation of momentum. Newton stated this principle quite simply:

If an object of mass, M, is subjected to an unbalanced force (F_{total}), it will undergo an acceleration, A, that is:

$$F_{total} = MA$$

We already applied this principle when we defined atmospheric pressure as the weight of the atmosphere. To do this, we took advantage of the fact that the atmosphere is often in hydrostatic balance. That condition is a special case of the above statement of Newton's principle. A mass of air is not accelerated either upward or downward if the total forces acting on it are balanced ($F_{total} = 0$).

With regard to horizontal motions of air, imbalances are common and horizontal accelerations often occur. In these cases, the acceleration is the change of the speed and/or direction of a mass of air as it moves along its path. F_{total} is the sum of all of the horizontally directed forces which act on a particular mass of air. Figure 4-4 illustrates how a parcel is affected if it is under the influence of balanced and unbalanced forces.

With this information, our question, "What makes the wind blow?" can be stated better as two questions: What are the forces that affect the air parcels? What are the causes of the forces?

The most important forces that affect air motions are

1. Pressure gradient force

2. Coriolis force

3. Frictional force

Because a "mass" of air is not an easy thing to visualize, meteorologists have found it useful to introduce the concept of an air parcel. An air parcel is a volume of the atmosphere that is small enough so that its mass can be treated as if it were concentrated at a single point.

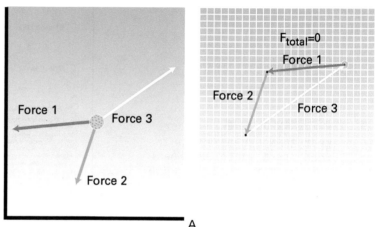

A

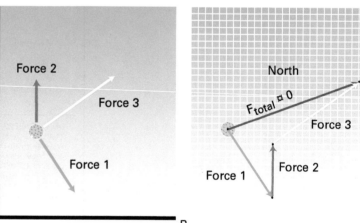

B

Figure 4-4. On the left are shown two parcels of air, each under the influence of three individual forces. Each force is represented as a vector with a magnitude and a direction. The force diagram constructed on the right shows the sum of the forces determined by simply adding the tail of one vector onto the head of the next. In diagram A, the head of the last vector ends up at the tail of the first. Therefore, the sum of the forces is zero. The parcel will not be accelerated. This is not true in diagram B. There is a gap between the first and last vector. The sum of the forces is not zero; therefore, the parcel is accelerated to the northeast, as indicated by the purple vector.

Section C

PRESSURE GRADIENT FORCE

The concept of a "gradient" was previously introduced in connection with discussions of temperature and pressure. Recall that a "pressure gradient" is simply the difference in pressure between two points divided by the distance between the points.

The fact that a pressure gradient has an influence on air movement is obvious when you deal with gases under pressure. For example, if you inflate a tire, you establish a pressure gradient across the thickness of the tire. If you puncture the tire, the air accelerates from the inside to the outside; that is, toward lower pressure. The larger the pressure difference, the greater the acceleration through the opening. The force involved here is known as the pressure gradient force. An example of this force and how it can be created in another fluid (water) is shown in figure 4-5.

In a similar way, the atmosphere causes air parcels to be accelerated across the surface of the earth toward low pressure; that is, when a horizontal pressure gradient force exists. Notice that, since we are dealing

specifically with the wind, we only need to consider horizontal pressure differences. When you study vertical air motions later in the text, the vertical pressure gradient force will be considered.

CAUSES OF PRESSURE GRADIENTS

The horizontal pressure gradient force is a root cause of wind. While both Coriolis force and the frictional force require motion before they become effective, pressure gradient force does not. Since pressure gradients are so essential to air motion, it is helpful to know how they develop.

Magnitude of the Pressure Gradient $= \dfrac{P_1 - P_2}{\text{Distance}}$

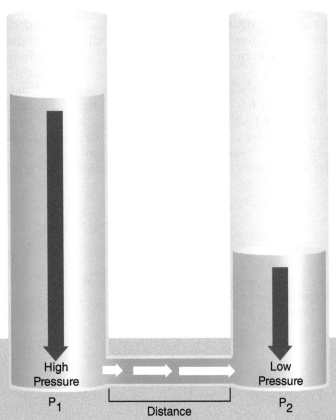

Figure 4-5. A pressure gradient develops in the pipe connecting the two reservoirs. This is due to the difference in water pressure generated by the difference in the depth (weight) of each water column, divided by the horizontal distance between the columns. The resulting pressure gradient force accelerates water through the pipe from the deep reservoir (high pressure) to the shallow reservoir (low pressure).

High Pressure P_1

Distance

Low Pressure P_2

The upper diagram in figure 4-6 shows a coastline sometime in mid-morning in the summer when the temperature of the land and sea are equal. In this ideal situation, there is no horizontal pressure gradient and no air movement across the coastline. As the sun continues to heat the earth's surface later in the morning (lower diagram in figure 4-6) the land temperature exceeds the water temperature. This happens because of the high heat capacity of water compared to land. In Chapter 2, you saw that it took much more energy to raise the temperature of water than that of dry soil. This is an example of the creation of a horizontal temperature gradient by differential heating.

The warmer land surface heats the overlying air by conduction and convection. The result is that the column of air over the land swells. That is, the mass of the heated air expands into a deeper layer than an equivalent amount of mass in the cooler air column over water. This is expected since we know from Chapter 3 that pressure decreases more rapidly with height in cold air than in warm air. As shown in figure 4-6, this process causes a horizontal pressure gradient aloft; warm air at that level starts to move toward the lower pressure over the sea.

There is more. In figure 4-6, as soon as the mass leaves the upper part of the heated column, the weight of that column (measured at the surface) decreases and the surface pressure goes down over the land. This creates a second horizontal pressure gradient between the columns of air, except that this gradient is at the bottom of the columns where the lower pressure is over the land. Air at this level starts to move across the coastline from the sea toward the land.

This is an interesting and useful result. By simply creating a temperature difference between two locations where the air was originally at rest, the air has been caused to move in one direction aloft and in the opposite direction at the surface. In general, the movement of air which results from differential heating is called a thermal circulation. Thermal circulations have two horizontal branches; an upper branch which is called the return flow, and a lower branch. The example shown in figure 4-6 is a sea breeze. Note the name indicates the source of the lower branch of the circulation; that is, the sea breeze blows from the sea. Some other thermal circulations are the land breeze, mountain breeze, and valley breeze. These will be described in a later chapter.

Thermal circulations of the type described above occur over distances of ten miles to a hundred miles or so. On larger scales, circulations are found which also have their roots in differential solar heating; however, the warm and cold air masses created by this process are often carried far from their sources. Additionally, in these large circulations, the rotation of the earth is important. As you would expect, the result is a bit more complex; but, with the help of Newton and a few simple diagrams, understandable.

The pressure gradient force is always directed perpendicular to the isobars toward lower pressure.

In a thermal circulation, the stronger the temperature gradient, the stronger the pressure gradient, and the stronger the wind.

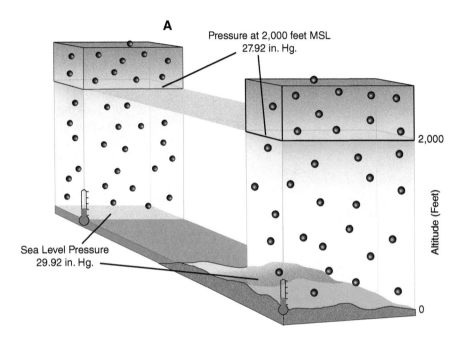

Figure 4-6. The development of pressure gradients by differential heating and the movement of atmospheric mass. Both diagrams represent three-dimensional cross sections through the atmosphere along a coastline. The upper diagram shows the conditions when the temperature of the land and water are equal. The bottom diagram shows the result of uneven heating. A few colored "molecules" are shown to indicate how the mass of the atmosphere is affected by the temperature. The numbers in the lower diagram indicate the sequence of events initiated by heating.

A

Pressure at 2,000 feet MSL
27.92 in. Hg.

2,000

Altitude (Feet)

Sea Level Pressure
29.92 in. Hg.

0

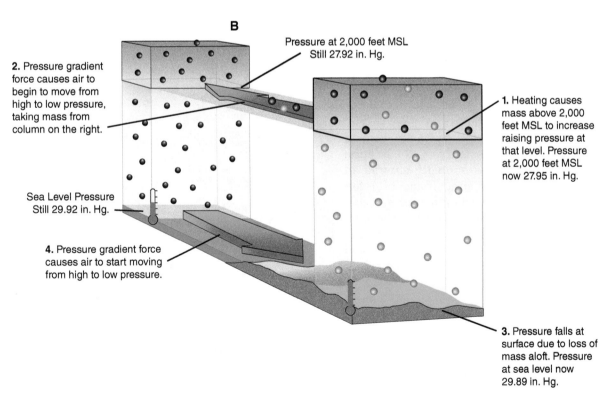

B

Pressure at 2,000 feet MSL
Still 27.92 in. Hg.

2. Pressure gradient force causes air to begin to move from high to low pressure, taking mass from column on the right.

1. Heating causes mass above 2,000 feet MSL to increase raising pressure at that level. Pressure at 2,000 feet MSL now 27.95 in. Hg.

Sea Level Pressure
Still 29.92 in. Hg.

4. Pressure gradient force causes air to start moving from high to low pressure.

3. Pressure falls at surface due to loss of mass aloft. Pressure at sea level now 29.89 in. Hg.

Section D

CORIOLIS FORCE

We live and fly in a rotating frame of reference. To us, the earth is fixed and the sun and stars move across the sky. Of course, you know that the movement of these celestial bodies is due to the rotation of the earth. Since we normally observe all motions from this rotating frame of reference, the effect of that rotation must be taken into account when we explain the observed motions. This is usually done by introducing the concept of Coriolis force, which is named for one of the first scientists to make an in-depth study of this effect.

Coriolis force affects all objects moving across the face of the earth. It influences ocean currents and the paths of airplanes. Most importantly, from our meteorological perspective, as soon as air begins to move, it is influenced by Coriolis force. Although a rigorous treatment of Coriolis force is beyond the scope of this book,

some important properties can be demonstrated with a simple experiment.

In figure 4-7, A man is shown standing on a merry-go-round which is rotating counterclockwise (ccw). The direction of rotation is determined by looking at the merry-go-round from the top. Imagine you are standing on the opposite side of the merry-go-round throwing a ball to the person in figure 4-7. As shown in the picture, you observe that the ball misses the target to the right. To you, a "force" acts on the ball, causing it to accelerate; that is, to change from the intended direction by curving to the right.

A person standing off to the side of the merry-go-round observes that the ball flies in a straight line after it leaves your hand. That person sees immediately that the ball is not being deflected, rather it is the position of you and the catcher that changes during the time it takes the ball to travel across the merry-go-round.

If the rotation rate is increased, the position changes are greater and

Figure 4-7. Coriolis force explains to the thrower why the ball appears to curve to the right of the intended target.

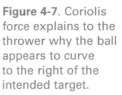

the deflection of the ball is greater, as observed by those on the merry-go-round. But to the observer off to the side, the path is still straight. Note that if the direction of rotation is clockwise (cw), the deflection of the ball is to the left.

When we attempt to describe the motion of the atmosphere (or anything else) relative to the rotating earth, we must also consider Coriolis force. However, things become a little more involved because the earth is a rotating sphere, rather than a rotating disk. In the case of the merry-go-round, it did not matter where the thrower and the catcher were located on the rotating platform. For a fixed rotation rate and a constant speed of the ball, Coriolis force was the same everywhere on the

platform. This is because the axis of rotation of the merry-go-round was vertical; that is, perpendicular to the platform across which the ball was moving. This is not the case with the earth. For a fixed rotation rate and speed of the ball,

Coriolis force is different at different latitudes. The variation is illustrated in figure 4-8.

If, as shown in figure 4-8, our merry-go-round is attached to the earth at the North Pole, it rotates counterclockwise. Note that the axis of the earth and the axis of rotation of the merry-go-round are parallel at the pole. If we let the earth's rotation rate and the speed of the ball be the same as in the previous example, then (considering only Coriolis force) we would see the same effect on the ball. At the equator, the situation is different. In that location, the axis of the earth is perpendicular to the axis of the merry-go-round, so the merry-go-round does not rotate about its vertical axis as the earth turns. Coriolis

Figure 4-8. For a given speed of the ball and a constant rotation rate, Coriolis force is a maximum at the poles and zero at the equator.

force is zero at the equator and the ball moves in a straight line.

Fortunately, the earth rotates much more slowly than our merry-go-round (one rotation per 24 hours); therefore, Coriolis force is much weaker. This is why we do not see all baseballs curving to the right in the Northern Hemisphere and to the left in the Southern Hemisphere. The effect is there, but it is only significant when an object moves over large distances (several hundred miles or more), allowing the weak force time to act. In the next section, we will see the impact of Coriolis force on very large atmospheric circulations. For smaller distances and times (for example, in a sea breeze), other forces such as pressure gradient, are much stronger. In those cases, the deflective effect of Coriolis force is not very noticeable, if at all.

Another aspect of Coriolis force is that it is opposite in the Southern Hemisphere. Motion there is deflected to the left. This difference between hemispheres is understood when our view of the earth is taken from the South Pole; the earth has clockwise rotation.

The most important characteristics of the effect of Coriolis force on the horizontal movement of air (wind) may be summarized as follows:

1. Coriolis force always acts 90° to the right of the wind in the Northern Hemisphere and 90° to the left in the Southern Hemisphere. Therefore, Coriolis force affects only wind direction, not wind speed.

2. Although Coriolis force does not affect the wind speed, it depends on the wind speed; that is, it requires the air to be moving. If the wind speed is zero, the Coriolis force is zero. The greater the wind speed, the greater the Coriolis force.

3. Coriolis force depends on the latitude. For a given wind speed, Coriolis force varies from zero at the equator to a maximum at the poles.

4. Although Coriolis force affects air motion on all scales, in comparison to other forces, its effect is minimal for small-scale circulations and very important for large-scale wind systems.

Navigation across large distances requires corrections for the influence of Coriolis force. Aircraft tracks must be corrected to the left in the Northern Hemisphere and to the right in the Southern Hemisphere to counteract the deflection due to the earth's rotation. These curved paths, in turn, affect some instruments used for celestial navigation, requiring further corrections for position computations. (USAF, 1985).

Section E
GEOSTROPHIC BALANCE

A very useful characteristic of the atmosphere is that the pressure gradient force and the Coriolis force tend to balance each other when the scales of atmospheric circulations are large enough. This means that when air travels over distances of hundreds of miles or more (the farther the better), Coriolis and pressure gradient forces tend to be equal in magnitude, but opposite in direction. This condition is known as geostrophic balance. The related wind is the geostrophic wind. The geostrophic wind is quite helpful in understanding the connection between wind and large scale pressure patterns.

"Geostrophic" is a useful memory device because the root of the word literally means "earth-turning," an obvious reference to the Coriolis effect of the earth's rotation. Since Coriolis force depends on the wind speed, geostrophic balance can only happen when the wind is already blowing. In the Northern Hemisphere, Coriolis force always acts 90° to the <u>right</u> of the wind, looking downstream. Therefore, geostrophic bal-

ance is only possible when the pressure gradient force acts exactly opposite; that is, 90° to the <u>left</u> of the wind. (Figure 4-9). Some useful properties of the geostrophic wind are summarized as follows:

1. In the Northern Hemisphere, the geostrophic wind is parallel to the isobars with the lowest pressure on the left. This condition is easily remembered with a well-known rule of thumb (Buys-Ballot's Law): *With your back to the wind, the low pressure is on your left (opposite in Southern Hemisphere).*

2. The closer together the isobars, the stronger the pressure gradient and the stronger the geostrophic windspeed.

3. In the Northern Hemisphere, winds tend to blow counterclockwise around low pressure centers (cyclones) and clockwise around high pressure centers (anticyclones). Therefore, counterclockwise motion is often described as cyclonic flow and clockwise motion as anticyclonic flow. The wind flow directions around lows and highs and this terminology are reversed in the Southern Hemisphere.

4. Geostrophic balance does not occur in small scale circulations such as sea breezes, thunderstorms, tornadoes, and dust devils because the pressure gradient force is much greater than the Coriolis force.

When the isobars on the surface analysis chart are close together, the pressure gradient force is large and wind speeds are strong.

Wind directions can be inferred from isobaric patterns.

Winds do not blow directly from large scale high pressure areas to low-pressure areas because of Coriolis force.

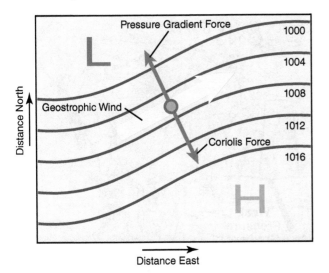

Figure 4-9. Solid purple lines are isobars (mb). Solid red arrows indicate forces acting on a parcel of air (small circle). The velocity of the parcel is indicated by the broad, yellow arrow. Geostrophic balance occurs when the pressure gradient and Coriolis forces are equal in magnitude and opposite in direction and are the only forces acting on the parcel of air.

ESTIMATING WINDS FROM ISOBARS AND CONTOURS

The geostrophic wind is a practical tool for the interpretation of large scale weather charts. It allows you to estimate the winds from the pressure field. This is very convenient because, typically, there are more pressure and altimeter setting reports than there are direct wind measurements. Examples of the approximate agreement of observed winds with the pressure field (as you would expect with geostrophic balance) are shown in figures 4-10 and 4-11.

Several characteristics of geostrophic winds are apparent: weak winds in areas with weak pressure gradients; strong winds in regions with strong pressure gradients; counterclockwise circulations of air around lows; and clockwise circulations around highs (in the Northern Hemisphere).

The tendency for the observed winds to be in geostrophic balance is stronger at 500 mb than at the surface. This is because surface frictional effects are small at the 500 mb level. (Figure 4-11) Friction is discussed in detail in Section F of this chapter.

The 500 mb constant pressure chart is suitable for flight planning at FL 180. Observed temperature and wind information give approximate conditions along the proposed route.

T/P ⊘	○ Station Location
	T Temperature (°F)
	P Pressure (220 = 1022.0 mb)
↗	Wind Direction (From the Northeast)
⊘	Wind Speed (15 knots: 1 barb = 10 Kts half barb = 5 Kts)
1028	Isobar (1028 = 1028.0 mb)

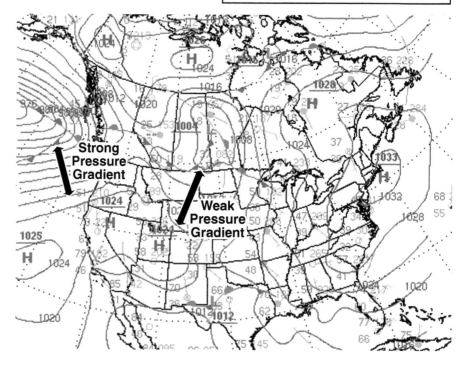

Figure 4-10. A portion of a Northern Hemisphere surface analysis chart. Three pieces of information important to our discussion of wind are plotted on the chart at each station location indicated by a small circle: temperature, observed pressure, and wind. Also, isobars are drawn every four millibars on the basis of the plotted pressure reports.

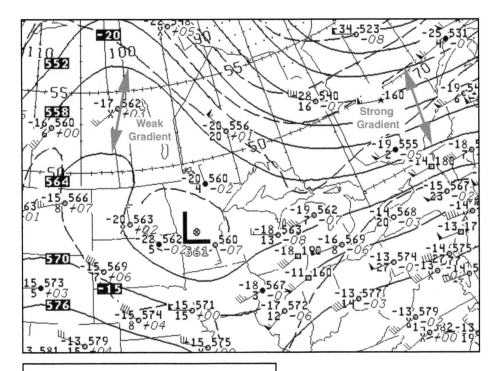

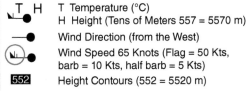

T   Temperature (°C)
H   Height (Tens of Meters 557 = 5570 m)

Wind Direction (from the West)

Wind Speed 65 Knots (Flag = 50 Kts, barb = 10 Kts, half barb = 5 Kts)

Height Contours (552 = 5520 m)

Figure 4-11. 500 mb constant pressure chart (~FL180). The important wind information plotted around the station locations includes observed 500 mb heights, temperatures, and winds. The solid lines on the charts are 500 mb height contours analyzed every 60 meters on the basis of the observed data. Notice that the winds are strongest where the contour gradient is strongest and that the winds are nearly parallel to the contours. These features are evidence of airflow that is nearly in geostrophic balance.

Prior to the widespread use of point-to-point navigation systems, such as GPS and INS, the geostrophic wind was a useful navigational tool, especially for long flights over water and when there were few navigational aids available. By determining the pressure gradient along the track, the crosstrack component of the geostrophic wind could be determined and the drift estimated. Important measurements for this calculation are the pressure altitude (PA) measured with the pressure altimeter set at 29.92 inches, and the true altitude (TA) measured, for example, with a radar altimeter. The difference between the two (TA – PA) is known as the D-value. The crosstrack geostrophic wind is proportional to the gradient in D-values along the flight track. Greater details about D-value measurements and procedures for drift calculations are given in navigation texts and manuals (USAF, 1985).

Section F

FRICTION

The root of the word friction is another useful memory device. It comes from the Latin word meaning "rub." Friction is the force that resists the relative motion of two bodies in contact. Friction also occurs within fluids, such as the atmosphere, and at the interface between fluids and solids (skin friction). In your studies of aeronautics, you have been introduced to drag as one of the primary forces affecting aircraft in flight. Drag is the resistance of the atmosphere to the relative motion of the aircraft. Drag includes skin friction as well as form drag which is caused by turbulence induced by the shape of the aircraft. Meteorologists use the term surface friction to describe the resistive force that arises from a combination of skin friction and turbulence near the earth's surface. The primary effects of surface friction are experienced through the lowest 2,000 feet of the atmosphere. This is called the atmospheric boundary layer. It is a transition zone between large surface frictional effects near the ground and negligible effects above the boundary layer. (Figure 4-12)

To understand the influence of friction, consider the following hypothetical situation. The wind at

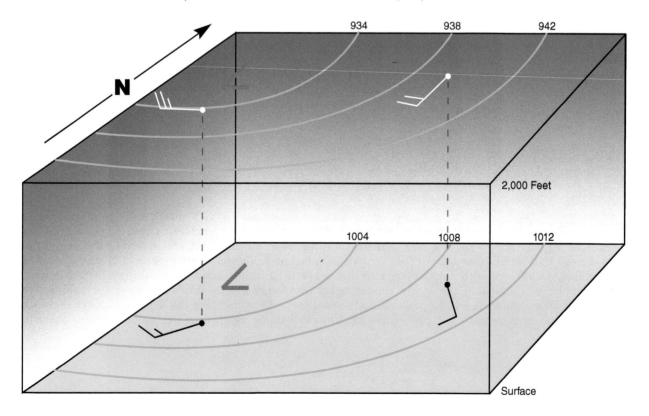

Figure 4-12. The influence of surface friction is greatest in the atmospheric boundary layer, which is typically the lowest 2,000 feet of the troposphere. Frictional effects are at a maximum at the surface and decrease to a minimum at the top of the boundary layer. The impact of this variation is illustrated here. Although the pressure gradient doesn't vary between the two levels, wind direction changes clockwise with increasing height and the wind speed increases. The direction change with height is counterclockwise in the Southern Hemisphere. Note isobars are labeled in mb (hPa).

anemometer level (10 meters or about 30 feet AGL) is initially in geostrophic balance (only pressure gradient and Coriolis forces exist). We then "turn on" the friction caused by the earth's surface and let all forces come into balance (pressure gradient, Coriolis, and friction). In the final balance, the wind speed is less than its original geostrophic value. Furthermore, the wind is no longer parallel to the isobars. It blows slightly across the isobars toward lower pressure. The angle between the wind and the isobars varies from about 10° over water to about 45° over land, depending on the roughness of the surface.

Keep in mind that this behavior is only approximate. It assumes, ideally, that a balance of forces is maintained. It doesn't include the effects of mountainous terrain. Also, in actual conditions, the slowing of the wind near the ground causes the air to form turbulent eddies that cause fluctuations in surface windspeed and direction. Details of these effects are described in a later chapter. The following is a summary of the effects of friction in the boundary layer.

1. Winds increase with altitude in the atmospheric boundary layer, with the greatest increases just above the surface.

2. The wind changes direction clockwise (veers) with increasing altitude.

3. When winds near the surface are strong, the boundary layer is turbulent and winds are gusty. As you descend into the boundary layer to land on a windy day, the air becomes rougher as you get closer to the ground.

4. The boundary layer is deeper during the day and in the warmer months of the year. It is shallower at night and during the colder months.

5. When winds are strong, the boundary layer is deeper over rough terrain.

6. Winds near the ground tend to spiral counterclockwise into cyclones and spiral clockwise out of anticyclones.

7. Some of the effects listed here may be masked in stormy conditions.

At the surface, winds cross the isobars at an angle toward lower pressure and are weaker than winds aloft. Because of the decrease of frictional effects with height, the winds at 2,000 feet AGL tend to parallel the isobars.

Wind is caused by pressure differences and modified by the earth's rotation and surface friction.

CE 180. No injuries. After a successful landing in a 10-12 knot crosswind, as the Cessna 180 slowed, the upwind wing was lifted by a gust of wind. While the pilot attempted to regain control, the opposite wing impacted the surface causing the aircraft to veer toward the upwind runway edge. The aircraft left the runway and nosed over onto its back in soft terrain.

Section G

OTHER EFFECTS

In most situations, pressure gradient force, Coriolis force, and friction explain the dominant, large scale characteristics of the winds. However, you should be aware of a few other influences that can modify that picture, sometimes significantly.

WIND PRODUCTION BY VERTICAL MOTIONS

In general, when an air parcel moves vertically for any reason, it carries its horizontal winds (actually horizontal momentum) to a different altitude, where it is mixed with the surroundings. This process changes the winds at the new altitude, causing the pressure gradient to change. One of the most frequent ways this occurs is when mechanical or thermal turbulence causes the boundary layer to become well-mixed. Stronger winds are brought from the top of the boundary layer to the ground, producing gustiness.

In some other atmospheric circulations, the effects of these processes can be quick and large, producing very strong horizontal winds at the surface. Examples occur in airflow over mountains and in thunderstorms. (Figure 4-13) Details about these phenomena, and flight hazards associated with them, are discussed later in the text.

ACCELERATED AIRFLOW

When air moves along a curved path, even if it is travelling at a constant speed, it is subjected to an acceleration; that is, the direction of motion is constantly changing along the path. This is known as centripetal acceleration. It is due to an *imbalance* in forces. When discussing this effect, some find it more convenient to refer to a "force" that produces the centripetal acceleration — the centrifugal force. In either case, large scale wind speeds are slightly modified from what we would expect according to geostrophic balance.

As the radius of the curved circulation becomes smaller, the effects of centrifugal force become larger. Where the scale is so small that the pressure gradient force is much larger than the

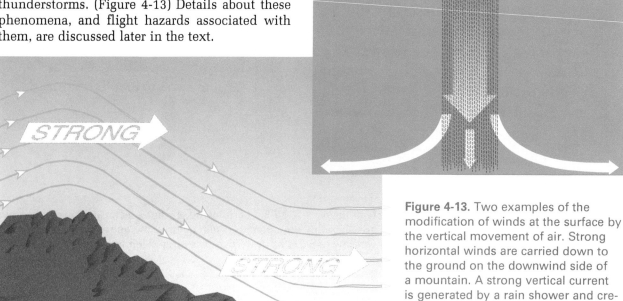

Figure 4-13. Two examples of the modification of winds at the surface by the vertical movement of air. Strong horizontal winds are carried down to the ground on the downwind side of a mountain. A strong vertical current is generated by a rain shower and creates strong horizontal winds near the ground.

Coriolis force, the pressure gradient and centrifugal forces may be in cyclostrophic balance and produce cyclostrophic winds. The most dramatic examples of these are dust devils and tornadoes. (Figure 4-14) More details of these particular phenomena are given in later chapters.

The geostrophic and other balances of forces that act on air parcels are idealizations. They are simple models that help us explain the causes and many of the characteristics of the wind and anticipate its behavior. The air is often accelerated by small imbalances in the sum of the forces. These are the sources of large changes in the wind and, as you will see, the production of weather in short time periods.

Figure 4-14. Tornados have winds that tend toward cyclostrophic balance. Because Coriolis force is much smaller than the pressure gradient force, winds can circulate either clockwise or counterclockwise. Tornado photograph courtesy of National Oceanic and Atmospheric Administration.

SUMMARY

The basic properties of horizontal motions of the atmosphere have been examined in this chapter. You should now understand that air responds to pressure gradients by being accelerated toward lower pressure. Furthermore, pressure gradients are caused by temperature gradients and the movement of atmospheric mass by the winds. Once the air is in motion, Coriolis force becomes important, especially in large scale atmospheric circulations.

The wind that results when Coriolis force is exactly in balance with the pressure gradient force is the geostrophic wind. Because the near balance of these two forces is common, the geostrophic wind has proven to be a very useful estimate of actual wind in a variety of applications ranging from the interpretation of isobars and contours on weather charts, to navigation. Friction modifies the geostrophic balance, especially in the atmospheric boundary layer where its effect is apparent in cross-isobar airflow, turbulence, and gusty winds.

Your knowledge of the basic causes and characteristics of wind will be of great value as you examine vertical motions, clouds, and weather in the next two chapters and, subsequently, specific atmospheric circulations.

KEY TERMS

Acceleration
Anticyclone
Anticyclonic Flow
Boundary Layer
Centrifugal Force
Coriolis Force
Cyclone
Cyclonic Flow
Cyclostrophic Balance
Cyclostrophic Winds
D-Value
Differential Heating
Drag
Form Drag
Friction
Geostrophic Balance
Geostrophic Wind
Gust
Horizontal Pressure Gradient Force

Parcel
Peak Wind
Pressure Gradient Force
Return Flow
Scalar
Sea Breeze
Skin Friction
Squall
Surface Friction
Sustained Speed
Thermal Circulation
True North
Vector
Veer
Wind
Wind Direction
Wind Speed
Wind Velocity

REVIEW QUESTIONS

1. What is the bearing of the center of a nearby low pressure area (assume it is circular) from your location if your measured wind direction at 2,000 feet AGL is
   1. northwest?
   2. 240°?
   3. south?
   4. 090°?

2. What would your answers to question number 1 be if the wind directions were measured at the airport weather station instead of 2,000 feet?

3. In cyclonic flow in the Southern Hemisphere, which way do winds circulate around the center of the pressure system? Is the central pressure relatively low or high in the cyclonic case?

4. A series of weather reports are listed below. Decode all wind information.

   METAR KDAY 050851Z 03003KT 5SM -RA BR OVC036 07/06 A3000=
   METAR KDAY 051405Z 10020G23KT 3SM BR SCT023 BKN037 OVC065 07/06 A2996=
   METAR KBAB 051755Z 00000KT 15SM FEW100 BKN200 12/03 A3028=
   METAR KSAC 051847Z VRB05KT 20SM BKN160 BKN280 13/02 A3027=
   METAR KVIS 051854Z AUTO 19006KT 10SM CLR 14/06 A3026=
   METAR KFTK 051755Z 21005KT 1 1/4SM -SHRA BR BKN003 OVC005 13/12 A2985=

DISCOVERY QUESTIONS

5. With the guidance of your instructor, obtain a surface analysis chart with well-defined high and low pressure systems. Select five or ten widely separated weather reporting stations for which wind data are available. Construct a table to record the answers of each of the questions below for each station.
   1. What are the observed wind speeds and directions?
   2. What is the most likely wind direction at 2,000 feet AGL?
   3. Which of the locations has the strongest surface geostrophic winds?

6. With the guidance of your instructor, select a 700 mb constant pressure chart for, preferably, a winter day. Select five observing stations for which wind data are plotted and in regions where the contours have different directions and gradients. Answer each of the questions that follow for each station.

   1. What are the observed wind speeds and directions?
   2. What are the geostrophic wind directions?
   3. Which of the locations has the strongest geostrophic winds?
   4. What is the approximate flight level of the chart?

7. Do some research on aircraft navigation and document the effects of Coriolis force in detail.

8. If the weather chart in question number 5 was in the Southern Hemisphere and the pressure pattern remained exactly the same, how would the winds be different? Redraw the map to illustrate your answer.

9. In the text, the development of a sea breeze was explained. Make a similar explanation of a land breeze, starting with (ideally) calm conditions after sunset. Draw appropriate diagrams. Be sure you explain how the pressure gradients are created both near the surface and aloft.

10. A Foucault pendulum is often used to demonstrate the Coriolis effect. Do some research and describe what a Foucault pendulum is and how it works.

CHAPTER 5
Vertical Motion and Stability

Introduction

In the previous chapter, we concentrated on the causes and characteristics of the wind; that is, the horizontal part of three-dimensional atmospheric motions. In this chapter, we examine vertical atmospheric motions. Although vertical motions are often so small that they are not felt by the pilot, they are still important in aviation weather. Very slow upward motions play a key role in the production of clouds and precipitation, and therefore, in the creation of flight hazards, such as poor visibilities, low ceilings, and icing. Gentle downward motions dissipate clouds and contribute to fair weather. But the atmosphere is not limited to weak vertical movements. Occasionally, turbulent upward and downward motions are large enough to cause injury, damage, and loss of aircraft control. Clearly, understanding the nature of vertical motions is a useful addition to your aviation weather knowledge. When you complete this chapter, you will understand not only how vertical motions are produced, but also what important effects atmospheric stability has on those motions.

Section A

VERTICAL MOTIONS

As we saw in the previous chapter, when an air parcel moves from one location to another, it typically has a horizontal component (wind) and a vertical component (vertical motion). Because of the hydrostatic balance of the atmosphere, vertical motions are usually much smaller than horizontal motions. However, there are some important exceptions. Small imbalances between the gravitational force and the vertical pressure gradient force arise in circulations such as thunderstorms and cause large vertical accelerations and vertical motions. When vertical motions are strong enough to affect aircraft motion, they are often referred to as "vertical gusts." (Figure 5-1)

CAUSES

Air may move upward or downward for a number of reasons. The most frequent causes are convergence and divergence, orography, fronts, and convection.

CONVERGENCE/DIVERGENCE

Convergence corresponds to a net inflow of air into a given area. It may occur when wind speed slows down in the direction of flow and/or when opposing airstreams meet. Divergence is the net outflow from a given area. Winds may diverge when the wind speed increases in the direction of the flow and/or when an airstream spreads out in the downstream direction. If either one of these processes occurs at some point in the atmosphere, air moves upward or downward. This interaction is common to all fluids; that is, motion in one region usually causes motions in a nearby region. You have observed this property many times in liquids; for example, when you dip a bucket of water from a lake, you don't leave a hole in the surface. The surrounding water rushes in to replace it.

The effect of convergence and divergence of the wind on vertical motions is easy to visualize near the earth's surface. When surface winds converge,

Vertical Velocities	Feet Per Minute	Turbulence Intensity
Average for the entire Atmosphere	0	
Nimbostratus Cloud	10	
Weak Thermal	200	
Growing Cumulus Cloud	500+	Light—Moderate
Thunderstorm	2,000+	Moderate—Severe
Strong Thunderstorm	5,000+	Extreme
Extreme Mountain Wave	5,000+	Extreme
Extreme Clear Air Turbulence	5,000+	Extreme

Figure 5-1. Typical and extreme vertical motions associated with various atmospheric phenomena. The right-hand column shows pilot-reported turbulence intensities. **Notes:** 100 fpm is approximately equal to one knot. Extreme cases of 10,000 fpm have been reported. **Caution:** What appears to be nimbostratus may contain regions of strong convection.

Embedded thunderstorms are obscured by massive cloud layers and cannot be seen.

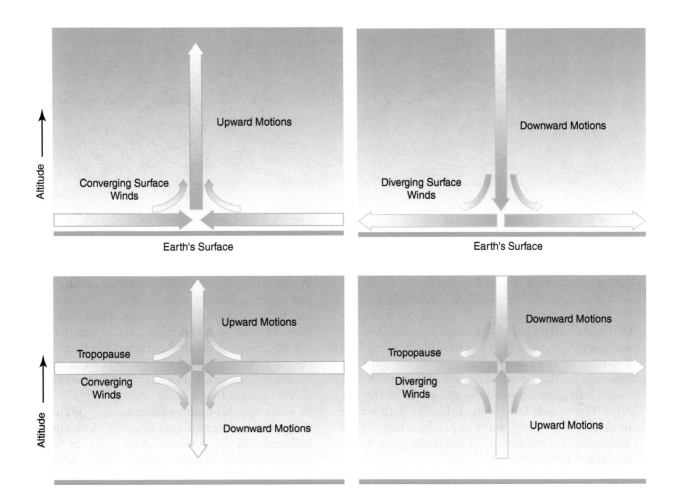

Figure 5-2. Patterns of vertical motions caused by convergence and divergence near the ground (top) and near the tropopause (bottom).

the inflowing air is removed by rising motions aloft. (Figure 5-2)

Conversely, divergence of surface winds causes air to sink from aloft to replace the air being removed at lower levels. Figure 5-2 also shows those vertical motions which may develop when the convergence or divergence occurs near the tropopause.

From the previous chapter on wind, recall that for large scale flow (nearly in geostrophic bal-

ance), friction causes the surface winds to blow across the isobars at a slight angle toward lower pressure. This means that around large low pressure areas, surface winds spiral into the centers (convergence). For high pressure areas, they spiral outward from the centers (divergence). As shown in the upper part of figure 5-2 and in figure 5-3, these processes force vertical motions. Air rises in low pressure areas and sinks in high pressure areas.

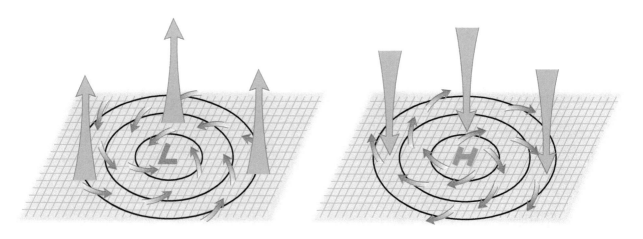

Figure 5-3. Left: Convergence of surface wind in the low pressure area causes upward motion. Right: Divergence of surface winds in a high pressure area causes downward motions.

OROGRAPHY

Air can be forced upward or downward when it encounters a barrier. A simple example is orographic lifting. When wind intersects a mountain or hill, it is simply pushed upward. On the downwind or lee side of the mountain, air moves downward. The strength of the vertical velocities depends on the speed of the wind perpendicular to the mountainside and the steepness of the terrain. (Figure 5-4) Orography interacts with winds in more complicated ways to produce turbulence and mountain lee waves. These flight hazards are described in Chapter 12.

FRONTS

When the atmosphere itself creates an obstacle to the wind, a barrier effect similar to a mountain can be produced. For instance, when a cold airmass is next to a warm airmass, a narrow, sloping boundary is created between the two. This is called a front. If either airmass moves toward the other, the warm air moves upward over the cold, dense airmass in a process called frontal lifting or, in some special cases, overrunning. (Figure 5-5) Air can also descend over fronts. Fronts and their influence in the production of aviation weather hazards such as clouds, precipitation, turbulence,

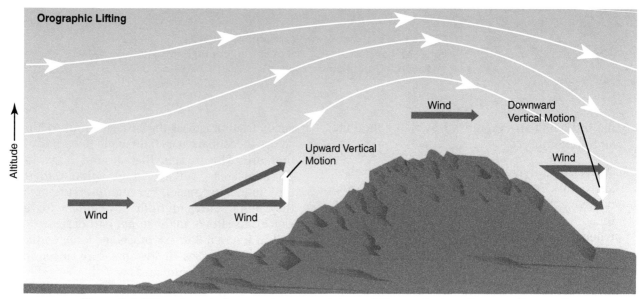

Figure 5-4. When the wind encounters mountains or hills, vertical motions are the result.

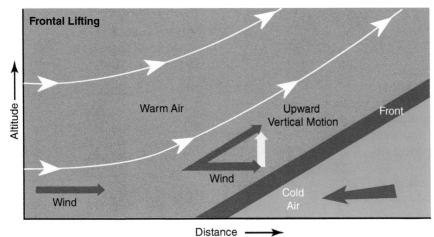

Figure 5-5. Frontal lifting. Vertical motion along a frontal boundary is caused by cold, dense air pushing under a warm airmass, or warm air moving over a cold airmass. The relative movements of airmasses can also cause air to descend near fronts.

Figure 5-6. Convective lifting. Air rises in discrete bubbles when the atmosphere is unstable. Relatively cool air sinks around the bubbles to replace the rising air.

and wind shear are discussed in greater detail in Parts II and III of this text.

CONVECTION

If air at a particular level in the atmosphere is warmer than its surroundings, it will tend to rise. As you know from Chapter 2, this is a form of convection. Although this word is used to describe a wide variety of processes involving vertical motions, it is most often used in reference to rising warm air and/or the clouds and weather associated with that process. We will use the latter meaning for convection throughout the remainder of the text.

As bubbles of warm air rise in the convective lifting process, the surrounding air sinks. (Figure 5-6) Convection, as described here, occurs under unstable atmospheric conditions. Stability and instability are discussed at length in the next section.

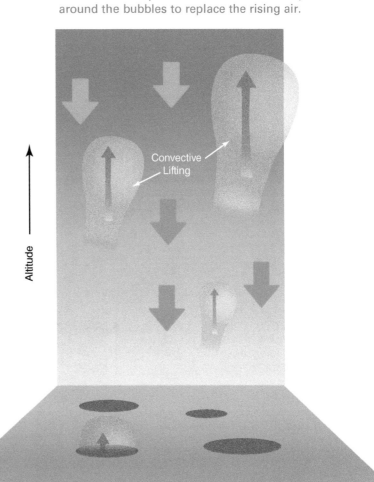

MECHANICAL TURBULENCE

When wind blows over the ground, friction causes the air to slow down in the lowest layers. The greater speed at higher altitudes causes the air to roll up into irregular circulations about horizontal axes. (Figure 5-7) These chaotic eddies are swept along with the wind, producing downward motions on their downwind side and upward motions on their upwind side. This is known generally as mechanical turbulence. Rough air experienced when landing on windy days is caused by these small scale circulations. More details about low-level turbulence are given in Chapter 12.

GRAVITY WAVE MOTIONS

Under certain circumstances, air may be disturbed by small scale wave motions; that is, parcels of air may be caused to oscillate vertically. (Figure 5-8) Such oscillations that move away from the source of the disturbance are called atmospheric gravity waves because the earth's gravity plays an important role in producing them. A mountain lee wave is one type of gravity wave. More details are given in Chapter 12.

Whereas convection occurs under unstable atmospheric conditions, gravity waves occur under stable conditions. Meteorologists use the concept of atmospheric stability to deal with gravity effects on vertical motions. We must examine the meaning and application of stability before we consider more of the details of gravity waves or convection.

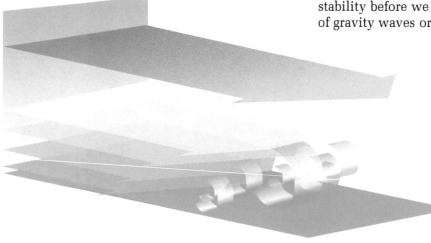

Figure 5-7. The rapid increase of wind velocity near the earth's surface causes mechanical turbulence. Turbulent eddies produce fluctuating (gusty) winds and vertical motions as they are swept along. The eddies have a three dimensional structure that is constantly being stretched and deformed by the wind.

Figure 5-8. Gravity waves are disturbances in which stable air, that was displaced vertically, oscillates due to the restoring force of gravity. In this diagram, the air is also moving horizontally. Note upward vertical motions occur upwind of the wave crest and downward vertical motions occur downwind.

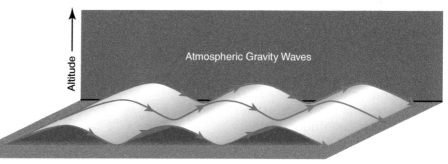

Altitude

Atmospheric Gravity Waves

Distance ⟶

Section B

STABILITY

Stability is a general concept applied to explain the behavior of mechanical systems. When discussing such systems, we may describe them as either stable or unstable. A stable system may be defined as one that, if displaced or distorted, tends to return to its original location and/or configuration. On the other hand, an unstable system is one that tends to move away from its original position, once it has been displaced or distorted. A system with neutral stability remains in its new position if displaced or distorted; that is, it neither returns to, nor is it accelerated away from, its original position. Some simple examples of stable, unstable and neutral systems are shown in figure 5-9.

Stable   Unstable   Neutral

Figure 5-9. Examples of stable, unstable, and neutral systems. Blue arrows indicate the initial, small displacement of a marble. Red arrows indicate the subsequent motion. In the neutral case there is no subsequent motion.

In the remainder of this section, stability and instability are applied to the atmosphere to understand and anticipate the influence of gravity on the development of vertical motions in the atmosphere.

ATMOSPHERIC STABILITY

As applied here, atmospheric *stability* is a condition that makes it difficult for air parcels to move upward or downward. In contrast, atmospheric *instability* is a condition that promotes vertical motions. Similar to the mechanical systems described above, atmospheric stability is determined by considering the behavior of a parcel of air after it receives a small vertical displacement. When an air parcel is displaced (upward or downward) and forces develop that cause it to return to its initial position, the parcel is said to be stable. On the other hand, if the forces develop that cause the parcel to accelerate away from its original position (upward or downward), the parcel is unstable. (Figure 5-10)

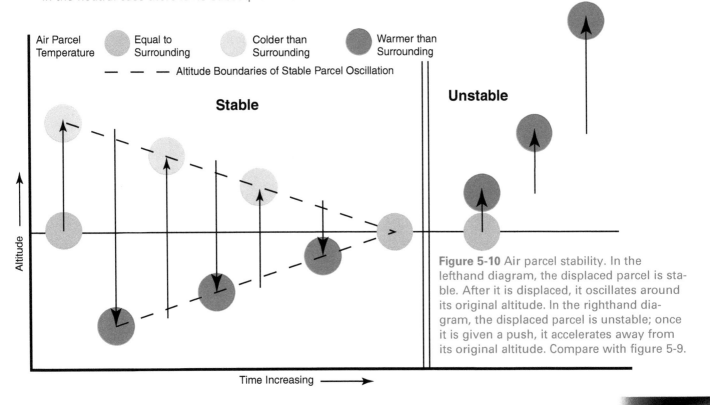

Figure 5-10 Air parcel stability. In the lefthand diagram, the displaced parcel is stable. After it is displaced, it oscillates around its original altitude. In the righthand diagram, the displaced parcel is unstable; once it is given a push, it accelerates away from its original altitude. Compare with figure 5-9.

How big is an "air parcel?" The size of the idealized air parcel used in the explanation and estimation of atmospheric stability is somewhat arbitrary. It is assumed to be large enough to be representative of the air at its original level but small enough so that single values of temperature and humidity are indicative of conditions for the entire parcel. Visualize something between the size of a breadbox and the size of a freight car.

BUOYANCY

In order to completely understand stability and instability of air parcels, we must understand the forces that arise when they are displaced. There actually is one primary force that must be considered: buoyancy force. Buoyancy is the property of an object that allows it to float on the surface of a liquid, or ascend through and remain freely suspended in a compressible fluid such as the atmosphere (Glickman, 2000).

Archimedes' Principle applies here. It simply states that when an object is placed in a fluid (liquid or gas), it will be subjected to a positive (upward) or negative (downward) force depending on whether the object weighs more or less than the fluid it displaces. This is where the gravitational force enters the picture. Weight is a force, defined as the product of mass and gravity. Since gravity varies little across the surface of the earth, differences in weight depend mainly on differences in mass or, in meteorological terms,

density. Archimedes' Principle can be thought of as the bowling ball/balsa wood-in-the-bucket-of-water concept. (Figure 5-11)

The density of a displaced parcel of air can be easily related to its temperature because the pressure of a displaced parcel adjusts to the pressure of its surroundings. Recall from the gas law that if two volumes of air are at the same pressure, the one with the lower density is warmer. This allows us to state Archimedes' Principle for air parcels in terms of temperature and combine it with the concept of stability.

1. If a parcel of air is displaced upward and becomes warmer than its surroundings, it is positively buoyant. It will accelerate upward (away from its original position); it is unstable.

2. If a parcel of air is displaced upward and is colder than its surroundings, it is negatively buoyant. It will be accelerated downward (back to its original position); it is stable.

DETERMINING ATMOSPHERIC STABILITY

Although mentally moving parcels of air around in the atmosphere helps us understand the concept of stability, in practice, it is not very convenient. Instead, meteorologists evaluate the stability of the atmosphere by taking atmospheric soundings and analyzing the soundings to determine stability conditions. Although you won't be doing this

Figure 5-11. The bowling ball in a bucket of water is much more dense than the water it displaces. It is said to have negative buoyancy. A downward-directed force accelerates the ball to the bottom of the bucket. If you push a piece of balsa wood down into the bucket of water, it is much less dense than the water it displaces; there is an upward-directed force. It has positive buoyancy. Once you release the block of balsa wood, it accelerates to the surface of the water.

very often yourself, you will be using information and terminology that comes from these analyses. Therefore, it is helpful to become familiar with the analysis process.

There are three concepts that you must be familiar with in order to understand how stability is determined:

1. Dry Adiabatic Process,

2. Atmospheric Soundings, and

3. Lapse Rates.

In order to understand stability, it is important to be aware of the difference between speed and acceleration. For example, a rising air parcel that slows down when it enters a stable environment has an upward speed and a downward acceleration.

DRY ADIABATIC PROCESS

Whenever a parcel of air changes its altitude, its temperature changes. The reason this happens is that it must change its pressure to match the pressure of its surroundings; so when an air parcel rises, it lowers its pressure by expanding. When the air parcel descends, it compresses.

In order to expand against its surroundings as it rises to a higher altitude (a lower pressure), an air parcel must use energy. The major source of parcel energy is in the motion of its molecules. As you know, the energy of this motion is measured by the temperature. Therefore, as the air parcel moves upward, its temperature decreases because it uses some of this energy to expand. Similarly, if an air parcel descends, its temperature goes up. This temperature change process, *cooling by expansion* and *warming by compression*, is called the dry adiabatic process. (Figure 5-12) It is called a "dry" process because it does not consider the influences of evaporation and condensation. This will be a topic of the next chapter.

Since pressure always decreases with height,

1. Adiabatic cooling will always accompany upward motion.

2. Adiabatic heating will always accompany downward motion.

The rate of temperature change associated with a dry adiabatic process is a constant: 3C° per 1,000 feet (5.4F° per 1,000 feet). As shown in the following paragraphs, this is a useful reference in the evaluation of atmospheric stability.

Unsaturated (cloud-free) air flowing upslope will cool at the rate of approximately 3C° per 1,000 feet.

SOUNDINGS

An atmospheric sounding is a measurement of meteorological conditions between the ground and some higher level in the atmosphere. Soundings are taken from a variety of instrumented platforms including satellites, rockets, and aircraft. Currently, the most common meteorological soundings are made via freely rising, unmanned, instrumented balloons called radiosondes or rawinsondes. Twice each day, at 0000 and 1200 UTC, hundreds of radiosondes are launched around the world to sample temperature, pressure, moisture, and wind at altitudes up to about 100,000 feet MSL. (Figure 5-13)

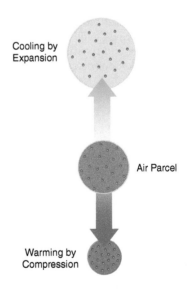

Figure 5-12. The dry adiabatic process causes air to cool when it rises and warm when it sinks.

Courtesy NWS/NOAA

Figure 5-13. Radiosonde sounding system. Winds are determined by tracking the balloon from a ground station or satellite. Pressure, temperature, and moisture measurements are made by the small instrument package which also carries a transmitter to send the information to a tracking station. Typical radiosondes rise at about 1,000 feet per minute.

Newer atmospheric sounding systems include microwave radars called wind profilers; vertically pointing, ground-based radiometers; lasers (LIDARS); space-based (satellite) radiometers; and devices based on sound measurements (SODARS and Radio Acoustic Sounders).

LAPSE RATES

An important stability measurement that can be determined from a sounding is the change of temperature with altitude for a given atmospheric layer. When defined as follows, it is known as the lapse rate (LR).

$$LR = \frac{T(bottom) - T(top)}{DELZ}$$

Where T(bottom) is the temperature at the bottom of the layer, T(top) is the temperature at the top of the layer, and DELZ is the thickness of the layer. Notice that LR can be positive or negative.

If temperature decreases with increasing altitude, LR is positive. From Chapter 1, you already know that the tropospheric lapse rate in the standard atmosphere is 2C° per 1,000 feet.

The rate at which the temperature of a dry parcel of air decreases as it ascends is also a useful reference in stability determinations. This is known as the dry adiabatic lapse rate (DALR). As noted in the last section, it is equal to 3C° per 1,000 feet. Figure 5-14 gives examples of these and other lapse rates that you may encounter in a particular sounding. Note the lapse rate corresponds with the slope of each temperature line.

In describing any layer in the atmosphere, the altitudes of the top of the layer and the bottom (base) are useful pieces of information. For example, in figure 5-14, the base of the inversion is relatively cold and the top is relatively warm. In the free atmosphere, the tops of cloud layers are frequently found near the bases of elevated inversions. It is also helpful to know if inversion

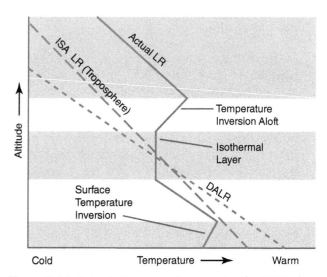

Figure 5-14. Actual atmospheric sounding (solid line), sounding with DALR (short-dashed line), and ISA tropospheric sounding (long-dashed line). Note the variation of LR from layer to layer in the actual sounding. Of particular interest are the isothermal layer where there is no change in temperature with height (LR = 0) and the inversion layers where the temperature increases with height (LR < 0).

layers are next to the ground. These "ground-based" or surface-based inversions often form at night and may be the source of wind shear problems, which will be covered in Chapter 11.

STABILITY EVALUATION

Given a sounding and your knowledge of DALR and LR, the determination of the stability of an atmospheric layer is a straightforward procedure. The steps are given below and the stability criteria are shown graphically in figure 5-15. An example is given in figure 5-16.

1. Select the layer in the sounding in which you are interested.

2. Within the layer, compare the actual LR and DALR.

3. Determine which of the following stability criteria are satisfied.

If	Then
LR > DALR	Absolutely Unstable
LR = DALR	Neutral
LR < DALR	Stable

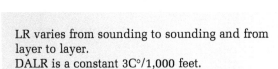

LR varies from sounding to sounding and from layer to layer.
DALR is a constant 3C°/1,000 feet.
ISA LR is a constant:
    2C°/1,000 feet in troposphere.
    0C°/1,000 feet in lower stratosphere.

When the observed lapse rate is referred to as "steep," it means that it approaches or exceeds the dry adiabatic lapse rate.

Figure 5-15. Stability criteria and lapse rates. In a dry atmosphere, all sounding curves with slopes that fall to the left of the curve labeled DALR (dashed) are absolutely unstable. All of those with slopes that fall to the right are stable. If a sounding curve and the curve labeled DALR are parallel, conditions are neutral. Inversions (negative LRs) are very stable. Absolutely unstable conditions, where LR > DALR, are sometimes called "superadiabatic."

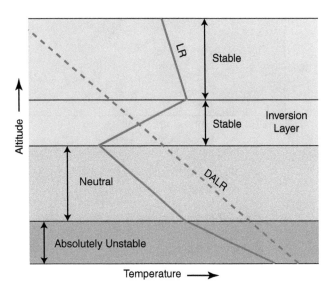

Figure 5-16. A sounding with layers of different stabilities is shown. Although both of the top two layers are stable, the inversion layer is more stable.

We have discussed two different ways to determine whether an air parcel is stable or unstable. The first involved determining whether the temperature of an air parcel would be warmer, colder, or the same as its surroundings after it was pushed upward. The second simply required the comparison of the actual (measured) lapse rate with the dry adiabatic lapse rate. Figure 5-17 gives an example that demonstrates that the two methods to determine stability are equivalent.

In figure 5-17, the diagram on the left shows an absolutely unstable situation by both measures;

LR is greater than DALR and when the parcel reaches 2,000 feet, it is one degree warmer than its surroundings. On the right, the situation is stable; LR is less than DALR and when the parcel reaches 2,000 feet, it is one degree colder than its surroundings.

If a cloud forms or dissipates during the upward or downward displacement of an air parcel, the stability of the air parcel will be modified. Moisture influences on stability are examined in the following chapter.

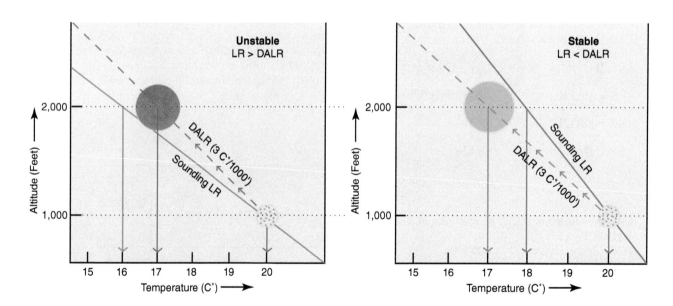

Figure 5-17. Layer stability determined by two methods for unstable (left) and stable (right) conditions. In each case, a parcel of air is displaced from an altitude of 1,000 feet to an altitude of 2,000 feet. The sloping solid lines (LR) indicate the actual sounding and the sloping dashed lines (DALR) indicate the temperatures a parcel would have as it is lifted adiabatically from 1,000 feet.

Section C
THE IMPACT OF STABILITY ON VERTICAL MOTIONS

Sections A and B have, respectively, given information about the development of vertical motions and the meaning and evaluation of stability. In this section, we look at how stability (and instability) influences vertical movements of the atmosphere.

A stable atmosphere does not necessarily prevent air from moving vertically, but it does make that movement more difficult. In a stable atmosphere, air parcels must be given "outside" help if they are to continue their ascent or descent. This "help" could come from convergence/divergence, orographic lifting, or frontal lifting. The air must be pushed or pulled. The stable environment is constantly working against vertical movements, so in most (but not all!) cases, vertical motions are very small and the airflow is smooth.

A stable airmass is more likely to have smoother air than an unstable airmass.

In an unstable atmosphere, convection is the rule. Air rises because it is positively buoyant. Aside from an initial "kick" from surface heating, or from any of the processes mentioned above, no outside help is needed. The air rises because it is warmer than its surroundings.

In comparison with vertical motions in a stable environment, unstable vertical movements are larger and the airflow is turbulent. Except in the vicinity of showers and thunderstorms, visibility is good in unstable conditions. The differences in unstable and stable environments are best seen in differences in cloud forms. (Figures 5-18, 5-19)

The formation of either predominantly stratiform or predominantly cumuliform clouds depends upon the stability of the air being lifted.

Other visual indications of stable conditions are the presence of fog, smoke, and haze which restrict ceiling and visibility. These conditions are frequently present near the ground in the nighttime hours and in daytime whenever a low-level inversion is present.

Figure 5-18. Differences in vertical motions between stable and unstable conditions are seen in the smooth, layered stratiform cloud (stable), above, and the very turbulent-looking cumuliform cloud (unstable), left. A thorough discussion of cloud causes and types is given in the next chapter.

Conditions favorable for the formation of a surface-based temperature inversion are clear, cool nights with calm or light winds.

Unstable air is associated with good visibilities and rough low-level flying conditions in the lower atmosphere in the afternoon and especially in the summer. At these times, ground temperatures tend to be much warmer than air temperatures; conditions in the lower troposphere near the ground are often absolutely unstable.

The stability of an airmass is decreased by heating it from below.

In many situations, it happens that an unstable layer of air is capped by a strong stable layer, perhaps an inversion. In this case, freely rising warm air in the unstable layer is blocked or suppressed when it reaches the stable layer. This effect is often made visible by vertically developing clouds, the tops of which flatten out at the base of a stable layer. (Figure 5-19)

Stability and vertical motions are intimately connected in another way. Not only does stability affect vertical motions as described above, but vertical motions affect stability. Sinking motions tend to make the atmosphere more stable and rising motions tend to make it less stable. Therefore, in high pressure areas where air is generally descending, the atmosphere is more often stable. Low pressure areas are more often associated with upward motions and unstable air. We will see the influences of these interactions on clouds and weather in the following chapters.

Figure 5-19. The low-level source of air feeding the cumulus clouds is an unstable layer. The tops of the clouds flatten out as they reach an overlying stable layer.

SUMMARY

Vertical motions in the atmosphere are critical for aviation because of their role in the production of turbulence, clouds, and associated phenomena. You have learned that upward and downward motions are forced by fronts, mountains, warm surfaces, and converging and diverging airstreams. Additionally, the resulting vertical motions are magnified or suppressed, depending on the atmospheric stability. The understanding of stability has required you to study and understand the concepts of buoyancy and the adiabatic process. With these tools, you have learned how atmospheric stability is evaluated by examining atmospheric temperature soundings. The information in this chapter is basic to later discussions of a wide variety of topics ranging from clouds and weather of large-scale cyclones, to thunderstorms, to small-scale clear air turbulence.

KEY TERMS

Adiabatic Cooling
Adiabatic Heating
Archimedes' Principle
Atmospheric Instability
Atmospheric Stability
Buoyancy
Convective Lifting
Convergence
Divergence
Dry Adiabatic Lapse Rate (DALR)
Dry Adiabatic Process
Front
Frontal Lifting
Gravity Waves
Inversion Layer
Isothermal Layer
Lapse Rate (LR)
Mechanical Turbulence
Negative Buoyancy
Neutral Stability
Orographic Lifting
Positive Buoyancy
Radiosonde
Rawinsonde
Sounding
Stable
Stability Criteria
Surface-Based Inversion
Unstable
Vertical Motion

REVIEW QUESTIONS

1. You are flying over a flat plain when you experience a significant upward gust (turbulence). List the possible causes of the upward vertical motion.

2. The air temperature at a particular station located at sea level is 77°F. The current sounding shows that the actual lapse rate is 2.5°C per 1,000 feet in the lowest 2,000 feet of the atmosphere. What is the air temperature at 1,500 feet AGL?

3. A wind of 25 knots blows against a mountainside that slopes upward from sea level to 2,000 feet AGL over a distance of 5 miles. If the temperature at the base of the hill is 50°F, what is the temperature of air parcels as they reach the top of the hill in °C? (Consider only adiabatic processes.)

4. A simple temperature sounding is shown opposite. Match the layers with the appropriate letters from the sounding. A layer may have more than one letter.

    1. Stable   ———-

    2. Unstable   ———-

    3. Neutral   ———-

    4. Inversion   ———-

    5. Isothermal   ———-

5. For the conditions in question 3, what will the magnitude of the upward vertical velocity (fpm) be along the side of the mountain? (Hint: In this case, vertical velocity = slope x wind speed. Be sure to keep your units consistent).

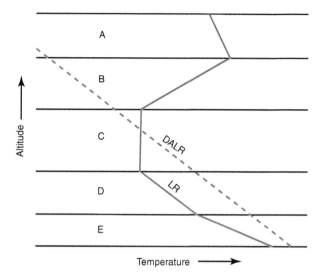

DISCOVERY QUESTIONS

6. How does the day/night surface temperature variation over land affect the stability of the lowest layers of the atmosphere?

7. Inversions aloft are sometimes called "capping inversions" or "lids." Why?

8. You are flying at 4,000 feet AGL over a city during the day. There are no clouds present. As you descend to land at a nearby airport, you notice that, although visibility was very good at 4,000 feet, there is a marked decrease just below 2,500 feet AGL. As you make your final approach, you observe a distinct increase in visibility near the ground. Give a reasonable explanation of the meteorological situation on the basis of what you know about stability.

9. Explain how air can rise when it is stable.

10. Under the conditions described in question 3, a parcel of air is lifted from the surface to 1,500 feet AGL. What is the parcel temperature at that level? Is it stable or unstable? Explain why, from the perspective of parcel temperature and lapse rate.

11. The surface air temperature at your airport is 86°F. There is no sounding, but an aircraft reports 80°F at 1,300 feet AGL on climbout. Do you expect turbulence on takeoff? Explain.

12. What happens to air parcels displaced downward in a stable atmosphere? Why?

CHAPTER 6
Atmospheric Moisture

Introduction

In Chapter 1, we learned that water vapor is a variable gas, occupying only a small percentage of the volume of the gases in the atmosphere. Although water vapor is around us in only small quantities, it has major consequences, not the least of which include icing, thunderstorms, freezing rain, downbursts, whiteouts, frost, and lightning.

In this chapter, we look at the basics of atmospheric moisture, a term which is used here to imply the presence of H_2O in any one or all of its states: water vapor, water, or ice. We examine the transformation between states and the importance of air temperature in that process. When you complete this chapter, you will understand the causes and effects of state changes, how clouds form and dissipate, and how precipitation is produced. You will also know how clouds and precipitation are classified and observed. In later chapters, we build on these important basic concepts to understand the occurrence and characteristics of moisture-related, aviation-critical weather phenomena.

SECTION A: MOISTURE CHARACTERISTICS
State Changes
Vapor Pressure
Relative Humidity
Dewpoint Temperature

SECTION B: CLOUDS
Cloud Formation
    Water Vapor
    Condensation Nuclei
    Cooling
    Latent Heat and Stability
Cloud and Visibility Observations
    Standard Cloud Observations
    Visibility
    Cloud Type
    Other Useful Cloud Observations

SECTION C: PRECIPITATION
Precipitation Causes
Precipitation Characteristics
    Types
    Intensity and Amount
METAR

Section A
MOISTURE CHARACTERISTICS

In Chapter 1, water vapor was identified as part of the small volume of gases other than nitrogen and oxygen that make up the mixture of atmospheric gases. Despite its relatively small amount, water vapor is the stuff that weather is made of — without it, the pilot's problems with the atmosphere would be greatly reduced and the aviation meteorologist would probably be out of business. Of course, this is not the case. The majority of serious weather hazards encountered in aviation operations owe their existence to water vapor. The reason is clear: unlike most other gases in the atmosphere, water vapor is able to change into other forms, or "states" (water and ice) in the normal ranges of atmospheric temperatures and pressures. Your ability to anticipate related flight hazards depends on your understanding of atmospheric moisture in all of its states and the transformation between states.

We begin with some useful definitions and the description of some basic physical processes. This essential information is applied in succeeding sections to explain the presence of clouds and precipitation.

STATE CHANGES

The three states that H_2O can take in the normal range of atmospheric temperatures and pressures are shown graphically in figure 6-1. Water vapor is a colorless, odorless, tasteless gas in which the molecules are free to move about, as in any gas. In the liquid state (water), molecules are restricted in their movements in comparison to water vapor at the same temperature. As a solid (ice), the molecular structure is even more rigid, and the freedom of movement is greatly restricted.

A change of state refers to the transition from one form of H_2O to another. These transitions have specific names as indicated in figure 6-1. The state changes indicated on the top of the diagram all involve the transition of the H_2O molecules to a higher energy state. They are melting (ice to water), evaporation (water to vapor), and subli-

The processes by which water vapor is added to unsaturated air are evaporation and sublimation.

mation (ice directly to vapor without water as an intermediate state).

On the bottom of figure 6-1, all of the transitions take the H_2O molecules to a lower energy state. They are condensation (vapor to water), freezing (water to ice), and deposition (vapor directly to ice without water as an intermediate state).*

As with most other substances, when H_2O is in one particular state, a change in molecular motion always corresponds to a temperature change. However, things are a little different when a state change occurs. At that point, there is a large change in molecular motion that does not correspond with a measurable temperature change. For example, if water evaporates, energy is used by the molecules to jump to the higher energy associated with the water vapor state. (Figure 6-1) If condensation occurs, energy is lost by H_2O molecules as they return to water, a lower energy state.

The amount of heat energy that is absorbed or released when H_2O changes from one state to another is called latent heat. It is absorbed and "hidden" (not measurable as a temperature change) in H_2O molecules in the higher energy states and released as sensible heat (heat that can be felt and measured) when the molecules pass to lower energy states. (Figure 6-1)

You have probably had experiences related to these processes. For example, when you step out of a swimming pool on a hot day, you experience cooler temperatures as heat is taken from your skin to supply the water with the energy to evaporate. So-called swamp coolers are very popular in dry climates; they operate on the principle of cooling by evaporation. The evaporative cooling effect is not limited to water. For example, alcohol evaporates readily. If you place rubbing alcohol or some other alcohol-based substance

---

*In older texts, "sublimation" is used for both ice-to-vapor and vapor-to-ice processes. To avoid ambiguity, "deposition" was adopted to represent the vapor-to-ice process while retaining "sublimation" for the ice-to-vapor transition.

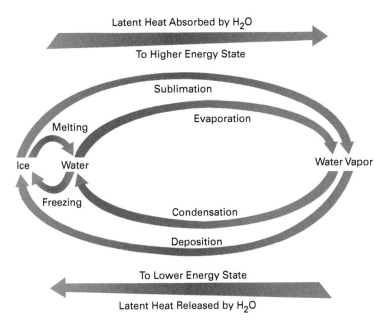

Figure 6-1. Changes of State of H_2O. The latent heat energy involved in the ice-to-water state change is only about 13% of the latent heat required in the water-to-vapor change.

on your skin, you will experience cooling as sensible heat is removed so the liquid can make the jump to the vapor state in the evaporation process.

The evaporation (also called vaporization) of fuel in the carburetor of your aircraft engine results in cooling. When that evaporative cooling is combined with cooling caused by expansion of air in the carburetor, induction icing may result even when the OAT is above freezing. This problem is covered in greater detail later in Chapter 13.

The release of latent heat when condensation occurs is a major energy source for many meteorological circulations. For example, heat released in the condensation process during cloud formation is an important factor in the production of the greater instability and stronger vertical motions of thunderstorms. Similarly, the heat taken from tropical oceans by evaporation becomes the primary energy source for hurricanes when it is released in condensation.

VAPOR PRESSURE

In the mixture of atmospheric gases, each individual gas exerts a partial pressure. When all of

the partial pressures are added together, they equal the total atmospheric pressure (29.92 inches of mercury, 1013.2 millibars/hectoPascals, at sea level in the standard atmosphere). The partial pressure exerted by water vapor (H_2O in gaseous form) is called vapor pressure (VP). It is the force per unit area exerted by the molecules of water vapor and is proportional to the amount of water vapor in the atmosphere. For example, if water vapor is added to the atmosphere, vapor pressure increases.

An important condition with respect to the presence of water vapor is saturation. It occurs when the same amount of molecules are leaving a water surface as are returning. The vapor pressure exerted by the molecules of water vapor in this equilibrium condition is known as saturation vapor pressure (SVP). (Figure 6-2)

Figure 6-2. Cross section of the interface between water and water vapor. The red dots indicate H_2O molecules leaving the water surface and the blue dots indicate H_2O molecules returning to the water surface. When the same number of molecules are going in both directions, the condition is said to be saturated.

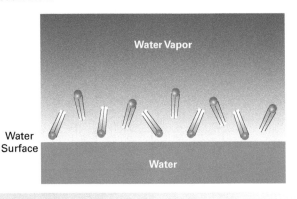

If the atmosphere is saturated at sea level under otherwise standard conditions, the pressure (SVP) exerted by the water vapor molecules in the atmosphere is only about 0.5 in.Hg. versus 29.92 in.Hg. for the total pressure.

The significance of the concept of saturation is that it serves as a practical upper limit for the amount of water vapor present in the atmosphere at a given temperature. SVP is a measure of that upper limit and depends primarily on the temperature. Saturation has many practical applications and is very useful in explaining several atmospheric processes involving changes of state. From theory, the relationship between SVP and temperature is well-known, so we can estimate SVP by simply measuring the temperature. (Figure 6-3)

Figure 6-3 shows two very important characteristics of SVP. First, saturation vapor pressure increases rapidly as the temperature increases. Consider, for example, air that is saturated (a cloud is present). Initially, there is no evaporation because the water vapor content is at its maximum for the observed air temperature. If the air is heated, SVP increases while the amount of water vapor remains the same, so the cloud evaporates. Expanded descriptions of cloud formation and dissipation processes are given in Section B.

The second important characteristic of figure 6-3 is that, for each temperature below 32°F (0°C), there are two possible saturation vapor pressures. This occurs because water does not necessarily

> The amount of water vapor needed for saturation largely depends on air temperature.

freeze at those temperatures; that is, it may be "supercooled." The SVP that applies for a given temperature in this range depends on whether the surface over which the vapor exists is ice or water. Note SVP is lower over ice than over water at the same temperature. This difference is very important in the generation of precipitation, which is discussed in Section C.

The concept of saturation vapor pressure helps explain why water boils. Boiling occurs when SVP equals the total air pressure. This occurs at standard sea level pressure when the water temperature is raised to 100°C. At that point, bubbles of water vapor form throughout the water and rise to the surface.

Recall from an earlier chapter that, without a pressure suit, exposed fluids will vaporize at very high altitudes. Similarly, water boils at lower temperatures at high altitudes because the atmo-

TEMPERATURE		SATURATION VAPOR PRESSURE Inches of Mercury	
°C	(°F)	Over Ice	Over Water
40°C	(104°F)		2.179
30°C	(86°F)		1.253
20°C	(68°F)		.690
10°C	(50°F)		.362
0°C	**(32°F)**	**.180**	**.180**
-10°C	(14°F)	.077	.085
-20°C	(-4°F)	.030	.037
-30°C	(-22°F)	.011	.015
-40°C	(-40°F)	.004	.006

Figure 6-3. The dependence of saturation vapor pressure (SVP) on temperature over ice and over water.

spheric pressure is lower at those levels. In other words, the temperature does not have to be raised as much as it does at sea level to make the saturation vapor pressure equal the total air pressure.

RELATIVE HUMIDITY

It is often useful to determine how close the atmosphere is to saturation. This information can help you anticipate the formation of clouds or fog. This is done by measuring the amount of water vapor in the atmosphere in terms of actual VP and then estimating SVP from a temperature measurement. (Figure 6-3) The degree of saturation is then computed by taking the ratio of VP and SVP and multiplying it by 100. The result is called relative humidity (RH). It expresses the amount of water vapor actually present as a percentage of the amount required for saturation.

$$RH(\%) = (VP/SVP) \times 100$$

For example, from figure 6-3, if the air temperature is 86°F and the actual vapor pressure is 0.627 inches of mercury, the relative humidity is 50%.

$$RH(\%) = (0.627 \div 1.254) \times 100 = 50\%$$

It is important to remember that RH is relative to SVP, and that SVP depends on the temperature. RH tells us nothing about the actual amount of water vapor present. For example, saturated air at -4°F in Alaska only has about one twentieth of the water vapor as that in saturated air at 68°F in Florida, although RH = 100% in both cases. This has some important ramifications. In another example, suppose the air outside your cockpit is

saturated (RH = 100%) at a temperature of -10°C. If that air is brought into the cockpit for ventilation, and heated to 10°C (50°F) along the way, the cockpit humidity will be less than 25 percent.

> In fair weather, near the ground, relative humidity is usually highest at the time of minimum temperature and lowest at the time of maximum temperature.

DEWPOINT TEMPERATURE

Dewpoint is the temperature at which condensation first occurs when air is cooled at a constant pressure without adding or removing water vapor. Dewpoint temperature is always less than the air temperature, with one exception. When the air is saturated (RH = 100%), the temperature and dewpoint are equal.

In aviation meteorology reports, dewpoint is given rather than relative humidity. Dewpoint is extremely useful in predicting precipitation amounts, thunderstorms, and icing. Also, changes in relative humidity are helpful for anticipating clouds, fog, and low visibilities. A very useful quantity that relates RH and dewpoint is the temperature-dewpoint spread (also called "dewpoint depression"). It is the difference between the air temperature and dewpoint. When the temperature-dewpoint spread is small, the RH is high. When the spread is very large, the RH is low. Examples of plotted reports of dewpoint and temperature-dewpoint spread are given in figure 6-4.

> Dewpoint refers to the temperature to which air must be cooled at a given pressure to become saturated.

> Because water vapor has a lower molecular weight than dry air, moist (humid) air is less dense than dry air at the same temperature and pressure and the density altitude is higher.

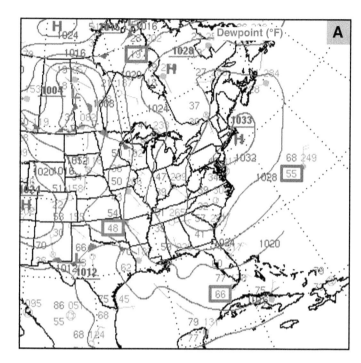

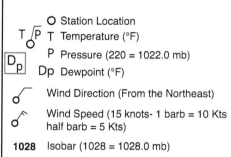

Figure 6-4. A: Surface analysis chart illustrating plotted dewpoint temperatures (°F). Note: similar charts for other regions often show both temperature and dewpoint in °C. **B**: 500 mb constant pressure chart (~18,000 feet MSL) showing temperature (°C) and temperature-dewpoint spread (C°). Other plotted data include wind, temperature, and pressure (A) or height (B). Solid lines are isobars in diagram A and contours in diagram B. Isotherms are dashed in diagram B.

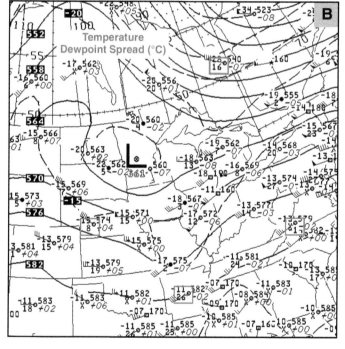

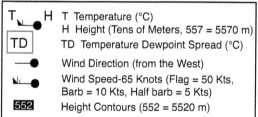

Dew is a condensation product that forms when the ground or other object (such as the wings of a parked airplane) loses heat energy through nighttime (nocturnal) radiation. Cooling reduces the temperature of the thin layer of air next to the object. When the temperature of the air reaches its dewpoint, dew condenses on the colder surface. If the temperature falls below 32°F (0°C) after dew is present, it will freeze (white dew).

In contrast with white dew, white frost is a deposition product. It forms under the same conditions favorable for dew, except that the dewpoint temperature is below 32°F (0°C). In this case, the critical temperature is technically known as the frostpoint. However, in operational usage the term "dewpoint" is always used, regardless of the air temperature.

Direct measurements of dewpoint are difficult. However, there are some practical indirect methods. One of the most common ways to determine dewpoint is from measurements with an instrument called a psychrometer. This instrument consists of two thermometers. One measures the air temperature (dry bulb thermometer). The second thermometer is covered with a wick saturated with water (wet bulb thermometer). When the wick is ventilated, evaporation occurs and the temperature decreases. The wet bulb temperature is the lowest temperature that can be reached by evaporative cooling. The difference between dry bulb and wet bulb temperatures (wet bulb depression) will be large if the atmosphere is dry and zero if the atmosphere is saturated. The relationship between dry bulb temperature, wet bulb depression, and dewpoint (and relative humidity) are well known.

Frost forms when the temperature of the collecting surface is at or below the dewpoint of the adjacent air and the dewpoint is below freezing. Frost is considered hazardous to flight because it spoils the smooth flow of air over the wings, thereby decreasing lifting capability.

Section B

CLOUDS

A cloud is a suspension of water droplets and/or ice crystals in the atmosphere. In and around clouds, several important physical processes unique to the saturated atmosphere take place. These processes not only contribute to the formation and dissipation of clouds, but they also produce precipitation as well as a wide variety of flight hazards. Knowledge of clouds and their causes is an essential step toward the understanding of those hazards. In this section, we examine cloud formation and cloud types.

CLOUD FORMATION

The three requirements for cloud formation are:

1. Water vapor
2. Condensation nuclei
3. Cooling

WATER VAPOR

Clouds don't form in dry air. Their development requires the presence of water vapor and conditions that will lead to a change of state from vapor to water droplets or ice crystals. Clouds are always more likely to form in air with high RH (small temperature-dewpoint spread) than in drier air.

CONDENSATION NUCLEI

Condensation nuclei are microscopic particles, such as dust and salt, that provide surfaces on which water vapor undergoes condensation to form water droplets or deposition to form ice crystals. These particles are also called "hygroscopic" nuclei because they have an affinity for water. Without them, it would be more difficult for the state changes to occur. Fortunately, an adequate number of condensation nuclei are almost always present in the atmosphere.

Fog is usually more prevalent in industrial areas because of an abundance of condensation nuclei from combustion.

COOLING

If air is not already saturated, either more water vapor must be added to bring it to saturation or it must be cooled in order to form a cloud. In either case, the RH must be raised to 100 percent. You know from our previous discussions that cooling is an effective way to reach saturation because the amount of water vapor necessary for saturation decreases as the temperature goes down.

Cooling of the air for cloud formation usually results from one or both of the following processes:

1. Contact with a cold surface
2. Adiabatic expansion

Cooling by contact with the earth's surface is primarily responsible for fog, dew, and frost. This contact cooling is the process by which heat is conducted away from the warmer air to the colder earth. You should also recall that contact cooling always causes the stability of the air to increase. Stabilization, in turn, influences the appearance of any clouds that form.

Contact cooling occurs when warm air is advected over a relatively cool surface. If there is adequate moisture, so-called advection fog forms. A classic example of the formation of advection fog occurs when air from the warm Gulf Stream waters of the Atlantic moves over the colder waters of the Labrador Current. Another example is found along the California coast where northwesterly winds bring moist Pacific air across the colder California Current and upwelling coastal waters. Both of these regions are notorious for low clouds and fog. (Figure 6-5)

Advection fog often forms in coastal areas.

Figure 6-5. A visible image from a Geostationary Operational Environmental Satellite (GOES), shows the tops of fog and low clouds caused by advective cooling over the cold water along the west coast of the United States.

Conditions favorable for the formation of radiation fog over a land surface are clear skies, little or no wind, and a small temperature-dewpoint spread.

Conditions favorable for contact cooling can also develop at night after the ground cools due to terrestrial radiation. These effects are greatest under conditions of clear skies and light winds. When the air temperature is reduced to the dewpoint by such cooling, so-called radiation fog will form. If the fog is very shallow (less than 20 feet deep), it is called ground fog. Radiation fog is a common phenomenon in wintertime when nights are long.

It is often found in river valleys (valley fog) where cool air pools and moisture is abundant. (Figure 6-6) Good examples are found in the valleys of the Appalachian Mountains in the eastern U.S. and the San Joaquin Valley in California. Specific flight hazards associated with fog are presented in Chapter 14.

The great majority of clouds that occur away from the earth's surface (in the free atmosphere) form in air that is cooled by adiabatic expansion; that is, in air that is moving upward. Whenever you see a cloud in the free atmosphere, most likely the air is either moving upward or has recently been moving upward. If a cloud is dissipating, it is often moving downward. It also may be mixing with its dry surroundings. In either case, the cloud evaporates (sublimates).

Figure 6-6. Valley fog forms when radiational cooling causes cool, dense air to pool in a valley. River valleys with ample supplies of moisture are favorite locations for this type of fog.

Adiabatic cooling can also contribute to cloud formation in the vicinity of sloping terrain. This is why there is increased cloudiness on the upwind (windward) side of mountains and decreased cloudiness on the downwind (leeward) side of the mountains. The drier, downwind side of the mountain is often described as a rainshadow. (Figure 6-7)

Contact cooling always produces stable air; whereas, adiabatic cooling can be associated with either stable or unstable air. The air that rises rapidly in thunderstorms is unstable. In contrast, wintertime fogs over the western plains of the U.S. often develop when moist air flows northward from the Gulf of Mexico. The air is cooled adiabatically, as it moves upslope, and cooled by contact with the cold ground, especially after sunset. This is sometimes called upslope fog. (Figure 6-8)

Figure 6-7. When moist air flows over a mountain range, clouds and precipitation normally form on the upwind (windward) side.

Figure 6-8. In winter, when warm, moist air is carried northward from the Gulf of Mexico across the coast of Texas, fog often forms inland. Although generally referred to as "upslope" fog, it is usually due to a combination of processes. The air cools adiabatically as its trajectory carries it over higher terrain (the upslope part); it cools by contact with colder ground (as advection fog); at night further cooling of the ground by nocturnal radiation enhances the process (as radiation fog).

The types of fog that depend upon wind in order to exist are advection fog and upslope fog.

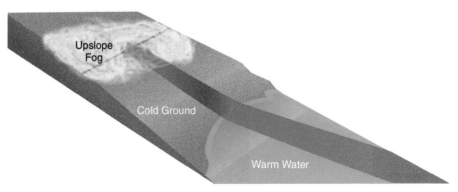

Clouds can also form when warm, moist air is mixed with cold air. A good example of this process is steam fog. When very cold, dry air moves over warm water, air very close to the surface picks up water vapor from the strong evaporation. Because the moist air in contact with the surface is warmer than the overlying cold air, convection develops, causing the moist air to mix with the cold air aloft. With the mixing, the air temperature is reduced below the dewpoint of the moist air. Condensation occurs in a shallow layer of wispy, plume-like columns. This process explains why steam fog is also called evaporation fog or sea smoke. (Figure 6-9)

Figure 6-9. Steam fog is common over unfrozen water bodies in the cold months of the year.

Under the right conditions, an aircraft can actually be a critical component in the cloud-forming process. Clouds known as condensation trails or contrails may appear around or behind an aircraft when the general requirements for cloud formation are met (water vapor, condensation nuclei, and cooling). There are two types of contrails:

Aerodynamic contrails form when pressure is lowered as air flows over propellers, wings, and portions of the aircraft fuselage. The pressure decrease causes adiabatic cooling which brings the air to saturation. Aerodynamic contrails may take different forms depending on what part of the aircraft they are generated. They are often vis-ible as thin, short-lived, corkscrew-shaped clouds in the core of wing tip vortexes on takeoff and landings in damp weather. (Figure 6-10A)

Exhaust contrails form when hot, moist exhaust gases are cooled by mixing with cold air. A critical condition for this type of contrail is the temperature: less than -24°C near sea level and less than -45°C at FL500. In comparison with aerodynamic contrails, exhaust contrails can be much more substantial in volume and far more persistent. (Figure 6-10B)

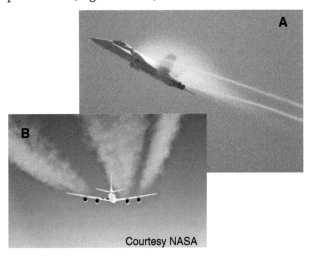

Courtesy NASA

Figure 6-10. A. Aerodynamic Contrails, B. Exhaust Contrails.

A **dissipation contrail** or **distrail** is a streak of clearing in a thin cloud layer that may form behind an aircraft flying near the cloud tops. The cloud dissipates due to heat added from the aircraft exhaust and/or mixing of dry air into the cloud in the aircraft downwash.

LATENT HEAT AND STABILITY

When air becomes saturated, further cooling results in a change of state (cloud formation) and a release of latent heat. This is particularly important when an air parcel is rising and cooling adiabatically. The additional heat can cause important changes in stability.

The rate of cooling of an air parcel during ascent in saturated conditions (in a cloud) is always less than in dry conditions.

The saturated adiabatic lapse rate varies between about 3C° per 1,000 feet for very cold temperatures and 1C° per 1,000 feet for very hot temperatures.

When condensation occurs in a parcel of rising air, adiabatic cooling is partially offset by warming due to the release of latent heat. Keep in mind that latent heat never completely offsets adiabatic cooling. A saturated parcel continues to cool as it rises, but at a slower rate than if it were dry. This is called a saturated adiabatic process and the rate of cooling of a rising, saturated parcel is called the moist or saturated adiabatic lapse rate (SALR).

Although DALR is a constant 3C° per 1,000 feet, SALR is variable. It is about the same as DALR at extremely cold temperatures (–40°C), but is only a third of DALR value at very hot temperatures (100°F). This is because, in saturated conditions, there is much more water vapor present at high temperatures, so there is much more latent heat to release when condensation occurs.

The condensation level is the height of the base of the cloud, that is, the altitude where a cloud begins to form in rising air. Below the condensation level the rising parcel cools at the DALR and above that level it cools at the SALR. Since parcel stability depends on the difference between the temperature of the parcel and the temperature of its surroundings, a saturated, rising parcel will be less stable than a dry parcel, all other conditions being the same. (Figure 6-11) Note that less stable does not necessarily mean unstable. The difference is apparent in the cloud forms described in the next section.

Figure 6-11 illustrates a fourth stability classification (in addition to absolutely unstable, neutral, and stable). In the example shown in the figure, if the parcel stays dry, it is stable; but, if it reaches

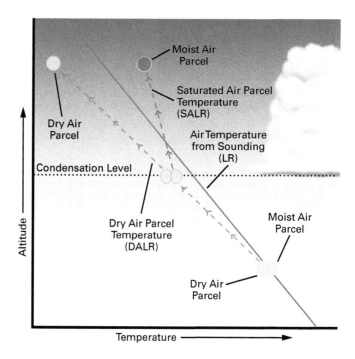

Figure 6-11. The solid red line indicates the measured temperature change with height (a temperature "sounding") while the dashed lines represent the temperature changes of two ascending air parcels (blue circles). The moist air parcel reaches saturation at the condensation level while the dry air parcel stays dry. Note the differences in temperature and stability that arise because of differences in the release of latent heat.

saturation, it becomes unstable. The outcome depends on whether latent heat is released. This is a case of conditional instability. The "condition" is that the air parcel must become saturated in order to be unstable.

A stability index is a single number that reflects the stability/instability conditions for a particular sounding at a given time. Two examples are the K Index and the Lifted Index (LI).

Since the 1990's, the number of surface weather observing stations has been expanded significantly with automated stations. Some of these are stand-alone (designated by "AUTO" in METAR code) while others are augmented with human observers.

CLOUD AND VISIBILITY OBSERVATIONS

Clouds and visibility are important indicators of the state of the atmosphere. They give visual clues about imminent weather changes, including the advance or retreat of large-scale weather systems, winds, turbulence, and stability. Learning to observe clouds and visibility is essential for proper interpretation of METAR and for flight safety.

STANDARD CLOUD OBSERVATIONS

Clouds are regularly observed and reported at weather stations. As a pilot, you will be using these observations for flight planning and to make in-flight decisions. It is important that you develop the ability to interpret an observation as if you were the observer who reported it. Cloud observations are made from the ground, where the view of the sky is different than what you see from the cockpit. In order to derive the most useful information from a cloud report, you must learn to "stand in the shoes of the observer."

The technical description of all of the clouds present in the sky at a particular location is called the sky condition. A complete observation of sky condition includes:

1. Cloud height
2. Cloud amount
3. Cloud type

CLOUD HEIGHT

A cloud layer refers to clouds with bases at approximately the same level. A cloud layer may be a continuous sheet of clouds, or it may be made up of many individual clouds. It is sometimes called a "cloud deck." There may be one or more cloud layers reported in a given observation.

Cloud height refers to the height of the base of a cloud layer above ground level (AGL). Heights are reported in hundreds of feet in the United States and other countries. Clouds with bases 50 feet AGL or less are reported as mist (visibility > 5/8 mile to < 7 miles) or fog (visibility < 5/8 mile). When cloud bases are very low, such as when mist or fog is present, the reported cloud height corresponds to the vertical visibility (VV); that is, the vertical distance that an observer or some remote sensing device can "see" into the cloud. (Figure 6-12)

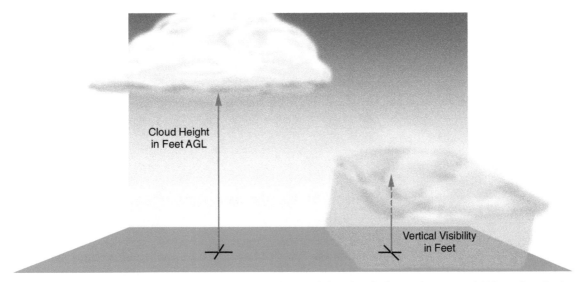

Figure 6-12. Cloud height is the height of the base of the cloud above the ground. When the sky is completely obscured, the reported cloud height is actually the vertical visibility.

Cloud Height in Feet AGL

Vertical Visibility in Feet

The heights of cloud bases can be estimated or measured. The measurements are determined from aircraft reports, reference to nearby landmarks (e.g. hills), or by means of a ceilometer. A ceilometer is a device with a vertical pointing light beam that locates and measures the height above the ground where the beam is brightest.

Vertical visibility (VV) or "indefinite ceiling" is the vertical distance that an observer or a remote sensing device on the ground can "see" into a low cloud or other obscuring phenomenon.

CLOUD AMOUNT

Cloud amount refers to the amount of sky covered by each cloud layer. It is usually observed in eighths of the celestial dome, which is the hemi-sphere of sky observed from a point on the ground. Cloud amount is reported as the total cloud cover at and below the layer in question. "At and below" implies a cumulative amount. Keep in mind that a surface observer cannot see higher clouds hidden by the lower cloud decks. (Figure 6-13)

When no clouds are present, the sky condition is reported as clear (SKC) for a manned station, and as clear (CLR) when no clouds are observed below 12,000 feet AGL for an automated station. If the clouds cover 1/8 to 2/8 of the sky, few (FEW) is reported. If the cloud amount for a particular layer is 3/8 to 4/8, the coverage is designated scattered (SCT). If the cloud amount is 5/8 to 7/8, the cloud layer is broken (BKN). If the coverage is 8/8, the layer is overcast (OVC). (Figure 6-13)

Manned weather stations may report a maximum of six cloud layers while automated weather stations only report a maximum of three layers up to 12,000 feet MSL.

Layer	Coverage (Summation Amt.)	Sky Condition
1	1/8	FEW
2	4/8	SCT
3	5/8	BKN*
4	6/8	BKN

*Ceiling

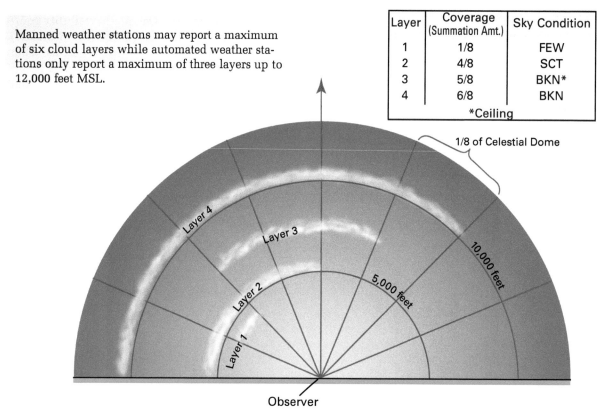

Figure 6-13. Cross section showing a ground observer's view of the celestial dome. The thick white curves represent cloud layers at different altitudes. Each "slice" of the celestial dome which intersects a cloud layer visible to the observer represents an eighth of total cloud amount. As shown in the box at the upper right, cloud amounts are reported for each cloud layer in the order of lowest to highest. The observed coverage of each succeeding layer is added to the cumulative coverage of the lowest layers.

VISIBILITY

Horizontal visibilities play an important role in the classification of sky conditions. Furthermore, sky conditions and visibility are critical for the specification of certain flight restrictions. For these reasons, it is important to pause here and define some useful terminology.

Visibilities reported in standard weather reports are horizontal surface visibilities; that is, they are measured by an instrument or a person standing on the ground or some convenient point of measurement, such as the roof of a building or a tower. The point of measurement is often near the local weather station. Tower visibility is the horizontal visibility determined from the control tower. In reports, it is identified as such only when the official surface visibility is determined from a different location.

Prevailing visibility is the greatest horizontal distance at which objects or bright lights can be seen and identified over at least half of the horizon circle. (Figure 6-14) Prevailing visibility is taken as the representative visibility at a particular location. Be aware that visibilities may be lower in other sectors of the horizon circle. Critical differences between prevailing and sector visibilities are reported at manned stations when the prevailing visibility is less than three miles. Standard reporting formats for visibility, as well as sky condition, weather, and precipitation are presented at the end of this chapter.

Runway visibility (RVV) is the visibility from a particular location along an identified runway. It also is reported in statute miles and fractions. Runway visual range (RVR) is the maximum horizontal distance down a specified instrument runway that a pilot can see and identify standard high intensity lights. It is reported in hundreds of feet.

In the U.S., visibility is reported in statute miles and fractions; internationally, it is reported in meters.

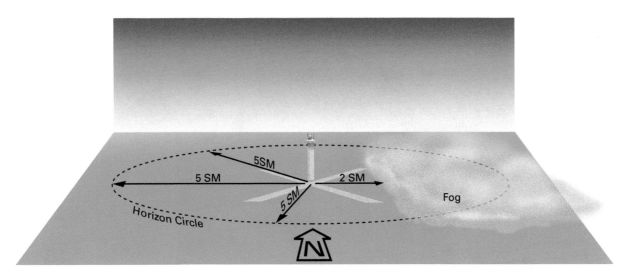

Figure 6-14. In this example, an observer can see and identify objects (day) or bright lights (night) at 5 s.m. except to the east where fog restricts visibility to 2 s.m. The prevailing visibility in this case is 5 s.m.

OBSCURATIONS AND CEILINGS

An obscuration is a weather phenomenon, other than precipitation, that hides part or all of the sky. Obscurations may be caused by fog, smoke, volcanic ash, widespread dust, sand, haze, or spray. Note that all cloud layers and obscurations are considered opaque. (Figure 6-15)

Other international conventions for reporting ceiling and visibility include CAVOK (ceiling and visibility OK), which is used when there is no significant weather **AND** the visibility exceeds 10 kilometers **AND EITHER** there is no ceiling less than 1,500 meters **OR** no ceiling below the highest ATC sector altitude, whichever is higher.

The height above the earth's surface of the lowest cloud layer which has 5/8 or greater coverage is designated as a ceiling. This is important to pilots because it has implications regarding VFR, IFR, and the associated flight rules. (Figure 6-16)

There are two broad classifications of ceiling and visibility conditions for aviation: VMC (Visual Meteorological Conditions) and IMC (Instrument Meteorological Conditions). The corresponding flight rules are VFR (Visual Flight Rules) and IFR (Instrument Flight Rules). The ceiling and visibility are further subdivided respectively into MVFR conditions (Marginal Visual Flight Rules) and LIFR (Low Instrument Flight Rules). These conditions are defined below in terms of ceiling and visibility. Chapter 14 contains more detailed information.

VFR Conditions
 VFR: ceiling > 3,000 feet AGL and visibility > 5 s.m.
 MVFR: ceiling 1,000 to 3,000 feet AGL and/or visibility 3 to 5 s.m.
IFR Conditions
 IFR: ceiling 500 to < 1,000 feet AGL and/or visibility 1 to < 3 s.m.
 LIFR: ceiling < 500 feet AGL and/or visibility < 1 s.m.

Figure 6-16. Terminology and criteria used to define visual and instrument weather conditions.

Figure 6-15. The sky can be totally obscured by a ground-based obscuration. The "height" of the lowest layer is the vertical visibility (arrow labeled "VV"). In this case, the vertical visibility is 500 feet. The upper layer cannot be seen by the observer.

Layer	Coverage (Summation Amt.)	Sky Condition
1	8/8	VV005
2	Not Seen	

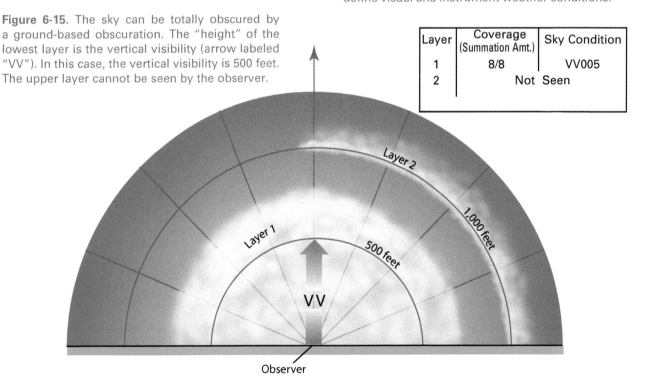

A ceiling is defined as the height above the earth's surface of the lowest layer reported as broken or overcast, or as the vertical visibility into an indefinite ceiling.

Prevailing visibility is used in North America. Outside that area, a METAR gives the sector with the lowest visibility in meters with the direction of that sector. For example, a reported visibility of 4000SE means the lowest visibility over the horizon circle is 4,000 meters to the southeast.

If the sky is totally covered (8/8) by a ground-based obscuring phenomenon, the base of the lowest cloud layer is an indefinite ceiling. Its reported height (AGL) is the vertical visibility.

If the sky is only partially covered by an obscuration (7/8 or less), the height of the lowest cloud layer is reported as zero. (Figure 6-17)

When clouds are observed in flight, a pilot weather report (PIREP) should be made of the heights of bases and tops of individual cloud layers whenever possible. Remember, weather observing stations are few and far between and surface observation systems (human or AUTO) do not have the in-flight perspective. Therefore, PIREPs are invaluable sources of cloud information. All cloud heights observed in flight are reported in feet MSL (not AGL) unless otherwise indicated. A PIREP of a broken layer of clouds with a base at 2,500 feet MSL and a top at 3,300 MSL would be coded: 025 BKN 033.

Layer	Coverage (Summation Amt.)	Sky Condition
1	7/8	BKN000
2	8/8	OVC010

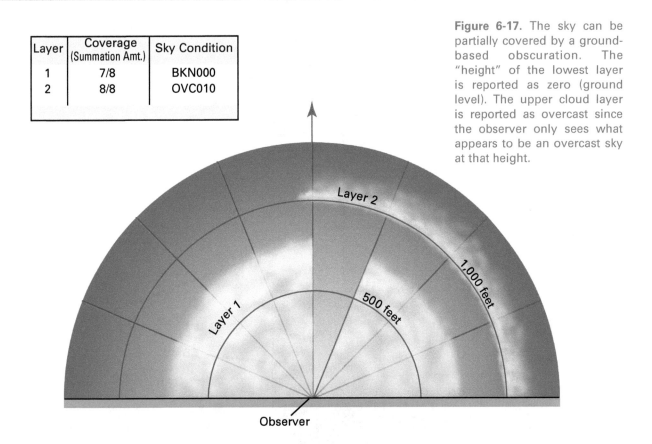

Figure 6-17. The sky can be partially covered by a ground-based obscuration. The "height" of the lowest layer is reported as zero (ground level). The upper cloud layer is reported as overcast since the observer only sees what appears to be an overcast sky at that height.

The four families of clouds are high, middle, low, and those with extensive vertical development.

CLOUD TYPE

Cloud type is determined on the basis of what a cloud looks like: its height, shape, and behavior. Clouds are classified as low, middle, or high clouds according to the height of their bases

Low Clouds	Middle Clouds	High Clouds
<6,500 feet AGL	6,500 to 20,000 feet AGL	>20,000 feet AGL
(ST) stratus	**(AC)** altocumulus	**(CC)** cirrocumulus
(SC) stratocumulus	**(AS)** altostratus	**(CS)** cirrostratus
(NS) nimbostratus		**(CI)** cirrus
Clouds with Vertical Development		
(CU) Cumulus		**(CB)** Cumulonimbus

Figure 6-18. International cloud classifications. Altitude ranges of cloud bases are given for each cloud category. Variations occur depending on season and geographical location.

Courtesy: George McCray

above the ground, and as clouds with vertical development. The ten basic clouds in these categories are listed in figure 6-18 and illustrated in figure 6-19.

Figure 6-19. Ten basic cloud types. International Cloud abbreviations are shown. The CB is a cloud of great vertical development. Notice in the center diagram that the CB base is in the low cloud range while its top is in the high cloud range. Also note that the CB is not drawn to scale. Typically, a single CB is about as wide as it is tall. (See CB Photograph)

Courtesy: Art Rangno

Cloud names are based on the following terms: cumulus (heap), stratus (layer), nimbus (rain), and cirrus (ringlet). In addition, the prefix "alto-" designates middle clouds; and the word "cirrus" and the prefix "cirro-" indicate high clouds.

The distinctive feathery appearance of high clouds is due to the fact that those clouds are composed primarily of ice crystals. Between temperatures of 0°C and -40°C, middle and low clouds are composed of water droplets and ice crystals. The proportion of droplets is much greater at higher temperatures. At temperatures above 0°C clouds are composed entirely of water droplets.

A high cloud is composed mostly of ice crystals.

Keep in mind that cloud height categories are approximate. For example, at high latitudes and in the winter, the tropopause and cirriform clouds tend to be lower, occasionally dipping into the middle-cloud range. Also, the difference between AS and NS is not always precise. Altostratus bases often lower with time; if precipitation begins, the cloud may be identified as NS even though the cloud base may not yet be in the low-cloud range.

Cumuliform clouds in all categories are indicative of some instability. However, well-developed CU, and especially CB, indicate great instability. Although their bases are usually in the low-cloud height range, well-developed CU and CB tops commonly extend well into middle- and high-cloud ranges.

The stability of the air before lifting occurs determines the structure or type of clouds which form as a result of air being forced to ascend.

Because of the extreme dryness in some areas, such as the intermountain western U.S., air must rise 10,000 feet AGL or more to reach the condensation level. High-based CU or CB are common in that area in the summer.

There are many other cloud forms besides the ten basic types discussed here. Some, such as lenticular clouds, are important visual indicators of possible turbulence and other flight hazards. These important cloud variations will be presented later in the text.

OTHER USEFUL CLOUD OBSERVATIONS

The development of your ability to estimate cloud heights and amounts, and to identify the basic cloud types is essential in connecting classroom aviation meteorology to cockpit aviation meteorology. Clouds are caused by specific temperature, wind, vertical motion, and moisture conditions. Their visual identification will help you anticipate, identify, and avoid many potential aviation hazards. You want to be able to "read the sky" from your aircraft as easily as you read this book.

Since cumulus clouds usually develop in air rising from the ground, the heights (H) of cumulus cloud bases (not altocumulus or cirrocumulus) can be accurately estimated from the measured surface temperature (T) and dewpoint (DP) with the formula

$$H = (T-DP)/4.4,$$

where H is in thousands of feet and T and DP are in °F. For example, if cumulus clouds are present with a surface temperature of 72°F and a dewpoint temperature of 50°F, the cloud bases will be at approximately 5,000 feet AGL.

Cloud watching is a good exercise to develop your skills, especially when you compare your observations with the official reports from a nearby airport. Another benefit of such an activity is that there is much more useful information in cloud observations than simply height, amount, and type. For example, by noting the time it takes clouds to grow, dissipate, or simply move across the sky, you will begin to understand time scales and life cycles. Furthermore, wind directions and relative wind speeds aloft can be estimated by watching the movement of clouds in various layers. Movement and the size of clouds (especially CU) can also be judged by watching cloud shadows. In later chapters, we will expand this list of meaningful cloud features.

Satellites provide us with almost continuous cloud observations from geostationary orbits at 22,000 miles above the equator and from polar orbits a few hundred miles above the surface. Onboard radiometers measure visible light reflected from the clouds and the earth and infrared radiation emitted by the earth, clouds, and certain gases in the atmosphere. Some examples are shown in figure 6-20.

In figure 6-20, the image in A is a visible picture, which depends on reflected light. Except for the lack of color, the cloud and ground features seen in A are about what you would see by eye from the same viewpoint. Visible images are usually only made in daylight.

Diagram B is an image acquired at the same time as A, but it is determined from measurements of IR radiation. It is essentially a picture of the pattern of the temperature of the earth's surface when skies are clear, or the temperature of the tops of the clouds when the sky is cloudy. Because the highest clouds are generally the coldest, they are easy to identify. In this image, the coldest temperatures correspond with the brightest white and the warmest temperatures correspond with black. Infrared images can be gathered 24 hours per day.

Figure 6-20. Examples of satellite images from the Geostationary Orbiting Environmental Satellite (GOES). Diagram A is a visible image for 1500UTC September 7, 2006. Diagram B is an infrared image acquired within 15 minutes of the visible image. See text for the explanation of the differences in the images. Source: ADDS.

A

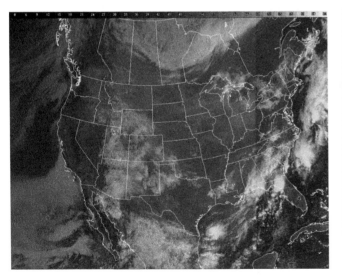

B

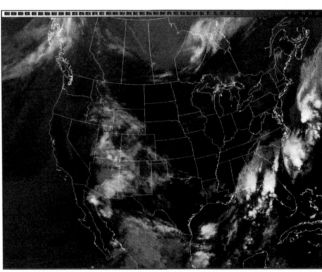

Section C

PRECIPITATION

For surface observations, precipitation is formally defined as all forms of H_2O particles, whether liquid or solid, that fall from the atmosphere and reach the ground. The point of view of this definition is important. Weather reports and forecasts of surface conditions don't necessarily include the falling particles that an aircraft in flight may encounter. These often evaporate before they reach the ground.

Precipitation contributes to many aviation weather problems. It can reduce ceiling and visibility, affect engine performance, increase braking distance, and cause severe wind shear. Under the right temperature conditions, precipitation can freeze on contact, affecting flight performance and aircraft ground handling. Your knowledge of the characteristics and causes of precipitation provides the necessary background to understand and deal with these and related flight hazards.

PRECIPITATION CAUSES

It is a common error for newcomers to meteorology to make the broad assumption that, since 100% RH means that clouds are present, then 100% RH also must mean precipitation! This is NOT necessarily true. Yes, a cloud usually forms when the atmosphere is saturated, but as you know from your own experience,

> MOST CLOUDS DON'T PRECIPITATE.

This statement is based on three important facts about clouds and precipitation:

1. Precipitation particles (water and ice) must be much larger than cloud particles so they can fall out of the cloud and exist long enough to reach the ground.

2. Most of the time, processes that produce small cloud particles are not very effective in producing large precipitation particles.

3. Efficient precipitation-producing processes mainly occur in certain cloud types (usually NS and CB).

In order to understand these limitations, we must examine the processes by which water droplets and ice crystals grow. There are three ways by which precipitation-size particles can be produced.

Condensation/deposition refers to the processes by which cloud particles are initially formed. (Figure 6-1) For precipitation to occur, the very small ice cloud particles must continue to grow through the addition of more molecules of water vapor by the same processes until the particles are large enough to fall out of the cloud and reach the ground.

In the second growth process, called collision/coalescence, two or more droplets collide and merge into a larger droplet. This happens because the initial sizes of the cloud water droplets are different. The larger drops fall faster, growing as they collide and capture the smaller ones. (Figure 6-21)

Neither condensation/deposition nor collision/coalescence can account for all precipitation. These processes are too slow to allow much precipitation to fall within the normal lifetime of a rain cloud.

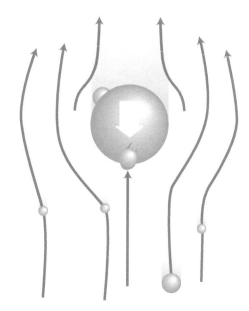

Figure 6-21. Collision/coalescence. Large droplets fall faster than smaller particles, capturing them as they descend.

There are two notable exceptions. Very low stratus and fog are known to produce precipitation that is very light and composed of very small droplets. In these cases, the collision/coalescence process is efficient enough to generate small amounts of precipitation. The cloud is so low that falling droplets, although small, do not evaporate before they reach the surface. Another exception is found in the tropical regions where large condensation nuclei (salt) from the oceans result in some large cloud droplets. These are numerous enough for the collision/coalescence process to work efficiently. But outside the tropics, conditions are different.

In middle and high latitudes, especially over continents, condensation nuclei are much smaller, water droplets are smaller and more numerous, and clouds are colder. Although collision/coalescence alone cannot produce significant precipitation under these conditions, there is another means of growth called the ice-crystal process. It can only operate in regions where water droplets and ice crystals coexist; that is, in clouds where the temperature is below 0°C.

Water droplets that exist in this environment are called supercooled water droplets. They are common in clouds with temperatures between 0°C and −10°C, but water droplets have been observed at temperatures near −40°C. Their existence illustrates why 0°C is technically referred to as the "melting" point rather than the "freezing" point.

The reason that the ice-crystal process works so well for cloud particle growth is that it takes less water vapor molecules to reach saturation over ice than over water at a given subzero temperature. Therefore, when water and ice co-exist at the same temperature, air in contact with the ice crystals can be saturated (RH = 100%), while the same air in contact with the water droplets is unsaturated (RH<100%). The impact of this mixed environment is that ice crystals grow by the deposition of the water vapor molecules given up by evaporating water droplets. This process is very efficient, allowing the crystals to grow rapidly to precipitation-size particles in relatively short time periods. (Figure 6-22)

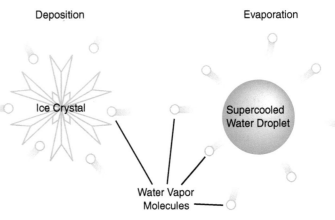

Figure 6-22. Ice crystals grow at the expense of supercooled water droplets in the ice crystal process.

In a mixed water droplet/ice crystal cloud, particles may grow even faster as supercooled water droplets collide with and freeze onto ice crystals. This growth process, known as accretion, is in addition to the process of collision/coalescence, which involves only water droplets.

The result of all of this is that, in middle and high latitudes, most precipitation begins as snow. It now becomes clear why most clouds don't precipitate. Some clouds may be too warm; that is, they have temperatures above 0°C so ice crystals cannot exist. Other clouds (such as cirrus) may be too cold so there are no water droplets present. In either case, the ice crystal process will not work.

Supercooled water droplets are a primary cause of aircraft icing.

PRECIPITATION CHARACTERISTICS

A complete precipitation observation includes type, intensity, and amount of precipitation. As a pilot, you should know how these observations and subsequent remarks are made so you can better interpret the weather you experience and the weather reported from other areas.

TYPES

The most common precipitation types include drizzle, rain, rain showers, snow, snow showers, snow grains, ice pellets, and hail.

Drizzle is distinguished by very small droplets (diameters less than 0.02 inches or 0.5 millimeters). It is commonly associated with fog or low stratus clouds. Rain has larger droplets which fall faster. Rain falls at a relatively steady rate; that is, it starts, changes intensity, and stops gradually. Rain showers refer to liquid precipitation that starts, changes intensity, and stops suddenly. The largest liquid precipitation droplets (diameters about 0.2 inches or 5.0 millimeters) and great-

est short-term precipitation amounts typically occur with rain showers associated with cumulus clouds and thunderstorms.

Freezing drizzle and freezing rain fulfill the definitions given above except they freeze upon contact with the ground or other objects, such as trees, power lines, and aircraft. Freezing rain produces black ice. This refers to difficult-to-distinguish clear ice on black pavement. It is a serious hazard for aircraft on the ground. Conditions under which freezing rain or drizzle form are illustrated in figure 6-23.

Ice pellets are transparent or translucent, globular, solid grains of ice that are formed from the freezing of raindrops or from the freezing of partially melted snowflakes before they reach the ground. They also may be hailstones smaller than 0.2 inches in diameter.

The presence of ice pellets at the surface is evidence that there may be freezing rain at a higher altitude.

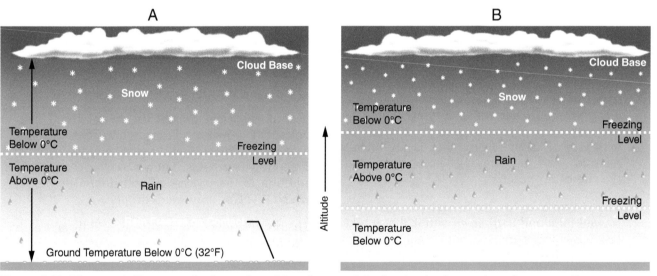

Figure 6-23. Diagram A illustrates the formation of freezing precipitation by the "warm layer" process. Temperatures close to the ground are below freezing. Just above this layer are temperatures above 0°C (the warm layer). A second freezing level is located well above the ground. Snow melts in the warm layer and then falls as rain to the surface. The rain freezes on contact with the ground. The result is freezing rain (or drizzle). In diagram B, conditions are nearly the same, except that the rain freezes before it reaches the ground. The result is ice pellets (sleet). Freezing precipitation and ice pellets may also form in a totally subfreezing environment when supercooled cloud droplets grow to precipitation sizes via the collision/coalescence process.

Snow is precipitation composed of ice crystals. Snow and snow showers are distinguished in the same manner as are rain and rain showers. Snow grains are the solid equivalent of drizzle. They are very small, white, opaque particles of ice. As distinguished from ice pellets (sleet, small hail) they are flatter and they neither shatter nor bounce when they strike the surface.

Hail is precipitation in the form of balls or irregular lumps of ice (0.2 inches or more in diameter) that are produced in the strong updrafts of cumuliform clouds. These are almost always cumulonimbus clouds. Hailstone sizes range to more than five inches in diameter with weights of more than one and one half pounds. The formation of hail and its flight hazards are examined in greater detail in the chapter on thunderstorms.

There are two other precipitation phenomena that you should be able to recognize. One is virga, which is precipitation that evaporates between the base of the cloud and the ground. (Figure 6-24) It is often associated with cumuliform clouds. In the upper troposphere, cirrus fallstreaks are ice crystals that descend from cirrus clouds. They are also called mare's tails or cirrus uncinus.

Figure 6-24. Virga near the top of the picture appears as a curtain of precipitation descending from the cloud base.

INTENSITY AND AMOUNT

At the ground, an observer estimates the intensity of precipitation as light, moderate, or heavy. A rainfall rate of 0.11 to 0.30 inches per hour (.011 to .03 inches per six minutes) is classified as moderate rain. As the intensity of drizzle or snowfall increases, visibility decreases. (Figure 6-25)

Intensity	Visibility (Statute Miles)
Light	> 1/2
Moderate	> 1/4 but < or = 1/2
Heavy	< or = 1/4

Figure 6-25. Drizzle or snowfall intensity and associated visibility.

The amount of liquid precipitation is usually expressed as the depth of water that would have accumulated over a given period of time if the water hadn't run off, soaked into the ground, or evaporated. If precipitation has occurred, but the amount is too small to be measured (the smallest reportable amount is .01 inches), then a trace is reported. On the other end of the scale, very large rainfall amounts can occur in certain situations. Figure 6-26 shows some extreme rainfall amounts for periods varying from a minute to a year.

Precipitation intensity can also be determined by the strength of weather radar echoes. The radar echo intensity level is a commonly available reflectivity scale used to judge the strength of radar echoes and the associated rate of precipitation. More details about weather radar and its practical applications are presented in Chapters 9 (Section C) and 12 (Section B).

If snow has occurred, snow depth is reported, that is, the depth of the snow actually on the ground is reported. In the U.S., snow depth is measured and reported in inches. The snowfall amount is also converted to a water equivalent for the

Observation Period	Rainfall Total (inches)
1 Minute	1.2
42 Minutes	12.0
12 Hours	53.0
1 Month	366.0
1 Year	1042.0

Figure 6-26. Some extreme rainfall rates observed throughout the world.

precipitation report. This is necessary because equal snowfalls can have substantially different water contents. A typical value is 10 inches of snow to 1 inch of water (10:1), but ratios of 2:1 for temperatures near 0°C and 20:1 for very cold temperatures are not unusual.

METAR

Standard aviation weather observations and reports document precipitation types, intensities, and amounts. This information is reported together with a number of other measurements related to atmospheric moisture. These include sky condition, weather, visibility, dewpoint, and related remarks.

Learning the common weather abbreviations, symbols, and word contractions contained in a METAR for the visibility, present weather, sky conditions, and temperature will help you understand this type of report and use it to your best advantage for flight planning. The following paragraphs cover the METAR elements discussed in this chapter. (Figure 6-27)

VISIBILITY

Prevailing visibility is reported in statute miles with "SM" appended. Examples are 1/2SM for one-half statute mile and 7SM for seven

A heavy snow warning indicates a snowfall of 4 inches or more in 12 hours or 6 inches in 24 hours. A blizzard denotes sustained winds of 35 mph (30.4 kts) and considerable falling or blowing snow, frequently reducing visibility to less than 1/4 s.m.

statute miles. In this element, whole numbers and fractions are separated by a space. For example, 1 1/2SM represents visibility one and one-half statute miles. There is no indication in the body of the report that visibility is variable. However, when certain criteria are met, the minimum and maximum reading are placed in the remarks.

When the visibility is less than seven miles, the restriction to visibility is shown in the weather element (item 6 in figure 6-27). The only exceptions to this rule occur when volcanic ash, low drifting dust, sand, or snow are observed. They are always reported, even if they do not restrict visibility to less than seven miles. If tower or surface visibility is less than four statute miles, the lesser of the two will be reported in the body of the report and the greater will be reported in the remarks section (item 10 in figure 6-27). Automated stations will report visibility less than 1/4 statute mile as M1/4SM and visibility ten or greater than ten statute miles as 10SM.

When runway visual range (RVR) is reported, it immediately follows the prevailing visibility in the METAR (item 5 in figure 6-27). RVR is reported whenever the prevailing visibility is one statute mile or less and/or the RVR for the designated instrument runway is 6,000 feet or less. The RVR element is shown with an "R," followed by the runway number, a "slash," and the visual range in hundreds of feet (FT). For example, R32L/1200FT means "runway 32 left visual range is 1,200

Visibility at an AUTO METAR site is estimated by sensor detection of the presence of obstructions to vision in a small volume of air. Conditions such as lower visibility in rain showers or fog near, but not at, the measuring site will not necessarily be reported.

Aviation Routine Weather Report (METAR)

METAR KTPA 122150Z AUTO 08020G38KT 1/2SM R36L/2400FT
+TSRA SCT008 OVC012CB 20/18 A2995 RMK A02 TSB24RAB24 SLP134

1 Type of Report

2 Station Designator and Date/Time

3 Modifier

4 Wind Information

5 Visibility

Prevailing visibility, statute miles (SM). Runway visual range: R, runway number, / , visual range in feet (FT).

6 Present Weather

Intensity: -light, +heavy, no sign for moderate.

Proximity: VC = weather 5 to 10 miles from airport center

Descriptor: for precipitation or obstructions to visibility:
TS Thunderstorm	DR low drifting
SH Shower(s)	MI Shallow
FZ Freezing	BC Patches
BL Blowing	PR Partial

Precipitation types:
RA Rain	GR Hail (1/4" increments)
DZ Drizzle	GS Small hail/snow pellets
SN Snow	PL Ice Pellets
SG Snow grains	IC Ice Crystals
	UP Unknown Precipitation (Automated stations only)

Obscurations:
FG Fog (vsby<5/8SM)	PY Spray
BR Mist (vsby 5/8 to 6SM)	SA Sand
FU Smoke	DU Widespread Dust
HZ Haze	VA Volcanic Ash

Other Phenomena:
SQ Squalls	SS Sandstorm
DS Duststorm	PO Dust/Sand swirls
FC Funnel cloud	+FC Tornado or Waterspout

7 Sky Condition

Amount of sky cover:
SKC Clear (no clouds)
CLR Clear below 12,000 feet
FEW (Less than 1/8 to 2/8 sky cover)
SCT Scattered (3/8 to 4/8 sky cover)
BKN Broken (5/8 to 7/8 sky cover)
OVC Overcast (8/8 sky cover)

Height: three digits in hundreds of feet AGL

Type: towering cumulus (TCU) or cumulonimbus (CB) clouds reported after the height of their base.
Vertical visibility (VV): height into a total obscuration in hundreds of feet.

8 Temperature/Dewpoint

Degrees Celsius, two-digit form. Prefixed "M" = minus (below zero)

9 Altimeter

10 Remarks

Prefixed by "RMK"
A01: Automated Station without Precipitation Descriminator
A02: Automated Station with Precipitation Descriminator
Volcanic Eruption: Plain Language
Tower Visibility or Surface Visibility: TWR VIS 1 1/2 (Tower visibility 1 1/2 sm)
Variable Prevailing Visibility: VIS1/2V1 (Visibility variable between 1/2 and 1 sm)
Sector Visibility: VIS NE 2 1/2 (Visibility 2 1/2 sm to the northeast of the airport)
Visibility at Second Site: VIS 2 RW 11 (Visibility 2 sm for runway 11)
Beginning and ending of Precipitation: RAB05E30 (Rain began 05 minutes past the hour, and ended 30 minutes past the hour)
Virga: VIRGA NE
Variable Ceiling Height: CIG005V010 (Ceiling variable between 500 and 1,000 feet AGL)
Significant Cloud Types: CB W MOV E (Cumulonimbus moving eastward)
Thunderstorm Location and Movement: TS SW MOV N
No Significant Clouds (International Convention): NSC
No Significant Change (International Convention): NOSIG
Plus any other information that will impact aviation operations.

DECODED REPORT: Routine observation for Tampa, FL, on the 12th day of the month at 2150 UTC. Automated Station. Wind from 080° at 20 knots with gusts to 38 knots. Prevailing visibility 1/2 statute mile, runway 36 Left visual range 2,400 feet. Thunderstorm with heavy rain. Scattered clouds at 800 feet AGL, overcast cumulonimbus clouds with bases of 1,200 feet AGL. Temperature 20°C, dewpoint 18°C. Altimeter setting 29.95 inches of mercury. Remarks: Automated station, precipitation discriminator indicated by A02, thunderstorm began 24 minutes past the hour, rain began 24 minutes past the hour, sea level pressure 1013.4 hectoPascals (Note: 1 hPa = 1 millibar).

Figure 6-27. METAR code for aviation weather information. Sections corresponding to topics discussed in this chapter are highlighted. The complete code is given in Appendix B.

feet." Outside the United States, RVR is normally reported in meters. Variable RVR is shown as the lowest and highest visual range values separated by a "V." When the observed RVR is above the maximum value that can be determined by the system, the value is prefixed with a "P," such as P6000. A value that is below the minimum value that can be determined by the system is prefixed with an "M," such as M0600. If an RVR should be reported, but is missing, "RVRNO" is included in the remarks section of the METAR. Manual stations may report only one RVR value for a designated runway. Automated stations may report up to four different RVR values for up to four designated runways.

Plain language METAR reports are available at ADDS. Use care when obtaining decoded information from commercial sites not approved as QICP or EWIN sources.

PRESENT WEATHER

When weather or obscurations to vision are present at the time of the observation, you will find them immediately after the visibility. The type of precipitation or obscuration is shown in codes, preceded by intensity symbols, proximity, and descriptor. Intensity levels are shown as light (-), moderate (no sign), or heavy (+). (Figures 6-27, 6-28, and 6-29)

Weather obscurations occurring between 5 and 10 statute miles of the airport are shown by the letters "VC" for vicinity. For precipitation, VC applies within 10 statute miles of the observation point. Next is a descriptor of the precipitation or obscurations to visibility. For example, blowing snow is reported as BLSN, freezing drizzle as FZDZ, and a thunderstorm in the vicinity of the airport with moderate rain is reported as VCTSRA. Some typical obscurations to visibility are smoke (FU), haze (HZ), and dust (DU). Fog (FG) is listed when the visibility is less than 5/8 mile; when it is between 5/8 and 6 miles, the code for mist (BR) is used. Note, 5/8 of a mile is approximately 1,000 meters or 1 kilometer; 6 miles is about 10 kilometers. When fog causes a visibility of 1/4 mile, it is reported as 1/4SM FG. If mist and haze reduce visibility to 1-1/2 miles, it is shown as 1 1/2SM BR HZ. Following the obscurations, other weather phenomena may be listed, such as sandstorm (SS), duststorm (DS), or a funnel cloud (FC). When the type of precipitation cannot be identified at automated observation sites, the contraction UP is shown for precipitation unknown. METAR contractions for various weather phenomena are given in figure 6-29.

SKY CONDITION

Item 7 in figure 6-27 is the sky condition section of the METAR code. As noted previously, the amount of cloud cover is reported in contractions representing eighths of cloud cover (FEW, SKC, CLR, SCT, BKN, OVC).

Estimating Intensity of Rain or Freezing Rain	
Intensity	**Criteria**
Light	From scattered drops that, regardless of duration, do not completely wet an exposed surface up to a condition where individual drops are easily seen
Moderate	Individual drops that are not clearly identifiable; spray is observable just above pavement and other hard surfaces
Heavy	Rain seemingly falls in sheets; individual drops are not identifiable; heavy spray to a height of several inches is observed over hard surfaces
Estimating Intensity of Ice Pellets	
Intensity	**Criteria**
Light	Scattered pellets that do not completely cover an exposed surface regardless of duration. Visibility is not affected
Moderate	Slow accumulation on the ground. Visibility reduced by ice pellets to less than 7 statute miles
Heavy	Rapid accumulation on the ground. Visibility reduced by ice pellets to less than 3 statute miles

Figure 6-28. This figure lists guidelines for determining the intensity of precipitation.

The height of clouds or the vertical visibility into obscuring phenomena is reported with three digits in hundreds of feet above ground level (AGL). To determine the cloud height in feet, add two zeros to the number given in the report. When more than one layer is present, the layers are reported in ascending order. Recall that the sky cover condition for any higher layers includes the sky coverage for all lower layers. For example, a scattered layer at 900 feet and a broken layer at 3,000 feet AGL would be reported as SCT009 BKN030. In addition, if towering cumulus clouds (TCU) or cumulonimbus clouds (CB) are present, their code is shown following the height of their base, such as BKN040TCU or OVC050CB.

In METAR code, a ceiling is the AGL height of the lowest layer of clouds that is reported as broken or overcast, or the vertical visibility into an obscuration, such as fog or haze. For example,

QUALIFIER				WEATHER PHENOMENA					
INTENSITY or PROXIMITY 1		DESCRIPTOR 2		PRECIPITATION 3		OBSCURATION 4		OTHER 5	
-	Light	MI	Shallow	DZ	Drizzle	BR	Mist	PO	Well Developed Dust/Sand Whirls
		PR	Partial	RA	Rain	FG	Fog		
	Moderate (No Qualifier)	BC	Patches	SN	Snow	FU	Smoke	SQ	Squalls
		DR	Low Drifting	SG	Snow Grains	DU	Dust	FC	Funnel Cloud
		BL	Blowing	IC	Ice Crystals	SA	Sand		
+	Heavy	SH	Showers	PL	Ice Pellets	HZ	Haze	+FC	Tornado or Waterspout
VC	In the Vicinity	TS	Thunderstorms	GR	Hail	PY	Spray		
		FZ	Freezing	GS	Small Hail or Snow Pellets	VA	Volcanic Ash	SS	Sandstorm
				UP	*Unknown Precipitation			DS	Duststorm

The METAR present weather group (item 6 in Figure 6-27) is constructed by considering columns 1-5 in this table, in sequence; i.e., intensity, followed by descriptor, followed by weather phenomena; for example, heavy rain shower(s) is coded as +SHRA.

* Reported by automated stations only

Figure 6-29. List of contractions for various weather phenomena.

in the sky condition report "SCT005 BKN015 OVC050" the ceiling is at 1,500 feet AGL. There can be only one ceiling in a given report.

At a completely automated (AUTO) site, cloud height and amount are determined by a time-averaged sensor measurement of the clouds vertically above the site and below 12,000 feet. Therefore, only *some* middle clouds and *no* high clouds will be reported. Also, nearby clouds that are below 12,000 feet but are horizontally removed from the observation site will not be reported.

TEMPERATURE AND DEWPOINT

The current air temperature and dewpoint are reported in two-digit form in degrees Celsius and are separated by a slash. For example, "18/09" indicates a surface temperature of 18°C and a dewpoint of 9°C. Temperatures below 0° Celsius are prefixed with an "M" to indicate minus. That is, 10° below zero would be shown as M10. Temperature and dewpoint also may be added to remarks in an eight-digit format showing tenths of °C.

REMARKS

The final part of the METAR code is the remarks section (Item 10 in figure 6-27). This is sort of a "catch-all" section for added data and comments to expand and/or clarify coded information reported in previous sections. Information that may be included in remarks are variable visibility, beginning and ending times of a particular weather phenomena, and temperature/dewpoint in tenths °C. In most cases, you will notice more remarks when the weather is bad and the airport is approved for IFR operations. For example, variable visibility is shown in remarks with the

minimum and maximum visibility values; VIS 1V2 indicates a visibility that varies between one and two statute miles. A sector visibility is shown when it differs from the prevailing visibility and either the prevailing or sector visibility is less than three miles. For example, VIS N 2 means the visibility to the north is two statute miles.

If differences in precipitation type (for example, snow versus rain) are not measured at an AUTO site, the METAR code will include the remark, "AO1." Those AUTO stations that have equipment to differentiate between precipitation types will carry the remark "AO2."

The beginning of an event is shown by a "B," followed by the time in minutes after the hour. The ending time is noted by an "E" and the time in minutes. For example, RMK RAE42SNB42 means that rain ended at 42 minutes past the hour and snow began at that time. The remark, T00081016 is temperature and dewpoint in tenths °C. The first zero indicates a plus value for temperature (+ .8 °C) and the leading "one" in the next sequence shows a minus value for dewpoint (−1.6 °C).

Except for Mexico and Canada, international METARs have fewer remarks than those listed in figure 6-27.

Plain language METAR reports are available from many private and public sources. Care should be taken in the use of these. Depending on the source, important aviation weather details such as ceiling height, cloud type, and obstructions to vision may be left out of the plain language format.

SUMMARY

In this final chapter of Part I — Aviation Weather Basics, you have learned some important details about H$_2$O and its three states in the atmosphere. Changes of state and the associated latent heat exchanges have important effects on cloud formation and dissipation and on atmospheric stability. You should now understand that there are important differences between the way clouds are formed and the processes by which precipitation is produced. On the very practical side, you should know the basic elements of cloud and precipitation observing and reporting. Your abil-

ity to recognize the 10 basic cloud types and the types and characteristics of precipitation give you valuable observational tools which will help you evaluate the state of the atmosphere and its likely effect on flight.

In the next part of the book, you will apply your knowledge of all of the basic physical processes gained thus far to understand how atmospheric storms and other circulations arise, and to determine their structures and future behavior.

KEY TERMS

Accretion
Advection Fog
Aerodynamic contrail
Atmospheric Moisture
Black Ice
Blizzard
Boiling
Broken (BKN)
Ceiling
Celestial Dome
Change of State
Clear (CLR, SKC)
Cloud
Cloud Amount
Cloud Height
Cloud Layer
Clouds of Vertical Development
Collision/coalescence
Condensation
Condensation Level
Condensation Nuclei
Conditionally Unstable
Conditional Instability
Contact Cooling
Contrail
Deposition
Dew
Dewpoint
Dissipation Trail
Distrail

Drizzle
Evaporation
Exhaust Contrail
Fallstreaks
Few (FEW)
Freezing
Freezing Drizzle
Freezing Rain
Frontal Fog
Frost
Frostpoint
Ground Fog
Hail
Heavy Snow Warning
High Clouds
Ice
Ice Crystal Process
Ice Pellets
Indefinite Ceiling
Instrument Flight Rules (IFR)
Instrument Meteorological Conditions (IMC)
Latent Heat
Low Clouds
Low IFR (LIFR)
Marginal VFR (MVFR)
Melting
METAR Qualifier: Intensity or Proximity
METAR Qualifier: Descriptor
METAR Weather Phenomena: Abbreviations
Middle Clouds

Overcast (OVC)	Snow
Partial Pressure	Snow Depth
Phase Change	Snow Grains
Pilot Weather Report (PIREP)	Snow Showers
Precipitation	Steam Fog
Prevailing Visibility	Sublimation
Psychrometer	Supercooled Water Droplets
Radiation Fog	Temperature-Dewpoint Spread
Rain	Trace
Rainshadow	Tower Visibility
Rain Showers	Upslope Fog
Relative Humidity (RH)	Vapor Pressure
Runway Visibility (RVV)	Vertical Visibility
Runway Visual Range (RVR)	Virga
Saturated Adiabatic Process	Visual Flight Rules (VFR)
Saturated Adiabatic Lapse Rate	Visual Meteorological Conditions (VMC)
Saturation	Water
Saturation Vapor Pressure (SVP)	Water Equivalent
Scattered (SCT)	Water Vapor
Sensible Heat	White Dew
Sky Condition	

REVIEW QUESTIONS

1. If the amount of water vapor present is 2/3 of the maximum possible water vapor at the observed temperature, what is the relative humidity?

2. The relative humidity is 100%. What is the Temperature-Dewpoint spread?

3. (True, False) Every time the relative humidity is 100% it will rain.

4. What are the meteorological conditions conducive to the formation of radiation fog after sunset?

5. The visibility is 5 sm in the north quadrant, 4 sm to the west, 3 sm to the south, and 2 sm to the east. What is the prevailing visibility?

6. Examine the METARs at the bottom of the page and determine the ceiling height in feet for each report.

METAR KHOU 100950Z 26002KT 1 3/4SM -DZ BR SCT001 BKN005 OVC007 19/19 A3013=

METAR KBGR 101250Z 15012KT 1/2SM R15/5000FT -SN BR VV005 M03/M04 A3003=

METAR KALI 102150Z 13017KT 10SM BKN018 BKN035 BKN075 25/18 A3003 RMK BKN035VOVC=

METAR KCDS 102153Z AUTO 21010KT 10SM CLR 24/03 A3000 RMK A02=

METAR KFVE 102153Z AUTO 16011KT 2SM -SN BR BKN008 OVC012 M04/M05 A2967=

METAR KMMV 102153Z AUTO 01005KT 5SM -RA BR FEW008 OVC016 05/04 A3012=

DISCOVERY QUESTIONS

7. It is often observed that relative humidity reaches a maximum near sunrise and a minimum in the afternoon. Why?

8. If a saturated parcel is descending, say in the middle of a rainshower, is the rate of heating of the parcel less than or greater than 3C° per 1,000 feet? Why?

9. Is there any truth in the adage, "too cold to snow?"

10. You are in a pressurized cockpit that undergoes rapid decompression. Fog forms suddenly in the cockpit, then dissipates. Explain.

11. You are standing next to your airplane preparing for a night flight. It is overcast and the visibility is very good. Rain starts abruptly. You notice the droplets are quite large. The rain stops after a minute or so. What can you say about flying conditions at cloud level?

12. You place a gallon can, partially filled with water, on a burner until it comes to a boil. You remove the can from the burner and cap it. After awhile, the can begins to collapse. Explain.

13. Observe and record sky conditions at the same time, every day for a week (cloud amount, height, type). Obtain official weather observations from a nearby airport and compare them with your observations.

14. You walk out to your aircraft for preflight just before sunrise. It is parked in the open. It has been clear all night. There is no moisture on the ground, but you find a thin layer of ice on your wing. Explain.

15. *Aerodynamic* contrails can often be seen streaming from aircraft wingtips on takeoff while *exhaust* contrails typically occur at high altitudes. Give a realistic example of a meteorological situation where exhaust contrails are produced from an aircraft on the <u>ground</u>. In what geographical location would such a situation most likely occur?

Part II

Atmospheric Circulation Systems

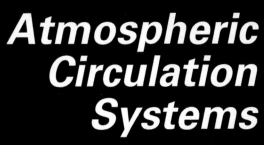

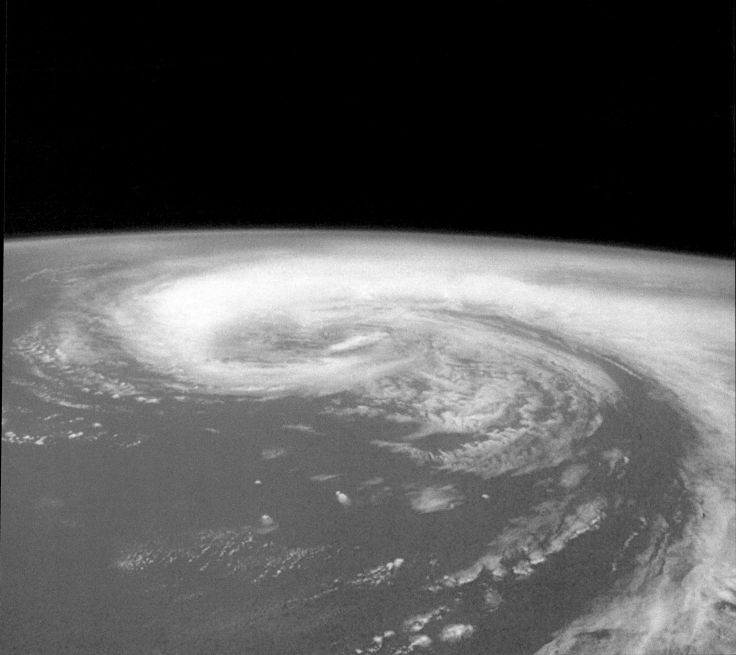

Part II
Atmospheric Circulation Systems

Part II uses your knowledge of "weather basics" to develop an understanding of circulations that occur within the atmosphere. These circulations produce temperature, wind, and weather changes that you must understand in order to plan and carry out safe and efficient flights.

When you complete Part II, you will understand how circulation systems of all sizes develop, move, and dissipate. You will know how they produce their characteristic global, regional, and local climate patterns. This knowledge will prove invaluable when you use observed and predicted weather information to anticipate flight conditions. Further, it will serve as an important background for Part III, Flight Hazards.

(Previous page: view of an ET cyclone from space, courtesy of NASA)

Chapter 7

Scales of Atmospheric Circulations

Introduction

Weather is not a random occurrence. Every weather event is the result of the development of some sort of atmospheric circulation. In this context, circulation means a more or less organized movement of air. The word eddy is often used in the same sense. The motion in a given circulation or eddy may be vertical, horizontal, or both. A very important characteristic of the atmosphere is that circulations occur with many different dimensions, ranging from organized motions on the scale of the entire earth to turbulent eddies as small as your hand. In this chapter, we formally introduce the concept of scales of atmospheric circulations to help you organize your study of various atmospheric weather phenomena. We then apply this idea to the examination of two important circulations of very different sizes: the general circulation and the monsoon circulation. When you finish this chapter, your knowledge of these two macroscale circulations will provide you with important background for understanding global climate and for your subsequent study of smaller scale circulations and their related weather.

SECTION A: SCALES OF CIRCULATIONS

SECTION B: THE LARGEST SCALE CIRCULATIONS
   The General Circulation
   The Monsoon Circulation

SECTION C: THE GLOBAL CIRCULATION SYSTEM
   The Global Circulation Aloft

SECTION D: GLOBAL CIRCULATION AND CLIMATOLOGY

Section A

SCALES OF CIRCULATIONS

A common way to study any system is to separate it into its component parts. Whether you are dealing with an airplane or the atmosphere, a complicated combination of parts becomes more understandable when you see what each of those parts does, how they fit into the whole, and how they interact to do what the system is designed to accomplish.

With regard to the atmosphere, if we measure the weather in a particular geographical region, the picture is often complicated, because many different physical processes are contributing to the total weather picture. To simplify things for better understanding, we want to be able to separate these processes.

One way of doing this is to consider the total circulation of the atmosphere as the sum of a number of individual circulations. The individual circulations are the parts of our system. By first studying the characteristics of each of them in isolation, the total picture will become more understandable.

Scales of circulations refer to the sizes and lifetimes of individual circulations. In your own experience, you have seen many examples of these. For example, the sea breeze develops during the day, reaches its maximum strength in the afternoon, and dies out at night. You might say it has a lifetime of about a half a day. Sea breezes typically extend 10 to 100 n.m. across the coast from the ocean side to the land side. This range can be taken as a characteristic spatial dimension. To summarize, the sea breeze has a "time scale" of about 12 hours and a "space scale" of 10 to 100 nautical miles.

Another familiar circulation is the dust devil. It has a typical time scale of a few minutes and a space scale of 5 to 100 feet (diameter of the circulation).

Figure 7-1 shows the approximate space and time scales of a number of atmospheric disturbances that are critical for aviation. Notice that the time and space scales of the various phenomena are roughly proportional; that is, as the sizes of the circulations increase, the lifetimes increase. This characteristic allows us to use a simple classification scheme that is based on space scale alone.

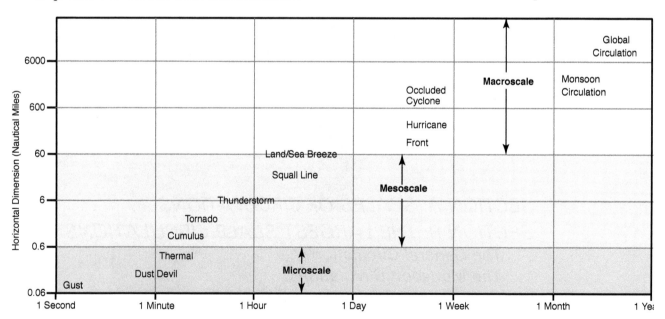

Figure 7-1. Horizontal dimensions and lifetimes of a selection of atmospheric circulations. Precise numbers for space and time scales cannot be given for each phenomenon because of variations caused by such things as local terrain, season, and larger scale weather systems. However, the range of the possible scales for each atmospheric circulation is clearly limited.

Figure 7-1 is separated into three segments labeled with the words "microscale," "mesoscale," and "macroscale." These are rather broad meteorological terms that are frequently used to describe atmospheric circulations. The term mesoscale refers to horizontal dimensions between 1 and about 1,000 nautical miles. Macroscale is greater, microscale is smaller. Clearly, macroscale circulations have the longest lifetimes and microscale circulations have the shortest.

Figure 7-1 is useful not only as a summary of atmospheric circulations, but also to help you develop the idea of embedded circulations. At any one time, several circulations may be present, with smaller ones embedded in, and often driven by, larger scale circulations. A good example is a macroscale cyclone associated with a front which produces a number of mesoscale thunderstorms, one of which generates a microscale tornado. The concept of embedded circulations will prove very useful in your interpretation of current and forecast weather conditions. (Figure 7-2)

Figure 7-2. GOES global satellite image showing cloud patterns produced by circulations of different sizes and time scales. Some examples: The bright clouds over the Pacific, east of Central America, mark the location of the Intertropical Convergence Zone between the Northern and Southern Hemispheres. The comma-shaped cloud mass over eastern North America shows the location of a cyclone near the polar front. The small white dots ("popcorn") over South America are the locations of thunderstorms in various stages of development. NOAA satellite image.

Section B

THE LARGEST SCALE CIRCULATIONS

In the following paragraphs, we use the concepts of scale and thermal circulation from chapter 4 to explain how global winds are affected by the equator-to-pole temperature gradient, the earth's rotation, the continents, and seasonal changes in solar radiation.

THE GENERAL CIRCULATION

The general circulation refers to the wind system that extends over the entire globe. The horizontal scale of this circulation is approximately 10,000 n.m. (macroscale). Aside from long term climatological changes, the time scale of the global circulation is one year. This is the period it takes the circulation system to go through a complete cycle of seasonal changes.

To help you understand the general circulation, we begin with a simplified version. Consider an idealized earth with a smooth surface (no surface friction) and no land-sea differences. Let the earth rotate in its usual direction (towards the east), but much slower than the real earth. In this case, and as you would expect from our previous discussion of a thermal circulation (Chapter 3), the equator-to-pole temperature gradients create pressure gradients. Surface high-pressure areas are located over each of the cold poles and a surface low pressure region is found around the warm equator. These features cause surface air to move from the poles toward the equator. The reverse occurs aloft where equatorial air moves toward the poles. (Figure 7-3) Each of these vertical circulation systems is called a circulation cell, or simply, a cell.

The simple general circulation cell that develops with slow rotation is similar to the thermal

circulation (sea breeze) cell with an important exception. Because the scale of the global circulation is many times larger, Coriolis force has an important modifying effect. Surface winds in the Northern Hemisphere are deflected to the right and become northeasterly. In the Southern Hemisphere, surface winds become southeasterly. Winds aloft have the opposite directions.

We now increase the rotation of our idealized earth to its normal rate of one rotation every 24 hours. The resulting wind circulation becomes more involved, but much more realistic. In the remaining discussion, we will concentrate on

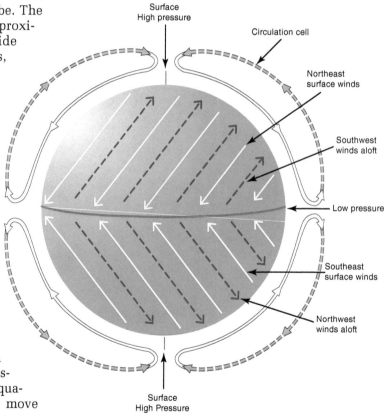

Figure 7-3. A slowly rotating earth has only one circulation cell in each hemisphere. Surface winds are indicated by solid yellow arrows and winds aloft are indicated by dotted blue arrows. Note how winds are changed from a strictly north-south direction by the Coriolis force. A cross section showing the vertical structure of the circulation cells in each hemisphere is shown on the edges of the globe.

the Northern Hemisphere pattern. Just remember the Southern Hemisphere circulation is a mirror image because Coriolis force acts in the opposite direction.

With the faster rotation rate, the single cell circulation breaks up into three cells. We find that air still rises at the equator and flows toward the pole aloft, but that branch of the circulation reaches only 30°N, where the air sinks. At the surface, between the equator and 30°N we again find northeasterlies. (Figure 7-4) This cell is called the Hadley Cell for an 18th century scientist who first proposed a model of the general circulation.

In the highest latitudes, a Polar Cell has developed. It is defined by air rising near 60°N and sinking over the pole. Coriolis force causes the cold surface winds in the polar cell to be northeasterly, and winds aloft to be southwesterly.

In the latitude belt between 30°N and 60°N, the faster rotation and strong north-south temperature gradient in midlatitudes favors the development of smaller scale eddies in that region. We will examine these eastward-moving disturbances in the next chapter. Their influence on the general circulation is to cause the average surface winds to be southwesterly in this latitude belt, and to remain westerly up through at least the tropopause. These average winds define a midlatitude circulation cell called the Ferrel Cell. It is also named for an early investigator of the general circulation.

The three-cell circulation generates some important and well-known features in the surface wind pattern. (Figure 7-4) These include the steady, northeasterly trade winds between the equator and 30°N; the prevailing westerlies between 30°N and 60°N, and the polar easterlies north of 60°N.

Other important surface features of the general circulation are found in the surface pressure distribution. The low pressure area near the equator is called the "Doldrums." Because of the convergence of trade winds from both hemispheres into that area, it is also known as the Intertropical Convergence Zone (ITCZ). The instability and

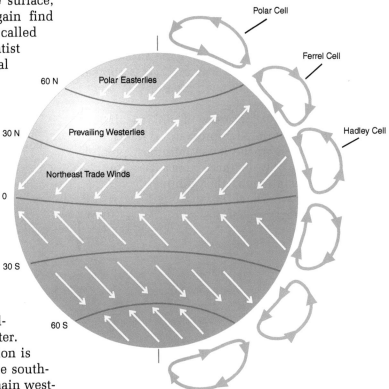

Figure 7-4. A three-cell circulation develops in each hemisphere of a smooth, homogeneous earth rotating at one revolution per 24 hours. A cross section showing the vertical structure of the circulation cells in each hemisphere is shown on the eastern edge of the globe. The related surface winds are shown with the yellow arrows. Note that the wind pattern in the Southern Hemisphere is a mirror image of the pattern north of the equator.

large moisture content of the air in the ITCZ, make it a favorite area for the development of thunderstorms. (Figure 7-5)

Air sinks in a region of diverging surface winds that correspond with a subtropical high pressure near 30°N. This part of the general circulation is known as the horse latitudes. Cloud formation is suppressed and precipitation is typically low in these areas.

Near 60°N, pressures are low and surface winds converge, bringing warm airmasses from tropical regions into contact with cold airmasses from polar regions. The line separating the airmasses at this location is called the polar front. It is another region of cloudiness and precipitation.

Finally, there are two areas of sinking air and diverging winds in high-pressure systems near the poles. As with the horse latitudes, precipitation is very low in these areas. Despite the low precipitation, the ground remains snow-covered because of the very low temperatures.

THE MONSOON CIRCULATION

Our discussion to this point has centered on an idealized general circulation on an idealized planet. The real picture is different because of the existence of oceans and continents. To construct a more realistic pattern of global winds, we must introduce the effects of surface differences and the monsoon circulation.

The monsoon circulation or, simply, the monsoon, is a macroscale wind pattern that undergoes a seasonal reversal in direction. The low-level winds of the "wet" monsoon of summer flow from the ocean to the continent. The "dry" monsoon flow is in the opposite direction (the continent to the ocean). A rough measure of the scale of a monsoon is 5,000 n.m or about the size of a continent.

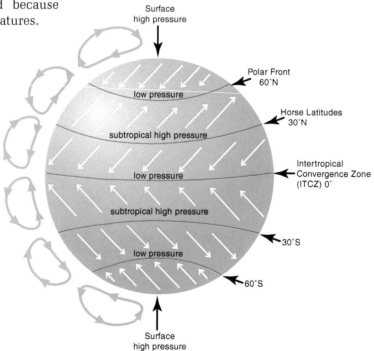

Figure 7-5. Surface pressure distribution associated with a three-cell circulation.

Summer

Winter

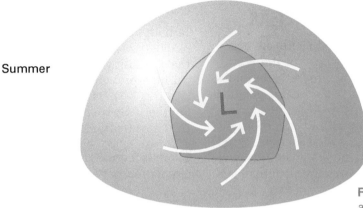

Figure 7-6. The summer and winter monsoon circulations for an idealized continent. These diagrams show the surface circulations caused by low sea level pressure over the continent in summer and high pressure in winter.

In order to understand how the monsoon works, we will look at another idealized situation. This time, we ignore the influence of the general circulation and consider a single continent with a simple shape in the Northern Hemisphere. (Figure 7-6) The monsoon has the characteristics of a thermal circulation. In the summer, the continent is much warmer than the surrounding ocean and the sea level pressure is lower over the land. Moist ocean winds sweep inland at that time. However, because the scale of the circulation is so large, Coriolis force is also important. With the added effect of friction, moist surface winds spiral counter-clockwise into the continental low.

In winter, the picture is reversed. The continent is cold relative to the surrounding ocean. High pressure prevails over the land and cool, dry surface winds spiral clockwise outward from the anticyclone. As you would expect, the directions of the circulations are opposite for a Southern Hemisphere continent.

On the real earth, the monsoon circulation is embedded in the larger general circulation. Additionally, continents vary in size, shape, and latitude. The results of these factors are that the monsoon is very well defined in some geographical areas (Southeast Asia), but is only barely noticeable in others (Europe). In the next section, we examine the effects of both the general circulation and monsoon circulations over the real earth.

Section C

THE GLOBAL CIRCULATION SYSTEM

Most global climatological wind charts are based on a monthly or seasonal average of the world-wide winds. This averaging process eliminates circulations with smaller time scales leaving what is called the global circulation system. It is a combination of the general and monsoon circulations. To illustrate, the average surface wind patterns for January and July are given in figure 7-7. The average sea level pressure patterns have been repeated from Chapter 3 to emphasize the relationships between pressure and wind.

In both January and July, the underlying general circulation is apparent over the oceans where the prevailing westerlies, trade winds, subtropical high-pressure regions, and ITCZ can be seen. (Figure 7-7) This is particularly true in the Southern Hemisphere where there is much less land area (less monsoon effect).

There is a strong seasonal variation in the global circulation pattern. In January, the Icelandic and

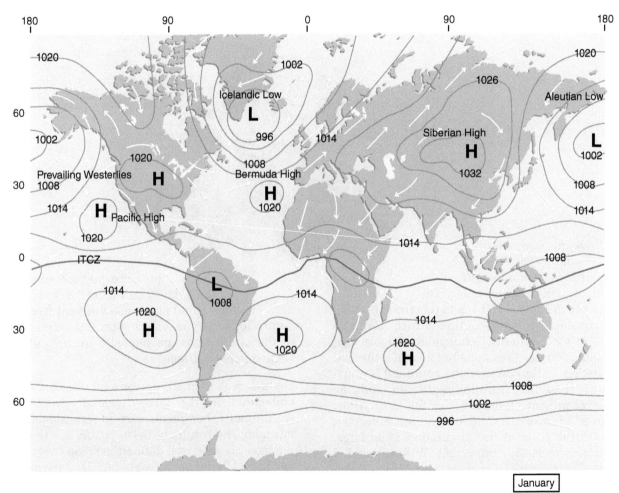

Figure 7-7. Global circulation for January and July. Average wind directions are indicated with arrows. Solid lines are mean sea level pressure in millibars.

Aleutian lows, which indicate the average position of the polar front, are stronger and farther south than in July. The subtropical highs are also farther south in January, but they are weaker than in July. The ITCZ tends to move northward in July and southward in January. In some regions of the globe, this north-south movement is much greater than in other regions. For example, in July, the ITCZ is north of the Indian subcontinent, while at the same longitude in January, it is just south of the equator.

In the vicinity of nearly all of the continents, the influence of the monsoon becomes evident. Nowhere is it so obvious as over Southeast Asia. (Figure 7-7) This is due to the location of the Asian landmass to the north of a very warm

ocean. There is well-defined cyclonic inflow into a low-pressure area over Asia in July and anticyclonic outflow from a cold continental high-pressure system in January. The Asian monsoon influence is so pervasive that winds over the Indian Ocean become southwest in the summer, rather than northeast, as would be expected when considering only the general circulation.

Monsoon winds also develop over Africa, Australia, and some parts of North and South America, especially in the lower latitudes and usually in combination with the seasonal shift of the ITCZ. Their strengths depend on the shape and size of the continents and the temperatures of the surrounding oceans.

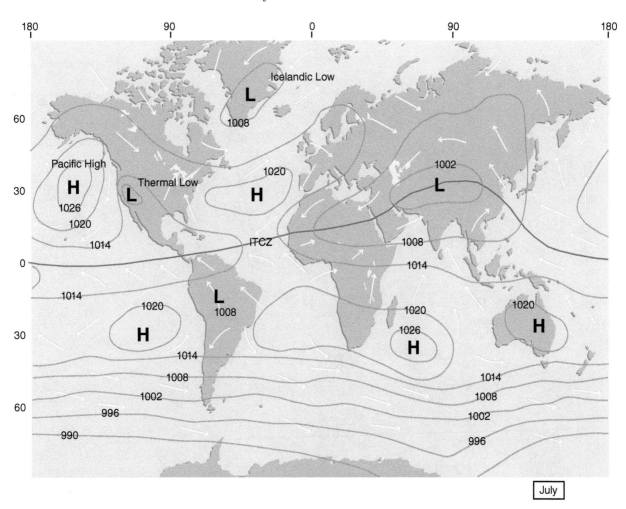

THE GLOBAL CIRCULATION ALOFT

The global circulation patterns aloft are far simpler than what you have just seen for the surface. Figure 7-8 shows average January and July 500 mb (18,000 feet MSL) charts with height contours and wind directions superimposed. Macroscale features of interest include wintertime cyclones over Western Siberia and the Canadian Arctic. These Northern Hemisphere lows are upper-level extensions of the Aleutian and Icelandic lows seen in the surface wind and pressure patterns. (Figure 7-7) The subtropical highs seen near the surface are also identifiable aloft where they are closer to the equator. These anticyclones are particularly noticeable in the summer, as shown in figure 7-8.

In figure 7-8, there is also a well-defined wave structure in the contour and westerly wind patterns, especially in the Northern Hemisphere. For example, in winter, there are wave troughs along the east coasts of both Asia and North America and a weaker trough over Europe. The three waves in figure 7-8 are examples of the largest scale wave disturbances that occur in the atmosphere. Appropriately, these are called long waves. They tend to move eastward much more slowly than the wind.

Long waves can be viewed as large-scale disturbances embedded in the basic westerly flow around the globe. The airflow through the upper-level waves causes storms and cold air to move to lower latitudes in the vicinity of the wave troughs; in contrast, warm air moves to higher latitudes in the wave crests (ridges). Long waves are necessary upper air links for heat exchange between equator and poles.

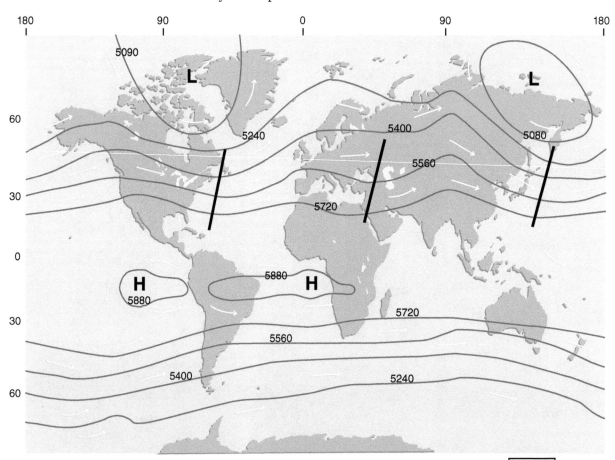

Figure 7-8. Average 500 mb heights and wind directions for January and July. The January chart also shows positions of three long-wave troughs along the east coasts of North America and Asia, and over eastern Europe.

January

An important characteristic of the flow patterns shown in figure 7-8 are the prevailing westerly winds in middle latitudes, which strengthen (tighter packing of contours) in winter and weaken in summer. In midlatitudes, typical westerly winds aloft are stronger and exist across a broader latitude belt than prevailing westerly winds near the surface.

Very important upper-air features known as jet streams are often embedded in the zone of strong westerlies. A jet stream is a narrow band of high-speed winds that reaches its greatest speed near the tropopause (24,000 to 50,000 feet MSL). Jet stream speeds range between 60 knots and about 240 knots. Jet streams are typically thousands of miles long, hundreds of miles wide, and a few miles thick.

Figure 7-9 shows the average positions of the two dominant jet streams in the Northern Hemisphere: the polar front jet stream and the subtropical jet stream. As the name implies, the polar front jet stream is found near the latitude of the polar front. Similar to the behavior of the polar front, it is stronger and farther south in winter and weaker and farther north in summer. The subtropical jet stream has no related surface frontal structure and shows much less fluctuation in position; it is typically found near 25°N to 30°N latitude near North America. The subtropical jet stream reaches its greatest strength in the wintertime and generally disappears in summer. A similar jet stream pattern occurs in the Southern Hemisphere.

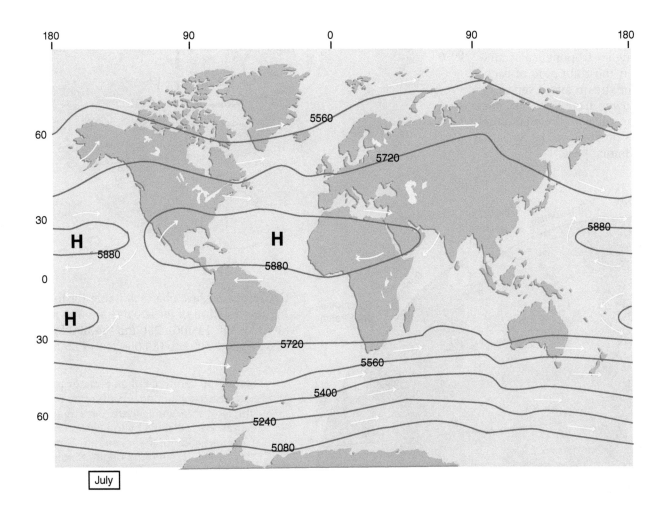

The polar front jet stream weakens and moves poleward in the summer.

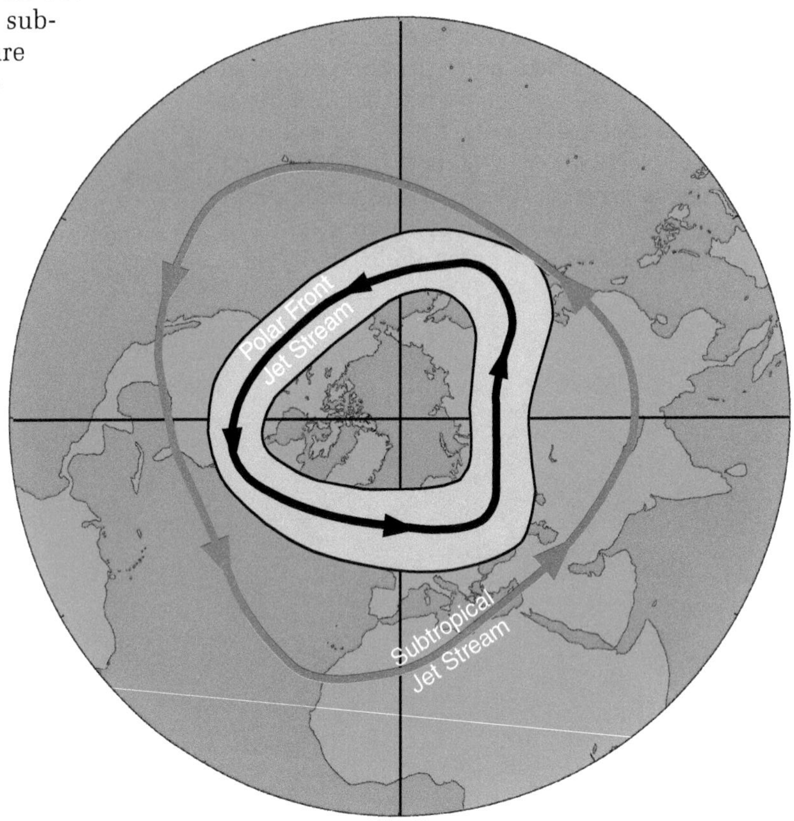

An equator-to-pole atmospheric cross section showing the polar front and subtropical jet streams is given in figure 7-10. Notice that the tropopause slopes upward from polar to tropical regions as described in an earlier chapter; but, upon closer examination, we find that the tropopause is not continuous. There is a break at the location of each jet stream. If you stand with the wind at your back, a distinctly higher tropopause occurs on the right side of each jet stream and a separate, lower tropopause occurs on the left. This structure is reversed in the Southern Hemisphere.

Figure 7-9. Approximate locations of polar front jet stream and subtropical jet stream near tropopause level in Northern Hemisphere winter. The polar front jet is enclosed within a broad zone, because its position varies widely from day to day. Similar conditions are found in Southern Hemisphere winter.

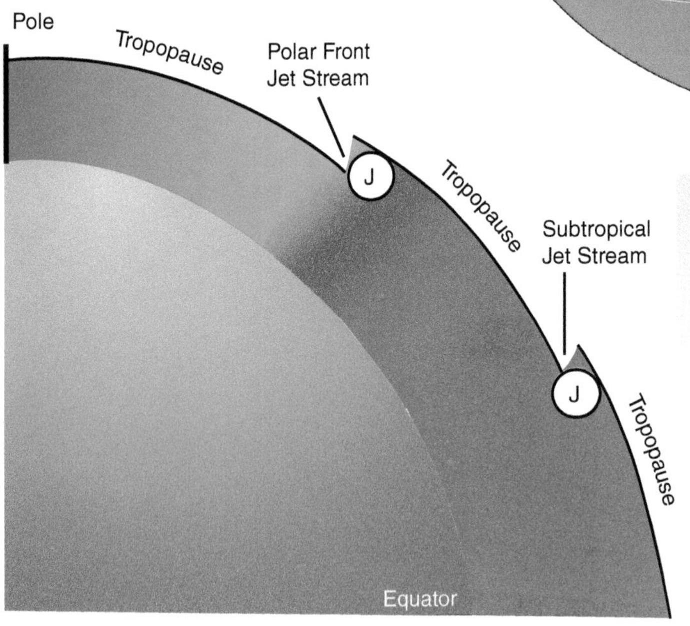

Constant pressure charts suitable for locating the position of jet streams are 300 mb (30,000 feet, FL300), 250 mb (34,000 feet, FL340), and 200 mb (39,000 feet, FL390).

Figure 7-10. Example of an equator-to-pole cross section on a winter day in the Northern Hemisphere. Jet stream cores are indicated by the letter, "J." The direction of the jet stream winds are westerly (into the page). Similar conditions are found in the Southern Hemisphere winter.

Section D
GLOBAL CIRCULATION AND CLIMATOLOGY

Climatology is the study of the average conditions of the atmosphere. Although an in-depth examination of climatology is not the purpose of this text, your understanding of the global circulation has provided you with some basic climatological background. You will find this information useful in a number of ways. First, it will help you to better understand the processes that produce the weather. Second, it will aid you in the deduction of average weather conditions for some distant destination from simple climatological charts. Finally, it will help you to understand the basic results of current research on climate change. In the following paragraphs, we consider some brief examples.

Your knowledge of global winds is very useful for explaining something as complicated as the unequal distribution of precipitation around the world. Arctic deserts, rainforests in the Pacific Northwest, desert canyons in Hawaii: all of these can be explained on the basis of your knowledge of the global circulation. (Figure 7-11)

In figure 7-11, the high precipitation near the equator is the result of large amounts of tropical moisture, convergence, and upward motions in the ITCZ. In both the Arctic and the subtropics (especially noticeable over North Africa and the desert southwest of the U.S.), downward motions forced by divergence of the winds in semipermanent, high-pressure regions minimize precipitation. Additionally, the Arctic atmosphere has low temperatures and, therefore, small amounts of water vapor.

Examples of the interaction of topography and the winds of the global circulation can be seen in western North America where a large area of low precipitation is found to the east of the Rocky Mountains. Since westerly winds dominate the middle latitudes, the eastern side of those mountains is subjected to downward motion, suppressing the formation of clouds. In contrast, in middle latitudes, clouds and precipitation are enhanced by upward motions on the western slopes of the north-south mountain ranges.

The climatology of winds, temperatures, storms, and other aviation weather hazards in your flying area should be reviewed at the beginning of each season.

Figure 7-11. Annual average world precipitation.

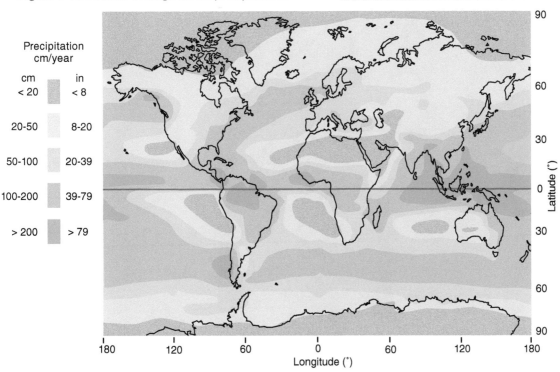

Precipitation cm/year

cm	in
< 20	< 8
20-50	8-20
50-100	20-39
100-200	39-79
> 200	> 79

An extreme example of the contribution of orographic lifting to precipitation is found along the southern edge of the Himalayas where the combination of the wet monsoon winds and orography causes large precipitation amounts. Cherrapunji, India, is in this area and has received over 1,000 inches of rain in a single year.

A similar example is found on Mt. Waialeale on the island of Kauai, Hawaii. Waialeale protrudes into the steady, moist trade winds that produce an average rainfall of about 460 inches at that location. Interestingly, not far downwind of Waialeale is Waimea Canyon, one of the driest spots in the Hawaiian Islands, yet another example of orographic effects and their interaction with a feature of the global circulation.

The scales of motion discussed thus far, and considered in future chapters, are associated with time periods of one year and less. Weather changes over longer periods do occur. For example, as you have probably noticed, some very wet years are followed by dry years. An occasional very warm or cold winter may occur between a couple of average winters. These "interannual" variations have been related to a variety of possible causes; such as, changes of ocean water temperatures (El Niño), long term oscillations in equatorial winds, fluctuations in solar output, and the interception of solar radiation by long-lived plumes from volcanic eruptions.

Much longer time scales of climate variation have also been identified. These include changes due to a gradual variation in the earth's tilt from 22° to 24.5° and back (cycle length: 41,000 years). This variation in tilt affects day length and seasonal changes. There is also a very gradual change in the shape of the earth's orbit around the sun from nearly circular to elliptical (cycle length: 100,000 years). This change affects the amount of energy received at the earth's surface and the length of the seasons. Also, there is a "wobble" in the axis of the earth (cycle length: 23,000 years). This causes a change in the time of year that the earth is tilted toward or away from the sun. Scientists generally believe that these fluctuations have been responsible for the ice ages during the last two million years.

Finally, there are scales of climate variations that are being driven by the impact of pollution caused by industrial growth, urbanization, and the demands of the earth's rapidly growing population. The ozone hole and greenhouse gases are but two concerns. The long term influences and time scales of these and other man-made climate modifications are not well known. Long-term changes in carbon dioxide levels in the atmosphere and parallel changes in global temperature are well documented. Projections of future levels of carbon dioxide indicate some serious impacts on global weather in the next decades.

SUMMARY

This chapter can be viewed as a transition between aviation weather basics and some useful applications of those basics. The concept of "scales of motion" has been introduced as a learning and organizing device. The observed state of the atmosphere is usually due to the effects of one or more individual circulations. By separating the variety of atmospheric disturbances according to their space and time scales, they become easier to understand. The interpretation of current and predicted weather also is much easier when you have an appreciation of the types and scales of the disturbances involved.

The scale approach has been applied in this chapter to describe the causes and characteristics of the general circulation and the monsoon. In combination, these largest circulation systems account for the average global winds, and help us explain many of the characteristics of global climatology.

KEY TERMS

Circulation
Circulation Cell
Climatology
Eddy
Embedded Circulation
Ferrel Cell
General Circulation
Global Circulation System
Hadley Cell
Horse Latitudes
Intertropical Convergence Zone (ITCZ)
Jet Stream
Long Waves

Macroscale
Mesoscale
Microscale
Monsoon
Monsoon Circulation
Polar Cell
Polar Easterlies
Polar Front
Polar Front Jet Stream
Prevailing Westerlies
Scales of Circulations
Subtropical Jet Stream
Trade Winds

REVIEW QUESTIONS

1. The islands of Hawaii lie in what surface wind regime of the general circulation?

2. The two jet streams commonly found near the tropopause in winter are the _____ _____ and the _____.

3. The dry monsoon occurs during what season?

4. Define "mesoscale."

5. Clouds and precipitation are typically greater on the western side of the Sierra Nevada mountain range in California than on the eastern side. Why?

6. What is the usual direction of the trade winds in the Southern Hemisphere?

7. One of the common reasons that both the ITCZ and the Polar Front are favored regions for bad weather is that surface winds in both regions _____, forcing upward vertical motions.

DISCOVERY QUESTIONS

8. You are responsible for advising an oceanic research group on the operation of an aircraft flight to do a low-level photo survey of the Atlantic between Panama and Gibraltar. You will be flying at about 1,000 feet MSL at an airspeed of 170 knots. Flights will be made one day a week for a year. There will be a full crew and scientific equipment going one way. The direction is arbitrary. The crew and equipment will return by commercial airline. It is up to you to minimize the cost of the missions (fuel, crew duty time, etc.). On the basis of average conditions in January and July, what would your meteorological advice be?

9. A minimum time track (MTT) is not necessarily the shortest path between two locations, but it is the fastest. Your company aircraft flies a daily, round trip flight from London to New York for a period of one year. The airspeed is 300 knots at an altitude of 18,000 feet MSL. On the basis of January and July conditions, give a rough estimate (draw a map) of the average annual MTTs for the out and return flights from London to New York. Discuss your reasoning. Would your answers change for flights at 300 mb? For an aircraft flying at Mach 3? If so, how?

10. You want to fly a balloon across the Atlantic. For technical reasons you must fly below 5,000 feet MSL. You want dependable (steady) winds. Where and when should you attempt your crossing? Discuss.

CHAPTER 8
Airmasses, Fronts, and Cyclones

Introduction

The general circulation and monsoon discussed in the previous chapter have very large horizontal dimensions and long time scales. In this chapter, we look at another collection of circulations that are different in at least three ways: they are smaller in size, have shorter life times, and they have significant movement. Examples are extratropical cyclones and tropical cyclones. They are the "weather makers" that have significant effects on aviation activities, producing a variety of flight hazards.

When you complete Chapter 8, you will be familiar with the causes and structure of extratropical cyclones and tropical cyclones, and the weather they produce. You will also have been introduced to a conceptual model of each type of cyclone, which will prove to be invaluable in the interpretation of meteorological observations, analyses, and forecasts.

Section A
EXTRATROPICAL CYCLONES

An extratropical cyclone is a macroscale low-pressure disturbance that develops outside the tropics. Extratropical cyclones draw their energy from temperature differences across the polar front, so they are also known as frontal lows or frontal cyclones. They move from west to east as macroscale eddies embedded in the prevailing westerlies. As shown in a later section, these disturbances distort the polar front into a wave shape; therefore, they are also referred to as wave cyclones and frontal waves.

In some circumstances, extratropical cyclones may simply be called "lows." We will use this term carefully because it can be ambiguous when taken out of context. Other, very different low-pressure systems develop in the tropics and elsewhere. These have different scales, different structures, different weather, and different behavior than extra-tropical cyclones.

Individual frontal lows have lifetimes of only a few days to a week as compared to time scales of months for the general circulation and the monsoon. Because of their movement and short lifetimes, extratropical cyclones are much easier to identify on weather charts for a given day and time rather than on seasonal average charts. Figure 8-1 shows the scale relationship of a frontal low to the global circulation. On any given day, there are always several of these lows around the globe in various stages of development, as shown in figure 8-2.

THE POLAR FRONT MODEL

The important characteristics of the development and structure of a frontal low are represented by the polar front model. The origins of this model date from research begun by Norwegian meteorologists about the time of WWI. Since that time, the model has been expanded and improved with better observations and understanding of the atmosphere.

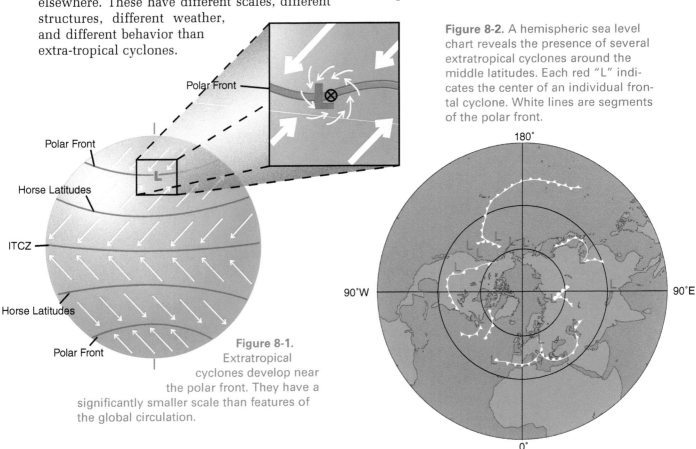

Figure 8-1. Extratropical cyclones develop near the polar front. They have a significantly smaller scale than features of the global circulation.

Figure 8-2. A hemispheric sea level chart reveals the presence of several extratropical cyclones around the middle latitudes. Each red "L" indicates the center of an individual frontal cyclone. White lines are segments of the polar front.

The modern polar front model has both a surface and an upper-air component. The surface model describes the structure and behavior of fronts and airmasses in the lower atmosphere. The upper air part of the model deals with the associated development of troughs, ridges, tropopauses, and jet streams. Both surface and upper air components contribute to unique cloud and weather patterns during the life cycle of the frontal low. We start our discussion with an examination of the surface components of the cyclone and work upward.

AIRMASSES

An airmass is a large body of air that has fairly uniform temperature, stability, and moisture characteristics. Typical airmasses are a few thousand nautical miles across. In terms of time scale, it is not unusual for airmasses to be identifiable over periods of several days to more than a week after they leave their area of origin.

Airmasses develop in regions where surface conditions are homogeneous and winds are light. This allows the air to adapt to the temperature and moisture properties of the surface. The locations of such regions are usually near the centers of semipermanent high-pressure systems over the snow and ice fields of polar regions and over the subtropical oceans. It follows that an airmass is generally identified by its airmass source region; that is, by the geographical area where it develops. Common airmass types are Arctic (A), Polar (P), and Tropical (T).

Once an airmass leaves its source region, it is also classified according to its temperature relative to the ground over which it is moving. A cold airmass is colder than the ground and a warm airmass is warmer than the ground over which it is moving.

As polar and tropical airmasses move away from their source regions they are further identified by their moisture content. They are classified as to whether their recent trajectories were over land

Arctic air only reaches the lower 48 states in the winter and initially has temperatures at or below 0°F. Maritime tropical air is common over Florida during the colder months and spreads northward in the spring and summer. It has dew-point temperatures of 60°F or more.

(continental) or over water (maritime). Figure 8-3 shows source regions and trajectories for North American airmass types.

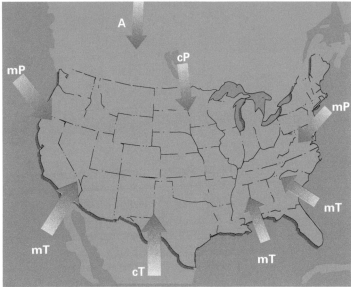

Figure 8-3. North American airmass source regions. Note standard airmass abbreviations: arctic (A), continental polar (cP), maritime polar (mP), continental tropical (cT), and maritime tropical (mT).

Airmasses undergo modification as they move away from their source region. If they move quickly, that modification will be small. For example, a fast-moving arctic airmass that moves through the prairie provinces of Canada will remain extremely cold as it penetrates the Central Plains of the U.S., because it has not had time to adjust to the new surface temperature conditions. In contrast, airmasses that move slowly and/or over great distances undergo large modifications. For example, a very cold airmass that moves from its source region over snow and ice often undergoes substantial modification as it moves over a large body of open water, such as the Pacific. (Figure 8-4)

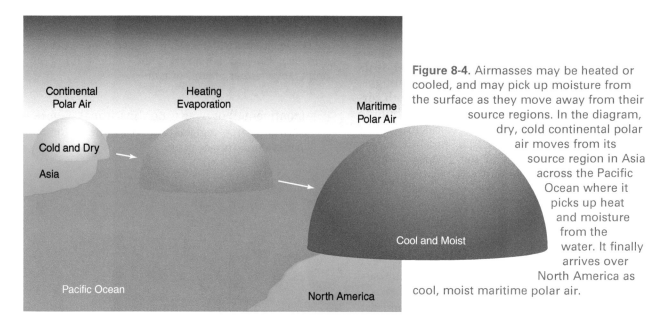

Figure 8-4. Airmasses may be heated or cooled, and may pick up moisture from the surface as they move away from their source regions. In the diagram, dry, cold continental polar air moves from its source region in Asia across the Pacific Ocean where it picks up heat and moisture from the water. It finally arrives over North America as cool, moist maritime polar air.

Another example of airmass modification is seen when a polar airmass moves from the eastern U.S. over the warm waters of the Gulf Stream along the Atlantic Coast. The moisture and temperature of the airmass increases and its stability decreases. Similarly, an arctic airmass moving slowly southward over the Great Plains will warm up rapidly during the day, especially if the skies are clear and the ground is not snow-covered. On a smaller scale, a cold airmass crossing the Great Lakes in fall, before the formation of substantial amounts of lake ice, often becomes very moist, resulting in heavy snow showers downwind of the lakes.

FRONTS

Airmasses tend to retain their identifying characteristics for long periods, even when they are in close contact with another airmass. Because two airmasses with different characteristics do not mix readily, there is often a distinct boundary between them. As you know from your earlier reading about the causes of vertical motions, that boundary is called a front. (See frontal lifting in figure 5-5.) Fronts are hundreds of miles long and have lifetimes similar to those of airmasses. As we will see, they are classified according to their movement.

A slow-moving, cold airmass that is unstable during the day because of surface heating will become stable at night due to cooling from below. This can result in a marked change in weather conditions from day to night. An example is a change from daytime heating with cumulus clouds and good visibilities to nighttime cooling with fog or low stratus clouds and poor visibilities.

When an airmass is stable, it is common to find smoke, dust, haze, etc., concentrated at the lower levels, with resulting poor visibility.

One of the most easily recognized discontinuities across a front is a change in temperature.

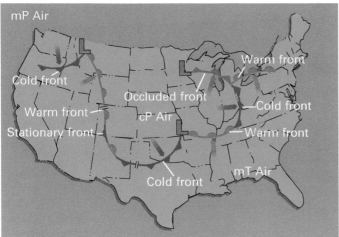

Figure 8-5. Colors and symbols used for weather front depiction. Airmasses are labeled in yellow. Frontal movements shown by red and blue arrows are also indicated by the location of frontal symbols (barbs) along each front.

it useful to identify and track fronts. Examples of identifying symbols used to indicate fronts on surface analysis charts are shown in figure 8-5. You should become familiar with these useful "road signs" that indicate the locations of possible aviation weather problems.

FRONTAL CLASSIFICATIONS

Fronts are assigned a name according to whether the cold airmass is advancing (cold front) or the warm airmass is advancing (warm front). If the airmasses show no appreciable movement, the front is designated a stationary front (or quasi-stationary front). Later, we will examine a situation where a cold front overtakes a warm front; the result of which is termed an occluded front.

When airmasses meet, their relative motion frequently leads to the lifting of moist air (frontal lifting). When sufficient moisture is present, fronts are often locations of clouds and precipitation. For forecasting purposes, meteorologists find

FRONTAL SLOPES

Whenever two contrasting airmasses come into contact, the more dense, cold air wedges under the warm air so that the front always slopes over the cold airmass. (Figure 8-6)

The frontal slope refers to the ratio of the altitude of the top of the cold air at some point in the cold airmass to the horizontal distance of that point on the surface from the nearest edge of the airmass. It is defined in figure 8-6. For the types of macroscale fronts described in this chapter, slopes of fronts are usually in the range 1:50 to 1:500. The understanding of the slopes of fronts is important because major changes in pressure, wind, temperature, and weather occur as a front passes you on the ground or as you fly through a front.

$$\text{Frontal Slope} = \frac{Z}{X} = \frac{1}{100}$$

Figure 8-6. Note that the cold airmass wedges under the warm airmass. This is the case for all fronts, regardless of their classification. If this is a warm front, it would be moving from right to left. A cold front would be moving from left to right. The slope of the front is the ratio of the altitude (Z) of the frontal surface to the distance (X) from the surface position of the front. The slope of this front is 1:100 since X = 100 n.m. and Z = 1 n.m. This slope is typical of a cold front.

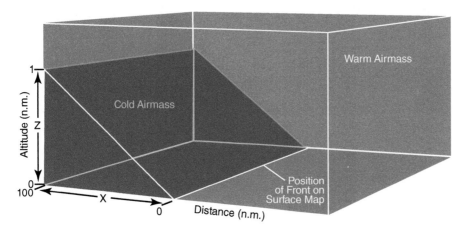

It turns out that cold fronts have steeper slopes (about 1:50 to 1:100) than warm and stationary fronts (about 1:200 or less) as shown in figure 8-7. Some rapidly moving cold fronts are steeper than 1:50 in the lowest 1,000 or 2,000 feet. Occluded fronts may have the slope of either a warm or cold front, depending on the type of occlusion. This is clarified in the section on cyclone structure.

Although fronts have a distinct three-dimensional structure, they are not usually identified on upper air charts as they are on surface analysis charts. Therefore, if your flight will pass through a front, you should be aware that the frontal position aloft will be different than its surface position because of the slope of the front. Remember these simple rules:

> The position of the front aloft is always on the cold side of the position of the front at the surface, regardless of the type of front. The steeper the front, the closer the positions.

FRONTAL ZONES

Another important concept to understand is that a front is not a thin line as shown on a chart, but is actually a narrow frontal zone through which there is a rapid transition of conditions from one airmass to the other. The width of the transition zone may be as little as 0.5 n.m. to more than 100 n.m. It is usually narrower near the ground than aloft. (Figure 8-8)

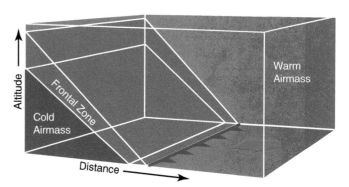

Figure 8-8. Perspective diagram of a cold front showing the frontal zone on the cold side of the line that indicates the front on a surface analysis chart. The front is moving from left to right.

On conventional surface analysis charts, single lines with appropriate symbols are used to represent the positions of the fronts. Because frontal zones are often the location of strong shears and turbulence, you should always be aware of their existence and location relative to the indicated frontal position. Remember,

> A frontal zone is always located immediately on the cold side of the position of the front shown on a weather map, regardless of type of front.

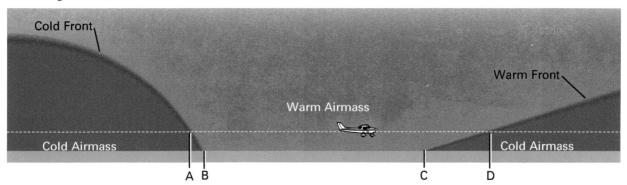

Figure 8-7. Cross sections through warm and cold fronts. For illustration purposes, the slopes are greatly exaggerated in this diagram. Both fronts are moving from left to right. The slope of a cold front is steeper than the slope of a warm front. The dashed line indicates the flight of an aircraft through both fronts. Notice the points of intersection along the flight path (A and D) versus the surface frontal positions (B and C).

EXTRATROPICAL CYCLONE STRUCTURE AND DEVELOPMENT

Extratropical cyclones are not accidental disturbances. They develop for a reason. As we saw in earlier chapters, there is an excess of solar energy received at the equator and a deficit at the poles. The resulting horizontal temperature difference (gradient) is concentrated along the polar front. If that temperature gradient becomes excessive at some place along the front, a disturbance will develop in the form of an extratropical cyclone. In the following description of its development and structure, it will become very clear how these frontal lows accomplish the task of mixing warm air toward the pole and cold air toward the equator to reduce the temperature gradient.

With regard to aviation, frontal cyclones can produce almost every weather flight hazard that you can think of, ranging from clear air turbulence to icing and wind shear. The importance of understanding these large scale circulations is that their dangers are not impossible to avoid. With a thorough knowledge of the structure of frontal lows, their associated fronts, and with good planning, you can often circumnavigate the problem areas while taking advantage of favorable winds.

CLIMATOLOGY

Frontal lows develop in areas of the globe where favorable conditions exist. For example, in winter, locally strong temperature gradients are found along some coastlines where cold continents are next to very warm oceans. This is the case for the U.S. just off the coast of the Gulf of Mexico and along the East Coast. When fronts move into these areas, the development of frontal lows is common. (Figure 8-9)

Vertical motions provided by large mountain chains and latent heat derived from moist air during con-

Figure 8-9. Frequent areas of cyclone development in North America are shaded. Regions of highest frequencies are dark red.

densation can also enhance cyclone development (cyclogenesis). These two processes frequently work together to produce frontal lows on the east slopes of the Rocky Mountains. (Figure 8-9)

CYCLONE STRUCTURE AND DEVELOPMENT NEAR THE SURFACE

The development of a frontal cyclone progresses through a distinctive life cycle. The incipient stage is shown in figure 8-10. Before the development begins in the most common case, a stationary front is present in the area, separating a cold airmass to the north and a warm airmass to the south. Pressure is generally lower along the front than in the airmasses on either side. The frontal zone is characterized by a change in wind speed and/or direction from the warm side to the cold side of the frontal zone.

As shown in figure 8-10, the cyclone development begins when pressure falls at some point along the original stationary front, and a counterclockwise

Figure 8-10. Development of a wave cyclone along a front. Diagrams are labeled chronologically. Red arrows represent winds in the warm air, blue arrows show winds in cold air. Isobars are drawn at 4 mb intervals. Note: only the last two digits are given (16 = 1016). Diagrams 0-2 represent conditions during the first 12 hours after the development begins (incipient stage).

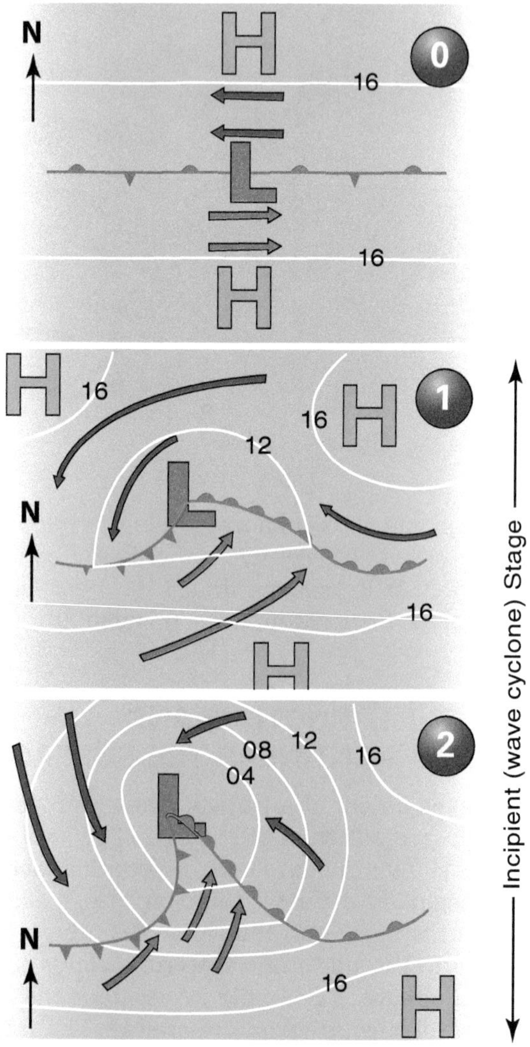

Pre-Development Stage

Incipient (wave cyclone) Stage

Wave cyclones do not necessarily develop beyond the incipient stage. These so-called "stable waves" simply move rapidly along the polar front, finally dissipating.

A variation that will always occur when flying across a front is a change in the wind.

circulation is generated (Northern Hemisphere). At this point, the cyclone is in the incipient stage; this is also called the wave cyclone stage because the previous stationary front has been distorted into a wave shape in response to the developing circulation. In addition to the motion around the low center, the entire low-pressure system typically moves toward the northeast at 15 to 25 knots. The speed of the cyclone will decrease in later stages of its development.

As the wave cyclone moves northeastward, the cyclonic circulation pushes warm air northward ahead of the low, and pulls cold air to the south behind it. The result of this process is first shown in diagram 1 of figure 8-10. The initial stationary front has been replaced by a warm and a cold front. The triangular region of warm air between the fronts and to the south of the cyclone is called the warm sector.

Both of the fronts in this idealized model lay in troughs of low pressure. This structure provides

Wind shear is the change of wind speed and/or wind direction over a distance. Shears may be vertical, horizontal, or both. A large change in wind over a short distance corresponds with strong shear. Wind shear is associated with a number of atmospheric disturbances. The strongest shears occur with mesoscale and microscale circulations, such as a microburst. Flight hazards associated with smaller scale wind shears are discussed in great detail in Chapter 11. When considering large disturbances, we often specify whether the shear is cyclonic or anticyclonic. Cyclonic wind shear means that changes in the wind speed or direction correspond with what you would find as you cross a low-pressure area. Anticyclonic wind shear is what you would expect when crossing a high-pressure area. The wind shear across a front (which often lies in a trough of low pressure) is cyclonic.

some useful indicators of the approach and passage of fronts.

1. As a front approaches a given location, the pressure falls. As the front passes, the pressure rises. This is more noticeable with a cold front than a warm front.

2. A sharp change in pressure gradient across a front corresponds with an equally sharp wind shift, an example of a cyclonic wind shear.

The winds change rapidly from a south or southwesterly direction just ahead of the cold front (in the warm sector) to northwesterly in the cold air. With the warm front, wind directions change from southeasterly in the cold air to southwesterly in the warm air.

Because a front has a distinct slope, wind shears are experienced during flight through the front, whether the penetration is made horizontally (level flight) or vertically (climb or descent). The vertical wind shear through a cold front is often visible from the ground. Just after a cold front passes, low clouds in the cold air will be moving from the northwest, while middle and high clouds move from the southwest.

> The approach of a warm front is indicated by southeasterly winds, falling pressures, and a gradually lowering ceiling. The progression of cloud types as the front approaches is cirrus (CI), cirrostratus (CS), altostratus (AS), and nimbostratus (NS) with stratus (ST), fog, poor visibilities, and continuous precipitation.

As the cyclone progresses northeastward, the central pressure continues to fall. This is an indication that the cyclone is deepening. The winds around the cyclone increase in response to the greater pressure gradient.

About 12 hours after the initial appearance of the frontal low, the cold airmass trailing the cyclone is swept around the low and overtakes the retreating cold air ahead of the cyclone. The warm sector air is pushed aloft by this occlusion process and the cyclone enters what is called the occluded stage.

(Figure 8-11) As noted previously, the combined frontal structure is called an occluded front. The central pressure of the low falls below 1,000 mb, and the cyclone slows down appreciably. The storm reaches its greatest intensity within about 12 hours after occlusion.

The central pressure begins to rise (the cyclone is filling) as the frontal low enters the dissipating stage of its life cycle. (Figure 8-11) Weakening

Figure 8-11. Development of an occluded cyclone. Diagram 3 represents the early occluded stage (12 to 24 hours after development began) when the cyclone reaches its greatest intensity. Diagram 5 shows conditions a few days after initial development when the system is dissipating. A weakening front (dashed) is shown near low center.

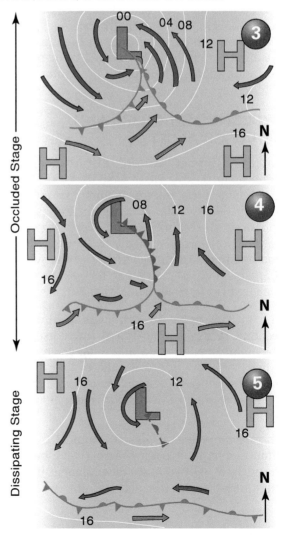

When a cyclone is in the wave cyclone stage, its direction of movement will parallel the surface isobars in the warm sector.

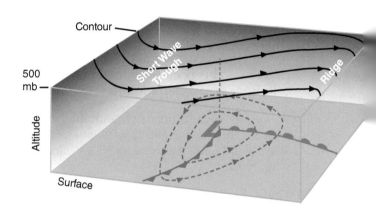

Figure 8-12. Perspective diagram of 500 mb (~18,000 ft) and surface charts for the case of a developing wave cyclone. Arrows have been added to the isobars and contours to show the wind directions at both levels.

usually begins 24 to 36 hours after the initial formation of the cyclone and lasts for another few days. The weakening is understandable if you recall that the low draws its energy from the temperature gradient across the front. In the occlusion process that gradient is destroyed, so the cyclone, now located entirely in the cold air, dies from the lack of an energy source.

Although the emphasis here is on the extratropical cyclone and its associated fronts, the frontal low development is usually accompanied by a well-defined, but shallow, cold high-pressure system behind the cold front. The center of this anticyclone is found near the center of the coldest air.

CYCLONE STRUCTURE AND BEHAVIOR ALOFT

Important upper airflow disturbances are troughs and ridges. These were first introduced in Chapter 3 as features commonly encountered in the middle and upper troposphere and stratosphere. In Chapter 7, very large macroscale (long wave) troughs aloft were identified as important characteristics of the wintertime global circulation along the east coasts of Asia and North America. (Figure 7-8)

In contrast, upper-level troughs, which correspond to developing frontal lows discussed above, are smaller scale than long waves. Also called short wave troughs, these disturbances move toward the east much more rapidly than long wave troughs, averaging about 600 n.m. per day.

The development of an extratropical cyclone often begins aloft before there is evidence at the surface. When surface development begins, the upper trough is located just upwind of the

surface low so development can proceed in an efficient manner. The ideal arrangement is shown in figure 8-12.

The position of the short wave trough to the west of the surface low allows mass to be removed above the low by strong winds ahead of the upper trough. This causes the pressure to fall at the surface and the deepening of the surface low. Two useful rules of thumb regarding a developing cyclone are:

1. There is a good chance of the development of a frontal low when an upper-level, short-wave trough moves to within 300 n.m. of a stationary front at the surface.

2. The east side of an upper-level, short-wave trough is the bad weather side.

Once the surface cyclone begins to develop, the upper-air system develops with it. There are no longer separate surface and upper air disturbances, but a single cyclone that extends from the surface through the tropopause.

Both the upper trough and the surface cyclone deepen through the wave cyclone stage. As seen in figure 8-13, about the time of occlusion, a closed cyclonic circulation develops aloft. At the same time, the upper cyclone becomes centered over the surface cyclone.

Figure 8-13. An occluded cyclone at the surface usually corresponds with a closed low aloft. Note the upper air low is directly over the surface low. Compare with figure 8-12.

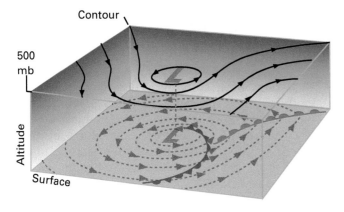

> While flying cross-country in the Northern Hemisphere, if you experience a continuous left crosswind which is associated with a major wind system, you are flying toward a low-pressure area and generally unfavorable weather conditions.

An important temperature feature of the extratropical cyclone is the location of the cold air. Aloft, the cold air is found near the center of the trough. At the surface, the low is initially located on the boundary between the warm and cold airmasses until occlusion occurs and the cold air reaches the center of the surface cyclone.

At every stage of development of the extratropical cyclone, the cyclone is stronger (as measured by the wind speeds) aloft than at the surface. The greatest wind speeds are in the jet streams near tropopause level.

In the troposphere, the polar front jet stream is on the edge of the coldest air; that is, it parallels fronts with the coldest air to the left of the wind, looking downstream. When an extratropical cyclone develops at jet stream levels, the segment of the jet stream that is found around the

upper trough intensifies as the trough develops. In the early stages of some cyclones, this jet streak of high winds may be more obvious than the upper-level trough. (Figure 8-14)

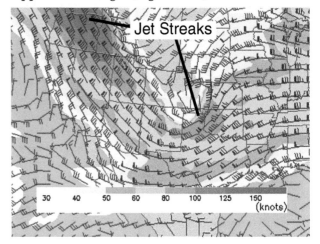

Figure 8-14. Winds at FL300. A jet streak is a segment of a jet stream where the winds are stronger than either upstream or downstream of that segment. The jet streak lies in a well-defined tropopause break. The tropopause is significantly lower to the left of the band of strongest winds along the jet stream axis and significantly higher to the right.

CLOUDS AND WEATHER PATTERNS

In moist areas around the frontal low, broad layers of clouds and precipitation are produced where upward motions occur. Rising air is generated at low levels by fronts and by the converging winds around the cyclone. Low-level cloudiness may also be produced in the warm and cold airmasses if there is sufficient moisture. The processes are contact cooling in stable air (warm airmass) or surface heating and convection in unstable air (cold airmass).

At higher levels, upward vertical motions are generated through a deep layer over the surface low, because mass is being removed by the winds at jet stream level more rapidly than it is being replaced near the surface. As noted in the previous section, this process causes the surface low to deepen. With adequate moisture, the resulting upward motions produce widespread cloud layers.

Frontal Clouds and Weather

In the lower half of the troposphere, clouds and weather tend to concentrate in the center of the cyclone and near the fronts and troughs. An idealized pattern is shown in figure 8-15.

Figure 8-15. Gray areas indicate the distribution of clouds and precipitation caused by an extratropical cyclone and its associated fronts in the wave cyclone stage (top) and in the occlusion stage (bottom). For clarity, jet stream cirrus and airmass cloudiness are not shown. White lines correspond to cross sections in figures 8-16 and 8-17.

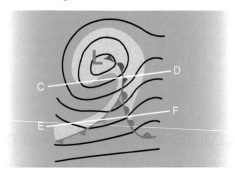

Clouds and weather caused by frontal lifting depend to a large degree on frontal type. Differences are illustrated with cross sections through warm, cold, and occluded fronts in figures 8-16 and 8-17.

In the idealized picture, the cold air lifts warm, moist, unstable air along the relatively steep cold front. This leads to deep convection, with a narrow line of CU and CB clouds and associated shower activity, as shown in figure 8-16. Meanwhile, along the warm front, warm, moist, stable air moves over the retreating wedge of cold air in what is frequently described as a "gentle, upglide motion" or overrunning. The result is that the warm front produces broad, deep lay-

ers of stratiform clouds (NS, AS, CS) and steady, continuous precipitation. In the stable, cold air below the sloping warm frontal zone, falling precipitation saturates the air; low ceilings and low visibilities with stratus, fog, rain or snow, and drizzle are common. The situation is made worse when freezing precipitation occurs (shown in figure 6-22).

The warm front cloudiness described above is modified when the warm, moist air moving over the front becomes unstable. This produces areas of convection. Thunderstorms embedded in otherwise stratiform cloudiness in the vicinity of a warm front are difficult to see and represent a serious flight hazard.

> Overrunning also occurs when moist, southerly flow intersects a stationary front east of the Rockies in the winter. Under these conditions, a region of bad flying weather with low clouds, poor visibilities and, occasionally, freezing rain and icing occurs over a distance of 400 n.m. or so on the cold air side of the front.

When a cold front overtakes a warm front in the occlusion process, the resulting occluded front combines cold and warm frontal cloudiness, depending on the type of occlusion. In a warm front occlusion (figure 8-17, left), the warm front remains on the ground because the cold

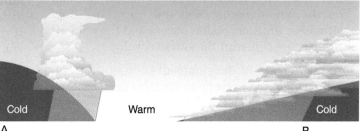

Figure 8-16. Idealized cross section showing the structure of cold front (left) and warm front (right), and associated clouds and weather in the vicinity of a cyclone in the wave stage of development along line A-B in figure 8-15.

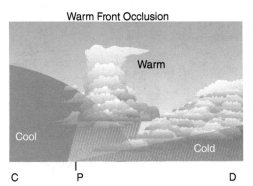 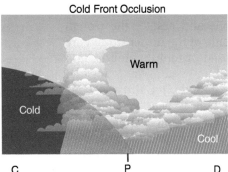

Figure 8-17. Idealized cross sections showing frontal cloudiness and weather in the vicinity of an occluded front. In both cases, fronts and airmasses are moving to the right. These diagrams are two possible vertical cross sections along line C-D through the occluded front on figure 8-15. Point P corresponds with the position of the occluded front on the ground. Note that a cross section along E-F in figure 8-15 would be identical to the diagram in figure 8-16.

air ahead of the warm front is much colder than the air behind the cold front. In this case, the cold front moves up the warm frontal boundary. Because of the flat slope of the warm front, the passage of this upper cold front with its showers and thunderstorms may precede the passage of the surface occluded (formerly warm) front by some distance. In comparison, the passage of a cold front occlusion (cold front remains on the ground) is followed fairly quickly by the passage of the upper warm front. (Figure 8-17, right) Both cases are subject to the hazard of embedded thunderstorms, especially during the warmer months of the year.

Behind the cold front, cold air moving over warm ground or warm water may become unstable. Visibilities are good except where the instability is so great that post-frontal showers occur. Convective cloud clusters in the cold air are often visible in satellite images over oceanic areas where moisture is plentiful. As the ridge or anticyclone centered in the cold air moves into the area, downward motion is dominant. Clouds and precipitation are suppressed and clear weather prevails.

Indicators of an approaching warm front are steady precipitation with stratiform clouds.

A common in-flight hazard associated with warm fronts is precipitation-induced fog.

In a cold front occlusion, the air ahead of the warm front is warmer than the air behind the overtaking cold front.

When the cold airmass following a cold front is moist and unstable, it is characterized by cumuliform clouds and showery precipitation.

A ridge or high-pressure area is characterized by downward motion.

A Space View of an Extratropical Cyclone

Images of clouds from weather satellites are very accessible via television and the internet. However, the space view of clouds offers a far different perspective than the view from the ground or the cockpit. To provide some interpretive guidance, a schematic satellite view of typical cloud patterns for a fully developed occlusion is presented in figure 8-18. In this example, the satellite image is in the infrared portion of the electromagnetic spectrum. Therefore, the gray shades correspond with actual temperatures of the object in the image. White is cold, black is warm.

From the images in diagrams A and B, we see three primary cloud features that support our earlier contention that the east side of a trough aloft is the bad weather side. A low-level, cold frontal cloud band is found to the south of the cyclone and east of the trough aloft. Also on the east side of the upper trough are a comma cloud composed of middle clouds, and a broad, curved band of jet stream cirrus located just to the right of the jet axis. Jet stream cirrus clouds are the highest clouds near the cyclone, and they will be the whitest (coldest) in a black and white infrared satellite image. They can usually be identified by the very sharp edge to the cirrus band near the jet stream axis; therefore the jet stream cirrus pattern is a useful indicator of the position and orientation of the jet stream in the absence of other data. Other cirrus clouds are also found near the comma cloud. These are lower "debris" cirrus clouds, not to be confused with jet stream cirrus. At lower levels, gray (warmer) clusters of cumulus clouds indicate the location of the cold air to the left of the jet axis, as shown in diagram B of figure 8-18. Large, cold-air cumulus clusters are common over oceans, but are usually absent over land. For clarity, the clusters are not shown in diagram A.

As shown in figure 8-18, at least a portion of cold frontal cloudiness can usually be seen from space. However, jet stream cirrus generally obscures warm frontal cloudiness. Also note that the tip of the comma cloud is a good indicator of the location of the upper trough or low center. In the early stages of extratropical cyclone development, the comma cloud may be separated from (upstream of) the cold frontal cloud band.

Both the polar front model presented on previous pages and the model of satellite-viewed cloud patterns around an occluded extratropical cyclone are very helpful for interpreting observed weather conditions, for understanding the surface analysis chart, and for anticipating future weather conditions. But keep in mind that neither model precisely describes the structure and behavior of every wave cyclone that occurs. For example, in some cases, a cyclone will deepen significantly, but the occluded front will not develop as previously described. Also, warm fronts in occluded cyclones approaching the West Coast of the U.S. are very difficult to locate near the surface and are often not shown on surface analysis charts.

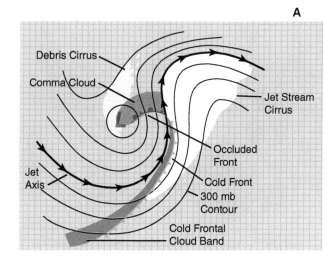

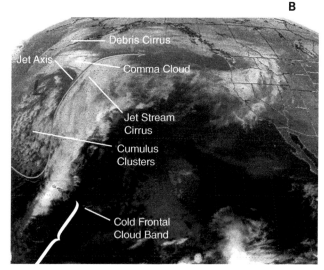

Figure 8-18. Diagram A: Schematic drawing of the main cloud features of the occluded cyclone shown in the infrared satellite image in diagram B. Locations of the cold and occluded fronts are also shown in A. The warm front position is not identified because it is obscured by a broad band of cirrus clouds to the right of the jet axis.

Furthermore, prominent mountain ranges and very warm water along coastlines may cause distortions in the various stages of wave cyclone development. For example, North American wave cyclones that develop on the eastern slopes of the Rocky Mountains often behave as occluded systems from their initial appearance.

These variations should not be difficult to deal with if you remember that all frontal cyclones typically retain their characteristics for several days, allowing you to identify variations from the idealized polar front model and adjust your interpretation accordingly.

Section B
TROPICAL CYCLONES AND HURRICANES

All cyclones that develop in the atmosphere are not exactly like extratropical cyclones. In many cases, the only similarity is that the winds blow cyclonically around a low-pressure area. Otherwise, behavior, structure, and energy sources are all different. Perhaps the best example of such a contrast is the tropical cyclone.

A tropical cyclone is a mesoscale, cyclonic circulation that develops in the tropical easterlies. In its most intense form, it becomes a hurricane with strong convection, exceptionally strong winds, and torrential rains. In this section, we briefly examine the climatology, structure, and behavior of hurricanes.

CLIMATOLOGY

The term "tropical cyclone" covers a number of similar tropical disturbances which are classified according to their maximum sustained wind speeds: tropical depression (33 knots or less); tropical storm (34 to 63 knots); and hurricane (64 knots or more). Hurricane-strength tropical cyclones are known by other local names, depending on the geographical location. For example, in the Western North Pacific, they are called "typhoons."

There is a large intensity range of tropical cyclones beyond the threshold of the hurricane definition; hurricanes with winds in excess of 100 knots are not uncommon. For this reason, the Saffir-Simpson scale was developed to rate the damage potential of individual hurricanes. (Figure 8-19)

When any tropical storm reaches hurricane strength, it is named from a list selected by international agreement. Examples of some of the strongest hurricanes to strike the U.S. in the past 20 years are Hugo, 1989, Andrew, 1992,

Figure 8-19. Saffir-Simpson scale of damage potential of hurricanes.

Category	Central pressure (millibars)	Winds (knots)	Damage
1	≥ 980	64 - 82	damage mainly to trees, shrubbery, and unanchored mobile homes
2	965 - 979	83 - 95	some trees blown down; major damage to exposed mobile homes; some damage to roofs of buidings
3	945 - 964	96 - 112	foliage removed from trees; large trees blown down; mobile homes destroyed; some structural damage to small buildings
4	920 - 944	113 - 136	all signs blown down; extensive damage to roofs, windows, and doors; complete destruction of mobile homes; flooding inland as far 6 mi (10 km); major damage to lower floors of structures near shore
5	< 920	> 136	severe damage to windows and doors; extensive damage to roofs of homes and industrial buildings; small buildings overturned and blown away; major damage to lower floors of all structures near the shore

and Floyd, 1999. 2005 saw a series of several very strong hurricanes including Katrina, which reached Category 5 in the Gulf of Mexico before striking the Gulf Coast as a Category 3 and causing disastrous flooding. Favored regions of development of tropical storms around the world and their local names are presented in figure 8-20.

The tropical disturbances that influence the continental U.S. are mainly produced in the Atlantic, the Caribbean, and the Gulf of Mexico. The areas of the U.S. that are most vulnerable to hurricanes are the Eastern Seaboard and the Gulf Coast. Hurricanes occur most frequently in the late summer and early fall.

Occasionally, the remnants of a dying tropical cyclone cross into the southwest U.S. from the Pacific. However, the great majority of storms produced in the Eastern Pacific move northwestward. They occasionally threaten the Hawaiian Islands, but more often they die over colder waters in the North Pacific.

DEVELOPMENT AND BEHAVIOR

As shown in figure 8-20, tropical cyclones develop within about 1,200 n.m. of the equator, over areas with water temperatures of about 27°C (~80°F) or greater. Each begins its life cycle as a poorly organized tropical disturbance. If conditions are favorable, it moves through the successively stronger stages of a tropical depression and a tropical storm. A relatively small number of tropical cyclones continue to intensify to hurricane strength. During the period of development, the cyclone usually moves westward or northwestward at about 10 knots.

Figure 8-20 shows that many tropical cyclones first move westward in the trade winds and then gradually turn poleward on the western sides of the oceanic subtropical highs. When these storms reach higher latitudes during this "re-curving" process, they weaken as they move over land or cold water. Some other dying tropical cyclones are caught up in the prevailing westerlies and move back toward the east. If a tropical cyclone encounters the polar front, it may undergo redevelopment as a strong extratropical cyclone. Some tropical cyclones may behave quite differently from the average picture given above, depending on differences in larger scale weather patterns and/or interaction with landmasses. Variations include tropical cyclones that remain stationary over long periods, storms with looping tracks, and hurricanes that weaken and then reintensify.

Figure 8-20.
Common tropical cyclone tracks and local names.

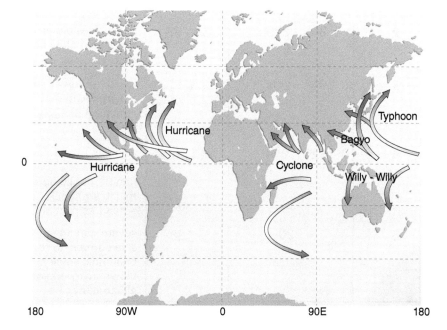

STRUCTURE AND WEATHER

When a tropical cyclone reaches hurricane strength, the storm is several hundred miles in diameter. Figure 8-21 gives different views of two hurricanes, one from space and one from weather radar. The horizontal scale (diameter) of the hurricane cloud signature is typically 300 n.m. or more. The clouds observed by satellite often cover a larger area than the most intense part of the storm. This happens because the cirrus spreads out in a high-level outflow region of the hurricane. The horizontal scale of the radar signature of a hurricane is much smaller than that seen in the satellite image because the radar doesn't observe the cloud structure. Rather, it senses the precipitation regions of the hurricane. A still smaller portion of the storm is the diameter of the region of hurricane strength winds; that distance is often less than 50 nautical miles. These are approximate scales. There are considerable variations from storm to storm, depending on overall strength.

Major features of the hurricane environment are the eye, the eye wall, and cloud bands spiraling into the storm. (Figures 8-21 and 8-22) The hurricane eye is the circular, nearly cloud-free region approximately 10 to 20 n.m. in diameter that is located in the center of the storm. It is the warm core of the hurricane, a region of relatively light winds, and the location of the lowest sea level pressure of the storm. As a matter of fact, the lowest sea level pressure ever measured anywhere in the world was in the center of a hurricane (870 mb in Typhoon Tip in 1979).

The eye wall is the cloudy region embedded with many thunderstorms immediately adjacent to the eye. It is the region of strongest winds and most intense convection. Because hurricanes occur in the tropics where the tropopause is very high, it is not unusual for the CB cloud tops to extend to 50,000 feet MSL or higher in the eye wall and elsewhere in the storm.

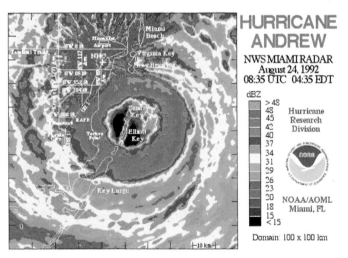

Figure 8-21. Hurricanes display distinctive cloud signatures in satellite images (diagram A) and distinctive echo signatures in radar images (diagram B). The hurricane eye and spiral band structure are clearly identifiable. (Hurricane photograph courtesy of NASA. Radar signature courtesy of National Oceanic and Atmospheric Administration.)

The rainbands that spiral into the storm are also lines of convergence characterized by thunderstorms and shower activity. They measure from a few nautical miles to about 30 n.m. in width and are spaced 60 n.m. to 200 n.m. apart.

As shown in figure 8-22, strong winds flow into the intense low-pressure area at the surface. High up in the storm (40,000 feet MSL or so) the circulation around the hurricane is reversed. This structure is a key characteristic of tropical cyclones: winds are strongest near the surface and weaken aloft, especially above 18,000 feet MSL. The same cannot be said about the convection associated with thunderstorms. More details on the structure of thunderstorms (CB) are given in the following chapter.

Although a hurricane may appear to be roughly symmetrical when viewed from a satellite, this is not true when considering the associated weather. For example, looking in the direction of the hurricane movement, the region of strongest winds is located to the right of the eye and the worst weather is located in the right front quadrant of the hurricane (Northern Hemisphere). Also, the spiral rainbands, depending on their velocity and width, can affect local winds and precipitation intensity. Although the strong, and often damaging, hurricane winds receive the greatest attention when a hurricane is initially described, the greatest damage is usually associated with coastal flooding caused by the storm surge.

Storm surge consequences were clearly demonstrated by the effects of Hurricane Sandy on the east coast of the U.S. in October, 2012.

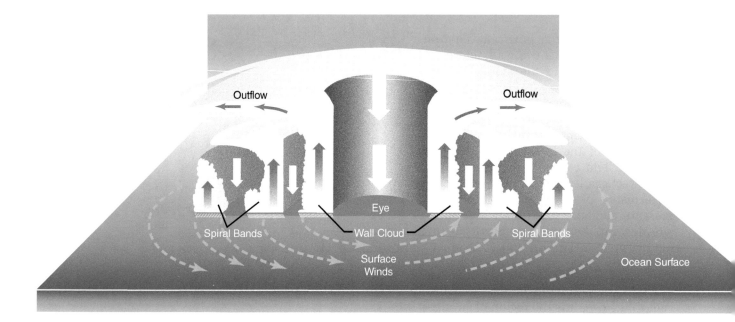

Figure 8-22. A cutaway diagram of a hurricane shows major features: eye, eye wall, inflow at low levels, spiral rain bands, and outflow near the top of the storm. Air rises in strong convection in the eye wall and rainbands. Strong sinking in the eye accounts for the warm core of the storm and the lack of clouds in the eye. Weaker downward motions occur between the spiral bands.

	Charleston Naval Station, SC	Charleston (City Site), SC	WSO Charleston Airport, SC
Date	September 21-22	September 21	September 22
Anemometer Height	118 feet	25 feet	20 feet
Peak Gust	137 mph @ 11:30-11:45 p.m., 9/21	108 mph @ 11:40 p.m.	98 mph @ 12:59 a.m.
Max. Sustained Speed	NA	87 mph @ 11:30 p.m.	78 mph @ 1:03 a.m.
Max. Mean Speed	15-minute average, 74 mph @ 1:00 a.m., 9/22	NA	10-minute average, 59 mph @ 1:10 a.m.

Figure 8-23. Surface wind observations from Charleston, South Carolina during Hurricane Hugo, which passed to the north of the city. The eye of Hugo crossed the coast about 0500 EDT, September 22, 1989.

With reasonable caution, flight is often possible in the vicinity of an extratropical cyclone; however, flight is never advisable in the immediate vicinity of a hurricane. Winds are strong, thunderstorms are common, and rain showers are heavy. When hurricanes reach land along the East or Gulf coasts of the U.S., they frequently set off severe convective weather, including intense thunderstorms and tornadoes. Figure 8-23 lists surface wind observations at Charleston, South Carolina, during the passage of Hurricane Hugo.

Clearly, it is not an environment for commercial or recreational flying. More detailed information about the structure and flight hazards of thunderstorms and low-level turbulence caused by strong winds are presented in the next chapter and in Part III.

When a hurricane approaches an area, the National Weather Service issues one or more special bulletins. A hurricane watch is issued when hurricane conditions are expected in a particular area within a day or more. A hurricane warning is issued when the arrival of those conditions is expected within the next 24 hours.

SUMMARY

Extratropical cyclones are important large scale disturbances that move eastward in the middle latitudes. They draw their energy from the polar front and involve the movement of large airmasses and fronts near the earth's surface, as well as the development of troughs and jet streaks aloft. The average wind, cloud, and precipitation patterns that evolve during the life cycle of the extratropical cyclone are captured by the polar front model. In contrast, slightly smaller scale tropical cyclones develop and move westward in low latitudes. Some of these develop into highly destructive hurricanes. Tropical cyclones, which are not characterized by fronts and airmass contrasts, instead draw their energy from warm waters and die over cold waters or land. Structurally, the extratropical cyclone has a cold core and intensifies with height. Tropical cyclones have warm cores and weaken with height. Both of these circulations are critical for aviation. Nearly every aviation weather flight hazard can be present at one time or another during the lifetimes of these phenomena, including thunderstorms, wind shear, turbulence, icing, and instrument meteorological conditions. These subjects will be examined in subsequent chapters in Parts II and III.

KEY TERMS

Airmass
Airmass Source Region
Anticyclonic Wind Shear
Closed Low
Cold Airmass
Cold Front
Cold Front Occlusion
Comma Cloud
Cyclonic Wind Shear
Cyclogenesis
Deepening
Dissipating Stage
Extratropical Cyclone
Eye Wall
Filling
Front
Frontal Cloud Band
Frontal Cyclone
Frontal Low
Frontal Slope
Frontal Wave
Frontal Zone
Hurricane
Hurricane Eye
Hurricane Warning

Hurricane Watch
Incipient Stage
Jet Streak
Jet Stream Cirrus
Occluded Front
Occlusion Process
Occluded Stage
Overrunning
Polar Front Model
Rainbands
Short Wave Troughs
Stationary Front
Storm Surge
Tropical Cyclone
Tropical Depression
Tropical Disturbance
Tropical Storm
Warm Airmass
Warm Front
Warm Front Occlusion
Warm Sector
Wave Cyclone
Wave Cyclone Stage
Wind Shear

REVIEW QUESTIONS

1. Why are extratropical cyclones more prevalent and stronger in mid-latitudes in winter than in the summer?

2. A typical short-wave trough line is just crossing the west coast of the United States. If it is moving directly eastward, when will it cross the Continental Divide?

3. A sea level pressure of 888 mb was reported in Hurricane Gilbert in September, 1988. If your altimeter was set at 29.92 inches of mercury, approximately what would your altimeter read if you were at sea level with an actual pressure of 888 mb?

4. List the indicators of an idealized cold front approach and passage.

5. List the indicators of an idealized warm front approach and passage.

6. You are at MIA. A hurricane is approaching from the east. If the eye passes directly overhead, in what sequence will the wind directions change during the passage of the hurricane from east to west?

7. In 1999, when hurricane Floyd crossed the southeast coast of the U.S., there was a tendency for clearing to the southwest of the storm center, while to the north, extensive clouds and heavy precipitation continued. Why?

DISCOVERY QUESTIONS

8. You are trying to land at an airport before the arrival of the weather associated with a cold front passage. The front is approaching the airport at a speed of 10 knots. You have been in the cold airmass for almost your entire flight and you manage to fly through the front into warm air at 3,000 feet AGL, about 5 n.m. from the airport. Your airspeed is 120 knots. Will you reach the airport before the front does? Discuss.

9. Obtain a U.S. surface analysis chart with a well-defined cold front between the Rocky Mountains and the East Coast. Identify the frontal zone.

10. Several years ago, when a typhoon was approaching an airfield on a Pacific island, it was determined that the eye of the storm would actually cross the base where several large aircraft were parked in the open. There was no hangar space and although it was too late to fly the aircraft to safety, minimum aircrews were placed in the aircraft. Why? Discuss.

11. Why does the front aloft precede the surface front by a large distance in a warm front occlusion and follow the surface front at a shorter distance in a cold front occlusion?

12. Make a table that contrasts the following characteristics of extratropical cyclones and hurricanes.
    1. Geographical region of development
    2. Initial direction of movement
    3. Energy source
    4. Altitude of greatest intensity
    5. Stages of development
    6. Scale
    7. Temperature structure
    8. Weather

CHAPTER 9
THUNDERSTORMS

Introduction

In this chapter, we continue our "scale approach" to the understanding of atmospheric circulations. Moving to smaller scales, our consideration is now the mesoscale phenomenon known as a thunderstorm. The thunderstorm is one of the most spectacular atmospheric circulations, and one that you must respect as a pilot. It can be bright, loud, violent, and dangerous in many ways. As with our study of macroscale circulations, we will begin with an idealized model of the thunderstorm. When you complete this chapter, you will understand thunderstorm structure and behavior as well as the wide variety of microscale phenomena that are frequently produced by a thunderstorm. You will also become familiar with larger mesoscale and macroscale circulations that provoke thunderstorms and organize them into lines and clusters. A thunderstorm is always a threat to aircraft operations. A wise pilot will be sure he or she understands the "what?" "why?" and "where?" of thunderstorms. This background will prepare you well for the study of specific flight hazards as detailed in Part III.

Section A

DRY CONVECTION

Observing a growing cumulus cloud provides clear evidence that the air in the cloud is going upward, quickly! Our study of thunderstorms concentrates on this buoyant, saturated air. However, we must keep in mind that the air in cumulus clouds or cumulonimbus clouds originally comes from the boundary layer. So-called dry convection is a common process within a few thousand feet of the ground. Since thunderstorms are rooted in dry convection, a discussion of their development would be incomplete without an examination of the important properties of convection below the cloud base.

When the ground becomes much warmer than the air above it, the lapse rate in the lowest layer often becomes "superadiabatic" (LR>3C°/1,000 feet). Under these absolutely unstable conditions, any air that receives the slightest vertical displacement, such as by a wind gust, will rapidly move in the direction of that displacement. After this process begins in the boundary layer, the air motion becomes organized into discrete "bubbles" of warm air rising from the ground. These bubbles are but another type of atmospheric circulation with a distinct range of scales and life cycles. They are more frequently called thermals, which are the cloudless roots of cumulus clouds.

Individual thermals have horizontal dimensions of a few hundred to a few thousand feet, lifetimes of a few minutes, and vertical speeds from a few hundred feet per minute to about 2,000 f.p.m. Thermals can develop day or night, as long as the ground is warmer than the overlying air. These conditions are often met in a cold airmass as it moves over warm land, such as following a cold frontal passage. Thermals are common over land in daytime, under clear skies, and during the warmer months of the year.

The size and strength of thermals varies greatly, depending on how much warmer they are than their surroundings. This, in turn, depends on the surface heating. Thermals tend to be smaller and weaker in the morning than they are in the afternoon. Daytime sources of thermals are those surfaces that heat up more rapidly than surrounding areas. Favorable surfaces include dry fields, paved roads, parking lots, and runways. Elevated terrain is also a producer of thermals, because it is often warmer than the surrounding air at the same altitude. High, bare hills generate thermals earlier in the day and for a longer period than in nearby valleys. Unfavorable thermal sources are forested areas, cool bodies of water, irrigated fields, and ground dampened by rain.

Close to the ground, thermals are elongated, plume-like structures of rising warm air, perhaps 100 feet across and a few hundred feet long. When winds are strong, thermals close to the ground become chaotic and difficult to identify. Otherwise, thermal plumes are often indicated by birds soaring over flat ground and/or by looping smoke plumes.

Occasionally, the wind is diverted by an obstruction, such as a stand of trees or a small hill. Air sweeping around the sides of the obstruction causes eddies to form downwind. If a thermal happens to form in the same area as the rotating eddies, it will also rotate. As the rotating thermal rises, it stretches vertically and shrinks horizontally. This causes a faster rotation. You see the same effect when a spinning skater pulls his arms in to his body. The result of the spin-up of a thermal is a vortex known as a whirlwind or dust devil, not to be confused with more violent tornadoes or waterspouts. Wind speeds up to 20 knots are not unusual within a dust devil; however, extremes of 50 knots have been reported. (Figure 9-1)

Cessna 152. No injuries. Pilot rushed his landing to avoid the effects of a nearby dust devil. After landing without mishap, the aircraft was taxied off the active runway where it contacted the dust devil. Control was lost and the aircraft nosed over.

Figure 9-1. A dust devil is a product of extreme surface heating and light winds. Photograph courtesy of Stan Celestian, Glendale Community College.

Dust devil formation is favored under light wind conditions over very hot surfaces, such as over barren desert areas in summer and in the early afternoon. Once formed, they have no preferred direction of rotation. They move with the speed and direction of the average wind in the layer that they occupy.

Dust devils are typically 5 to 100 feet in diameter and have lifetimes of 4 minutes or less, although extremes of hours have been reported. Dust lifted by the vortex often reaches altitudes of 100 to 300 feet AGL; although, the vortex itself may extend to a higher level. Over desert areas in the summer, dust devils occasionally reach altitudes of several thousand feet AGL. Remember, dust devils are a product of dry convection; they do not require the presence of CB or CU to form.

In contrast to dust devils, ordinary thermals develop a distinct internal circulation as they rise. An idealized model of a thermal is shown in figure 9-2. Superimposed on the overall rising motion of the thermal is a microscale circulation cell that is best described as an elongated vortex ring. Extending upward from the ground, the vortex ring has a relatively narrow core of upward motions surrounded by a broad region of weaker sinking motions. The horizontal dimension of the thermal also grows with altitude as outside air is mixed into the circulation.

The shape of the thermal is idealized in figure 9-2. Although the updraft is always the dominant feature, a real thermal twists and distorts as it rises due to internal temperature differences and external influences, such as wind shear. Furthermore, as thermals grow with altitude, they often merge.

Figure 9-2. A perspective diagram of an idealized thermal. The broad, vertical arrow indicates the warm air entering the thermal near the ground and the subsequent ascent of the thermal. The circular ribbons show the vortex ring that rises with the thermal. This circulation is similar to that of a smoke ring.

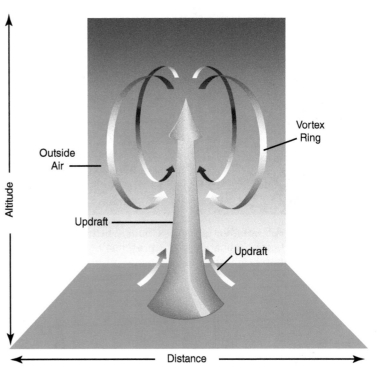

The vortex-ring circulation draws outside air into the thermal as it rises. This process reduces the temperature of the thermal and, therefore, its buoyancy. The rise of the thermal is often halted when it reaches a stable layer where it becomes colder than its surroundings. In a large high-pressure region, boundary layer air becomes unstable because of daytime surface heating, but thermals may only rise to 2,000 feet or so because of the presence of an elevated stable layer. If clouds form in this process, they are of the fair-weather cumulus variety. (Figure 9-3)

Thermals are a common source of lift for sailplanes. Many cross-country glider flights longer than 1,000 km (540 n.m.) have been made by using the thermal updrafts associated with dry convection.

Figure 9-3. Fair weather cumulus clouds which have formed at the tops of rising thermals. Notice the flattened cloud tops, indicative of the presence of an elevated stable layer. The horizontal dimensions of a single cloud are often larger than an individual thermal, because thermals tend to expand and merge as they rise.

Section B
CLOUDY CONVECTION

In its most common use, the term cloudy convection refers to saturated air that is rising because it is warmer than its surroundings. We also include in this definition saturated air that descends because it is colder than its surroundings. Therefore, cloudy convection includes all of the various forms of cumulus clouds and their updrafts and downdrafts. In order to better describe and explain thunderstorms, we begin by briefly examining the general process of convective cloud growth.

CLOUD GROWTH

The distinct appearance of cumuliform clouds reflects not only the saturation, but also the instability of the convective updraft. The characteristic flat bases of the clouds occur at the altitude where the rising, unstable air first reaches saturation and is called the convective condensation level. Above the convective condensation level, upward moving air cools at the saturated adiabatic lapse rate. You should recall that this cooling rate is less than the dry adiabatic lapse rate, because the adiabatic cooling due to expansion as the air rises is partially offset by the continued release of latent heat as the cloud forms. For this reason, an unstable updraft often becomes more unstable when the cloud begins to appear.

As shown in figure 9-4, above the convective condensation level, the cloudy updraft continues to accelerate upward. Clear air sinks around the cloud to compensate for the upward motion. The sinking is usually much weaker than the updrafts, typically taking place over a much broader area than that of the cloud. The updraft is similar to a jet of fluid pointed vertically. The strong shears between the updraft and its clear surroundings produce turbulent eddies marked by cauliflower-like protuberances on the edges of the cumulus cloud.

The cloudy updraft continues its upward acceleration until it reaches the equilibrium level; that is, the altitude where the updraft temperature is equal to the temperature of its surroundings. Above that level, the air continues to rise, but decelerates because it is cooler than its surroundings. The top of the cloud occurs at the level where the updraft speed decreases to zero. Because the cloud top is colder than its surroundings, it finally collapses and spreads out around the equilibrium level.

The upper limit of convective clouds depends strongly on the presence or absence of stable layers above the convective condensation level. A strong, elevated stable layer may stop the vertical growth of cumulus clouds at any stage, depending on the altitude of the layer. So-called fair weather cumuli typically have limited vertical extent because their growth is "capped" by a strong stable layer (often an inversion) within a few thousand feet of the ground. In this case, the

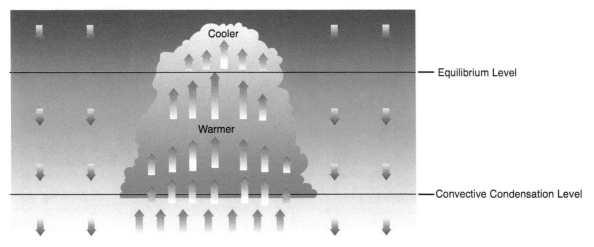

Figure 9-4. Schematic cross section of a growing cumulus cloud. Lengths of the arrows are proportional to the speed of the updrafts and downdrafts. "Warmer" and "cooler" indicate updraft temperatures relative to the temperature of the surrounding clear air.

convective condensation level (cloud base) and the equilibrium level (near cloud top) are close together. Cumulus clouds formed by this process look like those shown in figure 9-3.

Another example of limited cloud development is often found in a cold airmass behind a cold front. Although the convection may be strong in these circumstances, the vertical development of the clouds is frequently limited by the stable layer near the top of the shallow, cold airmass. (Figure 9-5)

DOWNDRAFT DEVELOPMENT

When the altitude of the cumulus cloud exceeds the freezing level, there is a rapid growth of cloud particles by the ice crystal process. At some point in this process, the updraft is no longer strong enough to support the weight of the large particles. They begin to fall, dragging air downward. This is the beginning of the precipitation-induced downdraft. These internal downdrafts are much stronger than the sinking motions outside the cloud.

The downward vertical motions are strengthened where unsaturated air outside the cloud is mixed across the boundaries of the cloud. Evaporation further cools the downdraft, increasing the negative buoyancy. As snow turns to rain at lower levels, melting also contributes to the cooling of the air and the intensity of the downdraft. As we will see in Section D, the precipitation-induced downdraft is a major component of the life cycle of the thunderstorm.

Strong upward currents in clouds enhance the growth rate of precipitation.

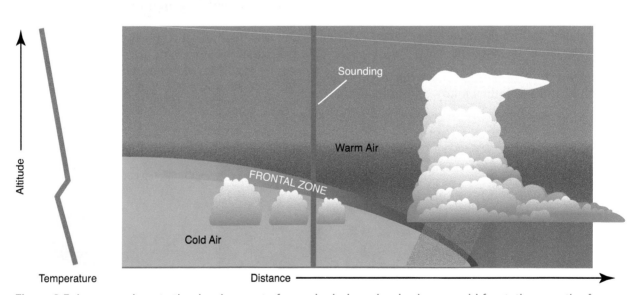

Figure 9-5. In comparison to the development of cumulonimbus clouds along a cold front, the growth of cumulus in the cold air behind the front is often limited by the stable layer that corresponds to the frontal zone at the top of the cold air. The diagram on the left shows the temperature sounding along the vertical red line through the front. Notice the inversion layer at the altitude of the front.

Section C

WEATHER RADAR

Before describing the development of a thunderstorm from a growing cumulus cloud, it is helpful to examine a useful thunderstorm detection tool: weather radar. Weather radar is used extensively to locate thunderstorms and to observe their structure and behavior. In general, radar, for Radio Detection and Ranging, is an instrument that uses electromagnetic radiation to detect objects and determine their distance and direction from the radar site. The objects, or radar targets, must be composed of matter that scatters or reflects electromagnetic energy in the frequencies of radio waves.

Radar consists of a transmitter and receiver, usually in the same antenna. (Figure 9-6) Electromagnetic energy from the transmitter is focused and emitted in a narrow beam by the antenna. Targets such as airplanes, buildings, and atmospheric particles reflect, scatter, and absorb the energy. A small fraction of the reflected/scattered radar signal returns to the radar antenna/receiver where it is intercepted. The received signal constitutes a radar echo. By monitoring the time it takes for the transmitted energy to travel from antenna to target and back, the distance or "slant range" from the antenna to the target can be determined. The direction of the target is simply determined by noting the direction the antenna is pointing when the echo is received.

Doppler radar has the capability to determine velocity of a target toward or away from the radar by measuring the frequency difference between the transmitted and received radiation. The returning frequency is lower than the transmitted frequency if the target is moving away from the radar, and higher if the target is moving toward the radar. You hear a similar Doppler effect when the pitch of the whistle of a train decreases as the train passes your location.

Weather radar operates at specific frequencies, or wavelengths, of electromagnetic radiation that are sensitive to scattering by ice and water particles. Most weather radars detect relatively large precipitation particles, such as rain and snow, better than cloud particles. Some precipitation types provide more substantial targets than others. For example, large water droplets and wet hail give better echoes than snow or drizzle.

The **Next** Generation Weather **Rad**ar network (NEXRAD) includes 164 WSR-88D Doppler radar installations in the U.S. and its territories. That network is enhanced by more than 40 Terminal Doppler Weather Radar (TDWR) sites at selected airports that are prone to severe weather.

The European weather radar network has expanded significantly to over 100 sites including a large number of Doppler installations. A consortium of 18 countries (EUMETNET) collaborates on stan-

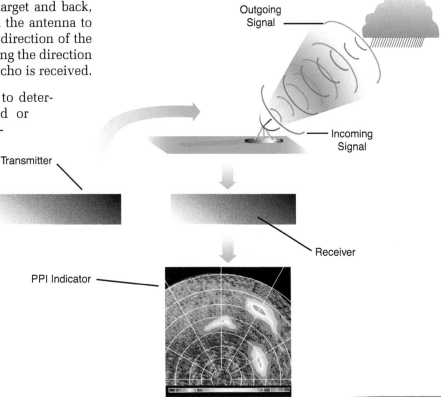

Figure 9-6. Radar transmits and receives a signal through an antenna. Radar data are processed and displayed in various formats including a plan position indicator (PPI) scope.

dardization of equipment and plans for continued improvement and expansion of the radar network.

Although not as powerful as modern surface-based radar, airborne weather radar has the advantage of observing the current conditions ahead of the aircraft. However, airborne weather radar does not have the power to detect extremely small targets. Most precipitation is detected, but cloud particles are definitely too small to cause significant scattering. This means that the horizontal cloud boundaries are wider and cloud tops are generally higher than shown by radar echoes. Also, the height of the base of a precipitating cloud is usually difficult to detect by radar because the echo often extends to the ground with the precipitation.

As a radar signal travels away from its source, it undergoes a process known as attenuation. This is a weakening of the signal that occurs as the signal is absorbed, scattered, or reflected along its path. Precipitation is an efficient attenuator of weather radar signals. In heavy rain, a radar signal may be partially or totally absorbed by the target (the rain) in the foreground, so that targets in the background cannot be seen very clearly, if at all. This is a critical feature for airborne radar. Your decision to fly across a line of echoes is usually determined by your ability to "see" across to the other side. This may not be possible with a very strong echo in the foreground.

Weather is observed continuously by the previously mentioned network of ground-based weather radars maintained by the National Weather Service (NWS), the Air Force Weather Agency (AFWA), and the Federal Aviation Administration (FAA). Common scales used by meteorologists and pilots to describe radar returns are shown in Figure 9-7A. These include echo intensity level, reflectivity, and precipitation rate. In a broader application, these classifications can be used to infer the strength of the turbulent circulation within a precipitating cloud. This is particularly important in evaluating flight conditions in developing cumulus and especially cumulonimbus (thunderstorms). Applications of radar to the evaluation of thunderstorm flight hazards is discussed in detail in Part III (Chapter 12, Section B).

Radar information is available in many different formats. Examples include real-time airborne radar systems, near real-time radar loops from individual radar stations, and the hourly weather radar summary chart (Figure 9-7B). An example of a radar chart constructed every 30 minutes from the coded reports of individual surface radar stations is given in figure 9-7C.

The contoured intensity levels on radar summary charts must be used carefully. The contours only describe the intensity of the echo in a particular area in very broad terms. As you will see in the next section, thunderstorms have short lifetimes, often less than the time between radar summary charts. For that reason, the NWS and FAA recommend a cautious interpretation of the radar summary chart. The maximum reported intensity level should always be used to estimate the severity of the storm.

You should also be aware that surface weather radar signals can often be blocked by mountainous terrain, or that a radar station may simply be inoperative at a particular time. The result is that some thunderstorm cells may be missed. Other modes of thunderstorm detection such as surface observations, satellite observations, and the monitoring of lightning discharges should also be used in these cases.

ALTERNATIVES TO AIRBORNE WEATHER RADAR

The size, weight, power requirements, and cost of airborne radar often require pilots of smaller aircraft to look to other thunderstorm detection systems. There are at least two alternatives:

Lightning detection equipment uses a magnetic direction finder to locate lightning discharges. This technique has been used by the ground-based National Lightning Detection Network (NLDN) for many years to augment surface radar

The radarscope provides no assurance of avoiding instrument weather conditions.

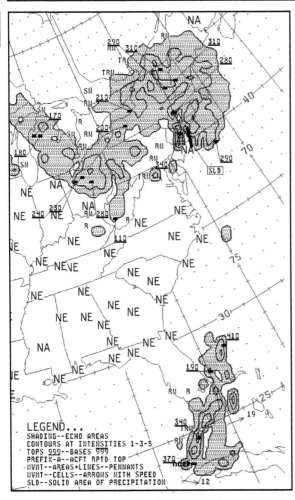

A

ATC Weather Radar Terms	Echo Intensity Level (1-6)	Echo Intensity (dBZ)*	Convective Rainfall Rate ** (in./hr.)
Light*	1	18-29	<0.1
Moderate	2	30-40	0.1 to 0.5
Heavy	3-4	>40-51	0.5 to 2.5
Extreme	5-6	>51	>2.5

Adapted from Soucy (2006)

* For operational purposes, radar reflectivity (Z) is expressed in decibels (dBZ)

**Precipitation from stratiform clouds may be significantly less for the same echo intensity

***ARTCC controllers do not use the term "Light" because, currently (2006), their systems do not display light intensities

B

LEGEND...
SHADING--ECHO AREAS
CONTOURS AT INTENSITIES 1-3-5
TOPS 999--BASES 999
PREFIX-A--ACFT RPTD TOP
MVMT--AREAS+LINES--PENNANTS
MVMT--CELLS--ARROWS WITH SPEED
SLD--SOLID AREA OF PRECIPITATION

observations of thunderstorms across the U.S. The low power requirements and compact size of airborne lightning detection equipment has made this tool a useful inflight thunderstorm detection tool for light aircraft. The user must keep in mind that this system does not detect precipitation such as showers and hail.

Rather than sensing thunderstorm activity directly from the aircraft, real-time information from surface weather radars can be relayed to an aircraft for display in the cockpit via communications systems such as Datalink. While such communications systems can help pilots avoid thunderstorms, use them with extreme care because of the degradation of information in data formatting and transfer processes. Rapidly changing conditions are not accurately represented by significantly delayed radar information ("data latency").

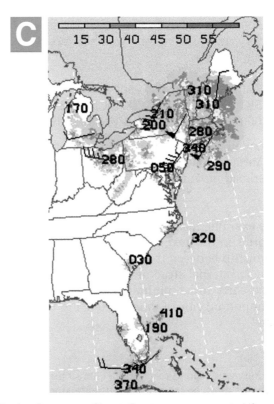

C

Figure 9-7. A. Weather Radar terminology. B. Weather Radar Summary Chart. Contours represent radar echo intensity levels of 1, 3, and 5. Wind barbs indicate directions and speeds of movement of radar echoes; three digit numbers are heights of echo tops in hundreds of feet MSL. C. Similar to B except echo strength is given in terms of color-coded intensity (dBZ) scale at the top of the map. (See AC 00-45 for more examples.)

Section D

THUNDERSTORM STRUCTURES

Based on surface observations, a thunderstorm is defined as a local storm produced by a cumulonimbus cloud, and always accompanied by lightning and thunder. It typically produces strong wind gusts, heavy rain, sometimes hail, and occasionally tornadoes. It is usually of short duration, rarely over two hours for a single storm. On the basis of flight experience, thunderstorms are also characterized by significant turbulence, icing, and wind shear.

Special (SPECI) weather observations are taken to mark the beginning and end of a thunderstorm, and to report significant changes in its intensity. Besides the standard coded information about sky condition, weather, visibility, pressure, temperature, and wind; evidence of the presence of thunderstorms is also found in the remarks section of surface weather reports. An example follows.

> SPECI KCVG 312228Z 28024G36KT 3/4SM
> +TSRA SQ BKN008 OVC020CB 28/23
> A3000 RMK TSB24 TS OVHD MOV E

Decoded Remarks: Thunderstorm began at 24 minutes past the hour. Thunderstorm is overhead moving east.

As we examine the growth and structure of thunderstorms in the next sections, we will stress the relationship between their visible characteristics and their internal structures. In this regard, it is not too early to be reminded of a practical and very important rule of thumb related to thunderstorms:

> If a convective cloud reaches the cumulonimbus stage, it should be considered a thunderstorm, whether or not any other evidence of thunderstorm activity is present.

THUNDERSTORM TYPES

There are two basic thunderstorm types: an ordinary thunderstorm, frequently described as an airmass thunderstorm, and a severe thunderstorm. A severe thunderstorm has a greater intensity than an airmass thunderstorm, as defined by the severity of the weather it produces: wind gusts of 50 knots or more and/or hail three-quarters of an inch or more in diameter and/or strong tornadoes.

The basic component of any thunderstorm is the cell. In the initial stages, this is the updraft region of the growing thunderstorm. Later in the thunderstorm development, it includes the precipitation-induced downdraft. A thunderstorm may exist as a single-cell, multicell, or supercell storm. A single-cell airmass thunderstorm lasts less than one hour. In contrast, a supercell severe thunderstorm may last two hours or longer.

A multicell storm is a compact cluster of thunderstorms. It is usually composed of airmass thunderstorm cells and/or severe thunderstorm cells in different stages of development. These cells interact with each other to cause the duration of the cluster to be much longer than any individual cell.

AIRMASS THUNDERSTORM

The life cycle of a single-cell, airmass thunderstorm is illustrated in figure 9-8. The cycle is divided into three stages: cumulus, mature, and dissipating.

CUMULUS STAGE

When atmospheric moisture and instability are sufficient, the evolution of the airmass thunderstorm begins. In the cumulus stage, an important change occurs in the nature of convection. There is a marked increase in the scale of the circulation. The size of the updraft region becomes larger than the size of any of the individual thermals that are feeding the region. This can often be seen in a field of cumulus clouds in which one particular cloud begins to grow more

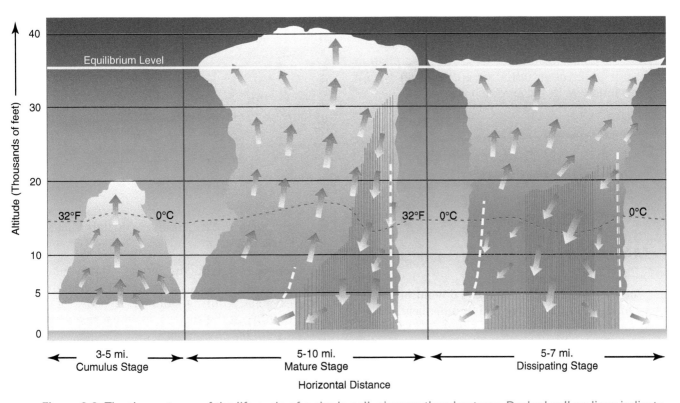

Figure 9-8. The three stages of the life cycle of a single-cell, airmass thunderstorm. Dashed yellow lines indicate boundaries of cool air descending with the rain shaft. Red dashed lines indicate the freezing level.

rapidly than the others. Around the developing cloud, the smaller clouds will frequently dissipate as the air starts sinking in response to the larger scale updraft.

In this first stage of development of the thunderstorm, air initially rises throughout the cloud. Upward growth is much greater in some portions of the cloud than in others, and the cloud grows in an unsteady succession of upward bulges as thermals arrive at the top. These can be seen as turrets on the top of the cloud in figure 9-9.

During the cumulus stage, the convective circulation grows rapidly into a towering cumulus (TCU) cloud which typically grows to 20,000 feet in height and three to five miles in diameter. The cloud reaches the next stage of development in about 15 minutes.

Figure 9-9. Towering cumulus clouds characteristic of the cumulus stage of an airmass thunderstorm.

As the cloud continues to grow, precipitation begins to develop, initiating a downdraft within the cloud late in the cumulus stage.

A continuous updraft is normally associated with the cumulus stage of a thunderstorm.

An indication that downdrafts have developed and that the thunderstorm cell has entered the mature stage is when precipitation begins to fall from the cloud base.

MATURE STAGE

As shown in figure 9-8, the mature stage begins when the precipitation-induced downdraft reaches the ground. Lightning and thunder begin as the thunderstorm cell grows to about 5-10 miles in diameter.

The circulation of the thunderstorm cell is well organized in this stage. The relatively warm updraft and the cool, precipitation-induced downdraft exist side by side. The downdraft reaches its greatest velocity below the cloud base, while the updraft reaches its maximum speed near the equilibrium level in the upper part of the cumulonimbus cloud.

The top of the mature cell often reaches into the lower stratosphere. The cumulonimbus cloud which is characteristic of this stage is easily identified by the appearance of its top. The highest portion of the cloud develops a cirriform appearance because of the very cold temperatures and the strong stability of the stratosphere. Vertical motions are dampened and the cloud spreads out horizontally, finally forming the well-known anvil shape. (Figure 9-10) When the anvil top forms, it points in the direction of the winds at the top of the thunderstorm. This is approximately the direction that the storm is moving.

Although the beginning of the mature stage of the airmass thunderstorm cell is usually indicated by the arrival of precipitation and wind gusts at the ground, there are exceptions. For example, a developing cumulus cloud may produce a shower and the associated downdrafts, but not reach the mature stage. In this case, lightning and thunder do not occur.

Another exception to the model of the mature stage is found in the arid regions of the western U.S., especially during summer. Because of the low humidity at the surface, air must rise a great distance to reach condensation. Thunderstorm bases can be as high as 10,000 feet AGL or more.

In high-based storms, lightning and thunder occur, but the precipitation often evaporates

Thunderstorms reach their greatest intensity during the mature stage.

Figure 9-10. A cumulonimbus cloud indicates that the thunderstorm has reached at least the mature stage.

before reaching the ground. In this case, only a veil of precipitation known as virga is observed immediately below the cloud base. (Figure 9-11) The combination of lightning and gusty winds in the absence of precipitation is often a cause of forest fires. Also, despite the lack of rain, the associated downdraft and gusty winds can still produce flight hazards such as strong downdrafts and turbulence. These and other flight hazards are discussed thoroughly in Part III.

If the precipitation-induced downdraft is exceptionally strong and small, it may be classified as a microburst, producing dangerous wind shear conditions on landing and takeoff. Furthermore, as the rain reaches the ground below the thunderstorm, the cool downdraft spreads out. The edge of the cool air behaves much like a micro-cold front with shifting winds and horizontal gusts moving outward, beyond the edges of the thunderstorm cell. While the outward moving air ultimately cuts off the energy for the single-cell thunderstorm, it will be seen that this so-called

Figure 9-11. Virga indicates precipitation falling from the base of a cumulonimbus cloud, but not reaching the ground. An invisible downdraft will often continue to the ground below the virga.

"gust front" plays a critical role in the development of multicell thunderstorms.

DISSIPATING STAGE

Thirty minutes or so after it begins, the single-cell airmass thunderstorm reaches the dissipating stage. As shown in the right hand panel of figure 9-8, precipitation and downdrafts spread throughout the lower levels of the thunderstorm cell, cutting off the updraft. Since the source of energy for thunderstorm growth is the supply of heat and moisture from the surface layer, the cut-off of the updraft spells the end of the storm. With no source of moisture, the precipitation decreases and the entire thunderstorm cloud takes on a stratiform appearance, gradually dissipating. Because the anvil top is an ice cloud, it often lasts longer than the rest of the cell.

Although the typical lifetime of a single-cell airmass thunderstorm is less than an hour, odds are that you have encountered thunderstorms that have lasted much longer. How can this be? In such cases, the explanation is that you were actually observing a multicell thunderstorm or a supercell thunderstorm, both of which last longer and affect larger areas than an airmass thunderstorm.

Virga

Photo courtesy of Paul Gallaway

In the life cycle of a thunderstorm, the dissipating stage is dominated by downdrafts.

MULTICELL THUNDERSTORM

The life cycle of any one of the cells of a multicell thunderstorm is much like any airmass thunderstorm. However, the life cycle of the multicell cluster is much different. Cell interaction produces more cells, thus sustaining the life of the cluster. (Figure 9-12)

The key to the long life of the multicell is the development of an organized thunderstorm gust front. The gust front is the sharp boundary found on the edge of the pool of cold air that is fed by the downdrafts and spreads out below the thunderstorm. Although most thunderstorms produce gust fronts to some degree, gust fronts are better organized with multicells because they develop in an environment where there is a significant wind increase with height. This wind structure allows the greater momentum of high-level winds

to be transferred downward in the downdrafts of the thunderstorm, influencing the movements of both the thunderstorm and the gust front.

The main updraft for the multicell is located just above the gust front at low levels, slanting upward into the mature cell. The warm updraft enters the multicell from the direction in which the storm is moving. A shelf cloud often indicates the rising air over the gust front. New cumulus cells also develop ahead of the mature cell as the gust front lifts unstable air. At the same time, the gust front is maintained by a supply of cool air from the precipitation-induced downdrafts of the mature and dissipating cells. This process of cell regeneration explains why the multicell thunderstorm influences a larger area and lasts longer than a single-cell thunderstorm.

A rough estimate of the movement of a thunderstorm cell is given by the speed and direction of the 10,000-foot (700 mb) wind.

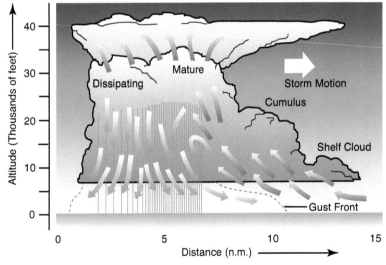

Figure 9-12. Multicell thunderstorm with cells in various stages of development. Small arrows indicate airflow. The vertical lines on the left indicate precipitation. The boundaries of the cool, downdraft air are shown by dotted lines below the thunderstorm base. Note: the right hand boundary is the gust front.

The strongest part of the gust front usually moves several miles ahead of the thunderstorm; that is, in the direction the cells are moving. When a gust front passes, it is much like a mesoscale cold front. There is a wind shift, the winds are strong and gusty, the pressure increases, and the temperature decreases. The gust front is also a region of turbulence and wind shear. More details about these and other flight hazards are given in Part III.

An outflow boundary is the remnant of a gust front that continues to exist long after the thunderstorms that created it have dissipated. On some occasions, outflow boundaries generated by thunderstorms late in the day have been observed to continue moving throughout the night, often covering well over one hundred miles. New convection may develop along an outflow boundary as it moves into unstable areas or intersects fronts or other outflow boundaries.

Multicell storms vary widely in intensity. They can produce severe convective weather, especially when organized into larger mesoscale convective systems. (Section E).

SUPERCELL THUNDERSTORM

While airmass thunderstorms occasionally produce severe weather, the supercell thunderstorm almost always produces one or more of the extremes of convective weather: very strong horizontal wind gusts and/or large hail and/or strong tornadoes. This difference in severity is due primarily to differences in thunderstorm structure.

The supercell storm can occur almost anywhere in middle latitudes, but the favored area is in the southern Great Plains of the U.S. in spring. This is because the supercell requires extreme instability and a special combination of boundary layer and upper level wind conditions that are most frequently found over Texas, Oklahoma, and Kansas at that time of year. These conditions cause the internal structure of a supercell thunderstorm to be more complicated than an airmass thunderstorm. Specifically, the supercell forms in an environment that tilts and twists the thunderstorm updraft. In order to illustrate the details of this airflow, it is necessary to use a three-dimensional, perspective model of the severe thunderstorm. (Figure 9-13)

The updraft enters the storm with low-level flow from the southeast. The air rises in a strong, steady updraft that slants upward toward the back of the thunderstorm, in this case, toward the northwest. Overshooting tops indicated by bulges on the top of the anvil show the location of the updraft. Under the influence of the strong westerly winds at upper levels, the former updraft, now mainly horizontal, twists toward the east where it exits the thunderstorm through the anvil.

A major precipitation-induced downdraft occurs north of the main updraft where the rain shaft can be seen in figure 9-13. Another downdraft (not visible in the figure) also spreads around to the west of the updraft as the supercell develops.

The gust fronts caused by these two downdrafts are indicated by a dashed line at the surface. The "flanking line," which parallels the gust front to the southwest of the updraft, is composed of growing cumulus towers.

There are two important differences between the structures of the single-cell airmass thunderstorm and the severe supercell thunderstorm. First, the supercell is much larger and, second, its updraft and precipitation-induced downdrafts remain separated. The change of the environmental wind direction from surface south-easterlies to upper westerlies is the key to this structure. In a severe thunderstorm, the downdraft occurs in a location where it does not interfere with the updraft as happens in the weaker airmass thunderstorm. This structure allows the supercell to develop a large, strong, steady updraft that lasts much longer than in an airmass thunderstorm. The longer lifetime also explains why some older aviation weather manuals refer to a severe thunderstorm as a "steady-state" thunderstorm.

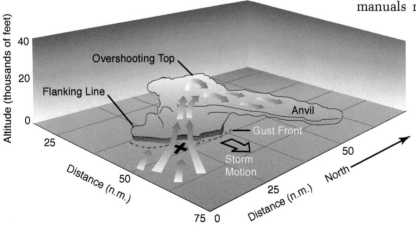

Figure 9-13. Perspective diagram of a supercell thunderstorm. For clarity, only the updraft is shown. The direction of movement of the supercell is toward the east in this example.

The horizontal separation of vertical drafts in a supercell can be better appreciated when observing the storm from the ground. Consider an observer looking at a supercell from the southeast (point X in figure 9-13). The view reveals the cloud features shown in figure 9-14. In addition to the anvil, the main storm tower, and the flanking line are also seen.

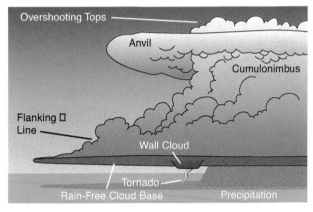

Figure 9-14. This is the ground view of the supercell thunderstorm at point "x" in figure 9-13.

In figure 9-14, the main downdraft location is indicated by the precipitation below the cloud base on the right side of the diagram. To the left of the downdraft is found the rain-free cloud base, and farther to the left, the flanking line. Precipitation may also occur on the far side of the storm (beyond the rain-free cloud base) but that feature is not shown here for clarity.

The rain-free cloud base in the middle of figure 9-14 is very close to the main updraft that slants upward and to the right. The top of the updraft is indicated by the overshooting tops above the anvil. A portion of the rain-free cloud base may appear lower in what is called a wall cloud. Significant rotation of that cloud is often observed. In fact, the wall cloud is the region where the strongest tornadoes descend from the severe thunderstorm. The bulges that appear under the anvil are known as mammatus.

Supercells may occur in isolation or in mesoscale convective systems with multicell airmass thunderstorms and other supercells. These large lines and clusters of thunderstorms are discussed in Section E of this chapter.

TORNADOES

A tornado is a violently rotating column of air which is found below cumulonimbus clouds. A tornado that does not reach the surface is called a funnel cloud. Tornadoes vary widely in intensity with the strongest most damaging tornadoes usually associated with severe thunderstorms. Most tornado diameters range from 300 feet to 2,000 feet, although extremes of one mile have been reported. Because of the macroscale weather conditions under which tornadoes develop in the U.S., they commonly move from southwest to northeast at a typical speed of 30 knots. Tornado lifetimes average only a few minutes, but unusual cases of over three hours have been documented. (Figure 9-15)

The strongest tornadoes are most often associated with severe thunderstorms. As described in the previous section, the supercell has an internal circulation that promotes the rotation favorable for tornado formation. The rotation first becomes visible in the vicinity of the wall cloud.

Much of the damage associated with a tornado is caused by the presence of one or more suction vortices. These are relatively small, intense whirls that rotate within the larger funnel of the tornado.

The Enhanced Fujita (EF) scale is the standard tornado intensity scale. It's a set of wind estimates (not measurements) based on the systematic examination of tornado damage. Wind speeds are stated in terms of three-second gust estimates

Figure 9-15. Tornado below a wall cloud at the base of a severe thunderstorm. (NOAA)

Figure 9-16. The Enhanced Fujita (EF) scale of tornado intensity.

EF Number	3-Second Gust		Expected Damage
	MPH	Knots	
0	65-85	57-74	Light: tree branches broken, sign boards damaged
1	86-110	75-96	Moderate: trees snapped, windows broken
2	111-135	97-117	Considerable: large trees uprooted, weak structures destroyed
3	136-165	118-143	Severe: trees leveled, cars overturned, walls removed from buildings
4	166-200	144-174	Devastating: frame houses destroyed
5	over 200	over 174	Incredible: structures the size of autos moved over 300 feet, steel-reinforced structures highly damaged

at the point of damage as opposed to standard one-minute wind measurements with anemometers located in exposed areas. High EF numbers are associated with severe thunderstorms. Weaker tornadoes may occur with non-severe thunderstorms. (Figure 9-16)

A tornado that occurs over water is called a waterspout. "Fair weather waterspouts" are common near the Florida Keys between March and October. These vortices form over warm water near developing cumulus clouds. In general, fair weather waterspouts are weaker than tornadoes, short-lived, and slow moving.

Near gust fronts and the edges of downbursts, tornado-like vortices known as gustnadoes sometimes occur. These phenomena are similar to intense dust devils caused by the strong horizontal wind shear and strong updrafts.

A cold air funnel is a weak vortex that occasionally develops after a cold front passage in association with rain shower and/or thunderstorm activity. These are not conditions associated with severe convective weather. Cold air funnels rarely reach the ground and are more frequent in the spring and fall.

HAIL

The water droplets observed in rain showers from convective clouds are notable by their sizes; that is, they are much bigger than the droplets that fall as rain from nimbostratus clouds. One of the main reasons for the large droplet size is the very strong upward motions in cumulus and cumulonimbus clouds. With strong updrafts, small water and ice

particles have a longer time to grow in a favorable cloud environment before they fall out as precipitation. Another product of strong upward motions is hail, which was first described as a precipitation form in Chapter 6.

> **Hail is most likely to be associated with cumulonimbus clouds.**

Large hail with diameters greater than three-quarters of an inch creates dangers to life and property on the ground as well as in the air. An understanding of hail formation is useful in anticipating and avoiding its hazardous effects.

When ice particles grow to precipitation sizes through the ice crystal process, we expect to see the largest snow or rain particles limited to sizes less than .2 inches in diameter (5mm). However, this is not always the case in a thunderstorm, which produces many large supercooled water droplets. From Chapter 6, we know that as snow collides with water droplets, the droplets freeze in the process known as accretion. In a thunderstorm, accretion may produce a larger particle that becomes the nucleus of a hailstone. If the updrafts in the thunderstorm are strong enough to keep the particle suspended in the cloud, it can continue to grow to significant sizes. In a thunderstorm with a tilted updraft, hail may be thrown out of the storm near the top, only to fall back into the updraft. If the updraft is strong enough, the hailstones are again carried up through the thunderstorm, growing still larger until they are so heavy that they finally fall to the ground. (Figure 9-17)

Figure 9-17 illustrates why hail has been observed at all levels throughout thunderstorms (up to about 45,000 feet AGL) as well as in clear air outside the clouds. These trajectories also explain why hailstones often have layers of alternating clear and opaque ice. The layered structure reflects variations in temperatures and in the amount of supercooled water in the droplets encountered by the hailstone along its path through the thunderstorm.

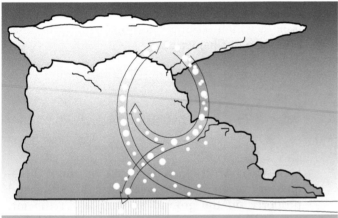

Figure 9-17. One way hail can grow to large sizes is by being re-circulated through the storm.

LIGHTNING

Lightning is the visible electric discharge produced by a thunderstorm. It occurs in several forms, including in-cloud, cloud-to-cloud, cloud-to-ground, and occasionally, between the cloud and clear air. There are also several less technical descriptions. For example, a branched lightning stroke is called "forked lightning." Lightning that occurs within a cloud and illuminates it diffusely, is described as "sheet lightning." Diffuse lightning that is observed in the distance, when no thunder is heard, may be called "heat lightning."

Whatever the form of lightning, all lightning discharges involve voltage differences of a few hundred thousand volts per foot (~1,000,000 volts per

Lightning is always present in (and near) a thunderstorm and occasionally occurs in the vicinity of volcanic plumes.

meter). Air along the discharge channel is heated to more than 50,000°F causing the rapid expansion of air and the production of a shock wave that moves away from its source, finally reaching your ear as thunder. Since the flash of lightning travels at the speed of light (186,000 miles per second) and the shock wave travels with the speed of sound (about 1,100 feet per second), the difference of the arrival times of these two thunderstorm indicators becomes greater the farther you are from the thunderstorm.

As with any electrical discharge, lightning requires a charge separation. One way this can come about is for large and small particles (water droplets, ice crystals, hail) to develop

The approximate distance (in feet) from your location to a thunderstorm is determined by counting the seconds between the lightning flash and the thunderclap and multiplying that number by 1,100. A five second lag between the lightning flash and thunderclap indicates the thunderstorm is about 5,500 feet or a little over one mile away.

opposite charges and then become separated by gravity or by convection. There are a number of ways by which charging can be accomplished before the charged particles are separated, although it is not clear which are the most important processes. For example, particles can become charged through collision, through a transfer of ions when a warm hailstone comes in contact with cold ice crystals, and a variety of other ways including freezing and splintering. In any event, the heavier, negatively charged particles end up in the lower part of the cloud with lighter, positively charged particles at the top. The negative charge distribution near the cloud base also induces a positive charge on the ground. (Figure 9-18)

Relatively high points on the earth's surface, such as mountain tops, tall buildings, treetops, antennas, and steeples are particularly vulnerable to lightning strikes because the lightning discharge favors the path of least resistance to the earth's surface. The closer the positively charged object is to the cloud, the more vulnerable it is to lightning strikes. In areas where there is a high frequency of thunderstorms, many buildings have lightning rods to carry the discharge harmlessly into the ground.

A typical thunderstorm produces three or four lightning flashes per minute. Only 10-25 percent of all lightning strokes are cloud-to-ground. Inflight lightning strikes are a definite flight hazard. Additional Details are given in Part III, chapter 15.

Figure 9-18. Charge separation in a convective cloud causes a region of positive charge at the top of the cloud and negative charge in the lower half. The photo inset shows the visible lightning discharge or return stroke. (National Oceanic and Atmospheric Administration)

When charge differences become large enough within the cloud, or between the cloud and its environment, lightning occurs. The lightning stroke is actually a series of events which begins with a nearly invisible stepped leader that carries electrons from the base of the cloud to the ground, creating an ionized channel for the subsequent discharge. Close to the earth, the stepped leader is met by an upward-moving positive charge. A bright return stroke occurs, marking the route of the positive charge along the original path of the stepped leader, back up into the cloud. The initial discharge is often followed by several so-called dart leaders and more return strokes. These individual events are so fast that the eye cannot resolve them.

Besides lightning, there exist other thunderstorm electrical phenomena that are rarely seen from the earth's surface but have often been observed at night by airline pilots. These include dim "red sprites" and faint "blue jets" that can extend 300,000 feet above the tops of active thunderstorms.

The more frequent the lightning, the stronger the thunderstorm.

In METAR reports from AUTO stations, thunderstorms are not necessarily reported. "TSNO" (no thunderstorm information available) indicates this situation. AUTO METAR stations with access to the National Lightning Detection Network report "TS" when a lightning strike is detected within 5 n.m.; "VCTS," within 5-10 n.m., and "LTG DSNT" (with the direction to the strike) for greater distances.

Section E

THUNDERSTORM ENVIRONMENT

Given the previous information about thunderstorm development and types, it is still difficult, if not impossible, to predict precisely where and when an individual thunderstorm of any type will develop. The size and lifetime of an individual thunderstorm are too small to predict its behavior until it is actually present. However, up to a day or so before thunderstorms occur, we can identify the larger areas where the thunderstorm activity will take place. The occurrence, type, and intensity of thunderstorms are determined by identifiable and more predictable larger scale weather systems with much longer lifetimes. In this section, we consider those large-scale environments to answer the questions, where, when, and why are thunderstorms likely to occur?

REQUIREMENTS FOR DEVELOPMENT

Two basic requirements must be met for the formation of thunderstorms: the air must have large instability and there must be a source of initial lift. The strongest thunderstorms develop with an unstable moist surface layer that is capped by a dry layer aloft. When the surface layer is lifted a sufficient distance, strong convection occurs. Initial lift is the minimum amount of vertical displacement necessary to release the instability.

The conditions necessary for the formation of cumulonimbus clouds are moist, unstable air and a lifting action.

Macroscale and mesoscale circulations in which thunderstorms are embedded provide instability by bringing in warm, moist air at low levels. Instability can also be caused or enhanced by bringing in colder air aloft. Initial lift can be provided by surface heating, orography, fronts, low-level convergence, and upper-level divergence. It follows that thunderstorms are favored in geographical areas that are close to moisture sources and sources of lift. Severe thunderstorms have stricter requirements that include not only great instability, but also a unique wind shear that provides the thunderstorm with the tilt and rotation needed to produce supercells.

Whether they contribute to airmass or severe thunderstorms, these influences organize thunderstorms into distinctive patterns. If you understand the relationships between thunderstorm occurrence, larger scale circulations, and geography, then you should be able to understand and anticipate thunderstorm development. In the next few paragraphs, we examine some of the more common of these relationships. A useful starting point is thunderstorm climatology.

CLIMATOLOGY

Figure 9-19 shows the worldwide pattern of the average annual number of thunderstorm days. Thunderstorms are most frequent over surfaces where there is a good supply of heat, moisture, and convergence of surface winds. These conditions are generally met in the ITCZ, and summer monsoon circulations, such as in Central Africa, South America, Central America, and Southeast Asia. Conversely, low frequencies of thunderstorms are found where at least one of those conditions is not met; that is, moisture is absent, surfaces are cool, and/or divergence of surface winds exists. Examples are the Sahara, and Middle East, and the Polar Regions.

Both mountains and coastlines play important roles in thunderstorm activity. A good example is the North American Continent. Notice in figure 9-19 that a region of relatively high thunderstorm activity stretches from Florida through Western Canada. The thunderstorm activity over Florida and the southeast reflects a maritime tropical environment enhanced by the frequent convergence of sea breezes along the coast. Potentially unstable air flowing onto the continent from the Gulf of Mexico is largely confined east of the Rocky Mountains.

There is a seasonal variation in thunderstorm activity that is not apparent from figure 9-19. However, the main variations can be easily deduced from your study of larger scale circulations in Chapters 7 and 8. Because of the decrease in solar heating, cold airmasses spread to lower latitudes and the monsoon circulations reverse (wet to dry) in the winter. The impact is dramatic: in Northern Hemisphere winter there are few thunderstorms north of 10° N, except along the U.S. coast of the Gulf of Mexico and in the Mediterranean.

Figure 9-19 also does not differentiate thunderstorm types. Although the highest frequency of thunderstorms in the U.S. occurs in Florida in summer, severe thunderstorms develop more often in the springtime in the area between the Rocky Mountains and the Mississippi River. Within that area, the states of Texas, Oklahoma, and Kansas are particularly susceptible to severe thunderstorms. This is due to their proximity to the very warm, moist air from the Gulf of Mexico and the tendency for extratropical cyclones (a source of initial lift and divergence aloft) to develop just to the northwest of that region in the spring.

Another useful consideration when describing "typical" thunderstorm activity, is time of occurrence. Thunderstorm activity reaches its peak in the afternoon in many areas because of the influence of solar heating and afternoon convergence such as sea breezes. However, this is not always

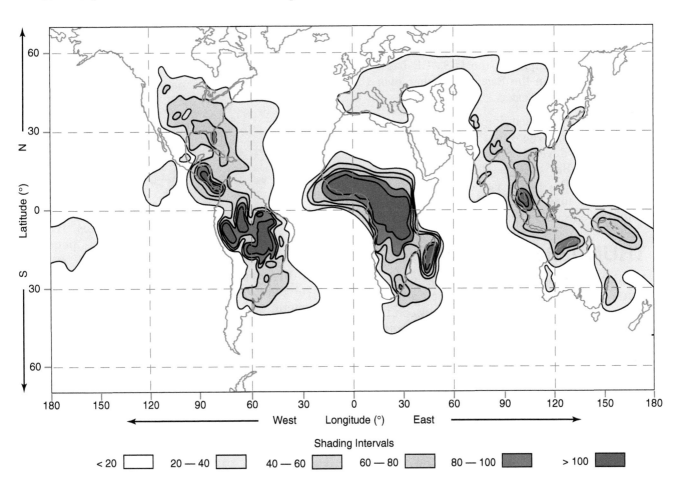

Figure 9-19. Average annual number of thunderstorm days.

the case. Off-shore convergence in land breezes may lead to nighttime thunderstorm occurrences (for example, along the U.S. Gulf Coast in summer). The Great Plains region of the U.S. has a nighttime maximum in thunderstorm activity during the summer. This condition is caused, in part, by strong, low-level southerly winds that frequently develop in a narrow band from south Texas into Oklahoma during nighttime hours. This low-level "jet" carries unstable air northward from the Gulf of Mexico. Finally, when thunderstorms are produced in connection with fronts and extratropical cyclones, they may occur any time of day or night.

Other seasonal climatological features of thunderstorms that are important to aviators are that CB tops tend to be lower in winter than in summer, and lower at high latitudes than at low latitudes. Also, cumulonimbus cloud bases are significantly lower in moist environments as compared to dry regions. For example, in the U.S., CB bases are typically lower in the East and higher over the mountains of the West.

Thunderstorm climatology provides a useful "first guess" of where and when thunderstorms are likely to develop, given the right macroscale conditions. But caution should be used in its application. Day-to-day variations from the average picture may be large. In the next few paragraphs, we examine some of these variations.

THUNDERSTORM LINES

Multicell thunderstorms often form along lines much longer than the diameter of any single storm. The processes by which wind conditions along lines can produce upward motions (initial lift) were introduced in Chapter 5. They include frontal lifting, surface convergence, and divergence aloft. Such lines may contain airmass and/or severe thunderstorms.

The most severe weather conditions, such as destructive winds, heavy hail, and tornadoes are generally associated with squall lines.

MACROSCALE FRONTS

A cold front is often the location of a line of abrupt lifting because it is fast moving and has a relatively steep slope. If the potential instability is sufficient, a line of frontal thunderstorms will be present. Thunderstorm production along fronts is particularly efficient when colder air aloft is advected over the area. (Figure 9-20)

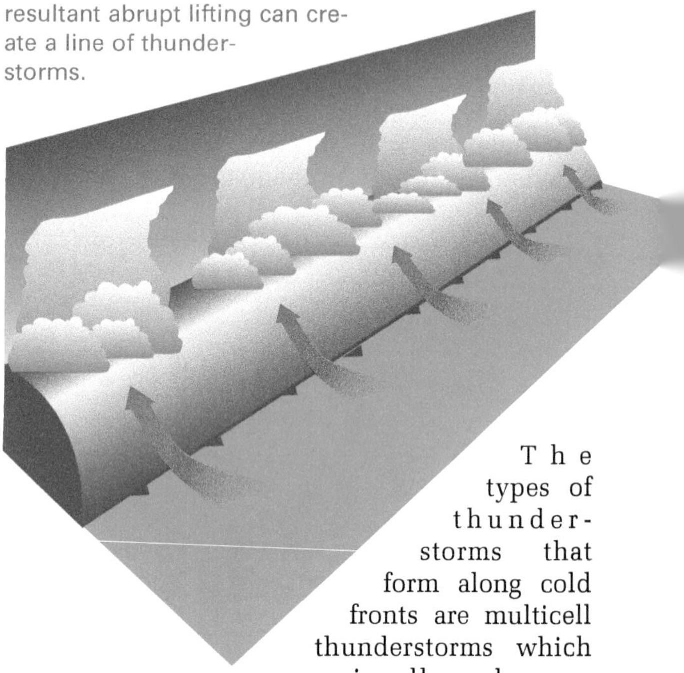

Figure 9-20. Fast moving cold front and resultant abrupt lifting can create a line of thunderstorms.

The types of thunderstorms that form along cold fronts are multicell thunderstorms which occasionally become severe, and severe supercell thunderstorms. The radar echo intensity level gives indications of thunderstorm type and strength.

Not all cold fronts produce thunderstorm activity. For example, some cold fronts may be dry (cloudless), while others will produce mainly nimbostratus with steady rain, or showers without thunderstorms. Because of these differences,

Embedded thunderstorms are thunderstorms that are obscured by massive cloud layers and cannot be seen.

it is important to examine other information than the surface weather analysis chart to determine if thunderstorms are associated with a front. Weather radar data, satellite imagery, and surface weather data provide many useful clues as to thunderstorm presence.

Thunderstorms may be aligned along warm fronts when unstable air overruns the wedge of retreating cold air at lower levels. Over land, this occurs more frequently in the warmer months of the year. It is a particularly troublesome situation, because the thunderstorms are often embedded in stratiform clouds and cannot be seen from the ground or from the air, unless you are above the cloud deck. This problem is also likely in occlusions.

MESOSCALE THUNDERSTORM LINES

A squall line, or instability line, is a broken or continuous line of thunderstorms not necessarily associated with a front. It ranges from about one hundred to several hundred miles in length. Depending on the degree of instability and the wind variation through the troposphere, thunderstorms along squall lines may be ordinary multicell, supercell, or a mixture.

A squall line frequently develops along or just ahead of a cold front in the warm sector of a cyclone. Once multicell thunderstorms form, their ability to regenerate new cells helps to maintain the line. A squall line generally moves across the warm sector in the direction of the winds at 500 mb. When a squall line approaches and passes a particular location, the effect is similar to an idealized cold front. Examples of the appearance of a squall line on a surface analysis chart, a radar summary chart, and a view from space are given in figure 9-21.

There are several other mesoscale phenomena that are known to contribute to the formation of thunderstorms along narrow bands. For example, in Chapter 10, you will see the lifting that is generated by a sea breeze front. If potentially unstable air is present, thunderstorms form in a line along

Squall lines are not necessarily associated with fronts and may contain either, or both, airmass and severe thunderstorms.

Squall lines most often develop ahead of a cold front.

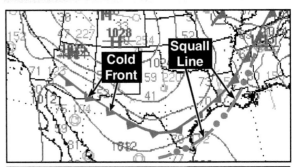

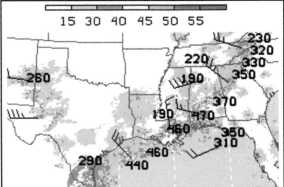

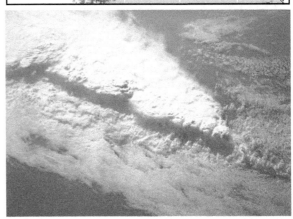

Figure 9-21. Three different examples of a squall line. Top: Section of surface analysis chart. Middle: Radar summary chart showing alignment of echoes along a squall line. Bottom: Photograph of a squall line from space. (Photo courtesy of Lunar and Planetary Institute, NASA Photograph)

that boundary. Similarly, outflow boundaries from thunderstorms produce favorable conditions for the formation of thunderstorm lines when those boundaries move into unstable regions.

In west Texas during late spring and early summer, there often exists a north-south boundary between moist tropical air flowing northward from the Gulf of Mexico and dry air over the higher terrain to the west. The moisture boundary is called a dry line. Weather radars in this area often show a long, narrow, clear-air echo known as a "fine line." This is where the moisture content of the air changes rapidly from one side of the dry line to the other. Dry lines are often the initial location of eastward moving squall lines.

When orographic lifting of potentially unstable air occurs, often with the added help of surface heating, thunderstorms will be aligned along mountain ranges. In some cases, these lines will remain stationary as thunderstorm cells keep forming in the same location. This condition can lead to local flooding. In other situations, the thunderstorm lines will move away from the mountains under the influence of winds aloft.

In all cases of thunderstorms along lines, thunderstorm development is enhanced when there is an upper-level disturbance in the area. Divergence near jet stream level and cold air aloft contribute to instability.

THUNDERSTORM CLUSTERS

Under certain circumstances, thunderstorms in middle latitudes develop into large clusters that are more circular or elliptical than linear. These include both macroscale and mesoscale clusters made up of multicell airmass and/or severe thunderstorms.

MACROSCALE CLUSTERS

There are many macroscale upper air circulations that can cause thunderstorm outbreaks over areas of thousands of square miles. A few of the more common patterns are described here.

As we saw in the previous chapter, when an upper air disturbance (short wave trough) influences a

surface front, an extratropical cyclone frequently develops with a surface low pressure region and warm and cold fronts. Thunderstorms are then distributed along the fronts or squall lines that develop as described earlier in this chapter.

Large areas of thunderstorms not clearly associated with fronts sometimes develop when an upper level disturbance moves over an unstable area. As viewed from a meteorological satellite, the associated thunderstorm cluster often appears as a comma-shaped cloud mass below and slightly ahead of a trough or low aloft. This pattern happens more often over oceans because of the availability of large amounts of moisture. (Figure 9-22)

Cumulus and
Cumulonimbus
Clouds

130   120

Figure 9-22. Comma-shaped region of convective activity below and slightly ahead of an upper-level short wave trough.

Other macroscale regions of thunderstorms observed to develop without any obvious frontal structure include those associated with old occluded cyclones, cold lows aloft, and tropical cyclones. For example, a macroscale low aloft will bring widespread thunderstorms to the southwestern U.S. during the warmer months. Also, the same region is subjected to extensive thunderstorm activity whenever a dissipating tropical cyclone moves across the area from the west coast of Mexico.

MESOSCALE CONVECTIVE COMPLEXES

Mesoscale convective complexes are nearly circular clusters of thunderstorms that develop primarily between the Rockies and the Appalachians during the warmer part of the year. Heavy rains and severe weather are not unusual. The complexes, as viewed by satellite, are typically a few hundred miles in diameter.

Mesoscale convective complexes typically form in late afternoon as a result of the interactions and merging of smaller groups of thunderstorms. They generally move eastward, reaching their maximum development about midnight, weakening in the early morning hours. An example of a mesoscale convective complex is shown in the satellite image of figure 9-23.

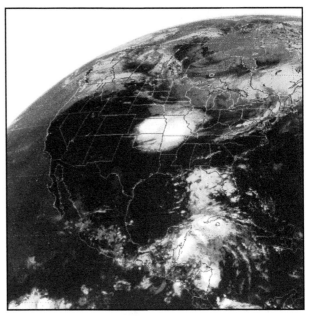

Figure 9-23. A large mesoscale convective complex covers Missouri and portions of Kansas, Oklahoma, and Arkansas. The area of major activity appears larger than it actually is due to the blow off of cirrus anvils from the thunderstorms.

SUMMARY

The thunderstorm, by itself, is a distinct mesoscale atmospheric circulation that begins as cloudless convection in the boundary layer and develops through a great depth of the atmosphere in a very short period of time. Thunderstorms have a range of structures. Some of these support the generation of new thunderstorms as well as the development of very intense and long-lived severe thunderstorms. It has become clear that in order to really understand thunderstorms, it is necessary to know about a variety of smaller and larger scale circulations that influence thunderstorm development and behavior. These include extratropical cyclones, fronts, squall lines, and individual thermals, as well as downdrafts, gust fronts, tornadoes, and suction vortices. Considering that thousands of thunderstorms occur over the earth's surface every day, and that a single thunderstorm may produce lightning, very heavy rain showers, hail, strong winds, low visibilities, wind shear, turbulence, and icing, it is not surprising that thunderstorms have a substantial impact on aircraft operations. You will examine the details of associated flight hazards beginning with Chapter 11 in Part III.

KEY TERMS

Airborne Weather Radar
Airmass Thunderstorm
Attenuation
Cloudy Convection
Cold Air Funnel
Convective Condensation Level
Cumulus Stage
Dart Leaders
Datalink
Dissipating Stage
Doppler Radar
Dry Convection
Dry Line
Dust Devil
Echo Intensity Level
Equilibrium Level
Funnel Cloud
Gust Front
Gustnadoes
Hail
Initial Lift
Lightning
Lightning Detection Equipment
Mammatus
Mature Stage
Mesoscale Convective Complex

Mesoscale Convective System
Multicell
Outflow Boundary
Precipitation-Induced Downdraft
Precipitation Rate
Radar
Radar Echo
Radar Summary Chart
Radar Target
Reflectivity (dBZ)
Return Stroke
Severe Thunderstorm
Shelf Cloud
Single Cell
Squall Line
Stepped Leader
Suction Vortex
Supercell
Thermals
Thunderstorm
Tornado
Towering Cumulus (TCU)
Virga
Vortex Ring
Wall Cloud
Waterspout
Weather Radar
WSR-88D (NEXRAD)

REVIEW QUESTIONS

1. Intense thermal activity over land is most common at what time of day?

2. What initiates downdrafts within growing cumulus clouds?

3. Your airborne radar may not "see" storm cells beyond an intense cell directly ahead of your aircraft because of _____.

4. An airmass thunderstorm cell lasts how long?

5. Why do multicell airmass thunderstorms last longer than single-cell airmass thunderstorms?

6. (True, False) Some Thunderstorms do not have lightning.

7. Define a severe thunderstorm.

8. Decode the following weather reports.

METAR KIAH 102353Z 34009KT 6SM –TSRA BR FEW019 BKN026CB OVC033 20/19 A3003 RMK A02 TSB35RAB27 SLP169 OCNL LTGIC NW-N TS NW-N MOV NE =

METAR KIAH 110022Z 33006KT 1 1/2SM +TSRA BR SCT023CB BKN033 OVC060 20/18 A3004 RMK A02 OCNL LTGIC N TS N MOV N =

DISCOVERY QUESTIONS

9. As you complete the preflight inspection of your aircraft, you notice lightning and rain south of the airport. You can't really see any movement of the storm. The airport winds are from the south. The airport is isolated and uncontrolled. You have no radar or other supplementary meteorological information. Discuss your options.

10. Convection also occurs at high levels producing altocumulus and cirrocumulus clouds. Surface heating obviously doesn't play a role. What is the source of the instability?

11. On a particular summer day, you notice that thermals are exceptionally strong. Fair weather cumulus clouds form, but there are no thunderstorms. Why?

12. Occasionally, aircraft will experience strong turbulence in a part of a convective cloud that does not show up on the radar. Give some reasonable explanations.

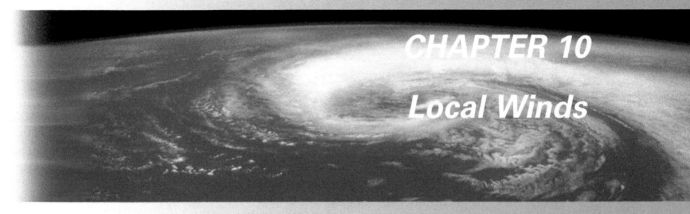

CHAPTER 10
Local Winds

Introduction

Local winds refer to a variety of mesoscale circulations other than thunderstorms. These circulations fall into two broad categories. Thermally driven local winds are caused by local differences in radiational heating or cooling. They are most noticeable when large-scale wind systems are weak or absent. Mountain lee waves and warm downslope winds are produced when strong winds interact with the local terrain. They are most noticeable when strong, large-scale wind systems are present. The phenomena discussed under these categories all have the potential to produce important flight hazards. It is imperative for you to know what their causes and characteristics are, and how to identify them and avoid their worst consequences. When you complete this chapter, you will have gained this knowledge and, additionally, you will have condensed it into some useful conceptual models of land, sea, mountain, and valley breezes; mountain lee waves; and downslope winds.

Section A

THERMALLY DRIVEN LOCAL WINDS

Thermally driven local winds include sea and land breezes, mountain and valley breezes, and slope circulations. Because they depend on radiational heating and cooling, these winds commonly develop in middle latitudes in the warmer part of the year. They may also develop in lower latitudes during any season as long as there are no effects of larger-scale circulations, such as extratropical or tropical cyclones. The dependence of thermally driven local winds on radiational heating and cooling causes directions and intensities of the circulations to be linked closely to the time of day.

SEA BREEZE

In Chapter 4, the concept of thermal circulation was introduced to help you understand how horizontal temperature gradients cause pressure gradients, which in turn, cause the wind to blow. The sea breeze was used as a brief example. To review, daytime heating along coastlines brings land areas to higher temperatures than nearby water surfaces. The temperature difference causes a redistribution of atmospheric mass and the pressure over the land falls, establishing a horizontal pressure gradient. Often, this pressure difference is so small that you can't observe it in the isobar patterns on a surface analysis chart. However, it is large enough to cause cool air to begin moving across the coastline toward land in late morning. This is the sea breeze.

In the sea breeze, and other circulations of this scale and smaller, Coriolis force is usually much less important than the horizontal pressure gradient force and frictional forces. Therefore, the wind tends to blow directly from high to low pressure.

The sea breeze continues to intensify throughout the day, reaching typical speeds of 10 to 20 knots in middle or late afternoon and decreasing thereafter. A well-developed sea breeze is usually 1,500 to 3,000 feet deep and capped by a weaker, deeper, and oppositely directed return flow aloft. The combined sea breeze and return flow are called the sea breeze circulation. (Figure 10-1)

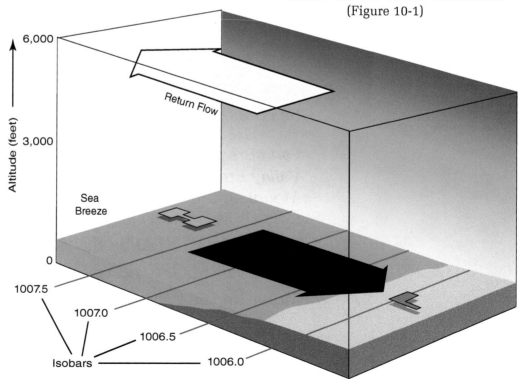

Figure 10-1. Sea Breeze Circulation. During the daytime, a low-level sea breeze flows from sea to land in response to a pressure gradient caused by the heating of the land. The sea level pressure pattern is shown by isobars labeled in millibars. Aloft, the pressure gradient is reversed and a return flow is directed from land to sea.

The sea breeze circulation is sometimes made visible by large differences in visibility at various altitudes. For example, over some urbanized coastlines, clear marine air moves inland at low levels with the sea breeze, while the return flow aloft is made visible by the offshore movement of polluted urban air.

SEA BREEZE FRONT

The boundary between the cool, inflowing marine air and the warmer air over land is often narrow and well defined. This feature is known as the sea breeze front. The frontal location may be identifiable by differences in visibilities between the moist and dry airmasses, or a broken line of cumulus clouds along the front. In locations where there is large conditional instability, the sea breeze front is marked by a line of thunderstorms. (Figure 10-2)

The sea breeze front moves inland more slowly than the winds behind it. Frontal speeds vary over a wide range (2 to 15 knots) depending on macroscale wind conditions and terrain. In some areas, the inland movement of the front is limited to a few miles by coastal mountains. In contrast, over regions with broad coastal plains, the front can move inland a hundred miles or more during the course of the day.

Certain coastline shapes and a favorable distribution of coastal mountains and hills promote the convergence of sea breezes. For example, sea breezes often converge from both sides of the Florida peninsula, producing lines of thunderstorms. Near coastal hills or mountains, gaps in the terrain allow the sea breeze front to move farther inland in those areas. Also, isolated hills may split the sea breeze into two parts which then move around the barrier and converge inland. (Figure 10-3)

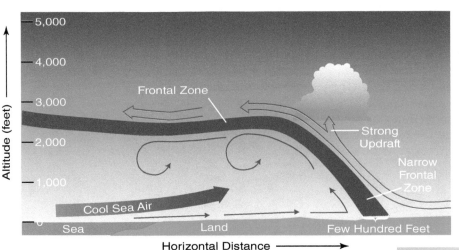

Figure 10-2. Cross section through a sea breeze front. The sea breeze is blowing from left to right. The front will be marked by a line of clouds only when adequate moisture is present.

Thermally driven local winds blow from cold to warm.

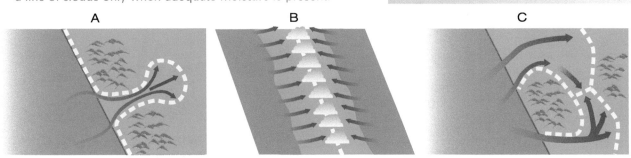

Figure 10-3. Examples of effects of topography on the sea breeze. The yellow dashed lines represent the sea breeze front. In diagram A, the sea breeze penetrates farther inland through a gap in the terrain. In diagram B, sea breezes from opposite sides of a peninsula converge. In diagram C, the sea breeze spreads around hills on a coastal plain and converges in a valley on the opposite side.

LAND BREEZE

A few hours after sunset, the land surface near a coastline has cooled much more rapidly than the nearby water surface. When the land becomes colder than the ocean, the pressure gradient across the coast reverses, so that the lower pressure is offshore. The low-level flow which begins to move from land to sea under the influence of this pressure difference is called the land breeze. The land breeze circulation is also made up of a ground level breeze and an opposite return flow aloft, the reverse of the sea breeze circulation. (Figure 10-4)

The land breeze continues to strengthen throughout the night, reaching its greatest intensity about sunrise. Because of the strong stability typical of nighttime conditions over land, the depth of the land breeze circulation is considerably less than that of the sea breeze. It normally reaches only a few hundred feet above the surface. The land breeze is weaker than the sea breeze with typical maximum speeds of about five knots. Some exceptions may occur when cold air moves down the slope of a mountain range located along the coastline. Details of such drainage winds are given in a later section.

Because a land breeze front occurs over water, it is not as well documented as the sea breeze front. However, in many coastal areas, a related convergence line is found offshore at night. The distance of the land breeze front from the coast varies widely between locations, from less than 5 nautical miles to over 100 nautical miles. The actual distance depends on the strength of the land breeze. In some cases, the offshore convergence zone is identified by a line of thunderstorms.

Noticeable land and sea breeze circulations are not restricted to ocean coastlines. For example, lake and land breezes are generated by the Great Lakes, as well as by smaller bodies of water such as Lake Tahoe and the Salton Sea in California. Wind speeds generated by such circulations are proportional to the area of the water surface and to the land-water temperature difference. They are stronger and more frequent in the summer.

> Thermally driven local winds are usually named for their source: sea breezes blow **from** the sea; land breezes **from** the land; valley breezes **from** the valley (upslope), mountain breezes **from** the mountains (downslope).

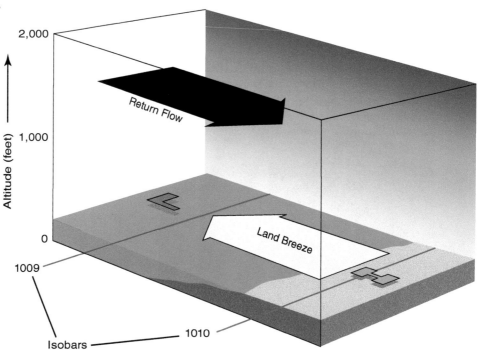

Figure 10-4. Land breeze circulation. Shallow offshore flow at low levels is capped by a weaker onshore return flow aloft.

VALLEY BREEZE

In mountainous areas that are not under the influence of large scale wind circulations, the daytime winds tend to be directed toward higher terrain. This primarily warm season circulation leads to rising air over mountains or hills and sinking air over nearby lowlands. It is often marked by cumulus clouds and greater thermal activity over the highlands than over the valleys.

These flow patterns occur because the hills and mountains are heated to temperatures that are warmer than air at the same level over nearby valley areas. Because of the horizontal temperature difference, a horizontal pressure gradient develops with the lower pressures over the mountains. Below the peaks, air responds by flowing toward the slopes of the warmer mountain. The hillside deflects the air, producing an "anabatic" or upslope wind. As expected, a return flow is found above the mountain. (Figure 10-5)

If the mountainside is part of a valley, the upslope flow may be part of a larger scale valley breeze which is also directed toward higher terrain. Above the mountaintops, a weak return flow known as an "anti-valley" wind is found. The valley breeze in combination with the return flow is called the valley breeze circulation. (Figure 10-6)

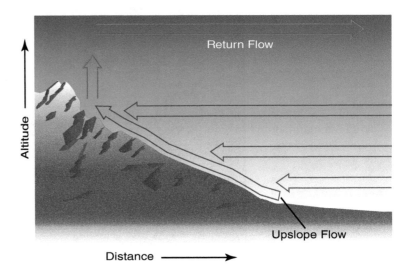

Figure 10-5. Upslope circulation. In the daytime, cooler air moves toward the warm slopes at and below ridge-top level while, aloft, there is a weak return flow.

The precise time that an upslope or valley flow begins depends on local sunrise. This time is determined not only by latitude and time of year, but also by the depth and orientation of the valley. In many valleys, upslope flow begins on one side of the valley while the other side is still in shadow. Similarly, in the afternoon, the upslope

Figure 10-6. The daytime valley breeze flows up the centerline of the valley and toward the warm slopes. An opposing return flow is found aloft.

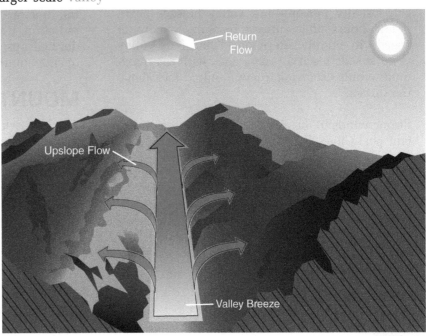

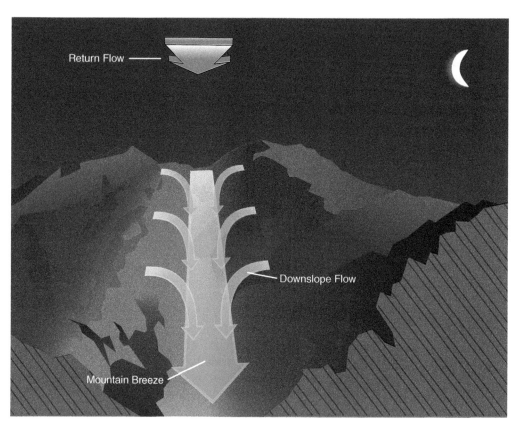

Figure 10-7. Mountain breeze circulation. As the ground cools at night, air flows away from the higher terrain. Winds are directed downslope along the mountain slopes and valley floor.

Return Flow

Downslope Flow

Mountain Breeze

circulation persists longer on sun-facing slopes. When the slopes become very warm, instability and convection make upward motion even stronger. Usually upslope and valley breezes begin a few hours after sunrise reaching maximum speeds in middle afternoon. Typical up-valley wind speeds reach 5 to 20 knots, with the maximum winds occurring a few hundred feet above the surface.

Strong winds in the atmosphere above the mountain peaks may disturb valley and slope circulations depending on the direction and speed of the upper winds and the orientation and depth of the valley. When winds above the mountains exceed about 15 knots, the valley circulation may be significantly modified. It may strengthen, weaken, or even reverse direction as strong winds aloft are carried down into the valley through mechanical mixing and/or by afternoon convection.

Over snow-covered terrain, heating of the high slopes is small due to the reflection of solar radiation by the snow. Therefore, over bare slopes, the daytime upslope flow does not usually extend beyond the snow line. However, if the hillsides are tree-covered, the flow may be different. When the treetops are snow free, they absorb solar radiation, warming the air and producing a well-defined upslope circulation despite the presence of snow on the ground.

MOUNTAIN BREEZE

At night, when the high terrain cools off, the air over the mountains becomes cooler than the air over the valley at the same altitude. The pressure gradient reverses and "katabatic," or downslope winds develop along the hillsides. On the larger scale of the valley, a mountain breeze blows down the valley with a return flow, or anti-mountain wind, above the mountaintops. This configuration is known as the mountain breeze circulation. (Figure 10-7)

As with the valley breeze, the size, depth, orientation of the valley, and the steepness of the slopes determine the intensity of the mountain

A.   Sea Breeze/Upslope

B.   Land Breeze/Downslope

Figure 10-8. In diagram A, a combined sea breeze/upslope flow with heating over the island produces cloudiness inland. In diagram B, the flow is reversed. The combined land breeze and downslope winds keep the island clear of clouds but converge offshore to produce clouds. These patterns might be significantly modified by asymmetrical island shapes.

breeze circulation. Prior to sunrise, speeds of 5 to 15 knots are common. It is not unusual to find greater speeds, sometimes exceeding 25 knots, at the mouth of the valley.

In locations where mountains are found along coastlines, the sea breeze enhances the upslope or valley breeze. Similarly, land and mountain breeze effects may combine to produce significant offshore winds. These effects are well developed on tropical islands where thermally driven circulations dominate. Because of the availability of moisture, the daytime circulation is often marked by convective clouds over the island. In contrast, the nighttime flow may produce a ring of cloudiness over the ocean around the island. (Figure 10-8)

Thermally induced breezes may be significantly affected by prevailing winds. For example, the sea breeze on an island in the northeast trade winds will be strengthened on the northeastern side of the island and weakened (possibly even reversed) on the southwestern side. If there is a mountain range on the island, there will be greater cloudiness and precipitation on the slopes facing the northeast. The overall effects depend on the size of the island and the height and orientation of the mountains.

COLD DOWNSLOPE WINDS

When air is cooled by contact with the ground, it becomes denser. Above sloping ground, gravity accelerates the dense air toward lower elevations. Concentrated in a relatively shallow layer, flows of this type are called drainage winds, one of several types of cold downslope winds. Just as a valley breeze can be intensified by rising thermals, the mountain breeze can be strengthened by drainage winds.

Drainage winds are very shallow. They can begin before sundown; that is, as soon as a slope becomes shaded. Their flow is similar to water, following the natural drainage patterns of the terrain. The cold air tends to pool at the bottom of the slope, unless it is caught up in a larger scale mountain breeze.

Besides the dependence of the downslope wind speeds on the amount of nighttime cooling of the mountain, speeds of winds in drainage flows are proportional to the steepness of the slope. Also, wherever large ice and snow fields exist, strong drainage flows may occur day and night. This effect is especially noticeable near the edges of glaciers. A shallow layer of cold, dense air flows rapidly down the sloping surface of the glacier. Gravity accelerates this glacier wind as it moves downslope, so the strongest winds occur at the lower end, or toe, of a glacier. The maximum speeds depend on the length and steepness of the slope of the glacier and the free-air temperature. Extreme glacier-driven winds are found along the coast of Antarctica.

Another example of an extreme cold, downslope wind is the Bora. It develops along the Dalmatian coast of Croatia and Bosnia in winter. The terrain slopes steeply from the Adriatic Sea to about 2,000 feet AGL. Gravity accelerates shallow, cold airmasses moving from the east, down the steep mountain slopes to the sea. In extreme cases, the cold air reaches the coast with speeds in excess of 85 knots. Many cold, downslope winds in other geographical areas are also called Bora, or described as "Bora-like." For example, during winter in North America, a very cold airmass will occasionally move from the Arctic over the mountains of British Columbia, Idaho, and western Montana. These conditions cause strong, cold winds to flow down the east slopes of the Northern Rocky Mountains in Alberta and Montana.

When the winds above the tops of the mountains blow in the same direction as the Bora, its strength may be enhanced. This is an example of "externally driven" local winds, the subject of the following section.

Section B

MOUNTAIN LEE WAVES AND WARM DOWNSLOPE WINDS

When large-scale circulations cause airflow across rugged terrain, numerous mesoscale circulations develop over and downwind of the mountains. Two of the most important are mountain lee waves and warm downslope winds.

MOUNTAIN LEE WAVES

When a stable airstream flows over a ridgeline, it is displaced vertically. Downwind of the ridge, the displaced air parcels accelerate back to their original (equilibrium) level because the air is stable. They arrive at the equilibrium level with some vertical motion and overshoot it. They again accelerate back to the equilibrium level and over-shoot, only to repeat the wave-like oscillation as they are swept downstream with the horizontal winds. The mesoscale wave pattern that they follow is known as a mountain wave or mountain lee wave. It is a particular form of an atmospheric gravity wave. These phenomena are so-named because, in a stable atmosphere, gravity (through stability) plays a major role in forcing the parcels to return to, and oscillate about, their equilibrium level. (Figure 10-9)

Because the mountain which initially displaces the air doesn't move, lee waves tend to remain stationary despite the fact that the air moves rapidly through them. Lee waves are relatively warm in the wave troughs where stable air has descended, and cold in the crests where stable air has risen. Once established in a particular locale, mountain lee wave activity may persist for several hours, although there are wide variations in lifetime.

Lee waves are impor-tant phenomena because they produce vertical motions large enough to affect aircraft in flight. Furthermore, they are often associated with tur-bulence, especially below mountaintop level and near the tropopause. The flight hazards associated

The formation of mountain lee waves requires movement of stable air across a mountain range.

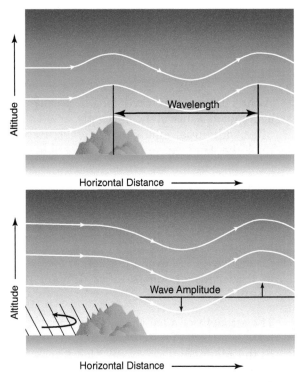

Figure 10-9. Two situations which contribute to the formation of lee waves downwind of a mountain ridge. In the top diagram, stable air flowing from left to right is lifted by the ridge. In the bottom diagram, the airstream is blocked at low levels in front of the mountain ridge, and stable air from aloft descends on the lee side of the mountain. In both cases, the vertical displacement of the stable air by the mountain causes lee waves.

with lee waves are discussed in detail in Chapter 12 (Turbulence). In the remainder of this section we will briefly describe the general features of lee waves.

Under typical mountain wave conditions, lee wave-lengths average about five nautical miles. (See upper diagram in figure 10-9) However, lengths can vary widely from a few miles to more than 30 n.m., depending on stability and wind speed. The stronger the wind speed, the longer the wavelength of the lee wave; the greater the stability, the shorter the wavelength of the lee wave.

Figure 10-10. A satellite image reveals lee wave activity as a "wash board" pattern of lenticular clouds over the western United States. The lenticular clouds are located in the crests of the lee waves.

Although the lee wave length is an accurate measure of the horizontal scale of an individual mountain lee wave, it must be kept in mind that effective scale may be quite a bit larger. This is because a single ridge often sets up a train of several lee waves, and a mountainous area may be composed of many parallel ridges, all capable of producing lee waves. Therefore, it is not unusual for lee waves to cover a horizontal area of thousands of square miles. (Figure 10-10)

The strength of a lee wave is indicated by the strength of the vertical motions it produces. In the more common "weak" lee waves, upward and downward speeds are a few hundred feet per minute or less. In contrast, in "strong" lee waves, vertical speeds can be 1,800 f.p.m. or more.

The strength of the vertical motions in the waves depends strongly on wave amplitude and on wind speed. The amplitude indicates how far an air parcel will deviate from a horizontal path as it moves through a wave pattern. Lee wave amplitudes may reach 4,000 feet or more in strong wave cases. If we compare two lee wave cases where the wind speed is the same in both cases, but the amplitudes are different, the wave with the larger amplitude will have the greater vertical motions. On the other hand, if the two waves had similar amplitudes, but different wind speeds, the wave with the greater wind speed would have the stronger vertical motions. Figure 10-11 illustrates the effect of wave amplitude on vertical speed.

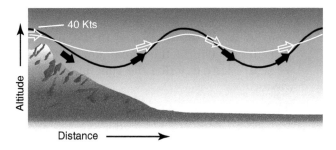

Figure 10-11. The influence of amplitude on the vertical speed of the wind. The wind speeds and wavelengths are the same in both cases. The yellow line indicates the path of an air parcel through a lee wave with a relatively small amplitude. The black line shows a case where the wave amplitude is greater and so the vertical speeds are larger.

To appreciate strong lee waves, assume that you were attempting to fly horizontally through a typical "strong" lee wave. The lee wavelength is 12 n.m. (stronger waves tend to be longer). Under these conditions, you would encounter a change in vertical wind speeds from +1,800 f.p.m. to −1,800 f.p.m. over a distance of only 6 n.m. (half of a lee wave length)! If your groundspeed was 480 knots, and your track was perpendicular to the waves, that change would occur over a 45 second period. It would be a memorable ride.

Tall, relatively narrow mountains are more effective in producing large lee wave amplitudes. For wide mountains, the steepness of the lee slopes, rather than the overall width of the mountain is important in determining lee wave strength. Two locations where exceptionally strong mountain waves are produced because of high, steep lee slopes are the Sierra Nevada range near Bishop, California, and the Rocky Mountains near Boulder, Colorado.

Winds nearly perpendicular to a ridgeline are more effective in the production of lee waves than winds nearly parallel to the ridgeline.

Significant vertical motions will occur in lee waves if the winds perpendicular to the ridgeline exceed 20 knots at the top of the ridge and the lee wave wavelength exceeds 5 n.m.

High, broad ridges with steep lee slopes often produce large amplitude lee waves. This is especially true when the height of the terrain decreases 3,000 feet or more downwind of the ridge line.

THE LEE WAVE SYSTEM

All lee waves, regardless of their geographic location, produce certain common flow features and clouds. These characteristics are captured in the idealized model of the lee wave system shown in figure 10-12. The lee wave system is divided into two layers, an upper lee wave region where smooth wave flow dominates and microscale turbulence occasionally occurs, and a lower turbulent zone from the ground to just above mountain-top level where turbulence is common.

This simple model is a valuable guide that helps you locate regions of wave action and turbulence from cloud observations and other visible indicators. The model also helps you deduce lee wave conditions from wind measurements and from macroscale airflow patterns shown on weather charts. For example, soundings taken during lee wave conditions show a number of similar features. Temperature soundings usually have a stable layer near mountaintop level with less stable layers above and below. Wind soundings display increasing wind speed with altitude.

In the lee wave portion of figure 10-12, the most intense lee wave is the first or primary cycle immediately downwind of the mountain. Successive cycles tend to have reduced amplitudes. Figure 10-12 shows that the lee waves have their greatest amplitudes within a few thousand feet above the mountains, decreasing above and below.

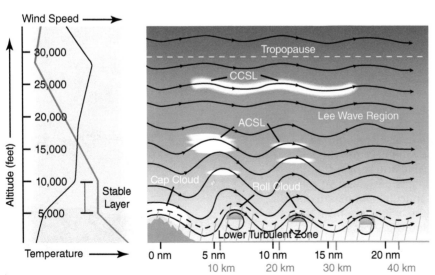

Figure 10-12. The lee wave system. Airflow through the lee waves is indicated by thin solid lines with arrows. The lower turbulent zone is shaded below the dashed line. Characteristic lee wave clouds are shown in white. A temperature sounding (red) and wind sounding (black) taken just upstream of the ridge are shown on the left. Altitudes and horizontal distances are indicated. Wide variations can occur.

The conditions most favorable to wave formation over mountainous areas are a layer of stable air at mountaintop altitude and a wind of at least 20 knots blowing across the ridge.

A major feature of the lower turbulent zone is the rotor circulation found under one or more of the lee wave crests. The altitude of the rotors is about mountain-top level. The rotor under the first wave crest is the most intense and is usually the major source of turbulence in the lower turbulent zone, if not in the entire lee wave system.

Crests of standing mountain waves may be marked by stationary, lens-shaped clouds known as standing lenticular clouds.

The lower turbulent zone is generally characterized by strong gusty winds with the strongest surface winds along the lee slopes of the mountain. These features contribute to the dominance of turbulence in this layer. Related flight dangers are examined in Part III on aviation weather hazards (Chapter 12).

When there is adequate moisture, the lee wave system produces one or more of three unique cloud forms. These are presented schematically in figure 10-12 and shown photographically in figure 10-13. They are the cap cloud immediately over the mountaintops; the cumuliform rotor, or roll cloud associated with the rotor circulation; and the smooth, lens-shaped altocumulus standing lenticular (ACSL) or lenticular clouds in the crests of the lee waves. Higher lenticular clouds are sometimes reported as cirrocumulus standing lenticular (CCSL) in METAR reports.

It is important to realize that clouds may be your only indication of the presence of lee waves. Because mountain waves are mesoscale phenomena, they escape detailed measurements in the regular network of weather stations.

Aside from pilot weather reports, the only direct evidence of lee wave activity comes from weather satellite images (see figure 10-10) and occasional surface weather reports of lee wave clouds. Automated METAR reports from unmanned stations have no such information. Some examples of METARs that indicate the presence of lee waves are shown in figure 10-14.

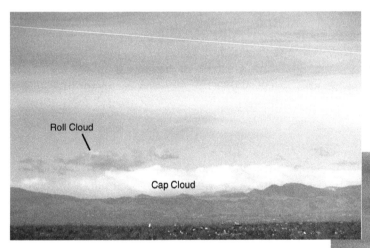

Roll Cloud

Cap Cloud

Lenticular

Figure 10-13. Mountain wave clouds are easily recognized by their proximity to mountains and by their unique shapes. On the left, the view is upwind. The cap cloud is over the peaks in the background and the filaments of the darker roll cloud are visible in the foreground. Lenticular clouds are not clearly defined. In the right-hand picture, winds are from the right. Neither the cap cloud nor roll clouds are present, but lenticular clouds are visible.

METAR KGFA 072054Z 24028G40KT 15SM SCT080 SCT100 OVC250 13/6 A2956 RMK A02 ACSL ALQDS=

METAR KTPH 152253Z 18003KT 30SM SCT120 4/M01 A2971 RMK A02 CCSL W ROTOR CLD SW=

METAR KDEN 221757Z 27014G23KT 20SM BKN100 OVC250 10/3 A2959 RMK A02 ACSL SW-NW=

Figure 10-14. METARs with remarks that indicate lee wave activity. Such important remarks are not available from weather stations that are completely automated.

The lee wave system shown figure 10-12 is a conceptual diagram based on observations of many different lee wave situations. Wide variations occur. For example, lee wave activity may be limited to the lower troposphere because the wind speed or direction changes radically with altitude, or because stability weakens at higher levels and wave action is no longer possible. In other cases, waves may intensify with altitude, leading to intense wave action near the tropopause and in the stratosphere. Significant mountain wave activity has been observed at altitudes of more than 60,000 feet MSL.

> The presence of lenticular, roll, and/or cap clouds indicate lee wave activity and locations of wave crests and rotor circulation. However, these observations should not be used to estimate the strength of the vertical motions or associated turbulence.

There are also horizontal variations in lee wave structure. Our model of the lee wave system is based on airflow across an idealized long ridge. In contrast, real mountain ridges are complicated by rugged peaks of different sizes and separations. Also, a typical mountainous area is more likely to be made up of several ridges which are not quite parallel and are irregularly spaced. This means that even when wind and stability conditions are generally the same across a particular geographical area, significant variations in wave characteristics may occur.

Despite these variations from the average lee wave system, the model is still a valuable reference, especially when used in combination with a good knowledge of local terrain and the latest METARs, PIREPs, and aviation forecasts.

> Cessna 150. One fatality, one serious injury. Substantial damage. Aircraft caught in downdraft. Stalled and crashed in trees. Exceeded capabilities to cross mountain.

WARM DOWNSLOPE WINDS

We have already seen that very cold air flowing down the steep slope of a mountain can produce a strong, cold wind called a Bora. In contrast, when a warm, stable airmass moves across a mountain range at high levels and descends on the lee side, it often produces a strong warm wind called a Chinook.

A Chinook, or Foehn, is defined as a warm, dry, gusty wind that blows from the mountains. It often occurs under the same conditions that produce mountain waves, although it can extend much farther downwind of the mountains than the wave activity. Surface winds in a Chinook are typically 20 to 50 knots, and extreme speeds near 100 knots have been measured. The strongest Chinook winds and greatest warming occur closest to the mountains. In the winter, especially in high latitudes, temperature changes with the onset of the Chinook can be very large; changes of 20F° to 40F° in 15 minutes have been widely documented.

The terms Chinook and Foehn are used widely to describe warm downslope winds in general, but such winds are identified by many local names. Examples are Santa Ana (southern California), the Zonda (Argentina), and Nor'wester (Canterbury, New Zealand).

> Fairchild FH227B. 13 fatalities. Aircraft destroyed. Aircraft flew into a downdraft in the lee of a mountain at an altitude insufficient for recovery. Wind 61 knots at 3,000 feet.

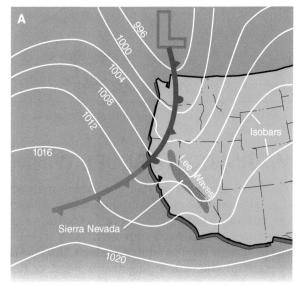

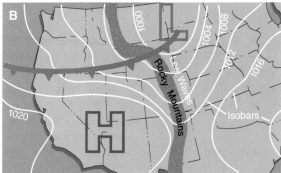

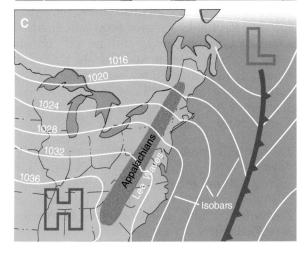

FAVORABLE MACROSCALE WEATHER PATTERNS

Large scale wind systems conducive to the development of lee wave and Chinook activity must satisfy two important requirements:

1. There must be a stable layer just above the mountain.

2. The wind speeds across the mountaintop must be at least 20 knots.

These conditions are frequently met when extratropical cyclones move across mountainous areas, bringing strong mountaintop winds and widespread stable layers associated with fronts. Lee waves occur most often during the cooler months of the year when extratropical cyclone activity is greater. Examples of large-scale weather patterns favorable for lee wave activity near the major mountain ranges of the contiguous U.S. are illustrated in figure 10-15.

In the western U.S., major mountain ranges are oriented north-south or northwest-southeast. Therefore, mountain waves occur when fronts and upper air troughs approach the mountains from the west. After the fronts and troughs pass, winds shift and significant wave activity ceases. In contrast, the Appalachian Mountains are oriented northeast-southwest. Lee wave activity is favored after the fronts and troughs aloft pass and the winds become northwesterly.

Figure 10-15. Surface analysis charts from actual lee wave situations along the east slopes of the Sierra Nevada (A), the Rocky Mountains (B), and the Appalachians (C). The mountains are shown in gray. Notice in all cases that the sea level pressure is higher on the west sides of the mountains and lower on the east. In A and B, the lee waves are prefrontal; while in C, they are postfrontal.

SUMMARY

Chapter 10 has shown how the simple concept of thermal circulation is used to explain the development and general features of sea and land breezes, mountain and valley breezes, and drainage winds. These small-scale circulations can certainly affect flight conditions, but their presence is not immediately obvious on surface analysis charts. The information you have learned in this chapter will help you anticipate winds produced by local terrain and land-water differences.

Additionally, when large-scale circulation systems such as extratropical cyclones make their way across rugged terrain, interactions of their winds with mountains and hills produce other unique mesoscale circulations including mountain lee waves and warm downslope winds. These phenomena offer many more serious problems to pilots than do most thermally driven circulations. An added difficulty arises because the conventional network of surface weather observ-

ing stations does not observe these mesoscale circulations very well. Therefore, there is not much detailed information available to the pilot to determine, for example, the location and strength of lee waves for flight planning and avoidance purposes. Your new knowledge of the model of the lee wave system and of large-scale patterns favorable for lee wave development will prove exceptionally valuable in your analysis of the presence and intensity of lee waves and the associated turbulence. (Chapter 12).

The completion of this chapter ends our formal consideration of atmospheric circulation systems. You have examined a wide spectrum of atmospheric phenomena, ranging from the macroscale general circulation to microscale dust devils. In Part III, we examine weather flight hazards and the larger scale circulations that produce them.

KEY TERMS

Altocumulus Standing Lenticular (ACSL)
Atmospheric Gravity Wave
Bora
Cap Cloud
Chinook
Cirrocumulus Standing Lenticular (CCSL)
Cold Downslope Wind
Downslope Wind
Drainage Wind
Externally Driven Local Winds
Foehn
Glacier Wind
Land Breeze
Land Breeze Circulation
Lee Wave
Lee Wave Region
Lee Wave System

Lenticular Cloud
Local Winds
Lower Turbulent Zone
Mountain Breeze
Mountain Breeze Circulation
Mountain Wave
Primary Cycle
Roll Cloud
Rotor
Sea Breeze
Sea Breeze Circulation
Sea Breeze Front
Thermally Driven Local Winds
Upslope Wind
Valley Breeze
Valley Breeze Circulation
Warm Downslope Wind

REVIEW QUESTIONS

1. The land breeze reaches its greatest intensity at what local time?

2. Where is the most intense wave action usually found in the lee wave system?

3. (True, False) Air involved in both the warm Chinook and the cold Bora experiences adiabatic warming while moving downslope.

4. Generally speaking, which flow has the greater depth, mountain breeze or valley breeze?

5. (True, False) A supersonic aircraft flying at 60,000 feet will never be exposed to lee waves, regardless of the terrain and weather conditions.

6. In a fully developed lee wave system, at what approximate altitude is the center of the rotor circulation located?

7. A typical lee wave length is _____ miles. How long will it take an aircraft flying at a ground speed of 150 knots to fly through one typical lee wave (assume that the flight is perpendicular to the wave front)?

8. In the absence of strong winds due to, for example, a passing cyclone, forest fires will usually burn _____ (uphill/downhill) during the day and _____ (uphill/downhill) at night.

9. List some evidence of the passage of a sea breeze front.

DISCOVERY QUESTIONS

10. Why shouldn't you use observations of lenticular, cap, or roll clouds to estimate the strength of the vertical motions in the lee wave system? How should you use such observations?

11. The island shown to the right is located in the trade winds of the Northern Hemisphere. It is about 60 n.m. in diameter and is low and flat. An airport is located at the point marked "X." A pilot lands at the airport twice in a given 24-hour period. Both final approaches were from the southwest. The first landing was accomplished with a 25-knot headwind. The second landing also experienced a headwind, but it was less than 10 knots. At what local times (24-hour clock) did the landings most likely occur? Explain.

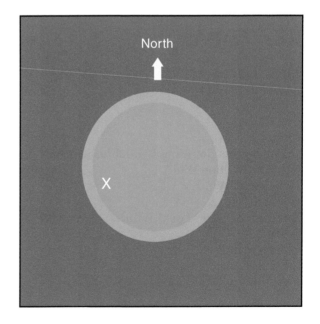

12. (True, False) A moist airmass from the Pacific moves across the Rocky Mountains producing Chinook conditions along the lee slopes. Clouds form during the passage of the air over the mountains, although there is no precipitation. The clouds dissipate as the air moves down the east slopes of the Rockies. The release of latent heat has contributed substantially to the warming of the air in the lee of the mountains. Explain.

13. You fly your aircraft well above the mountain peaks, upwind and downwind through a train of standing waves (lee waves). The wave conditions are exactly the same during both flights. You don't attempt to hold altitude, letting your aircraft "ride the waves." Draw cross sections along each flight track showing the airflow through the waves and the aircraft path. Be sure to indicate the flight direction.

14. A helicopter is carrying water to put out a fire along the east slopes of a ridge. Winds aloft are light. As would be expected, the flight is at low levels, so winds along the slopes are critical. It is mid-afternoon and, except for the smoke from the fire, the skies are clear. There are no significant large-scale wind systems in the area. As the pilot approaches the fire from the east, she notices that since her last run 15 minutes earlier, the fire has changed directions and is burning downhill. Give a reasonable explanation for the wind shift.

15. A dry, cool high pressure region has stagnated over Nevada in the early fall. For several days, the afternoon temperature at Tonopah, Nevada (elevation 5,425 feet MSL) has been 55°F. A dry, easterly wind is blowing over the beaches just west of Los Angeles. If the air in the latter region originated over Tonopah, what is its approximate temperature at the coast? Explain clearly, showing all of your work.

16. Sailplanes must often fly upwind in order to stay in the "up" portion of lee waves. Give a plausible explanation. (Note: there is more than one.)

17. In some circumstances, a large forest fire can set up its own circulation so that oxygen-rich air is circulated into the fire, actually making it worse.
    1. Explain how the circulation develops.
    2. Do a little research to find some cases where such fire behavior has been documented.
    3. Describe each case briefly.

18. The chart below is a simple topographic map that shows an airport at point "X" in a large valley. In this location, pilots claim that mountain waves occur over the valley both before and after the passage of a surface cold front and its associated trough aloft. Is this possible? Explain.

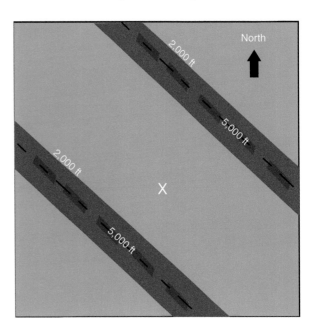

19. The abbreviated remarks below are abstracted from PIREPs given during flights through mountain wave situations. Write plain language interpretations.

LSV UA /OV CIM 270050/TM 1500/FL390/TP CL60/TB HEAVY/RM SEVERE UP AND DOWNDRAFTS 40 KTS CHANGE IN WIND

LSV UUA /OV CIM-CIM 270040/TM 1545/FL390/TP CL60/TB SVR/RM RAPID CHG OF WIND DIRECTION PLUS 500 FPM UDDFS

LSV UUA /OV CIM 270005/TM 1625/ FL 330/TP B767/TB SVR/RM ACFT ROLLED 30 DEGREES

PART III

Aviation Weather Hazards

PART III
AVIATION WEATHER HAZARDS

The background material presented in Part II has given you a broad view of the causes, structure, behavior, and weather of circulation systems of different sizes and lifetimes. Those circulations, often acting together, produce a number of specific flight hazards. Strong winds, low ceilings and visibilities, turbulence, wind shear, icing, and lightning are just a few of the phenomena that can threaten safety of flight. The purpose of Part III is to lead you through a careful study of aviation weather hazards in order to give you better tools to anticipate and avoid them whenever possible.

(Lightning photograph on previous page courtesy of National Oceanic and Atmospheric Administration)

Introduction

Strong wind shear is a hazard to aviation because it can cause turbulence and large airspeed fluctuations and, therefore, serious control problems. It is a threat especially to aircraft operations near the ground because of the limited altitude for maneuvering, particularly during the takeoff and landing phases of flight. In this chapter, we examine wind shear and its causes. When you complete the chapter, you will know what wind shear is and what its critical values are. You will also know how, why, and where it develops in the vicinity of thunderstorms, inversions, developing extratropical cyclones, fronts, and jet streams.

Section A

WIND SHEAR DEFINED

Wind shear was defined briefly in Chapter 8 in connection with fronts. Because of the critical nature of wind shear, we will review and refine that definition.

> Wind shear is best described as a change in wind direction and/or speed within a very short distance.

A wind shear is actually a gradient in wind velocity. It is interpreted in the same sense as a pressure gradient or temperature gradient; that is, it is a change of wind velocity over a given distance. It is commonly expressed in units of speed divided by distance; for example, knots per 1,000 feet. Since wind is a vector, with both speed and direction, wind shear can involve a change in either speed or direction, or both.

For flight considerations, the critical wind shear is the total shear along the aircraft path. However, when considering its causes, it is convenient to visualize wind shear as being composed of two parts: a horizontal wind shear (a change in wind over a horizontal distance) and/or a vertical wind shear (a change in wind over a vertical distance). Note that some other weather training publications refer to vertical wind shear as a "wind gradient." Figure 11-1 shows some examples of wind shear.

In diagram A, wind increases with altitude with no change in direction. Since the aircraft is flying into the wind, it experiences a decrease in headwind as it descends. In this example, the vertical wind shear over the entire layer is 30 knots per 300 feet.

In diagram B of figure 11-1, an aircraft is in level flight toward a point where the wind direction changes 180°. As you will see, this is the type of pattern expected when penetrating a microburst.

> PIPER PA-18-150 No injuries Landing on runway 34L, the aircraft touched down on the centerline with full flaps at 45 MPH. The airplane immediately "weather-vaned" to the left; the pilot overcorrected and the airplane departed the runway on the right side where it ground-looped. At the time of the accident, winds were 290/15 G20 and a Wind Shear Warning was in effect.

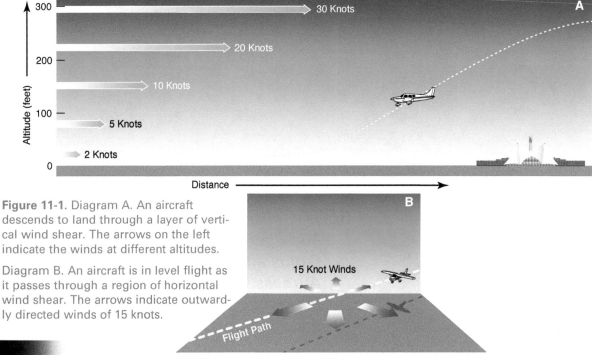

Figure 11-1. Diagram A. An aircraft descends to land through a layer of vertical wind shear. The arrows on the left indicate the winds at different altitudes.

Diagram B. An aircraft is in level flight as it passes through a region of horizontal wind shear. The arrows indicate outwardly directed winds of 15 knots.

We must be careful in evaluating the shear in this situation. The difference in wind speeds along the flight path is zero (15 knots – 15 knots). But this is not the total shear because it does not include the reversal in wind direction. The meaningful difference is the change from a 15 knot **headwind** to a 15 knot **tailwind**, which equates to a **30 knot loss** in airspeed. Technically, the wind shear is that change divided by the distance, say from one end of the runway to the other. However, wind shear information near an airport is usually given as a statement of the change in headwind in knots. In diagram B, the wind shear would be described as "minus 30 knots," a difficult, if not impossible situation for a light aircraft to handle on takeoff or landing.

> If the wind direction changes over a given distance, the actual wind shear is always greater than the change in the wind speed alone.

The two diagrams in figure 11-1 are idealized. More often, changes in wind speed occur simultaneously with changes in wind direction. Your concern as a pilot is how much the headwind or tailwind changes along your flight path, and in how short a distance the change occurs.

CHAMPION 7GCBC No injuries. While conducting an aerial survey of a hunting area, the pilot flew his aircraft upwind and then downwind at an altitude of 1000 feet AGL. From the pilot's GPS measurements of groundspeed made on the upwind and downwind legs, it is estimated that the windspeed was more than 60 knots, equating to significant vertical wind shear between the flight altitude and the ground.. During two attempts to fly crosswind, the aircraft rolled inverted. While recovering from the second roll, a downdraft pushed the aircraft into the treetops where it sustained major damage.

Wind shear below 2,000 feet AGL along the final approach path or along the takeoff and initial climbout path is known as low-level wind shear (LLWS). The influences of wind shear on aircraft performance during landing and takeoff are well known. If the pilot of an aircraft encounters wind shear on approach and fails to adjust for a sudden decreasing headwind or increasing tailwind, the airspeed will decrease and the aircraft may undershoot the landing due to loss of lift. Similarly, a suddenly increasing headwind or decreasing tailwind on approach can cause an overshoot.

When wind shear is encountered on takeoff and the headwind decreases or the tailwind increases, the angle of climb and rate of climb will be lower. In critical situations, obstacles near the airport may not be cleared. During both takeoff and landing, a strong wind shear with a crosswind component may cause the aircraft to deviate from the centerline of the runway. Close to the ground, clearance of nearby obstacles may become difficult or impossible. Figure 11-2 assigns severity categories to various ranges of low-level wind shear.

> During departure under conditions of suspected low-level wind shear, a sudden decrease in headwind will cause a loss in airspeed equal to the decrease in wind velocity.

Example of METAR wind shear remarks:

... /RM LLWS -15KT SFC-030 DURC RNWY 22 JFK.

This METAR remark is a pilot report. In plain language, it reads "Low level wind shear. Fifteen knots loss in airspeed experienced between surface and 3,000 feet during climb from runway 22 at JFK."

Low-Level Wind Shear(LLWS)	
LLWS Severity	**LLWS Magnitude (kts/100 ft)**
Light	< 4.0
Moderate	4.0 to 7.9
Strong	8.0 to 11.9
Severe	≥12

Figure 11-2. Severity categories of LLWS expressed in terms of vertical wind shear. According to these values, the vertical wind shear conditions in diagram A of figure 11-1 (30 knots/300 feet) corresponds to strong LLWS. Also note that the wind shear is stronger near the top of that diagram than near the bottom.

Section B

CAUSES OF WIND SHEAR

In the last few years, many in aviation have come to use the term "wind shear" almost exclusively to describe wind shear in the vicinity of a microburst. The reason that microburst wind shear has received so much attention is a simple one; it has been identified as the cause of a significant number of weather-related accidents with great loss of life and destruction of property. However, it is important to remember that microbursts are only one of several quite different causes of serious wind shear conditions.

An important characteristic of wind shear is that it may be associated with a thunderstorm, a low-level temperature inversion, a jet stream, or a frontal zone.

Critical wind shear for aircraft operations generally occurs on the microscale; that is, over horizontal distances of one nautical mile or less and vertical distances of less than 1,000 feet. These scales are so small that pilots may not have time to safely maneuver the aircraft to compensate for the wind change.

Although the dimensions of regions with significant shear are small, that shear is

caused by circulations on scales which range from macroscale low-pressure systems to microscale thermals. Some of the more important sources of wind shear are considered in the following paragraphs.

MICROBURSTS

The key to understanding development of wind shear below the bases of convective clouds is a good knowledge of the characteristics of a typical precipitation-induced downdraft. You were introduced to this phenomenon in Chapter 9. Its main features are summarized in figure 11-3.

Not all precipitation-induced downdrafts are associated with critical wind shears. However, there are two types of downdrafts that are particularly hazardous to flight operations because of their severity and small size. Tetsuya Fujita, who also developed the original tornado severity scale (Figure 9-16), was the first to identify and name the downburst, a concentrated, severe downdraft that induces an outward burst of damaging winds and dangerous wind shear near the ground. He also introduced the term microburst for a downburst with horizontal dimensions of 2.2 n.m. (4 km) or less. Note that, regardless of size, the term "microburst" is used more frequently

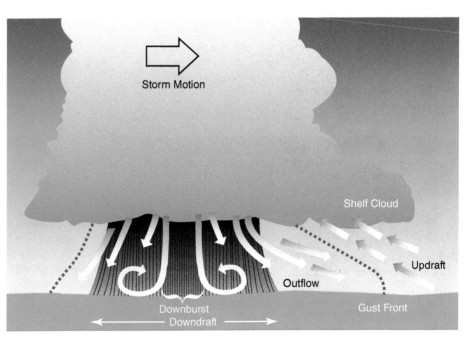

Figure 11-3. Conditions below the base of a thunderstorm. Wind shear and turbulence are found within the main downdraft; in smaller, stronger downdrafts occasionally embedded in the main downdraft (downbursts and microbursts); and at the boundaries of the outflow (the gust front).

in the general aviation literature to describe any precipitation-induced downdraft that produces critical wind shear conditions.

Microbursts form by the same processes that produce the more common and less intense downdrafts; that is, by precipitation drag and cooling due to the evaporation and melting of precipitation particles. In a microburst, the downdraft intensifies with heavy rain and when dry air is mixed into the downdraft causing evaporative cooling and great negative buoyancy.

Microbursts may occur in airmass, multicell, and supercell thunderstorms. Isolated, single-cell storms often present a greater hazard to aviation because they occur often, are small scale, and are not well observed; they develop rapidly and may reach intensities that may be easily underestimated, especially by eye. Larger multicell and supercell storms are usually easier to avoid because they occur on a larger scale and are better observed; they have longer lifetimes and are often already identified as severe.

Don't land or take off in the face of an approaching thunderstorm.

A perspective view of a microburst is shown in figure 11-4. The microburst is characterized by a strong core of cool, dense air descending from the base of a convective cloud. As it reaches the ground, it spreads out laterally as a vortex ring which rolls upward along its outer boundary. You can interpret this pattern as an upside-down version of a thermal. Typically, the microburst descends from the base of its parent cloud to the ground in a minute or so.

A cross section of an idealized microburst as it reaches the ground is

shown in figure 11-5. The shear of the horizontal wind across the base of the microburst is apparent. You now see why this shear is so dangerous. Wind speeds are strong and the directions reverse 180° across the centerline of the microburst. Furthermore, the strong downward motions and heavy rain in the center of the downburst also reduce lift. All of this takes place in a very short period of time, near the ground, and frequently with low ceilings and visibilities.

The lifetime of a microburst ranges from 5 to 30 minutes, once it reaches the ground. Most microbursts weaken significantly in only a few minutes. There is good evidence that some longer downburst events are a combination of successive microbursts a few minutes apart in the same location.

An aircraft that encounters a headwind of 45 knots with a microburst may expect a total shear across the microburst of 90 knots.

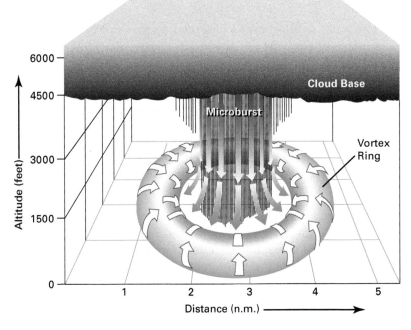

Figure 11-4. A symmetrical microburst. The broad arrows indicate airflow and the thin, vertical lines indicate precipitation.

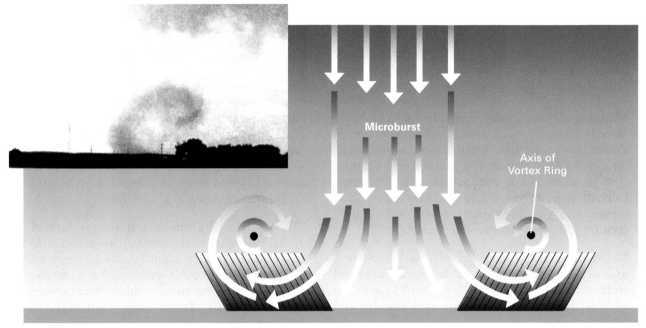

Figure 11-5. Microburst cross section. The flight hazards include the strong downdraft, often with heavy precipitation; gusty horizontal winds (shaded); strong horizontal wind shear from one side of the microburst to the other side; and turbulence in the vortex rings. The inset in the upper left is a photograph of the vortex ring of a microburst made visible by condensation. Photograph credit: NOAA Photo Library, NOAA Central Library

Within 100 feet of the ground, only a few seconds may be available for the recognition and recovery from wind shear associated with a microburst.

The peak outflow speed observed in an average microburst is about 25 knots. Winds in excess of 100 knots are possible. More critical is the change in wind speed across a microburst. An aircraft intersecting a typical microburst experiences an average headwind change of about 45 knots. This LLWS exceeds the capabilities of most light aircraft and is about the maximum that can be tolerated by heavy jet transports. The effect is illustrated in figure 11-6.

There are several variations in the formation and appearance of precipitation-induced downdrafts and microbursts. For example, a downdraft does not require a thunderstorm. As discussed previously,

On a July afternoon in 1982, a B-727 departed New Orleans, Louisiana, into a heavy rain shower near the end of the runway. The aircraft soon began sinking despite all the best efforts of the pilots to maintain takeoff climb. Less than twenty seconds after leaving the runway, the aircraft crashed killing 152 persons. An analysis of flight recorder and weather data by Dr. T. Fujita of the University of Chicago showed that the B-727 had flown into a strong precipitation-induced downdraft. During the penetration, a 14-knot head-wind at liftoff became a 27-knot tailwind just prior to the crash. Comprehensive analyses of this and other accidents by Dr. Fujita and his research team led to the identification of the microburst as a critical and identifiable aviation weather hazard. The subsequent development of flight techniques for wind shear situations and the installation of wind shear detection systems at airports received their impetus from Dr. Fujita's pioneering work on microbursts.

The duration of an individual microburst is seldom longer than 15 minutes from the time the burst strikes the ground until dissipation.

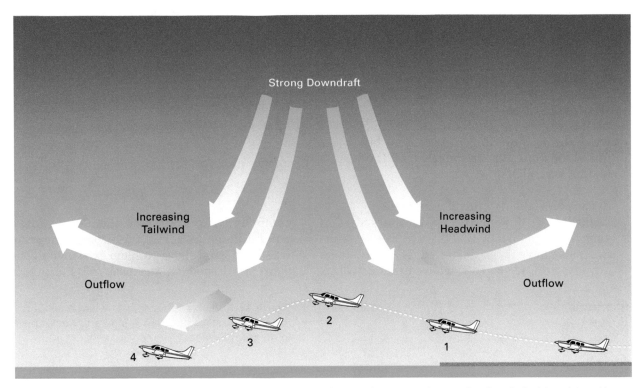

Figure 11-6. During a takeoff into a microburst, an aircraft experiences an increasing headwind (position 1), followed by a decreasing headwind and downdraft (position 2), and finally a tailwind (position 3). The most severe downdraft will be encountered between positions 2 and 3. Together with the loss of airspeed due to the tailwind, it can result in terrain impact or operating dangerously close to the ground (position 4).

showers are common from cumulus clouds that do not reach the cumulonimbus stage. Therefore, microbursts may also occur under these conditions.

Another variation on the ideal microburst model is that the microburst may move and be distorted under the influence of the larger scale wind field in which the thunderstorm is embedded. Such "traveling" microbursts have stronger winds on the downwind side; that is, in the direction in which the microburst is moving.

There are several visual indicators of the presence of large precipi-

tation-induced downdrafts, downbursts, and smaller scale microbursts. In humid climates, convective cloud bases tend to be low. These conditions produce "wet" downbursts and microbursts, which are closely associated with a visible rain shaft. However, in dry climates, such as in the deserts and mountains of the western U.S., thunderstorm cloud bases are often high and the complete evaporation of the rain shaft can occur. In this case, a "dry" downburst or microburst may be produced. All that may be visible is virga at the cloud base and a characteristic dust ring on the ground. Fortunately,

> When a shear from a headwind to a tailwind is encountered while making an approach on a prescribed glide slope, the pilot should expect an airspeed and pitch attitude decrease with a tendency to go below glide slope.

dry downbursts and microbursts occur mainly in the afternoon when these visible features can be identified. (Figure 11-7)

As the larger scale downdraft spreads out from one or more thunderstorms, strong shears persist in the gust front on the periphery of the cool air. Therefore, wind shear, including LLWS, may be found beyond the boundaries of the visible rain shaft.

Because of the low-level wind shear hazards of downbursts, microbursts, and gust fronts, low-level wind shear alert systems (LLWAS) have been installed at many large airports around the U.S. where thunderstorms

are frequent. LLWAS continuously monitors surface winds at remote sites around the airport and communicates the information to a central

If there is thunderstorm activity in the vicinity of an airport at which you plan to land, you should expect wind shear and turbulence on approach.

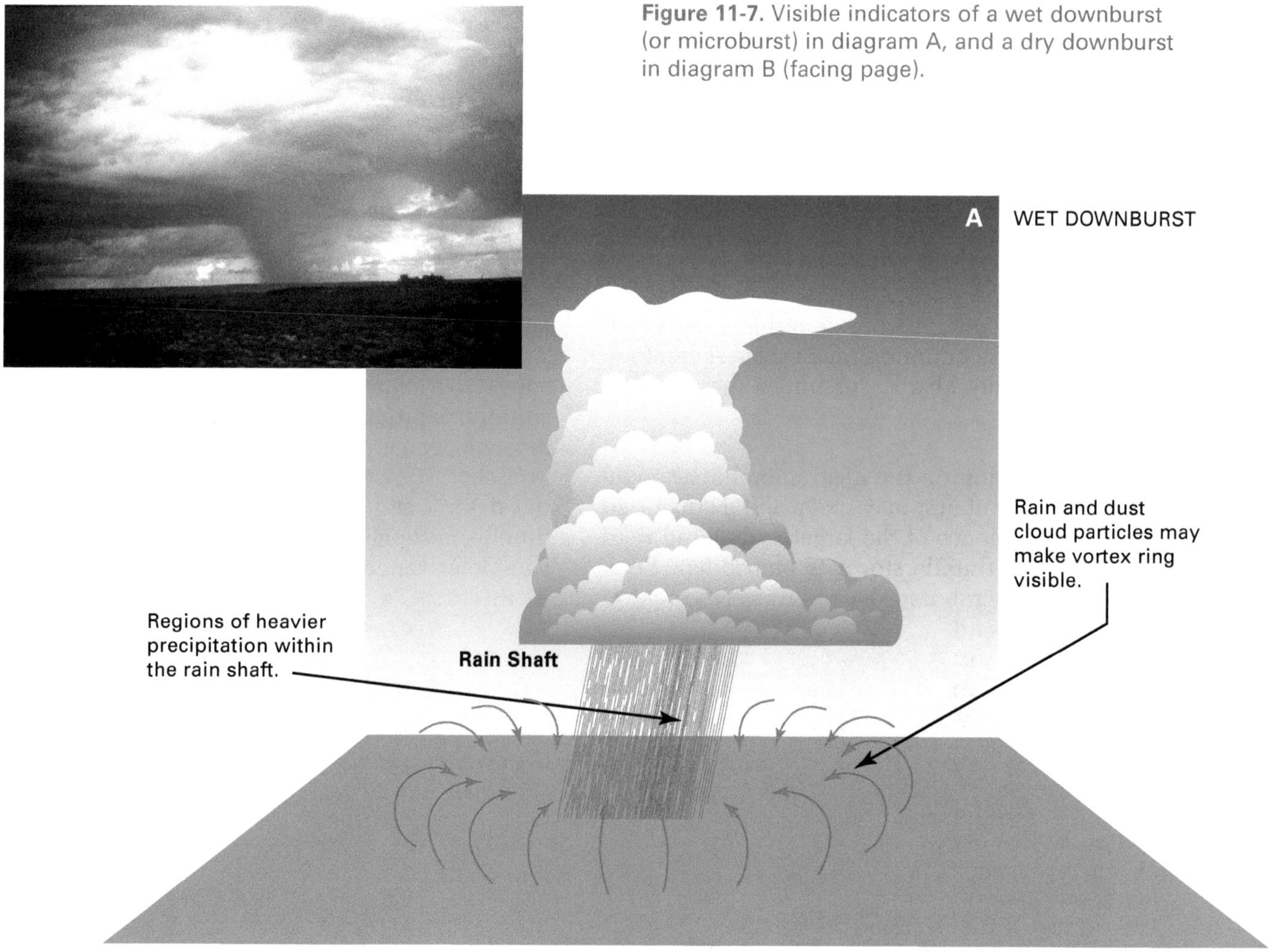

computer. The computer then evaluates the wind differences across the airport to determine whether a wind shear problem exists. Wind shear alerts are issued on the basis of this informa-

Figure 11-7. Visible indicators of a wet downburst (or microburst) in diagram A, and a dry downburst in diagram B (facing page).

A WET DOWNBURST

Rain and dust cloud particles may make vortex ring visible.

Regions of heavier precipitation within the rain shaft.

Rain Shaft

tion. Additionally, Terminal Doppler Weather Radar (TDWR) systems are installed across the U.S. at many vulnerable airports to provide more comprehensive wind shear monitoring. TWDR has greater power and a narrower radar beam than the WSR-88D, providing better detection of microbursts.

As we leave this brief discussion of microburst wind shear, it is important to note that a wide variety of information regarding microbursts and related flight techniques is contained in the FAA *Pilot Windshear Guide* and the FAA *Windshear Training Aid*.

Don't attempt to fly under a thunderstorm even if you can see through to the other side.

DRY DOWNBURST

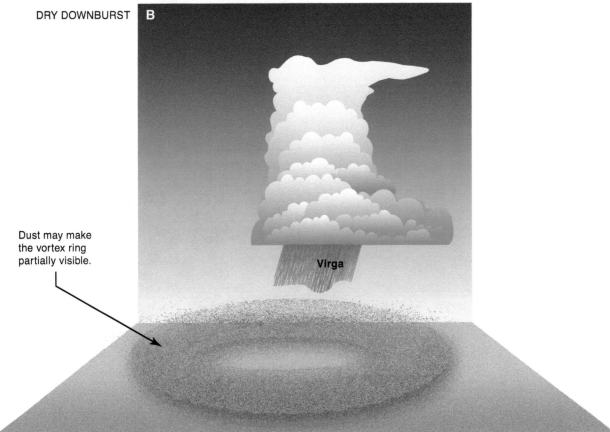

Dust may make the vortex ring partially visible.

Virga

Reports of wind shear and other flight hazards are often available through pilot weather reports (PIREPs). This may be the only direct evidence of these phenomena. Pilots are encouraged to use and to report PIREPs. A PIREP is disseminated in a standard coded format as shown with examples below and in Appendix B.

PIREP coded format:

UA (routine PIREP) or **UUA** (urgent PIREP)/**OV** (location)/**TM** (time UTC)/**FL** (altitude/flight level in 100s of feet MSL)/**TP** (aircraft type)/**SK** (sky condition)/**WX** (flight visibility and weather)/**TA** (outside air temperature °C)/**WV** (wind direction [°true] and wind speed in knots)/**TB** (turbulence intensity and type)/**IC** (icing intensity and type)/**RM** (remarks)

PIREP Example (Note: an actual coded PIREP will only contain those elements that are actually reported):

UUA /**OV** MIA/**TM** 1915/**FL** ON FNL APRCH/**TP** MD 080/**RM** LOSS OF 20KT AT 300FT APPROACHING MIDDLE MARKER RWY 27R

Urgent PIREP over Miami at 1915 UTC on final approach. Aircraft type MD-80. Aircraft lost 20 knots of airspeed at an altitude of 300 feet while approaching the middle marker, runway 27 right.

FRONTS AND SHALLOW LOWS

You already know from Part II that fronts are regions of wind shear. For example, when we inspect the surface analysis chart, we often use the wind shift across a front as an identifying feature of its location. You should also recall that a front is a zone between two different airmasses and frontal wind shear is concentrated in that zone. Since the cold air is more dense, it always wedges under the warm air. Therefore, the sheared frontal zone always slopes back over the cold air, *regardless of the type of front*. It follows that the sloping frontal zone contains both horizontal and vertical shear. (Figure 11-8)

A frontal passage is reported at a weather station when the warm boundary of the frontal zone passes the station. Therefore, the onset of LLWS follows a cold frontal passage and precedes a warm frontal passage. Typical periods for critical LLWS with frontal passages are one to three hours after a cold front and up to six hours before a warm front. Wind shear with a warm front causes the most problems because it lasts longer and frequently occurs with low ceilings and poor visibilities.

> The stronger the horizontal temperature gradient across the frontal zone, the stronger the wind shear.

> With a warm front, the most critical period for LLWS is before the front passes.

> Wind shear is not limited to macroscale fronts. It also occurs in the vicinity of mesoscale boundaries such as sea breeze fronts.

Figure 11-8. Perspective view of a cold front. Broad arrows indicate winds. Wind shears through the sloping frontal zone are both vertical shears, along line V, and horizontal shears, along line H. The shears are concentrated in the frontal zone. Note that the frontal slope is greatly exaggerated to show the details of the frontal zone. Actual fronts are much flatter.

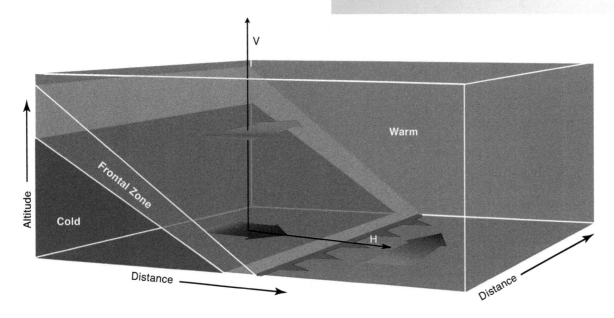

Strong wind shear often occurs in shallow wave cyclones during the cooler part of the year, especially in the vicinity of the warm front. In contrast with occluded cyclones, wave cyclones in their initial stages of development may not extend to 700 mb (10,000 feet MSL). An example is shown in figure 11-9.

During a two-hour period in the early evening of January 4, 1971, there were nine missed approaches to runway 04R at John F. Kennedy International Airport (JFK) in New York, NY. Several other aircraft reported difficulties on takeoff. During the same period, an accident occurred at La Guardia Airport (LGA) where one of the probable causes was identified as "The failure of the pilot to recognize a wind shear problem and to compensate for it." The cause of the wind shear was an approaching warm front with north-northeasterly winds at the surface changing to south-southwesterly winds within 1,000 feet of the ground. IFR conditions prevailed with low ceilings, poor visibilities, and rain or drizzle.

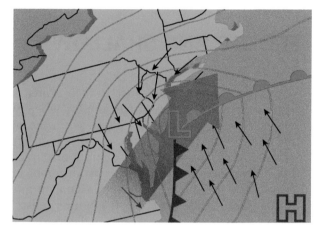

Figure 11-9. Example of wind shear in a shallow cyclone. Surface winds (thin arrows) are northeasterly ahead of the warm front, while just above the frontal zone, winds are strong southwesterly (broad arrow).

If a temperature inversion is encountered immediately after takeoff or during an approach to a landing, a potential hazard exists due to wind shear.

AIRMASS WIND SHEAR

Airmass wind shear occurs at night under fair weather conditions in the absence of strong fronts and/or strong surface pressure gradients. It develops when the ground becomes cooler than the overlying airmass as a result of radiational cooling. If the cooling is strong enough, a ground-based inversion results. In this case, the temperature increases with altitude from the surface to an altitude of a few hundred feet. This layer is also known as a nocturnal inversion. (Figure 11-10)

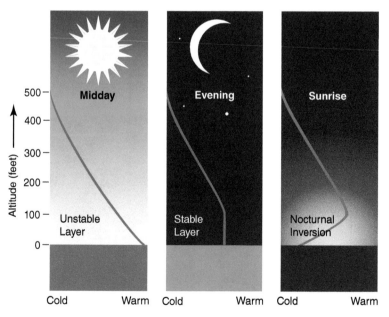

Figure 11-10. Low-level soundings taken throughout the day and night during fair weather conditions. A stable layer develops at night due to radiational cooling of the ground. By sunrise the stability has increased to a maximum as indicated by the nocturnal inversion.

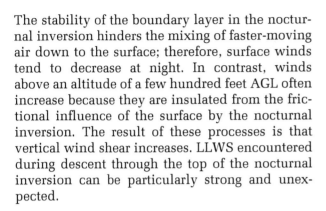

The stability of the boundary layer in the nocturnal inversion hinders the mixing of faster-moving air down to the surface; therefore, surface winds tend to decrease at night. In contrast, winds above an altitude of a few hundred feet AGL often increase because they are insulated from the frictional influence of the surface by the nocturnal inversion. The result of these processes is that vertical wind shear increases. LLWS encountered during descent through the top of the nocturnal inversion can be particularly strong and unexpected.

After sunrise, heating of the ground and the subsequent mixing of the air by convection destroys the nocturnal inversion. The connection between surface friction and the flow aloft is reestablished and the vertical shear weakens.

Over regions of snow and ice, surface-based inversions are particularly strong and tend to persist day and night. In any case of a surface-based

inversion, caution is advised during the landing and takeoff phases, especially when winds above the inversion are strong.

ELEVATED STABLE LAYERS

In addition to fronts and surface-based nocturnal inversions, wind shears may be found in the free atmosphere, in elevated stable layers. These layers are frequently found over shallow, relatively cool airmasses. Convection from the ground concentrates wind shear at the base of the stable layer.

A pilot can expect a wind shear zone in a surface-based temperature inversion whenever the wind speed at 2,000 to 4,000 feet above the surface is at least 25 knots.

Several years ago, departing aircraft from a busy California coastal airport were instructed to make a sharp turn soon after takeoff as part of a noise abatement program. During the warmer months of the year, that area is usually under the influence of an elevated inversion. The base of the inversion is typically located between a few hundred feet and 1,500 feet MSL. Winds below the inversion base are northwesterly, while above the base, they shift to southwesterly. No accidents occurred during the duration of the program, but occasionally, while executing the maneuver, the stall warning would sound in the cockpit of heavy, slow-moving aircraft, indicating a significant loss of airspeed due to wind shear near the base of the inversion.

After a cold airmass moves across a mountainous area, cold air may remain trapped in the valleys as warmer air moves in aloft. Under these conditions, an elevated stable layer is typically found just below the mountain peaks. If strong winds are present above the mountains, there are large vertical wind shears in the stable layer; that is, between the weak, cold airflow in the valleys and warmer air flowing across the mountains. (Figure 11-11)

> When a climb or descent through a stable layer is being performed, the pilot should be alert for a sudden change in airspeed.

JET STREAMS

Certain patterns of upper level, short wave troughs and ridges produce significant wind shear. The strongest shears are usually associated with sharply curved contours on constant pressure surfaces and/or strong winds. Stable layers near jet streams and within a few thousand feet of the tropopause have the highest probabilities of strong shears. Occasionally, the shear is strong enough to cause large airspeed fluctuations, especially during climb or descent. Since these sheared layers are also prime for clear air turbulence, this topic will be discussed in greater detail in the next chapter.

Figure 11-11. Vertical wind shear is often found in an elevated stable layer that caps cold air trapped in a valley.

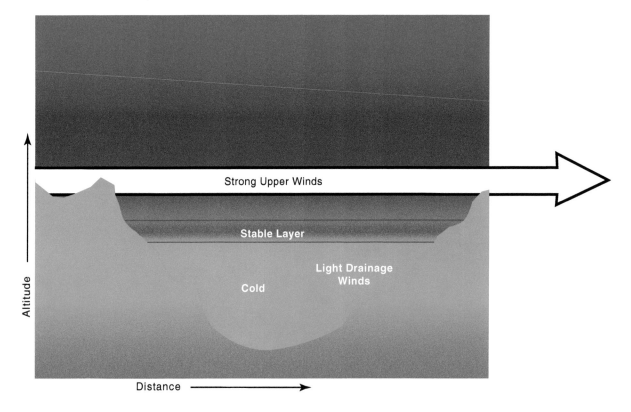

Strong Upper Winds

Stable Layer

Light Drainage Winds

Cold

Altitude

Distance

SUMMARY

Wind shear is one of the most serious low-level flight hazards in the atmosphere. Significant wind shear not only occurs with microbursts, but also with fronts and nocturnal inversions. Wind shear is also found in elevated stable layers in the free atmosphere, especially capping cold air masses and in the vicinity of jet streams and the tropopause. Failure to be aware of all causes and weather conditions that produce wind shear can lead to catastrophic results. An encounter with LLWS, in particular, is unforgiving because of the proximity of your aircraft to the ground. You now have some useful conceptual models and basic rules of thumb to help you recognize and, where possible, avoid potential wind shear conditions. In the next chapter, you will become aware of a number of situations where wind shear and turbulence are present at the same time in the same location.

KEY TERMS

Airmass Wind Shear
Downburst
Elevated Stable Layer
Frontal Wind Shear
Horizontal Wind Shear
Low-Level Wind Shear (LLWS)
Low-Level Wind Shear Alert System (LLWAS)

Microburst
Nocturnal Inversion
Terminal Doppler Weather Radar (TDWR)
Vertical Wind Shear
Vortex Ring
Wind Shear

REVIEW QUESTIONS

1. List five weather situations which favor the development of wind shear.

2. Where is the critical location for wind shear relative to an approaching warm front?

3. Assume that an aircraft is established on a set glide slope and encounters a wind shear where a headwind switches to a tailwind. What will happen to TAS, aircraft pitch, and altitude relative to the glide slope?

4. What is the difference between a downdraft, a downburst, and a microburst?

5. If the surface wind is calm and the wind at 2,000 feet AGL is 30 knots, what is the vertical wind shear in knots per 100 feet? What is the severity of the shear? Use figure 11-2.

6. If the outflow in a microburst is symmetrical and the outflow speed on one side is 10 knots, what will be the maximum airspeed change (indicate loss or gain) due to the wind shear from one side of the microburst to the other?

DISCOVERY QUESTIONS

7. The wind at 200 feet AGL is 330° at 15 knots. The surface wind is 240° at 15 knots.

   1. What is the wind speed difference over the 200-foot layer?

   2. What is the total wind shear (magnitude only) between the surface and 200 feet AGL?

   3. What is the severity of the LLWS?

8. You are taxiing out in preparation for takeoff from an uncontrolled airstrip. An isolated rain shower can be seen over the opposite end of the runway. There is no thunder or lightning.

   1. Should you take off?

   2. Why?

   3. If you elect not to take off, about how long will you have to wait until you can go? Explain.

9. Decode the following PIREPs. (See page 11-10.)

   A. UA/OV TOL/TM 2200/FL 240/TP UNKN/ TB MDT CAT 180-240.

   B. UA /OV DNV/TM 0030/FL 070/TP C206/ SK SCT 030 CA/TA 6C/TB LIGHT CHOP /RM LTGIC DSNT S-W

   C. UA /OV VNY-HEC/TM 1722/FL110/ TP P23A/SK SKC/WX FV99/TA 02/WV 25530KT/RM SMOOTH DURC-PPSN=

   D. UA /OV MOD/TM 1720/FL250/TP B737/ TB LGT-MOD CHOP/RM CHOP 250-190 NUMEROUS RPTS=

10. The critical period for a low-level wind shear hazard is longer for a warm front than for a cold front. Why? There are two reasons. A sketch will help.

11. Perform the following experiment to simulate the structure and behavior of a downburst. You need an eye-dropper of whole milk and a tall glass of water. Be sure the water is not moving. Place the end of the eye-dropper close to the surface of the water and release a single drop. Make a sketch and describe the results.

    1. What will happen if you use skim milk?

    2. What does this say about the intensity of downbursts?

12. List three causes of non-convective LLWS.

13. At just about sunrise, a pilot is descending to land on an island. The airstrip is on the north shore of the island, between the ocean and a range of volcanic peaks. The prevailing winds are easterlies. On final approach from the west, strong LLWS is encountered at 100 feet. Explain why this happened and provide appropriate sketches.

CHAPTER 12
Turbulence

Introduction

A characteristic of most naturally occurring fluids is that they contain some degree of turbulence. This means that you can usually find some part of the fluid where the velocities are fluctuating in a chaotic manner. The atmosphere is one of those fluids. The velocity fluctuations found within the atmosphere are often weak and barely noticeable in flight. Occasionally, however, atmospheric turbulence is so strong that passengers and crew are injured and the aircraft is damaged or destroyed.

The purpose of this chapter is to provide information that will help you avoid or at least minimize the effects of turbulence on your flight. When you complete this chapter, you will understand the basic types of turbulence and their causes, and you will know the large-scale conditions under which turbulence occurs. Also, you will have learned some rules of thumb that will help you to anticipate and deal with the turbulence problem.

Section A

TURBULENCE DEFINED

Based on descriptions from pilots, crew, and passengers, aviation turbulence is best defined simply as "bumpiness in flight." It is important to notice that this definition is based on the response of the aircraft rather than the state of the atmosphere. This means that the occurrence of aviation turbulence can be the result of not only disorganized turbulent motions, but also organized small-scale circulations. In addition, the magnitude of the bumpiness in flight depends on aircraft design and pilot reactions. For convenience, we will use the term turbulence for "aviation turbulence" except where the meaning is ambiguous.

AIRCRAFT AND PILOT RESPONSE

Since the identification of turbulence depends on its effects on the aircraft and pilot, we will begin our discussion by examining the nature of those effects. This will help you understand why certain atmospheric circulations are more closely associated with turbulence than others.

If the sizes of the atmospheric circulations (eddies) through which an aircraft is flying are large enough, the pilot has time to climb, descend, or divert in order to avoid any adverse effects. On the other hand, if the eddies are sufficiently small, the aircraft will pass through them before they can have any significant influence. The circulations that cause turbulence fall between these two size ranges. For most aircraft flying today, the horizontal dimensions (or scales) of turbulence-producing eddies are 50 feet to 8,000 feet. If turbulent eddies were circular or spherical (oversimplifications), these dimensions would correspond to the eddy diameters.

Atmospheric motions produced by turbulent eddies are often referred to as turbulent gusts. In general, vertical gusts are more likely to have a larger impact on flight than horizontal gusts, because they change the angle of attack and lift. Accelerations caused by strong vertical gusts can also cause pressure altimeter errors. Additionally, during takeoff and landing, horizontal gusts, such

as those produced by thunderstorms, lee waves, and rotors, may have serious impacts on aircraft control during those critical phases of flight.

Turbulence may affect the pilot in a number of ways. Turbulence of any intensity is, at best, uncomfortable. A pilot exposed to turbulence for long periods of time will experience greater fatigue. When aircraft shaking is large and rapid (4-5 cycles per second), the pilot cannot read the instruments. If the frequency of the turbulence is near one cycle per four seconds, air sickness may result. All of these effects, together with experience and ability, affect the pilot's response to the turbulence. If the pilot (or autopilot) overreacts, control inputs may actually add to the intensity of bumpiness. The latter actions are known as maneuvering.

TURBULENCE MEASURES

How is turbulence characterized? More practically, if you fly through a turbulent area, what do you report? By far, the most important property of turbulence is its intensity. The most common turbulence reporting criteria are shown in figure 12-1. Turbulence intensity varies from light to extreme, and is related to aircraft and crew reaction and to the movement of unsecured objects about the cabin.

The turbulence scale in figure 12-1 has been used for many years. The criteria are highly subjective and are dependent on aircraft type, airspeed, and pilot experience. PIREPs of turbulence should be cautiously interpreted.

Quantitative indications of turbulence intensity can be determined from the on-board measurements of g-load, airspeed fluctuations, and rate-of-climb. G-load (or gust load) is the force that arises because of the influence of gravity. Normal gravity corresponds to a g-load of 1.0g. A change in g-load above or below the normal value is a rough measure of the intensity of the turbulence. For example, if an aircraft experiences a total g-load of +1.5g, it means that associated turbulence (or maneuvering) caused an excess load of +0.5g.

Airspeed fluctuations refer to the largest positive and negative airspeed deviations from the

TURBULENCE REPORTING CRITERIA TABLE

Intensity	Aircraft Reaction	Reaction Inside Aircraft
Light 	Turbulence that momentarily causes slight, erratic changes in altitude and/or attitude (pitch, roll, yaw). Report as **Light Turbulence;** or Turbulence that causes slight, rapid and somewhat rhythmic bumpiness without appreciable changes in altitude or attitude. Report as **Light Chop.**	Occupants may feel a slight strain against belts or shoulder straps. Unsecured objects may be displaced slightly. Food service may be conducted and little or no difficulty is encountered in walking.
Moderate 	Turbulence that is similar to Light Turbulence but of greater intensity. Changes in altitude and/or attitude occur but the aircraft remains in positive control at all times. It usually causes variations in indicated airspeed. Report as **Moderate Turbulence;** or Turbulence that is similar to Light Chop but of greater intensity. It causes rapid bumps or jolts without appreciable changes in aircraft or attitude. Report as **Moderate Chop.**	Occupants feel definite strains against seat belts or shoulder straps. Unsecured objects are dislodged. Food service and walking are difficult.
Severe 	Turbulence that causes large, abrupt changes in altitude and/or attitude. It usually causes large variations in indicated airspeed. Aircraft may be momentarily out of control. Report as **Severe Turbulence**.	Occupants are forced violently against seat belts or shoulder straps. Unsecured objects are tossed about. Food service and walking are impossible.
Extreme	Turbulence in which the aircraft is violently tossed about and is practically impossible to control. It may cause structural damage. Report as **Extreme Turbulence**.	

Turbulence reports should include location, altitude, or range of altitudes, and aircraft type, and, when reported, whether in clouds or clear air. The pilot determines the degree of turbulence, intensity, and duration (occasional, intermittent, and continuous). The report should be obtained and disseminated, when possible, in conformance with the U.S. Standard Turbulence Criteria as shown above.

High-level turbulence (normally above 15,000 feet AGL) that is not associated with clouds, including thunderstorms, shall be reported as Clear Air Turbulence (CAT).
Source: AC 00-45

Figure 12-1. Turbulence reporting criteria. Standard turbulence symbols used on aviation weather charts are shown on the left side of the figure.

average during a turbulent event. For example, if your average airspeed is 140 knots with variations between 130 and 150 knots, you are experiencing fluctuations of ± 10 knots.

Rate of climb simply refers to the largest positive or negative values during horizontal flight through a turbulent region. Figure 12-2 relates various categories of these variables to the turbulence reporting criteria.

The indicated rate of climb induced by a turbulent gust can only be used as a very rough estimate of the vertical gust speed, because it includes both the effect of the vertical gust and the motion of the aircraft. "Derived gust velocity" is a theoretical estimate of the vertical gust required to produce a given incremental change in gust load.

Turbulence reporting suffers from several problems that affect the pilot's ability to anticipate turbulence and the forecaster's ability to predict it. A major difficulty is the lack of frequent reports, including those of "no turbulence." This has been overcome to some extent by the use of automated observing and reporting systems such as the Aircraft Meteorological Data Relay (AMDAR), common aboard commercial airliners worldwide.

But there are other problems. Turbulence-reporting criteria shown in figures 12-1 and 12-2 are subjective. They depend on pilot experience, control inputs during the turbulence encounter, and on aircraft type. For example, if the pilot of a Cessna reports "severe" turbulence according to Figures 12-1 or 12-2, a B-777 pilot would have no quantitative method to judge how that turbulence relates to the larger aircraft.

The subjectivity of turbulence (figure 12-2) has been addressed with the development of a system to measure the rate of decay of turbulent energy, that is, the Eddy Dissipation Rate (EDR). EDR has a simple interpretation ... if the atmospheric turbulence is large, EDR is large, and vise versa. EDR also has several advantages, the most important of which is that EDR is aircraft-independent. An EDR measurement for given turbulence conditions gives the same number whether measured by a small or large aircraft. That number might translate to "severe" turbulence for the small aircraft but only "light" turbulence for the large one. If you know your aircraft, you will know your turbulence limits as prescribed by EDR.

Because EDR values are automatically measured (pilot independent) and transmitted at regular intervals, many more turbulence and no-turbulence reports are available to be integrated into aviation forecasts. By 2012, EDR was regularly measured and reported by a few hundred foreign and domestic commercial airliners. Ground-based weather radars can also measure EDR distributions in the vicinity of thunderstorms to give even more coverage.

> Until actually flying in an area of reported turbulence, the severity of the turbulence should be interpreted as being at or above the reported values. Never downgrade reported severities.

	Airspeed Fluctuation (kts)	Change in G-load (g)	Vertical Gust (f.p.m.)
Light	5 – 14.9	0.20 – 0.49	300 – 1199
Moderate	15 – 24.9	0.50 – 0.99	1200 – 2099
Severe	≥25	1.0 – 1.99	2100 – 2999
Extreme	—	≥2.00	≥3000

Figure 12-2. Quantitative measures of turbulence intensity. Values may be positive or negative. "Vertical Gust" values are derived gust velocities.

> A study of nearly 4,000 VMC general aviation accidents by the Aircraft Owners and Pilots Association (AOPA) found that most of the accidents were due to loss of control during taxiing, takeoff, and landing in adverse wind conditions.

Section B
TURBULENCE CAUSES AND TYPES

Aviation turbulence can be divided into four categories, depending on where the turbulence occurs, what larger scale atmospheric circulations are present, and what is producing the turbulence. The categories are low-level turbulence (LLT), turbulence in and near thunderstorms (TNT), clear-air turbulence (CAT), and mountain wave turbulence (MWT).

LOW-LEVEL TURBULENCE (LLT)

For operational purposes, "low-level turbulence" is often defined simply as turbulence below 15,000 feet MSL. We will be a little more specific in order to concentrate on turbulence causes. Low-level turbulence (LLT) is defined here as that turbulence which occurs primarily within the atmospheric boundary layer. Recall from Chapters 4 and 9 that the boundary layer is the lowest few thousand feet of the atmosphere; that is, where surface heating and frictional influences are significant. LLT includes mechanical turbulence, thermal turbulence, and turbulence in fronts. Although wake turbulence may be encountered at any altitude, it is particularly hazardous near the ground, so it is also considered with LLT. For discussion purposes, turbulence which occurs near the ground in thunderstorms and in other moist convection is included with turbulence in and near thunderstorms. Turbulence which occurs near the ground in mountain wave conditions is included under mountain wave turbulence.

MECHANICAL TURBULENCE

Over flat ground, significant LLT occurs when surface winds are strong. This is called mechanical turbulence. It occurs because friction slows the wind in the lowest layers causing the air to turn over in turbulent eddies. (Figure 12-3) The turbulent eddies cause fluctuations (gusts) in winds and vertical velocities.

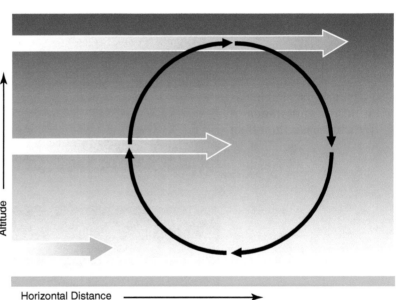

Figure 12-3. The broad arrows indicate sustained winds increasing with altitude. The circulation represents a turbulent eddy caused by surface friction. The observed wind field is a combination of the sustained wind and the eddy. Turbulent eddies mix stronger winds downward and weaker winds upward causing gustiness (LLT) and large fluctuations in wind shears. This effect increases with wind speed.

Maule M-5 235C. No injuries. The pilot reported that he experienced some wind shear on final approach to landing. Shortly after touchdown, a gust of wind caught the airplane. The pilot lost control and the aircraft ground looped. NTSB determined that the probable cause was the pilot's failure to maintain adequate control of the aircraft after touchdown.

Turbulent eddies which are swept along by the sustained wind also cause rapid fluctuations in wind shear near the ground. Fluctuating shears and turbulence contribute to rough approaches and takeoffs.

As the winds strengthen, the mechanical turbulence extends to greater heights above the ground. When surface wind gusts are 50 knots or greater, significant turbulence due to surface effects can reach altitudes in excess of 3,000 feet AGL.

The presence of obstructions such as buildings and stands of trees increase the effect of surface roughness and strengthen LLT and wind shear. (Figure 12-4) Typically, a trail of turbulent eddies is produced downwind of an obstacle with a sheared layer between the ground-based turbulent region and smooth flow aloft. This is generally referred to as a turbulent wake. In strong winds, hangars and other large buildings near a runway create a potential for control problems during takeoff or landing.

Hills can produce some very strong turbulent wakes with strong winds. In comparison with turbulence over flat ground, the turbulent eddies downwind of hills are larger because the obstructions

When the sustained surface wind exceeds 20 knots, airspeed fluctuations of 10 to 20 knots will occur on approach. When the surface wind over flat land exceeds 30 knots, mechanically produced LLT will be moderate or greater.

The type of approach and landing recommended during gusty wind conditions is a power-on approach and power-on landing.

Aeronca 7AC. No injuries. Substantial damage. Encountered wind shear just above a stand of trees after takeoff. Twenty-knot crosswind with gusts to 40 knots. Crashed in trees.

CE 172. No Injuries. While landing in a crosswind, a gust coming between hangars caused the airplane to veer off the runway and nose over.

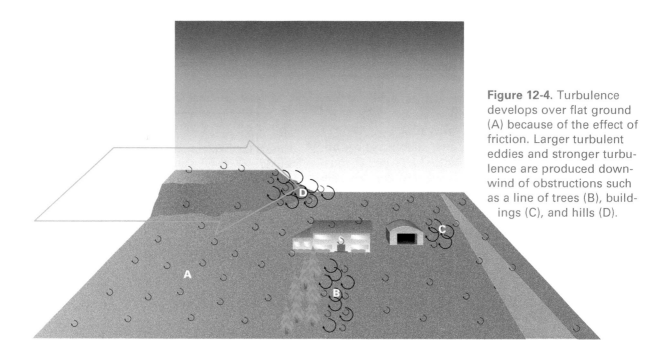

Figure 12-4. Turbulence develops over flat ground (A) because of the effect of friction. Larger turbulent eddies and stronger turbulence are produced downwind of obstructions such as a line of trees (B), buildings (C), and hills (D).

that cause them (the hills) are larger. The resulting wind shears and turbulence are also stronger. The nature of the turbulence also depends on the shape of the topography. Steep hillsides encourage the flow to separate from the surface, producing eddies, LLT, and sheared regions.

When taking off from a valley, climb above the level of the highest peaks before leaving the valley. Maintain lateral clearance from the mountains, sufficient to recover if caught in a downdraft.

PA-18. No Injuries. Substantial damage. Aircraft took off from a gravel strip in a river bed. Encountered turbulence from bluffs at approximately 50 feet AGL and crashed. Wind 20 knots and gusty.

Pilots must take care when flying in a valley with strong crosswinds aloft. There are often distinct updrafts and downdrafts on either side of the valley, as shown in figure 12-5. In a very narrow canyon, the nature of the turbulence becomes less predictable. With strong winds, turbulent gusts can be treacherous because of their strength and the limited space for maneuvering. Additionally, airflow within a narrow canyon is often turbulent at locations near the bottom, where there are sharp bends, and where side canyons intersect.

As an airstream crosses a ridge line, wind speeds and wind shears are frequently greater near the peaks than at the same altitude over the nearby flatlands because the depth of the airstream is reduced as it flows over the peaks. In order to move the same mass of air through the shallower layer, the wind speed must increase.

A related effect occurs on the edges of a narrow canyon when "along-canyon" winds are funneled through a narrow gap. When the winds are strong, significant horizontal wind shears and LLT are created, especially near the canyon

PA-28. Three fatalities. Aircraft destroyed when pilot encountered high velocity downdrafts during low altitude flight in a mountain pass. Wind speed 40 knots.

PARTENAVIA P.68. 3 Minor Injuries. Descending to about 200 feet AGL in a canyon, the airplane encountered a tailwind while in a turn, resulting in a rapid loss of airspeed and a further descent. Although the pilot leveled the aircraft and increased power, the aircraft was too slow and low to leave the canyon. It stalled and impacted the terrain.

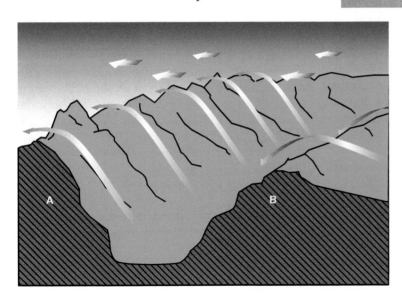

Figure 12-5. Winds across a gentle sloping valley produce updrafts on side A and downdrafts on side B. Whether or not the influence of the upper winds reach the valley floor depends on the valley width, depth, and the atmospheric stability.

walls. Strong winds due to this funneling effect may extend well downstream of the pass. (Figure 12-6)

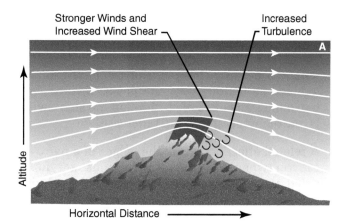

Figure 12-6. Cross section through a ridge line (A). Thin arrows indicate air flow. Winds and wind shears are stronger immediately over the mountaintop (shaded). Winds, turbulence, and wind shears are stronger through and downwind of the mountain pass (B).

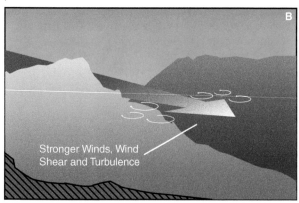

For larger hills and mountains, stable airflow across peaks and ridges creates lee waves in addition to the effects described in the preceding paragraphs. As you will see in a later section, the lee wave system is very effective in producing widespread turbulence in certain layers of the atmosphere.

CESSNA 170B. One Fatality and two serious injuries. Flying into a mountainous area, the pilot initiated a climb to clear elevated terrain along the intended flight path. However, increasing tailwinds reduced the effective altitude gain such that it was insufficient to overfly the mountain range ahead. Additionally, strong downdrafts directed along the mountain slopes were associated with a loss of altitude and speed. Flying too low and too slow to effect a reversal of course, the pilot elected to land in a meadow.

When there is a strong pressure gradient across a mountain range, flight through a mountain pass at low levels may expose the aircraft to strong winds (blowing toward the lowest pressure), strong shears, and turbulence.

The intensity of LLT increases with wind speed and steepness of the terrain. Over rough terrain, moderate or greater LLT is likely when sustained winds exceed 25 knots, and severe turbulence can be expected with winds of 40 knots or more.

THERMAL TURBULENCE

Thermal turbulence is LLT produced by dry convection in the boundary layer. As described in Chapter 5, it is typically a daytime phenomenon that occurs over land under fair weather conditions. Solar radiation heats the ground generating convection at the bottom of the boundary layer. During the morning and early afternoon, the convection intensifies and deepens. It reaches a maximum in the afternoon, then gradually dies out as the earth's surface cools. In contrast, where cool air moves over a warm surface, thermal turbulence can occur any time, day or night.

PIPER PA18-150. No injuries. Departing from an unimproved airstrip, as the airplane rotated for lift-off at 35-40 MPH, it was struck by a dust devil. Despite efforts to control the airplane, it rotated 90 degrees to the right and impacted the terrain sustaining major damage.

As indicated by the name, thermals are the basic elements of thermal turbulence. You were introduced to them in Chapter 9 as the main components of dry convection. They are an important source of LLT. Thermals initially develop in a seemingly random horizontal pattern dictated by the uneven heating of the terrain and the nature of the surface. Near the ground, the bubbles of warm air are somewhat chaotic, but soon take on distinct patterns. Thermal plumes, narrow curtains of rising air, and dust devils are common close to the ground, especially when the ground is very hot. All of these are LLT sources.

As thermals move away from the ground, they grow in size, and become more organized. The horizontal dimension of a thermal is proportional to its height above the ground. For example, at 500 feet AGL, it is about 500 feet across. Thermals may be arranged in patterns depending on winds and terrain. Over flat terrain, in light winds, thermals are often arranged in a "honeycomb" pattern. With stronger winds (about 20 knots) they frequently form lines along the wind. With very strong winds, thermal patterns are chaotic. In the latter case, the combination of mechanical and thermal effects usually produces strong LLT.

As you might suspect from our previous discussion of slope circulations, thermal turbulence is common over higher terrain. Thermals tend to be narrower and stronger over sun-facing slopes and LLT is stronger in these areas.

Glider pilots have long taken advantage of the upward motions in thermals to gain altitude and fly long cross-country distances. However, thermal sources of lift for slow-moving gliders are often sources of LLT for faster, powered aircraft. An aircraft flying through dry convection is commonly exposed to turbulence intensities ranging from light to moderate. Typical upward gusts in thermals range from 200 to 400 f.p.m., with

The characteristics of an unstable cold airmass moving over a warm surface are cumuliform clouds, turbulence, and good visibility. A stable airmass is most likely to have smooth air.

extremes of 1,000 to 2,000 f.p.m. reported. Flight through the boundary layer at midday in the summer will expose you and your aircraft to frequent (and uncomfortable) LLT due to thermals.

Relief from the continuous bumpiness of fair weather thermals can often be found by climbing into and above what is called the capping stable layer. This is a layer caused by a very slowly sinking motion aloft associated with a macroscale high pressure region. The capping stable layer is at the top of the dry convection. As your aircraft climbs through it, there is a sudden cessation of turbulence. The height of the capping stable layer is usually a few thousand feet above the ground. However, over desert terrain in the summer, the top of the dry convection can exceed 10,000 feet AGL.

The base of the capping stable layer is often visible as the distinct layer of haze and dust carried upward by thermals from below. If cumulus clouds are present, the haze layer is at the base of the clouds with the cloud tops extending into the lower part of the capping stable layer. Care must be exercised when descending into the convective layer from the smooth air above; the onset of turbulence is rapid and may cause problems for the unsuspecting pilot. (Figure 12-7)

It is not unusual for low-level flight over warm surfaces to be marked by extensive thermal turbulence. Here are two PIREPs from summer daytime flights over the deserts of southern California.

WJF UA/OV PMD/ 330020/TM 2118/FL 116/TP C172/SK CLR/TB LGT-MDT/RM UDDF 500-1000 FPM (Note: local standard time is 1318)

DAG UA/OV PMD-DAG/TM 2351/FL 095/TP MO20/ SK CLR/TB CONT LGT-MDT/RM STG UDDF (Note: local standard time is 1551)

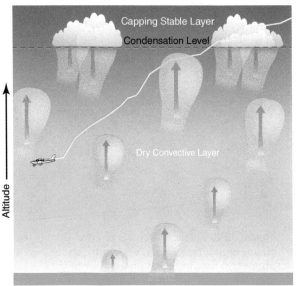

Figure 12-7. An aircraft descending from the capping stable layer through a layer of CU into the dry convective layer below cloud base will encounter persistent LLT due to dry thermals in the convective boundary layer. Your only visual cue to the existence of LLT may be a CU layer and/or a haze or dust layer aloft. The thermals may be tilted or otherwise distorted due to vertical wind shear.

Fair-weather LLT produced by thermals may be modified or interrupted by frontal passages, extensive cloud cover, and wet or snow-covered surfaces. When instability is very large, moist convection and thunderstorms are often the result. The boundary layer is greatly modified under these conditions and LLT is primarily the result of thunderstorm activity.

TURBULENCE IN FRONTS

Fronts may produce not only wind shear but also moderate or greater turbulence. In the boundary layer, fast-moving cold fronts are usually steeper than at higher levels, and updrafts may reach 1,000 f.p.m. in a narrow zone just ahead of the front. When these conditions are combined with convection and strong winds, LLT and wind shear can produce serious flight hazards over a broad area as illustrated in figure 12-8.

Mesoscale frontal zones such as the sea breeze and the thunderstorm gust front cause LLT in the same manner as the macroscale fronts previously described. The intensity of the turbulence also depends on the strength and speed of those fronts and any associated convection. The intense turbulence of the gust front is discussed in more detail under the topic of turbulence in and near thunderstorms.

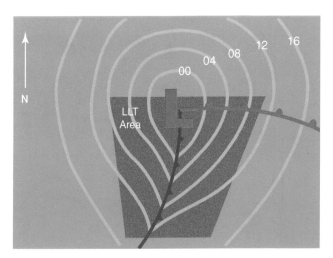

Figure 12-8. Surface analysis chart showing the primary LLT area associated with a typical wave cyclone (shaded). The area extends from about 200 miles behind the cold front (in the cold, northwesterly flow) through the region of strong southerly winds ahead of the front.

Generally, over flat ground, any front moving at a speed of 30 knots or more will generate moderate or greater LLT. However, over rough terrain, all fronts should be assumed to have moderate or greater turbulence, regardless of their speed.

WAKE TURBULENCE

As most pilots know, turbulent wakes are generated by aircraft in flight. This can be considered a form of mechanical turbulence. However, rather than the air blowing past an obstacle, the obstacle (in this case, the wing of the aircraft) is moving through the air. The result is still the same, a turbulent wake is produced behind the obstacle. The term wake turbulence is applied to the vortices that form behind an aircraft that is generating lift. (Figure 12-9)

In contrast to other types of mechanical turbulence, wake turbulence is somewhat more predictable since all aircraft generate lift and lift is a requirement to generate wake turbulence. Because most aircraft have the same basic shape, the vortices they produce tend to be similar; however, they vary widely in intensity and behavior, based on atmospheric conditions, aircraft size, wing configuration, weight, and speed. Heavy, clean, and slow aircraft produce larger vortices and stronger turbulence than small aircraft. Wake turbulence is caused by high-pressure air under the wing flowing toward lower pressure above the wing near the wingtip or at a flap edge. As shown in figure 12-9, this process creates two counter-rotating vortices that trail behind aircraft. Vortex generation begins near liftoff and ends at touchdown.

When fully formed at a distance of two to four wingspans behind the aircraft, the vortices are typically 25 to 50 feet in diameter; their actual size depends on the wing dimensions. They tend to remain about three-quarters of the wing span apart, centered inboard of the wingtips. Because of their interaction, the two vortices typically descend a few hundred feet below the generating aircraft within about two minutes and remain at that level until they dissipate. Upward motions caused by convection or mountain waves can distort wake vortices, actually causing them to rise. In general, any smaller scale atmospheric turbulence will hasten their dissipation.

When the generating aircraft is near the ground, vortices will descend and then move outward from the aircraft at one to five knots in calm wind conditions. If the wind is blowing, the net movement of the eddies will be the sum of the wind velocity and the "no-wind" motion of each vortex. Thus, a light crosswind could cause one vortex to remain nearly stationary over the runway while the other moves away at a few knots. Some wake vortices appear to "bounce;" that is, they actually begin to rise as they near the ground.

The flight hazard of wake turbulence is obvious, regardless of the phase of flight. A small aircraft following a large aircraft too closely may encounter vertical and horizontal gusts which cannot be compensated for by any flight maneuver. This is especially true when a trailing aircraft enters directly into a vortex. Maximum gusts in the wake of the aircraft occur in the cores of the vortices where gusts of 18,000 f.p.m. have been measured.

Figure 12-9. Wake vortices are created when lift is generated by the wing of an aircraft. A similar pattern is also created by the main rotor of a helicopter when it is producing lift.

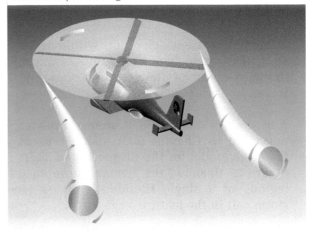

Piper Navajo. Three fatalities. Navajo pilot turned on final approach 250 feet below the glide path of a B737 that had passed that point 52 seconds previously. Shortly after the B737 landed, the Navajo was seen to roll from side to side, pitch up, roll inverted to the left and fly into the ground nose first.

The greatest vortex strength occurs when the generating aircraft is heavy, clean, and slow. Wake turbulence is near maximum behind a jet transport just after takeoff because of the high angle of attack and high gross weight.

The wind condition that prolongs the hazards of wake turbulence on a landing runway for the longest period of time is a light quartering tailwind.

The generation of wake turbulence is not restricted to "heavy" aircraft. Helicopters and light aircraft can cause significant wake turbulence. For example, there are cases where an aircraft involved in aerial spraying and flying near stall speed has crashed after intersecting its own wake from a previous spraying run. Specific flight procedures have been developed to avoid the effects of wake turbulence. The details of these have been published widely in FAA circulars, the *Aeronautical Information Manual (AIM)*, and other training media.

When landing behind a large aircraft, the pilot should avoid wake turbulence by staying above the large aircraft's final approach path and landing beyond the large aircraft's touchdown point. When departing behind a heavy aircraft, the pilot should avoid wake turbulence by maneuvering the aircraft above and upwind from the heavy aircraft.

TURBULENCE IN AND NEAR THUNDERSTORMS (TNT)

Turbulence in and near thunderstorms (TNT) is that turbulence which occurs within developing convective clouds and thunderstorms, in the vicinity of thunderstorm tops and wakes, in downbursts, and in gust fronts.

Helicopter wake vortices are larger, more buoyant, and longer lasting than those of a fixed wing aircraft of the same size and weight.

The best advice that can be given about flight in or near thunderstorms is "Don't!" But if you inadvertently fly into a thunderstorm, set your power for turbulence penetration speed and maintain a wings-level flight attitude.

A model of a developing thunderstorm was presented in Chapter 9. It also serves as the basic model for the discussion of TNT. Figure 12-10 shows the primary turbulence regions of a single thunderstorm cell in the mature stage.

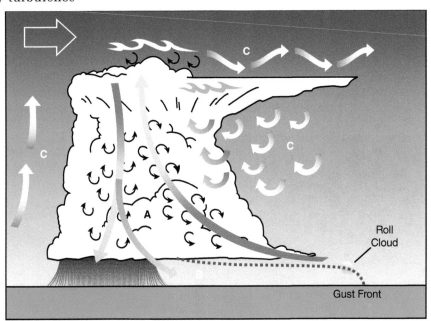

Figure 12-10. Turbulence in and near thunderstorms (TNT) occurs in three distinct turbulence regions: (A) within thunderstorms, (B) below thunderstorms, and (C) around and over thunderstorms. The dashed line below the cell indicates the position of the gust front.

Roll Cloud

Gust Front

TURBULENCE WITHIN THUNDERSTORMS

Turbulence within the thunderstorm cloud boundaries is caused by the strong updrafts and downdrafts. The most frequent and, typically, the most intense TNT is found within the cloud (although turbulence below the cloud may have more disastrous consequences). Furthermore, it is made worse because it occurs in instrument meteorological conditions with heavy rain, lightning, and possible hail and icing. The combination of these hazards increases the chances of disorientation and loss of control, major factors in many fatal general aviation accidents in thunderstorms.

Turbulence inside thunderstorms occurs on at least two different scales. The largest eddies have sizes comparable to the major updrafts and downdrafts. Small scale gusts are produced by strong shears on the edges of the vertical drafts.

In the cumulus stage of thunderstorm development, the turbulence inside the storm is due to the updraft, which usually occupies less than half the cloud volume. Updraft speeds increase from the base of the cloud to a maximum near the top of the cloud.

In the mature stage, updraft speeds accelerate through the depth of the storm, reaching a maximum in the upper part of the cell at the equilibrium level. This is often (but not always) near the tropopause. Because of the rapid rate of rise of the cloud tops, pilots flying just below the tropopause are occasionally surprised with a strong burst of turbulence as the top of a growing cumulonimbus cloud reaches flight level.

Updraft speeds in the mature stage of the airmass thunderstorm may vary from 400 to 1,200 f.p.m. near the base of the thunderstorm to 4,000 f.p.m. near the equilibrium level. Extreme vertical gusts of more than 10,000 f.p.m. have been reported in the strongest thunderstorms.

Although updrafts weaken above the equilibrium level, in intense thunderstorms, they may penetrate several thousand feet into the stratosphere before they are overcome by the stability. The strongest updrafts can often be identified by cumuliform bulges that extend above the otherwise smooth anvil top of the thunderstorm. These overshooting tops are useful visual evidence of a very strong thunderstorm and turbulence.

As expected, thunderstorm downdrafts are strongest in the areas of precipitation. Downdrafts typically reach their greatest intensities below the base of the thunderstorm. Extremes of near 5,000 f.p.m. have been reported.

Turbulence intensity increases with the development of the thunderstorm; that is, light and moderate intensities in the cumulus stage and moderate and severe (or worse) in the mature stage. When the thunderstorm cell begins to dissipate, turbulence within the thunderstorm weakens. However, a high degree of caution should be exercised in the visual evaluation of turbulence potential. For example, early in the dissipating stage, turbulence in some locations of the thunderstorm is as intense as it is in the mature stage. Late in the dissipating stage, isolated patches of severe turbulence may still be present. Also, in multicell thunderstorms, a nearby, mature cell may be obscured by the clouds of a dissipating cell.

> All thunderstorms should be considered hazardous, but if the thunderstorm top exceeds 35,000 feet MSL, it should be regarded as extremely hazardous.

> Mooney M20J. One fatal injury. The pilot was enroute at 11,500 feet and was receiving traffic advisories from Air Traffic Control (ATC), who advised him of heavy precipitation ahead. The pilot began a descent about 14 miles from his destination. ATC advised him to maintain VMC, which he acknowledged. The pilot reported later that he had encountered rain and turbulence and that he was not in VMC. ATC lost contact with the airplane soon afterwards. Witnesses reported a severe thunderstorm when they saw the airplane descend and crash. The investigation revealed that the airplane had an inflight breakup; wreckage was strewn for a distance of about two miles. There was no evidence of mechanical malfunction.

An estimate of the turbulence level within the region of the storm where precipitation is being produced can be made from the associated radar echo. (Figure 9-7A) Intensity Level 2 (30 dBZ) indicates that there is a significant chance of moderate turbulence and a slight chance of severe turbulence. By Level 3 (40 dBZ), the chances of moderate or greater turbulence are large. When the threshold for level 5 (50 dBZ) is exceeded, there is a high probability of severe and extreme turbulence as well as very strong surface wind gusts.

> Always use the HIGHEST observed echo intensity level or reflectivity value to judge the potential for turbulence in the vicinity of a weather radar echo.

TURBULENCE BELOW THUNDERSTORMS

The downdrafts, downbursts, and microbursts described in the last chapter define the primary turbulent areas below the thunderstorm. These phenomena produce intense turbulence as well as wind shear. Strong winds in the outflow from the downdraft generate mechanical turbulence, which is especially strong along the edge of any microburst and/or gust front. (Figure 12-11)

Of course, extreme turbulence is also to be expected near any funnel clouds, tornadoes, and other tornado-like vortices. The combination of turbulence and wind shear with heavy precipitation, low ceilings, and poor visibilities makes the area below a thunderstorm very dangerous.

TURBULENCE AROUND THUNDERSTORMS

Turbulence "around the thunderstorm" refers to that found outside the main region of convection. This includes turbulence in clear and cloudy air next to the main cumulonimbus cloud and turbulence in and over the anvil cloud.

For the most part, downdrafts in the clear air around airmass thunderstorms are a few hundred feet per minute or less. However, there are occasions when severe turbulence occurs in the clear

> Do not fly within 20 miles of a thunderstorm that is classified as severe or that has an intense radar echo (level 5 or greater).

Figure 12-11. A roll cloud along the leading edge of a thunderstorm gust front approaches an airport. Strong, gusty surface winds, wind shear, and significant turbulence are common in and around the front.

Photo courtesy Shawn Stewart

air. The causes of some of these events are not well understood, and those that are understood are not very well measured. These uncertainties are the primary reasons why you must always maintain a substantial separation between a thunderstorm and your aircraft.

Turbulence is produced outside the thunderstorm when the cell acts as a barrier to the large scale airflow. Multicell and supercell thunderstorms move more slowly than the winds at upper levels. Under these conditions, part of the prevailing airflow is diverted around the thunderstorm, producing a variety of turbulent eddies. This effect is greater with strong thunderstorms and with strong winds aloft.

> Do not fly in the anvil cloud. Your altitude should be 1,000 feet above the cloud for every 10 knots of wind at that level. For example, with a 50 knot wind, you should be 5,000 feet above the top. If this is above the ceiling of your aircraft, go around the thunderstorm.

A turbulent wake occurs under the anvil cloud downwind of the thunderstorm. This is one of the most hazardous regions outside of the thunderstorm and above its base. Sometimes referred to as the "region under the overhang (anvil)," it is well known to experienced pilots as the location of severe turbulence and, possibly, hail.

Near the top of the thunderstorm, several circulations are possible. The cumuliform appearance of the overshooting tops is a warning that this region is a source of significant turbulence due to the convective currents. Additionally, the interaction of strong winds in the stable stratosphere with the updraft can produce vertical shears, turbulent eddies, and atmospheric

> While deviating around a cell along the route at FL350, the aircraft suddenly encountered severe turbulence. The flight was clear of clouds and precipitation. The aircraft rolled approximately 45 degrees right, then 30 degrees left. Minor crew injuries.

gravity waves (similar to lee waves) over and downwind of the thunderstorm top. Flight near thunderstorm tops should be avoided wherever possible.

CLEAR AIR TURBULENCE (CAT)

Clear air turbulence (CAT) is that turbulence which occurs in the free atmosphere away from any visible convective activity. CAT includes high level frontal and jet stream turbulence, typically above 15,000 feet MSL. Its name is derived from early experiences of pilots who encountered significant high-level turbulence in clear skies; however, we now know that the processes that produce CAT can also be present in clouds. Nevertheless, the name remains "CAT."

Because we can't observe CAT very well, we often find it more convenient to describe it in statistical terms. For example, during a given flight anywhere in the atmosphere, an aircraft has about a 6 in 100 (6%) chance of encountering moderate or greater CAT. The chance of severe or greater CAT is less than 1 percent. The chances of encountering CAT are usually higher in regions near the jet stream. A 10% probability of encountering moderate or greater CAT is considered large. Therefore, keep in mind as we discuss "favored" areas and "higher" frequencies for CAT that these are relative terms. On

> Cleared to FL240, the aircraft encountered light turbulence at 21,000 feet. At 23,000 feet, it was like hitting a brick wall. Severe clear air turbulence, power to idle, speed brakes extended, aircraft shaking violently. Unable to see cockpit and instruments. Aircraft stopped climbing at 24,700 feet and was cleared to a lower altitude, FL230, which was then assigned by ATC. First officer had a hard time communicating as the mic was flying around the cockpit on its flex cord. Unable to see or reach the transponder. Aircraft pitched 10 degrees nose down and 20 degrees nose up while rolling 50-70 degrees right and left. No aircraft damage or passenger injuries.

an absolute scale, the chances of moderate or greater CAT are almost always small.

The chance of significant CAT increases rapidly when the vertical wind shear exceeds 5 knots per 1,000 feet.

stable layer are displaced vertically, atmospheric gravity waves develop. These waves can have wavelengths from a few hundred feet to a mile or two. If the vertical shear is strong, it causes the wave crests to overrun the wave troughs, creating a very unstable situation. The air literally "overturns" in the waves, often violently. (Figure 12-12). The result is a layer of CAT. Known as shearing-gravity waves, they are often superimposed on much longer mountain lee waves.

The reason you must be concerned about CAT encounters is that severe and extreme incidents do occur, causing injuries and occasionally damage to aircraft. It is your responsibility and the responsibility of the aviation weather forecaster to minimize significant CAT encounters, whenever possible.

CAT is found near high level stable layers that have vertical wind shear. When air parcels in a

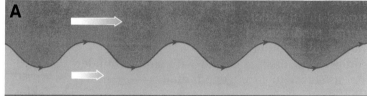

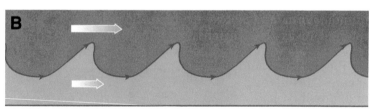

Figure 12-12. Left: Photographs of clouds that show evidence of shearing-gravity wave activity. The "herring bone" pattern of billow clouds in the upper left-hand photograph is a common feature in high cloud layers subjected to vertical shear. Right: Idealized cross sections through shearing-gravity waves at various stages of development. Diagrams A through C can be interpreted as a time sequence showing how wind shear may cause stable air to overturn as it moves along a wavy trajectory (thin lines with arrowheads). Wind velocities are indicated with the directions and lengths of the large arrows. Note that the wind speeds are greater in the wave crests than in the troughs. It typically takes a few minutes for an unstable shearing-gravity wave to go from stage A to stage C. If the atmospheric stability is too strong or, if the vertical shear is too weak, shearing-gravity waves will not develop beyond Stage A. Keep in mind that clouds do not have to be present for shearing-gravity waves and the related turbulence to occur. (Photograph A from NOAA, Photograph B courtesy D. Snyder.)

Jet streams, certain high level stable layers, and tropopauses are regions where strong vertical shears develop. This explains why these regions favor CAT. It also explains why the strength of vertical shear is used as a CAT indicator.

The jet stream, where about 2/3 of CAT occurs, is the focus of our model for CAT. Figure 12-13 is a vertical slice through an idealized jet stream.

Near the jet stream, there are three specific layers that favor the occurrence of CAT. Zone B in Figure 12-13 is the most common CAT layer. This is a high-level frontal zone, also called a jet stream

CAT occurs more frequently within a few thousand feet of the tropopause, over mountains, and in winter.

CAT tends to occur in thin layers, typically less than 2,000 feet deep, a few tens of miles wide and more than 50 miles long. CAT often occurs in sudden bursts as aircraft intersect thin, sloping turbulent layers.

Below the jet core, CAT is most likely in the jet stream frontal zone. On jet stream charts (300 mb, 250 mb, 200 mb), the frontal zone is on the left side of the jet axis, looking downwind.

When a pilot enters an area where significant CAT has been reported, an appropriate action when the first ripple is encountered is to adjust airspeed to that recommended for rough air.

front. Every atmospheric jet stream has a jet stream front with vertical and horizontal wind shears. The activation of other layers of CAT near a jet stream depends on whether or not the jet stream is embedded in a trough aloft (Zones A and B in figure 12-13), or in an upper ridge (Zones B and C in figure 12-13).

CAT forecasting has always been difficult because of the lack of good observations at the microscale where CAT occurs. Usually, the exact locations of CAT cannot be specified unless an aircraft

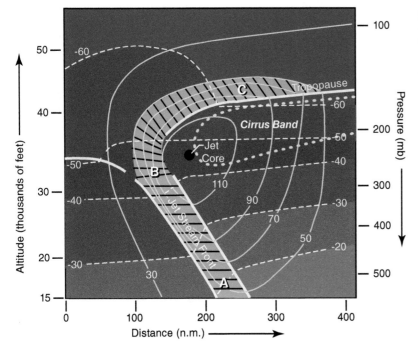

Figure 12-13. Idealized cross section through a jet stream (looking downwind). White lines represent wind speed in knots. Dashed yellow lines are temperatures in °C. Heavy solid lines are tropopauses and boundaries of the jet stream frontal zone in the upper troposphere. The dotted grey line indicates that a broad cirrus band is commonly found just below the tropopause on the right (warmer) side of the jet stream core. Note diagram extends from mid-troposphere into the lower stratosphere. Most likely zones of significant turbulence are hatched. CAT occurs more frequently in zones A and B in the vicinity of an upper trough, and in zones B and C in an upper ridge. Near an upper trough, zone A may extend all the way to the surface as a cold front. Note the slope of the front is greatly exaggerated, and altitudes of various features may be different, depending on latitude and season.

happens to encounter and report the turbulence. In the past, forecasts were made primarily on the basis of PIREPs and known statistical relationships between CAT occurrences and large scale weather patterns. Figure 12-14 shows some common high level patterns which favor CAT outbreaks. Familiarity with these patterns will aid you in anticipating potential CAT problems during flight planning.

The use of only PIREPs and large scale patterns has led to the problems of over-forecasting some turbulence regions and missing others. Although these problems still exist to some extent, forecasts are improving because of better on-board turbulence metrics, automation of PIREP reports from airliners, better use of satellite observations, the development of better forecast models with graphical outputs that are easier to interpret, and better understanding of the physics of CAT.

A sharply curving jet stream is associated with greater turbulence than a straight jet stream.

Significant CAT and wind shear in the vicinity of the jet stream is more likely when the speed at the core exceeds 110 knots.

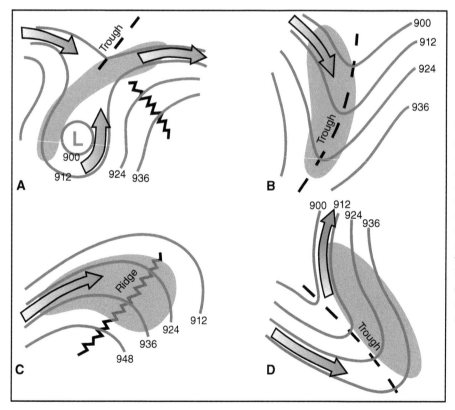

Figure 12-14. Idealized large scale flow patterns at jet stream level that are most frequently associated with CAT (shaded areas). Thin lines are 300mb contours (~FL300) and heavy arrows are approximate jet stream locations. The patterns are (A) cut-off low, (B) sharp trough, (C) ridge, and (D) unstable trough. With pattern D, CAT often occurs in or near thick cirrus clouds since this is a favorable pattern for cyclogenesis.

MOUNTAIN WAVE TURBULENCE (MWT)

The formation of mountain lee waves and a description of their structure was introduced in Chapter 10. Mountain wave turbulence (MWT) is that turbulence produced in connection with mountain lee waves. It is responsible for some of the most violent turbulence that is encountered away from thunderstorms. As illustrated in figure 12-15, wave action occurs throughout the depth of the lee wave system, but the worst turbulence occurs mainly in two well-defined layers: near the tropopause in the lee wave region and throughout the lower turbulent zone.

It is useful to keep in mind that the intensity of MWT (including wave action) depends on the wind speed near the mountain peaks. A simple rule is, the stronger the winds across the mountain at mountaintop level, the better the chances for turbulence. Moderate turbulence should be expected when winds directed across the mountain at mountaintop level are 25 to about 40 knots. Severe turbulence becomes more likely with greater speeds.

> Severe turbulence is likely in mountainous areas when the wind component is perpendicular to the ridgeline and the wind speed near the ridge top exceeds about 40 knots. The locations of the severe turbulence will be in the lower 5,000 feet of the troposphere, below the level of the ridge top, in the rotor circulation, and within 5,000 feet of the tropopause. Severe turbulence also may occur occasionally at the bases of other stable layers within the troposphere. Severe turbulence may extend downwind 50 to 100 miles in the lee of the ridge.

LEE WAVE REGION

Lee waves are more often smooth than turbulent, but if turbulence does occur in the lee wave region, it is most likely to occur within 5,000 feet of the tropopause. This happens because the winds reach maximum speeds near the tropopause, with strong vertical shears above and below that level. Mountain lee wave activity strengthens the shear, promoting the develop-

ment of shorter shearing-gravity waves, especially near stable layers. (Figure 12-12) The conditions for both mountain waves and CAT are more favorable when a jet stream is present over a mountainous area. This helps to explain why high level turbulence is reported more frequently over mountains than elsewhere.

> Smaller scale turbulence in the vicinity of smooth lee waves is often made visible by the sawtooth appearance of shearing-gravity waves on lenticular clouds. Avoid ACSL with ragged edges.

> To avoid mountain wave activity, change your route. If this is not possible, change your altitude away from the most likely layers of turbulence.

> When winds are strong, beware of significant turbulence downwind of isolated peaks.

MWT is usually strongest in the first wave cycle, just downwind of the mountain ridge. When lee waves have high amplitudes and the airflow is usually smooth, PIREPs often describe "...strong wave action..." rather than "...severe turbulence...." What the aircraft actually experiences depends not only on wave amplitude, but also on lee wavelength and aircraft speed.

The impact of lee waves on an aircraft is much different depending on whether the ridge line that generates the waves is approached upwind or downwind. An upwind approach will give you plenty of warning of the lee waves because the wave action typically increases as you fly closer to the ridge. A downwind approach, however, immediately puts the aircraft in the primary cycle. There is little or no warning as the most intense part of the lee wave is encountered first.

Except for the highest mountains, the following procedure is recommended. When approaching a mountain wave area from the lee side during strong winds, start your climb at least

Weak lee waves have updrafts and downdrafts of 300 to 900 f.p.m., while strong lee waves range from 1,800 to 3,600 f.p.m. Extreme vertical drafts of 5,000 to 8,000 f.p.m. have been reported. Caution: Altimeter readings may be inaccurate in strong lee waves.

In potential mountain wave areas, watch your altimeter, especially at night. Vertical motions in lee waves may be strong, resulting in large altitude excursions.

100 n.m. away from the mountains. Climb to an altitude that is at least 3,000 to 5,000 feet above the mountaintops before you cross the ridge. The best procedure is to approach the ridge at a 45° angle to enable a rapid retreat in case turbulence is encountered. If you are unable to make good on the first attempt, and if your aircraft has higher altitude capabilities, you may want to make another attempt at a higher altitude. Sometimes you have to choose between turning back and diverting to another, more favorable route.

LOWER TURBULENT ZONE

The lower turbulent zone is the boundary layer in the lee wave system. Strong winds and wind shears produce widespread turbulence there. In the typical case the worst turbulence occurs along the lee slopes of the mountain, below the first lee wave trough, and in the primary rotor. (Figure 12-15)

Close to the mountain, strong winds are directed downslope. The region of strong winds commonly

Flying mountain passes and valleys is not a safe procedure during high winds. If winds at mountain top level are 25 knots or more, go high, go around, or don't go.

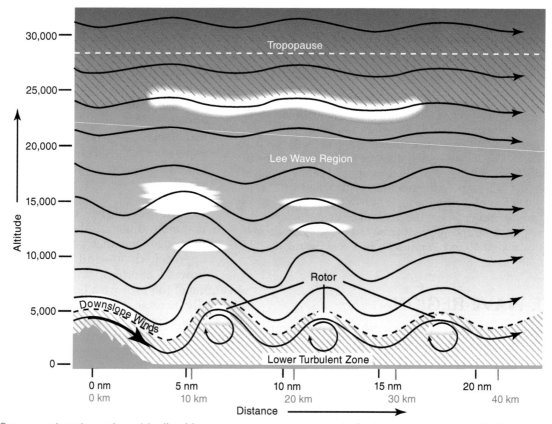

Fig. 12-15. Cross section through an idealized lee wave system composed of a lee wave region and a lower turbulent zone. Both the lower turbulent zone and a second layer favored for turbulence near the tropopause are hatched. Airflow is indicated by thin black lines with arrowheads. Lenticular-, cap- and rotor clouds are indicated in white.

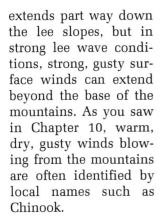

extends part way down the lee slopes, but in strong lee wave conditions, strong, gusty surface winds can extend beyond the base of the mountains. As you saw in Chapter 10, warm, dry, gusty winds blowing from the mountains are often identified by local names such as Chinook.

It follows from this description that you should avoid attempting a low-level flight across any substantial ridge when a mountain wave is present. If there is sufficient moisture, mountain wave clouds are useful indicators of such activity. (Figure 12-15) In particular, the cap cloud indicates strong downward motion over the lee

> An airliner at FL330 was flying upwind toward a major mountain range when it experienced increasing wave action and periodic bursts of light to moderate turbulence until the last cycle (closest to the mountains), where severe turbulence was experienced resulting in passenger injuries.

> One of the most dangerous features of mountain waves is the turbulent area in and below rotor clouds.

slopes. Remember, the absence of clouds does not guarantee the absence of MWT.

The greatest MWT typically occurs in rotor circulations which are found under the lee wave crests. The rotor associated with the first wave cycle downwind of the ridge is usually the most intense. The altitude of the center of the rotor circulation is about ridge top level. If present, the roll cloud is normally located in the upper part of the rotor. When strong and fully developed, a rotor is a closed circulation, producing a reversal of the winds in the lower levels.

The strength of the rotor is roughly proportional to the strength of the lee wave. In particular, the rotor will be strong where the mountaintop wind speed is strong, the lee slope is steep, and

CE 177. Two serious injuries, one minor injury, one uninjured. The pilot entered a 9,380-foot pass at 8,000 feet MSL. He said he encountered turbulence and downdrafts as he approached the summit, and the airplane "couldn't generate any lift" and stalled and crashed. Moments after the accident, another pilot reported occasional moderate to extreme turbulence in the vicinity. NTSB determined that the probable cause of the accident was the pilot's improper inflight decision to enter a mountain pass at an inadequate altitude, causing the aircraft's climb performance to be exceeded. Factors were turbulence and downdrafts.

If reported surface winds from a station on the lee slopes of a ridge are directed away from the ridge and exceed 20 knots, downslope winds and rotor activity should be suspected. Verification from other indicators should be sought: ACSL, roll cloud, cap cloud, blowing snow, or dust that is carried from the ground up into the rotor.

There are few eye witness accounts that give a more vivid description of the violence of very strong rotors than the destruction of pilot Larry Edgar's Pratt-Reid glider during the Sierra wave project (Holmboe and Klieforth, 1957).

"The flight path went to the very top of the little cloud puff. It seemed to swell up before the nose at the last moment. Suddenly and instantaneously, the needle went off-center. I followed with correction, but it swung violently the other way. The shearing action was terrific. I was forced sideways in my seat, first to the left, then to the right. At the same time, when this shearing force shoved me to the right, a fantastic positive g-load shoved me down into the seat. This positive load continued. Just as I was passing out, it felt like a violent roll to the left with a loud explosion, followed instantaneously with a violent negative g-load.

"I was unable to see after blacking out from the positive g-load. However, I was conscious and I felt my head hit the canopy with the negative load. There was a lot of noise and I felt like I was taking quite a beating at this time. I was too stunned to make any attempt to bail out.... Just as suddenly as all this violence started, it became quiet except for the sound of wind whistling by. I felt I was falling free of all wreckage except something holding my feet."

Edgar's parachute trajectory carried him around the rotor circulation first to the east, then westward, back toward the Sierra. During that time, he saw the wreckage of his glider carried past him, upward into the roll cloud.

where the mountain is high compared to the valley downwind. On some occasions, the rotor may exist only as a weak circulation or it may not be present at all. However, a conservative approach is always advised. When you suspect that lee waves are present, with or without roll clouds, you should assume that one or more strong rotors are also present.

SUMMARY

Aviation turbulence is caused by a number of different atmospheric phenomena. In this chapter we have considered the four most common types: turbulence generated in the boundary layer (LLT), turbulence caused by strong convection (TNT), turbulence in the vicinity of the jet stream (CAT), and turbulence caused by mountain waves (MWT). You now know why and where this turbulence develops. You have some useful conceptual models which help you connect the various types of turbulence to the larger scale circulations in which they are embedded. Finally, you have learned some rules of thumb to aid you in turbulence avoidance. In Part IV, we will cover some of the aviation weather products that are available from the NWS and the FAA to help you anticipate turbulent areas during preflight planning and in flight.

KEY TERMS

AMDAR
Aviation Turbulence
Billow Cloud
Capping Stable Layer
Clear Air Turbulence (CAT)
EDR
G-load
Jet Stream Front
Low-Level Turbulence (LLT)
Maneuvering
Mechanical Turbulence

Mountain Wave Turbulence (MWT)
Overhang
Overshooting Tops
Shearing-Gravity Waves
Thermal Turbulence
Turbulence in and Near Thunderstorms (TNT)
Turbulence Reporting Criteria
Turbulent Gusts
Turbulent Wake
Wake Turbulence

REVIEW QUESTIONS

1. What is the primary source of turbulence that you would expect while flying over land at 2,000 feet AGL around noontime on a summer day, far from any cyclones or fronts?

2. List the sources of turbulence below the base of a thunderstorm.

3. The majority of moderate or greater CAT occurs near what large-scale meteorological feature?

4. What are the approximate intensities of turbulence experienced under each of the following conditions?

   1. Your airspeed fluctuates ± 20 knots.

   2. Your g-meter registers 1.3g.

   3. While flying straight and level, your rate of climb jumps to 500 f.p.m.

   4. Unsecured objects are tossed about the cockpit.

5. You are approaching a field in flat terrain. The surface winds are reported to be 30 knots with gusts. Based on wind speed alone, what intensity of turbulence do you expect as you near ground level?

6. Interpret the following PIREP (refer to Appendix B):

   UA/OV MRB/FL060/SK CLR/TB MDT/RM TURBC INCRS WWD.

7. In your preflight preparation for a flight across a mountainous area in a light aircraft, you notice that a front is forecasted to be moving through the area at the time of your flight. It is a "dry" front (no precipitation or clouds), so icing and low clouds and ceilings are not a problem. Are there any other potential flight hazards?

DISCOVERY QUESTIONS

8. You are approaching a north-south mountain range from the east. Mountain top is 10,000 feet MSL. Your altitude is 12,000 feet MSL. 500 mb winds are 340° at 25 knots. 700 mb winds are 270° at 35 knots. Discuss. Consider the same situation but this time your approach is from the west.

9. You are diverting around a thunderstorm on the downwind side. The sky under the anvil is clear. If you fly under the anvil, it will save time and you might not have to stop for additional fuel. Discuss your options and risks of each option.

10. If you are flying over the North Pacific at 30,000 feet MSL with a strong tailwind and you encounter CAT, what would you do to get out of it? Explain.

11. The following are two rules of thumb for dealing with lee waves and rotors:

    "When there is a sustained loss of altitude while flying parallel to a ridge, rising air will often be found a few miles to the left or right of track. The exception is a downdraft close to the ridge. In that case, fly downwind."

    "In order to avoid rotors during arrivals and departures across rugged terrain in strong, low-level wind conditions, delay descent until clear of the area. If necessary, pass over the airport and make the descent from the other side."

    Draw clear and well-labeled diagrams of lee waves, rotors, and flight paths that show why this advice is good.

12. You are flying a Cessna 172 and the tower clears you to land behind a Boeing 757. The reported wind is a seven knot crosswind.

    1. Do you see any potential hazards in this situation?

    2. If so, what are your options and the risks associated with each option?

13. The internet address for the Aviation Digital Data Service (ADDS) is

    http://adds.aviationweather.gov/

    Access ADDS and go to the current turbulence information (the plot of turbulence PIREPs). Find a region of the U.S. with several turbulence PIREPs. With your instructor's guidance, obtain other supporting weather information and prepare a description of the large-scale weather conditions that contributed to the turbulence.

CHAPTER 13
Icing

Introduction

Aircraft icing can have serious negative effects on both the powerplant and the aerodynamic performance of your aircraft. As a pilot, your life and the lives of your passengers depend on your ability to understand icing and to take the proper preflight and inflight steps to deal with it safely. In this chapter, you will learn to identify and report the various types of icing, understand its causes, and become familiar with the meteorological conditions under which it is most likely to occur. When you complete the chapter, you should have a basic understanding of the icing threat and the knowledge of how to avoid it or at least minimize the problem.

SECTION A: AIRCRAFT ICING HAZARDS
    Induction Icing
    Structural Icing
      Ground Icing

SECTION B: OBSERVING AND REPORTING STRUCTURAL ICING
    Observations of Icing Type and Severity
    Icing PIREPs

SECTION C: MICROSCALE ICING PROCESSES
    Temperature
    Liquid Water Content
    Droplet Size

SECTION D: ICING AND MACROSCALE WEATHER PATTERNS
    Cyclones and Fronts
    Influence of Mountains
    Icing Climatology

SECTION E: MINIMIZING ICING ENCOUNTERS

Section A

AIRCRAFT ICING HAZARDS

Icing refers to any deposit or coating of ice on an aircraft. Two types of icing are critical in the operation of aircraft: induction icing and structural icing.

INDUCTION ICING

Induction icing is a general term which applies to all icing that affects the powerplant operation. The main effect of induction icing is power loss due to ice blocking the air before it enters the engine, thereby interfering with the fuel/air mixture. Induction icing includes carburetor icing and icing on air intakes such as screens and air scoops.

Carburetor icing occurs when moist air drawn into the carburetor is cooled to a temperature less than 0°C by adiabatic expansion and fuel vaporization. Ice forms on the internal surfaces of the carburetor by deposition; that is, by the transition from water vapor directly to ice. Ice in the car-buretor venturi and throttle value may partially or totally block the flow of the fuel/air mixture, resulting in a partial loss of power or in complete engine failure. (Figure 13-1)

Carburetor icing is much more common than many pilots realize. A 2010 FAA accident study for the period 2003-2007 revealed that carburetor icing was a factor in nearly 60% of all icing-related accidents. This particular icing problem is complicated by the fact that cooling in the carburetor can be so large that ice may develop under clear skies with an OAT well above freezing. (Figure 13-2)

The application of heat is essential for prevention of carburetor ice. The proper use of carburetor heat is dependent on aircraft type and phase of flight. General procedures and limitations for the use of carburetor heat are detailed in FAA Advisory Circular AC 20-113 Pilot Precautions and Procedures to be Taken in Preventing Aircraft Reciprocating Engine Induction System and Fuel System Icing Problems. Specific procedures for your aircraft are given in the Pilot's Operating Handbook.

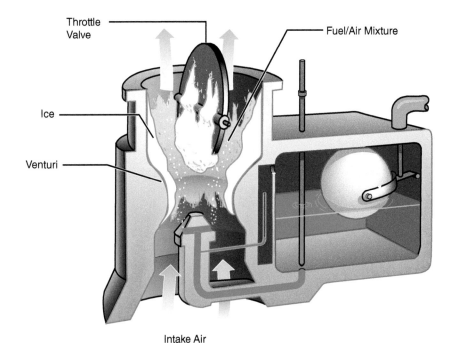

Throttle Valve

Fuel/Air Mixture

Ice

Venturi

Intake Air

Figure 13-1. Icing in a float-type carburetor. Ice forming in the venturi and throttle valve can effectively reduce the size of the air passage to the engine. This restricts the flow of fuel/air mixture and reduces power. If enough ice builds up, the engine can cease to operate.

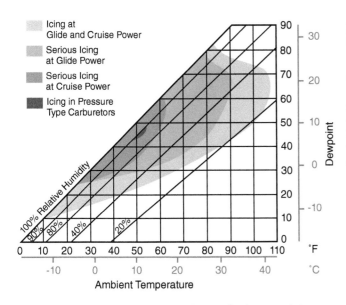

Figure 13-2. Carburetor Icing Chart. Carburetor icing depends on air temperature, dewpoint, and the power setting of your aircraft. This chart applies to float-type carburetors.

CE 150. One minor injury. The pilot had been fish spotting at 1,000 feet MSL when the engine suddenly quit, despite adequate fuel. He was able to get a restart, but only with partial power. Unable to maintain altitude, he ditched. The temperature and dewpoint at the closest reporting station were 87°F and 64°F respectively. These values are in the range of "Serious Icing at Glide Power" on the Icing Probability Chart in figure 13-2. NTSB concluded that the causes of the accident were engine failure due to carburetor ice and the pilot's improper use of carburetor heat.

In jet aircraft operations during taxi, takeoff, and climb, there are reduced pressures in the compressor air intakes. Air moving through the intakes is adiabatically cooled, which can cause induction ice to form by deposition when the outside air has high relative humidity. Similar to carburetor ice, this may happen even though clouds or liquid precipitation are not present and the outside air temperature is above 0°C. Air blockage and the reduction of engine performance may result. For a detailed description of this effect for your aircraft and engine type, consult the Pilot's Operating Handbook.

STRUCTURAL ICING

Airframe or structural icing refers to the accumulation of ice on the exterior of the aircraft during flight through clouds or liquid precipitation when the skin temperature of the aircraft is equal to, or less than, 0°C. The primary concern over even the slightest amount of structural icing is the loss of aerodynamic efficiency via an increase in drag and a decrease in lift. Also, there can be a decrease in aircraft stability and an increase in stall speed. Icing can interfere with propeller balance, jam landing gear, cover antennas, and reduce visibility through the windscreen. Additionally, structural icing on exterior components of the pitot-static system may cause instrument errors in the airspeed indicator, altimeter, and vertical speed indicator.

CE 182. One serious and one minor injury. Pilot received a weather briefing approximately one hour prior to flight during which "A chance of light icing" was forecast. Approximately 30 minutes after takeoff, while at 6,000 feet, a small amount of ice began to form on the strut in light rain. Although the aircraft was then cleared to climb above the cloud layer, heavy icing began to accumulate. The aircraft could not climb above 7,300 MSL and a 300 - 400 f.p.m. descent developed. The aircraft was cleared to an alternate airport via radar vectors. Over the runway at about 50 feet AGL, the aircraft uncontrollably veered to the left and struck the ground hard, collapsing the nose gear. A witness stated that there was 3/4 inch of ice on the leading edge of the wings, 1/2 inch on the fuselage and an inch on the belly. The aircraft was also loaded approximately 200 pounds over gross weight. NTSB cited the probable causes as icing, improper weather evaluation, and deteriorated aircraft performance.

In a given icing environment, the potential for structural icing also depends on the aircraft design and speed. At higher speeds, more droplets impact the aircraft. However, this effect is partially offset by heating due to friction and compression. Jet aircraft are usually less susceptible to icing because of their ice protection systems and the excess thrust capabilities, as well as the fact that in the cruise phase they usually operate at high altitude, out of the critical temperature range for icing and often above cloud tops. Many small general aviation aircraft with reciprocating engines are more vulnerable to icing because of their lack of icing protection and their frequent operation at altitudes within the range for icing. Helicopters are extremely susceptible to icing on the rotor blades which provide both thrust and lift.

There are two basic types of ice protection systems: de-icing and anti-icing. De-icing equipment removes ice after it forms, while anti-icing equipment prevents the formation of ice. The equipment includes the application of fluids such as glycol, the application of heat, and the use of inflatable boots. The Pilot's Operating Handbook for your aircraft describes the equipment available to you.

GROUND ICING

Another important form of structural icing to be considered is that which may occur prior to take off. The requirement for an aircraft to be ice-free is as critical for takeoff as it is in other phases of flight, if not more so. Causes of ground icing include freezing rain, freezing drizzle, and wet snow. Also, frost can be a significant hazard.

DC-9. Two Fatalities. The aircraft had arrived at a large international airport where some of its freight was unloaded and new cargo put aboard. During the 35-minute interval that the aircraft was on the ground, dry and blowing snow was observed. The reported temperature was 23°F and the dewpoint was 20°F. Witnesses observing the subsequent takeoff reported that, at 50 to 100 feet AGL, the aircraft underwent a series of rolling maneuvers, then rolled past 90° and crashed. NTSB concluded that the probable cause of the accident was the failure to remove ice contamination from the wings of the aircraft.

Conditions for freezing precipitation (FZRA, FZDZ) have been described in Chapter 6. It follows that, if a parked aircraft has a subfreezing skin temperature and water droplets strike that surface, the droplets will freeze on contact with the aircraft. "Wet" snow has a relatively high amount of liquid water and will freeze on surfaces with temperatures at or below 0°C.

A parked aircraft does not need clouds or precipitation to pick up ice deposits. At night, under clear skies, radiation heat loss reduces the temperature of the skin of an aircraft parked in the open. If the skin temperature cools to the dewpoint of the air, dew will form. This is not a problem unless, after the dew has formed, the temperature continues to fall to 0°C or less. In that case, the dew will freeze. More often, if the skin temperature cools to a subzero dewpoint (the frost point), frost will form by deposition. Although frost may not look very threatening in comparison to the bulk of structural ice accumulated in flight, the added drag and decreased lift caused by a thin coating requires a greater takeoff

Test data indicate that ice, snow, or frost having a thickness and roughness similar to medium or coarse sandpaper on the leading edge and upper surface of a wing can reduce lift by as much as 30 percent and increase drag by 40 percent.

A hard frost can increase the stalling speed by as much as 5 or 10 percent. An aircraft carrying a coating of frost is particularly vulnerable at low levels if it also experiences turbulence or wind shear, especially at slow speeds and in turns. Frost may prevent an airplane from becoming airborne at normal takeoff speed.

roll and may make it difficult, if not impossible, to take off.

Remove all ice, snow, and frost from your aircraft before takeoff.

Frost may also occur in flight when a "cold-soaked" aircraft with a skin temperature of 0°C or less descends or ascends into a warmer layer with high relative humidity. The frost is often short-lived as the aircraft warms up, but as long as it is present, the problem of increased stalling speed exists.

While minimizing the effects of induction icing is "primarily an engineering and operating problem" (having adequate heating systems and knowing when to apply them), minimizing the impact of structural icing is more complicated. In addition to dealing with the requirement for adequate de-icing and anti-icing equipment and knowing when to use them, other knowledge is critical. You must also be able to identify the type of structural ice that you encounter, evaluate its severity, and understand and anticipate a broad range of meteorological conditions that favor its formation. The next sections consider these topics.

Ground de-icing does not yield permanent results. There are limitations on holdover times prior to takeoff after de-icing is completed. The times, which range from a few minutes to 45 minutes, depend on the particular de-icing fluid, air temperature, aircraft temperature, and further icing threats due to frost, freezing fog, snow, freezing drizzle, or freezing rain.

Section B

OBSERVING AND REPORTING STRUCTURAL ICING

The visual identification of the presence of structural icing and the assessment of its intensity are critical steps in dealing with the problem in flight. In this section, conventions for the description and the evaluation of the intensity of structural ice are given together with guidance for the preparation and interpretation of icing PIREPs.

OBSERVATIONS OF ICING TYPE AND SEVERITY

Structural icing occurs when supercooled cloud or precipitation droplets freeze on contact with an aircraft. The freezing process produces three different icing types: clear, rime, and mixed ice. Rime ice is the most common icing type. It forms when water droplets freeze on impact, trapping air bubbles in the ice. This type of ice usually forms at temperatures below -15°C. As seen in figure 13-3, rime ice appears opaque and milky white with a rough, porous texture. Although rime icing has serious effects on the aerodynamics of the aircraft wing, it is regarded as the least

serious type of icing because it is lighter, easier to remove, and tends to form on the part of the aircraft where, if available, anti-icing and/or de-icing equipment is located.

Clear ice forms when large supercooled droplets impacting an airplane freeze slowly, spreading over the aircraft components. Air temperatures are usually between 0°C and -5°C. These conditions create a smooth, glossy surface of streaks and bumps of hard ice. Clear ice is less opaque than rime ice. It may actually be clear but often is simply translucent (clear ice is also called "glaze"). An example is shown in figure 13-4. Clear ice is the most dangerous form of structural icing because it is heavy and hard; it adheres strongly to the aircraft surface; it greatly disrupts the airflow over the wing; and it can spread beyond the location of de-icing or anti-icing equipment. When water or melting ice spreads beyond the ice protection equipment and subsequently freezes, it is referred to as runback icing.

Mixed ice is a combination of rime and clear ice. It forms at intermediate temperatures (about -5°C

Figure 13-4. Example of clear ice on the nose of a NASA research airplane. (Photograph courtesy of NASA.)

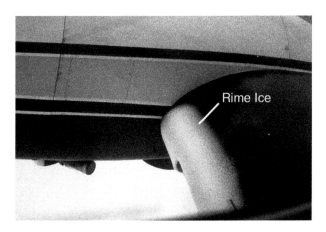

Rime Ice

Figure 13-3. Example of rime ice on a section of a wing between the nacelle and fuselage. (Photograph courtesy of Wayne Sand)

to -15°C) and has characteristics of both types. The variation in liquid water content in this temperature range causes an aircraft that is flying in these conditions to collect layers of both less opaque (clear) and more opaque (rime) ice.

The severity of icing is determined by its operational effect on the aircraft. Therefore, icing intensity (trace, light, moderate, severe) is related to the rate of accumulation of ice on the aircraft; the effectiveness of available de-icing/anti-icing equipment; and the actions you must take to combat the accumulation of ice. (Figure 13-5)

From figure 13-5, it is clear that icing encountered in flight will result in one of a variety of pilot responses, from no action to immediate action, depending on severity. In contrast, the occurrence of **any form** of ground icing has only one response: remove all ice contamination (including frost) before takeoff.

Intensity	Airframe Accumulation	Pilot Action
Trace	Ice becomes perceptible. Rate of accumulation of ice is slightly greater than the rate of loss due to sublimation.	Unless encountered for one hour or more, de-icing/ anti-icing equipment and/or heading and/or altitude change NOT required
Light	The rate of accumulation (0.25-1.0 in./hr or 6-25 mm/hr) may create a problem for flight in this environment for one hour.	De-icing/anti-icing required occasionally to remove/ prevent accumulation or heading and/or altitude change required
Moderate	The rate of accumulation (1-3 in./hr or 25-75 mm/hr) is such that even short encounters become potentially hazardous.	De-icing/anti-icing required or heading and/or altitude change required
Severe	The rate of accumulation is such that de-icing/anti-icing equipment fails to reduce or control the hazard.	Immediate heading and/or altitude change required

Figure 13-5. Icing intensities, accumulation, and recommended flight procedure.

ICING PIREPS

Pilot reports of structural icing are often the only direct observations of that hazard and, as such, are of extreme importance to all pilots and aviation forecasters. The critical information that an icing PIREP should contain includes location, time, flight level, aircraft type, temperature, icing intensity, and icing type. Figure 13-6 gives some examples.

Excellent aids to pilots in the diagnosis of icing conditions are graphical presentations of recent icing PIREPs. An example from the Aviation Digital Data Service (ADDS) is shown in Figure 13-7.

Accurate and timely PIREPs are good sources of icing information.

Figure 13-6. PIREPs illustrating a variety of icing types and intensities (highlighted). Coded PIREPs are followed by a plain language interpretation of the icing information. The PIREP format is detailed in Appendix B.

```
UA/OV ABI/TM 1700/FL 080/TP PA60/SK 024BKN040 OVC /TA -11/IC
     LGT-MDT RIME 050-075
```
   Icing: Light to moderate rime icing between 5,000 and 7,500 feet MSL

```
UA/OV YQB/TM 0445/TP DH8/IC LGT CLR 030-020/RM ON FINAL RWY 6
```
   Icing: Light clear icing between 3,000 and 2,000 feet MSL on final
   approach to Runway 6

```
UA/OV UJM225020/TM 1835/FL 210/TP DC 9/IC MOD MX
```
   Icing: Moderate Mixed Icing at Flight Level 210

Pilot Reports (PIREPs) of Icing
2048z – 2238z 03/27/**

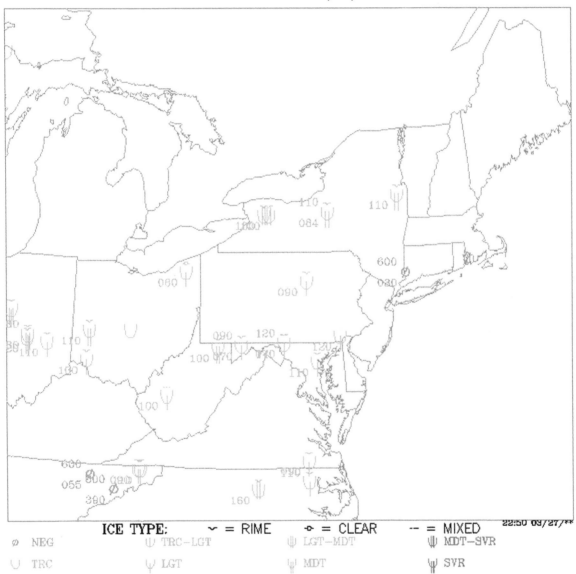

Figure 13-7. Icing PIREP map. Note that icing type and standard intensity symbols are defined in the legend. Flight level of reporting aircraft, in hundreds of feet, is plotted to the lower left of each icing symbol. If an icing layer is reported during climb or descent, the top of the layer is printed on the upper left of the icing symbol and the base is plotted on the lower left. The date and the period of time (UTC) when the PIREPs were reported are at the top of the map. Source: ADDS

Section C

MICROSCALE ICING PROCESSES

Instrument-rated pilots and those in training for an instrument rating must develop strategies to minimize icing encounters before they fly in clouds and precipitation. Even though you may never intend to fly in IFR conditions, it is still good operating practice to consider such strategies in case an inadvertent encounter occurs. To develop a strategy, you must understand the causes of structural icing and then use that information to identify conditions in which structural icing will or will not take place. The preflight questions you should ask in reference to structural icing along your route are, "Will icing occur?" If so, "Where?" "What type of icing will it be?" and "How bad will it be?"

With regard to occurrence, you already know that structural ice forms when water droplets freeze on the skin of an aircraft; that is, when the aircraft skin temperature is at or below 0°C and supercooled water droplets are present. These general conditions have led to a simple rule of thumb that addresses icing occurrence; that is, "Icing requires 'visible moisture' and subfreezing temperatures." Unfortunately, this rule, by itself, is very broad. There are many situations when such conditions exist, but no icing occurs. Also, this rule does not address either the type or severity (intensity) of icing. Icing occurrence, type, and severity depend on three basic parameters:
1. Temperature
2. Liquid Water Content
3. Droplet size.

TEMPERATURE

For as long as pilots and meteorologists have known of the threat of icing, close attention was given to cloud and liquid precipitation regions where air temperatures were 0°C or less. Through experience and research, it was found that the possibility of serious icing was highest at temperatures just below zero and became less of a problem at colder temperatures. Structural icing

probabilities are extremely small below -40°C because few supercooled droplets are present at those temperatures. Even in cumulonimbus clouds, there is not usually a great icing hazard at temperatures below about -20°C. Between 0°C and -20°C, the icing types fall into the temperature ranges listed in figure 13-8.

Icing Type	Outside Air Temperature Range
Clear	0˚C to -5˚C
Clear or Mixed	-5˚C to -10˚C
Mixed or Rime	-10˚C to -15˚C
Rime	-15˚C to -20˚C

Figure 13-8. Icing types and critical outside air temperature (OAT) ranges. Note that these guidelines are approximate, especially in the intermediate ranges between -5°C and -15°C. Also, rime ice may occur at temperatures below -20°C.

The skin temperatures of aircraft components are influenced by several factors including aerodynamic cooling due to lowered pressures near some portions of the wing and fuselage, and dynamic heating due to the compression of air along the leading edges. The resulting deviations of skin temperature from outside air temperature affect the formation of structural ice at various locations on the aircraft. However, because there are large variations in aircraft design and speed, critical icing temperatures are stated in terms of outside (true) air temperature. Differences between aircraft must be kept in mind when interpreting PIREPs. Details for your aircraft are described in the Pilot's Operating Handbook.

Given the presence of clouds, temperature only gives part of the icing picture. It does not tell you much about the severity of icing that may occur. The effects of the liquid water content of the cloud and the sizes of the supercooled droplets within the cloud must be considered.

LIQUID WATER CONTENT

Although you know that structural icing requires the presence of a cloud or precipitation with supercooled water droplets, research has revealed that clouds that often look alike may have very different icing intensities depending in part on the amount of liquid water that is present. Liquid water content (LWC) is simply a measure of the liquid water due to all the supercooled droplets in that portion of the cloud where your aircraft happens to be. Potentially severe icing conditions occur with high LWC.

> The icing process is rapid with high LWC and slow with low LWC.

> LWC is generally greater in clouds with warmer (usually lower) cloud bases and less in clouds with colder (usually higher) bases.

How does the LWC of a cloud evolve? Lifting of a moist airmass into a subfreezing environment by any of the means described in Chapter 5 (convergence, fronts, mountains, or convection) is usually sufficient to form clouds with supercooled water droplets. If the air is stable and the lifting is slow, stratiform clouds with lower values of LWC will develop. If the air is unstable and the lifting is rapid, cumulus clouds with higher values of LWC may form. Large variations in LWC values may occur both between clouds and within a single cloud. Cumulus clouds are characterized by pockets of higher LWC, which are conducive to intermittent, serious icing.

> Higher LWC and significant icing in cumulus clouds tends to occur in patches.

> Cirriform clouds do not usually present an ice hazard. An exception is found in the anvil cloud associated with a thunderstorm. Occasionally, icing will occur there as strong convective currents carry supercooled droplets to the top of the cloud despite the very cold temperatures.

DROPLET SIZE

At a given subfreezing temperature, supercooled small droplets will freeze more rapidly on impact with the wing of an aircraft than supercooled large droplets (SLD). However, because they freeze more slowly, SLD are associated with heavy icing and, especially, with runback icing problems. Supercooled droplets are considered SLD if their diameters are larger than about 0.04 mm. Droplets in this size range correspond with large cloud droplets, drizzle droplets, and rain droplets. The largest rain droplets have diameters of about 5 mm (0.2 inch).

How do small subfreezing cloud droplets grow into relatively large supercooled droplets? There are two basic formation processes: collision/coalescence and the warm layer process. In the first process, the drops are already supercooled; that is, they initially formed in subfreezing surroundings. You learned about the growth of cloud droplets by collision/coalescence in Chapter 6. This ordinarily promotes rather slow growth, especially when compared to the ice crystal process. However, if the large-scale environment provides adequate moisture and sufficient time for growth at temperatures warmer than -15°C, significant numbers of supercooled droplets can grow into SLD by means of collision/coalescence.

In Chapters 11 and 12, we saw that vertical wind shear and turbulence often occur with relatively stable layers, for example, at the tops of cold airmasses and in frontal zones. If clouds with supercooled droplets are also present, wherever the wind shear promotes turbulence, collision/coalescence and SLD growth may be enhanced.

> Relatively high LWC, large numbers of SLD, and more intense icing is often found near the tops of the stratus clouds with temperatures warmer than -15°C.

> ATR 72. 68 Fatalities. In the afternoon in late October 1994, over northwestern Indiana, an ATR commuter aircraft was in a holding pattern at an altitude 10,000 feet in an extensive cloud layer ahead of a surface warm front. While descending to a newly assigned altitude of 8,000 feet, it experienced an uncommanded roll excursion. It crashed following a rapid descent, killing all on board. The loss of control was attributed to a sudden and unexpected aileron hinge moment reversal that occurred after a ridge of ice accreted beyond the de-icing boots. Meteorological conditions at the time and location of the accident favored the development of SLD and clear ice in a cloud layer characterized by temperatures near -15°C.

The second way that SLD are created is when snow falls into a warm layer (temperature greater than 0°C) where ice crystals melt, and then fall into a cold layer (temperature less than 0°C) where the rain droplets become supercooled. As you also know from Chapter 6, if the SLD droplets subsequently freeze, ice pellets (PL) will be produced. If SLD survive to reach the subfreezing ground, they will freeze on contact as FZRA or FZDZ. If, in either case, you are flying within the cold layer and the skin temperature of your aircraft is at or below 0°C, you will experience significant icing.

> Structural ice will accumulate rapidly while flying in freezing precipitation.

> The presence of ice pellets (PL) at the surface is evidence that there is freezing rain at a higher altitude.

> About half the cases of freezing precipitation and ice pellets develop from the warm layer process, while the other half are due to the collision/coalescence process.

> Ice bridging is promoted when a pneumatic deicing boot deforms, rather than removes, a thin layer of ice. The ice retains its shape as the boot deflates. The deformed surface hardens and continues to accrete ice despite subsequent cycling of the boot.

Section D

ICING AND MACROSCALE WEATHER PATTERNS

Now that you are aware of the microscale factors that determine icing occurrence, type, and intensity, you must become familiar with the macroscale weather patterns that favor the development of those conditions. In this section, we will look at favored icing regions in cyclones and fronts, and the influence of mountains. Finally, we will see how all of these elements combine to explain the climatology of icing over the U.S.

CYCLONES AND FRONTS

Extratropical cyclones provide a variety of mechanisms to produce widespread, upward motions. These include convergence of surface winds, frontal lifting, and convection. Given a favorable temperature regime, the upward motions provide adequate LWC for the development of widespread icing. There are numerous possibilities for the development of SLD such as the presence of temperature regimes which favor the collision/coalescence process, the development of warm-layer regimes when warm air overruns cold air during the lifetime of the cyclone, and the presence of wind shears in fronts. In a word,

the chances of significant icing events in the vicinity of a wintertime extratropical cyclone are excellent.

Favored locations for icing in a developing wave cyclone are behind the surface position of the center of the low pressure (usually to the north and west) and ahead of the warm front (usually northeast of the low center). Less frequently, significant icing may also occur with cold fronts. When an extratropical cyclone reaches the occluded stage, moderate icing is common in the cloud mass circulating around the low center and ahead of the occluded front.

The distribution of icing reports in the vicinity of a wave cyclone for an actual case is shown in figure 13-9. Notice the locations where icing reports cluster relative to the position of the cyclone. In general, icing related to frontal lifting is closer to the surface position of the cold front because of the steeper frontal slope and the narrow, often convective, frontal cloud band in that area. Because of its flatter slope, wider frontal weather band, and slower movement, icing associated with a warm front tends to cover larger areas and last longer than cold front icing. Wide variations are possible.

Winter cyclones and their associated fronts provide optimum conditions for widespread icing.

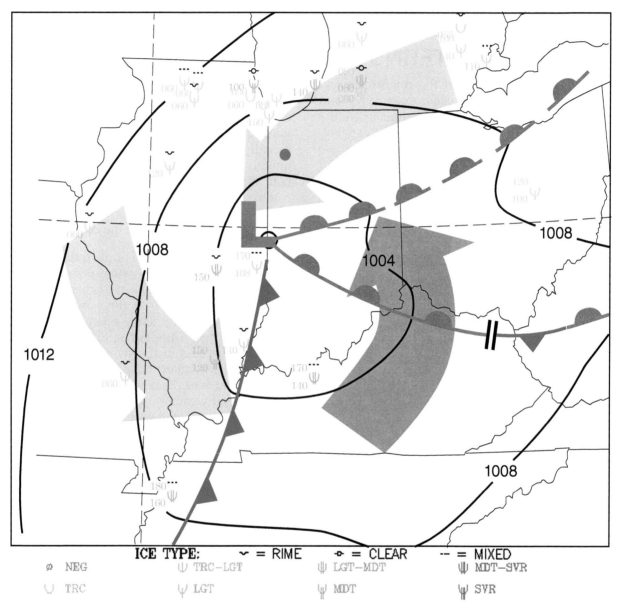

ICE TYPE: ⌣ = RIME   ⊶ = CLEAR   -- = MIXED

∅ NEG	⋃ TRC–LGT	⋓ LGT–MDT	⋓ MDT–SVR
⋃ TRC	⋎ LGT	⋓ MDT	⋓ SVR

Figure 13-9. Surface chart at about the time of the ATR icing accident described previously. The location of the accident is indicated by the red dot. Isobars and fronts are shown together with the locations of icing PIREPs for altitudes below 17,000 feet MSL and within about three hours of the accident. Surface wind directions are indicated with broad arrows (blue in the cold air, red in the warm air).

On some occasions in the winter, when cold air moves into the U.S. from Canada, a slow-moving warm front or stationary front will develop parallel to the coast of the Gulf of Mexico. Northward moving, warm, moist air from the Gulf overruns the front and the cold airmass to the north. These conditions often produce widespread freezing precipitation over the Southern Great Plains and/or the Midwest. Significant icing is common. (Figure 13-10)

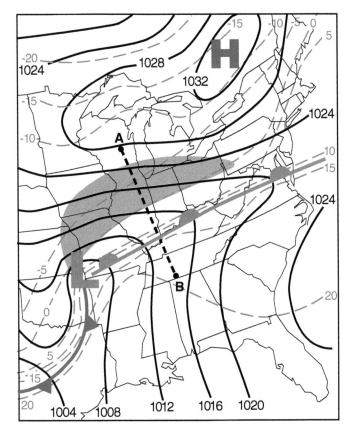

Figure 13-10. Surface analysis chart during a widespread freezing rain event (shaded area). Fronts are heavy solid lines with identifying symbols. Isobars (mb) are thin solid lines. Isotherms (°C) are dashed lines. Approximate freezing precipitation region is shaded. The isobaric pattern indicates that the warm air in the south is blowing toward the very slow-moving warm front, while in the cold air, winds are parallel to the front. A schematic vertical cross section through the warm front along line A-B is shown in the inset. Note that in the warm layer above the frontal zone, winds are parallel to the cross section (southerly), while in the cold air below the frontal zone, winds are directed out of the page (easterly).

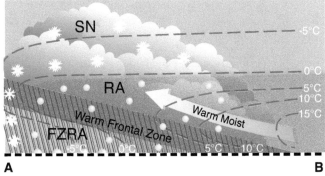

Heavy ice events in the Great Plains and Midwest of the U.S. may develop in winter when warm air from the Gulf of Mexico overruns a nearly stationary front oriented generally E-W.

INFLUENCE OF MOUNTAINS

Mountainous terrain should always be considered a source of icing hazards when subfreezing clouds are present. When winds force moist air up the windward slopes of mountains, the upward motions can supply moisture for the production of substantial liquid water in subfreezing regions. The worst icing zone is primarily above mountain ridges and on their windward sides. In addition, standing lenticular clouds downwind of ridges and peaks are always suspect for icing when the temperatures are in the critical subfreezing range. If the airmass crossing a mountain range becomes unstable, cumulus clouds may develop with their deeper icing regions.

When air from a substantial moisture source crosses a high mountain range, serious icing is possible, especially during the cooler months of the year.

When fronts carry moist air across mountain ranges, the potential for icing conditions exist. An icing encounter under these circumstances can be critical since other hazards are present such as obscurations of high, rugged terrain, wind shear and turbulence within frontal zones, lee wave systems, and embedded convection. Furthermore, if cold air is trapped in valleys as warmer air passes aloft, then precipitation through elevated warm layers and/or collision/coalescence processes in stratiform clouds near the top of the cold air can produce SLD and significant icing.

BE58P. One fatality. On a late winter flight over the Sierra Nevada, a BE58P descended and collided with mountainous terrain while in instrument meteorological conditions. The pilot was killed. A preflight weather briefing from the FSS forecasted IFR ceilings and occasional moderate turbulence over the entire flight. The briefing included a current SIGMET for severe turbulence and low-level wind shear, strong up- and downdrafts in the vicinity of mountains and passes, and occasional moderate mixed icing from the freezing level to FL200 over the entire route of flight. After receiving the briefing, the pilot decided to initiate the flight and filed an IFR flight plan. The airplane was observed on radar climbing through 11,400 feet MSL at a position that overlies a mountain range with peaks up to 8,000 feet MSL. Radio and radar contact was then lost. In the post-crash investigation, no mechanical problems were found. NTSB concluded that the probable cause of the accident was the pilot's loss of aircraft control due to his decision to initiate the flight after disregarding and poorly evaluating significant weather advisories forecasting adverse weather conditions along the route of flight.

ICING CLIMATOLOGY

An icing climatology refers to the average distribution of icing for a given area. It answers the question, "Where do various types and intensities of icing occur most often?" An icing climatology is a useful tool for illustrating the influences of the large-scale weather features discussed above. It is also helpful in familiarizing yourself with a new flight area and/or what to expect when transitioning from warm to cold season flying.

Some of the characteristics of an icing climatology are straightforward, especially on the largest scales. For example, consider the average global icing picture. The dependence of icing on temperature and cloudiness implies that conditions for icing occur more frequently in winter (colder), at higher latitudes (colder), near the tracks of extratropical cyclones (clouds and precipitation), and near major moisture sources. Icing occurs less frequently in the summer (except near CB), in cloud-free areas (for example, in subtropical highs), over deserts, and above 500 mb (~ 18,000 feet) where it is typically too cold.

Some aspects of icing require more detail to show the regional influence of moisture sources, land-sea boundaries, and mountains on the occurrence of icing. Icing associated with thunderstorms is a good example. The annual worldwide distribution of thunderstorms was illustrated in Chapter 9, in figure 9-19.

Another icing concern that requires more climatological detail is heavy icing that develops with freezing precipitation. Figure 13-11 is a map of the average annual hours of surface observations of FZRA, FZDZ, and PL over the continental U.S. Since these phenomena indicate the existence of SLD, figure 13-11 can be considered a climatology of conditions conducive to potentially serious low-level SLD icing.

Figure 13-11 shows that the most frequent low-level SLD icing events occur in the Northwest, especially in the Columbia Basin, and in the Northeast where cold air is often trapped near the surface while cyclones and warmer, moist air cross those areas aloft. Other favored areas include a narrow region just east of the Appalachians where cold air is occasionally trapped next to the mountains as warm air from the Atlantic overruns the area. A broad area of relatively frequent ice storms also stretches from West Texas through the Great Lakes. It owes its existence primarily to very cold, shallow airmasses that spread out of Canada and are overrun by warm, moist air from the Gulf of Mexico. Low-level SLD icing events are notably few (less than 10 hours per year) along coastlines, in the Rocky Mountains, over the western Appalachians, and throughout the Southwest States.

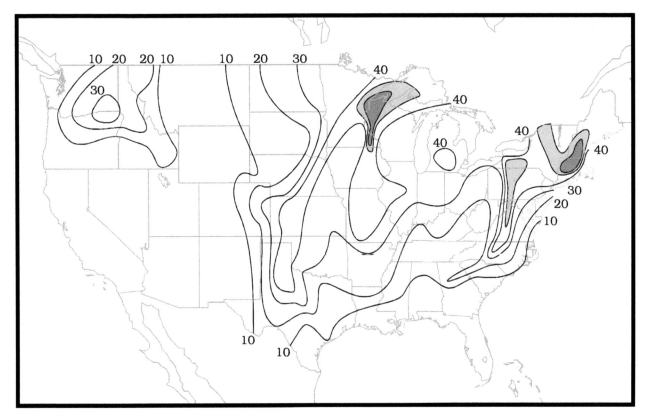

Figure 13-11. Average annual number of hours per year that freezing rain, and/or freezing drizzle, and/or ice pellets were observed at the surface. The shaded area is where the number of hours exceeds 50 per year. Averages are based on 30 years of observations from 207 weather stations. (Used with permission of Ben Bernstein, RAP/NCAR/NSF)

> Knowledge of the climatology of flight hazards such as icing leads to better flight planning.

> EMB 145LR. No injuries. While landing in a Midwestern city on a late January day, the aircraft departed the left side of the runway striking a runway distance marker and suffering damage to main and auxiliary gear doors and No. 2 main tire. Light snow was observed in the 14 minutes before the landing, and freezing rain began a few minutes prior to the accident.

Section E

MINIMIZING ICING ENCOUNTERS

The information provided in this chapter has included a variety of details related to atmospheric moisture, aircraft powerplants, cloud and precipitation microphysics, aerodynamics, large-scale weather systems, and climate. To put this information to good, practical use, you should organize it into useful checklists, standard procedures, and rules of thumb. However, this cannot be done as "one checklist suits all," because there is a strong interrelation between meteorological factors and the icing vulnerability of each aircraft.

> Know the capabilities of your aircraft and how and when to use the anti-/de-icing equipment.

As a simple example of how you might organize this information, consider planning a flight for an aircraft not certified for flight into known icing conditions and with only limited climb power. Figure 13-12 is an example of a flight planning decision tree for dealing with icing concerns.

The weather information required to use figure 13-12 is cloud amount, altitudes (AGL) of cloud bases and tops, type and location of precipitation, and temperature along the planned route. This information can be derived from the latest weather analysis charts, radar and satellite images, METARs, PIREPs, and forecasts along your route. An example of an icing PIREP graphic was previously shown in figure 13-6. Comprehensive graphics now available have enhanced a pilot's ability to assimilate current and forecast icing conditions along a planned flight track. The most

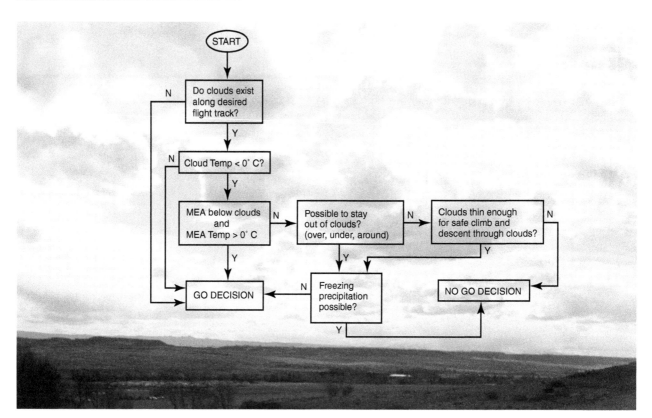

Figure 13-12. Decision tree for an aircraft not certified for flight into known icing conditions and with limited climb power available. Note: MEA means Minimum Enroute Altitude. (Diagram courtesy of Wayne Sand)

common displays are icing pilot reports (Figure 13-7) and freezing level information (Figure 13-13).

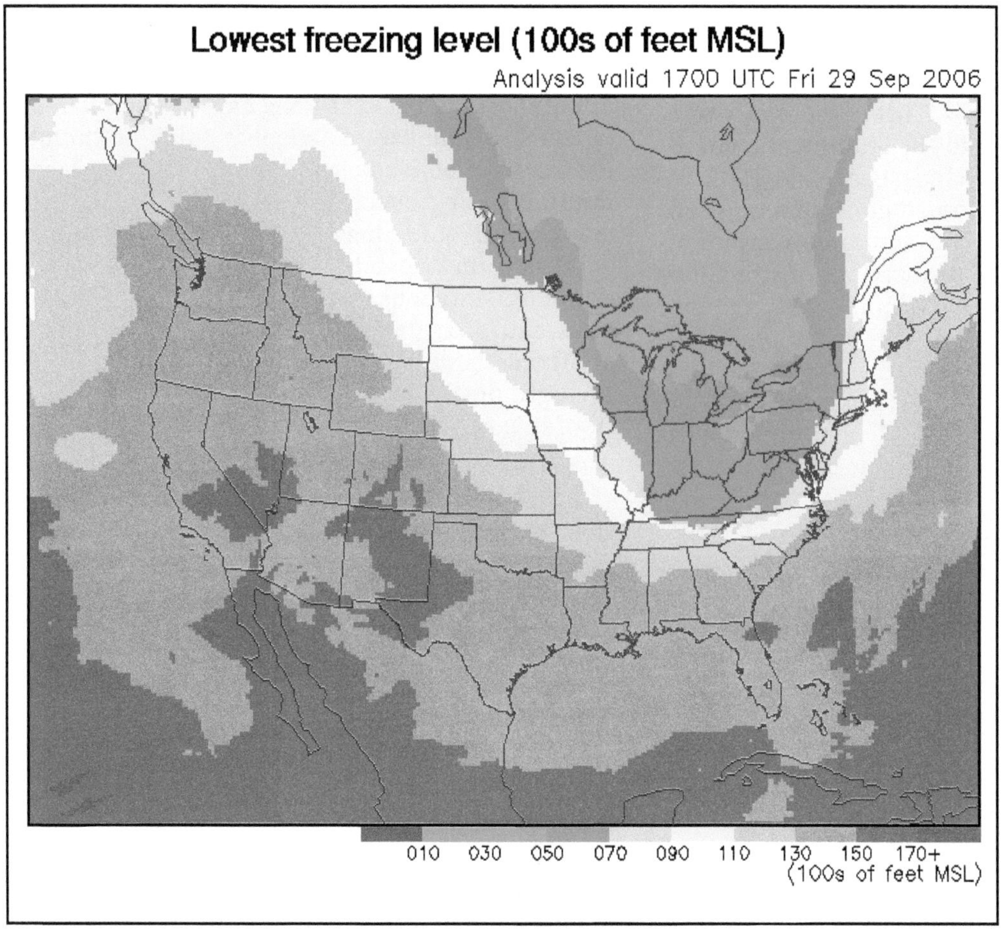

Figure 13-13. Lowest freezing level chart. Colors depict altitude ranges of freezing level according to the legend at the bottom of the chart. (Source: ADDS)

Locations of predicted structural icing conditions are found on aviation forecast charts and in Area Forecasts (FA), SIGMETs and AIRMETs. Details on the use of these and other forecast tools for general flight planning are presented in Part IV, Applying Weather Knowledge.

Once the "go" decision for any flight is made, whether or not your aircraft is certified for flight into known icing conditions, you must be prepared for an unexpected occurrence of structural icing. Icing can occur in any part of flight, given the right temperature and moisture conditions. The background knowledge and rules of thumb presented throughout this chapter will help you recognize and avoid or minimize structural icing. You are encouraged to build on those and on your flight training to develop decisive, safe procedures for encounters with icing in any phase of flight from takeoff and climb through approach and landing.

The icing analysis and forecast products that are available to pilots continue to undergo rapid development. These include the Current Icing Product (CIP) and the Forecast Icing Product (FIP). You can find detailed descriptions of these tools and how to use them in the most recent version of AC 00-45 and at the Aviation Weather Center (AWC)/Aviation Digital Data Service (ADDS).

The time available for making good decisions when flying in icing conditions decreases rapidly with icing severity.

SUMMARY

Icing can affect an aircraft in many ways, including the degradation of aerodynamics, and causing difficulties with control surfaces, powerplant operation, propeller balance, operation of landing gear, communications, instrument accuracy, and ground handling. An icing encounter does not leave much room for error. This is especially true when it is combined with the additional complications of turbulence, wind shear, and IMC. In this chapter, you have learned how induction and structural icing can form. You are now aware of the types and severity classifications of structural icing, and how temperature, liquid water content, and droplet size contribute to icing type and severity. You now understand that the production of supercooled large droplets, such as found in freezing precipitation, is of particular importance for severe icing. In addition, your brief examina-

tion of an icing climatology has demonstrated how extratropical cyclones, airmasses, and fronts interact with moisture sources and mountains to make some geographical areas more conducive to icing events than others.

Finally, on the basis of icing causes and characteristics, a number of practical rules of thumb have been established to help you avoid or at least minimize icing effects. Keep in mind that these are general guidelines; they have not directly addressed the capabilities of your aircraft to handle icing situations. More details with regard to tools and procedures for the general assessment of all weather conditions, including icing, in the preflight phase of flight will be presented in Part IV of this text.

KEY TERMS

Anti-icing Equipment
Carburetor Icing
Clear Ice
Collision/Coalescence
De-icing Equipment
Droplet Size
Freezing Level
Freezing Level Chart
Ground Icing
Icing
Icing Environment

Induction Icing
Icing Intensity
Liquid Water Content (LWC)
Mixed Ice
Rime Ice
Runback Icing
Structural Icing
Supercooled Large Droplets (SLD)
Supercooled Water Droplets
Warm Layer Process

REVIEW QUESTIONS

1. What is the aircraft type, aircraft altitude, icing type, and icing intensity reported in the following PIREP?

   UUA/OV UJM/TM 1841/FL 210-170
   /TP DC-9/TB MOD 180-150/IC SVR
   RIME

2. List the possible flight problems caused by structural icing.

3. Can carburetor icing be a problem at a temperature of 86°F?

4. (True, False) All clear icing is transparent.

5. Name the two meteorological processes by which SLDs can form.

6. (True, False) Frost covering the upper surface of an airplane wing usually will cause the airplane to stall at an airspeed higher than normal.

7. List the critical temperature ranges for clear, mixed, and rime ice.

DISCOVERY QUESTIONS

8. What is the danger of runback icing?

9. What are your chances of carburetor icing when the temperature is 30°C and the temperature-dewpoint spread is 12°C?

10. Several layers of clouds exist between 2,000 feet MSL and FL200. The freezing level is at 5,000 feet MSL. Use the standard atmosphere to estimate the top of the layer where icing would most likely accumulate during a climbout to 15,000 feet MSL.

11. Why do supercooled large droplets (SLD) often cause worse icing problems than smaller supercooled cloud droplets?

12. Why are wintertime warm fronts often producers of heavy icing events?

13. Why is icing usually not a problem in cirrus clouds?

14. Explain why ice pellets indicate that freezing rain or freezing drizzle exists at a higher altitude.

15. The Internet address for the Aviation Digital Data Service (ADDS) is

   http://adds.aviationweather.gov/

   Access ADDS and go to the current icing information (the plot of icing PIREPs). Find a region of the U.S. where several icing PIREPs occur. With your instructor's guidance, obtain other supporting weather information from ADDS and prepare a brief description of the large-scale weather conditions that are contributing to the icing problem.

CHAPTER 14

Instrument Meteorological Conditions

Introduction

Instrument Meteorological Conditions (IMC) refers to any state of the atmosphere where ceiling and visibility are below specific minimum values. Low ceilings and visibilities are common occurrences in the meteorological environment in which you fly. Unless the causes and properties of these weather conditions are understood and respected, serious flight problems can result. The purpose of this chapter is to describe the characteristics and primary causes of meteorological phenomena which limit ceiling and visibility.

When you complete this chapter, you will know the technical terminology used to specify current and forecast ceilings and visibilities; you will understand how they develop and the large-scale conditions under which they form. Finally, you will learn some useful rules of thumb that will help you deal with instrument meteorological conditions. As you read this chapter, keep in mind that a current instrument rating is required to operate in instrument conditions and that even experienced instrument-rated pilots will choose not to fly in some types of IMC.

SECTION A: BACKGROUND

SECTION B: CAUSES OF IMC
Fog and Low Stratus Clouds
Precipitation
Weather Systems
Smoke and Haze
Dust

SECTION C: CLIMATOLOGY

Section A

BACKGROUND

Instrument flight is governed by the Federal Aviation Regulations (FARs), which establish the minimum criteria for operating within the National Airspace System in weather conditions less than those required for visual flight. FARs govern IFR and VFR flights on the basis of weather conditions, aircraft equipment, pilot qualifications, airspace, and flight altitude. It is every pilot's responsibility to know and understand these regulations before beginning any flight. For further information on the regulations, consult FAR Parts 61 and 91.

A wide variety of weather information is available to you to help you make sound preflight and inflight decisions. In order to interpret this information efficiently and effectively, you must be aware of the important terminology and criteria that meteorologists use to define visual and instrument flight.

The counterpart to IMC is VMC (visual meteorological conditions). These two terms are rather broad classifications that are used to describe the state of the ceiling and/or visibility with regard to aviation operations. Specific ceiling and visibility categories were introduced in Chapter 6 and are repeated below for reference purposes. (Figure 14-1)

Figure 14-2 lists other key ceiling and visibility terms and measurements related to IMC that were defined in Chapter 6. This is very important background information for your understanding of flight hazards caused by low ceilings and visibilities. If you are unsure of any of these items, review them before proceeding with this chapter.

Ceiling	Relative Humidity
Cloud Amount	Runway Visibility (RVV)
Cloud Clearance	Runway Visual Range (RVR)
Cloud Height	Sector Visibility
Cloud Layer	Temperature-Dewpoint Spread
Flight Visibility	Tower Visibility
Obscuration	Vertical Visibility
Prevailing Visibility	Weather Depiction Chart
Radar Summary Chart	

Figure 14-2. Key terminology to be used in the evaluation of IMC conditions.

The determination of ceiling and visibility is not a perfect science; measurements are often rough approximations and large variations can occur over short distances and short time spans, especially with IMC. Because of these problems and the serious consequences that IMC can have on flight, a conservative interpretation of the measurements should be used when in doubt.

PA28. No injuries. Before departure, the non-instrument rated pilot observed patchy fog. The pilot did not receive a weather briefing; however, knowing that his destination was in VFR conditions, he elected to take off and observe the weather. Once airborne, the fog layer became solid. The pilot decided to return to the departure airport, but he could not locate it because of the fog. Fearing that he would become trapped on top of the fog layer, he decided to descend through an opening in the fog layer and make an off-airport landing in a field. During the landing, the nose gear and right main gear collapsed.

Keep in mind that the ceiling and visibility information given in METAR reports is determined by a ground-based observation. Uncertainties arise simply because of the way visibility is measured. The reported visibility

Category	Ceiling (feet AGL)	and/or Visibility (statute miles)
Visual Flight Rules (VFR)	None or > 3,000	and > 5
Marginal Visual Flight Rules (MVFR)	1,000 to 3,000	and/or 3 to 5
Instrument Flight Rules (IFR)	500 to < 1,000	and/or 1 to < 3
Low Instrument Flight Rules (LIFR)	< 500	and/or < 1

Figure 14-1. Ceiling and visibility categories that define VFR, MVFR, IFR, and LIFR conditions.

is the greatest horizontal distance over which objects can be seen and identified (daytime) or bright lights can be seen (nighttime). Under the same meteorological conditions, these two definitions can result in different distances being reported for the same meteorological conditions, the only difference being whether it is dark or light. In addition, visibilities often vary from one quadrant to another.

Another important consideration is slant range visibility or "slant visibility" on final approach. This is the oblique distance at which you can see landing aids, such as runway lights and markings. This value also is not necessarily the same as the visibility reported on the ground. These different visibilities are illustrated in figure 14-3.

Uncertainties in measurements are not limited to visibilities. Surface reports of the heights of cloud bases are subject to increasing estimation errors as the height of the cloud base increases. Automated stations in the U.S. do not detect clouds above 12,000 feet and do not report more than three cloud layers. Because of the differences between surface and pilot observations, surface observations should always be supplemented by current PIREPs whenever possible.

Although exact VFR minimums are well established by regulations, you should establish your own "personal minimums" based on your training, experience, proficiency, and currency. These can help you to make more objective "go/no-go" decisions.

PIREPs supplement surface cloud observations with information about cloud tops, cloud thickness, and higher clouds not visible from the surface. For example:

METAR:STL 231753Z 0000KT 8SM OVC015 03/01 A3011

PIREP: STL UA /OV STL/TM 1815/FLUNK/TP MD80/SK 010 OVC 033 CA=

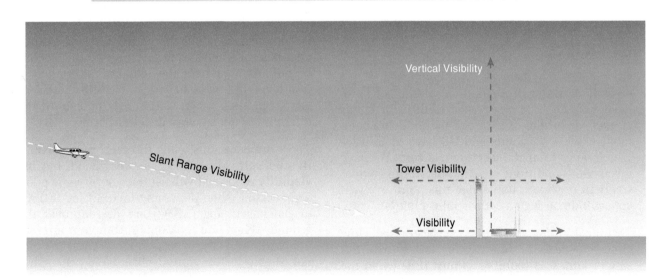

Figure 14-3. Slant range visibility. Other visibilities are shown for comparison. Visibility determined from the control tower is designated "tower visibility." When the surface visibility is also determined from another location, such as the weather station, it is called visibility. The height of an indefinite ceiling is reported as vertical visibility (VV).

Section B

CAUSES OF IMC

Visibility is decreased by particles that absorb, scatter, and reflect light. Such particles are always present to some degree in the atmosphere, but there are large variations. Sometimes they are too few and too small to have any significant effect on your ability to see and recognize objects at a distance. On other occasions, high concentrations of particles reduce the visibility to zero. In order to understand how these different conditions arise, it is useful to examine the types and behavior of particles that are found in the atmosphere.

For our purposes, we can separate atmospheric particles into two general groups: those composed of H_2O, such as water droplets and ice crystals; and dry particles, such as those from combustion, wind-borne soil, and volcanoes to name only a few sources. Both types of particles may be very large and fall rapidly (as rain or some volcanic debris), while others may be so small that they remain suspended (as cloud droplets or haze particles). The number and size of these particles influences not only the visibility, but also the color of the sky.

FOG AND LOW STRATUS CLOUDS

All clouds, whether they are composed of ice crystals or water droplets or a mixture of both, have varying influences on visibility. In cirrus clouds, visibilities of over one-half mile are common, while low clouds and CB have visibilities which range from 100 feet down to zero. We have discussed conditions in thunderstorms extensively in previous chapters; at this point, we will concentrate on fog and low stratus clouds.

Technically, fog (FG) is a surface-based, low cloud that reduces the visibility to less than 5/8 s.m. (1 km). It is reported as mist (BR) when the visibility is less than 6 s.m. (~10 km), but greater than 5/8 s.m.

In most cases, fog forms in stable air; that is, it is cooled to saturation by contact with the cold ground (radiation fog and advection fog). It is also caused by adiabatic cooling of stable air (upslope fog) or by some combination of contact cooling and adiabatic cooling. A situation where fog forms in unstable air (at least in the lowest layers) is steam fog. In this case, warmer water evaporates and mixes into the thin layer of cold air in contact with the water. Saturation results, as evidenced by a shallow layer of fog (also called "sea smoke").

C170B. One Fatality. The non-instrument rated pilot elected to take off at night in adverse weather conditions. After departing from runway 27, the aircraft climbed several hundred feet and turned left. A witness on the ground lost visual contact with the aircraft position lights after the left turn. Others on the ground reported they heard the aircraft flying low overhead. Engine sounds were reported until the time of impact. The aircraft crashed approximately 1.5 miles southwest of the airport. Witnesses near the accident site estimated the base of the clouds to have been approximately 150 feet AGL at the time of the accident, with the visibility less than 3 miles due to fog. NTSB determined that the probable causes were the pilot's poor decision to take off in adverse weather conditions, and the pilot's failure to maintain aircraft control due to spatial disorientation after encountering IMC.

In some cases, rather than advection fog, stratus clouds form when strong surface winds cause turbulent mixing, raising the height of the condensation level. In this case, surface visibility might be good, but slant range visibility is poor until the aircraft descends below the cloud base.

There are occasions when the slant range visibility and vertical visibility are very good, but the visibility reported by the surface observer is poor. This occurs when a shallow layer of fog (MIFG) or patches of fog (BCFG) are present near the ground. When you look down from your aircraft, you will often see objects on the ground that are not visible to the ground observer. In this case, there will be a progressive deterioration in visibility as the aircraft descends. (Figure 14-4)

In cold climates, ice fog may form. Ice fog is a radiation-type fog which, as indicated by its

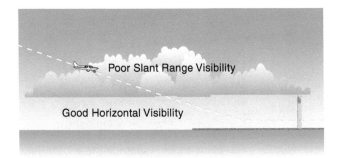

Poor Slant Range Visibility

Good Horizontal Visibility

Figure 14-4. Slant range visibility may be better or worse than surface visibility, depending on aircraft altitude and height of the cloud base (top) or the presence of some ground-based obscuring phenomenon (bottom).

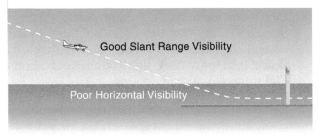

Good Slant Range Visibility

Poor Horizontal Visibility

> Be especially alert for fog or low stratus clouds when moderate or stronger winds carry stable, moist air up an extended slope. The smaller the temperature-dewpoint spread, the greater the chance of fog. The temperature-dewpoint spread will decrease 2.5C° (4.5F°) for every 1,000 feet that the air is lifted.

name, is composed of ice crystals. It forms at low temperatures (-22°F, -30°C or less) and may be quite persistent, especially in cities or industrial areas where many combustion particles are present to act as cloud nuclei.

PRECIPITATION

Precipitation can affect ceiling and visibility in a couple of ways. First, drizzle, rain, and snow particles are significantly larger than cloud droplets, so the effect on visibility can be significant. You have seen this in the dark rainshafts associated with heavy convective precipitation. Also,

recall that when the intensity of snow or drizzle is light or greater, the visibility will decrease significantly.

The second way that precipitation can affect ceiling and visibility is by saturating layers of the air between the cloud base and the ground. Ragged fractocumulus or fractostratus clouds (sometimes called scud) form below the original cloud base, causing the ceiling to lower over time. Also, precipitation fog may develop when rain saturates the layer near the ground.

> If fog occurs with rain or drizzle and the precipitation is forecast to continue, expect little improvement in visibility conditions.

Blowing snow (BLSN) is reported when the wind raises snow particles more than 6 feet above the surface and reduces the visibility to 6 s.m. or less. This is a particular problem in Polar Regions where the snow is dry and fine. Weather extremes are often reached under blizzard conditions. A blizzard exists when low temperatures combine with winds that exceed 30 knots and great amounts of snow, either falling or blowing.

> Ceiling and visibility conditions across the U.S. are mapped in different formats to enhance a pilot's ability to integrate multiple observations into a coherent picture for flight planning purposes. These include both the Weather Depiction Chart and the Ceiling and Visibility Analysis (CVA).

WEATHER SYSTEMS

Fog and low stratus clouds develop under identifiable larger scale weather conditions. Two of the most common are with warm fronts and when warm, moist air "overruns" a stationary front. These weather patterns typically occur in late fall, winter, and early spring and have similar structures. Air above the front is lifted in a stable upglide motion, producing clouds and precipitation. Precipitation fog and low clouds develop in the cold air near the surface with extensive IMC. You will recall from the previous chapters that icing and wind shear hazards may also be present under these circumstances. (Figure 14-5)

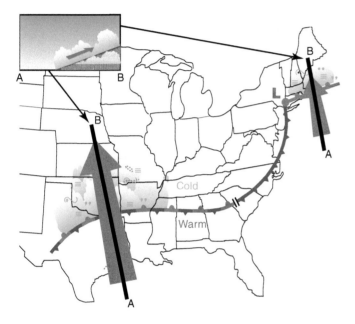

Figure 14-5. Weather map with cross sections showing precipitation falling from the overrunning warm air saturating the shallow cold air near the ground. Low clouds and fog occur in a broad band on the cold-air side of the front.

Be especially alert for low ceilings and visibilities with fog, low stratus clouds, and drizzle whenever a moist layer overrides a shallow, cold airmass.

Instrument meteorological conditions may also occur when warm, moist air overruns cold air trapped in valleys. Precipitation will saturate the cold air, producing low ceilings and visibilities in the valleys. These processes should sound familiar because, in the winter, they are also responsible for freezing precipitation and icing, recently discussed in Chapter 13.

The temperature-dewpoint spread is a useful index for possible fog formation. Here are two useful rules:

1. If, at dusk, the temperature-dewpoint spread is less than about 15F° (~8C°), skies are clear, and winds are light, fog is likely the next morning.

2. Fog is likely when the temperature-dewpoint spread is less than about 5F°(~3C°) and is decreasing.

Since radiation fog favors clear skies, cold ground, and light winds, it is commonly found in high pressure areas over land in the winter. It is not unusual for fog to form one or two nights after rain associated with a frontal passage dampens the surface. By this time, a stable, high pressure system has moved into the area with clearing skies, thus providing light winds and allowing nighttime radiational cooling.

Radiation fog typically dissipates after the sun rises, but there are exceptions. Under light wind conditions, damp, cold valleys are favorite sites for nighttime radiation fog in winter as cold air drains into the valley bottom. If the valley does not receive adequate solar radiation during the following day, the fog will not completely dissipate. If large scale wind and stability conditions remain the same, the fog will worsen with each succeeding night. The central valley of California is a good example. It is noted for its persistent wintertime "valley fog." In some winters, there have been weeks of IMC conditions in the Sacramento and San Joaquin Valleys as the valley fog persisted day and night. It usually takes a major change in the macroscale circulation (such as a frontal passage) to clear out the valley fog.

Expect little improvement in visibility when fog exists below heavily overcast skies.

Advection fog is common wherever warm, moist air is carried over a cold surface. Over land, this usually is a wintertime phenomenon. Advection fog may contribute to the precipitation fog ahead of a warm front. For example, when a warm front lies across the East Coast of the United States, easterly and southeasterly winds carry warm, moist air from the Atlantic over cold land surfaces to the north.

Advection fog also occurs when air over the warm Gulf Stream current blows across the colder waters of the Labrador current to the north. This causes the North Atlantic off the coast of Labrador to be an exceptionally foggy region.

In the warmer months of the year, the coast and coastal waters of Oregon and California are the locations of extensive advection fog and stratus clouds. These IMC conditions are caused by northerly and northwesterly winds carrying relatively warm, moist air from the North Pacific over a band of cold water along the Oregon-California Coast. The cold surface water in that area is the result of upwelling of bottom water. Under typical conditions, stratus clouds persist day and night over the coastal waters. The clouds tend to move inland at night and dissipate back to the coast during the day. This cycle is due to the radiational cooling and warming of land surfaces.

Although visibility below the bases of coastal stratus is often good, the altitude of the cloud bases is typically below 2,000 feet AGL. This can have an important impact on air traffic. For example, on a typical day, a large number of aircraft arrive at San Francisco International Airport (SFO) in late morning. Typically, the low stratus has dissipated in the vicinity of the airport by this time, but a later-than-normal dissipation can severely limit the aircraft landing rate, causing air traffic delays all the way back to the East Coast. This happens because side-by-side approaches to SFO are not allowed when the ceiling is below 2,000 feet AGL.

SMOKE AND HAZE

Smoke is the suspension of combustion particles in the air. A reddish sky as the sun rises or sets, and an orange-colored sky when the sun is well above the horizon often indicate the presence of large smoke particles. When smoke travels large distances (25 miles or more), large particles fall out and the smoke tends to be more evenly distributed. In this case, the sky takes on a more grayish or bluish appearance and haze, rather than smoke, is often reported.

The impact of smoke on visibility is determined by the amount of smoke produced at the source, the transport of smoke by the wind, the diffusion of the smoke by turbulence, and the distance from the source. In light winds, the most serious visibility reduction is in the vicinity of the source of the smoke. If winds are light, and the atmosphere is stable, visibilities remain low. Unstable conditions cause the smoke to be mixed through deep layers with less impact on visibilities, except near the source.

When smoke (FU) is produced by a large, hot fire, it rises to heights where it can be carried great distances in elevated stable layers. An example of a METAR remark from a weather station near a forest fire is "FU BKN020."

In large industrial areas, smoke provides many condensation nuclei. Fogs tend to be more dense and long lasting in those locations.

Smoke plumes from single sources may be carried far downwind. They are mixed with their environment, depending on the height of the plume, atmospheric stability, and wind speed. The height of the plume will not necessarily be the same as the stack height. If the effluent is hot, the plume will initially rise well above the stack until its temperature is equal to that of the environment. In unstable conditions, plumes will be mixed through deep layers. The instability is often visible as thermals cause a plume to take on a looping pattern as it leaves the stack. Under stable conditions, smoke plumes will maintain their shape, except for a tendency to fan out horizontally. A rough rule of thumb applicable for a few miles downwind of a smokestack is that the width of a smoke plume is about 1/20 of its distance from its source. These smoke problems can be complicated near the source where heat output in the stack is large enough to cause significant turbulence in the plume.

Haze (HZ) is a suspension of extremely small, dry particles. Individually, they are invisible to the naked eye, but in sufficient numbers can give the air an opalescent appearance. Haze particles may be composed of a variety of substances, such as dust, salt, or residue from distant fires or volcanoes (after large particles have fallen out). Haze tends to veil the landscape so that colors are subdued. Dark objects tend to be bluish, while bright objects, like the sun or distant lights, have a dirty yellow or reddish hue. When the sun is well above the horizon, haze gives sunlight a peculiar silvery tinge.

When the relative humidity increases beyond 60%, the dry haze particles begin to grow due to the presence of water vapor. The appearance of the haze changes; this "wet haze" layer takes on more of a whitish appearance with decreased visibility. These conditions (haze particles plus high humidities) often occur near the ocean where there is an abundance of moisture and salt particles. Also, a whitish, wet haze is often present early in the morning anywhere that temperatures are low and humidities are high. The whitish haze diminishes and visibilities typically increase in the afternoon as temperatures increase.

> When smoke or haze is present under overcast skies, there will be little improvement in visibility.

As with smoke, some of the worst haze problems occur in large industrial areas and cities where many air pollution sources add gases and more particulates to any naturally occurring haze particles. In some geographical areas, persistent elevated stable layers often combine with topographical barriers and light winds to trap pollutants. This results in the build-up of air pollution concentrations and further reduces visibility. Most of the primary gaseous pollutants are not visible, but they almost always exist in the presence of smoke and haze in large cities. One exception is nitrogen dioxide (NO_2), caused by the oxidation of nitrogen at high temperatures in internal combustion engines. In high enough concentrations, it has a reddish-brown color. Some well-known locations where air pollution problems are common are Los Angeles (where the term "smog" for smoke and fog was coined), Athens, and Mexico City. Flight into these areas usually means restricted visibilities, especially in the summer.

> When a persistent, weak pressure gradient and stable air (for example, in a stationary high) are located over an industrial area, low visibilities due to high concentrations of haze and smoke should be expected.

Besides generally reducing visibilities, haze also contributes to the problem of glare. This often causes visibility to be lesser looking toward the sun than away from the sun. For example, an observer on the ground may be able to see your aircraft when you can't see the ground because of the glare of the sun from the top of a haze layer. Glare can also be caused by snow and water surfaces and the flat top of a cloud layer.

DUST

Dust (DU) refers to fine particles of soil suspended in the air. If the actual source of the dust is far away from the point of observation, it might be reported as "haze." Dust gives a tan or gray tinge to distant objects. The sun's disk becomes pale and colorless, or has a yellow tinge. (Figure 14-6)

Blowing dust (BLDU) is dust raised by the wind to 6 feet (2 m) or more, restricting visibility to 6 statute miles (10 km) or less. Visibility is less than 5/8 s.m. (1 km) in a duststorm, and less than 5/16 s.m.(500 m) in a severe duststorm. Blowing sand (BLSA) is described similarly to blowing dust, but it is more "localized."

Blowing dust and sand occur when the soil is loose, the winds are strong, and the atmosphere is unstable. These conditions occur in some loca-

> When dust extends to high levels and no frontal passage or precipitation is forecast to occur, low visibilities will persist.

Figure 14-6. A wall of dust marks the leading edge of a cold airmass and strong winds. Photograph courtesy of Stan Celestian, Glendale Community College.

tions in the western U.S., such as desert dry lakes and areas of dry land farming.

One of the most useful charts for evaluating current ceiling and visibility conditions at a glance is the weather depiction chart. An example is shown in figure 14-7. These charts are available in different formats from different sources. The primary information presented is an estimation of those portions of the region that are VFR, MVFR, and IFR. These areas are determined from available METAR observations taken at the time indicated on the map. Depending on the source and the format of the chart, the information provided may include actual weather, cloud cover, ceiling, and visibility data at reporting stations. It is important to realize that weather depiction charts typically cover large areas. Since data do not include all METAR reporting stations, detailed conditions are not perfectly represented, especially where weather stations are far apart, the terrain is mountainous, or weather conditions are changing rapidly. The chart should always be supplemented with latest METARs and PIREPs for more recent data and greater detail.

Be alert for low visibilities due to dust and sand over semiarid and arid regions when winds are strong and the atmosphere is unstable. If the dust layer is deep, it can be carried hundreds of miles from its source.

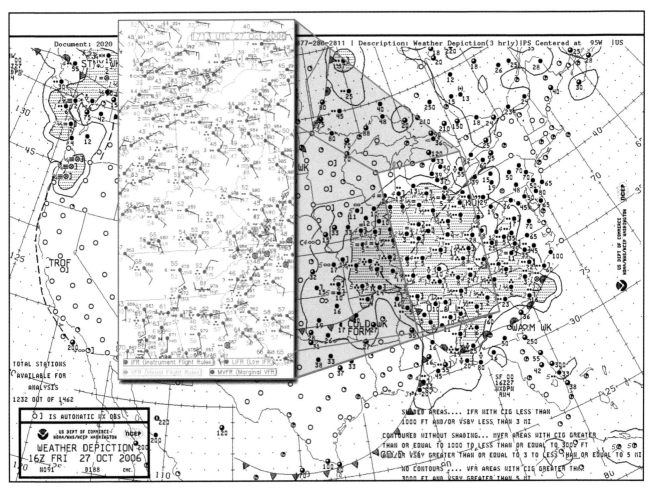

Figure 14-7. Weather Depiction Chart. VFR, MVFR, and IFR areas are explained in the lower right hand part of the map. Total cloud amount at each station is indicated by the coverage of the station circle. The number below the circle is ceiling height in hundreds of feet AGL. If the sky cover is SCT, the height of the lowest scattered layer is given. Visibility (SM) appears to the left of the station circle if it is five miles or less. Present weather is shown using standard symbols. Current positions of fronts and trough lines are also shown on the map. See Appendix B for complete description of symbols. Inset, portion of a plotted METAR chart. Note station circles are color-coded to indicate VFR, MVFR, IFR, and LIFR conditions. Source: ADDS

The Weather Depiction Chart is best used as a quick indication of areas that recently had ceiling and visibility problems. However, the chart should be used with caution for flight planning. In the case of rapidly changing conditions, the information shown on the Weather Depiction Chart may not be representative of current conditions. Always check the latest METAR/RADAR/satellite data.

During a night flight over a very dark surface such as water, an elevated haze layer may obscure the horizon which may lead to pilot disorientation.

Section C

CLIMATOLOGY

Knowledge of the favored areas of IMC is useful background for flight planning, especially in unfamiliar geographical regions. In this section, we will briefly consider the annual climatologies of dust and heavy fog over the continental U.S.

Figure 14-8 shows that lower visibility due to dust is common in the Texas Panhandle where dry land farming is extensive. Reduced visibilities occur there, especially in the spring, with southwesterly winds and with the passage of cold fronts that have little or no precipitation. In areas along the east slope of the Rocky Mountains, Chinook winds also cause blowing dust when ground conditions are dry.

Limited ceilings and visibilities due to fog can occur anywhere, but they occur more frequently in some locations than others. Figure 14-9 is a climatology of fog occurrences across the U.S. It may be interpreted as a good indicator of areas where IMC due to fog is frequent.

As would be expected, IMC due to fog is most frequent close to moisture sources; that is, along coastlines of the Atlantic, Pacific, and Gulf of Mexico, and near the Great Lakes. The greatest number of days with fog are found in the Northwest and Northeast and where the interaction of coastline, topography, and storm track produce optimum conditions for all fog types. The coast of Maine, with the strong influence of advection fog, has over 80 fog days per year. Inland valleys in Washington, Oregon, and California, and the west slopes of the Appalachians also have some of the highest numbers of annual fog days because of the trapping of cold, moist air in valleys and upslope effects. In fact, the average occurrence of

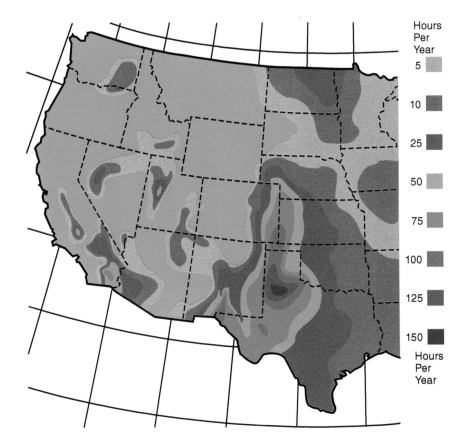

Figure 14-8. Annual average number of hours when visibility is reduced to 6 statute miles or less by dust.

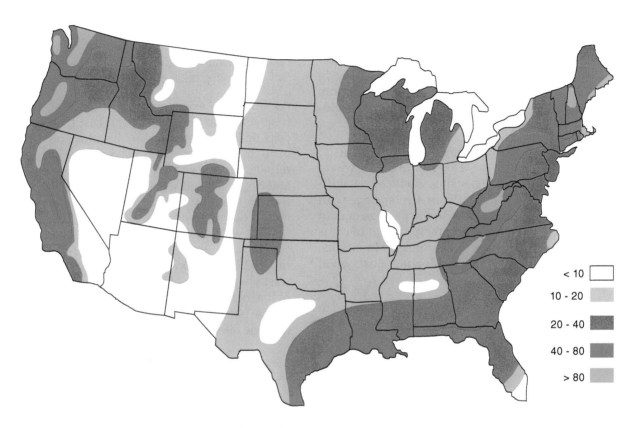

Figure 14-9. Annual average number of days with fog.

fog exceeds 100 days per year in some small areas of the inland valleys of Washington and Oregon. With the exception of the West Coast, the annual patterns of days of IMC due to fog in figure 14-9 are due mainly to fog days in the cooler part of the year. Notice that the patterns in figure 14-9 bear many similarities to figure 13-11. This is to be expected since the same large-scale processes

that cause fog will also cause freezing precipitation when temperature and droplet growth processes are favorable. During the warmer months of the year, West Coast airports such as SFO are commonly affected by low stratus clouds from the Pacific, especially in the morning hours. Although surface visibility may be good, ceilings are typically low, with major impacts on air traffic.

SUMMARY

IMC occurs when ceilings and visibilities are reduced by clouds, fog, precipitation, haze, and any other particles produced by natural or anthropogenic sources. Many of these conditions are associated with identifiable large-scale weather systems; occur during favored seasons of the year; and are more common in particular geographical areas.

Surface visibility and ceiling observations are critical to your assessment of IMC. Although the observations are made on the basis of certain definitions and procedures, they are, at best, approximations of a complex situation. Furthermore, surface observations alone give little information with respect to inflight conditions. Although imperfect, the system of weather observations is the only one that exists. The wise pilot knows IMC rules and regulations and the technical language and shortcomings of observations, reports, and forecasts of IMC conditions. When uncertain about conditions, the wise pilot takes a conservative approach to preflight and inflight decision making with respect to IMC. Antoine de Saint Exupery said in *Wind, Sand, and Stars*, "Navigating by the compass in a sea of clouds over Spain is all very well, it is very dashing, but — you want to remember that below the sea of clouds lies eternity."

KEY TERMS

Advection Fog
Air Pollution
Blizzard
Blowing Dust (BLDU)
Blowing Snow (BLSN)
Dust (DU)
Duststorm
Fractocumulus
Fractostratus
Haze (HZ)
Ice Fog
Instrument Flight Rules (IFR)
Instrument Meteorological Conditions (IMC)
Low Instrument Flight Rules (LIFR)

Marginal Visual Flight Rules (MVFR)
Precipitation Fog
Radiation Fog
Scud
Severe Duststorm
Slant Range Visibility
Smoke (FU)
Steam Fog
Upslope Fog
Visual Flight Rules (VFR)
Visual Meteorological Conditions (VMC)
Weather Depiction Chart

REVIEW QUESTIONS

1. List three causes of IMC.

2. In winter, what other weather hazards beside IMC are common in the conditions illustrated in figure 14-5?

3. What two flight hazards might you encounter in the vicinity of smoke plumes?

4. What does the following METAR remark mean? "FU BKN020"

5. On a calm, sunny day over a city, an inversion is present with its base at 1,000 feet AGL and its top at 1,800 feet AGL. When flying across the area, would you expect visibilities to be better at 900 feet AGL or 1,900 feet AGL?

6. It is 10 pm. Skies are clear, visibility is 7 s.m. and the wind is nearly calm. An hour ago the temperature-dewpoint spread was 4C°, now it is 3C°. What (if any) change in conditions do you expect in the next few hours?

7. Repeat question 6, but change the time to sunrise.

DISCOVERY QUESTIONS

8. If the surface temperature is 5°C and the dewpoint is 3°C, what is the RH?

9. If low clouds are present the next time you are at the airport, you can do a simple exercise that will illustrate the variability in cloud observations. Be sure to record the time for each observation.

    1. Before you look at any reports, estimate the altitude of the lowest cloud bases.

    2. Record the height reported in the latest METAR.

    3. Obtain an estimate of cloud height from the latest local PIREPs and/or your own inflight observations, both over the airport and 10 miles away.

    4. Discuss, explaining differences in measurements.

10. Construct an exercise similar to question 9, but for horizontal visibility, runway visibility, and slant range visibility.

11. You are "on top," well above a discontinuous cloud layer. You want to descend to a nearby airport. Discuss the applicable VFR rules.

12. You are at an isolated airport in a generally flat area far from the ocean. It is a fall evening, the skies are clear, and winds are light. There is no forecast for your local airport, but the forecast for a station 100 miles away indicates the chance of dense fog at the time you intend to take off (0600 the next morning). You are carrying a perishable cargo that you must begin loading four hours before takeoff. It is very expensive to load and to unload, so you want to make a decision before you begin to move the cargo. Aside from the previous forecast, you only have local observations. At 0200, it is clear. What should you do?

13. At sunrise on a clear, calm day, a whitish haze has reduced the visibility at the local airport. Ground fog exists along nearby creeks. Do you expect visibility conditions to improve in the next few hours? Explain.

14. It is midnight in winter. Large-scale weather conditions show a stagnant high pressure system over your area. Radiation fog occurred under clear skies last night and burned off at 0900 this morning. Fog has formed again this evening. The midnight sky condition is BR SCT000 OVC100. Will it be possible to fly VFR tomorrow morning at 0930? Discuss.

CHAPTER 15
Additional Weather Hazards

Introduction

In the previous four chapters, we have discussed windshear, turbulence, icing, and IMC, the most common and, often, the most lethal weather hazards. The current chapter provides detail on a number of other hazardous weather phenomena, some of which are encountered less frequently but all of which may be problematic. After you complete this chapter, you will understand the causes and effects of hazards as diverse as atmospheric electricity, ozone, solar radiation, volcanic eruptions, and whiteout.

Section A

ATMOSPHERIC ELECTRICITY

As described in Chapter 9, lightning is associated with every thunderstorm (and occasionally with volcanic eruptions). Lightning presents hazards for flight operations, both in the air and on the ground. Pilot knowledge of those hazards is crucial. (Figure 15-1)

LIGHTNING HAZARDS

Lightning strikes on aircraft result in a variety of adverse effects. Although most of them are minor, in some cases, the damage can be severe enough to result in an accident or incident. A lightning flash is extremely bright. Temporary blindness is not an unusual occurrence.

Aircraft structural damage is usually restricted to effects such as small holes in the fuselage, as illustrated in figure 15-1. Wingtips, engines, and other equipment protruding from the aircraft are also subject to lightning strikes. Problems include twisted and burned antennas and damaged pitot tubes.

During flight near thunderstorms, avoid looking directly at the storm to reduce the danger of temporary blindness due to lightning. Turn up the cockpit lights to full bright, even during daylight hours, to lessen the temporary blindness from lightning.

Although lightning is not typically associated with extensive visible damage, it may cause significant interference with electrical systems. Electric motors (for example, wing-folding motors)

Figure 15-1. Lightning discharges may be from cloud-to-cloud, cloud-to-ground, within clouds, and, occasionally, from cloud to clear air. The inset shows an aircraft nose cone with holes caused by a lightning strike. (Lightning photograph, National Oceanic and Atmospheric Administration)

have been known to operate spontaneously after lightning strikes. An increased reliance on digital flight control systems as opposed to analog or mechanical systems has made some aircraft even more vulnerable to the lightning problem. The damage in these situations results in errors in output from electronic processing equipment. Instruments, avionics, radar, and navigational systems can be influenced.

Potentially, one of the most serious effects of a lightning strike is the ignition of vapors in a fuel tank. However, the small number of suspected cases in the past, and improvements in fuel tank designs over the last 30 years or so, suggest that the probability of such occurrences is very small.

> After a lightning strike, all instruments should be considered invalid until their proper operation is verified.

The potential for aircraft strikes is high in the thunderstorm anvil, even after the main thunderstorm cell has weakened in the dissipation stage. However, the highest frequency of lightning strikes is found in the lower troposphere.

> All airports require suspension of refueling operations during nearby (within about 5 n.m.) lightning activity.

As explained in Chapter 9, the most common strikes are initiated from a negative charge center near the base of the thunderstorm. (Figure 9-18) But that is not the only source of lightning in a thunderstorm. Ten to twenty percent of cloud-to-ground strikes are generated from a positive charge center near the top of the thunderstorm.

> To reduce the chance of a lightning strike in the vicinity of thunderstorms, do not fly within ±5,000 feet of the freezing level or, alternately, do not fly in the layer where the OAT is between +8°C and −8°C.

Although fewer and farther between, a positive lightning strike is significantly more dangerous. It lasts longer and carries a charge that is 10 times that of a negative strike. Positive strikes often occur away from the main thunderstorm cell, for example, between the anvil and the ground. This is another reason why flight under the anvil is not recommended.

> Positive lightning strikes have been connected with the occurrence of sprites, one of several dim electrical displays that extend 18-60 miles (~30-100km) above thunderstorm tops.

Another word of caution: just because the chance of a catastrophic lightning strike is small doesn't mean that the problem should be considered "minor." The most frequent, and often the most serious, inflight problems are not caused by a single weather hazard, but rather by a combination of hazards. Lightning offers a good example of this rule of thumb. Consider a situation where you find yourself flying in a thunderstorm environment. Conditions are IMC with turbulence and icing. Clearly, your full attention is required to deal with the problems at hand. It is conceivable that a nearby lightning flash could temporarily blind and disorient you just long enough for you to lose control of the aircraft. Be prepared. Avoid thunderstorms.

PA28. One fatality. About 30 minutes before the accident, the pilot received an inflight weather briefing from Enroute Flight Advisory Service (EFAS). The pilot indicated to EFAS that he had received an AIRMET regarding icing conditions along his route. The pilot was then briefed on thundershowers, frequent cloud-to-ground lightning, and PIREPs of moderate turbulence and light mixed icing. The pilot continued on his flight route. Twenty-five minutes after his weather briefing, he reported airframe icing conditions to ATC. ATC advised the pilot of more severe weather ahead and recommended that he reverse course. Less than one minute later, the pilot reported being struck by lightning. ATC amended the pilot's clearance, instructing him to reverse course with a left turn heading 330°. The pilot read back the clearance. Afterwards, both radio and radar contact were lost. Radar data revealed that the airplane entered a left turn and climbed 200 feet. The airplane then descended about 1,200 feet in 35 seconds. The aircraft was not equipped with de-icing systems. NTSB concluded that the probable cause of the accident was the pilot's delayed inflight decision to reverse course to avoid forecast adverse weather conditions and that contributing factors were icing and lightning.

STATIC DISCHARGES

When an aircraft flies through an environment that encourages the build-up of the electrical field around prominent parts of the airframe, static discharges may result. A static discharge is the spark or point discharge that occurs when the electric potential between the aircraft and its surroundings becomes large enough. A common effect of static electricity is low frequency radio noise. Static can be particularly loud and bothersome in the 200 to 400 kHz frequency range. It can also be heard in the VHF range, although the effect is not nearly as bad as in HF range. Less frequently, a corona discharge, known as St. Elmo's Fire, appears as a bushy halo around some prominent edges or points on the aircraft structure and around windscreens. (Figure 15-2A)

Static discharge wicks are rods or thin wire-like devices that extend from the wingtips and at the trailing edges of control surfaces of some aircraft. All airliners have them. Wicks encourage static charges that build up on sharp edges of the airframe as well and those from lightning strikes to bleed off into the atmosphere. (Figure 15-2B)

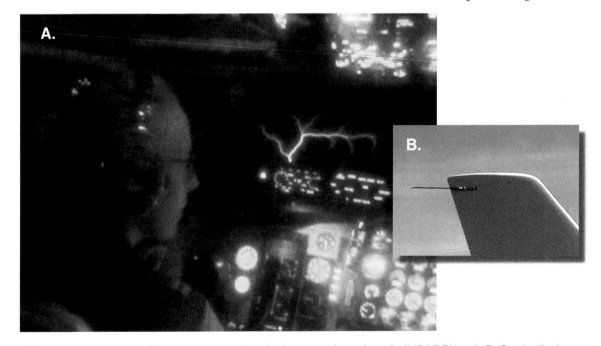

Figure 15-2. A: St. Elmo's Fire appears on the windscreen of an aircraft. (USAF Photo). B: Static discharge wick on the trailing edge of the winglet on a light twin.

Section B

STRATOSPHERIC OZONE

In Chapter 1, the ozone layer was described as a prominent feature of the lower stratosphere. Ozone (O_3), has both good and bad qualities. On the good side, it absorbs damaging UV radiation from the sun. On the bad side, it is not good in an environment where animals, people, and plants are present because it is toxic. In large enough concentrations, it has an acrid smell, it irritates the eyes, and can cause respiratory difficulties. These effects are well known in heavily populated areas, such as Los Angeles, where an ample supply of solar radiation interacts with oxides of nitrogen from automobile exhausts. This process produces "photochemical smog" of which ozone is a primary component.

In the lower atmosphere, the highest concentrations of ozone usually occur in the afternoon. If an elevated stable layer traps air pollutants, ozone concentrations tend to be relatively large and persistent just below the stable layer.

Naturally occurring ozone from the stratosphere may also create a hazard to flights at and above the tropopause. Exposure can occur in two ways. First, an aircraft may simply be so high in the stratosphere that it is close to the maximum concentrations in the ozone layer. (See Figure 1-9) Some military aircraft (and occasionally high-altitude balloonists) reach such altitudes.

Another way that aircrew exposure to ozone increases is when atmospheric motions bring stratospheric air with high concentrations of ozone down to altitudes near the tropopause where more aircraft fly. Such downward motions are found near jet streams, especially where extratropical cyclones are very strong or are rapidly intensifying. Typically, the tropopause is much lower over cyclones than over anticyclones, and ozone-rich stratospheric air is more likely to be found there, at the highest cruise altitudes of airliners (Bhangar et al., 2008). Also, stratospheric air is "injected" into the upper troposphere poleward of the jet stream axis (Northern Hemisphere). (Figure 15-3)

Typically, peak ozone concentrations occur near altitudes of 80,000 feet in the tropics and 60,000 feet in the Polar regions.

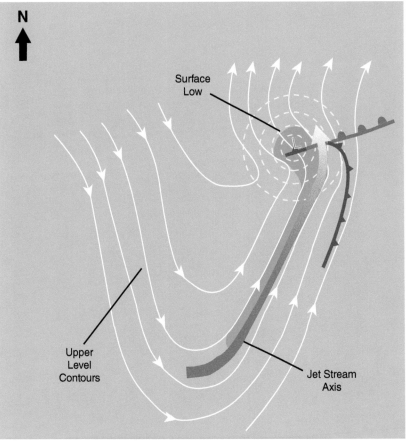

Figure 15-3. Ozone-rich stratospheric air (dark green shaded area) is brought down to the upper troposphere over an intense surface low-pressure area and along the left side of a strong jet stream (Northern Hemisphere).

When these processes take place at high latitudes, there is an increased probability of bringing higher-than-normal ozone concentrations to common airline cruise altitudes. This is because the average tropopause height decreases toward the poles. Some airlines may restrict flights to lower altitudes when ozone concentrations are estimated to be above some critical value. As Polar routes become more popular for airline flights, the exposure of aircraft to higher concentrations of ozone will increase.

There is no question that exposure of passengers and crew to elevated ozone concentrations will occasionally occur within the service ceiling of many corporate and airline aircraft. The amount and impact of the exposure is uncertain. Until there are regular measurements made in the free atmosphere and onboard aircraft, exposure on any given occasion can only be roughly estimated. Attention to the design of aircraft ventilation systems, knowledge of meteorological conditions, and the use of good flight procedures can minimize the potential problem.

Section C

VOLCANIC ERUPTIONS

Volcanoes are a fact of life around the world. On the ground earthquakes, explosive eruptions, heavy ash fallout, and lava flows may be the most important aspects of volcanic activity; but in the air, the primary feature is the ash cloud. So called "volcanic ash" also consists of gases and dust, as well as ash from an eruption. A volcanic ash cloud can spread around the world and remain in the stratosphere for months or longer. This volcanic material has important effects on the amount of solar radiation received at the earth's surface and, therefore, on the weather and climate.

Another major influence of volcanic ash clouds is the interruption of flight activities. (Figure 15-4)

VOLCANIC ASH HAZARDS

When an aircraft approaches an ash cloud some distance from a volcano, the cloud isn't always easy to distinguish from ordinary water or ice clouds. However, upon entering the cloud, the situation is distinctly different. Dust and smoke may enter the cabin, often with the odor of an electrical fire. Visible indications of the ash particles include lightning, St. Elmo's Fire around the windshield, and a bright orange glow around jet

Figure 15-4. Mount St. Helens eruption in Washington State, May 1980.

engine inlets. Because the ash is highly abrasive, particle impacts can pit the windscreen and landing lights to the point where they become useless. Depending on the conditions, there may be worse effects. Control surfaces can be damaged and the pitot-static system and ventilation systems can become clogged, causing instruments to malfunction. The ingestion of volcanic ash damages jet engines; it can cause compressor stalls, torching from the tailpipe, and flameouts.

> There have been more than 90 reported encounters of volcanic plumes by jet aircraft in the last 20 years. Many of those resulted in damage to the aircraft.

> Piston aircraft are less likely than jet aircraft to lose power due to ingestion of volcanic ash, but severe damage is almost certain to occur, especially with a volcanic cloud only a few hours old.

ASH CLOUD BEHAVIOR

Volcanic ash clouds are most dangerous close to the volcano when an eruption has just occurred because the ash particles are large. When the ash cloud is within 30 n.m. of the volcano, it may be identifiable with a nearby weather radar installation. Depending on the size of the ash cloud, radar sites as far away as 400 n.m. may be able to detect the cloud. However, the presence of precipitating clouds can mask the ash cloud.

> B747. No injuries. In 1989, a new B747-400 lost all four engines after an encounter with a volcanic ash cloud from the eruption of Mt. Redoubt. Although the crew was able to restart the engines and land safely, the initial estimate of damage to the aircraft was 80 million dollars including the replacement of all four engines.

The effect of the ash cloud on flight activities is not limited to the region of the largest particles. When volcanic material is injected into the stable

> It is most important to avoid any encounter with a volcanic ash cloud, especially those which are only a few hours old. Make every effort to remain on the upwind side of the volcano.

stratosphere, fallout is slow. In addition to the potential for continuing hazards for engine operation, the reduction of visibility at flight altitude may also persist as the cloud spreads out and is carried away by atmospheric winds. At a nominal speed of 25 knots, a typical ash cloud spreads downwind at 600 n.m. per day. If the cloud is near the jet stream, a more rapid movement may occur. As illustrated in figure 15-5, an ash cloud from an eruption in Alaska reached the lower 48 states in less than a day. After another day, it was causing disruption of air traffic in the upper Midwest.

> Volcanic clouds may extend to great heights and over hundreds of miles. Pilots should not attempt to fly through or climb out of the cloud.

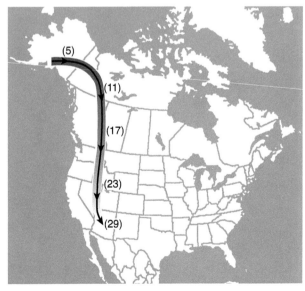

Figure 15-5. Estimated trajectory of the ash cloud from an eruption of Mt. Redoubt. Times in hours after the eruption are indicated in parentheses. Note that the ash cloud crossed major airline routes of the western U.S. and Canada in less than 30 hours.

METAR reports will occasionally carry volcanic eruption information in the remarks section. For example:

RMK MT. AUGUSTINE VOLCANO 70 MILES SW ERUPTD 231505 LARGE ASH CLOUD EXTENDING TO APPROXIMATELY 30000 FEET MOVG NE

REPORTS AND WARNINGS

Currently, volcanic eruptions are monitored internationally by means of pilot reports, radar, satellite observations, and volcanic observatories. Nine Volcanic Ash Advisory Centers (VAAC) have the responsibility for the preparation and worldwide dissemination of a Volcanic Ash Advisory (VAA) in a timely manner so that appropriate Meteorological Watch Offices (MWO) may issue SIGMETs. VAAC in the U.S. also prepare Volcanic Ash Forecast Transport and Dispersion (VAFTAD) charts. A Volcanic Ash Advisory gives the volcano location; describes the ash cloud; and provides a forecast of the plume. The statement is issued within six hours of an eruption and at six-hour intervals as long as conditions warrant.

VAFTAD charts show computer forecasts of the future locations and relative concentrations of ash clouds for a number of atmospheric layers up to FL550. If there has been an actual volcanic eruption, the charts will be labeled "ALERT." If the chart is issued for a potential eruption, it will be labeled "WATCH." See Appendix B for an example.

The VAFTAD chart is strictly for advanced flight planning purposes. It is not intended to take the place of SIGMETs regarding volcanic eruptions and ash.

One of the most important links in volcano observation and warning programs for aircraft is the pilot. Especially in remote areas, the pilot is often the first to see an eruption and, of course, any aircraft that inadvertently flies into an ash cloud becomes a direct sensor of the cloud location and effects. All pilots are advised to report volcanic activity.

If you see a volcanic eruption and have not been previously notified about it, immediately report it to ATC.

When landing at an airport where volcanic ash has been deposited, be aware that even a thin layer of dry ash can be detrimental to braking action. Wet ash may also be a problem.

Precautions should be taken to minimize reduction in visibility and ingestion of ash into the engine(s) when landing or taking off from an airport where volcanic ash is present.

Section D

SPACE WEATHER HAZARDS

The increasing dependence of aircraft navigation and communication systems on satellites and the opening of more airline routes in the North Polar area in the last few years have led to a greater concern with atmospheric hazards caused by solar disturbances. Instabilities such as solar flares cause increases in solar output of charged particles which subsequently reach the earth and the atmosphere. In the Northern Hemisphere, the visual indication of the interaction of these particles with the earth's magnetic field is the appearance of the beautiful aurora borealis (northern lights). (Figure 15-6A) A more critical impact of solar disturbances is interference with communication and navigation systems, with satellites, and surface power grids. Especially near the poles, intense geomagnetic storms also produce radiation increases which may impact the health of crew and passengers at and above flight altitudes of commercial airliners.

The state of the sun, variations of the transfer of energy from the sun to the earth, and conditions in the earth's magnetic field are collectively called space weather. Space weather is monitored by USAF and the Space Environment Center (SEC) of NOAA. Space weather conditions are regularly evaluated on the basis of specific impacts, which in turn govern the selection of flight routes and altitudes. (Figure 15-6B)

AIRLINE SOLAR RADIATION STORM SCALE — B.

Category	Effect
S_5 Extreme	High radiation hazard to passengers and crew (equal to 100 chest X-rays), loss of some satellites, complete blackout of high frequency (HF) communications possible in polar regions, which makes navigational operations extremely difficult.
S_4 Severe	Radiation hazard to occupants of commercial jets (equal to 10 chest X-rays), satellite star tracker orientation problems, blackout of HF radio in polar regions, and increased navigational errors over several days are likely.
S_3 Strong	Radiation hazard to jet passengers (equal to one chest X-ray), permanent damage to exposed satellite components, degraded HF in polar regions.
S_2 Moderate	Passengers and crew in high-flying aircraft at high altitudes may be exposed to elevated radiation risk, infrequent satellite event upsets, slight effect to HF in polar regions.
S_1 Minor	Small effect on HF radio in polar region.

RADIO BLACKOUT SCALE

Category	Effect
R_5 Extreme	Complete high frequency (HF) radio blackout on the entire sunlit side of the earth for a number of hours, navigational outages on sunlit side for many hours.
R_4 Severe	One- to two-hour HF blackout on sunlit side of earth, minor satellite navigation disruptions.
R_3 Strong	Wide area of HF blackout, loss of radio contact for en route aviators for about an hour, low frequency navigation degraded.
R_2 Moderate	Limited loss of HF radio, some low frequency navigation signals degraded.
R_1 Minor	Minor degradation of HF, minor low frequency navigation signals degraded.

GEOMAGNETIC STORM SCALE

Category	Effect
G_5 Extreme	Power grids can collapse, transformers are damaged, HF (high frequency) radio blackout in many areas for one to two days, low frequency radio out for hours.
G_4 Severe	Voltage stability problems in power systems, satellite orientation problems, HF radio propagation sporadic, low frequency radio disrupted.
G_3 Strong	Voltage corrections required on power systems, false alarms triggered on protection devices, increased drag on satellites, low frequency radio navigation problems.
G_2 Moderate	High latitude power systems affected, drag on satellites effect orbit, HF radio propagation fades at higher altitudes.
G_1 Minor	Slight power grid fluctuatuions, minor impact to satellites.

Figure 15-6. A. An example of **Aurora Borealis (Northern Lights)**. In the Southern Hemisphere, this phenomenon is called "Aurora Australis" or Southern Lights. B. Airline Solar Radiation Storm Scale, Radio Blackout Scale, Geomagnetic Storm Scale

Section E

RUNWAY HAZARDS

Another common hazard is a decrease of braking effectiveness when the runway surface is coated with wet snow, ice, frost, water, or volcanic ash. This problem occurs because friction between the tires and the surface is reduced by one of these hazards while taxiing or during landings. Frost may also be a significant hazard on some runway surfaces.

With water or wet snow, braking effectiveness may be greatly reduced by hydroplaning which occurs when a thin layer of water separates the tire from the runway surface. Heavy rain and/or slow drainage of the runway surface cause these conditions. This hazard is just one more reason why landing in the face of a downburst is inadvisable.

PA32. One minor injury. Upon touchdown, the pilot applied the brakes and the airplane skidded off the end of the runway into a wooded area. The airplane struck trees and the wings separated. According to the pilot's statement, "Runway was frost-covered grass. Brakes operated correctly, no mechanical malfunction." NTSB determined that the pilot did not attain the proper touchdown point on a grass runway covered with frost, which resulted in inadequate braking and runway overrun.

When you operate in conditions where braking effectiveness is poor or nil, be sure the runway length is adequate and the surface wind is favorable.

Section F

COLD CLIMATE HAZARDS

The differences between weather hazards encountered while flying during warm seasons in low and middle latitudes and those encountered in cold seasons, are large, especially in high latitudes. At very low temperatures, the performance of both pilots and aircraft can be compromised.

It is difficult for persons to function efficiently at extremely low temperatures; even at moderately low temperatures, physical activities are hampered by the combination of wind and temperature which produce a much lower windchill temperature. (Figure 15-7)

As discussed in the previous chapter, at temperatures less than -22°F (-30°C) in calm conditions, surface visibilities can be compromised by persistent ice fog. This problem is worse near towns and settlements, which act as water vapor sources. Nearby airports are vulnerable; in fact, the simple action of starting an aircraft engine may rapidly decrease visibility over the runway.

Takeoffs on snow and ice surfaces become problematic at extremely low temperatures. At -40°F, the structure of an ice surface begins to get "sticky." This condition affects aircraft equipped with skis. Longer takeoff runs and more power are required. At -60°F (-51°C), takeoff in a ski-plane is nearly impossible.

Wind Chill Chart

(°C)		0				-10				-20				-30				-40		
(°F) Calm	40	35	30	25	20	15	10	5	0	-5	-10	-15	-20	-25	-30	-35	-40	-45
5	36	31	25	19	13	7	1	-5	-11	-16	-22	-28	-34	-40	-46	-52	-57	-63
10	34	27	21	15	9	3	-4	-10	-16	-22	-28	-35	-41	-47	-53	-59	-66	-72
15	32	25	19	13	6	0	-7	-13	-19	-26	-32	-39	-45	-51	-58	-64	-71	-77
20	30	24	17	11	4	-2	-9	-15	-22	-29	-35	-42	-48	-55	-61	-68	-74	-81
25	29	23	16	9	3	-4	-11	-17	-24	-31	-37	-44	-51	-58	-64	-71	-78	-84
30	28	22	15	8	1	-5	-12	-19	-26	-33	-39	-46	-53	-60	-67	-73	-80	-87
35	28	21	14	7	0	-7	-14	-21	-27	-34	-41	-48	-55	-62	-69	-76	-82	-89
40	27	20	13	6	-1	-8	-15	-22	-29	-36	-43	-50	-57	-64	-71	-78	-84	-91
45	26	19	12	5	-2	-9	-16	-23	-30	-37	-44	-51	-58	-65	-72	-79	-86	-93
50	26	19	12	4	-3	-10	-17	-24	-31	-38	-45	-52	-60	-67	-74	-81	-88	-95
55	25	18	11	4	-3	-11	-18	-25	-32	-39	-46	-54	-61	-68	-75	-82	-89	-97
60	25	17	10	3	-4	-11	-19	-26	-33	-40	-48	-55	-62	-69	-76	-84	-91	-98

Frostbite Times: 30 minutes, 10 minutes, 5 minutes

Wind (knots) / Wind (mph)

Figure 15-7. Windchill Chart

Snow-covered ground can present some special visibility problems. The reflection of light by snow-covered surfaces and/or low blowing snow may reduce contrast on the ground, making it difficult to identify objects and estimate critical distances. The most serious version of this problem is whiteout. This is a situation where all depth perception is lost because of a low sun angle and the presence of a cloud layer over a snow surface. The diffusion of light from the sun by the cloud layer causes the light to be reflected

BE V35A. No injuries. The pilot reported that there was light snow blowing at the time of the accident. The airport environment and runway were covered with one to two inches of new snow. He cancelled IFR about 15 miles from his destination. He said he intended to make a low pass to observe the condition of the snow-covered runway. He lowered his landing gear and full flaps, turned onto the runway heading, and observed the altimeter indication. Before he realized it, the airplane impacted short of runway 33. NTSB concluded that the probable cause of the accident was the pilot's misjudgment of the actual altitude of the airplane. Contributing factors were the optical illusion caused by the environment of the snow-covered runway, and whiteout.

> An effect similar to whiteout (sometimes referred to as "grayout") may occur in desert regions when a sandstorm is present at the surface and cirrostratus clouds cover the sky.

from many angles when it reaches the ground. Repeated reflections between the ground and the cloud eliminate all shadows. The horizon cannot be identified and disorientation may occur. This is a particular problem in Polar Regions.

In Chapter 3, you learned that a pressure altimeter error will arise whenever the actual temperature is different than that of the standard atmosphere. In extremely cold locations, such errors are large; that is, the indicated altitude reads much higher than true altitude due to cold temperature alone. For example, considering only the temperature effect, at an indicated altitude of 6,000 feet with OAT of -28°C, the true altitude is 840 feet lower than indicated; at even lower temperatures at higher altitudes, the error grows. At an indicated altitude of 10,000 feet and OAT of -32°C, the true altitude is 1210 feet lower than indicated.

SUMMARY

This chapter alerted you to some additional aviation weather hazards, some of which are rare and others that are more often nuisances. However, all have the potential of contributing to serious difficulties when they occur with other flight problems. Also, a few of them by themselves can create critical flight conditions (for example, lightning, volcanic ash, whiteout, and hydroplaning). As with all weather hazards, your newly gained knowledge of their causes and of the conditions under which they occur should help you anticipate and avoid them where possible.

KEY TERMS

Aurora Borealis (Northern Lights)
Hydroplaning
Lightning
Positive Charge Center
Positive Lightning Strike
Ozone
St. Elmo's Fire
Space Environment Center (SEC)
Space Weather

Static Discharge
Volcanic Ash
Volcanic Ash Advisory Centers (VAAC)
Volcanic Ash Advisory (VAA)
Volcanic Ash Forecast Transport and
        Dispersion (VAFTAD) charts
Whiteout
Windchill

REVIEW QUESTIONS

1. List the potential adverse effects of an inflight lightning strike.

2. At 41,000 feet, would you expect ozone concentrations to be greater in a macroscale trough or ridge?

3. List the potential hazards of an encounter with volcanic ash.

4. Volcanic ash plumes become less hazardous as they "age" because _____.

5. How far will a volcanic ash cloud travel in 12 hours if the wind speed at plume level is 35 knots?

6. List the potential negative impacts of solar disturbances on flights near the Poles.

7. You are approaching a well-maintained but uncontrolled airport on a clear winter day. The airport is located in a flat area devoid of buildings, fences, or trees. The runway and surrounding roads are covered with fresh snow. What are the possible hazards during approach and landing?

DISCOVERY QUESTIONS

8. In whiteout conditions, it has been said that objects appear to "float in the air." What causes this?

9. What causes lightning to occur with volcanic eruptions?

10. Mt. St. Helens, which erupted in southern Washington State, caused much devastation on the ground. However, the ash cloud did not have the same long-term effects as ash clouds from either Mt. Pinatubo in the Philippines or El Chichon in Mexico. Why? (Hint: do some research on the description of the Mt. St. Helens eruption.)

11. An aircraft makes a wintertime flight from Seattle to Boston at FL410. Weather conditions included major low pressure systems and associated fronts on both coasts and a large high pressure center over the central U.S. Draw a diagram showing the aircraft track and the likely upper air patterns at flight level. Show contours and jet streams. Where would increased concentrations of stratospheric ozone most likely be encountered?

12. You are at an uncontrolled airport somewhere north of 30°N latitude. Because you are in a mountain valley, surface winds aren't a very reliable indicator of large-scale wind patterns. A volcanic eruption has occurred within a few hundred miles of your location in the last 12 hours. A light dusting of ash covers the airport. The pressure has been falling steadily during that period and clouds have increased significantly (the clouds are visible despite the falling ash). Based on this information alone, estimate the volcano location (distance and direction) relative to your location. Support your answer with a consistent description and sketches of the large-scale weather pattern.

Part IV

Applying Weather Knowledge

Part IV
Applying Weather Knowledge

Now that you understand weather-producing processes, the behavior of weather systems, and the flight hazards that weather phenomena generate, you can begin to apply this knowledge as a pilot. Part IV introduces the forecasting process, familiarizes you with useful forecast products, and provides an overview of weather information sources. It then uses an actual flight scenario with related weather data and graphics to demonstrate the development of a self-briefing procedure that integrates available weather information into a comprehensive mental picture of current and forecast weather.

When you complete Part IV, you will be able to interpret the information obtained in briefings, printed reports, graphic weather products, and other formats. You will also be given a method to help in the development of weather visualization skills to enhance your flight safety and prepare you to successfully use the innovative aviation weather products of the future.

(Challenger photograph on previous page, source: Bombardier Business Aircraft)

Introduction

Weather information and forecasts are beneficial in numerous ways. For example, a prediction of warm temperatures or the chance of rain helps us decide whether to plan a picnic or carry an umbrella for the day. More importantly, forecasts of severe weather such as blizzards, thunderstorms, or hurricanes, help communities prevent property damage and save lives. As a pilot, weather influences your life in a unique way. Determinations regarding weather conditions must be made before every flight, and crucial weather decisions may have to be made inflight. A wide variety of weather resources are available to assist you in this decision-making process. In this chapter, we describe the on-going process of collecting, transmitting, and processing weather data to produce a weather forecast. We then consider various formats of aviation weather forecasts, and the sources of aviation weather information.

When you complete Chapter 16, you should understand how weather information is compiled and processed, and some basic concepts of forecasting. You should also be familiar with the variety of aviation weather forecasts available to you, as well as the sources of aviation weather information to help you make safe preflight and inflight decisions.

SECTION A: THE WEATHER FORECASTING PROCESS
Collecting Weather Data
Processing Weather Data
Making the Forecast
    Forecasting Methods
    Forecasting Accuracy

SECTION B: AVIATION WEATHER FORECAST PRODUCTS
Forecast Products in Text Format
    Terminal Aerodrome Forecasts (TAF)
    Area Forecasts (FA)
    Inflight Weather Advisories (WS, WST, WA)
    Flight Information Service-Broadcast (FIS-B)
    Winds and Temperatures Aloft Forecasts (FB)
    Other Advisories, Watches, and Warnings
Forecast Products in Graphic Format
    Significant Weather Prognostic Chart
    Forecast Winds and Temperatures Aloft Chart

SECTION C: AVIATION WEATHER INFORMATION SOURCES
FAA Automated Flight Service Stations (AFSS)
Continuous Broadcasts of Weather Information (HIWAS, ATIS)
Weather on the Internet

Section A

THE WEATHER FORECASTING PROCESS

If the current state of the atmosphere is known, what will that state be in the future? This is the basic question that weather forecasters must consider every day. To fully comprehend and effectively use aviation weather forecasts, you must first understand the way forecasts are produced. Essentially, there are three important steps in the process: data collection, data processing, and forecasting.

COLLECTING WEATHER DATA

In order to develop a forecast for a specific location or region, the present weather conditions over a large area must be known. As shown in figure 16-1 observations of surface weather conditions are provided by a network of thousands of observing stations located throughout the world. Upper-air data are chiefly provided by radiosondes, wind profilers, aircraft, and satellites. Weather radar systems obtain additional information about precipitation, wind, and severe convective weather. The World Meteorological Organization (WMO), a United Nations agency, is responsible for the standardization of observations and the international exchange of weather data. Meteorological information from around the world is relayed through a network of national meteorological centers, regional centers, and global centers via the Global Telecommunications System (GTS).

Observations and forecasts for aviation are communicated internationally via the World Area Forecast System (WAFS). WAFS is a program developed by the International Civil Aviation Organization (ICAO) and WMO to improve the quality and consistency of enroute guidance provided to international aircraft operations.

PROCESSING WEATHER DATA

Global aviation weather products are produced at World Area Forecast Centers (WAFC) located in the U.S. in Washington, D.C. and in the U.K., in London. For the U.S. and environs, the National Centers for Environmental Prediction (NCEP) under NOAA/NWS handle weather forecasting. (Figure 16-1)

NCEP offices assimilate and quality-assure raw data and prepare computer analyses of temperature, pressure, wind, moisture, and a wide variety of other meteorological fields. By means of its large and fast computers, NCEP is able to prepare timely forecasts on both a national and worldwide basis. Typical NCEP products are national-forecast guidance products and discussions, public forecasts and warnings, and forecasts for special users such as the aviation community.

One of the components of NCEP is the Aviation Weather Center (AWC), which specializes in the preparation of aviation weather information. NCEP produces analyses, forecasts, and advisories in both graphic and alphanumeric formats. These products are distributed nationally and internationally to public and private agencies. Of particular importance for aviation in the U.S., are distributions of analyses and forecasts to Weather Forecast Offices (WFO), Air Route Traffic Control Centers (ARTCC), Automated Flight Service Stations (AFSS), airlines, and private weather companies. These organizations further develop regional and local forecasts and produce specialized products for the aviation industry. The most common aviation forecasts and advisories and their sources are discussed in Sections B and C.

MAKING THE FORECAST

Once the observed data are checked for errors and analyzed, the forecast can be made. It is important that you understand some of the basic elements of weather forecasting so that you can make intelligent use of forecasts. This under-

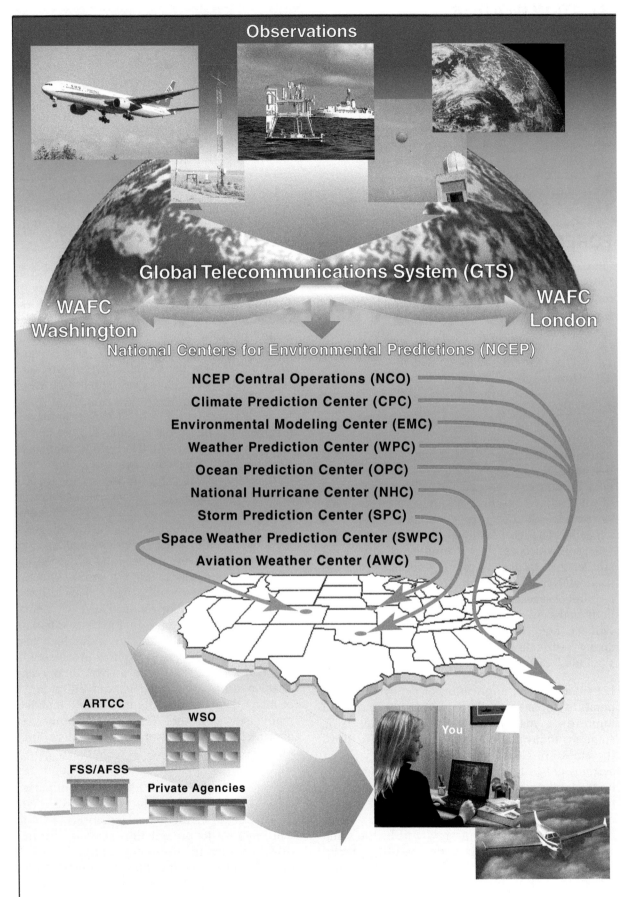

Figure 16-1. The Global Telecommunications System (GTS) acts as a two-way conduit for the gathering of worldwide weather observations by national and international weather centers and the subsequent distribution of analyses and forecasts from those centers to users.

standing is critical because, although forecasts are not perfect, they are invaluable for flight planning. A "good" forecast depends nearly as much on the user as on the forecaster. A pilot must understand the strengths and weaknesses of a forecast to use it properly.

FORECASTING METHODS

One way to begin to understand the weather forecasting process is by considering a simple temperature forecast problem, such as predicting the temperature at your location for tomorrow at this time. You can do this by answering two questions:
1. What is the temperature now?
2. How much will the temperature change over the forecast period (24 hours)?

Question one requires that you observe the temperature now. Question two requires that you determine the impact of any physical processes that will cause the temperature to change in the next 24 hours. Once you have these two pieces of information, the forecast temperature is equal to the sum of the current temperature and the expected change. Although quite simple, this forecasting process has a number of important similarities to the rigorous forecast processes used at NCEP and other forecast centers. Both require observations of current conditions, and both make an estimate of how the atmosphere will change during the forecast period. The change estimate in both cases can be considered a "model" of atmospheric processes.

Let's consider an application of our simple temperature forecast method to the prediction of tomorrow's maximum temperature. Say it is summer, today's maximum temperature is 30°C, the skies are clear, winds are light, no weather systems are in the vicinity. On the basis of your understanding of these conditions (your brain is the "model"), you forecast "no change" for the next 24 hours. In other words, the forecast maximum temperature for tomorrow will be the same as it is today, 30°C. This is the simplest prediction, known as a persistence forecast; that is, conditions at the time of forecast will persist through the forecast period. If, in another case, you base

your estimate of the temperature change upon your observation that the maximum temperature had been falling 3C° per day in the past few days, then your forecast would be today's temperature (30°C) minus 3C° for a forecast of 27°C. This technique is known as a trend forecast; that is, initial conditions will change at the rate observed in the recent past.

The simplicity of persistence and trend forecasting techniques for temperature or any other forecast variable is appealing. Those forecast techniques do work in periods of benign weather and for short periods of time, but life is more complicated. Put another way, if we want to consider all weather variables and their changes, then a more comprehensive model of atmospheric processes is required. For example, if we want to use a temperature forecast that is consistently accurate for all possible causes of temperature changes, then we must take into account advection, adiabatic processes, radiation, condensation and evaporation, conduction, and turbulent mixing. Additionally, interactions between temperature, pressure, wind, and moisture demand that the model should really consider all weather variables simultaneously. Professional meteorologists, who are well trained and experienced in forecasting, are able to use forecasting techniques that have better scientific bases than either persistence or trend forecasting. However, demands for even more accuracy in forecasts often reach beyond the capability of an individual meteorologist. Higher accuracy requires processing huge numbers of observations in a short time, comprehensive atmospheric models, and the production of many detailed forecasts in a timely manner for many areas and users. The use of computers is an absolutely necessary tool for the modern forecast process.

The most comprehensive forecast technique today is numerical weather prediction (NWP), which solves a set of mathematical equations (a "numerical" model) to predict the weather. The equations represent the well-known physical laws that describe the behavior of the atmosphere. Pressure, temperature, wind, clouds, and precipitation are predicted on a three-dimensional grid of points which cover the earth from the ground through the high atmosphere. Interactions with the surface such as evaporation, condensation, precipitation, latent and sensible heat exchange, and friction are accounted for in the model equations.

As you would expect from the previous paragraphs, the starting point for any NWP model forecast is the collection of current observations... the more observations, the better. Sophisticated numerical models not only use surface observations, but also upper air balloon soundings, satellite observations, and aircraft observations. The ingestion and processing of these data must be accomplished prior to the forecast process, requiring very large and fast computers at NWP centers around the world.

Once the forecasts are made, forecasters use numerical weather predictions as guidance. Then, they add detail based on their own scientific knowledge and experience. In this way, local terrain and small-scale influences can be taken into account.

FORECASTING ACCURACY

The previous section gave us a working definition of a forecast as the sum of current conditions (the observation) plus the estimated changes in the forecast period (based on some type of model). This concept helps us see where forecast errors can arise. If a bad observation is used to "start" (initialize) the forecast, the forecast is doomed even if the model is perfect.

> Forecast accuracy depends on the accuracy of the initial observations and the accuracy of the model. If either one or both of these are in error, the forecast will suffer.

Another type of observational error arises because of the large distance between weather stations and the long time between weather reports. It is difficult for a forecast to precisely describe a weather feature when the current observations cannot resolve that feature in space and time. This is a particular problem for the prediction of microscale and some mesoscale weather phenomena. A similar problem arises because the computer solutions represent the atmosphere at locations called grid points. The spacing of the grid points depends on the model. If an NWP model has a grid spacing much larger than a particular phenomenon, such as a thunderstorm, then that phenomenon can not be predicted precisely in computer-based analyses or forecasts, whether or not the thunderstorm is observed accurately. In the worst case, it is like trying to determine the future position of a particular aircraft when all you know is that it is in the sky.

On the other hand, if the observations are perfect, errors may still arise if the prediction method (the "model") is not perfect. Figure 16-2 shows that, considering all weather conditions and variables, a typical persistence forecast is good (that is, it has a small error) for only a few hours. In comparison to persistence forecasts, the accuracy of meteorological forecasts, which are based on scientific knowledge as used by NWP and weather forecasters, is much better and decreases much more slowly as the forecast period increases. However, for the longest forecast periods, the accuracy of meteorological forecasts is no better than that of climatological forecasts, which are based purely on past averages and are typically not very accurate at all.

> The accuracy of weather forecasts decreases as the forecast period increases.

In general, meteorological forecasts are quite accurate out to 12 hours. From 12 to 24 hours, predicting the movement of large-scale, extra-tropical weather systems and the variations in temperature, precipitation, cloudiness, and air quality associated with these systems are generally well forecast. Usually, forecasters can accurately predict the occurrence of large-scale circulation events such as cold waves and significant storms several days in advance. After about five days, however, the ability to predict details deteriorates rapidly. Due to the difficulty in making accurate predictions about specific weather conditions too far in the future, you can appreciate the importance of using the most current weather information for flight planning. It would not be wise to base today's go/no-go decision on a forecast that you received two days ago.

Weather forecasts tend to be more accurate when the weather is good than when it is bad.

The accuracy of a 36-hour forecast of large scale weather features such as lows and highs is much better than 36-hour forecasts of small-scale weather features such as clear air turbulence and thunderstorms.

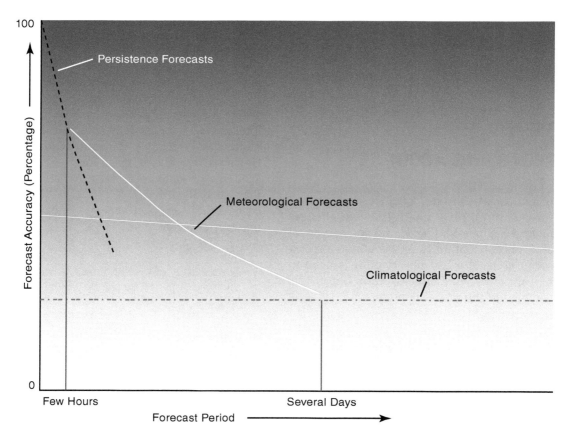

Figure 16-2. The accuracy of weather forecasts as a function of the forecast period and the forecasting method. This diagram schematically compares the accuracy of persistence, meteorological, and climatological forecasts for forecast periods from a few hours to several days. This diagram is very general. The actual rate of deterioration of the accuracy of forecasts for a given airport depends on its location, the season, and the forecast variable.

Section B

AVIATION WEATHER FORECAST PRODUCTS

One of your primary goals as a pilot is to be able to integrate available weather information into a coherent picture for planning and carrying out safe flight. Weather information can be divided into two parts: current conditions and forecast conditions. Weather products that describe current conditions have been considered in the previous chapters. You should already be able to interpret weather observations from the surface (METARs) and from the air (PIREPs). You also should be familiar with surface analysis, upper air, radar, and weather depiction charts, as well as satellite imagery. Now that you are familiar with the forecasting process, we will look at the products that describe forecast conditions. Specifically, we are interested in forecast material that is available to you as text and graphics.

Although the formats of bulletins, maps, and other forecast products may vary according to their source (public and private agencies) or their presentation (verbal, printed, or electronic), all have certain basic similarities. This discussion will concentrate on common forecast material available from government agencies. As an aid to the descriptions presented below, decoding keys for products are included in Appendix B. In addition, the most recent version of FAA *Advisory Circular 00-45, Aviation Weather Services,* contains further information.

The keys to efficiently using the weather information available to you are data selectivity and visualization. Selectivity requires that you know exactly what you need, what is available, and where and when it is available. For example, a pilot flying a light aircraft at 5,000 feet on a local flight doesn't need a High Altitude Significant Weather Prognostic Chart. Also, if the latest terminal forecast is five hours old, it may be better to wait for a short time until the next forecast is issued (they are issued every six hours). Visualization means forming a mental image of current and forecast weather conditions. This is particularly important if your weather information is from a telephone briefing or an inflight advisory text (no graphics).

FORECAST PRODUCTS IN TEXT FORMAT

Forecast products in "text format" include Terminal Aerodrome Forecasts (TAF), Area Forecasts (FA), Inflight Weather Advisories (WS, WA, WST), Transcribed Weather Enroute Broadcasts (TWEB), Winds and Temperatures Aloft Forecasts (FB), and a number of other advisories, statements, and warnings of interest to pilots.

TERMINAL AERODROME FORECASTS (TAF)

The terminal aerodrome forecast (TAF) describes weather conditions that are expected to occur within a 5 s.m. radius of an airport over a 24-30 hour period. In the U.S., routine TAFs are issued four times daily at 0000Z, 0600Z, 1200Z, and 1800Z. Schedules in other countries may differ. The TAF is one of your most valuable sources for the predicted weather at a specific airport. Predicted sky condition, visibility, weather and obstructions to vision, wind direction and speed, and expected changes during the forecast period can be derived from TAFs. TAF forecasts have a format and abbreviations very similar to METAR. An example of a TAF is shown together with a map of the locations of available TAFs in Figure 16-3.

Developments in technology continue to facilitate the acquisition of critical meteorological data. For example, TAFs and METARs are available in both coded and plain language formats, as well as from online clickable maps (http://www.wrh.noaa.gov/zoa/mwmap3.php?map=usa) for many sites in North America.

AREA FORECASTS (FA)

Expected VMC, clouds, and general weather conditions over an area the size of several states are described in an area forecast (FA). An FA is used to determine enroute weather, including conditions at airports that do not have terminal forecasts. An FA should always be used in conjunction with the most recent inflight weather advisories. Area forecasts are normally issued

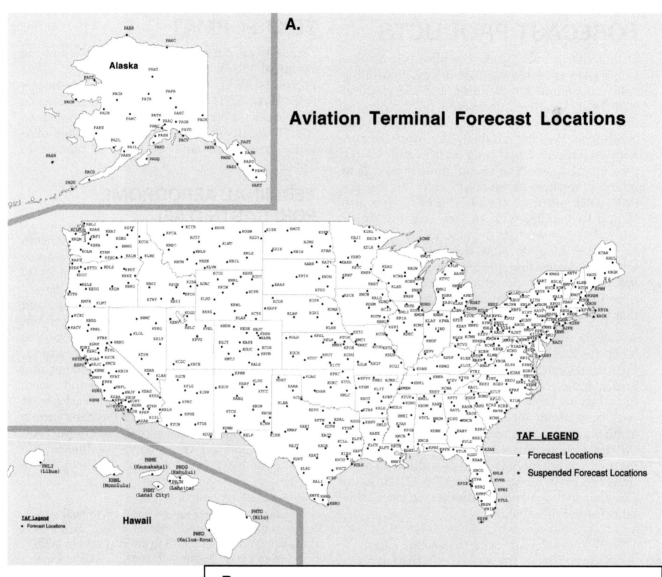

Figure 16-3. A. Locations for which Terminal Aerodrome Forecasts (TAFS) are available across the U.S. B. TAF for Syracuse, New York. See Appendix B for further details on U.S. and International TAFS.

three times daily and are valid for 18 hours. An FA has four sections:

1. A **Header** describes the source of the FA, the date and time of issue, the valid times, and the areas the FA covers.

2. **Precautionary Statements** describe IFR and mountain obscurations, thunderstorm hazards, and states that all heights are MSL unless otherwise noted.

3. A **Synopsis** is a brief summary identifying the location and movement of pressure systems, fronts, and circulation patterns for the 18-hour forecast period.

4. A **VFR Clouds and Weather** section lists expected sky condition, visibility, and weather for the next 12 hours and an outlook for the following 6 hours.

The area forecast covers an area of several states and can be used to determine enroute weather and conditions at your destination if no TAF has been issued.

FAs are issued by the Aviation Weather Center (AWC) for six regions in the contiguous U.S. as shown in figure 16-4. The Alaska Aviation Weather Unit issues an FA for the state of Alaska, while the Honolulu WFO handles Hawaii. Special FAs are also issued for the Gulf of Mexico and international airspace. Within its prescribed area, an FA describes weather features and conditions relative to common geographical regions and features. In addition to the forecast regions, figure 16-4 also shows commonly used geographical area designators for the contiguous states. An example of an FA is presented in figure 16-5.

To understand the complete weather picture, an FA should always be used together with the most recent inflight aviation weather advisories (AIRMETs, SIGMETs, Convective SIGMETs).

International Area Forecasts are provided for airspace from the surface to 25,000 feet for parts of the Caribbean Sea, the Gulf of Mexico, and parts of the Atlantic Ocean.

The FAA recognizes three sources of approved aviation weather information: the Federal Government; the Enhanced Weather Information System (EWINS); and Qualified Internet Communications Providers (QICPs). Be cautious if you use repackaged weather data, analyses, and forecasts from unapproved commercial sources.

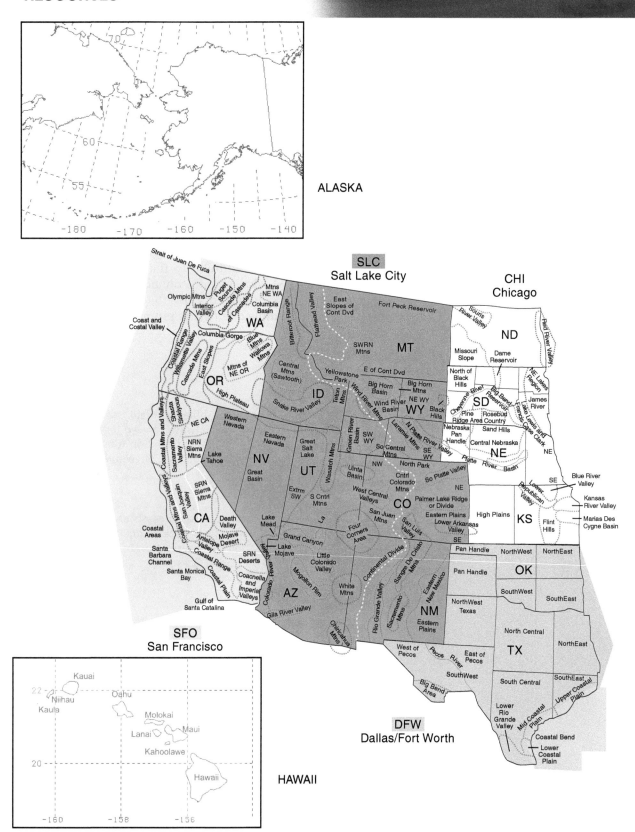

Figure 16-4. This geographical area designator map can be useful in determining the specific area described by an area forecast. The contiguous U.S. is divided into six forecast areas (color-coded) plus the Gulf of Mexico, Hawaii, Alaska, and the Caribbean. You may want to keep a copy of this map with your flight planning materials so that you have access to it when obtaining weather information.

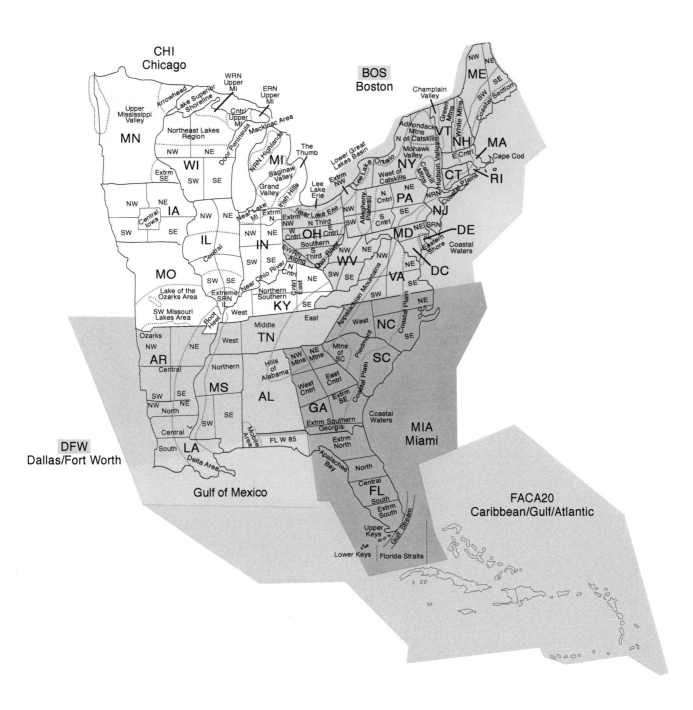

HEADER
```
FAUS44 KKCI 311045
FA4W
DFWC FA 311045
SYNOPSIS AND VFR CLDS/WX
SYNOPSIS VALID UNTIL 010500
CLDS/WX VALID UNTIL 312300...OTLK VALID 312300-010500
OK TX AR TN LA MS AL AND CSTL WTRS
```

PRECAUTIONS
```
SEE AIRMET SIERRA FOR IFR CONDS AND MTN OBSCN.
TS IMPLY SEV OR GTR TURB SEV ICE LLWS AND IFR CONDS.
NON MSL HGTS DENOTED BY AGL OR CIG.
```

SYNOPSIS
```
SYNOPSIS...11Z CDFNT ALG SSM-MBS-TTH-ARG LN THRU LOW NR DFW AND
CONT ALG ABI-30E ROW-CIM LM CONTG NWD AS STNR FNT. TROF FM LOW NR
DFW TO 50SE DLF. HIGH OVR CNTRL GA. 05Z CDFNT ALG BKW-40SE LOZ-
60W VXV LN CONTG AS STNR FNT ALG MSL-SQS LN TO LOW ARND 40NE MLU.
CDFNT FM LOW ARND 40NE MLU ALG MLU-40W LCH-PSX-50SSE DLF-70S FST
LN CONTG AS STNR FNT ALG 70S FST-60W INK TO LOW NR LVS. TROF FM
LOW NR LVS ALG TBE-40N GCK LN
```

VFR CLOUDS
AND WEATHER
```
OK
WRN 2/3...SKC. TIL 19Z NLY WND G25KT. 16Z SKC OR SCT CI.
   OTLK...VFR.
ERN 1/3...CIG BKN040 BKN100 TOP FL220 EXTRM SERN OK. CIG BKN025
   TOP 080 RMNDR. TIL 12Z ISOL SHRA EXTRM SERN OK. 17Z SKC OR SCT
   CI...VFR.

NWRN TX
SKC. 16Z SKC OR SCT CI. OTLK...VFR.

SWRN TX
ERN 1/2 TRANSPECOS...SCT100. BECMG 1214 SKC. OTLK...VFR.
RMNDR...SKC. OTLK...VFR.

N CNTRL TX
SERN 1/4...SCT120. BECMG 1416 SKC OR SCT CI. OCNL SCT120.
   OTLK...VFR.
RMNDR...SKC. 16Z SKC OR SCT CI. OCNL SCT120. OTLK...VFR.

NERN TX
CIG BKN050 TOP FL280. OCNL CIG BKN025. WDLY SCT SHRA/ISOL TSRA.
CB TOP FL350. 15Z CIG BKN040 TOP 150. OTLK...VFR.

S CNTRL TX
N OF LRD-40W IAH LN...AGL SCT040 BKN120 TOP FL180. ISOL SHRA. 16Z
   SCT080. OTLK...VFR.
S OF LRD-40W IAH LN...CIG BKN040 TOP 060 MID TX CSTL PLAIN. SKC
   RMNDR. 14Z AGL SCT030 SCT120. OTLK...VFR TSRA.

SERN TX
CIG BKN045 TOP FL250. AFT 14Z ISOL SHRA/TSRA. CB TOP FL350. 21Z
SCT120. SCT CI. OTLK...VFR.
```

Figure 16-5. An example of an area forecast with the sections of the forecast identified. Note: only a portion of the VFR Clouds and Weather section is shown for this FA.

INFLIGHT WEATHER ADVISORIES (WS, WST, WA)

Inflight aviation weather advisories consist of either an observation and a forecast, or just a forecast for the development of potentially hazardous weather. Although identified as "inflight," pertinent advisories are an important part of preflight weather planning as well. In the United States, the most commonly used inflight advisories are classified as a SIGMET (Significant Meteorological Information), Convective SIGMET, and AIRMET (Airman's Meteorological Information). Elsewhere, similar inflight weather advisories are referred to as International SIGMETs.

A non-convective SIGMET (WS) describes conditions which can pose hazards to all aircraft. SIGMETs are valid for up to four hours. If the following phenomena are observed or expected to occur, a SIGMET is issued.

1. Severe icing not associated with thunderstorms
2. Severe or extreme turbulence or clear air turbulence not associated with thunderstorms
3. Duststorms or sandstorms lowering surface or inflight visibilities to below three miles
4. Volcanic ash

> SIGMETs are issued as warnings of hazardous weather, such as severe icing, which is of operational interest to all aircraft.

A Convective SIGMET (WST) describes convective activity that is potentially hazardous to all categories of aircraft. Bulletins are issued hourly with special advisories issued as required. The forecast period for a WST is two hours or less. Criteria for issuance are any of the following conditions:

1. Severe thunderstorms (surface winds greater than or equal to 50 knots and/or hail at the surface greater than or equal to 3/4 inches in diameter and/or tornadoes)

2. Embedded thunderstorms
3. A line of thunderstorms
4. Thunderstorms producing precipitation with an intensity greater than or equal to "heavy" (level 4) and affecting 40% or more of an area at least 3,000 square miles

An AIRMET (WA) is issued for significant weather at intensities lower than those required for the issuance of a SIGMET.

> AIRMETs are intended for all pilots, but particularly for operators and pilots of aircraft that are sensitive to the weather phenomena described and to pilots without instrument ratings.

There are three different AIRMETs. AIRMET Sierra describes IFR conditions and/or extensive mountain obscurations. AIRMET Tango describes areas of moderate turbulence, sustained surface winds in excess of 30 knots, and areas of non-convective low-level wind shear. AIRMET Zulu describes moderate icing and provides freezing level heights.

AIRMETs are produced regularly every six hours with unscheduled amendments as necessary. Each bulletin contains any current AIRMETs that are in effect, an outlook for weather that is expected after the AIRMET valid period, and any significant conditions that do not meet AIRMET criteria.

Convective SIGMET bulletins are issued for the Eastern (E), Central (C), and Western (W) United States. AIRMETs and SIGMETs are issued for the regions highlighted in Figure 16-4. These "widespread" advisories must be either affecting or forecasted to affect at least 3,000 square miles at any one time. The total area influenced during the forecast period may be extremely large. For example, a 3,000 square mile weather system may be forecast to move across an area totaling 25,000 square miles during the forecast period. The affected areas are described by common VOR and airport identifiers (Figure 16-6) or by reference to well known geographical areas (Figure 16-4).

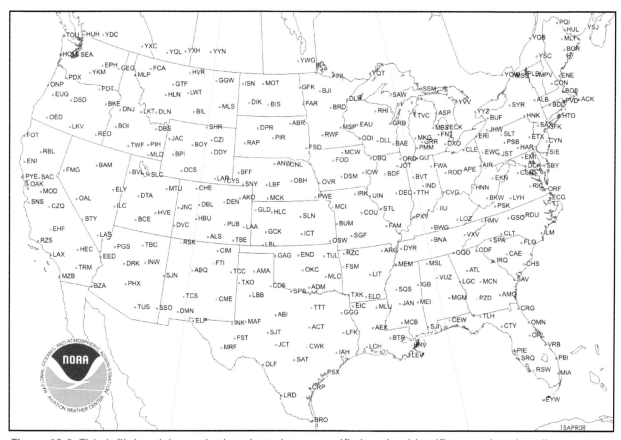

Figure 16-6. This inflight advisory plotting chart shows specific location identifiers used to describe areas affected by SIGMETs, Convective SIGMETs, and AIRMETs. Source: AWC.

Examples of SIGMET and Convective SIGMET texts are presented in figure 16-7. Examples of AIRMETs Sierra, Tango, and Zulu are given in figure 16-8.

International SIGMETs are issued worldwide by ICAO Meteorological Watch Offices (MWOs). Figure 16-9 shows an example. Note that the following criteria for international SIGMETs are broader than the criteria for either WS or WST for the United States.

1. Thunderstorms in lines, embedded in clouds, or in large areas producing tornadoes or large hail
2. Tropical cyclones
3. Severe icing
4. Severe or extreme turbulence
5. Duststorms or sandstorms lowering visibilities to less than 3 miles (5 km)
6. Volcanic Ash

A Graphical AIRMET (G-AIRMET) is a graphical display of hazardous weather. It is updated faster and with more precision than standard AIRMET text products, enabling pilots to maintain high safety margins while flying more efficient routes.

```
WSUS05 KKCI 301930
SLCQ WS 301930
SIGMET QUEBEC 2 VALID UNTIL 302330
SIGMET

CO
FROM 30E CHE TO 40SE CYS TO PUB TO HBU TO 30E CHE
OCNL SEV TURB BLW FL200 DUE TO MOD/STG WLY FLOW. STG UDDFS LKLY E
OF RDGLNS. RPTD BY ACFT W AND NW OF DEN DURG PAST 2-3 HRS. CONDS
SHFTG SLOLY SWD AND CONTG BYD 2330Z.


CONVECTIVE SIGMET 15E
VALID UNTIL 1855Z
OH MI IN LE LM
FROM 20N MKG-30SW CLE-50ENE IND-20W GIJ-20N MKG
AREA TS MOV FROM 31010KT. TOPS TO FL440.
OUTLOOK VALID 021855-022255
FROM 50E GRB-40WSW ASP-ECK-30SSE DXO-40W BUF-30SE ERI-APE-50E
IND-BVT-50E GRB
WST ISSUANCES POSS. REFER TO MOST RECENT ACUS01 KWNS FROM STORM
PREDICTION CENTER FOR SYNOPSIS AND METEOROLOGICAL DETAILS.
```

Figure 16-7. Examples of a SIGMET and a Convective SIGMET.

```
WAUS43 KKCI 291445
CHIS WA 291445
AIRMET SIERRA UPDT 5 FOR IFR VALID UNTIL 292100
AIRMET IFR...NE KS IA MO WI LM LS MI LH IL IN KY
FROM 70N SAW TO SSM TO YVV TO 40ENE ECK TO DXO TO FWA TO CVG TO
30NE ARG TO 30ESE OSW TO 60SE ICT TO 40ESE PWE TO 20NW GRB TO
80NNW RHI TO 70N SAW
CIG BLW 010/VIS BLW 3SM PCPN/BR. CONDS CONTG BYD 21Z THRU 03Z.


WAUS43 KKCI 291644 AAA
CHIT WA 291644 AMD
AIRMET TANGO UPDT 3 FOR TURB VALID UNTIL 292100
AIRMET TURB...ND SD NE KS MN IA
FROM 60SSE YWG TO INL TO 50NNW OVR TO 50W LBL TO GLD TO BFF TO
50NNW ISN TO 60SSE YWG
MOD TURB BTN 150 AND FL330. CONDS CONTG BYD 21Z THRU 03Z.


WAUS43 KKCI 291445
CHIZ WA 291445
AIRMET ZULU UPDT 2 FOR ICE AND FRZLVL VALID UNTIL 292100
AIRMET ICE...NE MN IA MO WI LM MI IL
FROM SAW TO 50ENE TVC TO 30S JOT TO 40ENE BUM TO 50NNW OVR TO
60SSW RHI TO SAW
MOD ICE BTN FRZLVL AND 170. FRZLVL SFC-090. CONDS CONTG BYD 21Z
THRU 03Z.
FRZLVL...RANGING FROM SFC-120 ACRS AREA
 MULT FRZLVL BLW 100 BOUNDED BY 30E MCW-50WNW DBQ …
```

Figure 16-8. Examples of AIRMETs Sierra, Tango, and Zulu. Note: Although these texts show examples of all of the pertinent parts of the AIRMETs, they are not necessarily complete texts for the date and time of issue. Some have been truncated because of space considerations.

```
WSNT03 KKCI 301815
SIGA0C
KZMA SIGMET CHARLIE 2 VALID 301815/302215 KKCI-
MIAMI OCEANIC FIR FRQ TS WI AREA BOUNDED BY 2510N07450W
2230N07220W 2110N07430W 2250N07640W 2510N07450W. TOPS TO FL490.
MOV NE 10KT. INTSF. BASED ON SAT AND LTG OBS.
```

Figure16-9. Example of an International SIGMET.

FLIGHT INFORMATION SERVICE-BROADCAST (FIS-B)

Systems that acquire and display current weather information for critical inflight decisions continue to undergo rapid development and improvement. An example is the Flight Information Service-Broadcast (FIS-B). FIS-B provides line-of-sight transmission of weather text and graphics directly to aircraft that are equipped with appropriate cockpit display systems. (Figure 16-10) The latest version of AC 00-45 gives more details.

WINDS AND TEMPERATURES ALOFT FORECASTS (FB)

A winds and temperatures aloft forecast (FB) furnishes a prediction of wind speed (knots), wind direction (° true), and temperature (°C) for selected altitudes at specific locations across the U.S., including Alaska, Hawaii, and over some U.S. coastal waters. Figure 16-11 shows the distribution of forecast stations.

A Transcribed Weather Enroute Broadcast (TWEB) and Synopsis is prepared three times daily for selected routes around the U.S. The morning and daytime broadcasts are valid for 12 hours; the evening broadcast is valid for 18 hours.

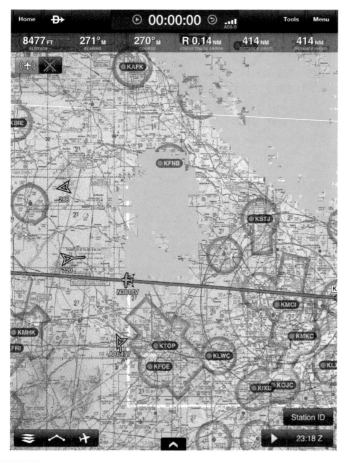

Figure 16-10. Example of a regional scale composite radar reflectivity product acquired via FIS-B. FIS-B can provide both textual and graphical weather information through your airplane's ADS-B equipment. Remember that FIS-B information is advisory only, and does not meet any regulatory requirements.

Figure 16-11. FB locations for the U.S. (Source: ADDS)

Depending on location, forecast wind and temperature information is available for up to 15 altitudes between 1,500 feet MSL and 53,000 feet MSL. Altitudes below 18,000 feet are true and altitudes at or above 18,000 feet are pressure altitudes. FB winds and temperatures are only given below 3,000 feet for Hawaii and the western Pacific. Forecasts are issued four times each day for use during specific time intervals, which are stated on the FB bulletin.

FBs are generally used to select flight altitudes, determine aircraft performance, and estimate groundspeed. In addition to flight planning calculations, an FB can add information to the overall weather picture. For example, strong winds aloft indicate a potential for turbulence. An example of an FB bulletin is presented in figure 16-12.

Winds and temperatures aloft contain wind direction in relation to true north, wind speed in knots, and temperature in degrees Celsius for a range of altitudes.

DATA BASED ON 151200Z

VALID 151800Z FOR USE 1700-2100Z TEMPS NEG ABV 24000

FT	3000	6000	9000	12000	18000	24000	30000	34000	39000
ALA			2420	2635-08	2535-18	2444-30	245945	246755	246862
AMA		2714	2725+00	2625-04	2531-15	2542-27	265842	256352	256768
DEN			2321-04	2532-08	2434-19	2441-31	235347	236056	236262
HLC		1707-01	2113-03	2219-07	2330-17	2435-30	244145	244854	245561
MKC	0507	2006+03	2215-01	2322-06	2338-17	2348-29	236143	237252	238160
STL	2113	2325+07	2332+02	2339-04	2356-16	2373-27	239440	730649	731960

Figure 16-12. An example of FB text for the locations along the left side of the table. The forecasts are based on data gathered at 1200 UTC on the 15th of the month. The FB is valid at 1800 UTC on the 15th; however, it can be used for the period 1700 UTC through 2100 UTC. Altitudes (feet MSL) are listed across the top of the table. In this example, forecast winds aloft over Denver (DEN) at 12,000 feet MSL are from 250° at 32 knots. The forecast temperature at that altitude is –8°C. Wind speeds between 100 and 199 knots are encoded so direction and speed can be represented by four digits. Decode these winds by subtracting 50 from the two-digit wind direction and adding 100 to the wind speed. For example, for St. Louis (STL) at 39,000 feet MSL, the code 7319 indicates a wind direction of 230° and a speed of 119 knots. Also, note that the forecast temperature is –60°C. The negative sign is not included for temperatures above 24,000 feet MSL. Although not used in this example, a wind coded of 9900 is interpreted as "light and variable" and forecast winds greater than or equal to 199 knots are reported as 199 knots.

OTHER ADVISORIES, WATCHES, AND WARNINGS

In order to facilitate close interaction between Air Route Traffic Control Centers (ARTCCs) and NWS, a Center Weather Service Unit (CWSU) is operated by NWS meteorologists within the confines of each ARTCC. Meteorological impact statements (MIS) and center weather advisories (CWA) are produced by the CWSU of each ARTCC. MIS is an unscheduled planning forecast for air traffic flow control and ATC flight operations. It is valid for 2 to 12 hours after it is issued. A CWA is a forecast for adverse weather conditions. It is valid for up to two hours. A CWA may be issued as a supplement to an existing advisory or when inflight advisory criteria are met but the advisory has not yet been issued. In the latter case, a CWA may be the quickest method to alert pilots to hazardous weather. A CWA also may be necessary when the criteria to issue an AIRMET or SIGMET have not been met but weather conditions exist that are affecting the safe flow of air traffic. A CWA is not a flight planning tool, but a short-term warning.

Hurricane advisories (WH) are issued to alert the aviation community to the presence of a hurricane located at least 300 n.m. offshore and threatening the coastline. WH gives only the position, projected movement, and maximum winds in the storm. Details of aviation weather hazards associated with hurricanes are given in TAFs, FAs, and inflight advisories.

Severe weather watch areas are regions where severe thunderstorms or tornadoes are expected during a specific time. Issued by the Storm Prediction Center (SPC), a severe weather watch bulletin (WW) is an unscheduled message that defines areas of possible severe thunderstorms or tornado activity. A severe weather watch alert (AWW) is a preliminary notice to alert forecasters, briefers, and pilots that WW is being issued. In contrast to severe weather watches and tornado watches, severe thunderstorm warnings and tornado warnings are public notifications that those phenomena have been sighted visually or by radar. SPC also produces a convective outlook (AC) for the occurrence of thunderstorms (non-severe and severe) five times a day for the next 24 hours (Day 1 convective outlook) and twice a day for the following 24 hours (Day 2 convective outlook).

FORECAST PRODUCTS IN GRAPHIC FORMAT

Graphic weather products make the development of an integrated picture of flight weather conditions much easier. Your visualization of weather problems and the areas and altitudes they impact are more rapidly digested than text material or audio descriptions via telephone or radio. A variety of aviation weather graphics are available via the internet from both public and private agencies. We have already touched on some graphics for current conditions, including the surface analysis chart, radar summary, weather depiction, and satellite imagery. With regard to forecasts of conditions along your planned flight track, in addition to Graphical AIRMETs there are many other useful products. Below, a few common forecast graphics are described.

SIGNIFICANT WEATHER PROGNOSTIC CHARTS

Significant weather prognostic (or "prog") charts are forecasts of conditions pertinent to aviation. In the U.S., the prog charts are prepared four times a day at 0000Z, 0600Z, 1200Z, and 1800Z. The forecasts for the first 24 hours (Day 1) are divided into 12- and 24-hour low-level significant weather progs and 12- and 24-hour high-level significant weather progs.

For the Day 1 forecast, each of the low-level significant weather progs consists of two charts: a surface prog of general weather conditions produced by NCEP's Hydrometeorological Prediction Center (HPC), and a second chart with a forecast of significant aviation weather from the surface to 24,000 feet MSL produced by AWC. Since both 12- and 24-hour progs are issued simultaneously, they are often presented as a four-panel chart with the two surface progs and two significant weather progs. Figure 16-13 shows only the 24-hour forecast charts.

Figure 16-13. Significant weather prognostic charts for 24 hours. The valid time of the forecast (VT) is indicated in the lower left-hand corner of each panel. The surface prog in the lower panel uses standard symbols to depict fronts, isobars, pressure centers, and areas of forecast precipitation. As shown by the map legend, the regions of continuous precipitation and unstable showery precipitation are within a solid green line with hatching, while intermittent precipitation is only enclosed with a solid green line.

The upper panel portrays forecast areas of IFR (solid red lines), MVFR (scalloped green lines), and VFR conditions. Areas and layers of expected moderate or greater turbulence are enclosed with dashed yellow lines. The highest freezing level (dashed green lines) and the intersection of the freezing level with the surface are also shown. All heights are in hundreds of feet (MSL).

See Appendix B for more detail. Source: AWC.

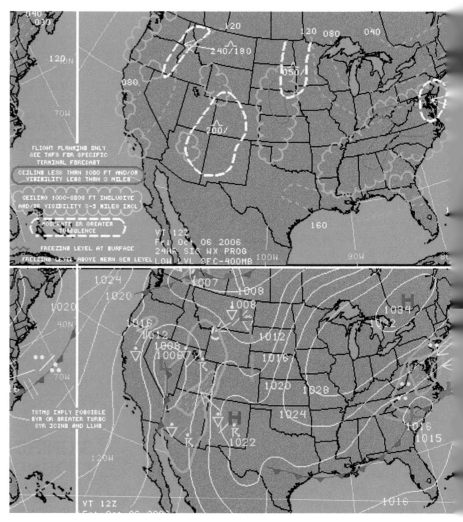

For the Day 2 low-level significant weather forecast, the available prog charts are the 36- and 48- hour surface progs. These are similar to the surface prog panels of the Day 1 forecast, with the exception that organized areas with BKN or OVC clouds are also shown and the graphic also includes a brief forecast discussion.

Low-level significant weather progs can greatly enhance your ability to visualize the potential weather systems and phenomena along your route of flight. Integrating prog chart information with other current reports, forecasts, and charts, as well as obtaining a standard briefing, enables you to create a comprehensive weather picture.

The high-level significant weather prog chart covers the airspace from 25,000 feet to 60,000

The significant weather prognostic chart can be used to determine areas to avoid, such as forecast locations of low visibilities or turbulence.

feet pressure altitude. Charts from some world area forecast centers (WAFC) cover the layer from FL240 to FL630. A wide range of information can be interpreted from this chart including forecast of thunderstorm areas, tropical cyclones, surface positions of well-defined convergence zones, movement of frontal systems, and the locations and speeds of jet streams. (Figure 16-14)

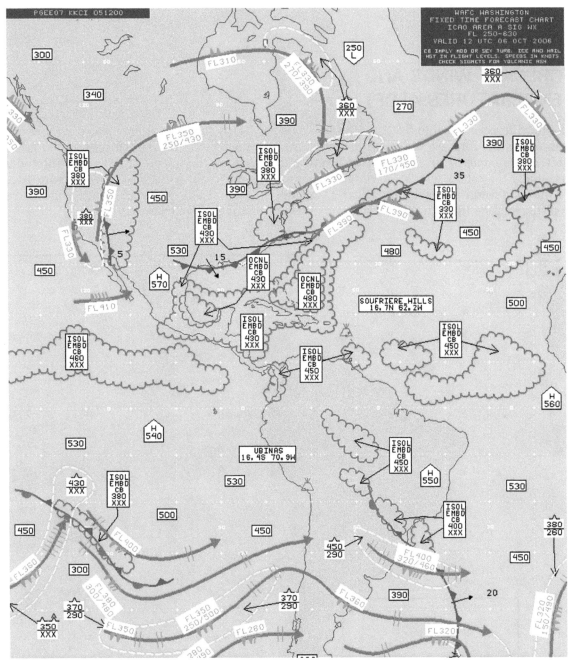

Figure 16-14. Example of a high-level significant weather prog chart for FL 250 to FL 630 feet, valid for the indicated day and time. All heights are in hundreds of feet (MSL). The positions of jet streams with speeds greater than 80 knots are indicated by long, heavy lines with arrowheads showing the direction of flow. Each jet is labeled with altitude; speed and direction of the maximum wind in the jet core is shown with conventional wind barbs. Heights of the tropopause are indicated in boxes; relatively high and low tropopause heights are indicated with "H" and "L," respectively. Areas of significant CB (thunderstorm) activity are enclosed in scalloped lines with heights of tops and bases indicated. If the base of the layer is below 25,000 feet, it is indicated by "xxx." These areas include CB embedded in clouds, haze, or dust. Areas of moderate and greater turbulence are enclosed in dashed lines. Predicted intensities and heights of bases and tops of the turbulent layers are also given. The high-level significant weather prog chart also includes positions of surface fronts, squall lines, and the location of volcanic eruptions. See Appendix B for more detail. Source: AWC/WAFC

FORECAST WINDS AND TEMPERATURES ALOFT

The third forecast graphic that is useful for flight planning is the forecast winds and temperatures aloft. These come in several different forms, but essentially they show winds and/or temperatures for one of several available flight levels ranging from the surface through the lower stratosphere.

These forecasts are not necessarily at observation sites, but at regular, closely spaced grid intervals across the map. This makes interpolation for your flight route fairly easy. Figure 16-15 shows examples of global and local wind and temperature forecast charts

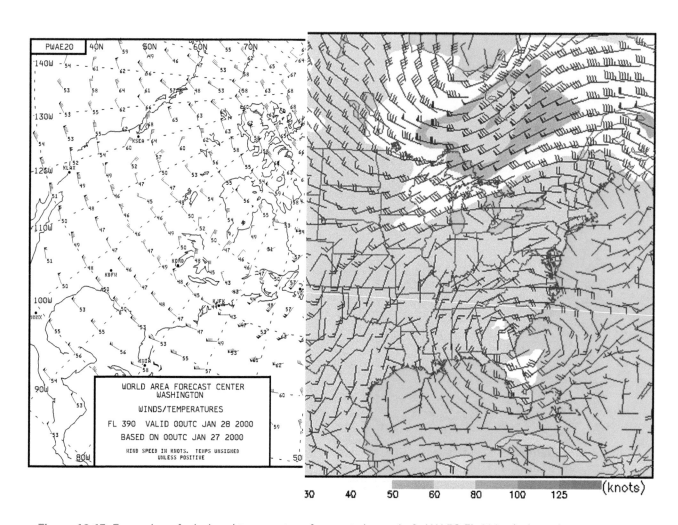

Figure 16-15. Examples of wind and temperature forecast charts. Left: WAFC FL 390 winds and temperatures. Right: AWC/ADDS 12,000 ft winds. See Appendix B and the most recent version of AC 00-45 for more details.

Section C

AVIATION WEATHER INFORMATION SOURCES

The final step in the forecasting process is disseminating the weather information to you, the user. A wide variety of resources are available to assist you in determining the weather for flight planning.

AUTOMATED FLIGHT SERVICE STATIONS (AFSS)

The Automated Flight Service Station (AFSS) is a primary source of official weather information for pilots in the U.S. All AFSS offices and data centers ("hubs") offer walk-in briefings, interactive briefings using the internet, and briefings by telephone (currently the most common). Additionally, after a briefing, email or text message updates on critical conditions are also available.

> An AFSS briefing can be obtained by dialing 1-800-WX-BRIEF.

A standard briefing provides you with the most complete weather picture tailored to your specific flight. Figure 16-16 lists the items included in a standard briefing together with examples of related weather data. For a telephone briefing, it is helpful to have examined these data ahead of time (for example, over the Internet) so you can better understand the briefing; formulate pertinent questions for the briefer; and develop a comprehensive picture of the weather affecting your flight.

An abbreviated briefing enables you to supplement mass disseminated data, update a previous briefing, or request specific information. If the proposed departure time of your flight is six or more hours in the future, an outlook briefing provides a general overview of forecasted weather.

Always use the latest weather information. You may be very skilled at interpreting meteorological conditions, but if you are using old information, the weather picture you formulate could turn out to be grossly inaccurate. Even what you may think are "current" observations may not be so current depending on the specific reporting station. For example, many smaller airports are not staffed to take late night and early morning observations. Old reports often remain in the current database until the next report is received. You should verify the time of the report, especially when planning early morning flights. The latest observation may be from the night before. An important rule is: **Always check the times of observations and analyses.** Most forecasts are issued at specific intervals and have specific valid times or cover specific time periods. Knowledge of the timing of those forecasts is invaluable in determining whether or not you have the latest information. There are always local exceptions; for example, terminal aerodrome forecasts for smaller airports may be delayed if the weather station is closed part of the night. Knowledge of the hours of operation for part-time weather stations is valuable information. An important rule is: **Always check the time of issue, and the valid time and period of a forecast.**

1. **ADVERSE CONDITIONS** — This includes the type of information that might influence you to alter your proposed route or cancel the flight altogether. Examples include such things as hazardous weather or airport closures.

2. **VFR FLIGHT NOT RECOMMENDED** — The briefer may skip this warning if your proposed flight is IFR. It is advisory in nature; the final decision whether to conduct the flight under VFR rests with you.

3. **SYNOPSIS** — The briefer will provide you with a broad overview of the major weather systems or airmasses that affect the proposed flight.

4. **CURRENT CONDITIONS** — This information is a rundown of existing conditions, including pertinent hourly, pilot, and radar weather reports. Unless you request otherwise, this item is omitted if your proposed departure time is more than two hours in the future.

5. **ENROUTE FORECAST** — The briefer will summarize the forecast conditions along your proposed route in a logical order from departure through descent for landing.

6. **DESTINATION FORECAST** — The briefer will provide the forecast for your destination at your estimated time of arrival (ETA). In addition, any significant changes predicted for an hour before or after your ETA will be included.

7. **WINDS AND TEMPERATURES ALOFT**—You will be given a summary of forecast winds for your route. If necessary, the briefer will interpolate wind direction and speed between levels and stations for your planned cruising altitude(s). Temperature information will be provided on request.

8. **NOTICES TO AIRMEN** — The briefer will supply NOTAM information pertinent to your proposed route of flight. However, information which has already been published in the Notices to Airmen publication will only be provided on request.

9. **ATC DELAYS**— You will be advised of any known air traffic control delays that might affect your proposed flight.

10. **REQUESTS FOR PIREPS** — The briefer may ask you to file a PIREP if the current conditions would benefit from additional inflight weather reports.

11. **EFAS** — You will be notified of the availability and appropriate frequency for Flight Watch for enroute weather updates.

12. **OTHER INFORMATION** — Upon requesat, the briefer will provide you with other information such as MOA and MTR activity within 100 n.m. if the flight plan area, ATC services and rules, as well as customs and immigration procedures.

Figure 16-16. A standard briefing consists of the presentation of information to you in the numerical order indicated. Examples of weather information useful to the pilot for evaluating various steps are listed where appropriate.

> You should request a standard briefing if you have received no preliminary weather information and plan to depart within the hour. To supplement mass disseminated data, request an abbreviated briefing. If your proposed departure time is six or more hours away, request an outlook briefing.

Recorded weather information is also available to you through flight service stations. The telephone information briefing service (TIBS) is an AFSS service that provides continuous telephone recordings of meteorological and/or aeronautical information 24 hours a day. TIBS provides route briefings and, depending on user demand, aviation weather observations, forecasts, and wind and temperatures aloft forecasts. TIBS information is frequently updated to ensure current and accurate weather data. With a few exceptions, the order of information given in TIBS recordings is similar to the order in the standard briefing. Local telephone numbers for TIBS are available in the *Airport/Facility Directory*.

In addition to the services supplied to pilots over the telephone, FSSs furnish weather information to pilots inflight. The en route flight advisory service (EFAS) is probably the most familiar inflight service to pilots. To use this service, contact the specific EFAS by using the words "Flight Watch." The frequency for Flight Watch below 18,000 feet MSL is 122.0 MHz. Upon your request, the flight watch specialist can provide aviation weather information and time-critical enroute assistance. If you are facing hazardous or unknown weather conditions, EFAS may recommend alternate or diversionary routes. The receipt and rapid dissemination of pilot weather reports is a primary responsibility of EFAS.

At Altitudes below 18,000 feet, you can contact Flight Watch on 122.0 MHz for information regarding current weather along your proposed route of flight.

CONTINUOUS BROADCASTS OF WEATHER INFORMATION

The hazardous inflight weather advisory service (HIWAS) provides a continuous broadcast of hazardous flying conditions over selected navigation aids to inform pilots of weather threats such as turbulence, icing, IFR conditions, and high winds. These advisories include SIGMETs, Convective SIGMETs, AIRMETs, severe weather forecast alerts, and center weather advisories.

The delivery of weather graphics directly to the cockpit is now a reality. Flight Information Services-Broadcast (FIS-B) now augments conventional weather information sources. See the most recent version of AC 00-45 for more information.

FAA air traffic control towers (ATCTs) are responsible for informing arriving and departing aircraft of pertinent weather conditions. At some locations, the NWS shares the duty of reporting visibility observations with the ATCT; while at other tower facilities, the controller has the full responsibility for observing, reporting, and classifying weather conditions for the terminal area. Automatic terminal information service (ATIS) is available at most major airports that have operating control towers. This service helps reduce frequency congestion and improves controller efficiency. ATIS is a prerecorded report, broadcast on a dedicated frequency, which includes information regarding current weather and pertinent local airport conditions. The ATIS broadcast is normally recorded every hour but may be updated any time conditions change significantly. ATIS frequencies are listed in the *Airport/ Facilities Directory* and on aeronautical charts. At some locations, ATIS can be accessed by telephone. The telephone numbers are listed in the *Airport/Facility Directory*.

The information provided by FIS-B is <u>advisory</u> in nature and should be used only to enhance standard weather briefings such as those from ATC and flight service stations.

A rapidly growing amount of weather information is available via television. In addition to weather forecasts provided in local news broadcasts, The Weather Channel and other cable news channels provide national and international weather information that can help you create a general weather picture over your planned flight route well in advance of a formal flight briefing.

WEATHER ON THE INTERNET

The Internet is a fast and dependable source of aviation weather information. Small, portable devices such as tablets and smart phones are now common and enable access to the Internet from anywhere internet service is available. These devices display weather information on the ground and in the cockpit.

The FAA supports the direct user access terminal service (DUATS). This computer-based program provides NWS and FAA products that are normally used in pilot weather briefings. Flight plans also can be filed and amended through DUATS. You can find more information about DUATs in the most recent version of AC 00-45.

Two important government sources of aviation weather products are Aviation Weather Center (AWC) and the Aviation Digital Data Service (ADDS). Observations, forecasts and advisories are available on the Internet as text and excellent graphics. Many displays are interactive, allowing the pilot to rapidly access pertinent information. In addition to standard products discussed in earlier sections of this chapter, "guidance" graphics are also available. These include, for example, Current and Forecast Icing Potential (CIP/FIP) and Graphical Turbulence Guidance (GTG). Two examples are presented in figure 16-17. Explanations of products are available on the AWC and ADDS websites.

> The FAA recognizes four sources of weather information: government sources; FAA-approved commercial sources that qualify as part of the Enhanced Weather Information System (EWINS); Qualified Internet Communications Providers (QICPs); and unapproved commercial weather information providers. Note that the quality and currency of weather observations and forecasts derived from unapproved sources might not be reliable and should be used with caution.

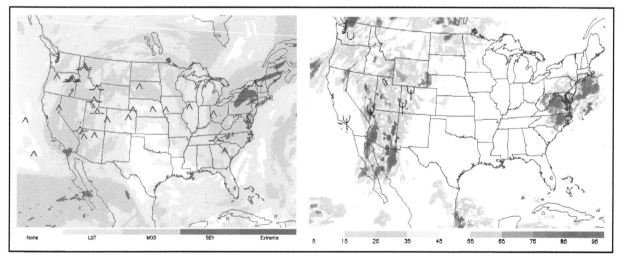

Figure 16-17. Left: Graphical Turbulence Guidance (GTG). Right: Current Icing Potential (CIP). These are composite analyses of current conditions for the indicated Flight Levels. Turbulence and icing PIREPS are indicated by standard symbols. As indicated at the bottom of each diagram, Icing Potential is color-coded in terms of the likelihood of icing on a scale of 0-100, and Turbulence Potential is color-coded according to turbulence intensity (Light, Moderate, Severe). These products are supplements to AIRMETs and SIGMETs. See AWC/ADDs website at http://adds.aviationweather.gov/ for further details.

SUMMARY

This chapter has provided an understanding of the procedures used to collect and process raw weather data, and to make weather forecasts. The discussion of forecast methods has given you some insight into the accuracy of forecasts. This knowledge should assist you in interpreting and effectively using weather data for flight planning. In addition, you are now familiar with the essential aviation weather forecast products in both text and graphic formats. You know of a variety of sources from which you can obtain observations and forecasts appropriate for your flying needs. The "standard briefing" is a useful guide in selecting pertinent information. Your knowledge of the three-dimensional structure and behavior of weather systems allows you to integrate available information into a comprehensive picture. This new information will help you practice "selectivity" and "visualization" in dealing with current and forecast flight weather. Some practical applications of your knowledge of aviation weather resources are explored in the final chapter.

KEY TERMS

Abbreviated Briefing
Air Route Traffic Control Center (ARTCC)
AIRMET (WA)
AIRMET Sierra
AIRMET Tango
AIRMET Zulu
Alert Severe Weather Watch (AWW)
Area Forecast (FA)
Automated Flight Service Station (AFSS)
Automatic Terminal Information Service (ATIS)
Aviation Weather Center (AWC)
Center Weather Advisory (CWA)
Center Weather Service Unit (CWSU)
Climatological Forecast
Convective Outlook (AC)
Convective SIGMET (WST)
Current and Forecast Icing Potential (CIP/FIP)
Direct User Access Terminal Service (DUATS)
Enhanced Weather Information System (EWINS)
Enroute Flight Advisory Service (EFAS)
Flight Information Services-Broadcast (FIS-B)
Global Telecommunications System (GTS)
Graphical AIRMET (G-AIRMET)
Graphical Turbulence Guidance (GTG)
Hazardous Inflight Weather Advisory Service (HIWAS)
High-level Significant Weather Prog Chart
Hurricane Advisory (WH)
Inflight Weather Advisories

International Civil Aviation Organization (ICAO)
International SIGMETs
Internet
Low-level Significant Weather Prog Chart
Meteorological Forecast
Meteorological Impact Statement (MIS)
National Centers for Environmental Prediction (NCEP)
National Convective Weather Forecast (NCWF)
Numerical Weather Prediction
Outlook Briefing
Persistence Forecast
Qualified Internet Communications Provider (QICP)
Selectivity
Severe Thunderstorm Warning
Severe Weather Watch Bulletin (WW)
SIGMET (WS)
Standard Briefing
Telephone Information Briefing Service (TIBS)
Terminal Aerodrome Forecast (TAF)
Tornado Warning
Trend Forecast
Visualization
Weather Forecast Office (WFO)
Winds and Temperatures Aloft Forecast (FB)
World Area Forecast Centers (WAFC)
World Area Forecast System (WAFS)
World Meteorological Organization (WMO)

REVIEW QUESTIONS

1. Name the three types of inflight weather advisories and give their standard abbreviations.

2. What are the four sections of an area forecast?

3. An area forecast is always used in conjunction with what inflight weather advisory?

4. What frequency do you use to contact Flight Watch (EFAS) for flights below 18,000 feet?

5. Consider the TAF given below for KDEN. What is the time period of the forecast? What conditions are predicted for the period, 1400 to 1600 **local standard time** on the 6th? (Hint: first find the time zone of KDEN.)

6. If there was such a thing as a "perfect" forecast model (there isn't), and NCEP used it to make a forecast for a 24-hour period, the forecast could still have errors. How?

7. What is the forecast at the bottom of the page?

8. What is the meaning of the highlighted numbers in the forecast below?

9. What is AWC?

10. What is the difference between a SIGMET and an AIRMET?

```
KDEN 061728Z 0618/0718 20012G20KT P6SM FEW080 SCT120 BKN220
     FM062100 18015G25KT P6SM SCT080 SCT120 BKN220
     FM070200 19015KT P6SM SCT120 SCT220
     FM070600 21012KT P6SM SCT120 BKN220
     FM071500 25012KT P6SM SCT120 BKN220
```

```
DATA BASED ON 121200Z
VALID 131200Z    FOR USE 0600-1700Z. TEMPS NEG ABV 24000
```

FT	3000	6000	9000	12000	18000	24000	30000	34000	39000
BRL	2017	2326+00	2436-03	2450-09	2463-21	2471-32	238748	249055	249261
DBQ	1608	2217-04	2328-06	**2438-12**	2457-22	2469-33	248150	248557	248961
DSM	1610	2217-02	2429-06	2438-11	2353-22	2362-33	236850	237255	247859

DISCOVERY QUESTIONS

11. Make a weather prediction for a nearby weather station using persistence, trend, and climatology methods. How accurate are your predictions using each method for different time periods? A few hours? 24 hours? Several days? A week? A month?

12. Prepare a list of all the weather observation and forecast sources for your local flying area. Include the information issue times, mode of acquisition (television, telephone, personal computer, facsimile, FSS) including pertinent information such as URLs, TV channel numbers, and telephone numbers.

13. Prepare a list of specific text and graphic weather products that provide observed or forecast information about the following phenomena.

    1. Turbulence

    2. Thunderstorms

    3. IFR conditions

    4. Icing

14. Completely decode the TAF in question 5.

15. From the forecast information in question 7, decode DSM winds and temperatures for all altitudes.

16. The Aviation Digital Data Service (ADDS) site has a link to "Standard Briefing." Access that link on the ADDS homepage (http://www.aviationweather.gov/adds/) and make a list of the specific weather information that can be used for the Standard Briefing outlined in Figure 16-16.

Introduction

A fact of aviation today is that you must have a better understanding of weather than your predecessors. There are at least two primary reasons for this. First, approximately 25% of aircraft accidents are weather-related. A weather-wise pilot is much less likely to become a statistic. Second, the rapid growth in the aviation industry and the increasing automation of weather information places a greater burden on you to obtain and interpret weather information pertinent to your flight. The concept of a "self-briefing" to augment official briefings requires that you develop a procedure to obtain and integrate weather observations and forecasts into your preflight preparations. This chapter provides guidelines to help you develop a self-briefing procedure. That procedure is then demonstrated by applying it to real weather situations. When you complete Chapter 17 you will understand how to use a variety of weather information to make wise preflight and in-flight weather decisions.

SECTION A
SELF-BRIEFING PROCEDURE

To improve your proficiency in weather evaluation, the development of a system for processing information during flight planning is valuable. We will refer to this system as the self-briefing procedure. A flow diagram outlining this process is shown in figure 17-1.

The self-briefing procedure does not begin an hour before your flight. It begins with weather awareness, familiarity with weather information, a clear understanding of your capabilities as a pilot, and knowledge of your aircraft's limitations. Weather awareness is achieved by learning the essentials of weather-producing processes and phenomena. Study of this, or similar textbooks helps provide you with a solid background in weather awareness. Your own flight experience as well as discussions with other pilots regarding their weather experiences will enhance this awareness. Keep in mind that, in addition to your understanding of basic meteorology, you must also know about available and relevant weather products. Previous chapters furnished you with information about some of the sources and specific materials that you can use. Given this meteorological background, the next step in the self-briefing procedure is self-evaluation.

Is your meteorological training adequate?

Are you familiar with relevant weather products and their sources?

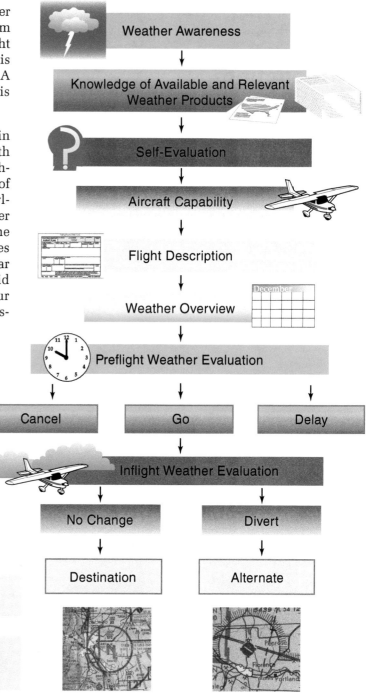

Figure 17-1. The flow diagram illustrates the self-briefing procedure.

Weather Awareness

Knowledge of Available and Relevant Weather Products

Self-Evaluation

Aircraft Capability

Flight Description

Weather Overview

Preflight Weather Evaluation

Cancel | Go | Delay

Inflight Weather Evaluation

No Change | Divert

Destination | Alternate

SELF-EVALUATION

As a pilot, you must be able to effectively assess your own abilities and limitations when making decisions regarding flight in specific weather conditions. The certificates and ratings you hold provide the most basic criteria for these decisions. Holding an instrument rating and maintaining IFR currency allows you to fly in a wide range of weather conditions. Even if the proposed flight is VFR, the option to file an IFR flight plan, or request a clearance to fly an instrument approach if weather deteriorates, may influence flight planning decisions. In addition to meeting regulatory requirements, you must honestly evaluate your own instrument flying skill level and be sure that you have the experience required to maintain that level. For example, your recent instrument experience may consist of approaches practiced only in a simulator without flight operations in actual IFR conditions. It is important to make a realistic evaluation of proficiency before departing on a lengthy flight in IFR weather that may be followed by an instrument approach at your destination.

Whether or not you are an instrument-rated pilot, the amount of your recent experience in specific flight conditions is still a factor that must be considered when making a determination about the weather. Setting personal limitations is an important aspect of flight safety. Lack of extensive flight experience in conditions such as strong gusty winds, crosswinds, turbulence, or low visibility must be considered.

> Are you current to fly in the weather conditions of the proposed flight?

Another element that affects the self-evaluation process is your ability to properly interpret weather data. You should be up-to-date with the products that you reference. Having easy access to a decoding key is necessary, especially if an extensive time period has passed since you last used certain information products. Keeping current on the content of new weather information products, as well as frequently reviewing material that you have used in the past is essential to maintaining a high level of proficiency in weather data interpretation.

The ability to simply decode weather data, however, is not enough. You must be able to make a competent decision about your flight based on your analysis of the weather situation. A go/no-go decision, a delayed departure, or a change in routing are all options you need to consider. Your decision must be based on not only formal studies, but also on your practice and experience with actual weather situations. You must possess the skills needed to visualize a complete weather situation, understand its causes and evolution, and anticipate the occurrence of hazards that may affect your flight. You will then be able to make a clear and informed flight decision based on your analysis.

> The evaluation of your ability to handle certain weather conditions in flight goes beyond ratings and weather knowledge. For every flight that you plan, self-evaluation must also take into account your mental and physical state. For example, a recent illness, a stressful personal experience, or simply the lack of adequate rest can negatively impact preflight and in-flight decisions. The IMSAFE personal checklist addresses these issues.

> Is your weather knowledge current. Are you up-to-date on the latest weather resources?

AIRCRAFT CAPABILITY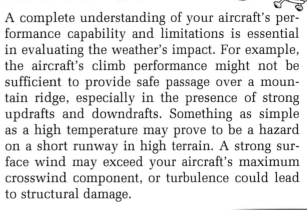

A complete understanding of your aircraft's performance capability and limitations is essential in evaluating the weather's impact. For example, the aircraft's climb performance might not be sufficient to provide safe passage over a mountain ridge, especially in the presence of strong updrafts and downdrafts. Something as simple as a high temperature may prove to be a hazard on a short runway in high terrain. A strong surface wind may exceed your aircraft's maximum crosswind component, or turbulence could lead to structural damage.

The equipment onboard your aircraft is another factor to consider when assessing aircraft capability. For example, an aircraft equipped with anti-icing/de-icing equipment, advanced navigation instruments, and weather radar would be capable of flying in a wider range of weather conditions than an aircraft without this equipment. Cabin pressurization or onboard oxygen may allow you to select an altitude above weather hazards such as icing.

Based on a complete assessment of yourself and your aircraft, you can set specific weather restrictions for your flights. Wind, ceiling, and visibility limitations can be determined as a foundation for flight planning. This allows for more efficient decisions regarding weather.

FLIGHT DESCRIPTION

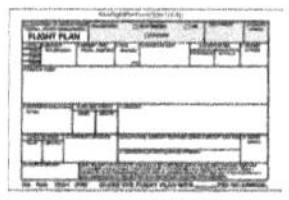

The next step in the self-briefing procedure is to establish a complete flight description. This focuses your preparation on the weather information that pertains specifically to your trip. Also, you will need to supply the details of your plan to a briefer or to any one of a number of automated services to obtain data tailored to your flight. The flight plan form can be used as a reference for the items that should be included in the flight description.

As practical examples, in the next section you will examine the flying weather for flight scenarios in two different geographical locations. You are the pilot in both cases. For each scenario, assume that you have a few hundred hours of flight time. In addition, although you are not instrument-rated, you fly as frequently as possible to maintain proficiency.

For each flight, your aircraft is a Cessna 182. Scenario A is a local flight in the area surrounding Lake Charles Regional Airport, Louisiana. (Figure 17-2) Scenario B is a cross-country flight between Ogden, Utah, and Fort Collins. Colorado.

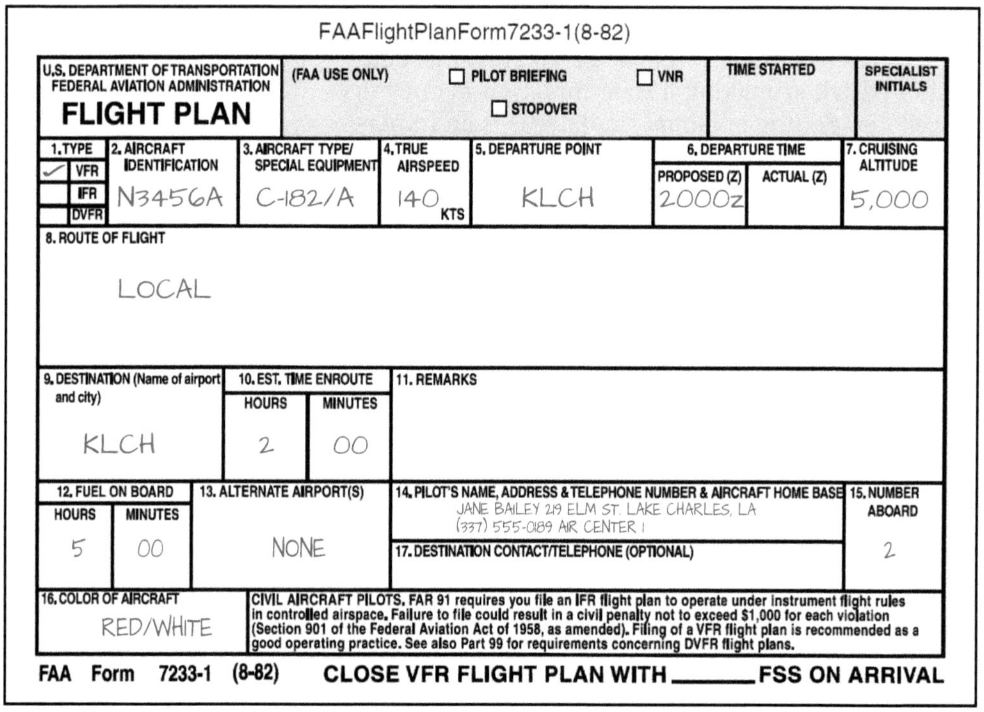

FAAFlightPlanForm7233-1(8-82)

U.S. DEPARTMENT OF TRANSPORTATION
FEDERAL AVIATION ADMINISTRATION
FLIGHT PLAN
(FAA USE ONLY) ☐ PILOT BRIEFING ☐ VNR ☐ STOPOVER
TIME STARTED
SPECIALIST INITIALS

1. TYPE: ✓ VFR / IFR / DVFR
2. AIRCRAFT IDENTIFICATION: N3456A
3. AIRCRAFT TYPE/SPECIAL EQUIPMENT: C-182/A
4. TRUE AIRSPEED: 140 KTS
5. DEPARTURE POINT: KLCH
6. DEPARTURE TIME: PROPOSED (Z) 2000z ACTUAL (Z)
7. CRUISING ALTITUDE: 5,000
8. ROUTE OF FLIGHT: LOCAL
9. DESTINATION (Name of airport and city): KLCH
10. EST. TIME ENROUTE: HOURS 2 MINUTES 00
11. REMARKS
12. FUEL ON BOARD: HOURS 5 MINUTES 00
13. ALTERNATE AIRPORT(S): NONE
14. PILOT'S NAME, ADDRESS & TELEPHONE NUMBER & AIRCRAFT HOME BASE: JANE BAILEY 219 ELM ST. LAKE CHARLES, LA (337) 555-0189 AIR CENTER 1
15. NUMBER ABOARD: 2
16. COLOR OF AIRCRAFT: RED/WHITE
17. DESTINATION CONTACT/TELEPHONE (OPTIONAL)

CIVIL AIRCRAFT PILOTS. FAR 91 requires you file an IFR flight plan to operate under instrument flight rules in controlled airspace. Failure to file could result in a civil penalty not to exceed $1,000 for each violation (Section 901 of the Federal Aviation Act of 1958, as amended). Filing of a VFR flight plan is recommended as a good operating practice. See also Part 99 for requirements concerning DVFR flight plans.

FAA Form 7233-1 (8-82) CLOSE VFR FLIGHT PLAN WITH ______ FSS ON ARRIVAL

Figure 17-2. A flight plan form can be used as a reference for the flight description items supplied to a briefer.

Section B
WEATHER EVALUATION PROCESS

After you complete the initial steps of the self-briefing procedure (as outlined in figure 17-1), begin to examine the weather conditions for your proposed flight. It is important to note that, although the decision process is similar for both scenarios, the sources, details, and formats of the weather data are different. Analyses and forecasts for the first scenario come from the Aviation Digital Data Service (ADDS), while the second scenario uses information from a QICP-approved vendor (DUATS.com).

WEATHER OVERVIEW
Scenario A

It is worthwhile to begin assessing the general weather situation a day or two before your flight. This task is not time-consuming and it goes a long way in preparing you to absorb the critical details of the Preflight Weather Evaluation a few hours prior to takeoff.

The Weather Overview step begins by documenting the large-scale weather patterns that may affect your flight. One way to start the process is simply by paying attention to general weather conditions as reported on radio and television. Keep in mind that large-scale weather features such as fronts and low pressure areas may move several hundreds of miles per day. Therefore your weather overview must examine these weather systems well upstream of the location of your proposed flight.

When you request a briefing, identify yourself as a pilot and supply the briefer with the following information: type of flight planned (VFR or IFR), aircraft number or pilot's name, aircraft type, departure airport, route of flight, destination, flight altitude(s), estimated time of departure, and estimated time enroute or estimated time of arrival.

The accuracy and timeliness of weather information becomes more critical within 24 hours of your planned flight. Be sure to obtain your data from government sources, EWINS-approved Commercial sources or commercial sources with QICP approval.

About 24 hours in advance of your departure you would like answers to the following questions:

1. What is the potentially adverse weather?

2. Where is the adverse weather located now?

3. How is the adverse weather moving? Developing? Dissipating?

4. Where will those areas be at your ETD?

For the proposed flight in the Lake Charles area, morning fog has been an occasional problem in the last few days, but it has been burning off by late morning. Of greater concern is a strong, N-S cold front moving eastward across Texas. The main part of the system with very cold temperatures and snow is staying to the north but the approaching front is producing thunderstorms and strong surface winds to the west of Lake Charles. That is a concern. At this point, it would be easy to cancel your flight for tomorrow on the basis of the likelihood of bad weather, but time-wise, it is your only "window-of-opportunity" for a flight in the next week. The flight is important, so you delay your decision in favor of looking closer at the timing of the frontal passage and the associated weather.

It is mid-morning on November 30th. You elect to use the Internet to obtain weather information. The 0900CST (1500Z) surface analysis obtained from ADDS shows the cold front approaching Lake Charles. (Figure 17-3A) The pressure gradient to the west of the front suggests strong northwesterly winds in that area. In addition, the 500mb chart reveals a trough with very strong southwesterly winds aloft associated with the surface system. (Figure 17-3B)

A wide cloud band in the vicinity of the front and the approaching trough aloft is the main feature of a satellite image a

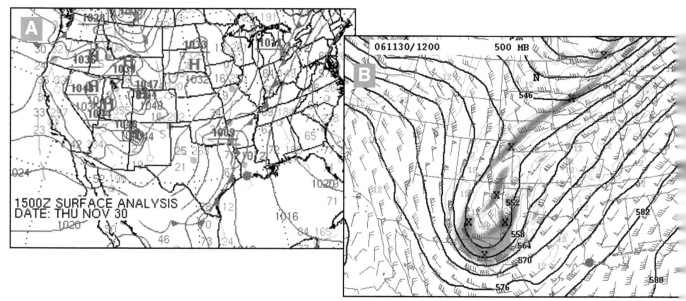

Figure 17-3 Portions of A. Surface Analysis Chart for November 30th at 0900CST (1500Z) B. 500mb chart (~ FL180) for November 30th at 0600CST (1200Z). The yellow and orange regions on the 500mb analysis chart are indicative of the intensity of cyclonic disturbances at that level. The darker colors correspond with stronger systems. Note the winds shown on this 500mb chart are not plotted at observation stations; they have been interpolated to regularly spaced grid points. KLCH location is identified by a pink dot. Source: AWC/ADDS

Before you can successfully interpret weather information for your flight, you must be familiar with Coordinated Universal Time (UTC) referred to as Zulu (Z) time in aviation. Because a flight may cross several time zones, estimating arrival time at your destination using local time at your departure airport can be confusing. By using the 24-hour clock system and UTC time, the entire world is placed on one time standard. Zulu time is local standard time at longitude 0° which passes through Greenwich, England.

Air traffic control operates on Zulu time, and aviation weather information valid times, forecast periods, and issue times are indicated in Zulu time. In the U.S., when you convert local time to Zulu time, you add hours. Converting Zulu time to local time requires subtraction of hours. You can reference the accompanying map and table to convert times as you interpret weather data in the self-briefing scenario.

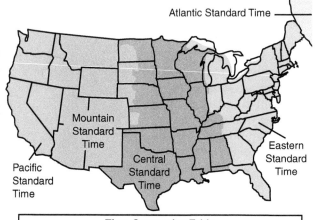

Time Conversion Table	
To Convert From:	To UTC (Zulu)
Eastern Standard Time	Add 5 Hours
Central Standard Time	Add 6 Hours
Mountain Standard Time	Add 7 Hours
Pacific Standard Time	Add 8 Hours

NOTE: For daylight saving time, subtract one hour from the conversion time before converting to UTC (Zulu).

Many of large scale troughs, ridges, and jet streams that have major effects on weather at the ground reach their greatest intensity near the tropopause. These "weather-makers" may exist with or without well defined surface cyclones and fronts. An examination of charts above 10,000 feet is a quick way to determine the location, intensity, and movement of weather systems aloft.

Your misinterpretation of a critical piece of aviation weather information is a pilot error.

Always use the latest weather information: TAFS valid for 24-30 hours are issued 4 times daily at 00, 06, 12, and 18Z plus amendments for significant changes in forecast conditions.

area. No place to be for an inexperienced VFR pilot. But the weather disturbance is moving rapidly. Will these conditions pass the area and improve significantly by your ETD?

By mid-afternoon on November 30th, the front has passed Lake Charles. Your suspicions about the development of bad conditions are validated by the METAR reports for KLCH and the surrounding area, as well as your own observation

few hours later. (Figure 17-4A) The radar chart for the same time shows bands of precipitation associated with the front and the trough aloft. (Figure 17-4B) This collection of information indicates a possibility of IFR/MVFR conditions with strong winds and turbulence at the surface and aloft as the systems move through the KLCH

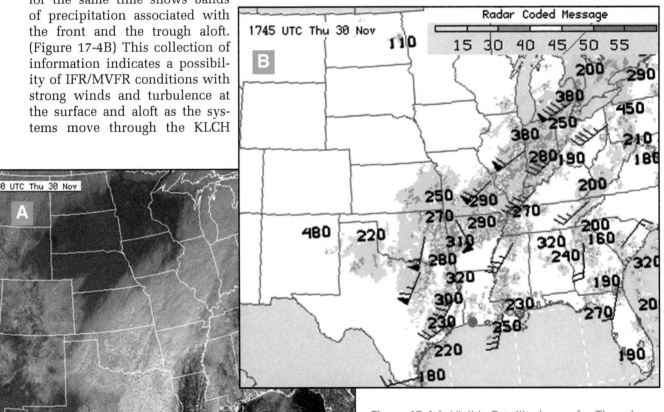

Figure 17-4 A. Visible Satellite Image for Thursday November 30th at 1130CST (1730Z)
B. Radar Chart for November 30th at 1145 CST (1745Z). Source: AWC/ADDS

of local conditions. (Figure 17-5) At 1513 CST (2113Z) Lake Charles is MVFR with gusty west-northwest surface winds and falling tempera-tures. These conditions extend well upwind with precipitation reported to the west and northwest. It is time to examine a forecast.

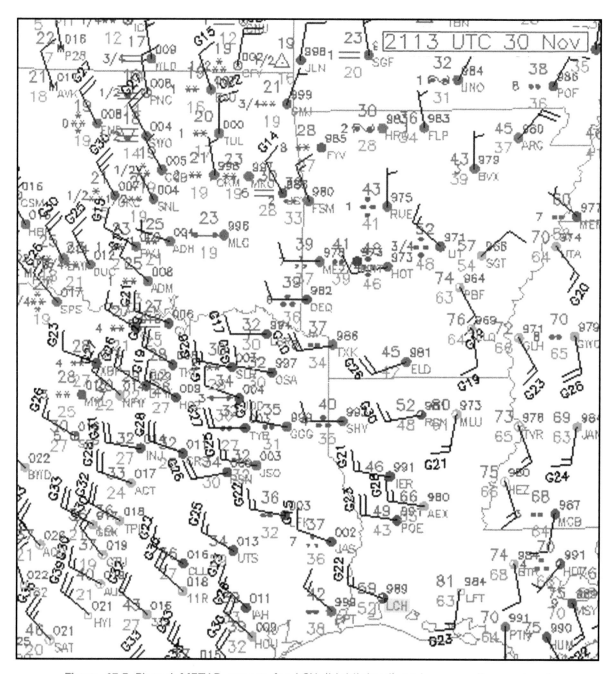

Figure 17-5 Plotted METAR reports for LCH (highlighted) and surrounding region for November 30th at 1513CST (2113Z). Source: AWC/ADDS

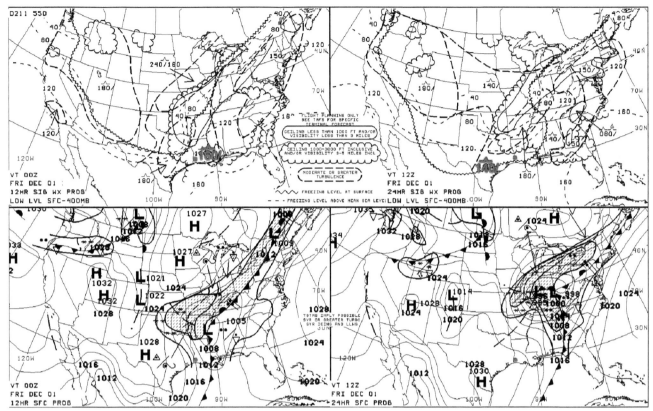

Figure 17-6 Low-Level Significant Weather and Surface Forecast charts valid at 1800CST today and 0600CST tomorrow (0000Z and 1200Z, December 1st). Source: AWC/ADDS. NOTE: Current prog charts are in color (see Figure 16-13, for example). This illustration presents the prog charts without color.

The surface forecast maps (Figure 17-6, bottom) place the front and the associated low pressure system well to the east and northeast of KLCH. Adverse weather shown on the Low-Level Significant Weather Progs (Figure 17-6, top) indicates a marked improvement in ceiling and visibility conditions over southern Louisiana between the times of the first and second forecast charts. You also note that the MVFR boundary is not far north of KLCH on the latest forecast chart. More importantly, moderate turbulence from the surface to 14,000 feet is predicted for the KLCH area. This turbulence corresponds with the strong northwesterly flow following the frontal passage.

If you had to make your final go/no-go decision now, on the basis of this information alone, it would obviously be "no-go." Moderate turbulence is not for you. However, you recognize that the 24-hour forecast charts in Figure 17-6 are based on information from 0600CST (1200Z) on November 30th. A more recent 1200 CST (1800Z) TAF for KLCH is now available. (Figure 17-7)

By tomorrow at 0900CST (1500Z), the KLCH TAF predicts that surface winds will subside in conjunction with clear skies and good visibility. Forecast conditions definitely look better. You will base your final go/no-go decision on the preflight weather evaluation tomorrow morning.

```
KLCH   301735Z 3018/0118 20015G20KT P6SM VCSH SCT010 OVC020
       FM302000 29015G25KT 3SM TSRA BR BKN008 OVC015CB
       FM302200 30015G20KT P6SM VCSH BKN008 OVC020
       FM010400 32015G20KT P6SM SCT015
       FM010900 32009KT P6SM SKC
       FM011500 36010KT P6SM SKC
```

Figure 17-7 TAF for Lake Charles LA Source: AWC/ADDS

PREFLIGHT WEATHER EVALUATION
Scenario A

Preflight Weather: What is the KEY weather information? What is available? When is it available? Where do you get it?

It is Friday morning, December 1st, just after 0700CST (1300Z). With an ETD of 1400CST (2000Z) for your flight, you begin to update yourself on current conditions and forecasts for the flight area via the Internet.

You can obtain an outlook briefing from AFSS when your ETD is six or more more hours away.

The 0653 CST (1253Z) KLCH METAR report agrees with your own observations: northwesterly winds, excellent visibility, and clear skies. (Figure 17-8) Although the temperature is just below freezing and there is some frost in low, damp areas, it does not pose a problem given that temperatures near ETD are expected to be above 50°F (10°C).

```
KLCH 011253Z AUTO 31004KT 10SM CLR M01/M03 A3032 RMK AO2 SLP275
T10061033 FZRANO
```

Figure 17-8. KLCH METAR for 0653 CST (1253Z) Friday, 1 December Source: AWC/ADDS

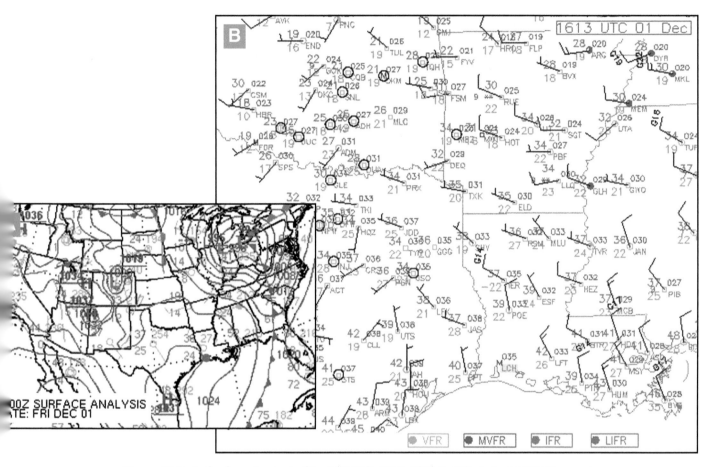

Figure 17-9. A. Surface Analysis Chart (1500Z, 0900 PST) B.16Z plotted METAR reports for 1600Z (1000CST) Compare with Figure 17-3A. Source: AWC/ADDS

The large scale features of the previous day's forecast are verified by the surface weather analysis for 0900 CST (1500Z). (Figure 17-9A) Bad weather and strong winds associated with yesterday's frontal passage have moved on leaving the Gulf States under the influence of a broad high pressure system. Details of the conditions at 1000 CST (1600Z) are given by the plotted METAR reports for the area. (Figure 17-9B)

You now check for possible adverse weather conditions as described by the latest weather hazard advisories (SIGMET, AIRMET). There are no current SIGMETs for the area of interest.

Only AIRMET TANGO (not shown) is in effect for turbulence above 14,000 feet. You plan to check for later advisories just prior to flight time.

The most recent FA available describes cloud and weather changes expected across the area from the time it is issued (0445CST, 1045Z) through late this evening. (Figure 17-10). Flight conditions continue to look acceptable.

By 1100CST (1700Z) you obtain the latest SIGMETs and AIRMETs. (Figure 17-12) There are no SIGMETs affecting the area of interest. The one AIRMET (TANGO) that includes the flight area is

```
DFWC FA 011045
SYNOPSIS AND VFR CLDS/WX
SYNOPSIS VALID UNTIL 020500
CLDS/WX VALID UNTIL 012300...OTLK VALID 012300-020500
OK TX AR TN LA MS AL AND CSTL WTRS
.

SEE AIRMET SIERRA FOR IFR CONDS AND MTN OBSCN.
TS IMPLY SEV OR GTR TURB SEV ICE LLWS AND IFR CONDS.
NON MSL HGTS DENOTED BY AGL OR CIG.
.

SYNOPSIS...11Z CDFNT FAR ERN TN-CNTRL GA-CONTG SSWWD INTO
GULF.


.

NERN TX
NR AR/LA BORDER...CIG OVC030 TOP 060. 13Z SKC. OTLK...VFR.
RMNDR...SKC. OTLK...VFR.
.

SERN TX
SKC OCNL SCT CI. OTLK...VFR.
.

LA
NRN...CIG BKN-SCT025 TOP 040. BECMG 1417 SKC OCNL SCT CI.
OTLK...VFR.
SWRN...SKC OCNL SCT CI. OTLK...VFR.
SERN...CIG BKN-OVC060 TOP 120 FAR SE..SKC RMNDR. 15Z SKC OCNL
SCT CI THRUT. OTLK...VFR.
```

Figure 17-10. FA issued December 1st at 1045Z (0445CST) Note that this FA has been edited to show information for the region of interest only. Source: AWC/ADDS

illustrated in figure 17-11. It indicates moderate turbulence above 14,000 feet MSL. Since your planned flight altitude is well below that altitude, it does not impact your flight.

If you have both text and graphical displays (maps) of the same weather observations and forecasts, the graphical displays are usually more quickly interpreted. It pays to be familiar with the formats of both.

The latest METAR and TAF for Lake Charles are now available. (Figure 17-12) You also want to check winds in the flight area near the intended altitude. The winds aloft forecast for KLCH are shown in Figure 17-13. Conditions are optimum for your flight.

Close to flight time, pilot reports from aircraft flying in the area are invaluable. Therefore, one of the last items in your preflight weather evaluation is to check for nearby PIREPs. (Figure 17-14) Between 1110CST (1710Z) and 1234CST (1834Z), five PIREPs are available from locations close to KLCH. Three reports document light-to-moderate, or moderate turbulence at FL350 and above. These reports are in line with the prediction of turbulence above 14,000 feet MSL as shown in the AIRMET graphic in Figure 17-12. Also in agreement with AIRMET TANGO, two PIREPs from flights close to your planned altitude document smooth conditions.

This completes your Preflight Weather Evaluation. On the basis of your detailed examination of weather conditions, the flight is a "go." Now it is time for an official briefing. Give Flight Service a call.

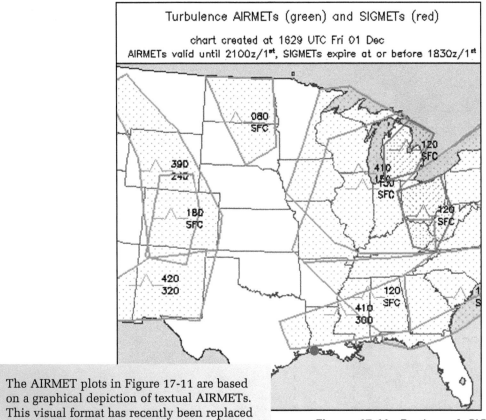

Turbulence AIRMETs (green) and SIGMETs (red)

chart created at 1629 UTC Fri 01 Dec
AIRMETs valid until 2100z/1ˢᵗ, SIGMETs expire at or before 1830z/1ˢᵗ

The AIRMET plots in Figure 17-11 are based on a graphical depiction of textual AIRMETs. This visual format has recently been replaced by Graphical AIRMETs (G-AIRMETs).

Figure 17-11. Portion of SIGMET/AIRMET Plot 1629Z (1029CST) Source: AWC/ADDS

```
KLCH    011720Z 0118/0218 33008KT P6SM SKC
        FM020000 VRB03KT P6SM SCT250

KLCH 011853Z AUTO 35008KT 10SM CLR 11/M05 A3027 RMK AO2 SLP256 T01061050
```

Figure 17-12. Top: KLCH TAF valid at 1800Z (1200CST); bottom: METAR for 1853Z (1153CST)

```
DATA BASED ON 011200Z
VALID 011800Z    FOR USE 1400-2100Z. TEMPS NEG ABV 24000

FT   3000    6000     9000    12000    18000    24000    30000    34000    39000
LCH 3612 2811+08 2622+09 2728+03 2652-09 2666-20 258834 259345 249756
```

Figure 17-13. Winds aloft Forecast (FB) for KLCH

```
LCH UA /OV LCH290030/TM 1710 /FL045 /TP C182 /SKC /TA 04 /RM SMOOTH
AEX UA /OV AEX170045/TM 1757/FL055/TP C180/SK SCT030/TA 08/TB NEG/RM
SMOOTH
SHV UA /OV DFW130040/TM 1819/FL350/TP B757/TB MOD CHOP
AEX UA /OV AEX135050/TM 1830/FL400/TP GALX/TB LGT-MOD CHOP
MLU UA /OV MLU225070/TM 1834/FL380/TP WW24/TB LGT-MOD CHOP
```

Figure 17-14. PIREPs in the vicinity of LCH between 1710 Z (1110CST) and 1834Z (1234 CST). Flight levels and turbulence reports are highlighted in yellow.

IN-FLIGHT EVALUATION
Scenario A

Your evaluation of the weather doesn't end if a "go" decision is made. The dynamic nature of weather makes in-flight weather evaluation essential to safety. The in-flight weather assessment is an on-going process that begins with your own observations. A visual assessment of your environment is made continuously in flight. In addition to scanning the sky for significant weather, changes in temperature and winds along your track can alert you to the presence of weather systems.

While enroute, you should also use in-flight weather services such as recorded surface observations and forecasts (HIWAS, ATIS, ASOS). Contacting Flight Watch (EFAS) is one of the most effective methods to receive updated weather information tailored to your flight. For example, if you observe developing thunderstorms along your route, a call to Flight Watch may provide you with the latest radar and pilot weather reports for the area. With this information, you can make an informed decision to continue along the route to your destination, change your route, or divert to an alternate airport. (Figure 17-15)

Figure 17-15. Flight Watch is a valuable in-flight weather service provided by flight service stations.

Courtesy NASA

WEATHER OVERVIEW
Scenario B

You are currently in Ogden, Utah.

It is early in the morning on February 21st. Personal business developments in the last few hours have made it important for you to attend a meeting in Fort Collins, Colorado, early tomorrow afternoon. Due to other commitments, you cannot leave earlier than 0900MST tomorrow morning, so driving is not an option. Based on this situation and the estimated flying time, you plan to depart Ogden (KOGD) for Fort Collins-Loveland (KFNL) tomorrow, February 22nd, as close to 0900MST (1600Z) as possible. You are considering a direct route, but, depending on the weather conditions, you might deviate to the north to avoid the highest mountains. Your aircraft is equipped with long-range tanks, so the added distance is not a concern.

Regarding to the self-briefing procedure (illustrated in Figure 17-1), the "weather overview" step begins about 24 hours prior to your desired ETD. This is when you acquire weather information appropriate to a standard outlook briefing. For this flight, you will obtain that information from a QICP-approved source, DUATS.com.

Regardless of the source of the information, in an outlook briefing, you answer the weather-related questions listed on the right hand side of page 17-5 somewhat generally with emphasis on the departure airport. For this flight, flying weather conditions are documented with both graphical and textual data.

For your anticipated flight from Ogden to Fort Collins, weather conditions in mountainous terrain play a key part in your final decision. For reference, topographic features along the proposed route are illustrated with an online flight planning chart in Figure 17-16.

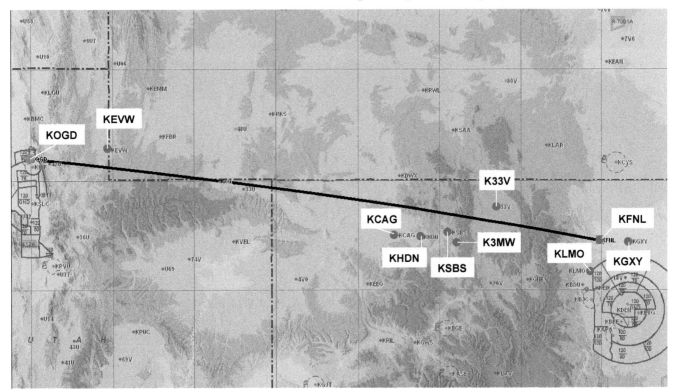

Figure 17-16. KOGD-KFNL flight track showing terrain and the locations of selected METAR reporting stations

A surface analysis chart early on February 21st is shown in Figure 17-17. For reference, your tentative flight track from KOGD to KFNL has been added to that chart and subsequent figures related to the current scenario.

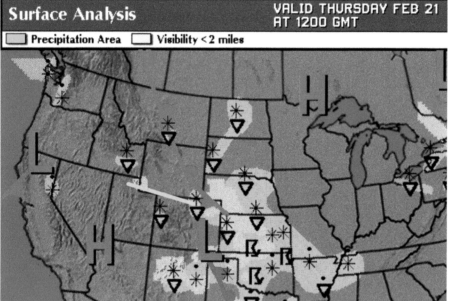

Figure 17-17. Surface Analysis Chart for 21FEB 1200Z (0500MST) Source: CSC.DUATS

the general surface wind directions from the location of the low center. Because the airflow around the low is broadly counterclockwise, the region north and east of the low pressure center is subjected to upslope flow due to the terrain. This situation is causing low clouds and snow showers in that area, including northeastern Colorado. Conditions look somewhat better to the west.

A Radar Summary Chart a couple of hours later emphasizes the precipitation across the area. (Figure 17-18) Not only does snow dominate the eastern slopes of the Rockies, it also penetrates across the mountains into northeastern Colorado. The situation does not

In contrast to the ADDS charts used to illustrate Scenario A, Figure 17-17 is a simplified surface analysis chart showing major low and high pressure areas, frontal positions, precipitation areas and types, and regions of low visibility.

The general weather conditions in the area of the planned flight are dominated by a low pressure area in southeastern Colorado and an associated front along the east slopes of the Rocky Mountains. Although isobars are not shown, you can infer

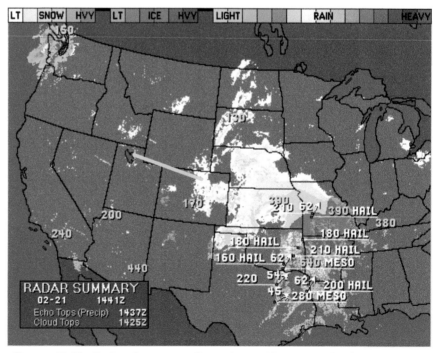

Figure 17-18. Radar Summary Chart for 21FEB 0741MST (1441Z) Source: CSC.DUATS

look good for your intended flight, but a 24-hour surface forecast chart (Figure 17-19) suggests improvement by early tomorrow morning. A more detailed evaluation of current conditions along the projected flight track is provided by a sampling of METAR reports at about 0700MST on the 21st (1400Z). (Figure 17-20) Reported conditions are far from VFR.

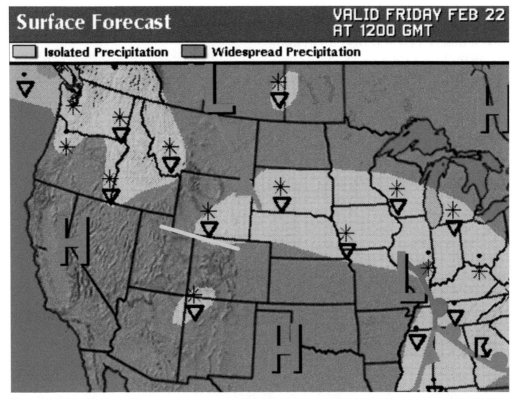

Figure 17-19. 24-Hour Surface Forecast valid 22FEB 0500MST (1200Z) Source: CSC.DUATS

```
Ogden UT 21/0705MST (1405Z)
KOGD Visibility 3 miles light snow, 2900 overcast, temperature -3C

Evanston WY 21/0653MST (1353Z)
KEVW Visibility 6 miles light snow, mist, 600 broken, 2400 broken, 3200 overcast -9C

Steamboat Springs CO 21/0709MST (1409Z)
KSBS Visibility 1¾ miles 1700 overcast -8C

Ft. Collins CO 21/0715MST (1415Z)
KFNL Visibility 1¼ miles 2000 overcast -10C
```

Figure 17-20. Selected METAR observations near the planned flight track (Note: Surface winds were 4 knots or less at these stations. See Figure 17-16 for station locations.) Source: CSC.DUATS

You now examine the latest FA. Information pertinent to your intended flight is found in the Outlook portion of that forecast. Currently, the Outlook is valid from this afternoon, (21/1700MST, 22/0000Z), through this evening (21/2300MST, 22/0600Z). Plain language information applicable to your flight is given in Figure 17-21. Available AIRMETS (not shown) also describe a mixed VFR and MVFR environment along the projected route.

Late in the evening on the 21st, you decide to obtain a standard briefing. Figure 17-22 shows the latest Surface Analysis Chart. The major low pressure system and its associated weather are now well eastward, although the chart shows some indications of continuing snow showers over northeastern Colorado.

You learn more details about weather in the vicinity of the proposed flight track from the

```
Utah
 Northwestern              VFR
 Northeastern              VFR

Wyoming
 Southwestern              VFR
 Southeastern              MVFR

Colorado
 Mountains Westward        VFR with snow showers
 Foothills                 VFR
 NE Plains                 MVFR due to ceilings and snow.
```

Figure 17-21. FA Outlook valid from 21/1700 MST (22/0000Z) to 21/2300MST (22/0600Z) Source: CSC.DUATS

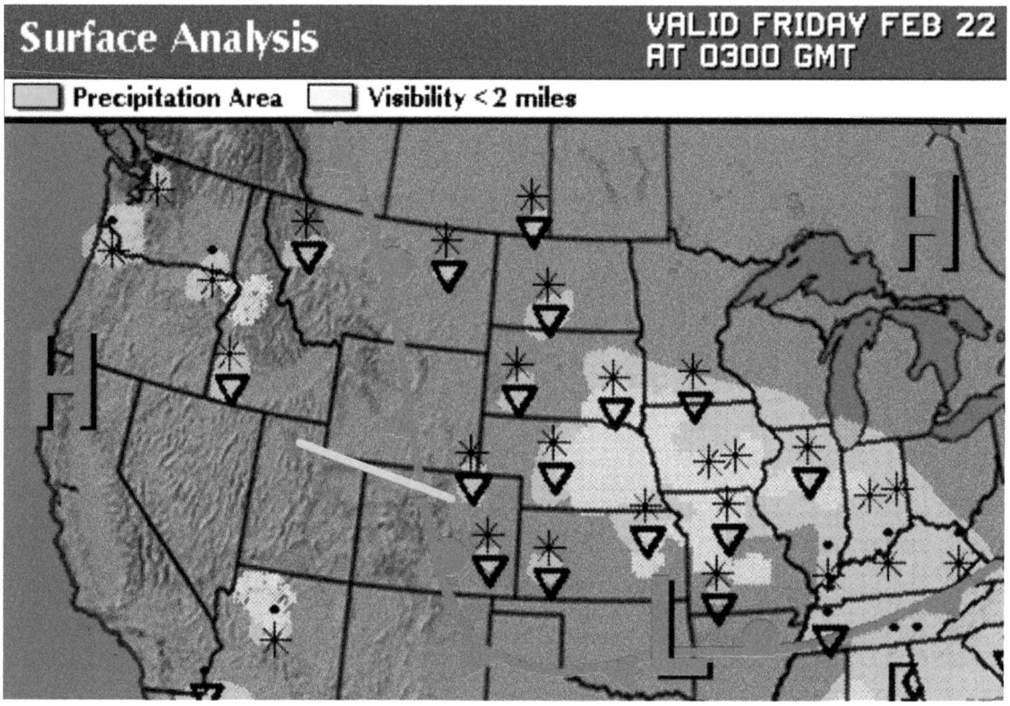

Surface Analysis   VALID FRIDAY FEB 22 AT 0300 GMT

Precipitation Area   Visibility < 2 miles

Figure 17-22. Surface Analysis Chart for 21/2000MST (22/0300Z) Source: CSC.DUATS

METAR reports about two hours later. (Figure 17-23) In agreement with the earlier FA Outlook discussion, scattered MVFR and IFR conditions are reported over both the mountains and the northeastern plains of Colorado.

Figure 17-24 is an abstract from the Outlook portion of the current FA Synopsis for the time and locations of your projected flight. The outlook is enhanced by AIRMET Sierra, which is valid until 22/0800MST (22/1500Z). That AIRMET outlines broad areas of Mountain Obscurations over Wyoming and Colorado. For your intended flight, the situation looks marginal at best. Although personal reasons tempt you to interpret the weather conditions more favorably than the conditions warrant, as you approach your intended ETD (22/1500Z), you make the sensible decision to obtain an abbreviated briefing.

```
KOGD  Ogden-Hinckley UT 0453Z          VFR
KEVW  Evanston WY 0501Z                VFR
KCIG  Craig CO 0453Z                   VFR
KHDN  Hayden CO 0515Z                  VFR
KSBS  Steamboat Springs CO 0532Z       MVFR
K3MW  Mt. Werner CO 0535Z              IFR
K33V  Walden CO 0533Z                  MVFR
KLMO  Longmont CO 0531Z                VFR
KFNL  Ft. Collins/Loveland CO 0535Z    MVFR
KGXY  Greeley CO 0535Z                 IFR
```

Figure 17-23. MVFR/IFR conditions deduced from 21/2223MST (22/0523Z) METARS (See Figure 17-16 for station locations.) Source: CSC.DUATS

```
Utah
  Northwestern            VFR
  Northeastern            VFR

Wyoming
  Southwestern            VFR
  Southeastern            VFR

Colorado
  Mountains Westward   VFR
  Plains Northern      VFR
```

Figure 17-24. FA Outlook valid until 22/0900-1500MST (22/1600-2200Z) Source: CSC.DUATS

PREFLIGHT WEATHER EVALUATION
Scenario B

The latest Surface Analysis Chart (Figure 17-25) indicates improving conditions as the low-pressure system that previously dominated weather over northeastern Colorado and the High Plains

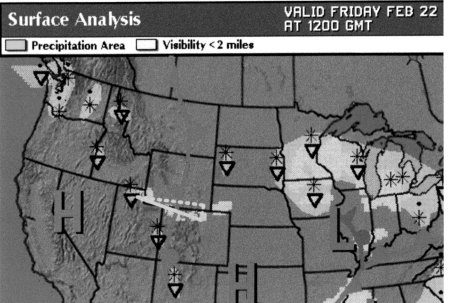

Figure 17-25. Surface Analysis Chart for 22/0500MST (22/1200Z) Source: CSC.DUATS

(Figure 17-17) has moved well to the northeast, which is a good sign. However, that chart also shows IFR conditions continuing in northern Utah and along the northern border of Colorado. By flying to Fort Collins via Cheyenne, Wyoming, you could possibly avoid the highest mountains and the associated obscurations. This modification would add time to the flight, but it is definitely worthwhile to consider in order to find VFR conditions.

You are now within two hours of your ETD. You request an abbreviated briefing. At about 0700MST, the weather in Ogden is MVFR in light snow, mist, with a ceiling at 1200 feet overcast. An Amended Terminal Forecast issued about two hours ago calls for improving weather throughout the morning. But the latest KOGD METAR reports clearly show that the "improvement" is

not occurring. In fact, during the next 40 minutes conditions at KOGD actually deteriorate to IFR with lowering visibilities. The 0700MST Weather Depiction Chart illustrates the extent of MVFR and IFR over a substantial area around your departure airport. (Figure 17-26)

You must make a decision now. Without question—your anticipated flight is a "no-go." Personal and business reasons aside, your thorough preflight weather evaluation has been a success that can be summed up in the words of an experienced and wise pilot. "It is better to be on the ground wishing you were in the air than to be in the air wishing you were on the ground."

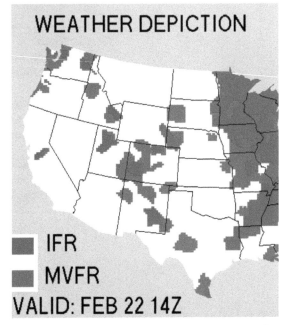

Figure 17-26. Weather Depiction Chart for 22/0700MST (22/1400Z) Source: CSC.DUATS

SUMMARY

The simple weather situations used here were chosen to demonstrate the value of the self-briefing procedure with real weather data. These are just a start. More complicated situations involving cross-country flying under marginal meteorological conditions require close attention to other weather information, especially in the preflight weather evaluation phase and in-flight. Also, be aware that data acquisition procedures and data formats will change depending on the source of aviation weather information and the method of acquisition.

The reader is encouraged to develop his/her own self-briefing procedure. Because there is an immense amount of weather information to choose from, the identification of key weather information and its sources is critical ... and sometimes confusing. Construction of your own self-briefing checklist is beneficial. The standard briefing is shown in Figure 16-16 of this text, in the latest version of AC 00-45, Aviation Weather Services, and is well illustrated on the ADDS website, http://www.aviationweather.gov/adds/

As with all aspects of flying operations, success requires continuing practice. Make it a point to use your checklist to prepare for simulated flights for different weather situations. With the Internet, it is easy to access the pertinent data. Include in-flight weather scenarios that might require in-flight decisions such as a request for a different altitude or the use of your alternate or a return to base. These practice sessions will help you to develop the ability to access and correctly interpret critical weather information rapidly and, most importantly, you will have a better understanding of aviation weather.

Finally, realize that the self-briefing procedure is also a summary of your weather knowledge to date. Unless you now know it all for all time, you need to continue to review and study the subject. Do it.

Fly safe. Fly smart.

KEY TERMS

Aircraft Capability
Available and Relevant Weather Products (Key
     Weather Information)
Flight Description
In-flight Weather Evaluation

Preflight Weather Evaluation
Self-Briefing procedure
Self Evaluation
Weather Awareness
Weather Overview

REVIEW QUESTIONS

1. List the first five requirements for an effective self briefing.

2. Does a self-briefing replace an AFSS briefing? Why?

3. You are flying from KLBB to KABQ. Your departure time is 1400 CST. What is the time in Zulu? Flight time is one hour. What is your ETA for KABQ? Express your answer in both local standard time and Zulu time.

4. What is the first piece of information that you expect to receive in a standard briefing?

5. What does "VNR" mean?

DISCOVERY QUESTIONS

6. Develop a checklist that organizes your own self-briefing procedure. The checklist should begin with a "weather overview" 24 hours before flight time. Include "key data" and its sources.

7. Construct self-briefings for three different, hypothetical flights using your checklist.

8. Obtain an Area Forecast (FA) in text format for one of the geographical areas in Figure 16-4. With no other information, sketch the weather systems described in the synopsis section on a blank map. Compare your sketch with an appropriate surface analysis chart and Low-Level Significant Weather Prog chart.

9. The National Transportation Safety Board (NTSB) places the records of aircraft accident and incident investigations online. (Key words "NTSB Accidents"). Find that site and, for any given year, pick a winter month and a summer month at random. Examine the daily "Accident Synopses" for each of those months and tabulate:

   1. the total number of accidents and incidents;

   2. the percentage of those reports in which weather contributed to the event; and

   3. the three most common weather problems.

Appendix A

Conversion Factors

LENGTH

1 meter (m)
   = 3.28 feet (ft)
   = 39.37 inches (in)
   = 100 centimeters (cm)
   = 1,000 millimeters (mm)
   = 1,000,000 micrometers (μm)

1 kilometer (km)
   = 3281 ft
   = 0.54 nautical miles (nm)
   = 0.62 statue miles (sm)
   = 1000 m

1 foot (ft)
   = 0.305 meters (m)
   = 30.5 centimeters (cm)
   = 305 millimeters (mm)
   = 12 inches (in)

1 statute mile (sm)
   = 1609 meters (m)
   = 1.61 kilometers (km)
   = 0.87 nautical miles (nm)
   = 5280 feet (ft)

1 nautical mile
   = 1853 m
   = 1.85 km
   = 1.15 sm
   = 6080 ft

AREA

1 square meter (m^2)
   = 10.76 ft^2
   = 1550 in^2

1 square kilometer (km^2)
   = 247 acres
   = 10,763,910 ft^2
   = 0.386 sm^2
   = 1,000,000 m^2

1 square foot (ft^2)
   = .093 m^2
   = 144 in^2

1 acre
   = 4047 m^2
   = 0.004 km^2
   = 43560 ft^2

1 square statute mile (sm^2)
   = 2.59 km^2
   = 640 acres

VOLUME

1 cubic meter (m^3)
   = 35.31 ft^3
   = 61023.8 in^3

1 liter
   = 0.26 U.S. Gallons
   = 1000 cm^3
   = 0.001 m^3

1 cubic foot (ft^3)
   = 0.028 m^3
   = 28316.8 cm^3
   = 1728 in^3

1 in^3
   = 16.39 cm^3

1 U.S. Gallon
   = 3.79 liters

SPEED

1 kilometer per hour (kmh)
- = 0.54 knots (kt)
- = 0.62 miles per hour (mph)
- = 0.91 feet per second (fps)
- = 54.68 feet per minute (fpm)
- = 0.28 meters per second (mps)

1 mps
- = 1.94 kt
- = 2.24 mph
- = 196.8 fpm
- = 3.28 fps
- = 3.60 kmh

1 knot (kt)
- = 0.51 meters per second (mps)
- = 1.85 kilometers per hour (kmh)
- = 1.0 nautical miles per hour (kt)
- = 1.15 statute miles per hour (mph)
- = 101.3 feet per minute (fpm)
- = 1.69 feet per second (fps)

1 mph
- = 0.45 mps
- = 1.61 kmh
- = 0.87 kt
- = 88 fpm
- = 1.47 fps

1 fpm
- = 0.0051 mps
- = 0.0183 kmh
- = 0.0099 kt
- = 0.0114 mph

1 fps
- = 0.305 mps
- = 1.097 kmh
- = 0.592 kt
- = 0.682 mph
- = 60 fpm

ACCELERATION

$1\ mps^2$
- $= 3.28\ fps^2$

1.0g (acceleration due to standard gravity)
- $= 32.17\ fps^2$
- $=\ 9.81\ mps^2$

$1\ fps^2$
- $= .305\ mps^2$

1.0g (acceleration due to standard gravity)
- $=\ 9.81\ mps^2$
- $= 32.17\ fps^2$

PRESSURE

1 hectoPascal (hPa)
  = 100 Pascals (Pa)
  = 1 millibar (mb)

1 hPa (mb)
  = 0.295 inches of Mercury (in. Hg.)
  = 0.0145 pound per square inch (lbs/in^2 [psi])
  = 0.750 millimeters of Mercury (mm. Hg.)

Standard Sea Level Pressure
  1013.25 hPa (mb)
  = 29.92 in. Hg.
  = 14.70 lbs/in^2
  = 1 atmosphere
  = 760 mm. Hg.

1.0 inch of Mercury (in. Hg.)
  = 33.86 hectoPascal (hPa [mb])
  = 25.40 millimeters of Mercury (mm. Hg.)
  = 0.491 pounds per square inch (lbs/in^2 [psi])

29.92 in Hg
  = 1013.25 hPa (mb)
  = 760 mm. Hg.
  = 14.70 lbs/in^2
  = 1.0 atmosphere

TEMPERATURE (T)

Conversion of a Celsius temperature (T°C) to a Fahrenheit temperature (T°F):

  T°F = [(T°C + 40) x 9/5] – 40   OR   T°F = (T°C x 9/5) + 32

Conversion of a Fahrenheit temperature (T°F) to a Celsius temperature (T°C):

  T°C = [(T°F + 40) x 5/9] – 40   OR   T°C = (T°F -32) x 5/9

Appendix B

Standard Meteorological Codes and Graphics for Aviation

Introduction

Appendix B is provided for easy access to the codes and graphics that are introduced throughout the text. In addition to descriptions of the commonly used domestic meteorological codes for METAR and TAF, generalized code breakdowns for international METAR and TAF codes are also given. The graphics section presents a brief explanation of the most common charts. Comprehensive descriptions of both domestic and international weather charts in other formats are provided in the latest version of AC 00-45, *Aviation Weather Services*.

Table of Contents...Page

STANDARD METEOROLOGICAL CODES

U.S. METAR CODE

An observation of surface weather which is reported and transmitted is called an aviation routine weather report (METAR). Learning the common weather abbreviations, symbols, and word contractions will help you understand this type of report, as well as others that are important for flight planning. Content may vary somewhat, depending on who, or what type of facility, issues the report. Although the METAR code is adopted worldwide, each country is allowed to make modifications or exceptions to the code for use in their particular country; therefore, you may notice some slight differences in coding. (Figure B-1)

A typical METAR may contain ten or more separate elements. Each element in the body of the report is separated with a space. The only exception is temperature and dewpoint, which are separated with a slash. When an element does not occur, or cannot be observed, the preceding space and that element are omitted from that particular report. A METAR report may contain the following sequence of elements in the following order:

U.S. Aviation Routine Weather Report (METAR)

1 METAR **2** KTPA 122150Z **3** AUTO **4** 08020G38KT **5** 1/2SM R36L/2400FT

6 +TSRA **7** SCT008 OVC012CB **8** 20/18 **9** A2995 **10** RMK A02 TSB24RAB24 SLP134

1 Type of Report

METAR Hourly Observation
SPECI   Special, unscheduled report

2 Station Designator and Date/Time

Four-letter ICAO location identifier
Date and Time of report in Zulu (UTC)

3 Modifier

Auto = Automated
COR = Corrected

4 Wind Information

First three digits = Direction, or VRB = Variable
Next two digits = Speed in knots (KT), or three digits if speed >99KT. G = highest gust, followed by speed. 00000KT = calm

5 Visibility

Prevailing visibility, statute miles (SM). Runway visual range: R, runway number, / , visual range in feet (FT).

6 Present Weather

Intensity: -light, +heavy, no sign for moderate.

Proximity: VC = weather 5 to 10 miles from airport center

Descriptor: for precipitation or obstructions to visibility:
TS Thunderstorm   DR low drifting
SH Shower(s)   MI Shallow
FZ Freezing   BC Patches
BL Blowing   PR Partial

Precipitation types:
RA Rain   GR Hail (1/4" increments)
DZ Drizzle   GS Small hail/snow pellets
SN Snow   PL Ice Pellets
SG Snow grains   IC Ice Crystals
                      UP Unknown Precipitation (Automated stations only)

Obscurations to visibility:
FG Fog (vsby<5/8SM)   PY Spray
BR Mist (vsby 5/8 to 6SM) SA Sand
FU Smoke   DU Widespread Dust
HZ Haze   VA Volcanic Ash

Other Phenomena:
SQ Squalls   SS Sandstorm
DS Duststorm   PO Dust/Sand swirls
FC Funnel cloud   +FC Tornado or Waterspout

7 Sky Condition

Amount of sky cover:
SKC Clear (no clouds)
CLR Clear (no clouds)
FEW (Less than 1/8 to 2/8 sky cover)
SCT Scattered (3/8 to 4/8 sky cover)
BKN Broken (5/8 to 7/8 sky cover)
OVC Overcast (8/8 sky cover)

Height: three digits in hundreds of feet AGL

Type: towering cumulus (TCU) or cumulonimbus (CB) clouds reported after the height of their base.
Vertical visibility (VV): height into a total obscuration in hundreds of feet.

8 Temperature/Dew Point

Degrees Celsius, two-digit form. Prefixed "M" = minus (below zero)

9 Altimeter

Inches of mercury, prefixed by "A".

10 Remarks

Prefixed by "RMK"
A01 or A02 = Station type (automated)
PK WND 28045/30 = Peak wind from 280°, 45 knots, at 30 minutes past the hour.
WSHFT 30 FROPA = Wind shift accompanied by frontal passage beginning at 30 minutes after the hour.
B (Began) or E (Ended) followed by time (minutes after the hour).
TS SE MOV NE = Thunderstorms southeast moving northeast
SLP134 = Sea level pressure in hectoPascals (1013.4 hPa)

DECODED REPORT: Routine observation for Tampa, FL, on the 12th day of the month at 2150 UTC. Automated Station. Wind from 080° at 20 knots with gusts to 38 knots. Prevailing visibility 1/2 statute mile, runway 36 Left visual range 2,400 feet. Thunderstorm with heavy rain. Scattered clouds at 800 feet AGL, overcast cumulonimbus clouds with bases of 1,200 feet AGL. Temperature 20°C, dewpoint 18°C. Altimeter setting 29.95 inches of mercury. Remarks: Automated station, precipitation discriminator indicated by A02, thunderstorm began 24 minutes past the hour, rain began 24 minutes past the hour, sea level pressure 1013.4 hectoPascals (Note: 1 hPa = 1 millibar).

Figure B-1. Aviation Routine Weather Report (METAR) for the United States.

---

1. Type of Report
2. ICAO Station Designator Date and Time of Report
3. Modifier (as required)
4. Wind
5. Visibility and Runway Visual Range (RVR)

6. Weather Phenomena
7. Sky Condition
8. Temperature/Dewpoint
9. Altimeter
10. Remarks (RMK)

Type of Report

The two types of weather reports are the scheduled METAR, which is taken every hour, and the aviation selected special weather report (SPECI). The special METAR weather observation is an unscheduled report indicating a significant change in one or more elements.

Station Designator and Date/Time of Report

Each reporting station is listed by its four-letter International Civil Aviation Organization (ICAO) identifier. In the contiguous 48 states, the letter "K" prefixes the three-letter domestic location identifier. For example, the domestic identifier for Denver is DEN, and the ICAO identifier is KDEN. In other areas of the world, the first two letters indicate the region, country, or state. Identifiers for Alaska begin with "PA," for Hawaii, they begin with "PH," and for Canada, the prefixes are "CU," "CW," "CY," and "CZ." A list of station designators is usually available at an FSS or NWS office. You can also use the *Airport/Facility Directory* to decode the identifiers.

Following the station identifier is a six-digit date/time group. The leading two digits are the date (day of the month) and the last four digits are the time of the observation. The leading two digits of the time group are the hours and the last two digits represent minutes. The time is given in UTC, or Zulu, as indicated by the Z following the time.

Modifier

When a METAR or a SPECI is created by a totally automated weather observation station, the modifier AUTO will follow the date/time element. These stations are grouped by the type of sensor equipment used to make the observations, and A01 or A02 will be noted in the remarks section of the report. RMK A02 indicates the weather observing equipment used has the capability of distinguishing precipitation type. The modifier COR is used to indicate a

corrected METAR which replaces a previously disseminated report. When the abbreviation COR is used, the station type designator, A01 or A02, is removed from the remarks section. No modifier indicates a manual station or manual input at an automated station.

Wind Information

The two minute average wind direction and speed are reported in a five digit group, or six digits if the speed is over 99 knots. The leading three digits represent the direction from which the wind is blowing, in reference to true north. If the direction is variable, the letters "VRB" are used. The next two (or three) digits show the speed in knots (KT). Calm winds are reported as "00000KT."

If the wind direction varies 60° or more and the speed is above six knots, a variable group follows the wind group. The extremes of wind direction are shown, separated by a "V." For example, if the wind is blowing from 020°, varying to 090°, it is reported as "020V090."

In addition to direction and speed, the character, or type, of wind may be reported. If the wind is gusty, ten knots or more between peaks and lulls, the wind is reported with a "G," followed by the highest reported gust over the last ten minutes. For example, wind from 080° at 32 knots with gusts to 45 is reported as 08032G45.

Visibility

Prevailing visibility is the second weather element in a METAR report. It is reported in statute miles with "SM" appended to the visibility. Examples are 1/2SM for one half statute mile and 7SM for seven statute miles. In this element, whole numbers and fractions are separated by a space. For example, 1 1/2SM represents visibility one and one half statue miles. There is no indication in the body of the report that visibility is variable. However, when the criteria exists, the minimum and maximum readings are placed in the remarks.

When the visibility is less than seven miles, the restriction to visibility is shown in the weather element. The only exceptions to this rule are if volcanic ash, low drifting dust, sand, or snow are observed. They are reported, even if they do not restrict visibility to less than seven miles. If tower or surface visibility is less than four statute miles, the lesser of the two will be reported in the body of the report and the greater will be reported in the remarks. Automated stations will report visibility less than 1/4 statute mile as M1/4SM and visibility ten or greater than ten statute miles as 10SM.

When runway visual range (RVR) is reported, it follows the prevailing visibility. RVR is reported whenever the prevailing visibility is one statute mile or less and/or the RVR for the designated instrument runway is 6,000 feet or less. The RVR element is shown with an "R," followed by the runway number, a slash, and the visual range in hundreds of feet (FT). For example, R32L/1200FT means runway 32 left visual range is 1,200 feet. Outside the United States, RVR is normally reported in meters. Variable RVR is shown as the lowest and highest visual range values separated by a "V." When the observed RVR is above the maximum value that can be determined by the system, the value is prefixed with a "P," such as P6000. A value that is below the minimum value that can be determined by the system is prefixed with an "M," such as M0600. If an RVR should be reported, but is missing, RVRNO is included in the remarks. Manual stations may report only one RVR value for a designated runway. Automated stations may report up to four different RVR values for up to four designated runways.

Present Weather

When weather or obscurations to vision are present at the time of the observation, you will find them reported immediately after the visibility. The type of precipitation or obscuration is shown in codes, preceded by intensity symbols, proximity, and descriptor. Intensity levels are shown as light (-), moderate (no sign), or heavy (+). Weather obscurations occurring between 5 and 10 statute miles of the airport are shown by the letters "VC" for vicinity. For precipitation, VC applies within 10 statute miles of the observation point. Next is a descriptor of the precipitation or obscurations to visibility. For example, blowing snow is reported as BLSN, freezing drizzle as FZDZ, and a thunderstorm within 5 to 10 statute miles of the airport with moderate rain is reported as VCTSRA. Some typical obscurations to visibility are smoke (FU), haze (HZ), and dust (DU). Fog (FG) is listed when the visibility is less than 5/8 mile; and when it is between 5/8 and 6 miles, the code for mist (BR) is used. Note, 5/8 of a mile is approximately 1,000 meters. When fog reduces visibility to 1/4 mile, it is reported as 1/4SM FG. If mist and haze reduce visibility to 1-1/2 miles, it is shown as 1 1/2SM BR HZ. Following the obscurations, other weather phenomena may be listed, such as sandstorm (SS), duststorm (DS), or a funnel cloud (FC). When the type of precipitation cannot be identified at automated observation sites, the contraction UP is shown for precipitation unknown. Definitions for the various weather phenomena contractions are shown in Table 1.

Sky Condition

The amount of clouds covering the sky is reported in eighths of sky cover. A clear sky is designated by SKC in a manual report and CLR in an automated report. FEW is used when cloud coverage is 1/8 to 2/8. However, any amount less than 1/8 can also be reported as FEW. Scattered clouds, which cover 3/8 to 4/8 of the sky, are shown by SCT. Broken clouds, covering 5/8 to 7/8 of the sky, are designated by BKN, while an overcast sky is reported as OVC.

The height of clouds or the vertical visibility into obscuring phenomena is reported with three digits in hundreds of feet above ground level (AGL). To determine the cloud height, add two zeros to the number given in the report. When more than one layer is present, the layers are reported in ascending order. However, the sky cover condition for any higher layers represents total sky coverage, which includes any lower layer. For example, a scattered layer at 900 feet and a broken layer at 3,000 feet AGL would be reported as SCT009 BKN030. In addition, if towering cumulus clouds (TCU) or cumulonimbus clouds (CB) are present, their code is shown following the height of their base, such as BKN040TCU or OVC050CB.

Although not designated by a METAR code, a ceiling is the AGL height of the lowest layer of clouds aloft that is reported as broken or overcast, or the vertical visibility into an obscuration, such as fog or haze. In general terms, a ceiling exists when more than half of the sky is covered.

Temperature and Dewpoint

The current air temperature and dewpoint are reported in two-digit form in degrees Celsius and are separated by a slash. For example, "18/09" indicates a surface temperature of 18°C and a dewpoint of 9°C. Temperatures below 0° Celsius are prefixed with an "M" to indicate minus. For instance 10° below zero would be shown as M10. Temperature and dewpoint also may be added to remarks in an eight-digit format showing tenths of °C.

| QUALIFIER | | WEATHER PHENOMENA | | |
Intensity or Proximity 1	Descriptor 2	Precipitation 3	Obscuration 4	Other 5
- Light Moderate (no qualifier) + Heavy VC in the vicinity	MI Shallow PR Partial BC Patches DR Low drifting BL Blowing SH Showers TS Thunderstorms FZ Freezing	DZ Drizzle RA Rain SN Snow SG Snow grains IC Ice Crystals (diamond dust) PL Ice Pellets GR Hail GS Small hail or snow pellets UP *Unknown Precipitation	BR Mist FG Fog FU Smoke DU Dust SA Sand HZ Haze PY Spray VA Volcanic ash	PO Dust/sand whirls SQ Squalls FC Funnel cloud +FC Tornado or Waterspout SS Sandstorm DS Duststorm

The weather groups are constructed by considering columns 1-5 in this table, in sequence; i.e., intensity, followed by descriptor, followed by weather phenomena; i.e., heavy rain showers(s) is coded as +SHRA.
   *Automated stations only

Table 1. List of contractions for various weather phenomena used in U.S. METAR

Altimeter

The altimeter setting is reported in inches of mercury in a four-digit group without the decimal point, and is prefixed by an "A." An example is A3012, indicating an altimeter setting of 30.12 inches.

Remarks

The remarks section begins with "RMK." Certain remarks are included to report weather considered significant to aircraft operations. Among this information are the sea level pressure to the nearest tenth of a hectoPascal (millibar). The remark "SLP134" refers to the sea level pressure of 1013.4 hectoPascals (hPa). The leading 9 or 10 is omitted. In order to interpret sea level pressure, prefix the number with a 9 or 10, whichever brings it closer to 1,000. When the pressure is rising or falling at a rapid rate at the time of the observation, remarks show PRESRR (pressure rising rapidly) or PRESFR (pressure falling rapidly) respectively.

A remark, "T00081016" refers to the temperature and dewpoint in tenths °C. The first zero in the sequence indicates a plus value for temperature (+ .8 °C) and the leading one in the sequence shows a minus value for dewpoint (–1.6 °C.)

At facilities that have a wind recorder, or an automated weather reporting system, whenever the maximum instantaneous wind speed since the last scheduled report exceeds 25 knots, the annotation "PK WND" (peak wind) is included in the remarks. The peak wind remark includes three digits for direction and two or three digits for speed followed by the time in hours and minutes of the occurrence. If the hour can be inferred from the report time, only the minutes are reported. When a wind shift occurs, WSHFT will be included in remarks followed by the time the wind shift began. If the wind shift is the result of a frontal passage, the contraction FROPA may be entered following the time.

Variable visibility is shown in remarks with the minimum and maximum visibility values. For example, VIS 1V2 indicates a visibility that varies between one and two statute miles. A sector visibility is shown when it differs from the prevailing and either the prevailing or sector visibility is less than three miles. For example, VIS N 2 means the visibility to the north is two statute miles.

The beginning of an event is shown by a "B," followed by the time in minutes after the hour. The ending time is noted by an "E" and the time in minutes. For example, RMK RAE42SNB42 means that rain ended at 42 minutes past the hour and snow began at that time.

The location of phenomena within 5 statute miles of the point of observation will be reported "at the station." Phenomena between 5 and 10 statute miles will be reported "in the vicinity," VC. Phenomena beyond 10 statute miles will be shown as "distant," DSNT. Direction of the phenomena will be indicated to the eight points of the compass. Movement of clouds or weather will be indicated by the directions toward which the phenomenon is moving. Distance remarks are in statute miles except for automated lightning remarks which are in nautical miles. The frequency of lightning is reported as occasional (OCNL) for less than one flash per minute, frequent (FRQ) for about one to six flashes per minute, or continuous (CONS) when more than six flashes per minute are observed. The contractions for the type of lightning are CG for cloud-to-ground, IC for in-cloud, CC for cloud-to-cloud, and CA for cloud-to air. More details and examples of domestic METAR code can be found in AC 00-45F, *Aviation Weather Services.*

INTERNATIONAL METAR CODE

The order of the information presented in figure B-2 was derived primarily from the World Meteorological Organization Handbook: *Aerodrome Reports and Forecasts, WMO-No. 792* (1996). The blue highlighted numbers correspond to the numbered sections in the U.S. METAR code description in figure B-1. Sections not included in the U.S. format are indicated with a blue highlighted "+" sign.

International Aviation Routine Weather Report (METAR)

1	2	3	4	5	6
METAR	EDDH	111320Z	29013G26KT	3500	DZRA

7	8	9	10
FEW003 BKN009	07/05	Q1006	NOSIG

1 Type of Report

METAR Routine observation
SPECI Special, unscheduled observation

2 Station Designator and Date/Time

Four-letter ICAO indicator
Day of month and time in hours and minutes UTC (Z)

3 Modifier

AUTO Fully automatic station
Since this report is not from an automated station, this modifier does not appear.

4 Wind Information

Mean wind direction in degrees true rounded to the nearest ten degrees
(VRB = variable)
Mean wind speed (units: KMH, KT, or MPS are given). If wind is calm, speed and direction are coded as 00000.
G, Indicator of gust, if necessary
Maximum wind gust (units: KMH, KT, or MPS are given)
If there is a variation of wind direction of 60° or more, another code group is added to document the extremes of direction variability (e.g., 230V350)

5 Visibility (may be replaced by **CAVOK)

Minimum horizontal visibility in meters. 9999 = 10 km or more. When there is a marked variation in horizontal visibility, the direction of the sector with the lowest visibility to eight points of the compass is given (e.g., 2000NW).
If the minimum sector visibility is less than 1500 m and the maximum sector visibility is greater than 5000 m, then the maximum and its direction to eight points of the compass is also reported (e.g., 1300SE 6000N). (Note differences with U.S. reports)

Runway Visual Range (RVR)

Runway Visual Range indicator (R) followed by runway designator and the RVR in meters. If more than 1500 m, P1500 reported. If less than 50 m, M0050 reported.
RVR is followed by RVR tendency in the last ten minutes (U = increasing RVR, D = decreasing RVR, N = no change). Tendency omitted if impossible to determine. When there are significant variations in RVR, the single value of RVR is replaced by the mean minimum RVR and the mean maximum RVR, separated by "V."

6 Present Weather (may be replaced by **CAVOK)

See Table 2

7 Sky Condition (Clouds) (may be replaced by **CAVOK)

Cloud Amount

(Oktas)	Code	
0	SKC*	(Sky clear)
1-2	FEW	(Few clouds)
3-4	SCT	(Scattered)
5-7	BKN	(Broken)
8	OVC	(Overcast)

* SKC used when **CAVOK is not appropriate.

If sky is covered (by a surface-based obscuring phenomenon such as fog). The Amount is reported as VV (Vertical visibility) when such information is available.
Cloud Height
Height of the base of each cloud layer is reported in units of 30 m (100's of feet).
Cloud Type
Only Cumulonimbus (**CB**) and Towering Cumulus (**TCU**) are reported.

+. **CAVOK.

Ceiling and Visibility OK (CAVOK) replaces visibility (including RVR), present weather, and sky condition if the following criteria are satisfied: 1) the visibility is 10 km or more. 2) No cumulonimbus cloud and no cloud below 1500 m (5,000 feet) OR below the height of the minimum sector altitude, whichever is greater. 3) No significant weather (Table 2).

8 Temperature/Dew Point

Temperature and Dewpoint in whole degrees Celsius (°C). If either is below zero, it is prefixed with an "M."

9 Altimeter (unless otherwise indicated)

If preceded by a "Q," units are hectoPascals, if preceded by an "A," units are inches of mercury
(e.g., Q0995 = 995 hPa, A2998 = 29.98 inches of mercury).

+. Supplementary Information

Note: The inclusion of this section **depends on regional agreements.**

Recent weather since the previous report indicated by "RE" plus the coded weather phenomenon (Table 2) (e.g., RERA)

Wind Shear indicated by "WS" plus runway (RWY) designator (e.g., WS RWY 20L or WS ALLRWY)

+. Trend Forecast for two hours beyond the time of the METAR.

Note: The inclusion of this section **depends on regional agreements.**

Change Indicator	BECMG	(Becoming)
	TEMPO	(Temporary)
	NOSIG	(No significant change)
Change and Time	AT	(At)
	FM	(From)
	TL	(Until)
	Time	(Time in hours and minutes UTC)

Forecast Wind See 4
Forecast Visibility See 5
Forecast Weather See 6. Replaced by "NSW" (No Significant Weather) when significant weather ends.
Forecast Cloud See 7. Replaced by "NSC" (No Significant Cloud) IF the forecast indicates no CB AND no cloud below 1500m (5,000 feet) or minimum sector altitude, whichever is greater, AND CAVOK and SKC are not appropriate.
CAVOK See 7.

10 Remarks

Formats of remarks vary regionally (e.g., see U.S. METAR)

DECODED REPORT: Routine observation from Hamburg-Fuhlsbuettel, Germany, (EDDH) on the 11th day of the month at 1320 UTC. Wind from 290° at 13 knots with gust to 26 knots. Minimum horizontal visibility 3,500 meters with drizzle and rain. Few clouds at 300 feet, a ceiling with a broken layer based at 900 feet. Temperature 7°C, Dewpoint 5°C. Altimeter Setting 1006 hectoPascals. Trend forecast over the two hours following this observation: no significant change expected.

Figure B-2. International Aviation Routine Weather Report (METAR).

SIGNIFICANT PRESENT, FORECAST, AND RECENT WEATHER

| QUALIFIER | | WEATHER PHENOMENA | | |
Intensity or Proximity 1	Descriptor 2	Precipitation 3	Obscuration 4	Other 5
- Light Moderate (no qualifier) **+** Heavy or well developed in the case of **PO** and **FC** **VC** in the vicinity	**MI** Shallow **BC** Patches **PR** Partial - covering part of the aerodrome **FZ** Freezing **DR** Low drifting **BL** Blowing **SH** Shower(s) **TS** Thunderstorm	**DZ** Drizzle **RA** Rain **SN** Snow **SG** Snow grains **IC** Ice Crystals (diamond dust) **PL** Ice Pellets **GR** Hail **GS** Small hail and/or snow pellets	**BR** Mist **FG** Fog **FU** Smoke **VA** Volcanic ash **DU** Widespread dust **SA** Sand **HZ** Haze	**PO** Dust/sand whirls (dust devils) **SQ** Squalls **FC** Funnel cloud(s) (tornado or water spout) **SS** Sandstorm **DS** Duststorm

NOTES:
1. The significant weather groups are constructed by considering columns 1 to 5 in the table above in sequence, that is intensity, followed by description, followed by weather phenomena.
   An example could be +SHRA (heavy shower(s) of rain).
2. Intensity is reported only with precipitation and with blowing DU, SA, SN, SS, and DS.
3. IC, FU, HZ, DU, and SA (except DRSA) are reported only when the visibility has been reduced to 5,000 meters or less.
4. GR used when hailstone diameter 5 mm or more. When less than 5 mm, GS used.
5. BR is reported when mist reduces visibility to 1000-5000 meters.
6. FG is reported when fog reduces visibility to less than 1000 meters.
7. VC may be used for precipitation within 10 km of the aerodrome and other phenomena between 5 and 10 km of the aerodrome.
8. UP reported for unknown precipitation type.

Table 2. International METAR contractions for various weather phenomena.

U.S. Terminal Aerodrome Forecast (TAF)

```
[1] TAF      [3]       [4]      [5]      [6]    [7]   [8]
[2] KSEA 041740Z  041818  15012KT  P6SM  -RA  SCT030 OVC045

              [9]
         TEMPO 2101 5SM -RA
                              [10]
         FM0100  15015KT 4SM -RA BR OVC020 WS020/20045KT
         FM0300  20018G25KT P6SM -SHRA BKN020 OVC050
         FM0900  20012KT P6SM VCSH SCT020 BKN050
```

[1] **Type of Report** – Routine terminal aerodrome forecast (TAF)

[2] **Location Identifier** – ICAO four-letter identifier

[3] **Issuance Date and Time** – Two-digit day of the month and the time in Zulu (Z)

[4] **Valid Period** – Two-digit date followed by the beginning and ending hours of the forecast period in Zulu

Forecast Elements:

[5] **Forecast Wind** – Three-digit direction, two- or three-digit speed in knots (KT), and gusts (G) coded as in METAR

[6] **Forecast Visibility** – Expected prevailing visibility in statute miles. Forecast visibility greater than 6 miles is coded as P6SM (plus 6 SM).

[7] **Forecast Weather** – Forecast significant weather coded as in METAR (Table 1)

[8] **Forecast Sky Condition** – Amount, height (CB) or vertical visibility
Cumulonimbus (CB) is the only type of cloud included in the TAF
North America TAFs will also include nonconvective low-level wind shear (WS), up to 2000 feet. When forecast, WS will appear after the cloud forecast group.

Significant changes expected during the forecast period:

[9] **Temporary Conditions** – (TEMPO) Fluctuations expected to last less than an hour in each instance and, in aggregate, to cover less than half of the period, two-digit beginning time, in hours, and two-digit ending time, also in hours.

[10] **Forecast Change Group** – Significant, permanent changes in conditions are indicated by "from (FM)" plus a four-digit hour and minute time (ZULU) when the change is expected to begin. Note: when necessary, the change group will also include a low probability of thunderstorms (30%), indicated by "PROB30."

DECODED TAF:
Routine TAF for Seattle WA on the 4th day of the month, at 1740Z ...valid for 24 hours from 04/1800Z to 05/1800Z ... surface wind from 150° at 12 knots ... visibility exceeding 6 statute miles in light rain ... scattered clouds with bases at 3000 feet and a ceiling with an overcast layer at 4500 feet.

Between 04/2100Z and 05/0100Z visibility is expected to decrease temporarily to 5 statute miles in light rain.

From 05/0100Z surface winds are expected to be 150° at 15 knots with visibility 4 statute miles in light rain and mist and a ceiling with an overcast layer at 2000 feet. Non-convective windshear is expected to exist from the surface to 2000 feet AGL with 2000 foot winds 200° at 45 knots.

From 05/0300Z surface winds will be 200° at 18 knots with gusts to 25 knots; visibility exceeding 6 statute miles in light rain showers with broken cloud layers at 2000 feet (ceiling) and 5000 feet.

After 05/0900Z surface winds will be 200° at 12 knots with visibility exceeding 6 statute miles, showers in the vicinity with a scattered cloud layer at 2000 feet and a broken cloud layer (ceiling) at 5000 feet.

Figure B-3. U.S. Terminal Aerodrome Forecast (TAF).

INTERNATIONAL AERODROME FORECAST (TAF)

The order of the information presented here was primarily derived from the World Meteorological Organization Handbook: *Aerodrome Reports and Forecasts, WMO-No. 792 (1996)*. Some regional differences in TAF format are illustrated by the differences between the International TAF description given in figure B-4 and the TAF description in figure B-3.

Figure B-4. International Aerodrome Forecast (TAF). The blue highlighted numbers here correspond to the numbered sections in figure B-3, U.S. Terminal Aerodrome Forecast.

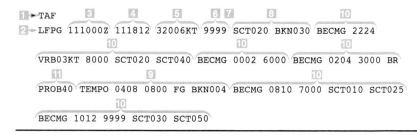

International Terminal Aerodrome Forecast (TAF)

```
1 ► TAF      3      4      5      6 7      8          10
2 ► LFPG 111000Z 111812 32006KT 9999 SCT020 BKN030 BECMG 2224
                10                  10              10
     VRB03KT 8000 SCT020 SCT040 BECMG 0002 6000 BECMG 0204 3000 BR
       11            9                        10
     PROB40 TEMPO 0408 0800 FG BKN004 BECMG 0810 7000 SCT010 SCT025
                    10
     BECMG 1012 9999 SCT030 SCT050
```

☐ **Type of Report** – TAF (Aerodrome Forecast) OR
   TAF AMD (Amended Aerodrome Forecast)

☐ **Station Designator** – Four-letter ICAO indicator

☐ **Date and Time Forecast was issued** – Day of month and time in hours and minutes UTC (Z)

☐ **Forecast Period** – Beginning day of month, beginning and ending times in hours UTC (Z)

☐ **Forecast Wind Information** – Mean wind direction in degrees true rounded to the nearest ten degrees (VRB = variable)
Mean wind speed (units: KMH, KT, or MPS are given). If wind is calm, speed and direction are coded as 00000. G, Indicator of gust, if necessary
Maximum wind gust (units: KMH, KT, or MPS are given)

☐ **Forecast Visibility** (may be replaced by **CAVOK)
Minimum horizontal visibility in meters. 9999 = 10 km or more (Note differences with U.S. TAFs)

☐ **Forecast Significant Weather** (may be replaced by **CAVOK)
Since no significant weather was forecast to occur in this TAF at that time, nothing appears in the coded message for item 7. However, between 02Z and 08Z, significant weather (mist, then fog) does appear in the coded message. (See Table 2)
Replaced by "NSW," Nil Significant Weather, when significant weather phenomenon is forecast to end during the forecast period.

☐ **Forecast Sky Condition (Clouds)** (may be replaced by **CAVOK)
Cloud Amount as in METAR
Cloud Height as in METAR
Cloud Type -- Only Cumulonimbus (**CB**) is indicated.

If agreed regionally, sky condition is replaced by "NSC," No Significant Cloud, when no cumulonimbus cloud is present AND there is no cloud below 1500 m (5,000 feet) or below the height of the minimum sector altitude, whichever is greater AND **CAVOK and SKC are not appropriate.

Note: **CAVOK (Ceiling and Visibility **OK**) replaces forecast visibility, weather, and sky condition if all of the following criteria are satisfied:
1. The visibility is forecast to be 10 km or more.
2. No cumulonimbus cloud and no other cloud are forecast below 1500 m (5,000 feet) or below the height of the minimum sector altitude, whichever is greater.
3. No significant weather is forecast.

☐, ☐, ☐ **Significant Changes in Forecast Conditions during the Forecast Period**

PROB -- Used to indicate the probability of occurrence of alternative elements and temporary fluctuations in conditions. Only PROB30 (30% probability) and PROB40 (40% probability) are used.

Period -- Beginning and end of period in hours UTC (Z)

International Terminal Aerodrome Forecast (TAF) cont.

Change Indicator

BECMG (Becoming) used when changes are expected to pass through specified values.

TEMPO (Temporary) used when fluctuations in conditions are expected to last less than one hour and, in aggregate, less than half of the length of the change period.

Period -- Beginning and end of period in hours UTC (Z)

FM (From) used when one set of weather conditions is expected to change completely to another different set of conditions, indicating the beginning of another self-contained part of the forecast. The time in hours and minutes (UTC) is appended to FM (e.g., FM1200). All forecast conditions before this group are superceded by forecast conditions after the group.

Note: The appearance and order of BECMG, TEMPO, FM, and PROB in any TAF depend strictly on IF and WHEN they will occur.

Regional Agreements

If agreed regionally, six-digit coded groups for icing and turbulence forecasts may be inserted in a TAF immediately after item 8. Also, a code group representing forecast surface temperature may be given at the end of the TAF. These additional forecasts are described as follows:

Forecast Icing

By regional agreement, a six-digit forecast icing group can occur at this point in the TAF. The group has the form $6I_ch_ih_ih_it_L$, where **6** is the forecast icing group indicator, I_c is the type of icing (see Table 3), $h_ih_ih_i$ is the base of the forecast icing layer in units of 30 m (hundreds of feet), and t_L is the thickness of the forecast icing layer in thousands of feet. If $t_L = 0$, the icing layer exists up to the top of the clouds.

Forecast Turbulence

By regional agreement, forecast turbulence information can occur at this point in the TAF. The six-digit group has the form $5Bh_Bh_Bh_Bt_L$, where **5** is the forecast turbulence group indicator, **B** is the type of turbulence (see Table 3), $h_Bh_Bh_B$ is the base of the forecast turbulence layer in units of 30 meters (hundreds of feet), and t_L is the thickness of the forecast turbulence layer in thousands of feet. If $t_L = 0$, the turbulence layer exists up to the top of the clouds.

Forecast Temperature

By regional agreement, the forecast surface temperature at a given time may be included in a TAF. The format is TT_fT_f/G_fG_fZ, where **T** is the forecast temperature group indicator, T_fT_f is the forecast temperature in Celsius (an M is appended if the temperature is below 0C) and G_fG_fZ is the time in UTC (Z) at which the forecast temperature is valid. For example, TM05/15Z is a surface temperature forecast of -5C valid at 1500 UTC.

DECODED TAF
The TAF for Charles DeGaulle International Airport was issued on the 11th day of the month at 1000 UTC. The TAF is valid from the 11th at 18Z to 12Z the next day.

• Forecast conditions are: surface wind from 320 at 6 knots, minimum horizontal visibility greater than 10 kilometers, a scattered cloud layer at 2,000 feet, a broken cloud layer at 3,000 feet.
• Between 22Z and 24Z (00Z), surface wind direction will become variable with a windspeed of three knots, minimum horizontal visibility will decrease to 8,000 meters, with a scattered cloud layers at 2,000 feet and at 4,000 feet.
• Between 00Z and 02Z, minimum horizontal visibility will decrease to 6,000 meters.
• Between 02Z and 04Z, minimum horizontal visibility will decrease to 3,000 meters in Mist.
(Between 04Z and 08Z, there is a probability of 40% that there will be a temporary decrease in minimum visibility to 800 meters in fog with a broken cloud layer at 400 feet.
• Between 08Z and 10Z, the minimum visibility will increase to 7,000 meters with scattered cloud layers at 1,000 feet and 2,500 feet.
• Between 10Z and 12Z minimum visibility will improve to greater than 10 kilometers with scattered cloud layers at 3,000 and 5,000 feet.

	0	1	2	3	4	5	6	7	8	9
I$_c$	no icing	light icing	light icing in cloud	light icing in precipitation	moderate icing	moderate icing in cloud	moderate icing in precipitation	severe icing	severe icing in cloud	severe icing in precipitation
B	no turbulence	light turbulence	moderate turbulence in clear air, occasional	moderate turbulence in clear air, frequent	moderate turbulence in cloud, occasional	moderate turbulence in cloud, frequent	severe turbulence in clear air, occasional	severe turbulence in clear air, frequent	severe turbulence in cloud, occasional	severe turbulence in cloud, frequent

Table 3.   Forecast type of icing (I$_c$) and turbulence (I$_B$) for international TAF.

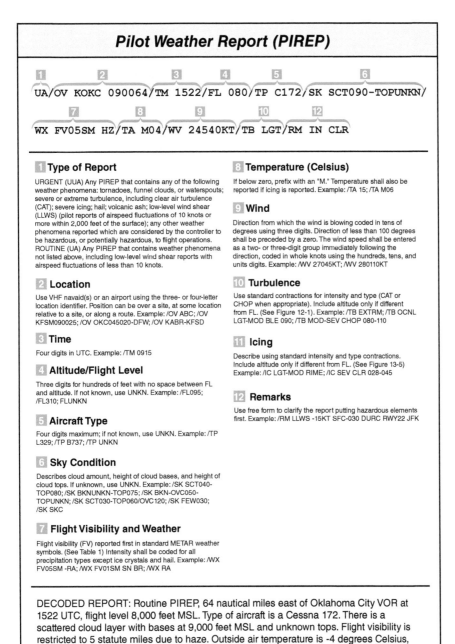

Pilot Weather Report (PIREP)

1 **2** **3** **4** **5** **6**

UA/OV KOKC 090064/TM 1522/FL 080/TP C172/SK SCT090-TOPUNKN/

7 **8** **9** **10** **12**

WX FV05SM HZ/TA M04/WV 24540KT/TB LGT/RM IN CLR

1 Type of Report

URGENT (UUA) Any PIREP that contains any of the following weather phenomena: tornadoes, funnel clouds, or waterspouts; severe or extreme turbulence, including clear air turbulence (CAT); severe icing; hail; volcanic ash; low-level wind shear (LLWS) (pilot reports of airspeed fluctuations of 10 knots or more within 2,000 feet of the surface); any other weather phenomena reported which are considered by the controller to be hazardous, or potentially hazardous, to flight operations. ROUTINE (UA) Any PIREP that contains weather phenomena not listed above, including low-level wind shear reports with airspeed fluctuations of less than 10 knots.

2 Location

Use VHF navaid(s) or an airport using the three- or four-letter location identifier. Position can be over a site, at some location relative to a site, or along a route. Example: /OV ABC; /OV KFSM090025; /OV OKC045020-DFW; /OV KABR-KFSD

3 Time

Four digits in UTC. Example: /TM 0915

4 Altitude/Flight Level

Three digits for hundreds of feet with no space between FL and altitude. If not known, use UNKN. Example: /FL095; /FL310; FLUNKN

5 Aircraft Type

Four digits maximum; if not known, use UNKN. Example: /TP L329; /TP B737; /TP UNKN

6 Sky Condition

Describes cloud amount, height of cloud bases, and height of cloud tops. If unknown, use UNKN. Example: /SK SCT040-TOP080; /SK BKNUNKN-TOP075; /SK BKN-OVC050-TOPUNKN; /SK SCT030-TOP060/OVC120; /SK FEW030; /SK SKC

7 Flight Visibility and Weather

Flight visibility (FV) reported first in standard METAR weather symbols. (See Table 1) Intensity shall be coded for all precipitation types except ice crystals and hail. Example: /WX FV05SM -RA; /WX FV01SM SN BR; /WX RA

8 Temperature (Celsius)

If below zero, prefix with an "M." Temperature shall also be reported if icing is reported. Example: /TA 15; /TA M06

9 Wind

Direction from which the wind is blowing coded in tens of degrees using three digits. Direction of less than 100 degrees shall be preceded by a zero. The wind speed shall be entered as a two- or three-digit group immediately following the direction, coded in whole knots using the hundreds, tens, and units digits. Example: /WV 27045KT; /WV 280110KT

10 Turbulence

Use standard contractions for intensity and type (CAT or CHOP when appropriate). Include altitude only if different from FL. (See Figure 12-1). Example: /TB EXTRM; /TB OCNL LGT-MOD BLE 090; /TB MOD-SEV CHOP 080-110

11 Icing

Describe using standard intensity and type contractions. Include altitude only if different from FL. (See Figure 13-5) Example: /IC LGT-MOD RIME; /IC SEV CLR 028-045

12 Remarks

Use free form to clarify the report putting hazardous elements first. Example: /RM LLWS -15KT SFC-030 DURC RWY22 JFK

DECODED REPORT: Routine PIREP, 64 nautical miles east of Oklahoma City VOR at 1522 UTC, flight level 8,000 feet MSL. Type of aircraft is a Cessna 172. There is a scattered cloud layer with bases at 9,000 feet MSL and unknown tops. Flight visibility is restricted to 5 statute miles due to haze. Outside air temperature is -4 degrees Celsius, wind is 245 degrees at 40 knots, light turbulence, and the aircraft is in clear skies.

Figure B-5. Pilot Weather Report (PIREP) format. The required elements for all PIREPs are type of report, location, time, flight level, aircraft type, and at least one weather element encountered. When not required, elements without reported data are omitted. All altitude references are mean sea level (MSL) unless otherwise noted. Distance for visibility is in statue miles and all other distances are in nautical miles.

Surface Analysis Chart

"L" indicates low pressure center. Central pressure 1004 mb.

"H" indicates high pressure center. Central pressure 1032 mb.

Observed Data. See Table B.

Stationary Front. See Table A.

"TROF" See Table A.

Isobar Label (1020 mb)

Sea Level Pressure Isobars at 4 mb Intervals.

Occluded Front. See Table A.

Cold Front. See Table A.

Warm Front. See Table A.

Observed Data. See Table B.

Chart ID

0600Z SURFACE ANALYSIS
DATE: MON NOV 06 2006
ISSUED: 0749Z MON NOV 06 2006
BY HPC ANALYST RUBIN-OSTER
COLLABORATING CENTERS: HPC, TPC, OPC

Source: ADDS

Table A

Symbols for Surface Fronts and Other Significant Lines Shown on the Surface Analysis Chart

Cold Front (blue)*

Warm Front (red)*

Stationary Front (red/blue)*

Occluded Front (purple)*

Squall Line

Trough Line (TROF)

Dry Line

*Note: fronts may be black and white or color, depending on their source. Also, fronts shown in color code will not necessarily show

Table B

Abbreviated Station Model
for the Surface Analysis Chart

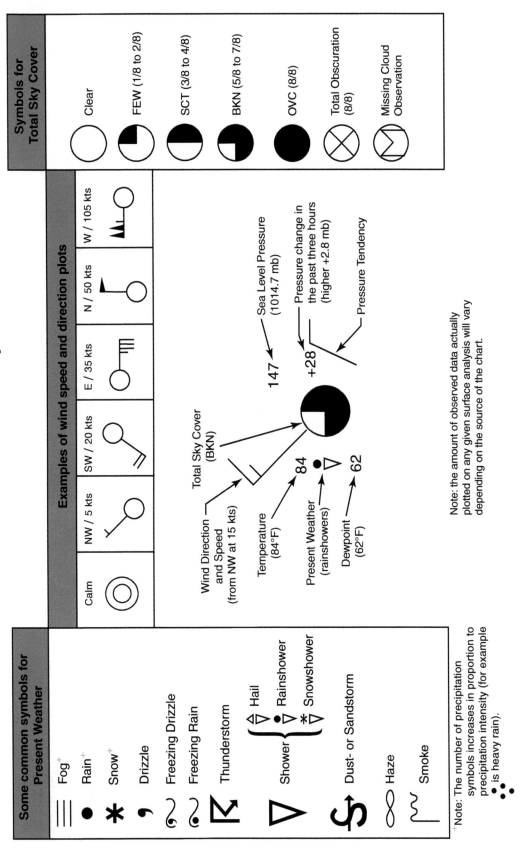

Some common symbols for Present Weather

≡ Fog[+]

● Rain[+]

✳ Snow[+]

, Drizzle

⌇ Freezing Drizzle

⌇ Freezing Rain

⎐ Thunderstorm

⎐ Hail

●▷ Rainshower

✳▷ Snowshower

} Shower[+]

⑀ Dust- or Sandstorm

∞ Haze

〜 Smoke

[+]Note: The number of precipitation symbols increases in proportion to precipitation intensity (for example •••• is heavy rain).

Symbols for Total Sky Cover

Clear

FEW (1/8 to 2/8)

SCT (3/8 to 4/8)

BKN (5/8 to 7/8)

OVC (8/8)

Total Obscuration (8/8)

Missing Cloud Observation

Examples of wind speed and direction plots

Calm	NW / 5 kts	SW / 20 kts	E / 35 kts	N / 50 kts	W / 105 kts

Total Sky Cover (BKN)

Wind Direction and Speed (from NW at 15 kts)

Temperature (84°F)

Present Weather (rainshowers)

Dewpoint (62°F)

147 — Sea Level Pressure (1014.7 mb)

+28 — Pressure change in the past three hours (higher +2.8 mb)

Pressure Tendency

84

62

Note: the amount of observed data actually plotted on any given surface analysis will vary depending on the source of the chart.

Weather Depiction Chart

Table C

Station Model for Weather Depiction Chart

Total Sky Cover
(see Table B)

Right bracket indicates automated station

Present Weather
(see Table B)

2½

25

Visibility (s.m.)
if 5 s.m. or less

Height in hundreds of feet (AGL) of ceiling or of lowest cloud layer when ceiling does not exist.

SHADED AREAS.... IFR WITH CIG LESS THAN 1000 FT AND/OR VSBY LESS THAN 3 MI

CONTOURED WITHOUT SHADING... MVFR AREAS WITH CIG GREATER THAN OR EQUAL TO 1000 TO LESS THAN OR EQUAL TO 3000 FT AND/OR VSBY GREATER THAN OR EQUAL TO 3 TO LESS THAN OR EQUAL TO 5 MI

NO CONTOURS.... VFR AREAS WITH CIG GREATER THAN 3000 FT AND VSBY GREATER THAN 5 MI

Observed Data
(see Table C)

Cold Front
(see Table A)

Contoured Areas Without Shading MVFR

Shaded Areas IFR

Occluded Front
(see Table A)

Observed Data
(see Table C)

Trough Line (TROF)
(see Table A)

VFR Area

Shaded Areas IFR

Chart Identification: Weather Depiction Chart
Valid Time/Date: 1300 UTC Wednesday March 8, 2000

US DEPT OF COMMERCE   NCEP
NOAA/NWS/NCEP WASHINGTON

WEATHER DEPICTION
13Z WED 08 MAR 2000

TOTAL STATIONS
AVAILABLE FOR
ANALYSIS
1194 OUT OF 1462

Source: ADDS Standard Briefing

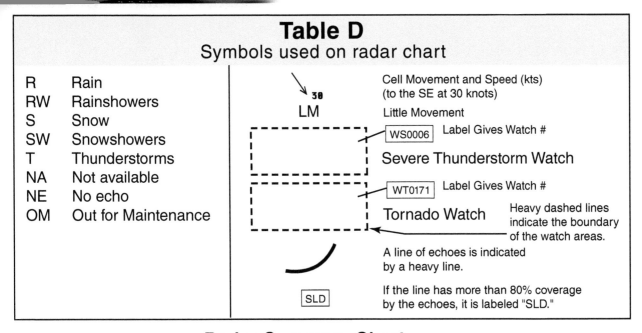

Table D
Symbols used on radar chart

R — Rain
RW — Rainshowers
S — Snow
SW — Snowshowers
T — Thunderstorms
NA — Not available
NE — No echo
OM — Out for Maintenance

Cell Movement and Speed (kts)
(to the SE at 30 knots)

30

LM — Little Movement

WS0006 — Label Gives Watch #

Severe Thunderstorm Watch

WT0171 — Label Gives Watch #

Tornado Watch

Heavy dashed lines indicate the boundary of the watch areas.

A line of echoes is indicated by a heavy line.

SLD — If the line has more than 80% coverage by the echoes, it is labeled "SLD."

Radar Summary Chart

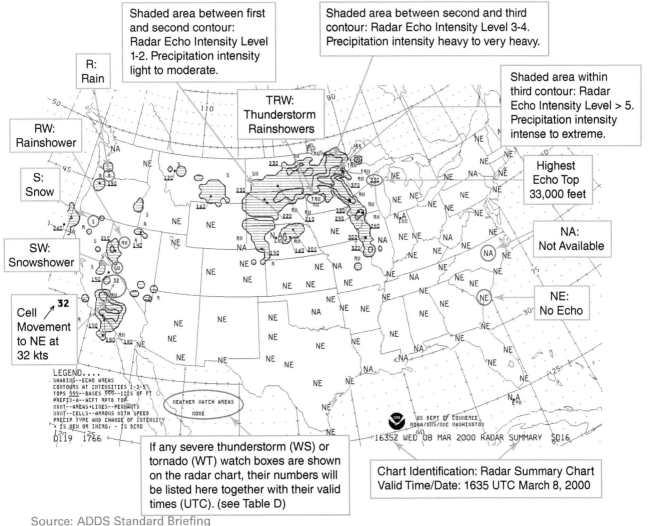

Shaded area between first and second contour: Radar Echo Intensity Level 1-2. Precipitation intensity light to moderate.

Shaded area between second and third contour: Radar Echo Intensity Level 3-4. Precipitation intensity heavy to very heavy.

Shaded area within third contour: Radar Echo Intensity Level > 5. Precipitation intensity intense to extreme.

R: Rain

RW: Rainshower

TRW: Thunderstorm Rainshowers

S: Snow

Highest Echo Top 33,000 feet

NA: Not Available

SW: Snowshower

NE: No Echo

Cell Movement to NE at 32 kts

If any severe thunderstorm (WS) or tornado (WT) watch boxes are shown on the radar chart, their numbers will be listed here together with their valid times (UTC). (see Table D)

Chart Identification: Radar Summary Chart Valid Time/Date: 1635 UTC March 8, 2000

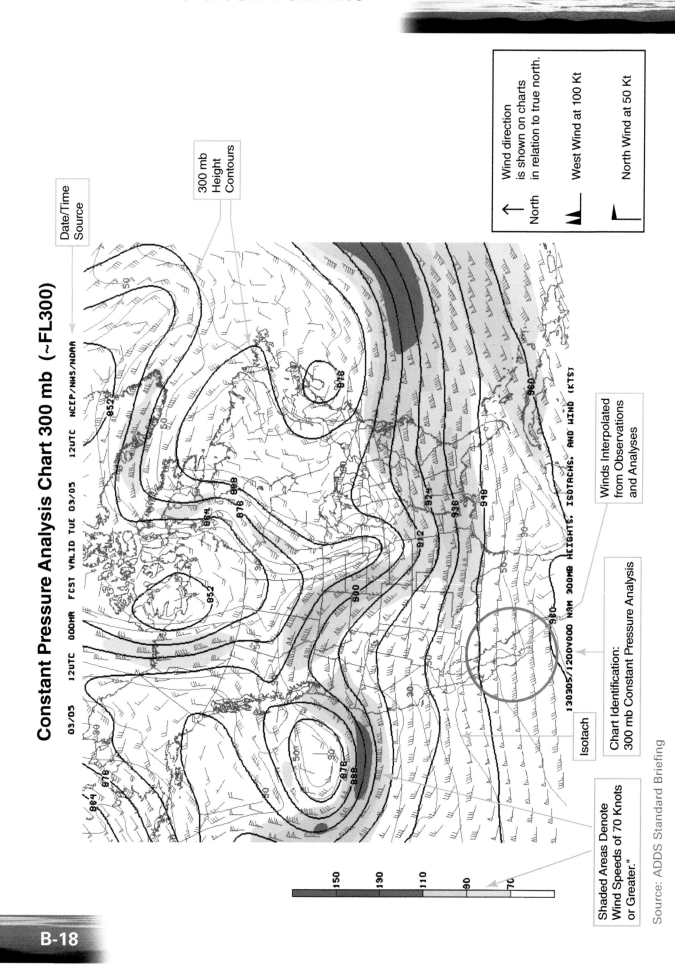

Constant Pressure Analysis Chart 300 mb (~FL300)

Date/Time Source

300 mb Height Contours

Winds Interpolated from Observations and Analyses

Chart Identification: 300 mb Constant Pressure Analysis

Isotach

Shaded Areas Denote Wind Speeds of 70 Knots or Greater."

Wind direction is shown on charts in relation to true north.

North

West Wind at 100 Kt

North Wind at 50 Kt

Source: ADDS Standard Briefing

Constant Pressure Analysis Chart 500 mb (~ FL180)

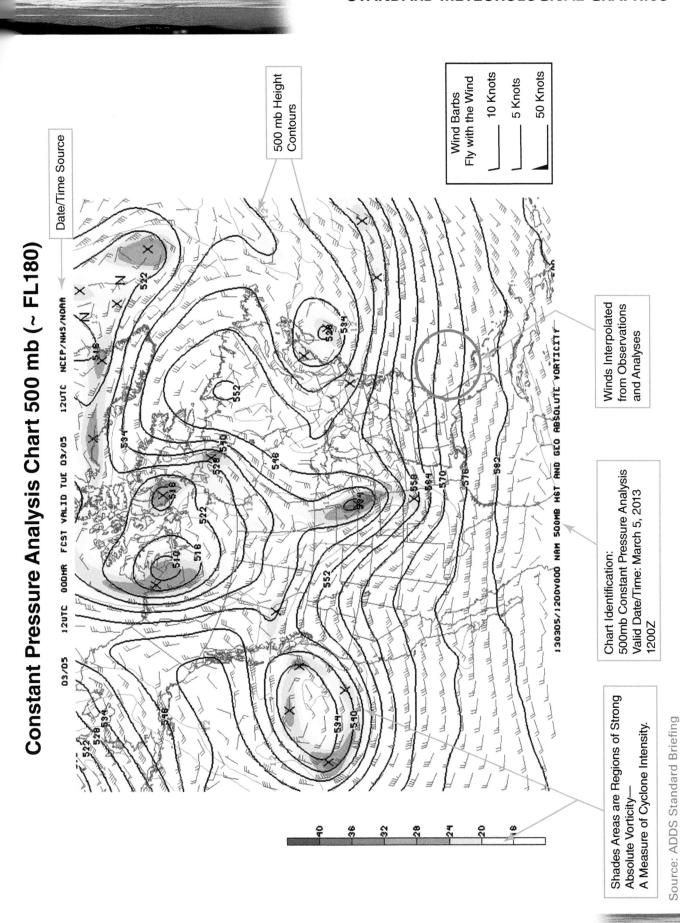

Date/Time Source

500 mb Height Contours

Wind Barbs
Fly with the Wind

10 Knots
5 Knots
50 Knots

Winds Interpolated from Observations and Analyses

Chart Identification:
500mb Constant Pressure Analysis
Valid Date/Time: March 5, 2013
1200Z

Shades Areas are Regions of Strong Absolute Vorticity—
A Measure of Cyclone Intensity.

Source: ADDS Standard Briefing

Forecast WInds and Temperatures Aloft Chart

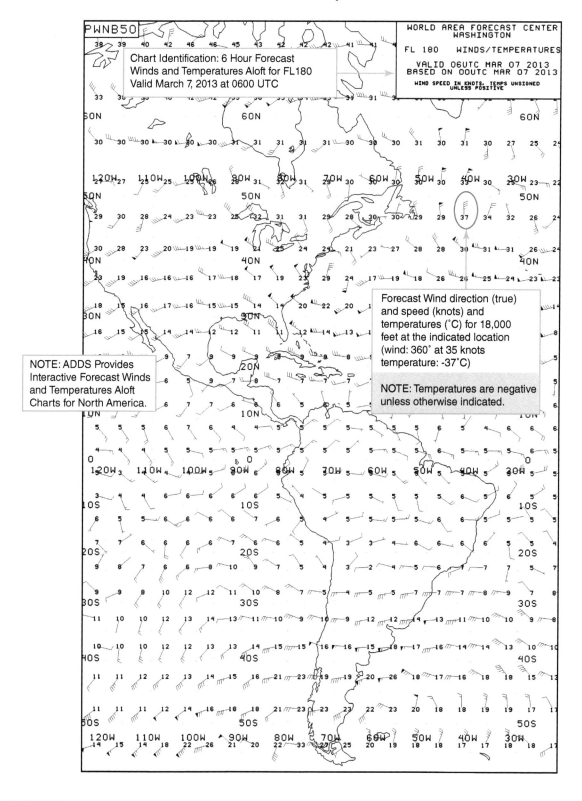

Chart Identification: 6 Hour Forecast Winds and Temperatures Aloft for FL180 Valid March 7, 2013 at 0600 UTC

WORLD AREA FORECAST CENTER WASHINGTON
FL 180   WINDS/TEMPERATURES
VALID 06UTC MAR 07 2013
BASED ON 00UTC MAR 07 2013
WIND SPEED IN KNOTS, TEMPS UNSIGNED UNLESS POSITIVE

Forecast Wind direction (true) and speed (knots) and temperatures (˚C) for 18,000 feet at the indicated location (wind: 360˚ at 35 knots temperature: -37˚C)

NOTE: Temperatures are negative unless otherwise indicated.

NOTE: ADDS Provides Interactive Forecast Winds and Temperatures Aloft Charts for North America.

Low Level Significant Weather Prognostic Charts

Freezing level contour label (4,000 feet MSL)

Green dashed lines indicate freezing level contours drawn at 4,000-foot intervals

The two charts on the right are identical to those on the left except they are 24-hour forecasts valid for 1200 UTC, Wednesday, March 6.

Dashed blue line separates precipitation types (for example ● from ✳) within a precipitation region.

Weather and frontal symbols are identical to those found on the Surface Analysis chart and Weather Depiction chart. (See Tables A and B)

Boundary of IFR Region

Boundary of MVFR Region

Green outlines indicate areas of forecast precipitation. Shading within these lines (not shown) indicates precipitation over 50-100% of the enclosed area. Lack of shading indicates precipitation covering less than half the area.

Purple zigzag line indicates the intersection of the freezing level with the ground

Region of moderate turbulence, surface to 18,000 feet MSL

Yellow dashed line is the boundary of an area of significant turbulence.

Chart Identification: Low Level (surface to 400 mb) Significant Weather Prognostic Chart (12-hour forecast) 0000 UTC, Wednesday, March 6

Chart identification: 12-hour Surface Prognostic Chart 0000 UTC, Wednesday, March 6

Orange dashed line indicates a trough of low pressure.

High Level Significant Weather Prog Chart

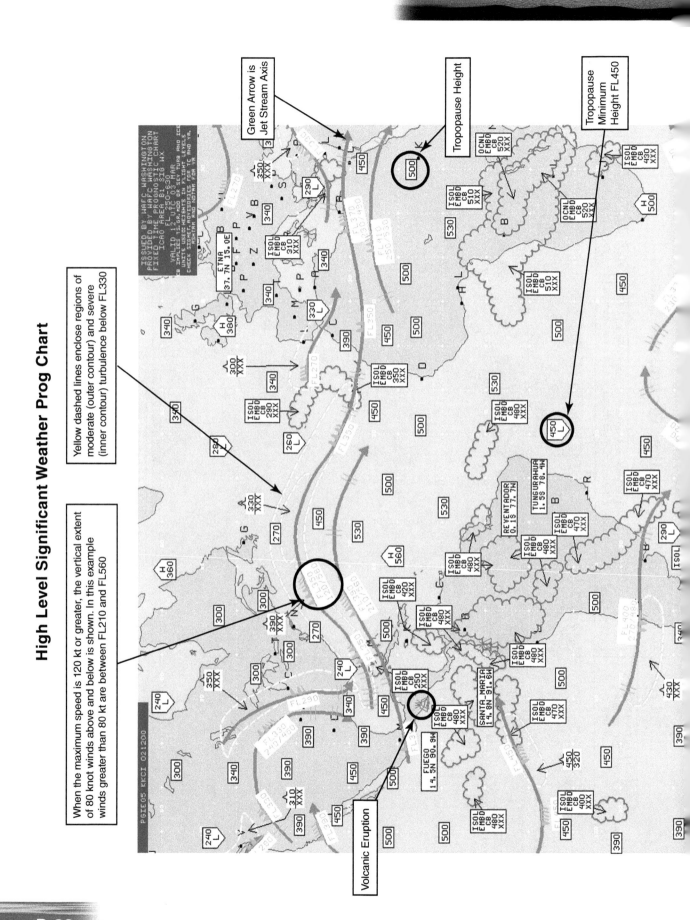

Green Arrow is Jet Stream Axis

Tropopause Height

Tropopause Minimum Height FL450

Yellow dashed lines enclose regions of moderate (outer contour) and severe (inner contour) turbulence below FL330

When the maximum speed is 120 kt or greater, the vertical extent of 80 knot winds above and below is shown. In this example winds greater than 80 kt are between FL210 and FL560

Volcanic Eruption

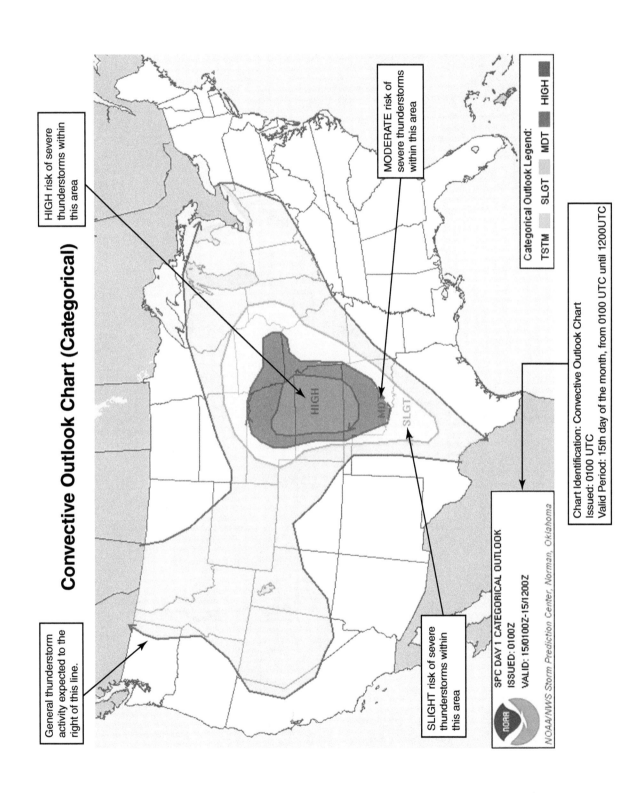

Convective Outlook Chart (Categorical)

General thunderstorm activity expected to the right of this line.

HIGH risk of severe thunderstorms within this area

MODERATE risk of severe thunderstorms within this area

SLIGHT risk of severe thunderstorms within this area

HIGH

MDT

SLGT

Categorical Outlook Legend:

TSTM   SLGT   MDT   HIGH

SPC DAY 1 CATEGORICAL OUTLOOK
ISSUED: 0100Z
VALID: 15/0100Z-15/1200Z

NOAA/NWS Storm Prediction Center, Norman, Oklahoma

Chart Identification: Convective Outlook Chart
Issued: 0100 UTC
Valid Period: 15th day of the month, from 0100 UTC until 1200UTC

Volcanic Ash Forecast Transport and Diffusion (VAFTAD) Chart

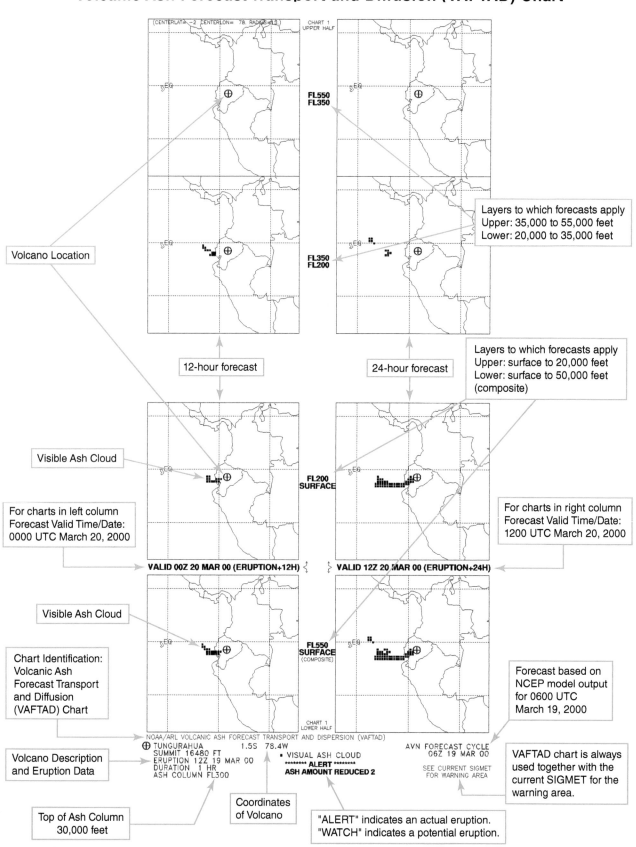

Volcano Location

Layers to which forecasts apply
Upper: 35,000 to 55,000 feet
Lower: 20,000 to 35,000 feet

12-hour forecast

24-hour forecast

Layers to which forecasts apply
Upper: surface to 20,000 feet
Lower: surface to 50,000 feet
(composite)

Visible Ash Cloud

For charts in left column
Forecast Valid Time/Date:
0000 UTC March 20, 2000

For charts in right column
Forecast Valid Time/Date:
1200 UTC March 20, 2000

Visible Ash Cloud

Chart Identification:
Volcanic Ash
Forecast Transport
and Diffusion
(VAFTAD) Chart

Forecast based on
NCEP model output
for 0600 UTC
March 19, 2000

Volcano Description
and Eruption Data

VAFTAD chart is always
used together with the
current SIGMET for the
warning area.

Top of Ash Column
30,000 feet

Coordinates
of Volcano

"ALERT" indicates an actual eruption.
"WATCH" indicates a potential eruption.

Appendix C

Glossary of Weather Terms

GLOSSARY OF WEATHER TERMS

> **Bold** is used to identify terms that are defined or cross referenced to another listing in the glossary. *Italic* is used for emphasis and to identify important terms that are not found elsewhere in the glossary.

AAWU: Alaskan Aviation Weather Unit.

Abbreviated briefing: A shortened **FSS** briefing to supplement mass disseminated data or update a previous briefing or to request specific information.

Absolute altitude: The altitude of an aircraft above the ground.

Absolute instability: The state of an atmospheric layer when the actual temperature **lapse rate** exceeds the **dry adiabatic lapse rate**. An **air parcel** receiving an initial upward displacement in an absolutely unstable layer will accelerate away from its original position. Compare with **neutral stability**. See also **instability, stability.**

Absolute zero: The temperature at which all molecular motion ceases (-273.16°C, 0°K).

AC: Convective Outlook (also Altocumulus).

Acceleration: The rate of change of speed and/or direction.

Accretion: The production of a precipitation particle when a supercooled water droplet freezes as it collides with a snowflake or a smaller ice particle. Such particles may become the nuclei of hailstones.

ACSL: Altocumulus Standing Lenticular.

ADDS: Aviation Digital Data Service.

Adiabatic cooling: Cooling of a gas by expansion.

Adiabatic heating: Warming of a gas by compression.

Adiabatic process: The change of temperature of a gas (e.g., the **atmosphere**) by expansion or compression. See **adiabatic cooling, adiabatic heating, dry adiabatic process.** Compare **saturated adiabatic process.**

Advection: The *horizontal* transport of atmospheric properties such as heat, moisture, and pollutants by the wind. *Vertical* transport is commonly referred to as *convection*.

Advection fog: Fog resulting from the transport of warm, humid air over a cold surface.

Aerodynamic contrail: An aircraft condensation trail that occurs when pressure is reduced in dynamic flow of moist air over the lifting surfaces of the aircraft. Adiabatic cooling brings the air to saturation. Aerodynamic contrails are usually generated by high-performance aircraft and are typically thin and short-lived. See also **condensation trail, exhaust contrail.**

AFSS: Automated Flight Service Station. See **Flight Service Station.**

AGL: Above Ground Level.

AIM: Aeronautical Information Manual.

Air density: The mass of air per unit volume.

Airmass: An extensive body of air within which the conditions of temperature and moisture are essentially uniform in a horizontal plane.

Airmass thunderstorm: A "nonsevere" or "ordinary" thunderstorm produced by local airmass instability. May produce small hail and/or wind gusts less than 50 knots, and/or **microbursts.** See also **severe thunderstorm.**

Airmass wind shear: Wind shear that develops near the ground at night under fair weather conditions in the absence of strong fronts and/or strong surface pressure gradients.

AIRMET (WA): Airman's Meteorological Advisory. Inflight aviation weather advisory pertinent to aircraft with limited capabilities, containing information on:

1. moderate icing, freezing level heights

2. moderate turbulence,

3. sustained surface winds of 30 knots or more,

4. ceilings less than 1,000 feet and/or visibility less than 3 miles affecting 50 percent of the area at one time, and

5. extensive mountain obscuration.

See also **G-AIRMET, SIGMET, Convective SIGMET, International SIGMET.**

AIREP: Abbreviation for aircraft report. See also **PIREP.**

Albedo: The reflectivity of a planet and its atmosphere.

Altimeter: An instrument that determines the altitude of an object with respect to a fixed level. See also **pressure altitude.**

Altimeter setting: The value to which the scale of a pressure altimeter is set so as to read true altitude at field elevation.

Altitude: Height expressed in units of distance above a reference plane, usually above mean sea level or above ground level. See also **absolute altitude, pressure altitude, true altitude.**

AMDAR: Aircraft Meteorological Data Relay.

Anemometer: An instrument for measuring wind speed.

Aneroid barometer: An instrument for measuring atmospheric pressure. Its key component is a partially evacuated cell which changes dimensions in proportion to the change in atmospheric pressure.

Anti-icing equipment: Aircraft equipment used to prevent structural icing.

Anticyclone: An area of high atmospheric pressure that has a anticyclonic circulation; i.e., when viewed from above, the circulation is clockwise in the Northern Hemisphere, counterclockwise in the Southern Hemisphere.

Anticyclonic flow: The clockwise circulation of air around an anticyclone in the Northern Hemisphere and the counterclockwise circulation of air around an anticyclone in the Southern Hemisphere.

Anvil cloud: Popular name given to the top portion of a cumulonimbus cloud having an anvil-like form. See also **overhang.**

Archimedes' Principle: When an object is placed in a fluid (liquid or gas), it will be subject to an upward or downward force depending on whether or not the object weighs less or more than the fluid it displaces. See also **positive buoyancy, negative buoyancy.**

Arctic airmass: An airmass with characteristics developed mostly in winter over Arctic surfaces of ice and snow. Typical surface air temperatures in an Arctic Airmass are 0°F (−18°C) or less. See also **Polar airmass, Tropical airmass.**

ARINC: Aeronautical Radio, Incorporated.

ARTCC: Air Route Traffic Control Center.

ASL: Above Sea Level.

ASOS: Automated Surface Observing System.

ATC: Air Traffic Control.

ATIS: Automated Terminal Information Service

Atmosphere: The envelope of gases that surrounds the earth.

Atmospheric moisture: The presence of H2O in any one or all of the states: water vapor, liquid water, or ice.

Atmospheric pressure: The weight of a column of air (per unit area) above the point of measurement.

Attenuation: In radar meteorology, any process which reduces the intensity of radar signals.

Aviation turbulence: Bumpiness in flight.

AVN: Aviation Model (numerical weather prediction model).

AWC: Aviation Weather Center. Part of **NCEP.**

AWIPS: Advanced Weather Interactive Processing System.

AWOS: Automated Weather Observing System.

Backing: Change of wind direction in a counterclockwise sense (for example, northwest to west) with respect to either space or time; opposite of **veering.**

Backscatter: Pertaining to radar, the energy reflected or scattered by a target; an **echo.**

Barometer: An instrument for measuring the pressure of the atmosphere; the two principle types are *mercurial* and *aneroid.*

Billow cloud: A cloud layer having a "herring bone" appearance, in which the nearly parallel lines of clouds are oriented at right angles to the wind shear.

Black ice: Transparent ice that forms on black pavement, making it difficult to see. It may be caused by the refreezing of melt water or by freezing rain. Also a thin sheet of transparent ice that forms on the surface of water.

Blizzard: A severe weather condition characterized by low temperatures and strong winds bearing a great amount of snow, either falling or picked up from the ground.

Blowing dust: Dust particles raised by the wind to a height of 2 meters or more.

Blowing sand: Sand raised by the wind to a height of 2 meters or more.

Blowing snow: Snow raised by the wind to a height of 2 meters or more.

Blowing spray: Water particles raised by the wind to a height of 2 meters or more.

Boiling: The process whereby water changes state to vapor throughout a fluid. Occurs when *saturation vapor pressure* equals the total air pressure.

Boiling point: The temperature at which pure water boils at standard pressure (100°C or 212°F).

Bora: Cold, downslope wind that develops along the coast of the former Yugoslavia in winter. See also **glacier wind, cold downslope winds.**

Boundary layer: The layer of the earth's atmosphere from the surface to approximately 2,000 feet (600 meters) AGL, where friction influences are large.

Buoyancy: The property of an object that allows it to float on the surface of a liquid, or ascend through and remain freely suspended in a compressible fluid such as the atmosphere. See also **Archimedes' Principle.**

Buys Ballot's law: If an observer in the Northern Hemisphere stands with his back to the wind, lower pressure is to his left. This rule applies to macroscale pressure systems.

Calm: The absence of apparent motion of the air. The windspeed is zero.

Cap cloud (also called cloud cap): A standing or stationary cloud crowning a mountain summit. Often associated with mountain lee wave activity and strong winds along the lee slopes of mountains.

Capping stable layer: The elevated stable layer found on top of a convective boundary layer. Usually marks a sharp transition between smooth air above and turbulent air below.

Capture/coalescence: The droplet growth process by which small droplets are swept up by faster-falling large droplets.

Carburetor icing: The formation of ice in the throat of a carburetor when moist air drawn into the carburetor is cooled to the frost point. Often detrimental to engine operation.

CAT: See **Clear Air Turbulence (CAT)** .

CAVOK: Ceiling and Visibility OK.

CAVU: Ceiling and Visibility Unlimited.

Ceiling: In meteorology in the U.S., (1) the height above the surface of the base of the lowest layer of clouds that hides 5/8 or more of the sky (BKN, OVC), or (2) the **vertical visibility** into an **obscuration.**

Ceilometer: A cloud-height measuring system. It projects light on the cloud, detects the reflection by a photoelectric cell, and determines height by triangulation.

Celestial dome: The hemisphere of the sky as observed from a point on the ground.

Centrifugal force: The component of apparent force on a body in curvilinear motion, as observed from that body, that is directed away from the center of curvature or axis of rotation.

Change of state: In meteorology, the transformation of H_2O from one form (i.e., solid [ice], liquid [water], or gaseous [water vapor]) to any other form. See also **phase change.**

Chinook: A warm, dry, gusty wind blowing down the eastern slopes of the Rocky Mountains over the adjacent plains in the U.S. and Canada.

CIG: Ceiling.

CIP: Current Icing Product

Circulation: The organized movement of air. Also called an **eddy.**

Cirriform: A term descriptive of high clouds composed almost entirely of ice crystals, such as cirrus. Compare with **cumuliform, stratiform.**

Clear air turbulence (CAT): Usually, high level (or jet stream) turbulence encountered in air where no clouds are present; may occur in non-convective clouds.

Clear icing (Clear Ice): The formation of a layer of hard, smooth, glossy ice on an aircraft. Clear ice is relatively transparent or translucent; synonymous with *glaze*. Clear ice is heavy and difficult to remove. Compare with **rime icing, runback icing.**

Climatology: The study of long-term average weather conditions. Compare with **weather.**

Climatological forecast: A forecast based on the average weather (climatology) for a particular location or region.

Closed low: A low-pressure center enclosed with at least one isobar (surface) or one contour (aloft).

Cloud: A visible collection of very small particles of ice and/or water suspended in the atmosphere at altitudes ranging up to several miles above sea level. Clouds of dry aerosols such as dust, smoke, and volcanic ash may also occur.

Cloud amount: For an individual cloud layer viewed from the ground, the amount of sky covered by that layer and all layers below. Usually expressed in eighths of the **celestial dome.** See also **total cloud cover, ceiling.**

Cloud height: The height of the base of the cloud layer above ground level (*AGL*).

Cloud layer: Refers to clouds with bases at approximately the same level.

Clouds with great vertical development: Cumulus and cumulonimbus clouds.

Cloudy convection: The upward movement of saturated air that is warmer than its surroundings.

Col: A point in the pressure pattern on a weather map between two lows and two highs (also called a neutral point or saddle point).

Cold air funnel: A weak, microscale vortex that occasionally develops with rainshowers and nonsevere thunderstorms behind a cold front.

Cold downslope winds: A **Bora**-type wind.

Cold airmass: An airmass that is colder than the ground it is passing over.

Cold front: The leading edge of a **cold airmass.** A line along which colder air replaces warmer air.

Cold front occlusion: An occlusion where very cold air behind a cold front lifts the warm front and the cool airmass preceding it.

COMET: Cooperative program for Operational Meteorology, Education, and Training.

Comma cloud: A cloud mass shaped like a comma as seen in satellite imagery.

Condensation: Change of state from water vapor to water. Compare with **Evaporation, Deposition,** and **Sublimation.**

Condensation level: The height at which a rising parcel or layer of air would become saturated if lifted adiabatically.

Condensation nuclei: Extremely small particles in the air on which water vapor condenses or sublimates.

Condensation trail (or contrail): A cloud-like streamer frequently observed to form behind aircraft. See also **aerodynamic contrail, exhaust contrail.**

Conditionally unstable air: Unsaturated air that will become unstable on the condition that it becomes saturated.

Conduction: The transfer of heat by molecular action through a substance or from one substance in contact with another; transfer is always from warmer to colder temperature.

Constant pressure chart: A weather chart that represents conditions on a constant pressure surface; may contain analyses of height, wind, temperature, humidity, and/or other elements.

Contact cooling: The process by which heat is conducted away from warmer air to a colder surface.

Contour: In meteorology, a line of equal height on a constant pressure chart; analogous to *contours* on a relief map.

Contrail: Contraction for **condensation trail.**

Convection: (1) In general, mass motions within a fluid resulting in transport and mixing of the properties of that fluid. (2) In meteorology, atmospheric motions that are predominantly vertical, resulting in vertical transport and mixing of atmospheric properties; distinguished from **advection.**

Convective cloud: A cloud with vertical development that forms in an unstable environment (stratocumulus, cumulus, cumulonimbus, altocumulus, cirrocumulus).

Convective condensation level (CCL): The lowest level at which condensation will occur as a result of **convection** due to surface heating.

Convective lifting: Occurs in unstable atmospheric conditions when a rising parcel of air is warmer than its surroundings. See also **convection.**

Convective SIGMET: An inflight aviation weather advisory of importance to all aircraft. Issued for thunderstorm occurrence. Implies severe or greater turbulence, severe icing, and low-level windshear.

Convergence: The condition that exists when there is a net horizontal inflow of air into an area.

Coriolis force: A deflective force resulting from earth's rotation; it acts 90° to the right of wind direction in the Northern Hemisphere and 90° to the left of the wind in the Southern Hemisphere.

Cumuliform: A term descriptive of all clouds exhibiting vertical development in contrast to the horizontally extended **stratiform** types. Such clouds are also known as **convective** clouds.

Cumulus stage: The initial stage in the development of a thunderstorm. The cloud grows from cumulus to **towering cumulus.** For an **airmass thunderstorm,** this stage usually lasts 10 or 15 minutes. See also **mature stage, dissipating stage.**

CWA: Center Weather Advisory issued by **CWSU.**

CWSU: Center Weather Service Unit. Also see **ARTCC.**

Cyclogenesis: Any development or strengthening of cyclonic circulation in the atmosphere.

Cyclone: An area of low atmospheric pressure that has a closed circulation. As viewed from above, the circulation is counterclockwise in the Northern Hemisphere, clockwise in the Southern Hemisphere. See **extratropical cyclone.** Also, a severe **tropical cyclone** in the Western South Pacific and Indian Oceans with sustained surface winds in excess of 64 knots. See also **hurricane, typhoon.**

Cyclonic flow: In the Northern Hemisphere the counterclockwise flow of air around an area of low pressure and a clockwise flow in the Southern Hemisphere.

Dart leader: In the evolution of a lightning stroke, a dart leader typically occurs after the first stroke (initiated by a stepped leader) and initiates each succeeding stroke. The composite flash is **lightning.**

dBZ: Radar echo reflectivity (Z) expressed in decibels (dB).

Deepening: A decrease in the central pressure of a low-pressure system. Usually corresponds with intensification of the circulation.

De-icing equipment: Aircraft equipment that is actuated to *remove* ice that has already formed on the structure of the aircraft.

Density: Mass per unit volume.

Density altitude: The altitude above mean sea level (MSL) at which the observed atmospheric density occurs in the standard atmosphere. See also **altitude, pressure altitude.**

Deposition: The change of state from **water vapor** directly to ice without passing through the water phase. Compare with **Sublimation, Condensation, and Evaporation.**

Dew: Water condensed directly onto grass and other objects near the ground from water vapor present in the atmosphere. Dew is not considered precipitation. Dew occurs when the temperature of the surface falls below the dewpoint temperature of the air. Compare with **frost.**

Dewpoint (or dewpoint temperature): The temperature to which a sample of air must be cooled, while the amount of water vapor and barometric pressure remain constant, in order to attain saturation with respect to water.

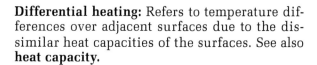

Differential heating: Refers to temperature differences over adjacent surfaces due to the dissimilar heat capacities of the surfaces. See also **heat capacity.**

Direct User Access Terminal Service (DUATS): A computer-based program providing weather products that are normally used in pilot weather briefings.

Dissipation contrail (distrail): A streak of clearing that occurs behind an aircraft as it flies near the top of, or just within a thin cloud layer.

Dissipating stage: The final stage in the life cycle of a thunderstorm cell. In an airmass thunderstorm, the dissipating stage begins as downdrafts spread throughout the lower levels of the cell cutting off its energy sources (surface heat and moisture). For an airmass thunderstorm, this stage lasts about 15 minutes. See also **cumulus stage, mature stage.**

Diurnal variation: The daily (24-hour) cycle that commonly occurs in meteorological variables such as temperature, wind, moisture, and cloud cover.

Divergence: The condition that exists when there is a net horizontal outflow of air from a region. The opposite of **convergence.**

Doppler radar: A radar system that has the capability to determine the velocity of a target toward or away from the radar site by measuring the frequency difference between the transmitted and received radiation. When the returning signal is a lower frequency than the transmitted frequency then the target is moving away from the site; if the return frequency is higher, the cell is moving toward the radar site.

Downburst: A concentrated, severe downdraft that induces an outward burst of damaging winds at the ground. See also **downdraft, microburst.**

Downdraft: A downward current of air. See also **downburst, microburst.**

Downslope wind: Wind blowing down a slope. A downslope wind can be either cold or warm depending on its cause. See also **Chinook, Bora, Foehn.**

Drainage wind: A shallow current of cold, dense air accelerated down a slope by gravity.

Drag: The resistance of the atmosphere to an object (such as an aircraft) in motion.

Drizzle: A form of **precipitation.** Very small water drops that appear to float with the air currents while falling in an irregular path (unlike **rain,** which falls in a comparatively straight path, and unlike **fog** droplets, which remain suspended in the air).

Dry adiabatic lapse rate: The rate of decrease of temperature with height when unsaturated air ascends adiabatically ($3°C/1,000$ feet).

Dry adiabatic process: The cooling of an unsaturated parcel of air by expansion (e.g., in rising air) and the warming of a parcel of air by compression (e.g., in sinking air). Compare with **saturated adiabatic process.** See also **dry adiabatic lapse rate.**

Dry bulb: A name given to an ordinary thermometer used to determine the temperature of the air; also used as a contraction for dry-bulb **temperature.** Compare with **wet bulb.** See also **psychrometer.**

Dry-bulb temperature: The temperature of the air. See also **Dry Bulb.**

Dry line: A mesoscale moisture boundary, where the moisture content of the air changes rapidly from one side to the other. Important in the development of lines of convection.

DUATS: See **Direct User Access Terminal Service.**

Dust: Small soil particles suspended in the atmosphere.

Dust devil: A small, vigorous **whirlwind**, usually of short duration, made visible by dust, sand, and debris picked up from the ground.

Duststorm: A severe weather condition characterized by strong winds and dust-filled air over an extensive area.

D-value: Departure of true altitude from **pressure altitude;** obtained by algebraically subtracting true altitude from pressure altitude.

Echo: In radar terminology:

1. The energy reflected or scattered by a *target*; and

2. The radar scope presentation of the return from a target.

Echo Intensity Level: ("VIP level" in older literature) A scale based on categories (1-6) of the amount of weather radar energy reflected from a target (water droplets) back to the antenna. See table 9-7A.

Eddy: An organized movement of air (atmospheric **circulation).**

Eddy Dissipation Rate (EDR): A true measure of the intensity of atmospheric turbulence. EDR is a metric that depends on the nature of the turbulence rather than on the aircraft response to the turbulence; that is, it is aircraft-independent.

EDR: See Eddy Dissipation Rate

EFAS: See **En route Flight Advisory Service.**

En route Flight Advisory Service (EFAS): A service provided by the FSS (Flight Watch) for pilots to get current enroute weather by way of the VHF aircraft radio.

Equilibrium level: The altitude where the temperature of a rising air parcel becomes equal to the temperature of the surrounding air.

Equinox: The day when, at noon, the sun's rays are perpendicular to the earth's surface at the equator and the lengths of day and night are equal at every point on the globe. First day of spring (*vernal equinox*) or first day of fall (*autumnal equinox*). Compare **solstice.**

Evaporation: Change of state from liquid to vapor. Compare with **Condensation, Deposition, Sublimation.**

Evaporation Fog: Caused when relatively cold, dry air moves over warm water. Evaporation from the water is followed quickly by condensation just above the water surface. The air being warmed from below is unstable, as revealed by the plume-like wisps in a shallow fog layer.

EWINS: Enhanced Weather Information System. An FAA-approved proprietary system for observing, reporting, and forecasting weather phenomena critical to flight.

Exhaust contrail: An aircraft condensation trail that forms at very cold temperatures (usually high altitudes) when water vapor in the aircraft exhaust is sufficient to saturate the atmosphere and exhaust particulates provide condensation nuclei. See also **condensation trail, aerodynamic contrail.**

Extratropical cyclone: A macroscale low-pressure disturbance that develops outside the tropics in the vicinity of the polar front. See also **polar front model.**

Eye: The roughly circular area of calm or relatively light winds and comparatively fair weather at the center of a well-developed **tropical cyclone. A wall cloud** marks the boundary of the eye.

FA: Area Forecast.

FAA: Federal Aviation Administration.

Fallstreaks: Ice crystals that descend from cirrus clouds.

FB: Winds and temperatures aloft forecast.

Filling: An increase in the central pressure of a low-pressure system; opposite of deepening. Usually corresponds with weakening of the circulation.

FIP: Forecast Icing Potential.

FIS-B: Flight Information Services-Broadcast.

Flight service station (FSS): Flight service stations are air traffic facilities that provide pilots with preflight and inflight weather briefings.

Foehn: A warm, dry, downslope wind. The warmth and dryness are due to adiabatic compression of air descending the lee slopes of a mountain range. See also **adiabatic process, Chinook, Santa Ana.**

Fog: A surface-based cloud consisting of numerous minute water droplets. The droplets are small enough to be suspended in the earth's atmosphere indefinitely. Unlike **drizzle**, fog droplets do not fall to the surface; differs from a cloud only in that a **cloud** is not based at the surface; distinguished from **haze** by its wetness and gray color. Consists of ice crystals at very low temperatures. See **ice fog**. See fog (FG) in Appendix D.

Form drag: Skin friction caused by turbulence induced by the shape of the aircraft.

Freezing: Change of state from liquid to solid.

Freezing drizzle: Drizzle that freezes on contact.

Freezing level: The altitude at which the temperature is 0°C (32°F).

Freezing level chart: A chart depiction of the freezing levels, reported in hundreds of feet.

Freezing rain: Rain that freezes upon contact with the ground or other objects.

Frequency: The number of waves that pass some fixed point in a given time interval, measured in cycles per second (cps) or Hertz (Hz).

Friction: The force that resists the relative motion of two bodies in contact.

Front: A transition zone between two adjacent **airmasses** of different densities.

Frontal cyclone: A macroscale low pressure disturbance that develops along the polar front and moves approximately west to east as a macroscale eddy embedded in the prevailing westerlies. Also called an **extratropical cyclone, frontal low,** or **wave cyclone.**

Frontal lifting: The lifting of a warm airmass over a relative cold airmass.

Frontal wind shear: The change of wind speed or direction per unit distance across a frontal zone.

Frontal zone: A narrow transition region between two airmasses.

Frost: Ice crystal deposits formed by sublimation when temperature and dewpoint are below freezing.

FSS: See **Flight Service Station.**

Funnel cloud: A **tornado** cloud extending downward from the parent cloud but not reaching the ground.

Funneling effect: An increase in winds due to airflow through a narrow mountain pass.

G-AIRMET: Graphical representation of hazardous flying weather conditions presented at short time intervals for more efficient flight-planning.

General circulation: The global **macroscale** wind system.

Geostrophic wind: A theoretical wind that would occur if **Coriolis force** and **pressure gradient force** are the only (horizontal) forces present and are equal and opposite. For macroscale circulations, the geostrophic wind gives a reasonable approximation of the real wind. When looking downwind, the geostrophic wind blows with low pressure on the left in the Northern Hemisphere and on the right in the Southern Hemisphere.

G-load: Gust load; the incremental change in vertical acceleration of an aircraft.

Glacier winds: One of the **cold downslope winds.** A shallow layer of cold, dense air that rapidly flows down the surface of a glacier.

Glaze: A coating of ice, generally translucent and smooth, formed by freezing of supercooled water on a surface. See also **clear icing.**

GOES: Geostationary Operational Environmental Satellite.

GPS: Global Positioning System.

Gradient: The change of any quantity (e.g., pressure, height, temperature) with distance at a point in time. On common weather charts, a gradient is strong where isobars (contours, isotherms, etc.) are tightly packed and weak where the lines are far apart. Rigorously defined, a gradient is a **vector,** commonly directed toward decreasing values with a magnitude proportional to the rate of decrease.

Gravity waves: Vertical oscillations of air parcels in a stable atmosphere. Gravity plays the major role in the return of displaced air parcels to their equilibrium level. The characteristics of gravity waves (speed, length, and direction of propagation) depend primarily on the magnitude of their initial displacement, atmospheric stability, and wind.

Greenhouse effect: The capture of **terrestrial radiation** by certain atmospheric gases. These gases are commonly called greenhouse gases.

Ground fog: In the United States, a **fog** that is generally less than 20 feet (6 meters) deep. A *shallow ground fog* is less than 6 feet (2 meters) deep. Usually a **radiation fog.**

Gust: A sudden brief increase in wind. According to NWS observing practices, gusts are reported as the maximum instantaneous speed when the variation in **wind speed** between peaks and lulls is at least 10 knots.

Gust front: The sharp boundary found on the edge of the pool of cold air that is fed by the downdrafts that spread out below a thunderstorm. A gust front is a key component in the formation of a **multicell thunderstorm.**

Gustnado: A tornado-like vortex that sometimes occurs near a **gust front** and/or the edge of a **downburst.**

Hadley cell: The tropical cell in a three-cell general circulation model. This cell exists between 0° and 30° both north and south of the equator.

Hail: A form of **precipitation** composed of balls or irregular lumps of ice, always produced by convective clouds which are nearly always **cumulonimbus.**

Hazardous Inflight Weather Advisory Service (HIWAS): This service provides a continuous broadcast over selected VORs to inform pilots of hazardous flying conditions.

Haze Fine, dry particles dispersed through a portion of the atmosphere. The particles are so small they cannot be felt or individually seen with the naked eye (as compared with the large particle of **dust**), but diminish the visibility; haze is distinguished from fog by its bluish or yellowish tinge.

Heat capacity: The amount of heat energy required for a specified increase in the temperature of a substance.

Height gradient: The rate of change of height per unit of distance on a constant pressure chart. See also **gradient, pressure gradient.**

High: An area of high barometric pressure, with its attendant system of winds; an **anticyclone.** Also called a *high-pressure system.*

HIWAS: Hazardous Inflight Weather Advisory Service.

Horizontal pressure gradient force: The force that arises because of a horizontal pressure gradient.

Horizontal wind shear: The change in wind direction and/or speed over a horizontal distance.

Horse latitudes: The areas near 30° latitude; characterized by sinking air, high-pressure systems, and low precipitation.

Hurricane: A **tropical cyclone** in the Western Hemisphere with sustained surface winds in excess of 64 knots. See also **typhoon, cyclone.**

Hurricane warning: Issued when the arrival of tropical storm-force winds (39-73 mph) or greater are expected within 36 hours.

Hurricane watch: Issued when the arrival of tropical storm-force winds (39-73 mph) or greater are expected within 48 hours.

Hydroplaning: In aviation, a condition that occurs on a runway when a thin layer of water separates a tire from the runway surface.

Hydrostatic balance: The balance between the downward-directed gravitational force and an upward-directed vertical pressure gradient force.

IAT: See **Indicated Air Temperature.**

ICAO: International Civil Aviation Organization.

Ice crystal process: Process by which cloud particles grow to precipitation size. Occurs where ice crystals and water droplets coexist at temperatures below 0°C. Ice crystals grow by **deposition** as water droplets lose mass by **evaporation.**

Ice fog: A type of fog composed of minute suspended particles of ice; occurs at very low temperatures.

Ice pellets: Small, transparent or translucent, round or irregularly shaped pellets of ice. They may be (1) hard grains that rebound on striking a hard surface or (2) pellets of snow encased in ice.

Icing: In general, any deposit of ice forming on an object, such as an aircraft. See also **clear icing, rime icing, mixed icing, glaze.**

IFR: See **Instrument Flight Rules.**

IMC: See **Instrument Meteorological Conditions.**

IMSAFE (I'M SAFE) checklist: A personal checklist developed by the FAA to help you evaluate your fitness for a flight. The letters remind you to check yourself for illness, medication, stress, alcohol, fatigue, and eating. See FAA H-8083-25, *Pilot's Handbook of Aeronautical Knowledge.*

Incipient stage: The time when **frontal cyclone** development begins as pressure falls at some point along the original stationary front and a cyclonic circulation is generated.

Indefinite ceiling: A ceiling classification denoting **vertical visibility** into a surface-based **obscuration.**

Indicated air temperature (IAT): The uncorrected temperature of the air as measured by the temperature probe on the outside of the aircraft. See also **true air temperature (TAT), outside air temperature (OAT).**

Induction icing: The formation of ice on aircraft air induction ports and air filters. See also **carburetor icing.**

Infrared (IR): Electromagnetic radiation having wavelengths longer than visible light and shorter than microwave (radar).

Initial lift: One of the two requirements for the production of a **thunderstorm,** the other is *unstable air.*

Instability: A general term to indicate various states of the atmosphere in which spontaneous **convection** will occur when prescribed criteria are met; indicative of turbulence. See also **absolute instability, conditionally unstable air.**

Instrument flight rules (IFR): Rules governing the procedures for conducting instrument flight. Also a term used by pilots and controllers to indicate the type of flight plan. Ceiling less than 1,000 feet AGL and/or visibility less than 3 s.m. (5,000 m). Compare with **VFR.**

Instrument meteorological conditions (IMC): Meteorological conditions expressed in terms of visibility, distance from cloud, and ceiling less than the minima specified for **visual meteorological conditions.**

International SIGMET: An inflight weather advisory issued worldwide by ICAO Meteorological Watch Office (MWO). See also **AIRMET, SIGMET,** and **Convective SIGMET.**

International standard atmosphere (ISA): A model atmosphere based on average vertical distributions of pressure, temperature, and density as prescribed by international agreement. See also **standard atmosphere.**

Intertropical convergence zone (ITCZ): The transition zone between the trade wind systems of the Northern and Southern Hemispheres; it is characterized in maritime climates by showery precipitation with cumulonimbus clouds.

Inversion: An increase in temperature with height; may also be applied to other meteorological properties.

Ionosphere: A deep layer of charged particles (ions and free electrons) that extends from the lower **mesosphere** upward through the **thermosphere.**

IR: See **Infrared.**

ISA: International Standard Atmosphere. See **standard atmosphere.**

Isobar: A line of constant barometric pressure.

Isotach: A line of constant **wind speed.**

Isotherm: A line of constant temperature.

Isothermal layer: A layer in the atmosphere where the temperature does not vary with height.

ITCZ: See **Intertropical Convergence Zone.**

ITWS: Integrated Terminal Weather System.

Jet streak: In the horizontal distribution of winds in the upper **troposphere** and lower **stratosphere,** a jet streak is a region centered on the axis of the **jet stream** where wind speeds exceed those up- and downstream. Jet streaks are several hundred to 1,000 miles long and move along the **jet stream** axis at speeds of about 600 n.m. per day.

Jet stream: In the horizontal distribution of winds near the **tropopause,** a jet stream is a relatively narrow band of high-speed winds (speeds exceed 60 knots). Normally found near the tropopause.

Jet stream axis: The line of maximum winds (>60 knots) on a constant pressure chart.

Jet stream front: High-level frontal zone marked by a sloping, stable layer below the jet core.

Jet stream cirrus: Anticyclonically curved bands of cirrus clouds that are located immediately to the equatorward side of the jet axis. Best observed in meteorological satellite images.

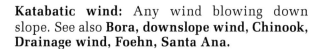

Katabatic wind: Any wind blowing down slope. See also **Bora, downslope wind, Chinook, Drainage wind, Foehn, Santa Ana.**

Knot: One nautical mile per hour.

Land breeze: A coastal nighttime breeze that blows from land to sea when the sea surface is warmer than the adjacent land.

Lapse rate: The rate of decrease of temperature with height. May be applied to any atmospheric variable. See also **adiabatic lapse rate, standard lapse rate.**

Latent heat: The amount of heat absorbed or released during a change of state. Compare with **sensible heat.**

Layer: In reference to sky cover, clouds or other obscuring phenomena whose bases are approximately at the same level. The layer may be continuous or composed of detached elements.

Lee waves: Atmospheric gravity waves that occur when stable air flows over a mountain barrier. Wave crests and troughs appear downwind of the ridgeline with typical wavelengths of about 10 km (6 s.m.). Under some wind and stability conditions, wave action may extend very far downwind of the mountains and to stratospheric altitudes. When sufficient moisture is present in the atmosphere, this wave will be identified with a lenticular **(ACSL)** clouds, cap clouds, and roll clouds; also called **mountain wave** or *standing wave*. See also**, lee wave system, rotor.**

Lee wave region: The upper layer of a **lee wave system** where smooth wave flow dominates and microscale turbulence occasionally occurs. See also **lower turbulent zone.**

Lee wave system: A system marked by two distinct layers. The upper layer is the **lee wave region**, which begins just above mountaintop level, and the lower layer is the **lower turbulent zone.**

LIFR: See **Low IFR.**

Lightning: Generally, any and all forms of visible electrical discharge produced by a **thunderstorm.**

LLT: Low-Level Turbulence.

LLWAS: See **Low-Level Wind Shear Alert System.**

LLWS: See **Low-Level Wind Shear.**

Long waves: Macroscale wave-like structures in contour and westerly wind patterns in the middle troposphere and higher. With typical lengths of 5,000 miles (8,000 km), long-wave troughs are frequently located along the east coasts of Asia and North America.

Low: An area of low barometric pressure, with its attendant system of winds. Also called a **cyclone.**

Lower turbulent zone: The lower layer of the **lee wave system**, extending from ground level to just above the mountaintop. It is characterized by turbulence due to strong winds and *rotors.*

Low IFR (LIFR): Weather characterized by ceilings lower than 500 feet AGL and/or visibility less than one statute mile.

Low-level wind shear: Wind shear below 2,000 feet AGL along the final approach path or along the takeoff and initial climbout path.

Low-level wind shear alert system (LLWAS): A system installed at many large airports that continually monitors surface winds at remote sites on the airport. A computer evaluates the wind differences from the remote sites and automatically provides alerts if a **low-level wind shear** problem exists.

Macroscale: Refers to atmospheric circulations with horizontal dimensions of 1,000 n.m. or more. See also **mesoscale, microscale.**

Mammatus: Bulges or pouches that appear under the anvil of a mature cumulonimbus cloud.

Maneuvering: Input by the pilot or autopilot in response to turbulence, resulting in an excess g-load.

Marginal Visual Flight Rules (MVFR): Weather characterized by ceilings 1,000 to 3,000 feet AGL and/or visibility three to five statute miles (5,000 to 8,000 meters). Compare with **VFR, IFR, LIFR.**

Mature stage: The most intense stage of a thunderstorm. Begins when the precipitation-induced downdraft reaches the ground. For an **airmass thunderstorm** cell, the mature stage usually lasts about 20 minutes. Much longer periods are expected for a **supercell thunderstorm.** See also **cumulus stage, dissipating stage.**

Mechanical turbulence: The turbulence produced when airflow is hindered by **surface friction** and/or an obstruction.

Melting: The change of state of a solid to a liquid, as in ice to water.

Melting point: The temperature at which pure water begins to melt. At standard pressure, 0°C.

Mercurial barometer: A **barometer** in which pressure is determined by balancing the weight of a column of air reaching from the point of measurement to the top of the atmosphere (atmospheric air pressure) against the weight of a column of mercury in an evacuated glass tube.

Mesopause: The upper limit of the **mesosphere,** slightly more than 280,000 feet MSL (85 km), the boundary between the mesosphere and **thermosphere.**

Mesoscale: Refers to circulations with horizontal dimensions of about 1 to 1,000 nautical miles. These dimensions are only guidelines. Other definitions use approximately 2 to 2,000 km as the limits of "mesoscale." See also **macroscale, microscale.**

Mesoscale convective complex (MCC): A nearly circular macroscale cluster of thunderstorms, 300 n.m. or more in diameter that develops in the area between the Rockies and the Appalachians during the warmer part of the year. MCCs typically develop late in the day and last into the night as they move eastward. Heavy rain and severe thunderstorms are common. Compare with **squall line.**

Mesosphere: A layer of the atmosphere where temperature decreases with height. The mesosphere is located immediately above the **stratopause,** between about 160,000 and 280,000 feet (50 km to 85 km).

METAR: Routine Meteorological Aviation Report.

Meteorology: The study of the atmosphere and its phenomena. See also **climatology.**

Microburst: A **downburst** with horizontal dimensions of 2.2 nautical miles (4 km) or less. See also **downdraft.**

Microscale: Refers to circulations with horizontal dimensions of 1 n.m. or less. See also **macroscale, mesoscale.**

MIS: Meteorological Impact Statement.

Mist: A popular term indicating **fog** and **drizzle.** In METAR code, mist (BR) is reported when fog restricts visibility to between 5/8 s.m. (1.0 km) and 6 s.m. (10 km).

Mixed icing: A combination of **clear icing** and **rime icing.**

Moisture: An all-inclusive term denoting water vapor, water, and ice in the atmosphere.

Monsoon: A seasonal reversal of a **macroscale** wind (i.e., on the scale of a continent). The summer monsoon cyclonically circulates inland, from the sea to a continental low-pressure area, often bringing copious rain. The winter monsoon blows from an interior anticyclone to the sea, resulting in sustained dry weather.

Mountain breeze: A **mesoscale** circulation that blows down-valley with a return flow, or anti-mountain wind, above the mountaintops. Typically, a nighttime phenomenon. Compare with **valley breeze.**

Mountain wave: An atmospheric **gravity wave** that forms in the lee of a mountain barrier. See also **lee wave.**

Mountain wave turbulence (MWT): Turbulence produced in conjunction with **lee waves.** See also **lower turbulent zone, lee wave system.**

MSL: Mean Sea Level.

Multicell thunderstorm: A group of thunderstorm cells in various stages of development. The proximity of the cells allows interaction that prolongs the lifetime of the group beyond that of a single cell. Compare with **airmass thunderstorm, severe thunderstorm.**

MVFR: See **Marginal Visual Flight Rules** Compare with **LIFR, IFR, VFR.**

MWO: Meteorological Watch Office.

MWT: See **Mountain Wave Turbulence.**

NAM: North American Mesoscale model designed to produce detailed forecasts in a relatively short time over limited areas such as the continental U.S., Alaska, and Hawaii. An earlier version was known as the ETA model.

NAS: National Airspace System.

NASA: National Aeronautics and Space Administration.

NCAR: National Center for Atmospheric Research.

NCEP: National Centers for Environmental Prediction.

Negative buoyancy: The tendency of an object, when placed in a fluid, to sink because it is heavier than the fluid it displaces. Applied to the atmosphere, negative buoyancy is the tendency of a parcel of air to sink because it is colder (more dense) than the surrounding air. Compare with **positive buoyancy, Archimedes' principle.**

NEXRAD: Next Generation Weather Radar (WSR-88D).

Neutral stability: A parcel of air is characterized by neutral stability if, when vertically displaced, it accelerates neither toward nor away from its original position. The atmosphere is in the state of neutral stability when the actual lapse rate is equal to the dry adiabatic lapse rate in unsaturated conditions. Compare with **absolute instability.**

NOAA: National Oceanic and Atmospheric Administration.

Nocturnal inversion: A surface-based stable layer caused by nighttime radiational cooling of the ground.

NOSIG: METAR code indicating that no significant change is expected in the next two hours.

NOTAM: Notice to Airmen.

NTSB: National Transportation Safety Board.

Numerical weather prediction (NWP): Meteorological forecasting using digital computers to solve mathematical equations that describe the physics of the atmosphere; used extensively in weather services throughout the world.

NWS: National Weather Service.

NWP: See **Numerical Weather Prediction.**

OAT: See **Outside Air Temperature.**

Obscuration: Denotes sky hidden by surface-based *obscuring phenomena.* Denoted by **vertical visibility(VV)** in METAR code.

Occlusion process: In a **wave cyclone**, the process by which the **cold front** overtakes the **warm front** pushing the warm sector air aloft.

Occluded front: The designation of the surface front that remains on the ground after a **cold front** overtakes a **warm front** in the occlusion process.

OFCM: Office of the Federal Coordinator for Meteorology.

Orographic lifting: The lifting of an airmass when it encounters a mountain or a hill.

Outflow boundary: The remnant of a **gust front** that continues to exist long after the dissipation of the thunderstorms that created it.

Outlook briefing: An aviation weather briefing requested from a certified FSS/AFSS weather briefer or via DUATS six hours or more before the aircraft departure.

Outside air temperature (OAT): The ambient air temperature outside the aircraft. The measured or **indicated air temperature (IAT)** corrected for compression and friction heating, also called **true air temperature (TAT)** .

Overhang: The anvil of a thunderstorm, under which hail may occur and an extremely turbulent wake may exist.

Overshooting tops: Cumulus towers that penetrate the otherwise smooth top of the **anvil cloud**. The presence of overshooting tops indicates an intense **thunderstorm** with very strong updrafts.

Overrunning: A condition that occurs when a warm, moist airmass moves over a cooler airmass, the boundary of which is marked by a **warm front** or a **stationary front.** In winter, this process often produces a broad, persistent band of low clouds, poor visibilities, and freezing precipitation.

Ozone: An unstable form of oxygen; greatest naturally occurring concentrations are in the **stratosphere (ozone layer)**; absorbs damaging ultraviolet solar radiation; prolonged exposure to high concentrations causes respiratory problems and causes some materials to deteriorate.

Ozone hole: The region of the **ozone layer** that has a lower-than-normal concentration of O_3.

Ozone layer: A layer of O_3 found in the lower stratosphere near 80,000 feet MSL (about 24 km). Characterized by a relatively high concentration of **ozone,** this layer absorbs damaging UV radiation and is the cause of the increase of temperature with height in the **stratosphere.**

Parcel: A volume of air, small enough to contain a uniform distribution of its meteorological properties, but large enough to represent the influence of all important meteorological processes. A simplifying concept particularly useful in the discussion/explanation of stability.

Partial pressure: The pressure exerted by any one of the gases that make up the mixture of gases that is the **atmosphere.** The total of all constituent partial pressures is the **atmospheric pressure.**

Particulates: Very small liquid or solid particles. When suspended in the atmosphere, they are called *aerosols.*

Peak wind: In the U.S., reported in the remarks section of a **METAR** observation whenever the maximum **wind speed**, since the last routine observation, exceeds 25 knots.

Persistence forecast: A weather prediction based on the assumption that future weather will be the same as current weather.

Phase change: A change of state. See also **condensation, sublimation, deposition, evaporation.**

PIREP: Pilot weather report.

Plan position indicator (PPI) scope: A radar indicator scope displaying range and azimuth of _targets_ in polar coordinates.

Polar airmass: An airmass with characteristics developed over high latitudes, especially within the subpolar highs. Continental polar air (cP) has cold surface temperatures, low moisture content, and, especially in its source regions, has great stability in the lower layers. Maritime polar air (mP) initially possesses similar properties to that of continental polar air, but in passing over water it becomes moist and may become unstable. Compare with **arctic airmass, tropical airmass.**

Polar easterlies: Surface winds generated by polar highs, poleward of about 60° latitude.

Polar front: The semi-permanent, semi-continuous **front** separating airmasses of tropical and polar origins.

Polar front jet stream: One of two westerly **jet streams** that commonly occur near the tropopause. Associated with the **polar front.** See also **subtropical jet stream.**

Polar front model: An idealized representation of the development of a frontal low **(extratropical cyclone).** The surface component of the model describes the structure and behavior of **fronts** and **airmasses** in the lower atmosphere. The upper air part of the model deals with the associated development of **troughs, ridges,** and **jet streams.**

Positive buoyancy: The upward acceleration experienced by an object placed in a fliud. It is caused by the difference in weight between the lighter object and the heavier fluid it displaces. Compare with **negative buoyancy.** See also **Archimedes' Principle.**

Positive charge center: The location of an intense positive charge usually near the top of a thunderstorm.

Positive lightning strike: Lightning discharge generated from a location high in a thunderstorm. Often more intense than a negative strike. (See Positive charge center.)

PPI: See **Plan position indicator (PPI) scope.**

Precipitation: Any form of water or ice that falls from the atmosphere and reaches the surface. It is a distinct class of hydrometeors that are distinguished from cloud, fog, dew, frost, and virga in that it must fall to the surface.

Precipitation attenuation: See **Attenuation.**

Precipitation fog: Develops when **rain** saturates the air near the ground.

Precipitation-induced downdraft: A downdraft produced by **precipitation** inside a **thunderstorm.** These downdrafts are enhanced by cooling due to **evaporation .**

Pressure: See **Atmospheric Pressure.**

Pressure altimeter: An **aneroid barometer** with a scale graduated in altitude instead of pressure using **standard atmospheric** pressure-height relationships; shows indicated, not necessarily true, altitude; may be set to measure altitude (indicated) from any arbitrarily chosen level. See also **altimeter setting, altitude.**

Pressure altitude: The altitude of a given pressure surface in the **standard atmosphere.** See also **altitude.**

Pressure gradient: Generally defined as a pressure difference over a known distance. As used in most applications in this text, pressure gradient is the horizontal difference in pressure between two points at a given time, divided by the distance over which the difference occurs (e.g., units of inches/statute mile or millibars/km). In the more rigorous definition, pressure gradient is a vector directed toward the lowest pressure. See also **gradient.**

Pressure gradient force: The force that arises because of a **pressure gradient.**

Prevailing visibility: In the U.S., the greatest horizontal visibility which is equaled or exceeded over half of the horizon circle; it need not be a continuous half. See also **visibility, sector visibility, minimum visibility.**

Prevailing westerlies: The dominant west-to-east motion of the atmosphere, centered over middle latitudes of both hemispheres.

Prevailing wind direction: Direction from which the wind blows most frequently.

PROG: Abbreviation for prognostication.

Prognostic chart (abbreviated **PROG** chart)**:** A graphic display (often a map) of forecast conditions.

Psychrometer: An instrument consisting of a **wet-bulb** and a **dry-bulb** thermometer for measuring wet-bulb and dry-bulb temperature; used to determine water vapor content of the air, **dewpoint**, and **relative humidity.**

QICP: Qualified Internet Communications Provider.

Quasi-stationary front (commonly called **stationary front**)**:** A **front** which is stationary or nearly so; conventionally, a front that is moving at a speed of less than 5 knots is generally considered to be quasi-stationary.

Radar: Contraction for radio detection and ranging. An electronic instrument used for the detection of distant objects and the determination of their distance from the radar site. The radar targets must be of such composition that they scatter or reflect radio energy.

RADAT: Radiosonde additional data. Includes observed height (MSL) of the **freezing level** and the observed **relative humidity** at that height.

Radar beam: The focused energy radiated by **radar.** Geometrically similar to a flashlight or searchlight beam.

Radar echo: See **Echo.**

Radar summary chart: A weather product derived from the national radar network that graphically displays a summary of radar weather reports at a given time.

Radiation: The transfer of energy by means of electromagnetic waves.

Radiation fog: Fog that occurs when radiational cooling of the earth's surface lowers the air temperature near the ground to or below its initial dewpoint on calm, clear nights.

Radiosonde: A balloon-borne instrument for measuring **pressure, temperature,** and **humidity** aloft. A radiosonde observation is a **sounding** made by the instrument. If radar, a radio direction finder, or GPS tracks the balloon, winds can also be determined.

RAFC: Regional Area Forecast Center.

Rain: A form of **precipitation**; drops are larger than **drizzle** and fall in relatively straight, although not necessarily vertical, paths as compared to drizzle which falls in irregular paths.

Rain bands: Lines of rain-producing cells; often lines of convergence associated with CB clouds; may spiral into the center of a cyclone, e.g., into a **tropical storm.**

Rain shadow: The drier, downwind side of a mountain.

Rain shower: See **Shower.**

RAOB: Radiosonde observation. See **Radiosonde.**

Relative humidity (RH): The ratio of the existing amount of **water vapor** at a given **temperature** to the maximum amount that could exist at that temperature; usually expressed as a percentage.

Return flow: The upper branch of a **thermal circulation.**

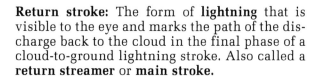

Return stroke: The form of **lightning** that is visible to the eye and marks the path of the discharge back to the cloud in the final phase of a cloud-to-ground lightning stroke. Also called a **return streamer** or **main stroke.**

RH: See **Relative Humidity.**

Ridge: On a surface analysis chart, an elongated region of high pressure. The same terminology is used to describe similar patterns in the height contours of constant pressure charts. The axis of a ridge is a "ridge line."

Rime icing (or rime ice): The formation of a white or milky and opaque granular deposit of ice on an aircraft. See also **clear icing, mixed icing.**

Roll cloud: A low-level line of cumuliform clouds occasionally found parallel to **gust fronts.** Vertical **wind shear** causes the cloud to have a rolling motion. Also used to describe the cloud associated with the **rotor** flow of a mountain **lee wave system.** Intense turbulence is associated with both phenomena. See also **lower turbulent zone.**

Rotor: A mesoscale circulation around a horizontal axis located parallel to a mountain ridge on the downwind side of the mountain. A common phenomenon in the **lower turbulent zone** of the **lee wave system.** When sufficient moisture is present, the rotor flow will be indicated by a **roll cloud.** May cause *extreme turbulence.*

RUC: Rapid Update Cycle (NWP forecast model).

Runback icing: Refers to **clear ice** that spreads beyond the location of **de-icing** and **anti-icing** equipment on an aircraft. A particularly dangerous form of icing.

Runway visibility (RVV): The *meteorological visibility* along an identified runway determined from a specified point on the runway; may be determined by a **transmissometer** or by an observer.

Runway visual range (RVR): An instrumentally derived horizontal distance that a pilot should see from the approach end of the runway; based on the sighting of high intensity runway lights.

RVR: See **Runway Visual Range.**

RVV: See **Runway Visibility.**

Saint Elmo's Fire: A more or less continuous, luminous electric discharge from various parts on the exterior of the aircraft (sometimes from the entire fuselage and wing structure). Also called a *corona discharge*, St. Elmo's Fire is typically experienced by aircraft that are flying through active electrical storms. May cause *precipitation static* in radio communications systems. Also may be observed on masts of ships in stormy weather.

Saturated adiabatic lapse rate (SALR): The rate of decrease of **temperature** with height as saturated air is lifted. SALR is less than the **dry adiabatic lapse rate.** SALR varies with temperature, being greatest at low temperatures. See also **saturated adiabatic process, dry adiabatic process, dry adiabatic lapse rate.**

Saturated adiabatic process: The process by which saturated air cools by expansion or warms by compression. It takes into account **adiabatic cooling** plus the *release of* **latent heat (condensation/deposition)** in the *expansion process*. In the compression process, it takes into account **adiabatic heating** plus the *absorption* of **latent heat (evaporation/sublimation)** . The related temperature change is not a constant as with the **dry adiabatic process** because the amount of latent heat released or absorbed depends on the amount of **water vapor** present which, in turn, depends on the temperature.

Saturated vapor pressure: The partial pressure of **water vapor** at saturation.

Saturation: A state of equilibrium where the same amount of H_2O molecules are leaving a water surface as are returning.

Scalar: A variable such as temperature or pressure that only has magnitude. Compare with **vector, pressure gradient.**

Scales of circulations: Refers to the typical horizontal dimensions and lifetimes of individual **circulations.** See also **macroscale, mesoscale, and microscale.**

Sea breeze: A coastal breeze blowing from sea to land. It occurs in the daytime when the land surface is warmer than the sea surface. See also **land breeze.**

Sea breeze front: The boundary between the cool, inflowing marine air in the **sea breeze** and the warmer air over land.

Sea level pressure (SLP): The **atmospheric pressure** at mean sea level.

Sea smoke: See **Evaporation Fog.** Also known as **steam fog.**

Sector visibility: *Meteorological visibility* within a specified sector of the horizon circle. See also **visibility, minimum visibility.**

Sensible heat: Heat that can be felt and measured. Compare with **latent heat.**

Severe thunderstorm: A **thunderstorm** having a much greater intensity, larger size, and longer lifetime than an **airmass thunderstorm.** Associated weather includes wind gusts of 50 knots or more, and/or **hail** three-quarters of an inch (2 cm) in diameter or larger, and/or strong **tornadoes.** Compare with **airmass thunderstorm, supercell thunderstorm, multicell thunderstorm.**

Shearing gravity waves: Short atmospheric gravity wave disturbances that develop on the edges of stable layers in the presence of vertical shears. Wave amplitudes may grow and overturn causing **turbulence.**

Shelf cloud: A cloud around a portion of a thunderstorm base that indicates the rising air over the gust front. Associated with the updraft of a **multicell thunderstorm,** it is located just above the **gust front** at low levels.

Short-wave trough: Troughs in the mid- and upper troposphere and lower stratosphere that correspond to developing frontal lows. Short wave troughs are **macroscale** in size but smaller than **long-wave** troughs. They move toward the east, averaging about 600 nautical miles per day.

Shower: Precipitation from a **cumuliform** cloud; characterized by sudden onset and cessation, rapid change of intensity, and usually by rapid change in the appearance of the sky.

SIGMET (WS): Significant Meteorological Advisory (WS). An inflight weather advisory describing conditions which pose hazards to all aircraft, including:

1. severe icing not associated with thunderstorms,

2. severe or extreme turbulence or clear air turbulence not associated with thunderstorms,

3. duststorms, sandstorms, or volcanic ash lowering surface visibilities to below three miles, and

4. volcanic eruptions.

5. See also **AIRMET, Convective SIGMET, International SIGMET.**

SLD: Supercooled Large Drops or *Solid* Line of Radar Echoes.

Sleet: See **Ice Pellets.**

Smog: A mixture of smoke and **fog.**

Snow depth: The depth of the snow actually on the ground.

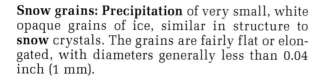

Snow grains: Precipitation of very small, white opaque grains of ice, similar in structure to **snow** crystals. The grains are fairly flat or elongated, with diameters generally less than 0.04 inch (1 mm).

Snow pellets: Precipitation consisting of white, opaque, approximately round (sometimes conical) ice particles having a snow-like structure, and about 0.08 to 0.2 inches (2-5 mm) in diameter; crisp and easily crushed, differing in this respect from **snow grains**; rebound from a hard surface and often break up. Also known as **sleet**.

Solar declination: The latitude where the noon sun is directly overhead.

Solar elevation angle: The angle of the sun above the horizon measured in degrees.

Solar radiation: The total electromagnetic **radiation** emitted by the sun.

Solstice: The first day of summer and the first day of winter when, at noon, the sun has reached its highest and lowest latitudes, respectively. Corresponds with the longest (*summer solstice*) and shortest (*winter solstice*) days of the year. Summer solstice in one hemisphere corresponds with winter solstice in the opposite hemisphere. Compare with **equinox**.

Sounding: In meteorology, a vertical probe of atmospheric conditions; e.g., a **radiosonde** observation.

Space weather: The state of the sun, variations in the transfer of energy from the sun to the Earth, and conditions in the Earth's magnetic field.

SPC: Storm Prediction Center.

Speed of light: The speed of propagation of electromagnetic **radiation** through a perfect vacuum. It is a constant of about 670 million mph (one billion kmh).

Squall: A sudden increase in windspeed by at least 16 knots to a peak of 22 knots or more, lasting for at least two minutes. Compare with **Gust**.

Squall line: Any nonfrontal line or narrow band of active **thunderstorms** that may or may not be severe. See also **mesoscale convective complex**.

Stability: A state of the **atmosphere** in which the vertical distribution of **temperature** is such that a **parcel** will resist displacement from its initial level. Compare with **instability**.

Standard atmosphere (ISA): An average **atmosphere** based on the following characteristics:

1. A surface temperature of 15°C (59°F) and a surface pressure of 1013.2 millibars (29.92 inches of mercury) at sea level;

2. A lapse rate in the troposphere of 6.5°C per kilometer (approximately 2°C per 1,000 feet);

3. A tropopause of 11 kilometers (approximately 36,000 feet) with a temperature of -56.5°C; and

4. An isothermal lapse rate in the stratosphere to an altitude of 24 kilometers (approximately 80,000 feet).

Standard briefing: A weather briefing provided by an FSS when you are planning a flight and you have not receved a previous briefing or are updating an outlook briefing. It is the most complete weather picture, tailored to your specific flight.

Standard lapse rate: In the **troposphere**, approximately 2°C per 1,000 feet, in the lower **stratosphere**, 0°C per 1,000 feet.

Standard sea level temperature: A surface temperature of 15°C (59°F). See also **standard atmosphere**.

Stationary front: Same as **quasi-stationary front**.

Station pressure: The actual **atmospheric pressure** at the observing station.

Steam fog: See **Evaporation Fog**. Also known as **sea smoke**.

Stepped leader: The first of a series of events that make up **lightning**. Nearly invisible to the eye, it is the path that carries electrons from the base of the clouds to the ground in a series of jumps, creating an ionized channel for the subsequent discharge.

Stratiform: Descriptive of clouds of extensive horizontal development, characteristic of stable air. Contrast with vertically developed **cumuliform** clouds.

Stratopause: Occurring at an altitude of about 160,000 feet MSL (about 50 km), the stratopause is the top of the **stratosphere**.

Stratosphere: The atmospheric layer above the tropopause, average altitude of base and top are 36,000 feet and 160,000 feet, or about 11 km and 50 km, respectively. It is very stable with low moisture content and very few clouds. Conditions vary with latitude and season. See also **standard atmosphere**.

Structural icing: The formation of ice on the exterior of an aircraft.

Sublimation: Change of state from **ice** to **water vapor**. Compare to **deposition**.

Subsidence: A slow descending motion of air in the atmosphere over a rather broad area; usually associated with a surface **anticyclone**, **divergence**, and stable air.

Subtropical jet stream: One of two major jet streams systems that circle the earth from west to east near the tropopause. In contrast with the Polar Front Jet Stream which is found near the location of the Polar Front, the Subtropical Jetstream is found near 30N and 30S and only exists during the cooler months of either hemisphere.

Suction vortex: A small **vortex**, about thirty feet (10 meters) in diameter, embedded in a **tornado funnel cloud**. There may be one or more suction vortices present in one funnel.

Superadiabatic lapse rate: A **lapse rate** greater than the **dry adiabatic lapse rate**.

Supercell thunderstorm: A **severe thunderstorm** that almost always produces one or more of the extremes of convective weather: Very strong horizontal wind **gusts**, large **hail**, and/or **tornadoes**. The supercell can occur anywhere in the mid-latitudes, but by far the favored area is the southern Great Plains of the United States. The supercell is so named because of its large size and long lifetime. See also **Airmass thunderstorm**.

Supercooled water droplets: Liquid cloud or precipitation droplets at subfreezing temperatures. See also **Supercooled large droplets (SLD)**.

Supercooled large droplets (SLD): Droplets with diameters larger than about 0.04 mm. The largest of these are precipitation-size droplets. These droplets contribute to some of the worst aircraft structural icing conditions including **clear icing** and **runback icing**.

Surface air temperature: In meteorology, the **temperature** of the air measured at 1.5 meters (about 5 feet) above the ground.

Surface-based inversion: An **inversion** with its base at ground level, often the result of surface cooling. See also **nocturnal inversion**.

Surface friction: The resistive force that arises from the combination of skin friction and turbulence near the earth's surface.

Surface visibility: Visibility observed from eye-level above the ground. See also **visibility**.

Sustained speed: The average **wind speed** over a one- or two-minute period.

TAF: Terminal Aerodrome Forecast. Provides weather conditions expected to occur within a five nautical mile radius of the runway complex at an airport.

TAT: See **True Air Temperature**. See also **OAT**.

Telephone information briefing service (TIBS): A service provided by **flight service stations** that is intended for preliminary briefing purposes. TIBS contains a continuous recording of area and/or route meteorological briefings, airspace procedures, and special aviation-related announcements.

Temperature: In general, the degree of hotness or coldness as measured on some definite temperature scale by means of any of various types of **thermometers**. Also, a measure of the direction that heat will flow; and a measure of the mean kinetic energy of the molecules.

Temperature-dewpoint spread: The difference between the air **temperature** and the **dewpoint**.

Temperature gradient: A difference in **temperature** between two points divided by the distance over which the difference occurs. See also **gradient**.

Temperature inversion: See **Inversion**.

Terrestrial radiation: The **radiation** emitted by the earth and its **atmosphere**.

TDWR: See **Terminal Doppler Weather Radar**. See also **radar**.

Thermal circulation: The movement of air resulting from **pressure gradients** created by **differential heating**.

Terminal Doppler weather radar (TDWR): Installed at many U.S. airports that are vulnerable to **thunderstorms** and **microbursts**. TDWR provides a narrower radar beam and greater power than so-called "network radars" (WSR-88D), and therefore give a more detailed measure of **wind shear** in the vicinity of the airport.

Thermal: A rising bubble of warm air. An element of **convection**; **microscale** in dimension.

Thermal turbulence: Low-level turbulence (LLT) that is produced by dry **convection (thermals)** in the **boundary layer**.

Thermosphere: The outer layer of the atmosphere that is directly adjacent to the **mesosphere** and where the temperature increases with an increase in altitude. The base of the thermosphere is about 280,000 feet (85 km).

Thunderstorm: A local storm invariably produced by a *cumulonimbus* cloud, which is always accompanied by **lightning** and thunder.

TIBS: See **telephone information briefing service**.

TNT: Turbulence in and Near Thunderstorms.

Tornado: A violently rotating, funnel-shaped column of air, which appears as a pendant extending from the base of a cumulonimbus cloud to the ground. **Microscale** in dimension, in its most intense form, it is the most destructive of all small-scale atmospheric phenomena. See also **funnel cloud**.

Total cloud amount: As observed from the ground, the amount of the sky covered by all cloud layers at and below the highest visible cloud layer. Usually expressed in eighths of the **celestial dome** (maximum eight-eighths). See also **cloud amount**.

Towering cumulus: A rapidly growing cumulus cloud; it is often typical of the **cumulus stage** of thunderstorm development. The cloud top may reach 20,000 feet AGL or more with a cloud width of three to five miles.

Tower visibility: Prevailing visibility determined from the control tower. See also **visibility**.

Trace: When **precipitation** occurs in amounts too small to be measured (i.e., less than .01 inches).

TRACON: Terminal Radar Control.

Transcribed weather broadcast (TWEB): A continuously broadcast weather information service on selected low and medium frequency nondirectional beacons, and on VHF omni-directional ranges. A TWEB includes a synopsis and route forecast and is based on a route-of-flight format specifically prepared by the NWS.

Transmissometer: An instrument system that shows the transmissivity of light through the atmosphere. Transmissivity may be converted automatically or manually into **visibility** and/or **runway visual range.**

Tropical airmass: An **airmass** with characteristics developed over low latitudes. Maritime tropical air (mT), the principal type, is produced over the tropical and subtropical seas; very warm and humid. Dewpoints in maritime tropical air are typically greater than 60°F (16°C). Continental tropical (cT) is produced over subtropical arid regions and is hot and very dry. Compare with **polar airmass, arctic airmass.**

Tropical cyclone: A general term for a **cyclone** that originates over tropical oceans. There are four classifications of tropical cyclones according to their intensity:

1. **Tropical disturbance:** winds less than 20 knots;

2. **Tropical depression:** winds 20 to 34 knots;

3. **Tropical storm:** winds 35 to 64 knots; and

4. **Hurricane or typhoon:** winds of 65 knots or higher.

Tropical storm: See **Tropical Cyclone.**

Tropopause: The boundary between the **troposphere** and **stratosphere,** usually characterized by an abrupt change of **lapse rate.** In the stan-dard atmosphere, the height of the tropopause is about 36,000 feet MSL (11 km). The height of the tropopause varies with season, latitude, and the presence or absence of local weather disturbances.

Troposphere: The atmospheric layer between the earth's surface and the **tropopause** at approximately 36,000 feet (11 km) MSL. The average troposphere is characterized by decreasing temperature with height; it is the atmospheric layer where the great majority of clouds occur.

Trough: In meteorology, troughs appear on surface analysis charts and constant pressure charts as elongated areas of relatively low **atmospheric pressure** or height. Troughs are generally associated with cyclonic curvature of the wind flow. Also called trough line; may be abbreviated "TROF."

True air temperature (TAT): See **outside air temperature (OAT).**

True altitude: The actual altitude of an aircraft above mean sea level (MSL).

True wind direction: The direction, with respect to true north, from which the wind is blowing.

Turbulence: In general, any irregular or disturbed flow in the **atmosphere;** in aviation, bumpiness in flight.

Turbulence in and near thunderstorms (TNT): That turbulence which occurs within, below, above, and around developing **convective clouds** and **thunderstorms.**

Turbulent gusts: Atmospheric **wind** and **vertical motion** fluctuations caused by **turbulent eddies.**

Turbulent wake: Turbulent eddies created when high surface winds are disrupted by obstacles. Examples are found behind aircraft in flight and when strong winds flow around and over **thunderstorms.**

TWEB: See **Transcribed Weather Broadcast.**

TWIP: Terminal Weather Information Program.

Typhoon: A severe **tropical cyclone** in the western Pacific Ocean with sustained surface winds exceeding of 64 knots. See also **hurricane, cyclone.**

UCAR: University Corporation for Atmospheric Research.

Ultraviolet (UV) radiation: Electromagnetic radiation with wavelengths shorter than visible light but longer than x-rays.

Unstable: See **Instability.**

Updraft: A localized upward current of air.

Upper air temperature: A **temperature** that is referenced to the height or pressure level where it is measured. See also **sounding, outside air temperature (OAT).**

Upper front: A **front** aloft not extending to the earth's surface.

Upslope fog: **Fog** formed when stable, moist air flows upward over higher terrain and is **adiabatically cooled** to or below its initial **dewpoint.**

Upslope wind: The deflection of the air by hills or mountains, producing upward motions.

UTC: Coordinated Universal Time (**Z**).

UV: Ultraviolet. See **Ultraviolet Radiation.**

VAA: Volcanic Ash Advisory.

VAAC: Volcanic Ash Advisory Center.

VAFTAD: Volcanic Ash Transport and Dispersion. Also refers to the numerical model used to predict volcanic plume trajectories and ash concentrations.

Valley breeze: A breeze that blows along the centerline of a valley, towards higher terrain.

Vapor pressure: The **partial pressure** of a particular gas in a mixture of gases. In meteorology, **water vapor** pressure is often referred to simply as vapor pressure.

Vector: A variable that has magnitude and direction. For example, wind or pressure gradient. See also, **scalar, gradient.**

Veering: Change of wind direction in a clockwise sense (for example, west to northwest) with respect to either space or time; opposite of **backing.**

Vertical motion: Movement of **air parcels** in an upward or downward direction.

Vertical visibility (VV): The distance one can see upward into a surface-based **obscuration**; or the maximum height from which a pilot in flight can recognize the ground through a surface-based obscuration.

Vertical wind shear: The change in wind speed and/or direction over a vertical distance. See also **wind shear.**

VFR: See **Visual Flight Rules.**

VHF: Very High Frequency.

Virga: Water or ice particles falling from a cloud, usually in wisps or streaks, and evaporating before reaching the ground.

Visibility: Meteorological visibility is a measure of horizontal visibility near the earth's surface, based on sighting of objects in the daytime or unfocused lights of moderate intensity at night. Compare with **runway visual range, vertical visibility.** See also **prevailing visibility, sector visibility, surface visibility, tower visibility, and minimum visibility.**

Visual flight rules (VFR): Rules that govern the procedures for conducting flight under visual conditions. The term "VFR" is also used in the U.S. to indicate weather conditions that are equal to or greater than the minimum VFR requirements: ceiling greater than 3,000 feet AGL, visibility greater than 5 s.m. (8,000 m). In addition, it is used by pilots and controllers to indicate a type of flight plan (such as VFR). Compare with **MVFR, IFR, LIFR.**

Visual meteorological conditions (VMC): Meteorological conditions expressed in terms of visibility, distance from cloud, and ceiling equal to or better than specified minimums.

Visual range: See **runway visual range.**

VMC: See **visual meteorological conditions.**

VNR: VFR not recommended

Volcanic ash: In general, particulates and gases from a volcanic eruption.

VOR: VHF omnidirectional range (Navigational aid).

Vortex: In meteorology, any rotary flow in the **atmosphere.** Examples: **Extratropical cyclone, hurricane, tornado,** and **dust devil.**

Vortex ring: The **microscale** circulation cell superimposed on the overall rising motion of a **thermal,** similar to a smoke ring. It has a relatively narrow core of upward motions surrounded by a broad region of weaker sinking motions.

WA: See **AIRMET.**

WAFC: World Area Forecast Center.

WAFS: World Area Forecast System.

Wake turbulence: Turbulence found to the rear of a solid body in motion relative to a fluid. In aviation terminology, the turbulence caused by a moving aircraft. See also **turbulent wake.**

Wall cloud: The well-defined bank of vertically developed clouds which form the outer boundary of the eye of a well-developed **tropical cyclone.** Also, in a **supercell thunderstorm,** that portion of the rain-free base that is lower in the vicinity of the main updraft. **Tornadoes** often develop there.

Warm airmass: An **airmass** characterized by temperatures that are warmer than the ground over which it is moving. Compare to **cold airmass.**

Warm downslope wind: A warm wind that descends a slope on the lee side of a mountain, often called a **Chinook** or **Foehn.**

Warm front: A **front** along which warmer air replaces colder air. Compare to **cold front.**

Warm front occlusion: In an **extratropical cyclone,** the frontal structure that evolves as a **cold front** overtakes a **warm front** and moves aloft over the colder air ahead of the warm front. Characterized by the warm front remaining on the ground.

Warm sector: In an **extratropical cyclone,** that portion of the surface that is covered by the warmest airmass; in the Northern Hemisphere, it is usually bounded by the **warm front** to the east or northeast and the **cold front** to the west or northwest.

Watch: A term used by NWS when the risk of hazardous weather or a hydrologic event has increased significantly, but its occurrence, location, and/or timing are still uncertain, It is intended to provide enough lead time for effective protective action.

Waterspout: A **tornado** that occurs over water. See also **tornado.**

Water vapor: The gaseous form of H_2O.

Wave cyclone: A **cyclone** that forms on a **front**. The circulation about the cyclone center tends to produce a wavelike deformation of the front. See also **extratropical cyclone.**

Wavelength: The distance between two successive, identical wave features, such as two wave crests.

Weather: The instantaneous state of the **atmosphere.**

Weather vane: A **wind vane.**

Wet-bulb temperature: The lowest **temperature** that can be obtained by **evaporation**; used together with the **dry bulb temperature** to compute **dewpoint** and **relative humidity.**

Wet-bulb thermometer: A **thermometer** with a muslin-covered bulb that is saturated with water and then ventilated to cause evaporative cooling. Used to measure **wet-bulb temperature.**

WFO: NWS Weather Forecast Office.

WH: Hurricane Advisory.

Whirlwind: A small (**microscale**) rotating column of air; may be visible as a **dust devil.**

White dew: Frozen dew.

Whiteout: A situation where all depth perception is poor. Caused by a low sun angle and overcast skies over a snow-covered surface.

Wind: The horizontal movement of air. Compare with **vertical motion.**

Windchill: The cooling of the human body by air movement. An effective temperature (Windchill index) is estimated from the observed temperature and wind speed.

Wind direction: The direction from which wind is blowing.

Wind shear: The difference in **wind velocity** (direction and/or speed) between two points divided by the distance between the points (e.g., units: knots per thousand feet); conventionally expressed as vertical or horizontal wind shear.

Wind speed: The rate of movement of the air (e.g., mph, knots, kmh).

Wind vane: An instrument to indicate wind direction. A wind vane points **into** the wind.

Wind velocity: A vector quantity that describes the horizontal motion of air in terms of **wind direction** and **wind speed.**

WPC: Weather Prediction Center. One of the eight national Centers for Environmental Prediction. Formerly the Hydrometeorological Prediction Center (HPC).

WS: See **SIGMET** or See **Wind shear.**

WW: Severe Weather Watch Bulletin.

WMO: World Meteorological Organization.

WSR-88D: Weather Surveillance Radar, 1988 Doppler. Also known as **NEXRAD.**

WST: See **Convective SIGMET.**

Z: Coordinated Universal Time (See **UTC).**

Appendix D

References

REFERENCES

The references provided here were used in the preparation of this text and/or are given as recommended reading for greater detail on the topics presented in the text. References that are also posted on the Internet are included along with the Internet address (URL) valid at the time the reference was obtained. Many publications listed below are available through the American Meteorological Society (AMS). Information on the availability of AMS publications may be obtained at *http://www.ametsoc.org/AMS* or by writing

American Meteorological Society
45 Beacon St., Boston MA
02108-3693
USA

Ahrens, C.D. *Meteorology Today, An Introduction to Weather, Climate, and the Environment.* Brooks/Cole/Thompson, 2012.

American Meteorological Society. *Preprints, 9th Conference on Aerospace and Aeronautical Meteorology.* Omaha, NE: American Meteorological Society, 1983.

American Meteorological Society. *Preprints, 3rd International Conference on the Aviation Weather System.* Anaheim, CA: American Meteorological Society, 1989.

American Meteorological Society. *Preprints, 5th Conference on the Aviation Weather System.* Vienna, VA: American Meteorological Society, 1993.

American Meteorological Society. Preprints, 7th, 8th, 9th, 10th, and 11th Conferences on Aviation, Range, and Aerospace Meteorology. 1997, 1999, 2000, 2002, 2004.

Anderson, J.D. *Introduction to Flight, 2nd Ed.* New York: McGraw-Hill, 560pp, 1985.

AOPA Air Safety Foundation. *Safety Review, General Aviation Weather Accidents, An Analysis and Preventative Strategies.* AOPA Air Safety Foundation, 421 Aviation Way, Fredrick MD 21701, 1996.

Atkinson, B.W. *Mesoscale Atmospheric Circulations.* Academic Press, 495pp, 1981.

Atlas, D. (Ed.): *Radar in Meteorology.* Boston: American Meteorological Society, 806pp, 1990.

Bernstein, Ben C., T. Omeron, M. Politovitch, and F. McDonough. "Surface Weather Features associated with freezing precipitation and severe in-flight aircraft icing,"*Atmospheric Research*, 46, 57-73. New York, Amsterdam, Tokyo, Singapore: Elsevier Science, 1998.

Bernstein, Ben C., and B. Brown. "A Climatology of Supercooled Large Droplet Conditions based upon Surface Observations and Pilot Reports of Icing," in *Preprints, 7th Conference on Aviation, Range and Aerospace Meteorology*, 82-87. Long Beach, CA: American Meteorological Society, 1997.

Bernstein, Ben C., T.P. Ratvasky, D.R. Miller, F. McDonough. "Freezing Rain as an In-Flight Icing Hazard," *Preprints, 8th Conference on Aviation, Range and Aerospace Meteorology*, 38-42. Dallas, TX: American Meteorological Society, 1999.

Bhangar, S., S. C. Cowlin, B. C. Singer, R. G. Sextro, and W. W. Nazaroff. Environmental Science and Technology, 42, 3938-3943."Ozone Levels in Passenger Cabins of Commercial Aircraft on North American and Transoceanic Routes." 2008.

Bluestein, H.B. Synoptic-Dynamic Meteorology in Midlatitudes. Volume I: Principles of Kinematics and Dynamics, 431pp. Volume II: Observations and Theory of Weather Systems. 594pp. New York, Oxford: Oxford University Press, 1993.

Bradbury, T.A., and J.P. Kuettner (Eds.). Forecasters Manual for Soaring Flight. Geneva: Organisation Scientifique et Technique International du Vol a Voile (OSTIV), 119pp, 1976.

Buck, R.N. *Weather Flying, 3rd Ed.* New York: MacMillan, 311pp ,1988.

Byers, H.R. *General Meteorology.* New York: McGraw-Hill, 1974.

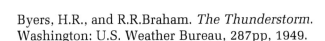

Byers, H.R., and R.R.Braham. *The Thunderstorm*. Washington: U.S. Weather Bureau, 287pp, 1949.

Caracena, F., R.L. Holle, and C.A. Doswell III. *Microbursts, A Handbook for Visual Identification, 2nd Ed*. NOAA, ERL, NSSL, 35pp, 1990.

Chan, W., and P. Lester. "The Wingrove Parameter: A Real Time Turbulence Metric," *Journal of Aircraft*, 33, 363-368, 1996.

Chambers, E. "BOAC experience with turbulence," *Flight in Turbulence*. AGAARD Conference Proceedings No.140, p6-1 to 6-13, NATO, 1973.

Collins, R.L. *Thunderstorms and Airplanes*. New York: Delacorte Press/Eleanor Friede, 280pp, 1982.

Crossley, A.F. and A.G. Forsdyke. *Handbook of Aviation Meteorology. M.O. 630 (A.P.3340)*. London: Her Majesty's Stationery Office, 1960.

Edgar, L. "Frightening Experience during the Jet Stream Project," *Soaring (July-August)*. 20-23, Soaring Society of America, 1955.

Elsberry, R.L. (Ed.), W.M. Frank, G.J. Holland, J.D. Jarrel, R.L. Southern. *A Global View of Tropical Cyclones*. USNPGS, Monterey: Publication sponsored by Office of Naval Research, Marine Meteorological Program, 185pp, 1987.

FAA. *Aeronautical Information Manual (AIM)*. Washington, D.C.: U.S. Department of Transportation, Federal Aviation Administration, 2006. http://www.faa.gov/ATPubs/AIM

FAA. *AC 00-6A Aviation Weather*. Washington, D.C.: U.S. Department of Transportation, Federal Aviation Administration, and U.S. Department of Commerce, National Oceanic and Atmospheric Administration, National Weather Service, 219pp, 1975.

FAA. *AC 00-24B Thunderstorms*. Washington, D.C.: U.S. Department of Transportation, Federal Aviation Administration, 7pp, 1983.

FAA. *AC 00-45G Change 1, Aviation Weather Services*. Washington, D.C.: U.S. Department of Transportation, Federal Aviation Administration, and U.S. Department of Commerce, National Oceanic and Atmospheric Administration, National Weather Service, 405pp, 2010. NOTE: Always refer to the latest version of AC 00-45.

FAA. *AC 00-54 Pilot Wind Shear Guide*. Washington, D.C.: U.S. Department of Transportation, Federal Aviation Administration, 56pp, 1988.

FAA. *AC 20-113 Pilot Precautions and Procedures to be Taken in Preventing Aircraft Reciprocating Engine Induction System and Fuel System Icing Problems*. U.S. Department of Transportation, Federal Aviation Administration, and U.S. Department of Commerce, Washington, D.C., 1981.

FAA. *AC 90-23F Wake Turbulence*. Washington, D.C.: U.S. Department of Transportation, Federal Aviation Administration, 2002.

Fleagle, R.G., and J.A. Businger. *An Introduction to Atmospheric Physics. 2nd Ed*. New York: Academic Press,. 346pp, 1980.

Fujita, T. *The Downburst. SMRP Research Paper 210*. The University of Chicago, 154pp, 1985.

Fujita, T. *DFW Microburst. SMRP Research Paper 217*. The University of Chicago, 122pp, 1986.

Geer, R.W. (Ed.). *Glossary of Weather and Climate*. American Meteorological Society, 272pp, 1996.

Glickman, T.S. (Ed.), *Glossary of Meteorology 2nd Edition* American Meteorological Society, Boston, 855 pp. 2000

Hildore, J.J., and J.E. Oliver. *Climatology: An Atmospheric Science*. New York, Toronto, Singapore, Sydney: MacMillan Publishing Company, 423pp, 1993.

Holmboe, J., and H. Klieforth. *Investigation of Mountain lee Waves and the Airflow over the Sierra Nevada.* Final Report Contract AF 19(604)-728. Los Angeles: Department of Meteorology, University of California, 290pp, 1957.

Hurt, H.H. *Aerodynamics for Naval Aviators. NAVWEPS 00-80T-80.* Office of Chief of Naval Operations, Aviation Training Division, 416pp, 1965.

Jeppesen Sanderson. *Instrument Commercial.* Englewood, CO: Jeppesen Sanderson, Inc., 920pp, 2006.

Jeppesen Sanderson. *Private Pilot Handbook.* Englewood, CO: Jeppesen Sanderson, Inc., 744pp, 2004.

Johnson, D.L. (Ed.). *Terrestrial Environment (Climatic) Criteria Guidelines for use in Aerospace Vehicle Development, 1993 Revision. NASA Technical memorandum 4511.* Marshall Space Flight Center: NASA Office of Management, Scientific and Technical Information Program, 472pp, 1993.

Jones, T.N. *"Density Altitude." FAA Aviation News. September, 11-13, 1994.*

Kessler, E. (Ed.). *Thunderstorm Morphology and Dynamics, 2nd Ed.* Norman, OK: University of Oklahoma Press, 411pp, 1986.

Knecht, W.R., and M. Lenz, Causes of General Aviation Weather-Related, Non-Fatal Incidents: Analysis using NASA Aviation Safety Reporting System Data. Final Report, DOT/FAA/AM-10/13, 2010.

Krause, K.A. *"Aspects of the influence of low-level wind shears on aviation operations,"* Preprints, International Conference on Aerospace and Aeronautical Meteorology. Washington, D.C.: American Meteorological Society, 332-333, 1972.

Kupcis, E.A. *"The FAA Sponsored Wind Shear Training Aid,"* Preprints, Third International Conference on the Aviation Weather System. American Meteorological Society, 317-322, 1989.

Lester, Peter F. *Turbulence, A New Perspective for Pilots.* Englewood, CO: Jeppesen Sanderson, Inc., 286pp, 1993.

Lindsay, C.V. and S.J. Lacy. *Soaring Meteorology for Forecasters, 2nd Ed.* Soaring Society of America, 1976.

Marwitz, J.D., M. Politivitch, B. Bernstein, F. Ralph, P. Neiman, R. Ashenden, and J. Bresch. "Meteorological conditions associated with the ATR-72 aircraft accident near Roselawn, Indiana, on 31 October 1994," *Bulletin of the American Meteorological Society,* 78, 41-52, 1997.

Miller, E. *"Volcanic Ash and Aircraft Operations,"* Preprints, Fourth Annual Confer-ence on Aviation Weather Systems, Paris. Boston, MA: American Meteorological Society, 1991.

Morris, D. "Over the Top Weather" *Weatherwise* May/June 2006.

NRC. *Weather for Those Who Fly.* National Weather Service Modernization Committee, Commission on Engineering and Technical Systems, National Research Council. Washington, D.C.: National Academy Press, 100pp, 1994.

NTSB, NASA. Turbulence accident and incident descriptions were acquired from the NASA Aviation Safety Reporting System (ASRS), NTSB accident reports, and NTSB Aviation Accident Synopses, 1999. http://www.ntsb.gov/aviation/months.htm

Office of Federal Coordinator of Meteorology (OFCM). *Federal Meteorological Handbook #1(FMH1) Surface Weather Observations and Reports.* FCM-H1-1995, September, 2005. http://www.ofcm.gov/Homepage/text/pubs.htm

Office of Federal Coordinator of Meteorology (OFCM). *Federal Meteorological Handbook #12 (FMH12) United States Meteorological Codes and Coding Practices.* FCM-H12-1998, September, 2005. http://www.ofcm.gov/Homepage/text/pubs.htm

Palmen, E. and C. Newton. *Atmospheric Circulation Systems.* New York: Academic Press, 1969.

Pantley, K. and P.F. Lester. "Observations of Severe Turbulence near Thunderstorm Tops," *Journal of Applied Meteorology,* 29. 1171-1179, 1990.

Peixoto, J. and A. Oert. *Physics of Climate.* New York: American Institute of Physics, 1994.

Politovitch, M. *"Forecasting Aviation Icing: Icing Type and Severity,"* in COMET/UCAR forecaster education modules. *http://meted.ucar.edu/whameted.htm*

Rauber, R.M., M.K. Ramamurthy, and A. Tokay. *"Synoptic and mesoscale structure of a freezing rain event: The St. Valentine's Day Ice Storm,"* Weather and Forecasting, *9, 183-208.* American Meteorological Society, 1994.

Riegel, C.A. *Atmospheric Dynamics and Thermodynamics.* World Scientific Press, 1989.

Rolt, I.T.C. *The Aeronauts.* New York: Walker and Company, 1966.

Sand, Wayne R. and C. Biter. *"Pilot Response to Icing: It Depends!" Preprints, 7th Conference on Aviation, Range and Aerospace Meteorology,* 116-119. Long Beach, CA: American Meteorological Society, 1997.

Schneider, S.H., (Ed). *Encyclopedia of Weather and Climate.* Oxford and New York: Oxford University Press, two volumes, 1996.

Schroeder, M.J. and C.C. Buck. *Fire Weather.* USDA USFS Agricultural Handbook 360, 1970.

Scorer, R.S. *Clouds of the World.* Harrisburg PA: Stackpole Press, 176pp, 1972.

Scorer, R.S. *Environmental Aerodynamics.* Chichester, England: Ellis Horwood, Ltd., 1978.

Scorer, R.S. *Natural Aerodynamics.* Chichester, England: Ellis Horwood, Ltd., 488pp, 1978.

Serebreny, S.M., *Personal Communication,* 1995.

Soucy, C. "Weather to Go" *FAA Aviation News* July/August 2006

Storm Prediction Center (SPC) "Enhanced Fujita Scale" *http://www.spc.noaa.gov/efscale/* 2006

Stull, R.B. *An Introduction to Boundary Layer Meteorology.* Kluwer Academic Publishers. 666pp, 1988.

Trollip, S.R. and Richard S. Jensen. *Human Factors for General Aviation.* Englewood, CO: Jeppesen Sanderson, Inc, 308pp, 1991.

USAF. *Air Navigation. AFM 51-40 (Also* NAVAIR 00-80V-49*).* Reprint with change 1 included. Washington, D.C.: Departments of the Air Force and Navy, 379pp, 1983.

USAF. *Weather for Aircrews. AFM 51-12. Volume 1.* Washington, D.C.: Department of the Air Force, Headquarters, 137pp, 1990.

U.S. Department of Transport. *Wake Turbulence.* Computer based training (CBT) package. CD available from Research and Special Programs Administration, Volpe national Transportation Center, Surveillance and Sensors Division, DTS-53. 55 Broadway Kendall Square, Cambridge MA 02142, 1999.

U.S. Navy. *U.S. Naval Flight Surgeon's Manual.* Department of the Navy, 871pp, 1968.

Wallington, C.E. *Meteorology for Glider Pilots, 2nd Ed.* London: John Murray, Ltd., 284pp, 1966.

Williams, J. *The USA Today Weather Book.* New York: Vintage Books, Random House, 212pp, 1992.

WMO: *Aerodrome Reports and forecasts: A Users handbook to the codes.* Geneva: Secretariat of the World Meteorological Organization (WMO), 2005.

Wolfson, M. M. "Characteristics of Downbursts in the Continental United States," *The Lincoln Laboratory Journal,* Volume 1, No. 1. MIT, 49-74, 1988.

Appendix E

REVIEW QUESTION ANSWERS

CHAPTER 1

1. Troposphere
2. Approximately 36,000 feet MSL
3. Approximately −57°C
4. Stratosphere
5. Approximately 18 hours
6. 18,000 feet (506 mb), Approximately 34,000 feet (253 mb)
7. 316 mb (9.33 in. Hg.)
8.
    1. 13.0°
    2. 12.0°
    3. 8.4°C
    4. 0.2°C
    5. −49°C

CHAPTER 2

1.
    1. −76°F
    2. −40°F
    3. +5°F
    4. +41°F
    5. +95°F
2.
    1. −269°C
    2. −73°C
    3. −18°C
    4. −4°C
    5. +45°C
3.
    1. −4.5° (below horizon)
    2. 19.0°
    3. 40.5°
    4. 47.0°
    5. 57.5°
    6. 75.0°
    7. 23.5°
4.
    1. 19.0°
    2. 42.5°
    3. 64.0°
    4. 70.5°
    5. 81.0°
    6. 51.5°
    7. 0.0°
5. About 8.3 minutes

CHAPTER 3

1. 2116.8 pounds
2. About 4,000 feet
3. 4,703 feet
4. 5,379 feet
5. 700mb
6. Not necessarily
7. The true altitude would be less.

CHAPTER 4

1.
    1. NE
    2. NW
    3. W
    4. S
2.
    1. ENE
    2. NNW
    3. WNW
    4. SSW
3. Clockwise, low
4.
    KDAY 05851Z from 30° at 3 knots
    KDAY 031405Z from 100° at 20 knots with gusts to 23 knots
    KBAB wind is calm
    KSAC variable at 5 knots
    KVIS from 190° at 6 knots
    KFTK from 210° at 5 knots

CHAPTER 5

1. Mechanical turbulence, convection, orographic lifting, gravity waves
2. 21.25°C (70.25°F)
3. 4°C (39.2°F)
4.
    1. Stable: A, B, C
    2. Unstable: E
    3. Neutral: D
    4. Inversion: B
    5. Isothermal: C
5. For 5 n.m. 1.645 knots (~165 f.p.m.)

CHAPTER 6

1. 66.66%
2. Zero

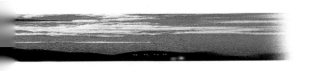

3. False
4. Small temperature-dewpoint spread, clear skies, light winds
5. 4 sm
6. 500 feet, 500 feet, 1800 feet, no ceiling, 800 feet, 1600 feet.

CHAPTER 7

1. Northeast Trade Winds
2. The Polar Front Jet Stream and Subtropical Jet Stream
3. Winter
4. A term referring to circulations with horizontal dimensions of one to one thousand miles
5. The Sierra Nevada mountain range is oriented SE-NW in the prevailing westerlies. Therefore, airflow is upslope on the west side with adiabatic cooling and more clouds and precipitation, and downslope on the east side with adiabatic warming and less clouds and precipitation.
6. Southeast
7. Converge

CHAPTER 8

1. The winter pole is colder and the polar front, from which extratropical cyclones draw energy for development, is stronger in mid-latitudes in winter.
2. At a typical speed of 25kt, a short wave will cover the approximately 800 n.m. in 32 hours.
3. 888 mb (26.22 inches of mercury) corresponds with an altitude of 3,700 feet in the ISA (29.92 inches at sea level).
4. **Cold Front Approach**: pressure fall, southwesterly winds, CB to the northwest and west.
   Cold Front Passage: pressure rise, wind shift to northwest, temperature decrease, dewpoint decrease, rainshowers and thunderstorms.
5. **Warm Front Approach**: pressure fall, southeasterly winds, cloud and weather sequence: Cirrus, cirrostratus, altocumulus, altostratus, nimbostratus, rain or snow, stratus, fog, temperature begins to rise.
   Warm Front Passage: slight pressure rise, temperature increase, dewpoint increase, wind shift to the southwest.

6. Taking the effects of friction and pressure gradient into account, the winds would shift from NW on the west side of the storm; to variable in the eye; to SE on the east side of the storm.
7. Winds circulating around the southwest of the hurricane were directed from land to sea, reducing the moisture available for producing clouds and rain.

CHAPTER 9

1. Afternoon
2. Precipitation
3. Attenuation by heavy precipitation
4. 45-60 minutes
5. Because the thunderstorm gust front produced by one thunderstorm provides lift that generates new thunderstorm cells.
6. False
7. **A** thunderstorm that produces wind gusts of 50 knots or more and/or hail 3/4 in (2cm) or more in diameter and/or strong tornadoes
8. **KIAH** 10th day of the month at 2353Z. Winds from 340° at 9 knots, prevailing visibility 6 statute miles, thunderstorm with light rain and mist. Few clouds at 1,900 feet, ceiling at 2,600 feet broken with cumulonimbus, 3,300 feet overcast. Temperature 20°C, dewpoint 19°C, altimeter setting 30.03 inches. Remarks: Automated station with precipitation discriminator and with an observer present; thunderstorm began 2335Z; Rain began 2327Z. Sea level pressure 1016.2 mb (hPa), occasional lightning in cloud northwest through north of KIAH; thunderstorm located northwest through north of KIAH and moving northeastward.

   KIAH 11th day of the month at 0022Z. Winds from 330° at 6 knots, prevailing visibility one and one half statute miles, thunderstorm with heavy rain and mist. Scattered clouds at 2,300 feet with cumulonimbus, ceiling at 3,300 feet broken, 6,000 feet overcast. Temperature 20°C, dewpoint 18°C, altimeter setting 30.04 inches. Remarks: Automated station with precipitation discriminator and with an observer present. Occasional lightning in cloud to the north. Thunderstorm located north of KIAH and moving north.

CHAPTER 10

1. Sunrise
2. In the first lee wave downwind of the ridge line
3. True
4. Valley breeze
5. False
6. At the altitude of the crest of the upstream ridge
7. 5 n.m., two minutes
8. Uphill, downhill
9. Increase in wind speed from the sea, possibly with a wind shift, temperature decrease, visibility increase (especially in urban areas), sometimes the passage of a line of cumuliform clouds parallel to the sea breeze front

CHAPTER 11

1. Elevated stable layers, ground-based inversions, microbursts, fronts, shallow cyclones, jet streams
2. In the frontal zone PRIOR to the frontal passage
3. TAS decreases, a stable aircraft pitches down, aircraft descends below glide path
4. See Glossary
5. 1.5 knots per 100 feet, Light
6. –20 knots (loss in airspeed)

CHAPTER 12

1. Thermals
2. Downdrafts (downbursts, microbursts), mechanical turbulence due to strong surface winds, gust front, and tornadoes
3. The Jet Stream
4.
   1. Moderate
   2. Light (incremental change is 0.3g)
   3. Light
   4. Severe
5. Moderate or greater
6. Routine pilot report over MRB at 6,000 feet MSL. Sky clear, turbulence moderate with increasing intensity westward
7. Moderate or greater turbulence

CHAPTER 13

1. DC-9, between 21,000 and 17,000 feet MSL, Rime, Severe
2. Decreased lift, increased drag, higher stall speed, aircraft instability, interference with movement of control surfaces, propeller imbalance, communications interference, decrease in visibility, pitot-static blockage, jammed landing gear
3. Yes
4. False
5. Collision/coalescence and the warm layer process
6. True
7. See figure 13-8

CHAPTER 14

1. Fog, smoke, precipitation, dust, sand, volcanic ash, etc.
2. Icing, wind shear
3. IMC, turbulence, toxic gases, abrasive particulates
4. Smoke layer covering 5/8 to 7/8 of the sky, base of smoke at 2,000 AGL
5. 1,900 feet AGL
6. Fog will form
7. Fog will probably not form as the spread typically increases with rising temperatures after sunrise.

CHAPTER 15

1. Small holes in fuselage, damage to wingtips, antennas, pitot tube, malfunctions of electrical systems, avionics, instruments, radar, navigation systems, small chance of fuel tank ignition
2. Trough
3. Engine malfunctions, pitting of the windscreen and landing lights, jamming of the pitot system, clogging of the ventilation system, damaging of control surfaces
4. Because of the fallout of large ash particles
5. 420 nm

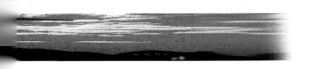

6. Interference with communication and navigation systems, satellites, and surface power grids; and radiation impacts on the health of crew and passengers
7. Whiteout and a lack of braking effectiveness

CHAPTER 16

1. AIRMET (WA), SIGMET (WS), CONVECTIVE SIGMET (WST)
2. Header, Precautionary Statements, Synopsis, VFR Clouds and Weather
3. AIRMET SIERRA
4. 122.0 MHz
5. The forecast is valid from 1800Z on the 6th through 1800Z on the 7th. For the period from 1400 to 1600 MST (2100Z -2300Z) on the 6th, forecast conditions are: surface winds from 180° (true) at 15 knots gusting to 25 knots; visibility exceeding 6 statute miles (unrestricted); scattered cloud layers at 8,000 and 12,000 feet AGL and a broken layer (ceiling) at 22,000 feet AGL.
6. The observations used to "start" the model could be in error
7. Forecast winds and temperatures aloft (FB) valid on the 13th at 1200Z and for use on the 13th from 0600Z through 1700Z

8. At DBQ the forecast winds at 12,000 feet MSL are from 240° at 38 knots and the forecast temperature is -12°C
9. The Aviation Weather Center at Kansas City, Missouri (part of NCEP)
10. A U.S. domestic SIGMET is an inflight advisory of non-convective weather potentially hazardous to all aircraft. Hazards included are different than those in a Convective SIGMET or an International SIGMET. An AIRMET is also an inflight advisory of significant weather conditions, but at intensities lower than those which require the issuance of a SIGMET.

CHAPTER 17

1. Weather awareness, knowledge of available and relevant weather products, self evaluation, aircraft capability, flight description
2. No. It enhances an AFSS briefing.
3. ETD: 1400CST (2000 Z), ETD: 1400MST (2100 Z)
4. Adverse conditions
5. VFR not recommended.